Gideon's People, Volume 1

The Iroquoians and Their World

EDITORS

José António Brandão

William A. Starna

Gideon's People
Volume 1

Being a Chronicle of an American
Indian Community in Colonial
Connecticut and the Moravian
Missionaries Who Served There

TRANSLATED AND EDITED BY
CORINNA DALLY-STARNA AND
WILLIAM A. STARNA

UNIVERSITY OF NEBRASKA PRESS | LINCOLN AND LONDON

© 2009
by the
Mashantucket Pequot Tribal Nation
All rights reserved
Manufactured in the United States of
America
(∞)
Library of Congress
Cataloging-in-Publication Data
Gideon's people : being a chronicle
of an American Indian community in
colonial Connecticut and the Moravian
missionaries who served there / translated
and edited by Corinna Dally-Starna and
William A. Starna.
p. cm. — (The Iroquoians and their
world)
Includes bibliographical references and
index.
ISBN 978-0-8032-2427-8 (cloth : alk.
paper)
1. Scaticook Indians—Missions—
Connecticut—History. 2. Scaticook
Indians—Connecticut—Religion.
3. Scaticook Indians—Connecticut—
Social life and customs. 4. Moravians—
Missions—Connecticut—History.
5. Missionaries—Connecticut—Diaries.
I. Dally-Starna, Corinna.
II. Starna, William A.
E99.S252G53   2009
974.6′02—dc22
2009004675

Set in Quadraat by Kim Essman.
Designed by R. W. Boeche.

Contents

Illustrations

Acknowledgments

A work of this scope and duration cannot be completed without the generosity of colleagues and friends. Over the more than a decade's worth of work it has taken to translate and edit the diaries and other materials that the Moravians who served at Pachgatgoch left behind, we have greatly benefited from the cooperation and contributions of others, all of which makes *Gideon's People* truly a team effort.

Kevin McBride was the first to express an interest in the translation of the diaries, hoping that they might provide much-needed insight into the mid-eighteenth-century life of the native people of Connecticut, an idea that was seconded by Jack Campisi. A first-draft translation, as well as a preliminary annotation, was funded by the Mashantucket Pequot Museum and Research Center, Theresa H. Bell, executive director (1994–2006). We are extremely grateful for Terry's support and enthusiasm in seeing the project to completion. *Gideon's People* would not have happened without her. Other assistance has continued through the offices of the museum's newly appointed executive director, Kimberly Hatcher-White. In addition, the museum's director of research, Kevin McBride, arranged for funding that allowed us to travel to the Moravian archives in Herrnhut, Germany, and Bethlehem, Pennsylvania, to conduct research.

The staffs of several libraries and archives were of critical importance to this project. We first would like to extend our thanks to Vernon Nelson, former executive director and archivist of the Moravian Archives in Bethlehem. It was the German script seminar conducted by Vernon Nelson and Lothar Madeheim that provided Corinna with the skills to engage with this type of primary source. At Herrnhut, Corinna was assisted by Rüdiger Kröger, the head archivist of the Unitätsarchiv der Evangelischen Brüder-Unität. She also was welcomed at Staatsarchiv Bremen and, in particular, by the friendly staff headed by Monika Schulte at Kommunalarchiv in Minden. We would like to thank the staffs of the Steven-German Library at Hartwick College, Oneonta, New York, and the Interlibrary Loan Office at Milne Library, State University of New York, College at Oneonta. At Milne, the librarians Andrea Gerberg and Dawn Gage never failed us in searching out a large number of often obscure written works needed for the project. We very much appreciate their efforts.

On numerous occasions, Charles Gehring provided invaluable technical advice and generously shared his extensive experience with matters of translation. Thank you, Charly. The introduction to the translation and many of the annotations benefited from careful readings by Jack Campisi and Martha Dickinson Shattuck.

We received considerable assistance, and, we would add, needed instruction, on the native languages of western Connecticut and eastern New York from Ives Goddard. Marianne Mithun and Hanni Woodbury answered our queries on Iroquoian languages.

Francelia Johnson not only shared with us her vast knowledge of the colonial families that settled in the region surrounding Kent, Connecticut, but she also furnished us with copies of early maps of the area and led us on a tour along the stretch of the Housatonic River where Pachgatgoch was once located.

And then there are the many persons we contacted who had something to teach us about regional and local history, genealogy, the Dutch of the Hudson Valley, basket making, geology, architecture, native people, geography, earthquakes, editing, and the myriad topics that the Moravians just happened to make mention of in their diaries. We thank them one and all: Raymond Beecher, Jack Campisi, Michael Stephen Cummings, Frank Doherty, John Ebel, James Folts, Charles Gehring, Robert Grumet, George Hamell, Edward Hogan, Paul Huey, Ross Kilpatrick, Mark Louden, Marge McAvoy, Kevin McBride, Martha Millington, Patricia Morrow, David Poirier, Harald Prins, Wayne Sherrer, Elizabeth Shapiro, Dean Snow, Robert Thorson, William Turnbaugh, Christopher Vecsey, and Anita Whitehead.

On a personal note, Corinna wishes to acknowledge her parents, Hans and Terry Dally, and to thank Karin and Jürgen Stubbe for their gift of the multivolume collection of Grimm's *Deutsches Wörterbuch*, that indispensable tool for anyone who translates the German language.

Translation and Editorial Comments

Various measures have been applied to maintain the linguistic integrity as well as the texture, that is, the pace and "voice" of the German diaries.

Lengthy sentence structures have been largely retained, although in keeping with the rules of English grammar and syntax. Unwieldy sentences have been silently separated to ensure intelligibility. Tense shifts have not been amended.

Words that in the original were written in a language other than German have been faithfully transcribed and italicized. However, capitalized English common nouns have been silently reduced to lowercase.

The German words *"Wilde"* or *"Wilden,"* and *"Wilder,"* often translated as "savages" and "savage," are at times used by the Moravian diarists. "Savage" is generally applied to a person who is regarded as uncivilized, primitive, or fierce. *"Wilder"* carries similarly complex meanings that range from indicating a "cultureless" condition to life in a state of nature in far-away places. Many times *"Wilder"* denotes a non-Christian person. Because the terms *"Wilder"* and "savage," and variations thereof, are not wholly comparable in meaning, and to allow for more nuanced readings within the context of the Moravian mission records, the German has been retained throughout.

The appearance of a superscript *d* attached to a noun marks the use of the diminutive in the German text. This notation permits various interpretations on the part of the reader, given that it is difficult to determine whether the diarist meant to communicate size, youth, affection, familiarity, disdain, or paternalism with respect to the person or object in question, or a combination of any of these qualities. Moreover, where nouns cannot take the English suffixes -let, -kin, or -et, only adjectives that signal fondness or smallness, such as, for example, "dear" or "little," could be applied. These limited choices would have rendered most English translations of the German diminutive unsatisfactory.

Much of the religious language in the diaries is characteristic of the "Sifting

Period" of the Moravian Church, which occupied most of the 1740s. This specialized idiom, created by the church's founder, Nicolaus Ludwig, Graf von Zinzendorf, was intended to portray the very intimate bond believed to exist between the faithful and Christ himself. Highly emotional, effusively sensual, and visceral in the extreme, this was a vocabulary of blood and wounds underlain with childlike expressions and sentimentality. Prohibited by Zinzendorf in about 1750, the language of the Sifting Period nonetheless remained in use by many Moravians in America, hence its appearance in the diaries.

We have used *Young's Analytical Concordance to the Bible*, by Robert Young (Peabody MA, 1984), to standardize the spellings of the Christian names carried by many of the Indians. The names of colonists that we could securely identify in published records have also been standardized. All other personal names, that is, the names of Indians and colonists we could not identify, are as they appear in the Moravian Records. German Christian names are as written and are standardized where there are variations: for example, Henrich becomes Heinrich, Nicholas becomes Nicolaus. In only a few instances do we have documentation showing the original spelling of the German name. We have left initials for names as is but in most cases have completed names that were abbreviated. The feminine endings -*in* and -*en* in several German surnames — "Macken," "Sensemannin," and others — identifying a Moravian's wife, have been removed.

There are numerous instances where the Moravians wrote verses from the Bible in their diary entries — whether in German or English — either verbatim, incompletely, in modified form, or inaccurately. Accordingly, we have left most of the German language passages untranslated in the text, placing the appropriate verse, with its biblical citation, in an endnote. Passages in English are as the Moravians wrote them. This most readily enables the reader to see the connections the Moravians sometimes tried to draw between events or situations developing in the community and biblical analogues or lessons.

All other translation and editorial matters are addressed in the endnotes.

Gideon's People, Volume 1

N

Lake
Champlain

LAKE ONTARIO

Albany •

Connecticut R.

Hudson R.

Housatonic R.

Hartford
•

Delaware R.

Pachgatgoch •
(Schaghticoke)

Gnadenhütten • • Nazareth
Bethlehem •

• New York

Susquehanna R.

0   25   50   75 mi

Map 1. Northeast region

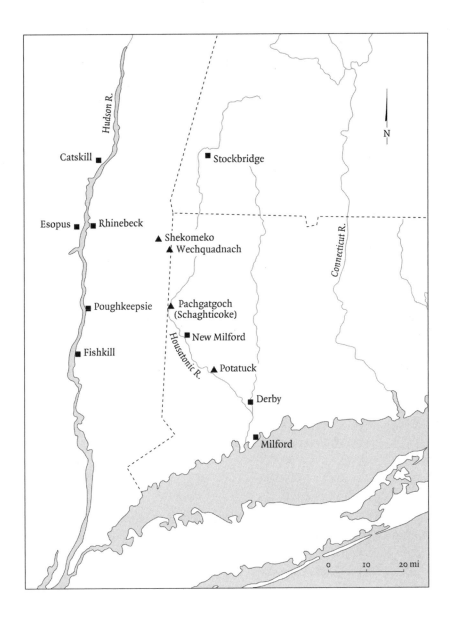

Map 2. New York and New England

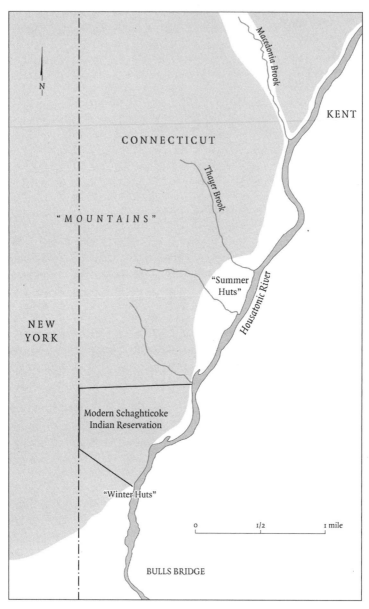

Map 3. Pachgatgoch and vicinity

Introduction

> In this way our settlements will gradually circumscribe and approach the
> Indians, and they will in time either incorporate with us as citizens of the
> United States, or remove beyond the Mississippi. *The former is certainly the
> termination of their history most happy for themselves.*

These words, excerpted from a longer but equally candid description of federal Indian policy, were from the pen of a man widely viewed as a humanitarian. In this context, then, they might seem revelatory, although in fact, they are not. President Thomas Jefferson was simply stating what, if it had not been official policy, seemed assuredly to be design, ever since the *Mayflower* bumped its prow against that now-famous rock. According to Jefferson, extending settlements into Indian homelands would cause "the decrease of game rendering their subsistence of hunting insufficient," which in turn would "draw them to agriculture," and then spinning and weaving, tasks better pursued indoors. "When they withdraw themselves to the culture of a small piece of land," the president continued, "they will perceive how useless to them are their extensive forests, and will be willing to pare them off from time to time in exchange for necessaries for their farms and families."[1]

Aided by warfare, disease, famine, and racism, the strategy that Jefferson so well articulated, one that had been tested and refined in southern New England decades earlier, was in most ways realized. By the mid-eighteenth century, Indian communities throughout much of that region were in sharp decline, having retreated into praying towns or other enclaves separated from, but economically and sometimes socially intertwined with, surrounding colonists. Most found themselves engaged in a holding action, determined to secure their identities, a way of life, and what little remained of their lands.

The mission to the American Indians initiated by Old World Moravians, who were rebounding from their own experiences with adversity, was following a more favorable trajectory, having just taken its very first steps. The Thirty Years' War had forced members of the fifteenth-century Unitas Fratrum, or Church of the Brethren, whose Protestant members mostly lived in Moravia and Bohemia, underground or into exile. Many fled to Poland, while others sought refuge in Saxony on the lands of Nicolaus Ludwig, Graf von Zinzendorf. It was from there that he would found the Herrnhuter Brudergemeinde (Community of Brethren at Herrnhut) and, in 1727, lead the spiritual renewal of the Moravian Church, and it was from Herrnhut that the ecumenical missionary movement in Europe and into the Americas was launched. Thus begins our story.

The Indians living near New Milford, Connecticut, early in the eighteenth century had probably anticipated a move farther up the Housatonic River. Over the previous several decades, their landholdings had been sold or otherwise lost to encroaching and ever more numerous colonists.[2] Wood to warm their homes, fields in which to plant their corn, and game to cook in their kettles had become increasingly scarce, and there was no reason to believe that things would get better. Taking themselves and their belongings somewhere else made perfect sense. So it was that in 1736, the Connecticut General Assembly reported that the Indians had left what they called Weantinock in favor of "a bow on the west side" of the river, "upon a piece of plain land there, and [they] have a desire to continue at said place."[3] This place, which sat in the valley between where the modern Macedonia Brook and Tenmile River flow into the Housatonic, was Pachgatgoch, also known as Schaghticoke, signifying "the confluence of two streams" in two of the local native languages.[4]

Indians in southern New England had been on the move for some time, most noticeably since the fury and brutality of King Philip's War (1675–76) and the deep and widespread devastation to people and towns it had wrought.[5] Yet scholars have produced conflicting assessments of the war's impact on native people. Some maintain that the Indians, reduced to "demoralized and dispirited remnants," "sank deeper into subjection and debauchery" or simply fled the scene, while others cite their "adaptability and persistence," their ability to redefine their communities, and their forging of "regional ethnic networks."[6] Missing from this picture, with just a handful of exceptions, are thorough and thoughtful studies of the war's survivors that would allow such assessments to be better examined.[7]

Also on the move were Protestant missionaries, who, beginning early in the seventeenth century, had come to New England with the inalterable goal of "reduc[ing]" the Indians from savagery to "civility."[8] A century later, they were preaching from Indian churches and in dozens of praying towns and reservations throughout the region, sometimes side by side with native clerics they had cultivated. In the remoteness of western Connecticut, however, there were no missions. Indian people were ministered to, if at all, on the run, mostly by ecclesiastically hard-nosed Presbyterians planted in towns and farming villages in the more populated southern reaches of the Housatonic Valley. Holding firm to their faith and flocks, it is doubtful that these groups envisioned the arrival of pious interlopers of a different stripe. But they did come, from another place in the Old World, and with their own way of doing things.

The Setting

The Housatonic River flows 150 miles from its multiple sources in southwestern Massachusetts, first south and then southeast, to Long Island Sound. In northwestern Connecticut, the gradient increases and the river gathers steam, rushing through narrow limestone and granite-lined gorges, through rapids and over cascades, broken by long, broad, slower-moving stretches. Of great importance to the lives of the Indian people of Pachgatgoch were the falls at Bulls Bridge, which they called Sasaksuk; the "Great Falls" below New Milford; and the rich floodplains bordering the river from Kent south to Bulls Bridge.[9] Today, as in the past, the Housatonic watershed is marked by a great diversity of plants and animals, a factor that was of no little importance to its native inhabitants.

Scattered up and down this river valley were the homes and farmsteads of Indian people, about whom, until the end of the seventeenth century, little is known, with existing information sketchy and often unreliable.[10] Nonetheless, it is safe to assume that the way of life there had been similar to that of natives elsewhere in southern New England and in southeastern New York.[11] The picture that emerges after 1700, however, is framed by the familiar triad of warfare, nearly a century's worth in coastal and eastern New England; the calamitous effects of epidemic disease; and the colonial juggernaut, colored by the cold language found in the documentation of land loss.

Attempts to locate and identify the Indian people of western Connecticut, along with those adjacent in New York, in conformance with presumptive rules of social theory and political organization have been met with only limited success. Much the same can be said about efforts to generate a regional archaeological framework, one buttressed by high-resolution data and against which systems of adaptation and change could be discerned and models tested. In each case, a large part of the problem is the general lack of evidence. The primary sources on the region's history are scattered and spotty, and the secondary literature is weak and of questionable worth. Archaeological data are incomplete, tentative, or unreported. And there remains the tyranny of the ethnographic record, in which Indians have been shoehorned into ill-fitting and unrealistic sociopolitical units such as "bands," "tribes," and "confederacies."[12] Most discouraging is the near absence of a renewed, if not refocused, scholarly interest in the region and its native people.

Although King Philip's War forever altered the face of much of native New England, leaving those who escaped its ruin to grapple with an unpromising future, it was not the root cause of the shift in ground in the Housatonic Valley; indeed, there is little to connect Indian people there to the conflict. The clashes that did occur were over lands claimed by Connecticut and coveted by New York, whose governors saw the war first in terms of opportunity; other conflicts were largely local squabbles, frequently manufactured, about what Indians might do.[13] Certainly the Indians at Weantinock wanted no part of it, taking the noteworthy step in September 1675 of offering the colony assurances of their friendship.[14] Thus, change that is evident in the form and function of native societies at the turn of the century is more readily explained by the early and unremitting loss of population to the ravages of European-introduced disease and the rapid and aggressive pace of settlement, which exerted pressure on Indians to adapt to a radically different environment—for them, the very transformation of self.

With the move of the Weantinock Indians to Pachgatgoch in 1736, only a handful of what could be described as consolidated Indian communities were to be found in the Housatonic Valley. There was Wechquadnach in the town of

4

Sharon, close-by Indian Pond on the New York–Connecticut border, and several hamlets in the vicinity of Milford and Long Island Sound, one of which was called Turkey Hill.[15] Potatuck, which rivaled Pachgatgoch in population, was adjacent to the river in the town of Southbury. Otherwise, individual native families erected their dwellings in the valley wherever they could. Over the hill in New York Colony, just south of Pine Plains, was Shekomeko, and north across the border in Massachusetts, the praying town of Stockbridge, which was established at the same time as Pachgatgoch. To the west of Stockbridge was the enigmatic Westenhook. To this mix can be added references to Indians in the Salisbury, Connecticut, area; in the Hudson Highlands; and to a couple of poorly known settlements in Dutchess County, closer to the Hudson River.

Other, more distant native communities with which Pachgatgoch had some degree of interaction included Kaunaumeek, southeast of Albany, and another at Farmington, Connecticut. Finally, across the Hudson, a short distance up the Catskill Creek, was a hamlet of Indians at Freehold. This is the way it was when, in August 1740, Christian Heinrich Rauch made his way up the height of land separating the Hudson and Housatonic Valleys and to the Indians at Shekomeko.

Moravians, Indians, and the Colonies

Rauch, a twenty-two-year-old laborer in the Moravian Church, had landed in New York City from London via Heerendyk, Holland, in mid-July 1740. Five years earlier, a small contingent of his brethren had undertaken the church's first mission effort in the colonies on the Ogeechee River of coastal Georgia.[16] Scarcely off the ground, it fell victim to the ravages of dysentery and other maladies, internal disputes, and also to the Moravians' pacifistic inclinations, which rendered them a liability to a colony under threat of invasion by the Spanish in adjacent Florida. Their plans to teach and preach to the local Creek Indians went nowhere, and talk of going to the Cherokees farther inland remained just that. There would be no mission to the Indians here, at least for the moment.[17]

Rauch had been sent by the bishops at Marienborn, Hessen, perhaps at the urging of David Nitschmann, and also Augustus Spangenberg, who later would head the North American church, to minister to the Indians in New York Colony, about whom Rauch seemed entirely uninformed.[18] He had no idea which Indians he was to contact or where they might be living, or even whether there would be interest in hearing a missionary's message if he managed to find any. In his wanderings around New York City, Rauch encountered two Mahicans, Shabash and Tschoop.[19] Somehow he persuaded these natives, who described themselves, it was said, as being from a very wicked people, to invite him to their village in the Hudson Valley. They assured him that he would be met at Martinus Hoffman's place near Red Hook.[20] But when Rauch knocked at his door, Hoffman told him the Indians had left word that they had gone hunting, and he pointed the way to Stissing Mountain and the home of Johannes Rau, on the eastern edge of Dutchess County.[21] Rauch set out alone toward the highlands.

Johannes Rau was one of the hundreds of Palatine Germans who had flooded into the region thirty years earlier.[22] As Rauch laid out his plans to him, Rau offered up his own sentiments, suggesting that conditions among the natives were such that they were quite beyond salvation. But Rauch was not to be deterred. His initial contacts with the Indians, with whom he lived, as well as with a few of their German and also Dutch neighbors, who reportedly were anxious to hear the word of God, were mostly positive. However, meddling by other colonists, who threatened Rauch with all sorts of harm, including lynching, and whose interests did not lie with seeing the Indians become Christians, much less receive wise counsel from someone who was, helped foster from within Shekomeko a belligerent opposition to his presence.[23] Withdrawing to the relative security of Rau's home, which for nearly two years he would use as a base, Rauch spent his days with the Indians, just a short walk away, and his evenings tutoring his host's children in exchange for room and board.[24]

Nothing is known about Shekomeko in the time before Rauch's arrival. Although the bulk of its inhabitants were identified as Mahicans, this was a mixed Indian community formed also of Esopus (Sopus) and Highland Indians, Wompanoos, Minisinks, and possibly others.[25] A prized, detailed sketch of the place, drawn by the Moravian John Hagen in 1745, survives (fig. 1).[26] The only other information we possess about the community concerns a suggestion of Shekomeko's political relationship to other Mahican or Housatonic communities, and the existence of a few kinship ties, mostly to Indians at Stockbridge and to several native families living in the vicinity of or closer to the Hudson River.

In the meantime, its attempt to establish an Indian mission in Georgia abandoned, the church turned its attention to the north and Pennsylvania. A number of the displaced Moravians found temporary employment erecting a building at Nazareth, a tract that had been purchased by the evangelist George Whitefield for a "Negro school." Shortly thereafter, Bishop David Nitschmann arrived from Europe with orders to establish a Moravian community in the area.[27] In spring 1741 a log house was raised on land where the Monocacy Creek flows into the Lehigh, and with a founding population of seventeen brethren, Bethlehem was born. These numbers grew when a party of Moravians from Herrnhut, Saxony, the home of the mother church, landed the following October. Among them was Nicolaus Ludwig, Graf von Zinzendorf, a bishop of the Unitas Fratrum and the head of the renewed church. He would not only inaugurate the community but bestow its name. Also in this company was a lesser soul, one Gottlob Büttner, an unmarried brother from Silesia.

Back in Shekomeko, Rauch's persistence and fervor had yielded results. Two Wompanoos and a Mahican in Shekomeko had responded to his teachings and expressed a desire to be baptized.[28] But Rauch was not ordained, which made it impossible for him to administer the sacrament. As chance would have it, however, Zinzendorf had just then ordered Büttner to travel to Shekomeko, where he arrived on New Year's Day 1742. Wanting in part to know more about this distant mission, and perhaps hoping to use the opportunity to demonstrate his church's vitality, Zinzendorf instructed Büttner to have Rauch travel to Oley, Pennsylvania, where an all-Protestant synod had been scheduled. He was to make sure that Rauch brought an Indian with him, and to remain at Shekomeko if he was unable to find someone trustworthy to keep an eye on things. Büttner sought out Jacob Maul, a freeholder living near Rhinebeck and a member of Rauch's fledgling colonist flock, to take his place. The pair made their way to the Hudson River and south. Instead of one Indian, they brought along the three candidates for baptism.[29]

The arrival of the party of Moravians and Indians in Oley may have generated some apprehension among the congregation and its supporters there. Rauch and Büttner reported that their trip had been difficult. They had been refused lodging, overcharged for purchases, and ridiculed by locals and passersby for being in the company of Indians. Zinzendorf was unhappy that neither of his charges could tell him whether the minister at nearby Westenhook (here a reference to Stockbridge), a potential obtruder and canonical competitor, was affiliated with the "high church."[30] He proposed to make a trip to Shekomeko that summer to take stock of the mission himself.[31]

Rauch was ordained a minister of the Moravian Church by Bishop David Nitschmann in Oley on 11 February, and on the same day, he baptized his Indian companions, the first native baptisms in the North American church.[32] Shabash, Seim, and Kiob became Abraham, Isaac, and Jacob.[33] The most noteworthy of the three was Abraham, who asserted a claim, around which swirled considerable controversy, to the land on which Shekomeko stood, and from all indications was a man of influence. A few years later, as one of Shekomeko's many emigrants, he would assume headman status among the refugee Indians in Pennsylvania and in New York's Susquehanna Valley, and play a role in colonial-Indian politics.[34]

In September 1742 Gottlob Büttner and his wife of just a few days, Margarethe Bechtel, were sent to head the mission at Shekomeko. There they joined Rauch and his assistant, Martin Mack, who had been a member of the second contingent sent to Georgia and was himself newly married to Jeannette/Johannetta Rau, Johannes's daughter. Before long came several other Moravians who would spend time in the community, which was destined to become a missionary training ground.[35]

Life at Shekomeko was hard. The brethren were often shorthanded, the supply of food was more scarce than not, and there were debts to pay and little ready money with which to do so. Nonetheless, the mission thrived, at least in the eyes of the brethren, and there were additional baptisms.[36] Moreover, the activity there increasingly drew the attention of Indians from the surrounding area, including the headman and a number of the people from Pachgatgoch, a several hours' walk to the southeast. There would be some thirty years to come of social and spiritual interaction between Indians and Moravians in this part of colonial America, all marked by life's peaceful moments and well attended by its vicissitudes.

Visits by Indians in the neighborhood had undoubtedly been part of an ongoing pattern for as long as Shekomeko had existed.[37] But there is no doubt that they took on an added significance with the arrival of the Brethren. Soon, the

8

Moravians began taking note of the numbers of Indians who stopped by and where they had come from, which suggests something other than mere curiosity. As promised, Zinzendorf arrived at Shekomeko in mid-August 1742. After deliberating with his followers, he presented his plans, most of which had to do with the task at hand—converting natives. Zinzendorf's primary goal was to see a congregation organized at Shekomeko that would be strengthened not only by the appointment of Indian assistants but also by seeking counsel from his native acolytes, Isaac, Abraham, and Jacob, to whom of late had been added Johannes.[38] Büttner was even more expansive, declaring that Shekomeko should be the "Rendivouz" for the "heathen messengers of these eastern parts."[39] Also on Zinzendorf's list was the need "to explore Albany and New England." This meant looking into the disposition of the Mohawks, west of Albany, one of the six Iroquois nations that he had made arrangements to visit after a chance meeting with a number of their headmen in Tulpehocken, Pennsylvania, two weeks earlier.[40]

Viele Fremde, many Indian strangers, from Wechquadnach, Pachgatgoch, Potatuck, and elsewhere in the region made their appearance in Shekomeko, and in turn played host to the Moravians intent on widening their search for souls. The initial contacts were made with the residents of Wechquadnach, about ten miles distant; in October 1742 they went to Rauch with the news that, after conferring among themselves, they had agreed to ask the Moravians to come and assist them as well. To smooth this new relationship, they intended to move their houses to the west side of Indian Pond, closer to the mission.[41] The following January, Rauch traveled to the Mohawks' country, not to preach, but to explore, find a place to live, and then learn the language. He stopped first at Fort Hunter, the Mohawks' easternmost location at the mouth of Schoharie Creek. This was no easy trip for the Moravian, and certainly unsettling. The daily exercise of the Indians at the fort, he reported, was to paint their cheeks red and their eyes and noses black, making themselves look quite frightful. They laughed at him whenever he spoke. Still, his meeting with Henry Barclay, the minister in charge, was businesslike, and shortly thereafter, Rauch headed west toward the Mohawk town of Canajoharie. On the way, he ran into a thoroughly disagreeable and churlish minister who hounded him at every step. He also met with the hostility of farmers fearful of losing their lands as the threat of war loomed. The only Indians he managed to see were shy, apprehensive, and unapproachable. Rauch cut short his trip, deciding to return via Albany. But once there, he learned that there were constables on his trail bent on arresting him because he did not have a pass to travel in the area. Upon his return, Shekomeko must have been a very welcome sight to him.[42]

Rauch's journey to the Mohawks was one of several undertaken by Moravian brethren as part of the reconnoitering effort that Zinzendorf had ordered the previous summer. Two weeks after his return to Shekomeko, Rauch left for Kaunaumeek, an Indian community southeast of Albany, stopping off at Stockbridge on the way. Brother Shaw traveled to the Highlands on the east side of the Hudson in August 1743; a month later, he and Brother Sensemann set out for Schaghticoke, the refugee Indian settlement above Albany. Also in August, Sensemann went into New England in search of Indians with Brother Mack.[43]

In January 1743, Indians from Potatuck and Pachgatgoch arrived at Shekomeko requesting a Moravian of their own.[44] Within the week, the Macks were dispatched to explore these two places, both of which were located south along the Housatonic.[45] After losing their way in the deep snows and spending the night in a barn along the trail, they reached Pachgatgoch and were welcomed by the headman Maweseman (var.), with whom they lodged. The next day an English "New Light" preacher appeared and harangued the Indians for some two hours about how angry God was with them and told them that He would cast them all into hell. The Indians were left uneasy, telling Mack how different this message was from what they had heard at Shekomeko. In fact, when Mack spoke to these Indians about his God, they responded, *"Gahene, Gehene"* (That is true, that is true).

Just then at Pachgatgoch was the unnamed headman from Potatuck, considered to be a particularly bad person who, Mack was told, "shot or beat dead every one who spoke of the Savior." This play at menacing could only have been for effect. Considering the circumstances of Indians in southern New England at this time, and even in the previous two decades or more, it is doubtful that any such acts would have been carried out, not without reprisals.[46] Mack was undaunted by the threat and went ahead and asked the headman whether he could pay his people a visit. The discussion that followed was mostly one-sided, with the headman first wavering about whether there would be any Indians at Potatuck who would care to listen to him and then making doubly sure that Mack understood that white people had on other occasions tried to deceive him. Finally, he did consent, and he and Mack shook hands on their agreement, much to the surprise of Maweseman, who allowed that no such thing had ever happened before. Before leaving for Potatuck, Maweseman, along with his wife and two children, who Mack declared were no longer considered to be "dead people" or unawakened, approached him, asking to be baptized. Mack relayed this news by messenger to his brethren at Shekomeko.

From Pachgatgoch the Macks made their way to the vicinity of Potatuck, some twenty-five miles down the valley. Although Potatuck was by itself a village, a collection of Indian houses, the Macks also happened upon a number of nearby dwellings in which lived Indians who were part of the larger community. As she had done on occasion at Pachgatgoch, Jeannette Mack translated. When asked, the Indians said they understood her quite well.[47] Mack discovered that the Indians at Potatuck had had dealings with surrounding "New Light" preachers long before they had ever seen a Moravian. And as they had at Pachgatgoch, the Indians expressed some doubt about the Moravians' message. The "New Lights" instructed them not to sin or work on Sundays if they expected God to take them in. For their part, the Moravians welcomed the Indians as sinners, saying that for as long as they believed in God and had Jesus in their hearts, they would experience happiness. The headman of Potatuck became especially sour when several Englishmen, evidently also preachers, appeared; he reproached them for the years when they had come to the Indians only to babble, pray, and read books, while Brother Mack spoke to them about what he experienced in his heart. He invited Mack to live in Potatuck. For Indian people, at least for the moment, the differences in religious perspectives among the missionaries could not have been more stark.

Returning to Pachgatgoch, the Macks found a very ill brother Büttner, who had struggled through deep snow and intense cold from Shekomeko to reach them. On 13 February he baptized six Indians, including Maweseman, to whom he gave the name Gideon. Gideon's son became Joshua.[48] Gideon soon repaid the visit, accompanied by nearly thirty Indians from Pachgatgoch and Potatuck, and requested that a brother be sent to live in his community.

A few days later, without Jeannette, Mack left for Pachgatgoch with a party of twenty Indians.⁴⁹ Her skills at translating were not required, Mack recounted: the natives spoke English. The Indians again asked that a Moravian come to live with them so that they too could live and be much like those at Sheko-meko. The headman from Potatuck was there as well, and showed himself to be friendly. Mack then made his way in the direction of Long Island Sound and Milford, where a considerable number of Indians lived. His escort was Joshua, who took the time to visit his grandmother during a stopover at Potatuck. Before long, the convert Johannes from Shekomeko joined them and preached to the gathered Indians with great effect. From here, Mack and his companions traveled farther south along the river, visiting Indians wherever they found them, finally reaching the scattered dwellings of those living at "the seaside." Once again, Joshua met with a relative, this time one of his brothers, either Chuse or Martin.⁵⁰

With one or two exceptions, Mack was greeted everywhere by friendly and receptive Indians. Nearly as common as the Indians were Protestant clergymen. Because there were so many, Mack remarked, it was difficult *not* to come across one. But these may have been more than chance meetings. While Mack was absent from Potatuck, a Presbyterian minister, a justice of the peace, and ten other men came to speak with him. They instead questioned the Indians and left, apparently satisfied with what they had heard.

Returning once again to Potatuck, Mack saw that the headman was not his usual self and arranged to meet with him. He was, Mack discovered, in a fix and fearful. Now that the headman had befriended the Moravian, the English made sport of him. In the past, he reminded Mack, he had threatened to shoot any minister who came to Potatuck, but now that had changed, and people had noticed. He assured Mack that while he would prefer to remain on good terms with him, he could not bear the ridicule. Mack interpreted the headman's quandary as a lack of commitment, a kind of spiritual waffling, and concluded that he could not or would not be converted. He nonetheless decided to regard him as a friend.

It was probably as much the fact that English ministers lower down the Housatonic far outnumbered them, as it was the Potatuck headman's distress, that brought the Moravians to their decision. With the promise of garnering more souls for Christ, including doing whatever they could for those at Potatuck,

Martin and Jeannette Mack packed up and moved their belongings to Pachgatgoch in mid-April 1743 to assume their duties as resident missionaries.[51] This was the second Indian mission established by the Moravian Church in North America. Yet as events rapidly unfolded, this beginning was but a flash in the pan.

Gideon's request for a missionary at Pachgatgoch had followed on the heels of that from a headman on the other side of the Hudson, a certain "Governor Corlaar" whose Mahican name was Metoxson (var.).[52] In response, the Moravians sent Cornelius, a former headman at Shekomeko, to gather information. During their conversation on the topic of hosting a Moravian preacher, Cornelius reminded Corlaar of their mutual old age and what might lie just around life's corner for them, a reality that seems to have struck a chord.[53]

Corlaar was part of a community whose name the Moravians recorded as Tetechtak, Teteching, but also Letechgoth, although his house was situated a mile from the others. As did the colonists living in the vicinity, the Moravians spoke of the place as Freehold; it was situated northwest of Catskill and, by their own estimate, about fifty or sixty miles from Shekomeko.[54] The size and population of the community are unknown, although it was large enough to merit a second headman, and Rauch, often accompanied by his wife Anna, spent more than a year there as the resident missionary. His time at Freehold was fraught with hardship, which seems to have been a constant companion to this brother. For several months, the Rauchs lived uncomfortably in a cramped, smoky hut near the Indians, where, as Büttner put it, Anna bravely acted as if she had all of the conveniences of a king's palace. Some weeks after their arrival, and in spite of his initial friendliness and invitation to the Moravians, Corlaar turned against Rauch. Said to have been influenced by surrounding colonists opposed to the Moravian's presence, Corlaar first forbade the daughter of Freehold's headman to stay with Anna during her husband's absences, warning that the devil would come and take her and anyone near her. He would not so much as look at Rauch, nor would he acknowledge other visiting Moravians. He had a truly fiendish appearance, said Büttner, and the Indians thought him to be a sorcerer and were afraid of him, as were his own sons. Making matters worse, Rauch learned that a price had been placed on his head: some locals had offered the Indians rum if they would kill him. Evidently, someone tried to do just that, for the brother bore a scar on his face after being struck with a firebrand.[55]

The goals that the Moravians had set for themselves — to further inspirit and anchor their missions at Shekomeko, Pachgatgoch, and also Wechquadnach, and to continue with their efforts to reach Indian communities elsewhere in the region — were soon thwarted by colonial governments. The first such occasion was in Connecticut, where the Moravians' movements had been shadowed closely by the local and exclusionary Protestant clergy. Although the record is thin, it may have been these men of the cloth who pushed for the passage of a May 1743 Connecticut act to provide "Relief against the evil and dangerous Designs of Foreigners and Suspected Persons" who were spreading "false and dangerous doctrines of religion" meant "to alienate and estrange the minds of the Indians from us." Obvious to anyone who was paying attention, the statute had been conceived with the Moravians in mind, and it was quickly brought to bear on them.[56]

In June 1743 Brother Joseph Shaw assumed his duties as the schoolteacher at Pachgatgoch. Almost immediately, he received a visit from John Mills of Kent, an officer in the local militia, who inquired by what authority the Moravians were in New England. Complaining that the Indians milling around them "was very lowsy," Mills invited Shaw to his home, apparently to continue the discussion. Shaw declined, and then discovered that Mills was an outright opponent of the Moravians, a prejudice that mirrored much of the local sentiment. Alarmed, Brothers Mack and Johann Christopher Pyrlaeus, who had just then arrived at the mission, went to Abel Wright, a friend in Kent, to ask him about the new law. In the meantime, Sheriff William Drinkwater (1710–1758) of New Milford, along with three other men, appeared at Pachgatgoch and, after some preliminary questioning, arrested Shaw and Sister Mack "under the law." Setting out for Kent, the party ran into Martin Mack and Pyrlaeus on their way back to Pachgatgoch. Drinkwater arrested them as well, taking his four prisoners to Abel Wright's home, where a group of local citizens awaited them, shortly to be joined by Cyrus Marsh, the Congregational minister.[57] After some debate, and then lunch with the Wright family, the Moravians were walked to New Milford, where they were questioned further by justices Samuel Canfield and Lemuel Bostwick, and the sheriff, about their activities among the Indians.

From New Milford, but without Sister Mack, whom the justices had "acquited," they were marched some forty miles downriver to "Old Milford," where they appeared before a tribunal consisting of Governor Law, several other colonial officials, one of whom was Justice Canfield, and a couple of Protestant clerics. The three were thoroughly examined, the governor finding that since Pyrlaeus had not preached and nothing had been found in his disfavor, no charges would be brought. Brothers Shaw and Mack, however, were required to sign a "Bond of Recognisance" promising "to keep the Laws of this Land under the penalty of 100 pounds (if hereafter they brake them)."[58]

With the governor's admonition to comply with the law, which included a de jure instruction not to teach or preach "among white or brown people," Shaw, Mack, and Pyrlaeus were permitted to return to Pachgatgoch.[59] There, they met again with the Reverend Mr. Marsh, behind whom stood some of Kent's citizens. His straight-ahead message to the Moravians — "It is impossible to stay amongst them [the Indians at Pachgatgoch] and not be liable to the punishment of the Laws" — was delivered with sufficient force that Shaw and Pyrlaeus left the colony the same day, to be followed by the Macks shortly afterward.[60]

Events across the border in New York were a good deal more complicated and dangerous for Moravians and Indians alike. The usual dustups that stemmed from the unavoidable proximity of colonist and Indian were now intensified by the presence of the Moravians, who themselves saw enemies all around; there were also other, more pressing and ultimately related issues.[61] The first sure sign of trouble was a rumor that the Moravians were attempting to enslave the Indians and sell their children abroad. Meanwhile, a few colonists made certain that the Indians were delivered enough alcohol so they would commit all sorts of "follies," perhaps even against the brethren, and then be harassed for having done so. The obvious aim was to drive a wedge between the Indians and the missionaries.[62] A second rumor went to the heart of the matter — the Moravians themselves. Sometime in early or mid-spring 1744, New York's governor George Clinton received information, most likely from one of the many well-connected persons in Dutchess County, that "the Moravians had Endeavoured to seduce the Indians from their Allegiance which in this Time of Warr would be of most dangerous Consequence."[63] King George's War (1744–48) was in its beginning stages, and whether there was an immediate threat to anyone in the

Hudson Valley, colonist or Indian, did not seem to matter much. That June, Henry Beekman, a justice of the peace, member of the colonial assembly, and a major landholder in the county, received instructions from the governor to question the Moravians. In addition, and wearing another one of his hats, this time as colonel of the militia, he was to go to Shekomeko in a search for contraband arms and ammunition, and "to Cause the said Indians to be dispersed."[64]

Near the end of June, Beekman did as he had been instructed, reporting that at Shekomeko, there were four resident missionaries among a large number of Indians. A search for arms and ammunition had turned up nothing, and there was no further mention of dispersing the Indians. However, Beekman also disclosed that a party of men mobilized by Henry Filkin, the high sheriff of the county, which included his brother Judge Francis Filkin, had gone to Shekomeko on the nineteenth of the month before the order from the governor had reached him. Their intent was to look into rumors rampant among Poughkeepsie's citizens that they were about to be attacked by five hundred Indians who allegedly were gathered at Shekomeko and joined, if not led, by the Moravians.[65] A small number of Indians had indeed fled there from Wechquadnach following what turned out to be a bogus report that marauding French Indians had murdered three families of colonists in the area of Weataug, on the west side of the Housatonic River, near the Massachusetts border. The residents of Wechquadnach not only feared the French Indians but also expected to suffer reprisals at the hands of Sharon's colonists, who, Büttner had learned, had armed themselves against what they also believed would be an attack by the Indians at Shekomeko.[66] He quickly sent off a letter to Peter Pratt, the minister of Sharon, with whom he was on speaking terms, assuring him that "the Indians here to my knowledge so long as I have been acquainted with them in any such a Manner had not had such an Intention."[67]

When the Filkins and their posse arrived at Shekomeko, they noted that Büttner and the Indians, who were busily working in their fields, "seemed in Consternation" at their approach "but received them Civilly." "As few Arms as Could be Expected for 44 men" were discovered, although, Büttner recounted, there were only about twenty Indians in the village that day. Stymied, Judge Filkin nonetheless took full advantage of the situation, rebuking the Moravian, who, he said, was "Suspected to be disaffected to the Crown," an imputation Büttner denied, explaining that he and the other missionaries were also in dread of the French and their Indian confederates. The Moravians' interests, he said, lay only with gaining "Souls among the Heathens," and furthermore, they had in hand a commission from the Archbishop of Canterbury authorizing them to do so. Filkin then demanded that Büttner swear two oaths he put before him. He refused, "through a Scruple of Conscience against Swearing," an act of defiance that would later lead to his being detained by the authorities.[68]

Weeks earlier, on 14 May, the Moravians had been given a notice to report to a military muster in Poughkeepsie, which they promptly ignored because of a technicality they spotted: their names were not included on the roll. A second notice was handed them on 9 June, with instructions to appear in Rhinebeck. With this, Büttner paid a visit to the militia captain, informing him of the Moravians' pacifist principles and their objections to taking oaths before whatever jurisdiction. If anything, there was confusion among local officials about how best to respond to the Moravians' stance, and also in their assessment of the risk the brethren might pose to the local citizenry; at the same time, summonses began to fly in all directions. In the first week of July, the Moravians were brought before a panel of judges, one of whom was Francis Filkin, where they heard testimony presented against them, some of which was countered by that of their old friend Johannes Rau. Among the disapproving witnesses were, not surprisingly, a local clergyman and also the Sackett brothers, John and Richard Jr., whose father, Richard Sr., was one of the patentees of the Little Nine Partners patent, within the borders of which Shekomeko was located.[69] Finally, the missionaries were bound over and ordered to appear at a hearing in New York City before Governor Clinton, Chief Justice James DeLancey, and colonial council members Philip van Cortlandt, Daniel Horsmanden, Joseph Murray, and Archibald Kennedy.

The brethren gave their initial depositions on 1 August. First up was Joseph Shaw, followed by Joachim Heinrich Sensemann and then Büttner. Each was questioned about his background, secular and religious, and why he had gone to Shekomeko in the first place. In addition, they were asked to spell out their duties, the manner in which they supported themselves, and whether they spoke the Indians' language. Very little, was their response to the last question. In the end, each of the brethren was asked to take the oaths, with Shaw and Büttner twice given the opportunity. To the man, they refused, although Büttner did offer "to take an affirmation."[70]

After the hearing, the Moravians were told to remain in the city, and on 11 August, Clinton directed them to return to Shekomeko and await further instructions.[71] Meanwhile, the colonial assembly was in the process of drawing up a bill to deal with the matter, which was passed and signed into law on 21 September. With the hazy title "An Act for Securing of his Majesties Government of New York," it nonetheless contained the pointed proviso that "no Vagrant Preacher, Moravian or Disguised Papist, shall Preach or Teach Either in Publick or Private without first takeing the Oaths appointed by this Act, and obtaining a Lycence from the Governour or Commander in Chief."[72] The Moravian Bishop Spangenberg was not to be fooled, describing the act as "directed against the Brethren who are at work among the Indians" and claiming that it "was published due to the malice of several preachers, who are called Presbyterians, and other politicians who carry on Jezebel's artifices contrary to all fundamental English principles."[73] On 27 November 1744 the governor directed the sheriffs of Albany, Ulster, and Dutchess counties to give notice to the Moravians "to desist from further teaching or preaching and to depart this province or that the said Act will be immediately put into Execution."[74] In early December, Henry Filkin and his undersheriff, along with three justices, rode to Shekomeko to do just that, and they also ordered the Moravians to appear in court in Poughkeepsie several days later.[75] On 9 January 1745 the congregation in Bethlehem received word from Büttner that the brethren had been ordered to leave Shekomeko.[76]

The response to the expulsion of the Moravians from Connecticut the previous year was twofold. First, now without a resident missionary, the Indians at Pachgatgoch made more frequent trips to Shekomeko so they could maintain their ties to the brethren. Second, local Protestant clergy attempted to take advantage of the void left by the Moravians, one of whom proposed to go to Pachgatgoch to preach and to baptize. The Indians refused the offer. Then, Reverend Marsh in Kent tried to persuade the Indians to attend his church—Shekomeko was too far away, he told them, and besides, he would give them money if they did.[77] The response from Gideon was blunt. Shekomeko was not too far away, his people did not want to hear what Marsh had to say, and the promise of money was an affront. "Well then, don't," was Marsh's spiteful reply; he also raised the specter that before long, there might not be any brethren at Shekomeko to whom the Indians could go.[78]

The Moravians, however, had not abandoned the Indians at Pachgatgoch, nor would they any time soon. Throughout the summer and fall of 1743 the Macks and Brothers Post and Büttner continued to cross the border into Connecticut to visit the Indians. Over the years that followed, so would others. For the most part, it seems, the Moravians followed the letter of the law and did not preach or conduct services of any kind. But they did spend their time talking with the Indians, most assuredly about spiritual matters, and on one occasion, they helped with the corn harvest, which provided yet another opportunity for close interaction. On 13 August, Büttner, accompanied by Jeannette Mack, slipped into Pachgatgoch just for the day, where he baptized Gideon's ailing wife, giving her the name Lazara. She would die at the end of September and be laid to rest in the woods a short distance from where the Moravians, a few years later, would build a mission house.[79]

In late December 1743, after conferring with his people, Gideon went to the Moravians to discuss the question of not having a teacher at Pachgatgoch. Gideon's solution, Büttner reported, was that either his people would move to Shekomeko, or, in an alternative assuredly reflecting a Moravian's coaching, he would dictate a letter to the Archbishop of Canterbury formally requesting that a brother be returned to Pachgatgoch. Shekomeko, though, would probably not support additional Indians, certainly not the large number of Gideon's people, and there is no doubt that surrounding colonists would not only take notice but be alarmed by any influx. Whether this, in fact, had any bearing on the final decision is unknown. A few days later, a delegation of Indians left for Bethlehem, intending while there to address the issue of soliciting the archbishop's assistance. Making the journey were Gideon; his betrothed daughter Maria; his son Joshua; a son-in-law Andreas; Lucas, the father of Rachel, who had married Brother Post the previous September; and Benjamin, an Indian from Pachgatgoch who may have been named Schabat.[80]

The party arrived in Bethlehem on 19 January 1744 and was immediately caught up in the religious and social goings-on, which included the wedding of Gideon's daughter to the Pachgatgoch Indian Samuel. There is no specific mention of discussions that might have taken place between Gideon and the brethren in regard to the need for a missionary at Pachgatgoch, yet an outcome of sorts was made known. Just before their return home in late February, "hope was given to our dear Pachgatgoch brethren and sisters that permission would be sought by Br. Spangenberg from the bishop in England for a brother to remain there to minister to them." It was left to Bishop David Nitschmann to contact Spangenberg, who at the time was in Europe. In March, in the company of a number of brethren, Nitschmann boarded the Moravian-owned ship *Little Strength* in New York. With him were Maria and Samuel.[81] The initiative taken by the congregation in Bethlehem to seek assistance from a person with connections was significant whether or not it bore fruit immediately, as it signaled the Moravians' first steps to exert political influence in London as a means of insuring a future for their mission effort in the colonies.

Unaware that his followers were about to be expelled from Shekomeko but nonetheless prompted by the passage of the September 1744 New York act and that in Connecticut the previous year, Bishop Zinzendorf went on the offensive. His first attempt was to appeal not only on principle but also on the basis of what he believed to be the law. Writing to the Lords of Trade in December 1744, he petitioned for the issuance of two directives. The purpose of the first would be to keep the "honest people" of America "from being chicaned with and plagued without the least reason & as if it were only *de gayeté de Coeur*."[82] The second was much less obtuse: "no body but least of all the Indians shall be hindered from joyning with any Protestant Church whatsoever," in accordance, he argued, with "measures taken for encouraging Foreigners to settle in the British Colonies in America."[83] There does not appear to have been an immediate response. However, in a letter to Governor Clinton the following June, the lords broached the topic of the New York statute. They told Clinton they had in hand a letter from Baron von Gersdorf, one of Zinzendorf's closest advisors and a relative. Writing on behalf of himself and the Moravian congregation in New York City, von Gersdorf had complained about the statute and then paid a personal visit to the lords in the company of two ministers of the church, where his objections were discussed further. Chiding Clinton about the fact that they had received a bundle of twenty-four other laws from New York's provincial secretary without the required letters of transmittal, the lords asked him to explain "what the behaviour of these Moravians has been in Yr province and whether any ill practices on their part gave occasion to there being inserted by name in the said Act."[84]

When the lords dispatched their letter to Clinton in late June 1745, the Moravians had already been told to leave Shekomeko. But the lords again wrote to Clinton in January 1746, apparently to remind him of von Gersdorf's complaint and repeating their desire to see a justification for the law's enactment. Clinton was polite in his reply, which was five months in the making, with the total delay now amounting to a full year. With it, he enclosed a committee report "upon the subject matter of your letter, to which I beg leave to refer, and hope it will prove satisfactory."[85] It was at this juncture that the Lords of Trade and the Moravians decided to conduct their negotiations far from New York and Clinton's dragging, if not designing, feet.

Goings and Comings

The order to expel the Moravians from Shekomeko, issued near the end of 1744, did not result in the immediate abandonment of the mission. On the contrary, it would take some time to pack up and transport their meager belongings to Bethlehem, and then, there was the question of the Indians. Still, the pressure on the Moravians to move was there, and it was not always in line with the letter of the law. Büttner voiced his concerns in late January 1745, writing: "'It is reported that they [local officials] are going to take everything away from us; if that is done, all right, then we shall have just as much as our Savior possessed on earth.'" Some two weeks later the congregation in Bethlehem was told that New York's governor had ordered Büttner, Rauch, and Mack imprisoned.[86] But by this time, Büttner was deathly ill and would succumb to chronic tuberculosis on 24 February 1745. His body was washed by Mack, Abraham, and Abraham's son Jonathan, dressed in clean clothes, and buried alongside the Indian child Lazara, who had been the first to be laid to rest in the small God's acre at Shekomeko. Büttner was in his twenty-eighth year.[87]

The piecemeal exodus of the Moravians from Shekomeko was not without incident. In the first week of March 1745, Martin and Jeannette Mack, their nine-month-old little girl, Post's wife Rachel, her infant son, and the pregnant and now widowed Margarethe Büttner left Shekomeko to begin what would be a trying journey back to Bethlehem. On crossing the river to Esopus, they were beset by what to all appearances was an altogether unhinged justice of the peace, one "Johanis Lameter" [Johannes Delameter], who seems to have been tipped off about their coming. "You dogs, you traitors!" he bellowed. "You pack of whores, you go there, you made a gang—that Mack—you shall not go there; I shall have you thrown in jail at once. . . . You keep the company of Negroes and *Wilden* [Indians]. What are you doing here with this *Wilden* [Indian woman]." Hustled off to a nearby tavern, the Moravians found themselves in front of several magistrates who asked them "several strange Questions and raged so much, that they continually stamped on the Ground and called us Traitors, Deceivers." Mack was asked to take the oaths, which he refused. At this point appeared a "Colonel Löbenstein," a member of the powerful Hudson Valley Livingston family, who allowed that Mack's party could continue its journey without further interference.[88] But the harassment continued. Outside the tavern stood the justice who had met them at the landing, still in a fury; he "tore open his coat, closed it again, and this he did 5 or 6 times one after another." Finally, he let them proceed, although their troubles did not end there. A short distance outside of town, the Moravians ran into a constable whose angry words drew an equally angry crowd. "Meanwhile, they got through it," reads the terse entry in the Bethlehem diary.[89]

The Moravians who remained at Shekomeko continued to quietly minister to the Indians, while assuredly looking over their shoulders. Not permitted by law to preach or hold services, they turned to their Indian acolytes, in particular Johannes, Isaac, and Jacob, to do their preaching for them, something they also attended to at Wechquadnach and Pachgatgoch. Others, such as Brothers Hagen and Bischoff, who spent lengthy periods of time at Shekomeko held love feasts, helped the Indians practice their singing, and met with them in conferences.[90] Yet, as Pyrlaeus tells it, there was still plenty of room for Satan to do his work, and a number of the Indians who had trouble resisting his temptations went spiritually adrift.[91]

In May 1745, Martinus Hoffman, who a short five years before had kindly directed Rauch to the Indians near Stissing Mountain, "let the Brethren at *Checomeko* know that they should not take anything from their house that is attached or nailed down. He [Hoffman] is one of the partners who are taking over the land of the Indians and everything built upon it and pretending it is theirs."[92] Reconciling itself to the fact that the days of the mission were now truly numbered, the congregation at Bethlehem resolved to do something about its Indian charges. Brothers Spangenberg, David Zeisberger, and John Bull were dispatched to Onondaga to request permission from the Iroquois to move the Indians from Shekomeko to Wyoming, at least those who were prepared to go.[93] They followed along behind Pennsylvania's Conrad Weiser, an acquaintance of Spangenberg who was on an involved diplomatic mission to end the war between the Iroquois and the Catawbas. The Moravians returned in July, and although the record of the council at Onondaga is silent on the question, permission for the move seems to have been granted. But for the Indians at Shekomeko, a move to Wyoming was out of the question. Instead, in the face of the disruption to their lives engendered by the closing of the mission, they strove to maintain their contacts with the Moravians by making frequent trips to Bethlehem. This produced fresh problems for the brethren, who found themselves accused of amassing the Indians for motives other than religious and secretly stashing firearms in coffins buried in the local cemetery, allegations which, reported Pyrlaeus, even drew the attention of the governor.[94]

In September 1745 the Moravians petitioned New York Colony and asked to return to Shekomeko, but the request was denied.[95] For their part, many of the Indians concluded that they could no longer stay without a guarantee that the Moravians would return. Moreover, the intense and increasingly hostile pressure to move coming from colonists who claimed the land on which Shekomeko stood quashed any hope of remaining. Taking the initiative, these Indians sent a delegation to Bethlehem to ask the brethren for refuge, and there they ran into an unexpected snag. The Moravians, they were told, could not care for them just then. They tried hard to convince the Indians to stay at home, knowing full well that this was asking too much. By early 1746, however, a solution was reached, and in April, a reported ten Indian families left the Hudson Valley and made their way to a temporary home at Friedenshütten, located just outside of Bethlehem. Before long, they were led to a section of land the Moravians had purchased, roughly thirty miles to the northwest at the junction of the Mahoning Creek and the Lehigh River, and began at once to clear and plant fields, hoping for a good harvest to get them through the coming winter. That summer the settlement, a dedicated Moravian mission, was fully operational. It was called Gnadenhütten. The knowledge that a more secure place for them to live now existed drew additional Indians from Shekomeko and nearby communities. On 25 July 1746 the Moravians officially closed the mission at Shekomeko, signing it over to the Indians. Those who had chosen not to travel to Pennsylvania would continue to live there and in the neighborhood.[96]

As things began to wind down in Shekomeko, life continued at Pachgatgoch and Wechquadnach. Brother Post and Rachel, the Indian woman from Pachgatgoch he had married, lived there from the closing of Shekomeko until late February 1747. Post passed the time much like the Indians among whom he was now considered family, making baskets, brooms, and canoes, and fishing. He also gathered flax and spun yarn for himself. These homely activities allowed him to engage in religious conversations and to monitor their effect, for many of the Indians going out to work for surrounding farmers were sorely tested by drink given them as wages. Such "worldly" matters also affected the spiritual fiber of some of the residents of Wechquadnach, who were said to have "fallen asleep." "Sometimes there is light and sometimes there is darkness," Post lamented.[97]

The departures, first of the Moravians and then of the Indian families from Shekomeko, created an uneasiness that extended into Pachgatgoch and Wechquadnach. Much of this, of course, was owing to the absence of the Moravians' spiritual guidance, which many of the Indians had come to rely on, although for most, it also meant having to cope with the loss of kith and kin who had followed the brethren. It was no surprise, then, when talk in these communities turned to the possibility of joining those in Pennsylvania. In late May 1747 Brother David Bischoff traveled to Pachgatgoch to escort a number of Indians to Bethlehem and thence to Gnadenhütten, speaking to several others at Shekomeko and Wechquadnach who expressed a wish to move as well. But a few days later, when Bischoff showed up at the spot on the Hudson River where they had agreed to assemble to begin the journey, there were no Indians to greet him, and he returned to Bethlehem.[98] The record suggests that disorganization among the Indians preparing to move prevented their meeting with the brother; apparently solving whatever problems there were, twenty-six of their number arrived in Bethlehem near the end of June.[99]

Shortly after their introduction to the congregation, the Indians announced that they had come not merely to visit but to stay, a point Gideon drove home with his declaration that he intended to remain in Gnadenhütten "for the rest of his life." But they quickly discovered that Bethlehem was not at all like home. The Moravians laid out to them the same offer they had made to the party that had come down from Shekomeko the previous year: each Indian family would go to Gnadenhütten, clear a piece of land, plant corn, and become self-sufficient, although for now, since the time for planting had passed, the brethren would provide for them. In the meantime, the Indian men were directed to go to Gnadenhütten and build a house for their families on a height of land called Gnadenhügel. The women and children would remain in Friedenshütten until this work was finished. Gnadenhütten, however, did not prove satisfactory to the Indians, and in September they removed to Nazareth.[100]

In early October, several of the leading men from Pachgatgoch, Shekomeko, and Wechquadnach sat down with the brethren. Framing their argument in terms they perhaps believed the Moravians would understand, they said that being at Gnadenhütten had caused them to "stray from their hearts," which in part explained why they had come to Nazareth. Nevertheless, now that they were there, they wanted to know if the brethren would give them land that they could call their own, and whether there would be a brother to look after their children. In reply, the Moravians insisted that the Savior wanted them in Gnadenhütten, where there was a place for them. They would not permit Nazareth to become an "*Indian-town*," although, conceding that the Indians were no longer able to hear the voice of the Savior, the brethren would, just this once, give them a parcel of land on which they could farm. For all that, this land would not be the Indians'.[101] Denied the opportunity to hold property and shackled to an economic system that was alien to them in its form and regimentation, not to mention the fact that the hunting was poor, many of the Indians from Pachgatgoch once again gathered their belongings and made the journey back to their former homes.[102]

Reestablishing Contact

On 24 June 1749, after an intensive lobbying effort by the church's senior clergy and politically connected friends in London, which had been initiated by Bishop

Spangenberg and then Zinzendorf himself in 1744, the Moravians were, by an act of parliament, declared to be members of the "ancient Protestant Episcopal Church." This edict, which substituted a "solemn Affirmation or Declaration" for the oath and set aside the requirement of military service on "Application to the Governor or Commander in Chief of the said Colony," permitted the brethren to again operate freely in New York and Connecticut. Given the dissolution of much of the Shekomeko community, however, the Moravians did not return there.[103] Instead, they focused their attention on the Housatonic Valley.

The pending return of the Moravians to Connecticut was preceded by the journey of Bishops Johannes von Watteville and Johann Christian Friedrich Cammerhoff to Shekomeko, Wechquadnach, and Pachgatgoch in December 1748, which had as its purpose the official rekindling of ties with the Indians in the region. At Shekomeko they found a handful of Indians living in a single large house close to the "barren places" where the mission village had stood, now partly sown in wheat. They visited God's acre and its more than a score of graves, among which was Brother Büttner's, and found them fenced and in good order, von Watteville observed. Wechquadnach, its four winter houses sited in the Oblong, west of Indian Pond, was clearly the busier of the two settlements. Living there, without the consent of the church, was Brother Post, who had returned to the area the previous March after the death of his wife Rachel in Bethlehem. He explained that he had come to be with the Indians until the congregation was in a position to care for them again. In a joint effort, Indians from Wechquadnach and Pachgatgoch had built a meeting house there, which also served as Post's residence.[104]

Many of the Indians Cammerhoff and von Watteville encountered were from the contingents that had removed to Gnadenhütten in 1746 and 1747 and then returned. Despite their largely negative experiences, a few expressed sentiments suggesting that they not only missed being in that Indian town but might consider moving back. The feelings of the others were mixed; this may have stemmed from the general uncertainty they faced about their future. This was clearly the case at Shekomeko, but also at Wechquadnach, where in addition to problems of simple survival, questions had been raised about the ownership of the land they were on. Whatever the details, it is generally recognized that the mid-eighteenth century was a very bad time for Indian people all through the

Northeast. Native communities were badly shaken by the combined assault of disease and famine, the ruin of alcohol abuse, and poverty—all of which were underwritten by colonization and the cant of civilization. King George's War had not helped, but much worse would be the havoc wrought by its transformation into the Seven Years' War, known in the colonies as the French and Indian War (1756–63). In this conflict many native groups would be beaten into submission, while others, most notably the six Iroquois nations, would resist and survive to fight another day. In southern New England, however, those who remained were little more than shadows of their former selves.

Shekomeko managed to hang on for a time, although virtually nothing is known of the day-to-day life of the small number of Indians who lived there or in the immediate area. With the out-migration of its remaining residents to Gnadenhütten in 1753, Wechquadnach would cease to exist as an Indian community.[105] At Pachgatgoch, things were entirely different. The promise made by von Watteville and Cammerhoff in 1748 to send the brethren to the Indians was followed the next year by visits from Cammerhoff and Gottlob Pezold, David Bruce, Nathanael Seidel, and Bernhard Adam Grube, as well as Mattheus Renz and Abraham Büninger. By late 1749 Pachgatgoch again had a resident missionary.[106]

Locating Pachgatgoch

A remarkably full description of Pachgatgoch can be constructed from the diaries, letters, and travel journals left by the Moravians.[107] These documents cover the period from January 1743, when the Macks made their first journey there, to October 1770 and the official closing of the mission.[108] But there are gaps and irregularities in the record. Expelled from Connecticut in mid-1743, the Moravians were not officially permitted to minister there until 1749. As we have noted, however, they continued to visit from their base at Shekomeko, and also from the church's home congregation in Bethlehem. From early 1750 until the end of July 1763, the record for Pachgatgoch is essentially continuous, with the few short interruptions occurring during changeovers in missionaries or when a brother would return to Bethlehem for a rest. There is one exception: there are diaries missing for the period of November 1757 to March 1758. A more serious problem exists for the last seven years of the Pachgatgoch mission, for which only one diary has been located following searches in the

Moravian Archives in Bethlehem and the Unity Archives in Herrnhut. What survives otherwise from this period are scattered correspondence by the resident missionaries and other records containing references to them, namely, Joachim Sensemann from 1763 to 1766, and then Edward Thorp from 1766 until 1770.[109] After 1770, Francis and Anna Böhler, the lone Moravians serving what was a large colonial congregation at Sichem, near Indian Pond, paid the occasional visit, which ended with their recall to Bethlehem in 1772.[110] On 5 April 1773 Brother John Ettwein traveled to Pachgatgoch, where he found "the church and all the huts quite empty. In one hut outside the place, I found Johanna, Gideon's daughter, and Josua's daughter. Josua died 2. years ago, Samuel has moved to Stokbridge, and some wish to migrate to the Ohio. Most of the time the place is quite empty."[111]

The earliest surviving, if brief, portrait of the setting of Pachgatgoch is found in a letter from the Moravian Gottlob Büttner to a colleague in early 1743. Pachgatgoch, he wrote somewhat poetically, "is in a beautiful location; it is entirely surrounded by mountains and rocks, as if enclosed by walls."[112] Almost six years later, Cammerhoff furnished a more expansive description.[113] He and his companions had come from near Shekomeko, and after wending their way down Macedonia Brook, they reached the Housatonic River on 20 December. Moving south along the river on the west side, the party came to "Pachgatgoch, that is, the place where they [the Indians] have their summer huts and fields," making note of thirteen "huts," "most of which are still new and quite spacious, and there are also several houses built on English footing[s], with fireplaces."[114] The Moravians visited a few of the Indians, one of whom "lives in a pleasant house built in the English *fashion*." They continued on to where, it seemed, most of the Indians were residing at the time, "in their winter huts 3 miles farther down on the *kill*."[115]

> And then we set out right away toward the winter huts, continued down along the *kill* past very large rocks, and then finally came to the place where they have encamped behind a rock. Martha, Gideon's wife, noticed us first, welcomed us in front of her hut, and was so overjoyed that she immediately began to weep quite heartily for joy.[116] Gideon also joined us at once, being very glad to see

us, and led us into his hut, where he had fixed up everything quite
beautifully and had laid out the skin of a panther for us on which
we were to take a seat.

Gideon made a count of the Indian people there, telling Cammerhoff that there
were sixty, "big and small."

The next day Cammerhoff and the others were taken to a falls in the river
near the winter huts, "where the water forces itself through the narrow rocks
with a loud roar, shooting down from very high up, which the Indians call
Sasaksuk."[117] Cammerhoff also was shown a structure "that the Indians generally build for their boys to sleep in, where they, to wit, usually make a low
hut from brushwood with earth on top, almost in the shape of a sweating oven
[sweat house], only larger and more spacious."[118]

The division of the Pachgatgoch community into "winter huts" and "summer huts" is significant to an understanding of how and where the people there
placed themselves on the land, and for what purposes. We assume that the
Moravians learned of this named distinction from the Indians. We also assume that the "winter" and "summer" designations had their origins early on
in the Indians' seasonal occupation of principally the west side of the Housatonic. Based on the information Cammerhoff provides in which he mentions
going past "very large rocks," the high and sheer rock faces abutting the river
in the southeastern corner of the Schaghticoke Reservation, the winter huts
were most likely on the flat north of Bulls Bridge.[119]

Where the winter huts might have been located before 1748 is unknown, although there is a hint in the record. In early 1752 the resident missionary was at
the winter huts when he was asked by an Indian to go with him "across the ice
to the other brethren and sisters to visit them now as well." Several weeks earlier, this same Moravian had gone "into the winter huts on this and the other
side of the river to visit."[120] One possible location for these Indians was on the
flat on the opposite side of the river, just to the northeast of where we believe
the winter huts were, and where they may have been built in previous years.

By late 1751, however, the site of the winter huts on the west side of the river
had become permanent, and it was thereafter used as a place of year-round residence for many of the Indians at Pachgatgoch. That September the Indians had

gathered in Gideon's house at the summer huts to discuss where they would build their winter huts for the approaching season. They had come "to be all of one mind . . . and tomorrow [they] wanted to choose the suitable place for this purpose." The next day, accompanied by the missionary, the Indians went out to search for a location but "along the way they changed their minds and resolved to make a sledge-path [so] that during the winter they are able to bring the wood down from the mountain."[121] The availability of and access to firewood appears to have been of primary concern in selecting a site for the winter huts. With the building of the sledge-path, which involved the entire community, took six weeks to complete, and insured for the Indians a supply of firewood, a considerable number could remain at the summer huts while others lived at the winter hut site downriver. "Often we had to move very large stones out of the way," explained Brother Abraham Büninger. "Anyone who sees it will be amazed that the Indians ventured to make a path up this rocky mountain."[122]

The Moravians provided an early account of "winter huts" in a context different from that presented thus far, that is, as one of the two permanent residential loci of Pachgatgoch. At the end of 1751 Brother Sensemann wrote that he had gone "on the mountain" to visit a sick Indian woman "and the other brethren and sisters" living there.[123] For the next eight years the diaries are silent in regard to similar mentions, until Brother Bernhard Grube reported that two Indian women had moved into their winter house six miles from Pachgatgoch and were planning to return in the spring. Several days later, "Our dear old Gideon moved with his family into his winter house on the mountain, because here [at Pachgatgoch] it is much too difficult for him to go and get the [fire] wood."[124] Over the next few winters, a number of other Indians also moved to the mountain and returned in the spring, "for the warm weather is now beginning to set in."[125]

The placement of the community's residents in chiefly two settlements—the winter huts and the summer huts—distanced from each other reduced the extractive pressure on nearby but limited sources of firewood. At about the same time, the Moravians ceased employing the designation "summer huts" but continued with their use of "winter huts." A decade later, the terms "Lower Schaghticoke" ["*das unttere* Scatticok"], "lowermost town," and "lower town" appear, with the diarist recording that the first was a term "the English" applied to the winter hut location.[126] What is important, however, is that the name "Pachgatgoch," and at times "Schaghticoke," was applied in an inclusive manner, embracing the locations of the "winter huts," the "summer huts," and everything in between.[127]

The probable site of the summer huts can be determined by taking into account several lines of evidence. In 1748 Cammerhoff placed the huts near the Indians' fields, which would have been on relatively flat, arable land. There are frequent mentions in the diaries of local colonial farmers bringing in their teams to plow both the Indians' and the Moravians' fields. On one occasion, following a particularly heavy rain, a farmer was unable to plow because of "the great amount of water on the low land," which clearly indicates that the fields were on a floodplain.[128] This broadly limits the area of the summer huts to that stretch of the Housatonic River between the mouth of Macedonia Brook downriver to the second rivulet running out of the mountains south of Thayer Brook.

Other details useful in siting the summer huts are found in the same diary in which, during the harsh winter of 1761, Brother Mack wrote that a storm had deposited "nearly 2 feet of snow, which lay pretty much that deep also on my entire brook."[129] As will be established later, the area of the summer huts was where the Moravians erected several structures of their own and had their kitchen gardens. For reasons also to be explained later, the brook Mack mentions is most likely the first rivulet south of Thayer Brook. In addition, in 1754, "the [Indian] brethren helped Samuel put his house in a different spot, because the old one is standing too close to the public road for him."[130] Samuel's house was presumably on the mountain side of the road that runs along the Housatonic River between Kent and Bulls Bridge, roughly following that shown on the map. The Indians used this road to reach the winter huts and other locations, but it also was a thoroughfare for colonists. To be on the road's east side probably would have placed Samuel's house on a low-lying floodplain ten or more feet down a steep bank, a rather unlikely setting.

Evidence that appears to firmly establish the location of the summer huts is found in a sequence of events beginning with a May 1752 petition of the Pachgatgoch Indians to the Connecticut assembly asking for a piece of land south of the mouth of Macedonia Brook and lying adjacent to the Housatonic River. They wished to use it for planting corn, and the hill behind it as a wood lot. In response, the assembly granted the Indians the whole of lot 25 and one-half of lot 24 of the colony's lands west of the Housatonic River. In 1755 the remaining or northern half of lot 24 was purchased by one of Kent's early settlers, who appropriated more than his share, thus depriving the Indians of their use of "a Certain Notch in the Mountains which is the Outlet or Walk for us into ye woods."[131] This "Notch in the Mountains," the only notch or cut anywhere near the probable location of Pachgatgoch, is that through which Thayer Brook flows.

Thayer Brook formed the northern limit of Pachgatgoch in the mid-eighteenth century. The lands to its north were in private hands. Thus, based on what we have presented to this point, the most likely location of the summer huts and the Moravian mission is on the interval of land between Thayer Brook and the first rivulet to its south, perhaps extending for a short distance downriver from this rivulet. This determination of the location of the summer huts and the mission is supported by an early and credible source that states: "About a mile and a half below" the Episcopal Church in Kent, "on the opposite [west] side of the river, the Moravian Church or mission house was standing 30 or 40 years since, near the house of Mr. Raymond."[132] This point is midway between the aforementioned brooks.

A final note on the summer huts. This locus of the Pachgatgoch community where the Moravians, with Indian help, built their mission, appears to have been at least a semipermanent settlement dating to the time of the initial move of the Indians from Weatinock to the west side of the Housatonic River in 1736. "The first land that they [the Indians] cultivated has been planted now for 17 consecutive years," wrote Brother Büninger in 1754.[133] With the knowledge that the summer huts were near the Indians' fields, it may be assumed, in the absence of evidence to the contrary, that their location there dates to about 1736.

From what we believe to be the relatively secure site of the summer huts and the Moravian mission, that of the winter huts can be reaffirmed without resorting to circular reasoning by using distance measurements provided in the diaries. In January 1761 Brother Mack reported that he had spent a day "visiting the Indians in the winter huts at [the] Bulls," the home of the colonial family from which Bulls Bridge derives its name, and that "most of it [firewood] is now brought from 1 1/2 miles away, down at the Indians' winter huts; presently nothing can be rolled down the mountains due to the deep snow."[134] Bulls Bridge is on the map. The place where the firewood was being collected was probably on the sloping land near the river later made part of the Schaghticoke Indian Reservation. In the spring of that year Mack announced the birth of a son to an Indian couple who lived "2 miles from here [the summer huts], in Lower Schaghticoke," and the next February, Brother Sensemann "visited the brethren and sisters at the river, two miles down."[135] These distances place the winter huts past where the firewood had been collected, past the sheer rock faces in the southeastern corner of the Schaghticoke Reservation, and on the flat just below the reservation's southern boundary.

The Indian Settlement

There is no more concise and to-the-point statement on the variety of dwellings built and used by the Indians at Pachgatgoch than that of Brother Eberhardt writing in 1756: "Today the brethren helped [the Indian] Br. Martin build a new *wigwam*, just as they had earlier helped Samuel lay up his house, and had helped re-erect Solomon's *frame* house that the wind had knocked over this spring."[136] For all this, the Moravians provide only very limited descriptions of these dwellings or how they were constructed.

On his visit to Pachgatgoch in the winter of 1748, Bishop Cammerhoff mentioned an Indian house built in the "English fashion." We take his observation to mean that this was a bark-covered half-pole frame structure with vertical or near vertical side walls and perhaps a pitched roof. The drawing of Shekomeko made by Brother John Hagen in 1745 depicts a number of such dwellings, complete with smoke holes suggesting a single, central hearth, although at Pachgatgoch, the Indian Andreas's house is reported to have had two hearths.[137] The houses are shown with gabled ends, below which are doors. The roofs of several houses appear to be covered with sheets of bark running from peak to eave.[138] Stone footings, structural features that are found elsewhere in eighteenth-century native southern New England, were incorporated in a few of the Indians' houses in Pachgatgoch, whether half-pole frame or wigwam.[139] Wigwams, another house type at Pachgatgoch, were also covered with sheets of bark. There is no evidence that woven mats, a commonly found covering, were so used.

The remaining, wholly native structures at Pachgatgoch are the boys' hut that Cammerhoff described during his 1748 visit, and the frequently mentioned sweat houses, which figured prominently in the lives of Indians. The records suggest that there was a sweat house at both the winter and the summer hut locations; unfortunately, no information is given about their placement or the details of their construction. Presumably they would have been near running water, as was historically the case in the region.

Perhaps following the Moravians' lead, two Indians are reported to have built log houses, and another a frame house, evidently some form of post-and-beam construction. That the Indians helped "lay up" [*aufblocken*] Samuel's house, mentioned earlier, is a reference to laying up hewn logs. Like Samuel's house, the Indian Joshua's frame house was roofed with wooden shingles. It also had a stone chimney. No other details of construction for either the log or frame houses are provided, although they may in part be inferred from what is known of the building methods of the Moravians.

The Moravian Mission

Initially, it seems, the Moravians may have lived in bark-covered houses. "I worked on my winter house," Brother Büninger reported. "I have had to build it twice now, for I had torn it down in the spring, taking of it what was usable for the summer house."[140] The Indian Jeremias helped put on the roof, and a month later, Büninger went out and cut wood suitable for a floor, offering no other details. But on 9 April 1750, the Moravians and the Indians began constructing a building that would serve them for the next two decades as a residence, a place to hold meetings, and a schoolhouse. Two years later, a larger room was added that they sometimes referred to as the "hall" or the "church."

The first building was of logs that had been felled and then rolled down the mountain to the area of the summer huts. Brother Büninger reported it being fourteen by sixteen feet. Indian men first laid up the walls and framed the roof, which was probably covered with sheets of bark, while women carried in water and clay that had been mixed together and used it to chink the firewall, the roof, and around the outside. That August, the Indians helped Büninger build a catted chimney. The Indians also helped split chestnut logs into rough planks for the main floor. Büninger intended to use planks that he had split himself to lay a floor in the loft, but deciding that they would not work to his satisfaction, he went to Kent to get what were evidently saw-cut boards, which he and several Indians floated down the river to the summer huts. The following year he purchased glass from a merchant a short distance below Bulls Bridge to close up at least two window openings in the house. In a humorous episode that took place during a visit to Pachgatgoch in 1760, the Moravian George Sölle recounted being awakened one night by the sound of breaking glass. Thinking that someone was about to crawl through the window, he called out, "Who's there?" His answer was the fading gait of the perpetrator, "an old Indian horse" that brazenly returned the next night and broke another pane.[141]

In fall 1751 Büninger concluded that the log structure was not large enough and that an additional room was needed. Under the supervision of Brother Christian Frölich, construction would begin the following spring before it was time to plant the fields. Brother Rundt described the scene:

> Several brethren from the winter huts were called here for assistance, and with that, they marched into the woods. . . . In the afternoon an extraordinarily delightful procession of Indians could be seen. Our whole town (I should like to say) — young and old — had gone, without having been pressed by us, onto the high mountain behind our house, to carry hither from the woods there the wood for our construction, that which previously had been cut down and belongs to the Indian Brother Christian, as well as the wood that was cut by the brethren today, and now they came marching down all at once. This was delightful to watch, as each one came trundling down with joy, carrying hither his large and small pieces on his back. Many a large beam needed to be carried by about 8 to 10 men.[142]

First the sills were laid, Brother Rundt later wedging stones under what was apparently a low side to maintain a level. Then the workers raised the walls, which had been assembled from joined wood. The Indians made it a point to remark that this was the first house that they had built in this manner. Architectural features included framed glass windows built into each of the three walls, shutters, a split shingle roof, clapboard siding, hung doors, and a boarded interior. The Moravians delivered the first sermon in the addition on 21 May 1752; the room was barely large enough for the eighty Indians, not including the children, who were present.

There are indications in the diaries that sometime after the attached log-and-frame buildings were constructed, the Moravians may either have added a cellar or built yet another house with a cellar for which there is no description. It is difficult to resolve this question because of the significant gap in the records, mentioned earlier, from November 1757 to March 1758. In any case, the Moravians were worried that if the cellar wall or walls were not taken care of, this house might collapse on them.

The Moravians, at times assisted by Indian people, erected several other structures at their mission. In 1751 Brother Büninger laid up a pigsty that he covered with a bark roof. The next year Sensemann, a baker by trade, decided to build an oven so that the Moravians would not have to go to local colonists to buy bread. And in 1756, several Indians cut poles and peeled bark, which they used to build a new wigwam, repair another, and to help the Moravians put up some sort of a structure to use as a kitchen. Finally, before 1760, a cow barn had been built at Pachgatgoch.

Death at Pachgatgoch

Indian people at Pachgatgoch died in all of the ways and manners familiar to the human experience. Infant mortality was high, and so were rates of death in early childhood as influenza and other maladies took their toll. Writing from Stockbridge in January 1747, John Sergeant observed: "Near half that are born die in infancy or childhood, which I attribute to their manner of living, and want of suitable medicines in time of sickness. The grown people abundantly die with consumptions, begun with violent colds."[143] Tuberculosis was not uncommon in native communities, and neither were dysentery, measles, smallpox, typhus, syphilis, salmonellosis, and other forms of food poisoning. Deaths due to drowning, injuries, or, on occasion, violent altercations also occurred.

The diary entry for 12 May 1755 reads: "In the afternoon, Br. Christian [Seidel] had Brothers Gideon and Joshua give him the names of the brown brethren and sisters who are lying here in our God's acre, and made a drawing of God's acre."[144] This drawing of the cemetery at Pachgatgoch affords an intimate look into the community and its genealogical and demographic profiles, while at the same time reflecting the influence of Moravianism on its social fabric (see fig. 4). Still, the story of life and death it tells is incomplete.

There are forty-eight burials depicted on the drawing, nearly all of which are labeled with the name of the person interred. The three lines of graves plus the single grave, numbers 1–34, are, with three known exceptions, those of baptized Indians.[145] They are arranged in rough correspondence with the "choir system," the stratification of the Moravian community according to age, sex, and marital status, which would vanish in the American church under the secularizing influence of the nineteenth century. Von Watteville described a similar arrangement for Shekomeko's God's acre in 1748: "the newer graves [were] right nice and orderly separated by the choirs, as at our other congregations."[146]

Burials 1–15 are of male children; 16 is the headman Gideon.[147] With the exception of one female child, the deaths recorded for burials 17–25 are of older girls and adult women, married, unmarried, and widowed. Documentation is lacking for three of the burials in the row numbered 27–34. The remainder is a mix of female children and probably older girls and single sisters; however, number 31 may be that of a stillborn boy. Although graves in Moravian cemeteries are traditionally marked by a stone laid flat on the ground, none are mentioned for Pachgatgoch. Many of the dead were buried in wooden coffins the Indians made themselves. The last recorded interment shown took place on 10 August 1760, demonstrating that there was at least some attempt to keep the drawing up to date for five years after it was made.[148]

The burials on the top third of the drawing are of unbaptized Indians. Included in this section of the cemetery is Gideon's mother, who, together with the headman and the deceased children of Joshua, Martin, and Chuse, his three sons, represent four generations of this family at Pachgatgoch. Buried "about a couple of 100 paces" behind the Moravians' house "in the woods" were two baptized women: Lazara (d. 1743), Gideon's wife, and his daughter Maria, Samuel's wife (d. 1744).[149]

Of the forty-eight burials on the drawing, twenty-seven of the deaths they represent are recorded in the mission diaries or in the Pachgatgoch catalog of baptisms. The remaining twenty-one are otherwise undocumented. There are an additional forty-five deaths recorded in the diaries or in the catalog absent corresponding graves on the drawing.[150] Nothing is known about deaths that may have occurred when Brother Sensemann was at Pachgatgoch from 1763 to 1766. But even if we assume that no one in the community died over this three-year period, there is nonetheless a minimum number of ninety-three baptized and unbaptized persons buried in God's acre.[151] This figure must be regarded as conservative, not only because of the absence of information from 1763 to 1766, but also because it is possible that the deaths of other Indians in the community, especially the unbaptized, may have gone unrecorded. Moreover, it is likely, though not proven, that Indians who died in the community after the closing of the mission in 1770, and until the move to the present-day reservation at the turn of the century, a period of thirty years, continued to be buried in this God's acre.

The location of God's acre is not known, although there are a few clues. The Moravians' diaries suggest that it was near the mission station, a relatively short walk from their "hall" or "church." This fits the pattern found at other Moravian Indian missions, where the cemetery is just outside the settlement.[152] In summer 1859, members of the Moravian Historical Society traveled into eastern New York and the Housatonic Valley of Connecticut to trace the path taken by their brethren more than a century earlier. Reaching Kent, they were joined by several local men, including John Raymond (1793–1867), whose farm was just north of the reservation; Wells Beardsley (1770–1860), a physician and formerly Kent's postmaster; Alden Swift (1793–1867), whose grandfather Reuben was the state-appointed overseer of the Schaghticoke Tribe for a short time in the early 1770s; and Rufus Fuller (1809–1881), who had been serving as overseer since 1852. The party first rode to "the Pachgatgoch place, two miles to the southwest of Kent," which once again sites the mission between Thayer Brook and the first rivulet to its south. Continuing down the west bank of the river, they soon reached "the 'Reserve,'" where they spent some time in conversation with Eunice Mahwee, Gideon's aged granddaughter.[153]

On the party's return to Kent from the reservation, Beardsley "pointed out the site of the Pachgatgoch graveyard, lying in a meadow near the bank of the river, on the farm of Mr. John Raymond."[154] In assessing Beardsley's credibility as a witness, we note that he was a prominent citizen of Kent who had been born the year the mission closed. His first wife Chloe's father Barzilla was the son of Reuben Swift, a former overseer of the Indians. However, Beardsley was an elderly man in 1859—in a few months, he would turn eighty-nine—and it had been six decades since the Indians had lost their lands at the summer huts where the God's acre was located.

As Reichel reports it, Beardsley told him that the cemetery was "near the bank of the river." This would put it somewhere on the floodplain on the east side of the road that stretches from a point just north of the reservation boundary to about Thayer Brook; that is, between the winter huts, and the summer huts and mission. This area is today low-lying ground, most of it sitting below a ten-foot contour line that also marks the steep face of a terrace above the present floodplain. Although we recognize that the present river surface is somewhat higher than it was in the mid-eighteenth century, there is no doubt that the floodplain was low-lying ground then. As the Moravians noted, a heavy rainstorm had once soaked the fields to such an extent that they could not be plowed.[155] Placing a cemetery where it might be subject to periodic flooding, or at the very least, where the water table was high, would be an unusual choice.[156]

In addition, an unknown portion of the floodplain was cultivated by the Indians, the Moravians, and, somewhat late in the life of the mission, neighboring farmers. By 1752 the Moravians were farming two plots of land, about two acres in all, which had been allotted them by the Indians. The Indians' fields must have been much more extensive. To illustrate, in spring 1761, "Five plows from the neighborhood came here to plow the land for the Indians for planting corn, and spent nearly the entire week here going about this work."[157] By 1765 local farmers were cultivating a part of the Indians' land in exchange for plowing their fields.[158] Despite this activity, sections of the floodplain may have been left untouched, and Beardsley may have been correct in pointing out the cemetery somewhere near the bank of the river. Of course, if Beardsley was mistaken, then other areas of conceivably higher potential should be considered; for example, the raised section of land on the ten-foot contour east of the road, just to the south of the first rivulet, and the area west of the road below this rivulet.

Although no obvious signs of the eighteenth-century God's acre remain, another cemetery, located directly east of the notation "Indian Reservation" on the map, west of the road, is still in use by Schaghticoke people. Here there are more than fifty grave markers, most of which are plain, upright fieldstones suggesting eighteenth- to mid-nineteenth-century interments. There is, though, a late-nineteenth-century description of this cemetery mentioning that the graves were "mostly marked by wooden head-boards, and many have not even this memorial."[159] A smaller number of headstones are inscribed with dates of death ranging from 1860 to the present. By all accounts, this cemetery was at one time closer to the river. But when the construction of the hydropower plant at Bulls Bridge began in the early 1900s, the operation of which would inundate lower-lying lands, the burials were allegedly moved to their present location. For many years, however, there have been questions about what exactly was moved: grave stones and the burials they marked, or just the stones, if there had been any in the first place. In any event, it remains to be fully determined what the plain headstones in this cemetery represent. We would only add that, for a variety of reasons, we do not presently believe this cemetery contains burials from a time before the arrival of the Moravians.

Deaths most assuredly had occurred in the Pachgatgoch community between the move of the Indians across the river in 1736 and the establishment of the God's acre in about 1749. The average number of deaths per year in Pachgatgoch, calculated from the ninety-three deaths recorded from 1749 to 1770, discussed earlier, is about four. Thus, over the thirteen-year period from 1736 to 1749, there could be as many as fifty deaths and burials that are unaccounted for, excepting those of Lazara and Maria in 1743 and 1744. This assumes a relatively stable population, which is known to have remained at around one hundred for much of the life of the mission.[160]

With the knowledge that from Pachgatgoch's beginnings its people resided chiefly in two areas, the winter huts and the summer huts, there arises the prospect that there also are burials at these two locations dating to before the mission period. What has been reported on native mortuary practices in southern New England generally, and western Connecticut and southeastern New York specifically, reflects a pattern commonly found elsewhere in the Northeast: Indian people buried their dead in proximity to where they lived. For the residents of Pachgatgoch, the constraints placed on their land base, or the reduction thereof owing to the encroachments of colonists, would have insured that this was the case. Although the Moravians often reported that the bodies of persons who had died at the winter huts were carried upriver to the mission house, where they were sometimes laid out and mourned and then taken in a procession to the cemetery, we are hesitant to conclude that this was native practice.[161] It is likely that before the establishment of the God's acre, the Indians buried their dead at both the winter and summer huts rather than using a single communal cemetery.

This brings us back to that second, present-day cemetery. The historical record suggests that its original site, closer to the river, before the construction of the hydropower plant, may not have come into use until the beginning of the nineteenth century. There is no doubt that Indians remained in the vicinity of the summer huts following the closure of the mission and Brother Ettwein's visit in 1773, although for the same period of time nothing is known of the situation at the winter huts. And while we cannot be sure that the Indians continued to bury their dead in or near the God's acre after the mid-1770s, there is no obvious reason to conclude otherwise. What is known is that in 1801, the whole of the Indians' lands at and surrounding the summer huts and the former mission was sold, compelling them to withdraw downriver to the area of what is today the Schaghticoke Reservation.[162] This loss of land would have denied the Indians access to the God's acre.

Life in Pachgatgoch

Understanding what went on in Pachgatgoch is possible only through a reading of the materials left by the Moravians, who lived, worked, and worshipped with the Indians for much of the mid-eighteenth century.[163] There is no comparable Indian record of this encounter or of their world as they knew it. Unfortunately for the ethnologically minded, the brethren did not have a lot to say about native kinship and marriage, leadership and status, religion and ideology, ceremony and ritual, medicine and curing, or death and mourning. And despite what had to have been their exotic mien, there is scarcely a whisper about the Indians' dress, hair styles, ornamentation, tattooing, or physical appearance.[164] The lack of curiosity displayed in the Moravians' writings—what is left unsaid—is a bit of a surprise, especially considering that outside of the experience of a few brethren at the Shekomeko mission, Pachgatgoch was for many a first-time venture with Indian people of any persuasion. Yet at other times and other places, the Moravians did pay attention. On a visit to Shekomeko in fall

1745, for example, two brethren walked into the mission house to find it "full of Indians, some in Bead [bed] some, Eating, some painted and Dressed out with Beads and Feathers."[165] At the funeral of Michael, a Minisink Indian who had died in Bethlehem in 1758 and who had resided in Shekomeko when the mission was in full swing, it was reported that

> he also had (as one still sees on the very old Indians) a face with figures painted in gunpowder so that it [sic] would not come off, and his cheerful look with the figures gave a pleasing appearance in the coffin. The figures that he had on his face were a large snake on the ~~one~~ right side at the temple, and ~~from~~ starting at the lips a pole that [ran] between the eyes and nose and up the forehead onto the head, on which pole there was every quarter of an inch something of a round figure, like a scalp. On the left cheek he had 2 spears crosswise, one over the other, and at the jaw line the head of a wild boar. All of it done very neatly.[166]

Aside from what the Moravians provided about Indian economy, housing, and material culture—what survives are mostly mentions without description—we are left, in general, with impressions woven around a chronicle of religious goings-on. This is not news in the narrative of Indian-colonial relations or mission histories from the eighteenth-century Northeast, where accounts of native communities are routinely absent the particulars of cultural practices. Still, the Moravians must have known something of the people they chose to serve, even if they often failed to report what they saw, for some level of understanding of the Indians was necessary if their mission was to succeed. In this circumstance, it is entirely possible that the Moravians had decided whatever differences in worldview and demeanor there did exist would neither impede their religious message nor prevent them from putting the Indians on the right path. In the final analysis, these differences may not have been considered worthy of comment.

To complete this picture, however, it is not known to what extent or how strongly the "traditional" cultural practices of the Indians at Pachgatgoch were likely to capture the Moravians' notice, although the brethren were quite vocal about what pained them most. A working assumption must be that their cultural system—subsistence, settlement, and sociopolitical behavior—was different to an unknown degree from what had existed in the Housatonic Valley at an earlier point in time. This is almost certainly the case counting forward from the heady days of first sustained contact with Europeans in about 1630, when Indians in southern New England are described as living in relatively small, autonomous farming communities led by one or possibly more headmen. Both patrilineal and matrilineal descent systems seem to have been present, although the emphasis on horticulture suggests the prevalence of the latter.[167] Marriage preferences and postnuptial residence rules are only hinted at; the same can be said for social units beyond the extended or compound family, such as lineages, clans, or phratries. Somewhat more is known about cosmology, religion, and ritual, yet many questions remain.[168]

It is likely, given the history of decisive and even inducing factors such as depopulation, loss of land, and shifts in economy, all of which accompanied the enveloping nature of colonial expansion, that by the early eighteenth century, native cultural systems had changed, but the Moravians provide precious little information on this count. On the whole, they leave the impression that the community at Pachgatgoch consisted of several related, extended families rather informally organized, which, in most ways, practiced an economy that was not very different from that of their colonial neighbors. But the diaries contain more than data meant to fit formalist ethnological classifications. Their portrayals of the almost daily, blow-by-blow accounts of activities in and around Pachgatgoch, the broad historical context in which they occurred, and the people who participated in them—Indian, Moravian, and colonial—provide one of the most intimate pictures of community dynamics known for the region from any time period.

Although the Indians and Moravians at Pachgatgoch stood culturally in contrast to one another, their dissimilarities were partially conciliated by the social intimacy that arose from their being virtually in each other's laps for the period of the mission. Moreover, they exhibited affinities that may have rendered the conduct and attitude of the brethren not only familiar to Indians but also understandable and ultimately acceptable. At the same time, it is conceivable that consciously or unconsciously, the brethren took some comfort in observing these affinities among the Indians. In the most obvious example, Moravians organized their religious communities into collectives or sodalities known as "choirs." Here church members were assembled into groups and assumed their roles and responsibilities on the basis of age, gender, and marital status: children, boys and unmarried men, girls and unmarried women, married people, widows and widowers. The full range of Moravian behaviors, experiences, and obligations took place within these segregated social units.[169]

A less doctrinaire variant of this kind of social organization was widespread among American Indian people, including those residing at Pachgatgoch. As with most nonstate polities, native communities customarily exhibited a relatively well-defined gender-driven division of labor and forms of age-grading within the general population. Among adult Indians, the roles assumed by women and men were distinct. The obligations of seventeenth-century native women in southern New England, for example, included childcare, food gathering and preparation, and making clothing. Men hunted, fished, and took part in raids and warfare. This division of labor persisted at Pachgatgoch into the eighteenth century, although by then the variety of tasks had changed, both by choice and through necessity in the face of decades of contact.

The existence of the choir system may provide the best explanation for the inattention Moravians paid to native kinship, the rudiment upon which the workaday duties, rights, and reciprocal obligations that permeated all aspects of native life were ascribed. Beyond segregating members of Moravian congregations, choir living deemphasized kinship ties and, for all intents and purposes, abolished the nuclear family.[170] If the brethren viewed the community at Pachgatgoch in the same fashion, and there is clear evidence in the record that they did, this may have acted to mask or make irrelevant the manner in which the Indians recognized kin and kindred.[171]

There may be an additional set of factors at work to explain the general absence of detail on Indian life at Pachgatgoch. As early as 1738, brethren dispatched to the missions were cautioned against filling their diaries with descriptions of the difficulties they might encounter or how bad things were going while among the "heathen." Zinzendorf's order issued from Marienborn two years later, also in regard to keeping diaries, emphasized recording matters of religious import, including the texts and spiritual topics addressed and instances where the Savior would reveal something new to a person. And in 1756,

Bishop Spangenberg made explicit his preferences for what should be included in diary entries, wanting to know more about the children's religious growth, what went on in the occasions, and how the Indians declared themselves in preparation for communion, matters of this sort being "a sweetmeat" to him. "I also wish," he wrote, "that the work of the Holy Spirit, that one observes every day when occupying oneself with the souls, is noted," adding that the diaries "must not be too *general* rather the *specialia* [Latin: particulars] make them pleasant and edifying for reading."[172] Insofar as diary keeping was concerned, these church leaders were directing that religious matters were to be given priority, suggesting that any other information would be viewed as incidental or nonessential.

In certain situations, men and women joined together to form work groups. Both sexes tended village fields, planting corn and beans, adding later a few new crops such as grains and root vegetables. Fishing, too, appears to have been a communal activity, although there are indications that fishing parties were sometimes composed exclusively of men. When the Moravians arrived, the Indians at Pachgatgoch were already deeply involved in a cash economy by means of two traditional pursuits made easier and more efficient by metal tools: woodworking and basket making. Teams of men or women or of both sexes were mobilized to go into the forest and nearby swamps to cut and gather materials used to fashion splint and perhaps twined baskets, wooden buckets, spoons or ladles, short-handled splint brooms, and dugout canoes, all of which were sold to colonists up and down the Housatonic Valley. Money the Indians received for these items was used to purchase clothing, shoes, blankets, and food staples. Men and women, sometimes accompanied by their children, also hired themselves out to local farmers, especially during planting and harvesting times. They were paid in corn as well as in meals and drink, often, to their detriment, hard cider and rum.

The social intimacy that evolved at Pachgatgoch can also be accounted for by examining two key factors: Moravian religious practices and language. In keeping with the tenets of their church, the Moravians worked to encourage the Indians to reflect on their own spiritual lives. This could only be accomplished through fervent, ceaseless, and often lengthy dialogues over the "state of their hearts," a central theme in Moravian theology. When not busy in their homes and gardens, teaching school, or holding services, the Moravians were talking to Indians, individually or in small groups, wherever and whenever they could. Often assisted by their wives, the brethren probed into the lives and thoughts of the Indians, scrutinizing and questioning family relationships, marital responsibilities, the rearing of children, or any other issue that they could tie to moral and spiritual well-being.[173] Frequently at the center of these discussions was alcohol and its pernicious effects, a topic to which we will return.

No one doubts the centrality of language in negotiating the intricacies, and the misreadings, that attend the meeting of dissimilar cultures. As the Jesuits in Canada had learned a century earlier, there were but two courses open to them in this regard: "they could teach their numerous hosts to speak French or church Latin, or they could themselves learn a native tongue."[174] They chose the latter, albeit with varying degrees of success. Among the Indians in the Housatonic Valley, however, there was a somewhat more complicated set of factors at work.

The Indians of the region conversed in several native languages and dialects. An unknown number of Mahicans and other River Indians living in the Hudson Valley spoke some Dutch, having had decades of practice that followed from their trading relationships with the residents of what once was New Netherland and, later, New York Colony. At the same time, contact with Yankee settlers and missionaries in southern New England obliged many Indians there to learn English, and to the degree required of them, they did. With but a few exceptions, the Moravians' first language was German, although most also spoke English. The outcome was that at Pachgatgoch, the Moravians preached to the Indians in English, often with the help of native interpreters who translated the sermons into a language identified as "Wompona." The importance placed on the use of English is illustrated by the experiences of Brother Büninger. Shortly after his return to Pachgatgoch in 1750, the Indians approached him, complaining that he had not held a meeting with them in two days. When Büninger confessed that he could not preach because he was without his interpreters, both of whom had gone to the seaside, the Indians asked why it was that he needed interpreters. After all, he spoke English (and obviously, so did they)! But when they chose to, the Indians would take a different tack, which drew the following comment from Bishop Spangenberg: "I wish the Indians would speak English when conducting a homily," he fretted, "otherwise you cannot observe them."[175]

In the beginning, perhaps following the lead of their brethren in Gnadenhütten, the Moravians tried teaching German to some of the children at Pachgatgoch, although this effort was short-lived. "It would be looked into how their present German school could be changed into an English one," reported Brother Rundt in the spring of 1752, "because it had been learned that the brethren and sisters would like it that way, and almost all of them knew English ~~themselves~~ (but not German), and also [because they] always had dealings with such people who spoke English."[176] And while there may have been some earnest attempts to learn the Indians' language, it is doubtful that any of the Moravians exceeded barely adequate levels of fluency. None of the brethren spent sufficient enough time among the natives to do otherwise. As the scholarly Jesuits had discovered, they, like the Moravians, were in age beyond the best years for learning a language. The linguistic skills the Moravians did manage to acquire, while perhaps acceptable for everyday conversation, were not enough to convey theological abstractions or ecclesiastical missives. Revealing what may have been his own understandable linguistic frustrations, and perhaps inadequacies, Brother Büninger observed that "the dear brethren are lacking suitable words in their language to express themselves when interpreting. For example, they do not have any suitable words for *grace, blessing, and redemption*. We advised them to incorporate these particular words into their language, as one language often borrows one word from another language."[177]

It is noteworthy that in mid-1746, just as the Moravian Indian mission in Pennsylvania was getting started, the questions of language and difficulties with translations were raised, resulting in an intriguing proposal, one that was actually put into practice:

> Only now is it becoming truly apparent what an obstacle the lack of language is creating. Because even when a brother is fluent in the language of an Indian nation, he still cannot make it clear to them what he wants to say, for there are 1000 words in the German language of which they cannot translate even a single one. Therefore, we have in the end come to the conclusion that we want to mix

German and Indian, also when composing hymns, to make the matter clear to them that way. This, then, will provide us with a new
language, such as our Negro language on St. Thomas.[178]

The religious discourse between Indian and Moravian did little to cloud the
cultural differences between the two groups, which although conceded, would
not be reconciled. But neither did these differences generate significant intolerance, provoke a disruptive incivility, or deter the occasional cooperative effort or
thoughtful gesture. What is also worth observing is the degree of separateness
that, at the same time, characterized many aspects of their secular lives. Outside of the daily routine of religious activities, the Indians and their Moravian
guests expended a substantial measure of their energy on economic pursuits.
Farming, of course, was critical for their survival. In carrying out this task, the
brethren and the Indians cultivated and kept separate fields. The Moravians
planted corn, beans, and oats on land the Indians allotted them, and they cut
meadow hay and cornstalks to use as winter feed for their livestock. Turnips,
potatoes, cabbages, and currants were grown in small kitchen gardens.

The physical separation of their fields (and to some extent, their homes) was
often bridged by the Indians with offers of assistance, which included working the Moravians' crops. There are only a handful of instances in which the
brethren reciprocated in kind. It was nearly always the case that, in exchange
for their labor, the Moravians offered the Indians cooked meals. Indian hunters
at times supplied the Moravians, who typically did not hunt or fish themselves,
with deer and bear meat as well as fish. Other courtesies the Indians extended
included gifts of apples, flat corn bread, white bread, and beans.

Firewood was a critical and increasingly scarce resource in the Housatonic
Valley and elsewhere in southern New England. On a number of occasions, Indians, particularly single or widowed women and the elderly, tried to ease this
situation by moving in the fall to live on the mountain west of Pachgatgoch,
where supplies were more readily available. Gathering firewood dominated
community life, and it was no different for the Moravians, whom the Indians
often assisted in this task. In January 1751 Brother Sensemann wrote that during the course of a fierce and cold wind, he tried to dissuade the Indians from
cutting firewood for him. The men nonetheless insisted and hauled in three

sleds full. In return, Sensemann gave the headman's wife some dried beans, corn, and meat with which to prepare a meal, which was held at the brother's house. The next winter, Sensemann reported: "Because our firewood was almost used up, the other day an Indian sister had secretly carried a load of wood to the front of our house."[179]

It is difficult to determine whether the Indians' actions in supplying the Moravians with labor, food, and firewood were demonstrations of altruism, expressions of a traditional pattern of reciprocity, or an unadorned strategy to meet real and immediate needs: most likely, the answer is to be found in a combination of these factors. For decades, Indians had suffered the effects of expanding colonial settlement, which accelerated the pace of forest clearing to meet the demand for lumber to build homes, farmsteads, and towns; for fields to plant crops; and, of course, for firewood, sharply reducing Indian access to the land and restricting their movements. In turn, these activities altered the habitat of game animals, in particular the white-tailed deer, for a while increasing their number. The overhunting that resulted, in addition to the introduction of livestock—cattle, sheep, and pigs—that usurped the deer's space and fodder, led to a rapid decrease in their population. Indians responded by keeping livestock for themselves, which furnished them with the meat they no longer could obtain by hunting. By the time of the Revolution, the once ubiquitous white-tails had nearly vanished in much of southern New England and adjacent New York.[180]

There is no question, then, that in part, the assistance the Indians provided the Moravians, occasionally in the face of their strong opposition, was calculated to serve a singular purpose: to allow them to be fed as payment for their labor. In most instances where groups of villagers either delivered firewood or planted, hoed, and harvested for the Moravians, they were provided with a meal. The Indians' unyielding resolve to bring Sensemann firewood in the dead of winter may have been contrived to get badly needed food. Late winter and spring were generally the hungry times for Indian people. Stored surpluses would be in short supply or exhausted and wild plant foods unavailable. Going to the Moravians with offers of assistance in return for desperately needed provisions made perfect sense.

Gestures of goodwill toward the Moravians may also have served to maintain or enhance the status of the headman Gideon, the first to be baptized, and perhaps other influential people in the community who are known to have played a central role in organizing these activities. The formation of alliances between native and preacher that then could be used for political gain is nothing new in the history of missions.[181] Furthermore, the Moravians understood, as had the Jesuits before them, that in order to gain admission to and remain in a native community, and ultimately, to be permitted to promote their religious teachings in it, they would have "to create a rock-ribbed Christian faction among the tribesmen, preferably from leading families and lineages who could withstand the disdain of their more conservative neighbors."[182] Economic exchange helped shape and solidify these vital relationships.

The one or two Moravians stationed at any one time at Pachgatgoch were not in the best position to exercise a great deal of largesse to the Indian population there. Their food supplies were limited: they grew what they could, raised a few livestock, and, with their meager funds, purchased staples and meat from local merchants. If there was a choice and the means, they preferred eating familiar dishes, such as bread soup and turnips. And although Indian corn, whether sweet, roasted, or cracked, was a part of the Moravians' diet, it was not always appreciated. A case in point is Brother Sensemann's complaint that Indian bread upset his stomach. He also did not relish the hard work of pounding dried corn into flour using the Indians' heavy wood mortar and pestle. "The pounding is very toilsome," he wrote on the same day that he intended to borrow an Indian woman's horse to haul two bushels of corn to a nearby mill to have it ground.[183]

There are several likely explanations for the Moravians' hesitancy to participate any more than they did in task- or subsistence-sharing relationships with the Indians. Perhaps it was because even when the Moravians were accompanied by their wives, there were simply not enough of them present at any given moment. The requirements of their religious duties may have left them with little time to spare for much else, including helping the Indians. But they also were very hard-pressed to do what was needed to feed and shelter themselves, and in general, keep their fields, fences, and lodgings in good repair, which was a never-ending grind. The work took its toll on the Moravians, who suffered injuries and lived with stiff and aching joints.[184] With other tasks, however, such as building and repairing the school and meeting house, the brethren and the Indians worked side by side.

A few Moravians took a greater part in the everyday affairs of the Indians than did some of their brethren. In winter 1751, Brother Sensemann labored hard helping to dig out the village spring and line it with stones. That evening he prepared his own supper and ate alone. In the end, the secular lives of the Moravians remained very much removed from those of the Indians. Still, whatever inferences can be drawn about the sharing and redistribution of resources and labor at Pachgatgoch, by Indians or Moravians, there nonetheless remains the plain and poignant language of Brother Büninger: "Here I must praise the Indian Brethren and Sisters' readiness to serve others, for they are, on all occasions when I am in need of their help, willing with all their heart[s]. A good many [times] they have done [things] for me without [being] asked . . . because they saw that it was necessary."[185]

The parallel lives that the Moravians and Indians led extended also to features of their religious conduct. In contrast to the earlier Jesuits and their Protestant competitors in New England, who strove mightily, for example, to undermine native religious systems, the Moravians at Pachgatgoch appeared unusually indifferent on this point.[186] It is difficult to link this attitude to any particular philosophical underpinning of the church, which did not explicitly stress, or practice, forbearance toward the "heathen." A more realistic and useful answer might lie in examining the situation in which the Moravians found themselves. Pachgatgoch was not, and would never be, a Moravian Indian town, a "praying town" such as those that the church created in eastern Pennsylvania beginning in the late 1740s and then later in the Ohio country. It was an *Indian* town into which the Moravians had been invited, and they could remain there only at the pleasure of its residents. Here the Moravians did not set the rules, and they could not play the role of enforcers. Their success, or lack of it, depended entirely on how they behaved toward the community and in the delivery of their religious message; it was always on their minds that any untoward act would almost certainly put their mission in jeopardy. Thus, there is little evidence to suggest that the Moravians openly confronted or challenged the Indians' culture or discounted or disparaged their way of life; they apparently recognized that, at least in the short term, they could not dissuade the people of Pachgatgoch from doing what they always had done. Yet they did not hesitate to publicly level criticisms at the Indians when it came to drinking or the behavior of Indian children, whom they schooled and fittingly considered their most likely candidates for conversion. However, when it came to proposing changes they thought would be beneficial for the adult members of the community, the Moravians wisely employed an indirect approach, one that involved the "helpers' conference." This was a small group of the most influential Indians at Pachgatgoch with whom the Moravians periodically met to discuss matters concerning the good management of the community, in particular, conduct appropriate to a Christian people or those wishing to become Christians. From all indications, the helpers were Gideon and his wife Martha; Gideon's son Joshua and his wife Elisabeth; Samuel, the husband of Gideon's late daughter Maria; and perhaps Martin, another of Gideon's sons. Together they formed the core of the "rock-ribbed Christian faction" critical to the Moravians and the operation of their mission.

The most troublesome and divisive factor affecting relations between Moravians and natives at Pachgatgoch was alcohol. It was both an impediment to Moravian accomplishments and a recognized threat to the survival of the community. The devastation it wrought in the Americas is well known and has been extensively chronicled, and the Indians in New England fared no better than the rest.[187] Drinking and its dreadful effects were a constant source of controversy, strife, and struggle.[188] It was a wedge issue that frustrated the Moravians' efforts to draw the Indians to Christ, and it was often a force that unraveled many of their hard-fought victories. To keep the Indians away from drink and "close to the Lamb" was an unending battle. "Before they knew the Savior," the Indians unabashedly told Brother Sensemann, they came together "to drink, to dance, to fight, and for all kinds of indecent ways of life."[189]

Complicating matters for everyone were the frequent trips the Indians made outside of Pachgatgoch to work as farm laborers and to sell their handcrafted goods. This not only kept the Indians from their fields and other routine food producing and gathering activities, but it also put them in regular and not always righteous contact with outsiders and, again to their detriment, within easy reach of alcohol, causing them to "stray from their hearts," as the Moravians dolefully put it. The risk alcohol posed, absent the supportive presence of the Moravians and their religious message, was one the Indians understood and feared, and against which they tried to protect themselves.

Discord, squabbles, and the occasional brawl intruded on the peace of Pachgatgoch, and alcohol-induced illnesses and death were hard realities. It is here that the interests of Moravian and native converged, with the Indians taking advantage of the presence and the religious teachings of the brethren to help shield themselves from drink's lethal impact. This is not to say that natives in western Connecticut were little more than religious cynics or only nominally receptive to the Christianity the Moravians brought to them. But we agree with the historian James Axtell, who, with ethnological insight, argues that Indian societies in colonial America were "pragmatically incorporative" when it came to other faiths, not to mention the cultural practices of non-Indians.[190] The Moravians' diaries suggest that Indians took what they believed to be useful from the religious culture presented to them and fashioned for themselves a means of maintaining the solidity and well-being of their community. They listened and frequently took to heart the counsel and cautions the Moravians regularly offered; nonetheless, leaving Pachgatgoch to hunt, fish, work, or sell their goods was for some a test of their sobriety, one that they are reported to have failed many times. Even so, the Indians seem to have understood that. On coming home again, they would be met by the forgiving brethren and, equally important, by their own people. There is every indication that the Moravians' teachings and their concern for the spiritual welfare of their "brown flock" were not simply passively or casually received by the Indians but were instead turned to good use: to appeal for temperance in the form of a religious message and thereby help ensure their survival.

Moravians, Indians, and Christianity

The essential ecclesiastical goal of the Moravians did not vary in any way from that of their Roman Catholic and other Protestant compeers. "In our labour among the heathen," wrote Bishop Spangenberg, "we will particularly endeavor, that they become converted to Christ Jesus with all their hearts."[191] Yet there were differences in the way each denomination introduced Indians to the concepts of Christianity, and at which point in this process they would baptize Indians into the faith. A century earlier, the Jesuits in Canada had likened their religious venture to a military exercise, employing "the ancient metaphors of evangelical Christianity and religious crusade."[192] Thousands were baptized in the first four decades of their campaign, a third of whom were infants, children, and adults anointed virtually on their deathbeds as victims of European diseases. Healthy natives, on the other hand, faced a rigorous course of instruction and probation before they were believed fit to receive the holy waters, for to do any different, the Jesuits feared, would result in "'making more Apostates than Christians.'"[193]

Most English Protestant missionaries in New England, until the 1760s, also elected not to administer the sacraments before the appropriate, orderly schooling had taken place. But they departed philosophically and materially in one important way from the Jesuits. Indians would not be baptized in the church without first having to endure a lengthy and trying cycle of *resocialization*. The "savages," went the drill, had to be "civilized" before they would be admitted into Christianity: they were to be made "men." Their transformation into sentient human beings was, in Cotton Mather's distasteful turn of phrase, "'*To bring an idiot unto the Use of Reason.*'"[194] Yet it was precisely this "*Kopf-Bekehrung*," a conversion of the mind instead of the heart, that the Moravians openly disputed.[195]

For their part, at least in the first decades of their missions, the Moravians conducted themselves in ways reminiscent of the Jesuits: they lived in Indian communities; made some attempt to learn native languages; and moved to baptize, first, adults in the communities, later shifting their sights to the more impressionable and less renitent children. And until they abandoned the Pachgatgoch mission in 1770, having earlier organized their own praying towns in Pennsylvania and then in the Ohio country, the Moravians adopted a culturally relative posture, making only weak attempts to work their influence on certain of the Indians' cultural practices such as marriage, medicine, and family structure. Their toleration of these and other expressions of native life were of considerable benefit to the brethren at Pachgatgoch, for to have done otherwise would surely have meant their expulsion.

The most obvious doctrinal difference between the Moravians, and the Jesuits and English Protestants was in the administration of baptism, that singular act meant to dissever convert from pagan. For the brethren, it was not so much a matter of time before an Indian could be anointed but rather a matter of the heart and individual desire. Required was the volition to open one's self to hearing about the Lamb and his wounds, a recognition by the initiate that he or she was a sinner, and a willingness to appeal to the Savior on that basis. From this, baptism could follow. One illustration of the relative ease with which the sacrament might be forthcoming is from Bishops von Watteville and Cammerhoff's journey to the Indians in 1748. Nearing Shekomeko, they came upon Adrian Okaiasegkamen, his wife Atschiak, and one of their daughters and had the opportunity to speak to them about Christ with the help of the Indian Joshua, their interpreter. After a short while, as von Watteville described this encounter in his travel journal, "Our hearts were quite warm, and theirs [were] feeling, and we could scarcely keep ourselves from baptizing them that very instant."[196]

In the second year of the mission's operation, which was cut short by the Moravians' banishment from Connecticut colony, they baptized eleven adults. Gideon was first, followed by several of his kin and his wife Martha. A short year after the Moravian's return to Pachgatgoch in 1749, twenty adults and one child were besprinkled. But soon the brethren seem to have had something of a change of heart, and they moved to set the bar a bit higher when it came to dispensing this sacrament. Although baptisms in the community continued, along with the admission of deserving adults to Communion, they no longer occurred with the alacrity of the early years. In fact, over time, the brethren seem to have dug in their heels, demanding that Indian initiates behave more in a manner befitting the spiritual status they were seeking. An instructive example is that of Brother Carl Gottfried Rundt.

In a plainly worded protest to his superior, Bishop Spangenberg, in October 1755, Rundt voiced his strong opposition to baptizing Indian children at Pachgatgoch, because in his view, their upbringing "before the Savior is being neglected so incredibly by their parents." Complaining of spiritual inconsistencies and failings, licentiousness, and the generally iniquitous behavior of the Indians, Rundt refused to "subject the Savior and the congregation to the dishonor, my conviction to the disloyalty, and my conscience to the torture of baptizing their children under circumstances of this nature."[197]

Although there are obvious signs that things did not always go as hoped for in the community, the diaries from Pachgatgoch are absent the very forceful objections that Rundt raised. On this basis alone, his grousing could easily be interpreted, and then dismissed, as extreme, perhaps that of an ill-tempered, reactionary cleric. Still, whatever Rundt (and possibly others) would not commit to his diary about the Indians' conduct and his own scruples, he did not hesitate to put in a private letter to his bishop.

Severe as it was, Rundt's assessment may not have been far from the mark, at least for the period of time he was at Pachgatgoch. Or, and equally revealing, it perhaps reflects the pragmatic outlook of the brethren, who—unlike their Protestant rivals elsewhere in New England, it has been claimed—did not take for granted their "conversions" of native people.[198] In any event, Rundt's views do not square with what had occurred at Pachgatgoch in the first years of the mission, when most of the adult Indians, constituting a third or more of the entire community's population, were baptized over a short span of time. We hasten to add that the Moravian Church did, in fact, encourage infant and, in special cases, child baptisms, although families were under no doctrinal obligation to follow suit. Instead, it was hoped that parents who themselves were baptized and followed the Lamb would come forward and ask that their children be anointed as well. At Pachgatgoch, many did.

But following the spiritual euphoria and exhilaration that accompanied the opening of the mission, marked by the flurry of baptisms and then a period of relative stability in the community, there came a downturn. In religious terms, this is best measured by the falloff in the number of Indians who were permitted to attend Communion and the increasing number of instances in which the Moravians judged that no one was considered worthy to receive the Lord's Supper when it was offered. Something was changing at Pachgatgoch.

Religion and Its Use

It has only been recently that historians of religion and missions in colonial America have raised questions about the form and degree of religious conversion among American Indians. Works especially relevant to the mission at Pachgatgoch are those by James Axtell and Neal Salisbury.[199] Where Axtell argues that in New England there indeed were bona fide Indian conversions, if amid moments of doubt and apostasy, Salisbury suggests that since the terms "conversion" and "convert," noun and verb, are rooted in the language and judgments of missionaries, they should therefore be abandoned by contemporary ethno-historians. "What we as scholars have failed to appreciate," Salisbury writes, "is the extent to which natives could embrace what the Euro-American tradition could and can comprehend only as ambiguity." This ambiguity, he explains, characterized chiefly by a "psychological distance" between natives and new-comers, arose from Europeans who "distinguished constantly and most fundamentally between themselves and native people rather than between Christians and non-Christians."[200] There is a strong signal that such was the case in the Moravian Indian missions, albeit with a twist. Whether it was at Pachgatgoch or any of their other stations, the Moravians invariably drew a distinction between persons in their religious community, pointedly referring to "*Indian* brethren and sisters" and then "brethren and sisters," the latter intending *white* people.

The detailed record of life at Pachgatgoch the Moravians left provides an opportunity to examine the ambiguity that Salisbury postulates. But it also allows for a contemplation of the culture-based choices that emerged from the differing material needs and contradictory ideological sentiments of the Indians at Pachgatgoch and their Moravian visitors. Moreover, the diaries provide a means of measuring the effect Christianity had on the community, along with the manner in which it may have been practiced and used by numerous of its native residents.

To start with, there is no way to know the religious preferences of the Indians at Pachgatgoch, save for falling back on unsatisfying ethnographic analogies and generalizations found primarily in the secondary literature. What can prudently be said is that they most likely structured their way of life in a manner similar to that of other native North Americans, that is, around locally produced modes of diverse, uncompartmented, and, importantly, dynamic relationships to persons and powers in their environment. Unfortunately, over the more than two decades that the Moravians lived in the community, they failed to mention a single example of native religious practice. There are no descriptions of planting or harvest ceremonies, curing rituals, divination, hunting magic, rites of passage, or anything else that might be broadly regarded as religious behavior. The one or two references to native "doctors" are equivocal, suggesting either shaman or less supernaturally invested herbalists. Although we noted earlier that the Moravians may have been inattentive observers of or have chosen not to record native customs and conduct, it is nonetheless curious that they would have nothing to say about practices that might have impeded the delivery of their own religious message.

The Moravians' frequent mentions of sweat houses and the Indians' use of these structures, however, deserve further consideration. It is widely accepted that among native people in the Northeast, sweating fulfilled several vital and related functions. It could serve to prevent disease and thereby sustain health; as a curative for both body and mind; as an act of purification and life renewal; and to promote social solidarity, all in the broad context of religious behavior. It is interesting, then, that the Moravians raised no objections to the existence or the natives' use of sweat houses at Pachgatgoch. There is, as well, a similar indifference to sweat houses found throughout the literature on mission history from any period and place.[201] But assuming for the moment, on the basis of the conventional wisdom surrounding this practice, that the Indians did perceive sweating as a form of religious activity, it is unlikely that they would have withheld such information from the brethren. The mix of pagan and Christian Indians in a community the size of Pachgatgoch would make concealing such activity impossible. Equally improbable is to think that the Moravians were either blind or oblivious to what the Indians may have been up to, or that they looked the other way. What the record does reveal are the numerous instances in which one or the other brethren postponed or canceled altogether a meeting or religious service he had planned so that the Indians could attend a sweat. Whatever the Indians may have thought about their sweat-house activities, they did not provoke a negative reaction from the Moravians, who did not see them as religious behavior and thus a threat to their efforts.

The absence of religious elements, whether unrecognized or unnoted, in the Moravians' writings raises the provocative question of Indian nonbelief or, perhaps more accurately, religious indifference on the part of the people of Pachgatgoch. Largely absent from the literature on American Indian religions, any resolution of this matter is made difficult by the scarcity of or an inability to interpret the evidence, but also by the absence of literacy in traditional native societies, and thus, written doctrine or other commentary from which an assessment might be made.[202] Yet the idea that religion, in whatever form, may have been of little or no concern to many native minds cannot be dismissed as a possible explanation for what is not found in the Moravians' writings.

Matters of this sort also raise the question of how "pure" a Christian the Indian convert would have been or could become.[203] To this we would add others: To what extent did the Moravians offer their Indian "converts" access to their church; that is, how far might a baptized Indian proceed in assuming the cloak of a Moravian? Was there more to being of the faith than accepting baptism, Communion, and finally, a resting place after death?[204] If the experience of Indian converts elsewhere in the Northeast is any gauge, the distance traveled did not extend much beyond the boundaries of their own communities. But the reasons for this had little to do with leading pious and exemplary Christian lives. The greatest obstacle to full admittance to any church and the fellowship it served was that they were Indians, and as such were viewed with a widespread prejudice that "often exceeded cultural arrogance and fell clearly into the category of racism."[205] English Protestant clergy in New England, even the most open minded, knew that their native charges were not likely to join English society, either by election or with consent. But bigotry had an unintended positive consequence. The social barriers it helped to erect, which compelled natives to live in praying towns or other ethnic enclaves, kept the Indians on their own lands, even if but a small portion of what they once held. This attachment to land and place, even with the acceptance of Christianity to whatever degree, allowed natives to preserve a cultural core, defined and shielded by distinctive ethnic boundaries, so that in the end, they remained "Indians" and were recognized, if disparaged as such, by the dominant colonial society.[206]

There is scant evidence that the Indians at Pachgatgoch were the targets of racism on the part of their colonial neighbors, at least not until the Seven Years' War and the efforts by officials in the town of Kent to extend their jurisdictional reach into the community. In this, the good citizens of Kent and the surrounding region were no different from their compatriots in other parts of New England and the middle-Atlantic colonies. Their prejudices stemmed largely from an enmity toward and fears long held of Indian people that had been fed by presumptions of cultural superiority and, not infrequently, religious intolerance; another source for prejudice was the ruin Indians had suffered from war, disease, and famine, which left them badly weakened, vulnerable, and then disdained.

The existence of English bigotry (and following in its tracks, exploitation) directed at the Indians did not escape the notice of the Moravians at Pachgatgoch, who, in harmony with their own designs, could use it to their advantage.[207] The brethren recognized early on that much was to be gained by restricting the Indians' movements, encouraging them to remain in Pachgatgoch and away from the contaminating influences of surrounding colonists, which included easy access to alcohol and many other things that might undo their ecclesiastical successes. A backdoor approach was to use the intimidating effects that racism, often under the guise of colonial laws, had on the Indians as one means by which to keep them home and close to the Lamb.

Gideon and Company

The record suggests that while there were undoubtedly bona fide and perhaps even "pure" converts at Pachgatgoch, the reasons the Indians sought baptism and Communion were more complex than a straightforward acceptance of Christ. A useful illustration in this regard is that of the headman Gideon and his coterie.

The site of the second-earliest Moravian mission, Pachgatgoch bore little similarity to those that followed, whether at Gnadenhütten, Friedenshütten, and Nain in Pennsylvania, or the later stations of Schönbrunn and Lichtenau in the Ohio country. Pachgatgoch was first and foremost an Indian community, and it sat smack in the middle of several colonial settlements. The other localities mentioned, actually a shortlist of mission towns, had all been created by the Moravians: they were manufactured communities of Indians rather than Indian communities. Moreover, the newly formed mission towns, ideally located at a distance from the profanities of Euro-American society and "wild," nativist Indians, were subject to the brethrens' form of social organization, physical layout, and economy, as well as to "statutes and rules" that regulated the conduct of residents. At all of these places, authority was in the hands of the missionaries, flowing either directly from them or indirectly through the "helpers' conference" and appointed Indian officers. Resident Indians, all of whom were refugees from near and far, were obliged to abide by the rules or face expulsion.

At Pachgatgoch, however, there existed the kind of native leadership that was not permitted to flourish in the Moravian-generated mission towns. Here the brethren were compelled to tailor their efforts to fit the workings of a native community on its home turf, replete with a functioning leadership discharged principally through the headman Gideon. The result of what was plainly a cultural compromise at Pachgatgoch was a symbiosis of sorts, a mutually beneficial interdependence of purpose. Gideon exploited the Moravians' presence from the outset to strengthen and further validate his political status and authority, by which the unity of the community was maintained. In turn, he and several key family members provided the brethren with a core of converts whose standing and influence in Pachgatgoch would be of considerable assistance in the delivery of their religious message.

As the first Indian, and the leader to boot, from Pachgatgoch to be baptized, Gideon was the muscle behind a good deal of the Moravians' successes. But he was much more than a convert tailor-made for their benefit. He was the headman of his people, which raises the question of who, exactly, may have been the users and those used. Although the Moravians may not have known, in May 1742, nearly a year before Gideon's "conversion," the Indians at Pachgatgoch and Potatuck had presented a petition to the Connecticut assembly. Claiming that a number of them had been awakened by local Presbyterians, they asked to be taught to read English and to have a minister appointed to "preach the Gospell of Jesus Christ unto us; and Instruct us in the Principles of the Christian Religion." Gideon was among the petition's signatories. The assembly's response was favorable, with the Reverends Daniel Boardman and Samuel Canfield appointed and funds appropriated "for the support of the said Indians when at school or attending on the ministry," although there is no indication of what happened next. An entirely credible suggestion has been made that this demonstration of the Indians' willingness to become Christians, at least those at Pachgatgoch, was a strategy employed to secure the lands on which they were living, the title to which was unsettled.[208] Perhaps the Indians believed that should they take up the cross with the blessing of the local clergy, who had strong ecclesiastical and, of course, political ties to the surrounding (and acquisitive) colonists, they and their lands would be afforded some protection. If so, the spiritual life that Gideon and the others were outwardly seeking was thus motivated by an overriding material and pragmatic rationale.

Gideon's independent bent and, without doubt, his heedfulness for his people (predicated, assuredly, on the safeguarding of his status as headman) were once again on display in the context of land and in pursuit of a way of life. As mentioned earlier, following the Moravians' banishment from Connecticut and New York, and shortly after the mission at Shekomeko closed in mid-summer 1746, Gideon and several members of his family joined others in following the brethren to Pennsylvania. There, things soon turned sour. Gideon first balked at living in what was a large communal residence with other Indians, wanting his own house much in the manner that he had enjoyed in Pachgatgoch. Furthermore, he wished to live in Nazareth, where he might have a piece of land to call his own and that he could pass on to his heirs.

Gideon had earlier told the brethren that "he did not see how he could live here [in Gnadenhütten] and earn something for himself. Yet in Pachgatgoch he had his beautiful land and, in addition, would be able to earn something for himself, and in his heart he had also been more calm there than here." Brother Rauch, ever the critic, questioned Gideon's lament, suggesting that worldly matters were what was really drawing him away from the fold. Frustrated in his efforts to find the peace he wanted and had known in Pachgatgoch, and sensing that he would likely be denied any opportunity to do so in Gnadenhütten or any other Moravian Indian town, Gideon made a decision. In mid-October 1747, turning his back on his spiritual mentors and the Moravian Church, Gideon and his followers returned to Pachgatgoch. Again, Gideon's position as headman, and the immediate material, if not cultural, needs that he and his people faced had won the day.[209]

A year later, anticipating changes in the laws that had enjoined them from preaching and teaching in New York and Connecticut, the Moravians made their way back to Pachgatgoch. Assembling in Gideon's house, the brethren relayed the message that they "had come to them in the name of the Lambkin and the congregation to announce and impart new grace and complete absolution for all their sins up to this time," and that they were prepared to send brothers to minister to them.[210] In September 1749 the mission at Pachgatgoch was once more up and running.

Gideon, wrote August Gottlieb Spangenberg three years later, was "an old Indian captain, who reigned with much authority and is still held in great esteem by his people." "He . . . cared for his people faithfully," attested Brother Bernhard Adam Grube on the day of Gideon's passing in 1760, at about age seventy.[211] But as Gideon lay awaiting his death in his winter hut on a cold January day, he might have looked back on the previous two decades with mixed feelings. Maintaining the unity of the people at Pachgatgoch and their land base, along with his own headman status, had come at a price: He had had no choice but to share his authority with the missionaries and also the local government. Throughout, not only Connecticut authorities but also the Moravians had employed the tried and tested tools of the colonial venture to extend their influence over the community, sometimes in uncomfortable collaboration with each other. In the final analysis, however, Gideon may have taken some consolation and pride in the fact that Pachgatgoch had indeed survived, and it had done so remaining relatively intact. This was no small feat in those turbulent and trying times.

That the Moravians had followed Gideon's invitation to come and stay in the community had served him and the people of Pachgatgoch well. If we reflect on what Gideon's aims might have been at the time and how he thought the Moravians might have been able to help him realize them, we can see that there is every reason to believe that his expectations were met. With his support, the missionaries had, in truth, contributed to a more orderly atmosphere at Pachgatgoch, which Gideon had hoped for.[212] In keeping with their views of shared, harmonious living, the Moravians had sought frequent face-to-face interactions with all of the Indians, including the unbaptized, had mediated family disputes, engaged in marriage counseling, treated illnesses, collected food supplies for those in need, and had given from their own meager resources. Their presence and religious teachings worked to keep the Indians from deserting the community, which helped it to maintain its viability; at the same time, the Moravians also acted as a draw for others to join. Moreover, through frequent spiritual counseling of the Indians and direct interventions with the local farmers for whom they sometimes worked, the brethren often were able to limit the consumption of alcohol, the scourge of the community. Most important, the Moravians had, though not unselfishly, assisted the Indians in securing their remaining lands and petitioning, however unsuccessfully, for more.

To assist in the pursuit and management of the souls they had gathered around them at Pachgatgoch, the Moravians had introduced elements of their communal social and religious organization into the community, the "helpers' conference" being a prime example. This presumably compliant circle of influential converts was seen as well-suited to the Moravians' purposes, for it was here where discussions and much of the decision-making in the community took place. Acting as an arm of the missionaries, as was intended, these converts would exert influence on other Indians consistent with the brethren's wishes and also provide them with information on the state of affairs in Pachgatgoch.[213] Perhaps in passive resistance to such meddling with the traditional workings of the community, Indians continued to use the sweat house, where they might confer away from the ears of the brethren, and held the occasional open community meeting.

The Moravians undertook to use Gideon's authority to mitigate or preferably eliminate unacceptable behaviors and to help add names to the list of the baptized. Conferring on him the title of "steward," securing his place in the helpers' conference, and having him hold services were means to those ends. At the same time, Indians would sometimes use Gideon's favorable standing with the missionaries, making application through him to be baptized and admitted to the congregation.

The reasons many of these and other persons in the community sought the holy waters and a place in the fledgling congregation were often quintessentially native and not necessarily founded on the singular desire to follow the Lamb. Nor did they conform to the standard explanations that have typically been offered. Some historians argue that the principal inducements for Indians to choose to be baptized were economic, political, and military: through joining the church, they could put themselves in favorable positions for trade, cultivate and maintain alliances with standing colonial administrations, and obtain guns. Others have found an explanation in the devastation wrought by European-introduced diseases, alleging that this tragedy resulted in an undermining of native religious systems, causing them to be seen as unequal to the dual tasks of healing and prevention in their wake. This sent Indians scrambling to seek more powerful supernatural forces than their own, even if they were Christian. To these arguments about the undermining of native religion and belief systems can be added the uncertainties tied to land loss, which resulted in the erosion of sovereignty, security, and a way of life. And there were for Indians as well such elusive motivations as curiosity and a longing for psychological assurance accompanied by purposeful change and accommodation within their own cultures as a rational response to events swirling about them.[214]

The situation of the Indians at Pachgatgoch, however, matched with few of these inducements. By the mid-eighteenth century, Indians in western Connecticut were actively and without serious hindrance fully involved in an economic system of their own making, which in many ways resembled that of their colonial neighbors, with all of the associated successes and failures. In their isolation, their political bonds, however strained or tenuous, were with the colony. And they had long had easy access to guns, which they used for hunting. Moreover, they suffered from the same diseases with the same degree of recovery and mortality as did surrounding populations.

Although the evidence is hard to read or nonexistent, the attraction of the Indians at Pachgatgoch to Christianity may very well have stemmed from an inquisitiveness attached to a desire for some sort of metaphysical solace. But the Moravians did not provide these natives with their first glimpse of Christians and Christianity; the Indians had lived in the midst of adherents to that faith for many years. For reasons known only to the Indians, they had not previously felt any need to abandon their own belief system and embrace another. Still, there did come a change of heart, at least for many natives, suggesting there was surely something more to their search.

From all signs, the paramount concern of the Indians at Pachgatgoch was, not surprisingly, to hold on to their land, and in so doing, preserve their community. Their move to the secluded area below Kent in 1736 distanced them from the fast-expanding settlement of New Milford; perhaps they hoped that the hardscrabble, craggy lands farther upriver would not attract attention. And there, the Moravians' presence and being Christian would be of considerable advantage. But there is more.

Also of significance to the Indians was the weight attached to status and family. As for the former, Gideon was again key. His ability to maintain his headman position and the status that went with it was fully dependent on his links to the adult members of the community and on everyone appropriately fulfilling a set of reciprocal obligations. Simply put, he was headman because he was able to effect decisions, in counsel and with the support of other influential persons at Pachgatgoch, that were perceived to be of benefit to the majority, and, of course, to himself. And as did headmen elsewhere, he fostered consensus with a practiced persuasion and, when needed, some arm-twisting, accompanied by no little measure of personal charm. To what extent Gideon's achievement of status and the role he played as headman reflect earlier, traditional practices is unknown. In the absence of the needed evidence, going beyond what was happening in the mid-eighteenth century is an incautious exercise. Recall for a moment that before Gideon's lifetime, change had come swiftly, and in whatever manner he had become headman, he was to face what those who had served a century and more before him did not: an ever-increasing, aggressive, and avaricious colonial population whose presence spelled land loss, dislocation, the fragmentation of Indian communities, and inevitable social turmoil. His advantage, as he must have seen it, was the Moravians' presence. So, at the same time that Gideon, the acknowledged and respected headman, and his kin sought and obtained baptism, they were consciously binding themselves to the Moravians and what that might gain for them beyond salvation. And from this, others followed, intent not only on following their leader but also maintaining their own place and their material security in the community, linked, as it was, to their obligations to Gideon and his to them.

It is impossible to know what went on in the minds of the Indians at Pachgatgoch or in the discussions that took place within families, but there seems little doubt that once a person decided on baptism, other family members and closely attached relatives—spouses in particular—frequently followed. The reason for this progression may, of course, have been entirely religious, as one after the other native decided to follow the Lamb. However, there were already strong bonds of kinship that worked to keep families together, thus meeting their and the larger community's needs. It would not be a surprise, then, should a family member become baptized, that others would follow suit, if only to remain together with their kin. As the historical record frequently attests, to be separated or otherwise estranged from family, in life or in death, was to native groups everywhere the worst of all possible situations.[215]

Moravians in Pachgatgoch

Aware of their standing as guests, and careful not to act counter to Gideon's interests, the missionaries were cautious in deciding how much control they would attempt to exercise over the Indians' lives. Formal edicts, such as those they later employed in their mission towns to control behavior, dress, the use of alcohol, and who would be permitted to settle in the community, were never instituted in Pachgatgoch. Although Brother Eberhardt at one point suggested that something should be done to deal with disorderly newly arrived Indians, there was no follow-up. The imposition of rules, of course, would have implied that sanctions be levied for noncompliance. At Pachgatgoch, with its several related, extended families, the Moravians most likely understood that any attempt on their part to expel the Indians' errant kin would not be tolerated.

The brethren, together with a number of the Indians, worked hard to keep alcohol out of Pachgatgoch, but they did not have any visible control over who was to live there, and they could not direct the Indians to carry out tasks. In truth, Gideon's skills at persuasion were quite enough to organize work parties, making a rule to that effect unnecessary. Although the children's conduct was lamented and the parents were advised on how to better deal with their offspring, the Moravians realized that there would be no interfering with the Indians' permissive child-rearing practices.

A Community Struggles

The evangelical achievements of the Moravians at Pachgatgoch, at least initially, were equal to and may have exceeded those of other Protestant missions in New England. In large part, this success can be attributed to their restraint in the exercise of the "civility must precede Christianity" mandate of their competitors, a certain casualness toward orthodoxy, and, in many situations, the practice of a brand of cultural relativism, without losing sight of their spiritual goals, that echoed the approach of the Jesuits.[216] But in 1770 it all came to an end.

Five years earlier, Brother Sensemann had suggested that something was amiss at the mission, writing: "It seems to be agreed before the Savior that we shall give up the plan, and there is also not much to be done here, but sometimes such things change."[217] Sensemann's reserve—he must have been biting his tongue—could not hide the fact that Pachgatgoch was coming apart at the seams. The one diary that is known from the period provides a glimpse of the hell it had become. Drinking and dancing were the order of the day. Word of Indian women prostituting themselves to surrounding colonists, some at the prompting and for the financial gain of Gideon's son Joshua, came as disturbing news to the resident brother Johannes Rothe. Kinsmen beat, deceived, and stole from one another, keeping the local justices busy. Whereas in times past, the Moravians' meeting house would be filled with Indians, now only a handful attended services. "There is not a soul here about whom one can say, this is a brother or a sister—they all drink," reported a pained and despondent Rothe.[218]

But the Moravians did not act until 1768. Expressing their dismay that the Indians had reverted to all of their former abominations and heathenish ways, the Moravians threw up their hands, first in frustration and then in resignation, and turned to the lot. Central to the process of decision-making in the church during the eighteenth century, the lot was employed "to accept and allocate persons into various positions in the status structure of the community and to determine issues of communal policy." In its basic form it consisted of blindly drawing one of three ballots, one marked affirmative, one negative, and one blank, to determine whether or how to implement a given action. It must be said, however, that its use allowed for a considerable degree of "human manipulation."[219]

Edward and Grace Thorp were the last missionaries to serve at Pachgatgoch, relieving Brother Sensemann in 1766 after completing a three-year tour of duty with the non-Indian congregation at Sichem, just across the border in Dutchess County. The little correspondence that survives from both stations points to Brother Thorp having been a tortured soul who saw himself as spiritually inadequate, incapable of preaching or teaching, physically ill, and terribly homesick for Bethlehem. "I am quite ashamed of my Self," he lamented from his post at Sichem. "I have got so litle to say and Many times according to my own feeling [I am] as dry as a stick of wood."[220] After two years with the Indians, he wanted out. Accordingly, in October 1768 the lot was employed for the first time, although not in Thorp's favor. To the question of whether to abandon the mission, the answer was to continue at Pachgatgoch, leaving the Thorps where they were. One year later, Thorp raised the same question, only to be told that the

Savior had given instructions to maintain the mission, at least for the time being. The following May, Thorp wrote to Brother Ettwein, adding a note on the state of the Indians at Pachgatgoch: "as to there Char.r in general I think you are aprised of, here is not much alteration excepting for the Worse as to personals I will not enter upon." The letter ends with his heart's wish: "What we think about our Plan here is this, That we are here with our Saviours approbation and Shall be glad to be Dissmist with the same when HE and his Congregation Shall think fit."[221] In July 1770 the lot was called on for the last time, first on the question of whether to consider closing the mission. The answer was yes. The second draw went directly to the point: Should the mission at Pachgatgoch be closed and the Thorps recalled? "Yes," came the answer.[222] The Indians were notified of the outcome on 25 September, and in early October were told that, should they desire to hear good words again, they could find a Moravian at Sichem. Their reaction to this news, if there was any, was not recorded. The Thorps said their goodbyes at Pachgatgoch on 13 October.[223]

The first signs that there were problems with the mission had surfaced more than a decade earlier with the onset of the Seven Years' War, followed in 1760 by the death of Gideon. The war did more to throw Indian communities in the Northeast into tumult and disarray than had any before. Indian men, occasionally accompanied by their families, left their communities to fight as mercenaries or work as laborers building and repairing colonial fortifications meant to keep the enemy at bay. If they managed to survive the skirmishes, pitched battles, and disease-ridden garrisons, they were laid low by the free flow of alcohol. Many returned to their homes bringing contagions with them, and all too frequently, addicted to drink.[224]

A number of men from Pachgatgoch, baptized and unbaptized, voluntarily joined the fray, recruited by colonial militias or sometimes other Indians. For some, it was thought, this would be a chance to escape the debts owed to local colonists. Months after Gideon's death, for example, the Indian Samuel told the story that Gideon had once taken a bribe to give "all of the young people the liberty, indeed he advised them, to go to war; there they would be able to get plenty of money."[225] At any rate, Indians from Pachgatgoch went to the front in far fewer numbers, and with much less enthusiasm, than their fellows at Stockbridge, who gained a rather tenebrous reputation as guerilla fighters in

"Roger's Rangers."[226] None of the Pachgatgoch Indians are recorded as dying in battle, although Gideon's son Martin was taken by dysentery while at Crown Point, and another Indian, Nanaush, died of unknown causes somewhere outside of Albany. But the war was perilous in other ways. In May 1759, on his way to be a soldier, the Indian Paulus and his wife Quāhnpēhmāhs, who had gone with him, got drunk and quarreled. He beat her so badly that she lost the baby she was carrying; while being tended to by a physician in nearby Dover, she died. Her body was carried home and buried alongside the unbaptized in God's acre.[227] Paulus eventually deserted the army, and continued to drink.

Gideon's death was a blow not only to the Indians at Pachgatgoch but also to the Moravians, who had depended heavily on his leadership, secular and religious. As headman, he had taken the community from its uncertain future at Weantinock to the relative security of Pachgatgoch, was instrumental in recruiting the Moravians, insured as best he could the cooperation and good intentions of the Indians in all of their and the brethren's endeavors, and acted to manage and mediate the interactions between his people and outsiders. He was, without doubt, a person of considerable ability, persuasive power, and influence.

Some historians have haphazardly hung handles of sorts on native people like Gideon, but also on colonial players, dubbing them "cultural brokers" and "go-betweens," although in the real-world context of many of these so-styled persons, the terms "political entrepreneurs," "survivors," or "self-servers" might just as well be thrown into the mix.[228] The utility of any of these labels, however, is subject to question, as they serve no obvious analytical purpose and do not render historical explanations any more convincing. But Gideon's effectiveness as headman is a matter of record, and in most ways it was he, working with two or three others, who fashioned and implemented the strategy that for many years had kept Pachgatgoch intact and functioning.

Still, following the example of leaders the world over, Gideon was not at all shy about taking care of himself. His name and mark appear with those of presumably other senior men or heads of families on a number of land sale agreements, the first in 1716. And he may on other occasions have privately engaged in selling land in the vicinity of Pachgatgoch to colonists, all of which must have left him with some sort of a return, undoubtedly in goods, cash, or both.[229]

A few years later Gideon, his son Joshua, and several other men were co-opted by officials from the town of Kent. Perhaps for reasons best explained as a necessary accommodation, a process of cultural backing and filling intended to secure their future, they became the agents through which colonial rule was infused into the community, although in the first instance it was with the apparent collaboration of a Moravian, Brother Jungmann. This, too, carried with it some kind of prize.

In 1757, at the Indians' request, Gideon was officially made "Captain" of Pachgatgoch, a title, however, that had been linked to his name earlier in the mission records. This move came at the same time that the colony appointed its first overseer to the Indians. Shortly before Gideon's death, "captain" became "steward," while his son Joshua was named "constable." The titles of "steward" and "tithingman" were bestowed on several other men later on, along with the responsibility and authority to act, at least on the face of it, on behalf of the community. Assuredly, however, the prosecution of their duties was frequently at the bidding and in the interests of local and colonial authorities.

That local and colonial governments were able to extend their reach into Pachgatgoch and exercise indirect control over its affairs was largely a consequence of the Seven Years' War, aided by the absence of an effective leader after Gideon's death. The war fueled the fears that surrounding colonists had long held, or, for their own purposes, often concocted about the Indians, who they saw as their unpredictable and one-step-from-savage neighbors. And it gave rise to their acts of belligerency and bigotry. At Pachgatgoch, the to-and-fro movements of men carrying arms put a strain on families and disrupted village routine. Badly rattling Moravians and Indians alike were the drunken frolics of returnees and foreign Indians passing through the area. Accompanying all of this were destitution, sickness, and famine, maladies found in Indian communities all through the region.

In the short run, the Seven Years' War emboldened the colony and its citizens to further their attempts to entirely subjugate the Indians at Pachgatgoch, and to reduce their already meager land holdings. In the not-so-long run, the war spelled doom for the mission, leaving the Indian community to go it alone.

The closing of the mission at Pachgatgoch sent the Moravians back to their headquarters in Bethlehem, although a brother would remain posted at Sichem until it too was abandoned in 1773, the pleas of the congregation there notwith-standing.[230] A few of the Indians talked about joining the brethren at Friedenshüt-ten, and there is the possibility that a handful of others moved north to Stock-bridge.[231] Some families drifted off to live in places here and there in western Connecticut and immediately adjacent in New York. However, a large number stayed put to face a difficult, uncertain, and poverty-ridden future. Little more can be said about the Indians at Pachgatgoch until after the Revolution.[232]

In the years following the Revolution, Pachgatgoch, now known in the re-cords only as Schaghticoke (var.), appears to have been led, in part, by Chuse, Gideon's son. Joshua, whose attempts to replace his father were, at best, erratic, had died in 1771. Throughout, however, Connecticut maintained its oversight and recognition of the Indians and their lands, as it would continue to do for the next two centuries, up to and including the present day. In 1801 the Indi-ans' lands surrounding the "summer huts" and the former mission were sold, compelling them to withdraw a short distance downriver to what is now offi-cially designated the Schaghticoke Reservation.[233] For much of the nineteenth century, the number of Indians in the community appears to have remained around fifty, about a score of whom resided on the reservation at any one time. They earned their modest livings mostly as basket makers, hired hands, colliers, and housekeepers, keeping small kitchen gardens near their homes. In the early 1880s a visitor to the reservation saw "six little, brown, clap-boarded one-story houses tenanted by some seventeen persons." An elderly woman living there told him that most of her people were "'scattered like grasshoppers.'"[234] With the turn of the century, the on-reservation population began to decline, and members of the larger community who lived elsewhere withdrew into them-selves. Yet the reservation remained a place where a few Schaghticoke Indians continued to live, or from time to time would visit, and so it is today.

Epilogue

In December 1981 the "Schaghticoke Indian Tribe" filed a letter of intent with the Department of the Interior, Bureau of Indian Affairs (BIA), to petition for federal acknowledgment; a documented petition would not be submitted until December 1994. Thus began a more than a decade-long effort by the Schaghti-cokes to gain status as a federally recognized Indian tribe. The administrative process, in many ways reflecting events that typified the 270-year history of the Schaghticoke community, had its ups and downs. In December 2002 the BIA issued a proposed negative finding, concluding that the tribe had failed to meet two of the seven criteria required for federal acknowledgment. Two years later, after evaluating the tribe's response to the finding, which had been bolstered by additional research, the BIA reversed itself, acknowledging the Schaghticokes as a tribe within the meaning of federal law and establishing a government-to-government relationship between the tribe and the United States. But a short five months later, May 2004, that decision was vacated, and in October 2005, the BIA published a reconsidered final determination to decline to acknowledge the Schaghticoke tribe. Appeals filed within the Department of the Interior and before a federal court have proved unsuccessful.

Johann David Bischoff

18 May to 5 June 1747

Diarium of the visit of David and Zacchaeus, the Indian, to Shekomeko, Wechquadnach, and Pachgatgoch — *st. vet.*[1]

☽ [Monday], May 18, 1747

We traveled in a state of heartiness from Bethlehem to Gnadenthal and Nazareth.

♂ [Tuesday], May 19

We went as far as Samuels Green's place,[2] where a Negro lives who has an Indian woman for a wife, [and] who is free and has been to Bethlehem.[3] Always talks about moving to Bethlehem. His name is Anton Robert; [he] served us in accordance with his means.

☿ [Wednesday], May 20

We went through the wilderness. Zacchaeus asked me if I did not think that he should come along to Germany. Answer: He had to leave such thoughts to the Savior and the congregation; if it were beneficial to him, it would surely happen. There was a man who had 2 horses free; he wanted to take us on them for another 5 miles to his house. But Zacchaeus did not want to, saying he was not able to ride. Hence I stayed behind with him in a house where even Zacchaeus said, These are indeed an entirely different sort of people. The man with the horses was the same where Br. Seidel had once stayed overnight, and the [same] people [who] pretty nearly came to meet me, Br. Rauch, and Hannes, the Indian, out in the road, giving us apples. Today I felt something special in my heart—I thought my brethren and sisters are praying for us.

♃ [Thursday], May 21

It rained all day today, but we nonetheless advanced a fair distance. We came upon a good many heathens in the woods; we thought they were [some] of our brethren and sisters, but they were not. Some women came into our quarters [and] got completely drunk. They spoke English. I was able to understand them well, but it was nothing more than an incredible boasting.

♀ [Friday], May 22

We reached the river.[4] A Presbyterian *mennister* [minister] came, wanting to question me [about] what *law* we were subject to. Answer: Subject to the English [law]. He asked what we believed. I asked what he believed. However, given that he wanted to move on, I said I did not know English well and was not able to express myself toward him in such a way that he would not misunderstand me. He rode across with us and we remained good friends. Today my Zacchaeus turned stubborn. I was concerned; I wanted to put up here and there, to take up lodgings for his sake, yet he would let me continue on and [then] he would always walk by. Thus I followed him until late into the night.

♄ [Saturday], May 23

We traveled on. [I] was concerned about getting bread and butter at [such] a very early hour. Came to a house; the people were still asleep. Finally, they sent [out] a boy. I asked if we could have bread. He said, No. Zacchaeus said I should go to the house at once. I said it will not work this way—I would get bread [somewhere], not to worry. He said if I would not get any there, I would not get any at all. I said, with *afrot* [affront], Dear Zacchaeus, let us not act this way. We have a *plan*[5] now, hence we must speak with each other lovingly. Answer [from Zacchaeus]: I should shut up. I went into another house [and] received all the necessaries. I asked him to wait, but he ran away from me and I did not know the way. I did finally find him, however. I asked the dear Savior that, where I failed, He shall please make amends for everything. We walked in silence. I did not stir up anything but tried as much as I could to win him over. We came to Hannes Rauch.[6] He asked that we stay with him. We went to visit Shekomeko; we found Martha and Deborah at home. They did not look up, neither did Shau Beenu. Judith also was not the way we had hoped. I visited Brother Büttner's grave; I was able to speak with him as if in person. My heart was soft and almost in tears on this occasion. I went into our former house.[7]

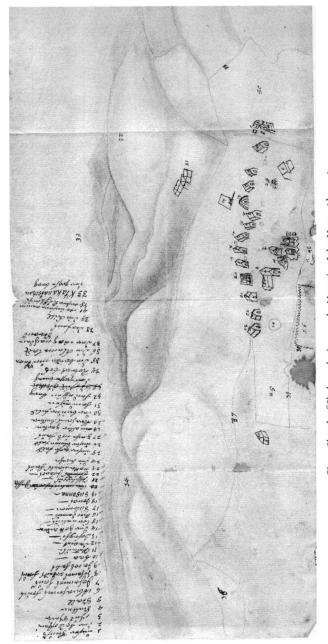

Fig. 1. Sketch of Shekomeko in 1745, by Moravian John Hagen (d. 1747). From the collections of the Moravian Archives, Bethlehem, Pennsylvania.

My heart had been uneasy before this, [but] then I became well and was able to sing a couple of verses with joy; with them I thought I brought about sighs from the brethren and sisters.

☉ [Sunday], May 24

I concluded with Zacchaeus that he should go ahead to Pachgatgoch, for I had learned that not all of them [the Indians] were home, and in the meantime I stayed here with Hannes Rau, now and then going to Shekomeko, praying and weeping, also working some. I occupied myself with Timotheus until the 26th. I had some effect on him; he was very openhearted with me.

☿ [Wednesday], May 27

I went to Wechquadnach.[8] The watchword[9] read: *O Her[r] hilff o Her[r] laß wohl gelingen.* Verse[d]: *Ja zu unßern Thaten hilff selbst daß beste Rathen den Anfang Mittel u Ende Her[r] alles zum besten Wende.*[10] I trusted the Lamb would carry out everything. I came upon Jonathan who right away was prepared to go with me to Pachgatgoch. Moses received me with kindness and affection. I delivered my message to Jonathan. He said [that] he had never had any other intention but to follow his father; he wanted to hurry now to ready himself. He went with me to Pachgatgoch. [There] I found Zacchaeus happy. Gideon, who received me kindly, was readying himself. It went on in the same way with Simon's family, but [they] were not yet ready. I lodged in the house of Zacchaeus's brother. We had all of them assemble and saluted them from the congregation and from several brethren and sisters. In particular, we assured them that they would not be forgotten by the white brethren and sisters; we had now been sent here in everyone's name to see what they were doing. They thought I should hold a meeting, but I did not feel up to it. I sang a verse and let them go.

♃ [Thursday], May 28

I was quiet in Pachgatgoch, but Zacchaeus went and reported to me continuously. Everyone stirred today. The wind of life went into the dead bones. Simon and his entire family resolved today to go to Bethlehem. I only impressed upon Zacchaeus that he tell everyone the *plan* correctly, as well as the reason for the

change, which he did. There even came to us from Wechquadnach Bartholomew's brother young Johannes, Moses's son.[11]

♀ [Friday], the 29th

We again were quiet here throughout the day. In the evening Simon held a love
feast for all who were present in Pachgatgoch. I sang a verse[d]. Gideon addressed
everyone in a moving manner. I heard it [Gideon's address] praised much, but
was unable to understand the words. I also expressed myself plainly in the presence of everyone, that I saw and heard that many were preparing themselves to
go to Bethlehem. Thus it was so, then, that all of them had in their hearts evidence from the dear Savior that their souls could not prosper here but would
die again and be corrupted, and [they] therefore came to us solely for the sake
of their souls. Those we would take in as children and brethren and sisters, but
they would also have to submit themselves to our rules, [and] also find satisfaction in work, and like us, be able to manage everything necessary—that we
white brethren also had to work diligently, yet show patience in poverty. However, those who had a different purpose shall please stay away from us. Moreover, those who would go there [shall] not bring along any of this kind, and
rather spare them the journey, for they themselves could not stay there anyhow, and we reserved to ourselves the liberty to send them away again. Jonathan interpreted this for me but added himself that one could well imagine that
one would have to work there, given that no white people lived there.[12] I said
that was not the reason, but they knew themselves how it had been, especially
in Shekomeko and elsewhere, that once they had felt the dear Savior and His
blood in their hearts, and had felt well, they were obliged to go out among the
people, and there they had lost everything again and the enemy had deceived
them.[13] That is what was our concern, that we could stay together and hold our
meeting every day and remain preserved.

♃ [Thursday], May 30

Sherman, who is [the head of] a large family, came and said [that] his heart
~~would have to~~ was telling him he did not have to stay here, but he had no money
[to get] across the [North] river. I gave him some to get across. Right away
his entire house stirred. Abel's wife, her husband not being home, said, I am

79

not staying behind. I said she could not leave her husband; she had to pray for him. She assured me, however, that he would follow and [that] they had fondly agreed on this beforehand. At this I left it up to them. The wife of Joshua—who also is not at home—acted in like manner; she would go, her husband would follow. Likewise the wife of Jeremias, but she said her husband would come along. Samuel wants to come as well. I was not able to wait for Andreas and Lucas. I also spoke with Jacob [about] how matters stood with him—what should he say when the Indians in Gnadenhütten asked about him [and] what he was doing? Answer: He would come soon, but first he had to go to Sheko-meko and Rhinebeck and sell his belongings. We went in the house where I had slept, they [the Indians] were unbaptized. The woman said about me that she could tell that we were very different people. The husband was the brother of Zacchaeus. We still went to Wechquadnach today. Jonathan and the others went ahead. Moses again rendered us every service. [He] said that he wanted to sell everything soon and come too, although I do not think this year. Jo-hannes very much wanted to go with Jonathan, which I noticed. I could see that his wife did not want to, thus, he could not say anything, and Jonathan, whose wife is still looking forward to coming to us, apparently does not hin-der him. However, when it did not seem to work out with Johannes, he [Jon-athan] too could not give me any clear information, other than that he will come soon. We slept in Moses's house.

☉ [Sunday], May 31

We once again went to Judith in Shekomeko, who did not pay much attention to us, however, saying instead, very *indeverent* [indifferently], that she would look to Jacob. Indeed, Abraham has told us very clearly that Jacob is the man who is working against us. We went to Rhinebeck, to Jacob Maul and Zacharias Haber; I saluted them and inquired about the school.[14] Thus I learned that Jacob Maul apparently has assurances from Merteins[15] to get a piece of land there in per-petuity, but saw that they prefer that the school be set aside for now.

☽ [Monday], June 1

I went to Friederich Streit's [house] to stay overnight. When I had the opportu-nity and said something to Zacchaeus—because he wanted to sell something, first having asked less from Jacob Maul and now asking more from his sister—that he should not do this, [that] they were brethren and sisters, he lashed out at me, [saying] that I was a liar. I asked that he not take me wrong, I only meant well. He said he would not stay with me, and with that [he] up and left. I asked him not to do this, please. But [he] proved himself more and more unseemly. I could not run after him, I did not feel like doing so, yet my heart burst into tears and supplications to the dear Savior. Streit, who otherwise is a member to be banned from the school, told me that he wanted to give two pounds for it if only his children went to Bethlehem. I had the opportunity to express the congregation's *plan*. Thus Jacob Maul tells me that [Christian] Führer had come into his house determined to take either Martin's wife, or his, and the children of both, and take them to Bethlehem, which had also upset his, Maul's wife. I said, Bethlehem was not so open that anyone who wanted to could simply flock to it. Did not the brethren have more sense than to press the congregation that hard?

♂ [Tuesday], June 2

I followed [and] found my companion drunk on the way. I walked with him awhile. Finally, he fell down [and] I laid down with him. Having waited awhile, I remembered that we had summoned the brethren and sisters from Pachgatgoch to definitely meet at the [North] river this evening, and I wanted to assist them when it came to changing the money, in case they were lacking some. Thus, I thought, as long as this Zacchaeus still has money, he will not allow himself to be led now, but I thought nonetheless he would soon follow, for it was not far from the [North] river. However, I did not find the ones [we had] summoned [there]. I waited at this out-of-the-way place for half a day today, and [on] June 3 until noon, but no one came. In the meantime, I occupied myself with 2 Negroes. First, I asked what they believed. They said, what all the people hereabouts believed. I said that we particularly loved the Negroes and [that] our brethren had been among them for a long time, teaching them the word of life, which has been manifested in their hearts. I told them about the difference between Christians. They understood me and loved me very much. Thus, I departed alone and came to Bethlehem on June 5.

The families who were ready to come are:[16]

First, Gideon and she[17]	2
One daughter as widow who [has] a girl of 9 or 10 years	2
One grown daughter, unmarried	1
One grown boy	1
Joshua's wife, she and 3 children	4
Andreas and she and 2 children	4
Lucas and she and 3 grandchildren[18]	6 and the old mother
Simon and she and 3 children	5
Simon's married brother and his wife and 2 children	4
Sherman and she and one grown girl	3
Abel and she and 2 or 3 children	4
Jeremias and she and 3 children	5
Samuel and she and his mother	3
Jonathan and she and 1 child	3

David Bruce

6 March to 5 May 1749

☽ [Monday], March 6, 1749[1]

Returning from Shekomeko, I brought the greetings from our dear hearts Cammerhoff and Gottl[ieb] [Pezold], [and] our dear Indians greatly rejoiced at that.[2] I found them blissful and in good spirits. In the evening we had [a] blissful singing service to learn several of the newly composed verses in Indian,[3] throughout which all of us were lively and cheerful, and the feeling of grace, which they had enjoyed so recently, was fresh in all of their minds, and this could be very well seen and sensed about each one.

♂ [Tuesday], March 7

This morning I spoke with Brother Jacob with Br. Abraham.[4] He was soft and sensible, and wept, and wished that he may once again feel like he had in the beginning. I held school with the children today, also spoke with Timoth[eus]. But he was sullen and very angry, and seeks to blame his wife, and because his wife did not want to give herself up to the Savior as well, he had to be of one mind with her. We found he was still hard and had no intention of giving himself up to the Savior. Thus, he was left to the Savior. The two newly baptized ones, Elenora and Catharina, were quite blissful and feeling, and were cleaving to the Savior.

☿ [Wednesday], March 8

I spoke with several more brethren and sisters today. They also told me of their intention to go to the sugar hut tomorrow.[5] I held school that forenoon. Elenora desired to hear something of her own. I told her, as a mother does with her child, that is how the Savior did it with us, and it was in this way that He wanted to bring her to the breast of the wounds and into the side hole.[6] I went to Salisbury that afternoon and visited several English people on whom the Savior is working. They left the church of the Presbyterians, and the Savior made it happen that I chanced to speak with them when they were just in the beginning of their separation, and came to speak of many extraordinary matters. The Savior gave me from His blood and wounds so as to speak with them in such a way that they have demonstrated a great love ever since, and there is reason to be hopeful that through the blood they will be preserved from many peculiar extremes into which a great number of their fellow brethren in New England are being led. There are some among them who [have] a soft heart for the wounds, [so] that when I [recite] to them a fervent English hymn, they cannot keep from weeping. But it is to be seen how the Savior wants to proceed with them.

♃ [Thursday], March 9

I came home this morning and spoke with several brethren and sisters, with Abr[aham] and Sarah, [and] Mo[ses] and Miriam, who had readied themselves to go into the *zugar* swamp.[7] They were blissful and full of light. Elenora too was childlike and blissful. Johannes went along to Pachgatgoch, where we arrived that evening, at which our dear hearts greatly rejoiced. In the evening we had an anointed and blessed singing service during which we sang several Indian verses[d]. When we sang the verse *Seitenhöligl. du bist mein,*[8] dear mother Erdmuth told us that she had dreamed that she was amid a delightful company that sang so beautifully, and also with these same words: *Leib u Seel färt in dich hinein.*[9] Brother Martin said, When we arrive at the Savior above, we will not have to take such great pains with learning how to sing. Then [he] said, I believe the singing will become very natural to us. The breeze of grace coming from the corpse and blowing among the dear hearts was most palpable.

♀ [Friday], March 10

Today we made preparations to speak with our brethren and sisters in Gide[on's] house, first with those who had partaken of Communion, and thereafter with the newly baptized ones. However, the shame and abasement that this occasioned, and also the joy at seeing what the Savior is affecting in the dear hearts, cannot be described, for with the exception of some few hearts, it is a body fully permeated by blood and wounds. Old mother Rachel was not as blissful, and [neither was] Lucia; but [some] of the others were, such as Erdmuth. She had truly enjoyed Communion with the others, in spirit. Gottlieb, Magdalena, Martin, and Justina were so hungry for it [Communion] that it will not [be] possible to deprive them of this very fare, for they hungered greatly. To our great joy, our dear Leah was happily delivered of a young son this evening, between 9 and 10 o'clock at night. The watchword was of great comfort to us today.

♄ [Saturday], March 11

I spoke with Brother Gideon and Joshua today, whose hearts were in very good spirits, and I visited all the huts[10] and also our dear Leah, who along with her husband desired that their little son[d] be baptized with the blood and water from the side hole[d], which I promised them as soon as a brother would come from Bethlehem. Thereupon I departed with my heart[d] Johannes [and] arrived in Wechquadnach at 2 o'clock. I spoke some with our dear Elenora, and comforted her in the Savior and His wounds with regard to her circumstances. She wept, but I told her the Savior would help her through [so] that her little heart[d], whom He had thus blessed in her womb with His blood when He had baptized her with blood and water, should be brought happily into this world as well. Her husband told her this in Indian, and [I] was very glad for the opportunity, for the poor hearts were both distressed. Afterward, I went to the sugar huts and had the opportunity to speak with several more hearts[d].

☉ [Sunday], March 12

Today we stayed at the sugar huts because the weather was terrible, and I also held our meeting here. We were together in bliss. In the evening I went and stayed overnight at Belius's [house].

☽ [Monday], March 13

I held school with the children and worked in my house today.

♂ [Tuesday], March 14

I held school again. In the afternoon Joseph Skinner came to me, who is putting forth *pretension*[s] to the land on Gnadensee, where the Indians are living. He was one of the New Lights,[11] and said [that] the Lord had first used him as an instrument unto the Indians, and because they were stirred, our Brother

Christian [Rauch] came to them. Yet he had loved them so much that he had purchased their land so that they would not be driven out, but now he was forced to sell it, yet wanted to let them [the Indians] have it for a reasonable price. Perhaps the Brethren would assist them with it. But he wanted one hundred pounds for the one hundred acres, to which I hardly responded, and dismissed him. I told this to Br. Moses in the evening; left the matter up to the Savior, however.[12] This evening a messenger came to the Indians who told them that the poor and unfortunate Papenõha lay dead in Rhinebeck, but for fear of the Indians, he did not want to say how he had perished. That caused a terrible uneasiness in everyone's mind. I entreated the Lamb[d] to avert harm this evening. Already during the night some set out with the intention to bring the body [of Papenõha] to Shekomeko to bury [it] there. Tonight I had the opportunity to speak with our dear Catharina. Her heart was suffering a great deal of distress because her husband is trying with wicked tricks and many things to be a hindrance to her and to cause her to stray from the feeling. This saddened me very much, and I deeply entreated the Savior to preserve her from this, because she was very agreeable and feeling.

☿ [Wednesday], March 15

In the forenoon I held school. In the afternoon I went to Salisbury and had the opportunity to speak further with several of the souls there; I stayed overnight with them.

♃ [Thursday], March 16

This morning Ephraim Colver came to the house where I was lodged. He was very tenderhearted, and one has good reason to hope [that] he will become entirely the Savior's. They would be only too happy to have several of our English hymn books. I came home and went with Br. Abraham to Shekomeko, yet no one had arrived from Rhinebeck. All of the brethren and sisters had gone [from] here and to Rhinebeck. However, we knew nothing more except that it was said that he [Papenõha] had been shot dead by a Low German white woman.[13] I stayed overnight with Hannes Rau, and together with his son, young Hannes, who intends to leave for [New] York tomorrow. I wrote one letter to Br. Horsefield and one to the brethren.

♀ [Friday], March 17

During the night Timotheus had arrived from Rhinebeck. He brought word that he [Papenõha] was already buried in Rhinebeck, and because I could see that I would not be able to go to Pachgatgoch today, I went home. Tonight our dear Elenora was happily delivered of a young daughter.

♄ [Saturday], March 18

Today I went and worked, and all of the others came home from Shekomeko and Rhinebeck. Our Sister Martha had conducted herself very nicely when, in council, she was to answer whether she desired revenge for her son's blood.[14] She said, Our God showed mercy on us and forgave us, and the Brethren teach us not to be revengeful, and this disobedient son of mine has thus perished by misfortune. My other son, who also is a murderer, is still alive; therefore, we likewise want to forgive this woman just as the Savior forgave us. Since we cannot help the matter through revenge, let her live.[15]

☉ [Sunday], March 19

This morning [I] spoke heartily and most thoroughly with our dear Jacob in the presence [of] Abrah[am] and Mos[es]. We affectionately pointed out his conduct to him. He was soft and sensible, thus, we dismissed him heartily. I also spoke some with Rachel; in her heart, she was on tender terms with the Savior. We also spoke with Timotheus; he was somewhat more candid, yet still in a state of confusion. Thereafter we gathered for the meeting and delivered an address on today's watchword, blessed with a feeling of grace and very suitable to the situation here.

☽ [Monday], March 20

This morning I took the opportunity to speak with Moses and Abraham and to deeply entrust to them the matter concerning the Savior, about which our hearts revive. I also spoke with our Catharina; spoke with Judith and Abigail as well. They were on quite childlike terms with the Savior; we rejoiced at that. I took leave of Moses and Abraham and went to Pachgatgoch, where I arrived in the evening. Our dear hearts were very glad at that. I found that it was in the nick of time, for our dear Leah was deathly ill.

♂ [Tuesday], March 21

I visited Leah this morning, and thus spoke with her of dying and going to the Savior. She was very agreeable, and one could clearly see that the Savior will soon prepare her for dying. In Brother Gideon's house we spoke again with all our dear hearts, with [the help of] Br. Joshua;[16] first with the communicants, [and] afterward with the newly baptized ones. Some small matters had gotten in the way of several [of the Indians]. Yet the dear Lamb[d] bestowed upon us the grace to prevent further harm, so that they were once again shown the path of the blessed blood and side hole, causing all our hearts to be very happy and revived in regard to them. Elisabeth was very blissful, and [so were] Andreas, Martin, and Justina. He[17] has only one complaint; he was troubled that he [has] some debts here and there that amounted to nearly 20 pounds New England money. I consoled him about it and said he should not torment himself over it; the Savior would assist him. She[18] said she had experienced that when previously she was about to do something: she would think on it upon going to bed; she also dreamed about it; and when she awoke or went to eat, she would continuously think on it. Now, she is the same way with the Savior; she was occupied with His wounds and blood by day and night and in her dreams. Gottlieb and Magdalena likewise were very blissful. Gottlob too was agreeable. However, when we called his wife—as we had already a mind to speak with her in this way, and had seriously enjoined him to do so before—and when she then tearfully asked to be baptized, he was completely beside himself. Paulus has an unmarried brother; she and the Savior led onto the right path.[19]

☿ [Wednesday], March 22

This morning I again visited our dear Leah. She was very ill and said, Now I have given my whole heart to the Savior, and I feel that I have no worries concerning this world or the affairs here; and she left her children and [her] husband and everything to the Savior. She desired to go to the Savior now. She was so weak she could not sleep. However, when she closed her [eyes] and slumbered, she thought she saw near her a man, and he was so very friendly and had wings on his sleeves, and she thought [that] she too would get such wings, and with them she would fly with him to the Savior. I told her yes, she shall soon receive the grace to go to the Savior and to fly all the way into His side hole[d], and to kiss the beautiful wounds that ~~beautiful wounds~~ have warmed her heart here so often, and there she should report to the Savior a great many things about the Indians, and especially [about those] here in Pachgatgoch. And she should entreat the Lamb[d] that He may deliver into Joshua's and her father's heart a great amount of blood so that they may also help the others, and that all of the souls here may be drawn very deeply into the wounds. Thus, I took leave with a happy heart. Because I had heard that the preacher in this area wanted to visit her today to give her some medicine, I did not feel that I should stay. With that I recommended everything to the Savior, to His faithful hands, and went to Wechquadnach. I found our dear hearts there and told them that if someone wanted to go to Pachgatgoch to see Leah before she died, they should go tomorrow. We then had a blessed singing service.

♃ [Thursday], March 23

Today many readied themselves to go to Pachgatgoch. But because I thought that the preacher might [be] there, or otherwise, someone from among the white people [who might engage me in a] quarrel or some other talk with them, I did not intend to go, but instead set out on my journey, this time to Rhinebeck. Having talked with Abrah[am], Moses, and Jacob, I readied myself, and at 8 o'clock our dear heart Gottlob came from Pachgatgoch, bringing us word that our dear Leah had flown home[20] blissfully one hour before daybreak. Hence the brethren left so that they could get to the funeral. But because I did not want to create a stir, nor did I want to give the white people occasion to hinder our other work among our dear Indians, I went to Rhinebeck and arrived at Jacob Maul's [house] in the evening. He was very glad to see me again.

♀ [Friday], March 24

I felt especially comfortable about our watchword today. This forenoon we went to hear the Lutheran preacher. He preached plainly and also fairly agreeably in his own way, but not so anointed and bloody. He touched upon a matter (of which I could ask the Lamb[d], with all my heart, that it may become so in his heart and those of his hearers) that one should not think of the Savior's sufferings only during Passiontide,[21] but, like the first Christians, keep them in view at all times and in constant remembrance. This evening I intended to hold a meeting among strangers, but set it aside because Jacob Maul wanted to visit young Streit,[22] for we heard [that] he was very ill. Hence I went along as well. However, we had little opportunity to say anything, given that there is no one in the house who takes much pleasure in hearing something about the Savior, except for the boy.

♄ [Saturday], March 25

Very early today we set out and returned home. There I occupied myself and wrote a bit, also [I] thought of Bethlehem a good deal, and of my brown hearts at home. I also spoke with David Führer a little, who, however, is in a very bad way, having fallen into carnal lust up to his neck, so that for now matters are no longer any good with him, nor does he intend to go to the congregation unless the Savior performs an extraordinary miracle on him.

☉ [Sunday], March 26

I continued writing today. Toward 3 o'clock I went to [Zacharias] Haber's [house] where a meeting had been arranged. A number of strangers attended it as well. When I spoke to them about today's epistle, which the Lamb[d] had inspired in me as He was near me with His wounds, our friends were very glad about the occasion,[23] but several of the strangers grumbled that they were unable to gain [from it] what they had expected.

☽ [Monday], March 27

I set about soling my shoes today and accomplished it.[24] The remaining time I wrote. Haber visited me in the evening; thus, I had the opportunity to speak with him of his heart. There is indeed something of the Savior among the people, but it is indeed very weak and in great need of care.

♂ [Tuesday], March 28

Today I once again prepared myself for traveling and [also] spoke a little with Jacob Maul and his wife, saying something to them about their children. With that I took leave, and he [Maul] and Haber accompanied me a few miles through the woods. Shortly before sunset I came to Hannes Rau. He told me about our dear heart Joshua,[25] that he had arrived here from Bethlehem on Sunday. Thus I hurried so that my horse could feed a little so that I could get home this very day, for I had brought some things with me from Rhinebeck that I could not carry on my own. Arriving at home, I was very glad to see our dear Joshua, and also to receive the delightful letters, allowing me to enjoy something from the congregation [in Bethlehem].

☿ [Wednesday], March 29

Today we visited the huts a bit, and let Abraham and Sarah and Moses know of Jonathan's intention to go and live in Gnadenhütten. They were altogether pleased with it, but at the same time told me what they thought would be in the way. I said I wanted to write to Bethlehem about the circumstances. Thus we wanted to see if perhaps a brother could come soon, and if it were possible, also baptize them. Joshua went with me to my house and he told me what he had noticed about this or that person in the course of his visit here. The delightful news of our dear Jacob especially gave me great joy. In the evening we had [a] singing service in Moses's hut.

♃ [Thursday], March 30

Today Brother Joshua went along to Pachgatgoch. Our dear hearts were very glad to see our Joshua here again, and furthermore, that they once again had a visit from [an] Indian brother from the congregation. Our dear Gideon had fallen and struck his side hard, so that, as a result, he was somewhat indisposed. Martha had gone to Potatuck.[26] This evening we visited in all of the huts, also Benjamin's father, with whom I had the opportunity to speak, and it appears that the Savior is working on his heart. In the evening we had a blessed singing service during which they also learned to sing several of the new verses. They usually are in the habit of getting together every evening.

♀ [Friday], March 31

Today I made arrangements to speak with our dear hearts [in preparation for Communion]. Something had interfered with a number of them so that they did not have free access to the wounds in a true childlike manner. However, the Lamb[d] helped us portray to them His side hole[d] in such a way that they again took heart and summoned the courage to [approach] Him. Old mother Rachel and Lucia are now beginning to understand the grace that they had first

91

felt, and to get on the wounds' path. I greatly rejoiced at that. Old mother Erd-muth was ill, but very blissful. Samuel had gotten into something, yet the Savior blessed the instruction of him and also of his wife. This evening we again had [a] singing service on our blessed watchword, and we portrayed to them the side hole[d] as their temporary and eternal dwelling. The letters from the congregation were most savory and weighty to them, and they were hardly able to express their joy and gratitude about them.

♄ [Saturday], April 1

Today all of our dear hearts paid a visit, and they came to us in Gideon's hut and had their letters to the congregation written. Afterward, we took leave, and I and Joshua went to Wechquadnach. On the way we visited Lazara. She was much better and was now able to walk upright, in one place. Joshua spoke with her some as I did not have a favorable opportunity because of the people in the house. Moses and Abraham were also there just then, so we went home together. Today for the first time I went to sleep in my house alone, because I wanted to work on writing my letters to Bethlehem early tomorrow. The Lamb with His angels watched over me, so that I slept cheerfully and blissfully in the side hole.

☉ [Sunday], April 2

We had a meeting today; Joshua interpreted. Afterward, those here also wrote their letters to the congregation. I continued with my writing until about evening. After that I went and stayed with Abraham today so that I would still have more of an opportunity [to speak] with them.

☽ [Monday], April 3

I wrote until about noon today. Then I was done, and I right away sent off our dear Joshua, and we accompanied him on his way for a short distance. The farewell at Moses's and Abraham's was quite passionate, and one could feel and see the love swelling in their hearts for the dear hearts in Gnadenhütten and [this was also evidenced by] the heartfelt greetings that they sent on to them through Joshua. Next we went to talk to Timoth[eus] and his wife, but he was not at home. We had the opportunity to speak with her, but we found that the Savior has to first make matters even more serious for her before something can happen. We also took the opportunity to speak with Esther, for the Savior has vigorously worked on her heart. I held school this afternoon.

♂ [Tuesday], April 4

I went with Abraham and Moses this morning to visit our dear Jacob and Rachel. On the way I spoke with Moses [about] what he now thought regarding the land, because the white people are set on taking it away.[27] He said he knew nothing, yet whenever he thought about this, and especially last night and this morning when he and his wife spoke to each other about her wanting to go to Bethlehem, he felt in his heart an indescribable joy about this. At this point I had the opportunity to help him somewhat with that, but gently to be sure, so as to let the Savior work on this matter Himself. From here onward it was noticeable that the Savior was working not only with the outward circumstances but also was working vigorously on the hearts, that they all shall leave here together and come to the congregation. I greatly rejoiced at this, but I kept quiet as much as possible, except when this or that person spoke of it of his own accord. Our Jacob was somewhat better today, but was still weak, yet the state of his heart was agreeable. The Savior continued to work on him quietly. Rachel also was very agreeable. The Savior affected both of them in such a way that they shall go to the congregation [in Bethlehem]. Timotheus happened to come here to us just then; we spoke with him, but he was still in as bad a state as before. We could not do anything else but only ask the Lamb[d] that He may seize his heart again. Held school again today.

☿ [Wednesday], April 5

Held school again that forenoon. That afternoon I went to Salisbury and visited the people there. It is bad with their poor souls, however. They torment themselves in so many roundabout ways and because of their own *praxi* [Greek: deeds or actions] and teaching, and also their [keeping] company with the other lawful,[28] corrupted people, they continuously stray from the simple path of the gospel. In the course of a talk, I had the opportunity to again tell them something about the wounds, and to direct them thereto, in a simple and childlike manner. Stayed overnight with Jonathan More.[29] He and his very much desire to hear something, but it does not appear to penetrate them all too deeply.

The New Englanders are very corrupted through and through, and have much brain but no heart.

♃ [Thursday], April 6

I went home [to Wechquadnach] this morning. There I found our dear Jonath[an] and Anna, who had come yesterday evening. I was very glad to see him again. I was also very much gladdened by our watchword today. At this time it can be felt that more of what the Savior wanted to have happen with the souls here is coming about, thus things are strongly moving toward virtually all of them intending to leave together. And this afternoon they had to go to take *posess* [possession] of their summer houses,[30] so that the same person who purchased the land would not take *posess* first and drive them out in a body, all at once. Thus they moved out of the *zugar schwammp* [sugar bush] and into the summer houses today. I deeply entreated the Savior that He may achieve His end. Yet my journey to Pachgatgoch was hampered today. Jonathan wanted very much to come along, but he was very tired. Moreover, I wanted very much to be on hand so that everything would go well when they moved out, also because Moses had been threatened that the *constable* would come from Sharon.

♀ [Friday], April 7

Today I stayed in my house and again refreshed myself with the letters that Jonathan had brought me from the congregation. Also, I felt that my heart longed for Bethlehem and I hoped [that] I would soon get the opportunity to go there again myself.

♄ [Saturday], April 8

Today I stayed home again and occupied myself. I stayed away from the summer houses because the *justice* from Sharon and others wanted to go there to speak with the Indians about their land and to get them off it.[31] Also, Moses was still expecting the *constable*. I comforted him a little, but I myself went to my house.

☉ [Sunday], April 9

This morning our Johannes came to me. He had returned from the shore, but had conducted himself badly there.[32] He came and admitted it to me; I spoke with him warmly and directed him as a poor sinner to the wounds, hoping that there will be an end to this soon, once he came to the congregation. He said he felt [that] here it was not possible for him to stay long. We held our meeting and Jonathan interpreted. However, on every occasion one could feel that it was finished here, and the Savior did not inspire me to speak with joy, and one could see and grasp that the Savior did not want to encourage the Indians in the least to stay here.[33]

☽ [Monday], April 10

This morning I prepared myself for traveling and went to Pachgatgoch. Jonathan and Moses went with me. Along the way we had a number of blissful talks. I could indeed see what the Savior has done in Jonathan's heart with respect to the congregation, and this was made apparent at every opportunity. When we came to Pachgatgoch, many brethren and sisters were not home, thus I could tell that this time our usual [act of] speaking[34] would not take place; moreover, their plantation work[35] happened to be such that those who were home could not easily participate. We visited all the houses and talked with those who were there. It was noticeable that the Savior continued to affect their hearts so that they keep within their bounds. And the old stock, such as Erdmuth, Maria, Rachel, Hannah, and Priscilla, [as well as] Petrus and Thamar, were also very blissful. In the evening we had a blessed singing service; Jonathan interpreted and also passed on greetings by word of mouth, which pleased the brethren and sisters greatly.

♂ [Tuesday], April 11

I held school with the children this morning. However, because the brethren and sisters were not at home [at Pachgatgoch], we thought it necessary to go home [to Wechquadnach] that afternoon, also because the circumstances there appeared so perilous. We departed at 1 o'clock and arrived home in the evening, blissful and in good spirits.

☿ [Wednesday], April 12

This morning Sarah and Abraham visited me. They wanted to have something written to the congregation. That afternoon I went to Salisbury to speak with several of the people there and stayed overnight. There are several hearts at this place who are open to hearing something about the Lamb[d] and His wounds.

♃ [Thursday], April 13

I arrived home this morning, and because I now had Jonathan [with me], I applied myself to learning the language with more diligence, for although I have tried it many times, I still have not been able to quite catch on. Moreover, all of the work here was at a standstill until one could see how the matter concerning the land would turn out, and regardless of how it may turn out, there are still and all so many in favor of leaving that I could do nothing else but stand still and watch what the Savior would do.

[No entry for April 14]

♄ [Saturday], April 15

Today Skinner and the *depute schrieff* [deputy sheriff] came to me at my house because of the Indians — that they should get off the land — and he wanted me to point out to them [the Indians] the danger if they let matters go to extremes, for the *justice* wanted to prosecute them. I told them that it was not my business here to meddle with the Indians in matters such as these, and in no such situation [did I want to step] between them and the white people; hence I asked to be spared this, for they could come to terms with them through others. And so they left me in peace, and I was very glad, and they went away cordially. All of those of ours from Pachgatgoch came here yesterday to settle their affair concerning Wanachquaticok. For that reason we held a singing service each evening, which felt blessed and anointed to us.

☉ [Sunday], April 16

Today those from Pachgatgoch asked that I hold an English service for them without translation, which I did. That afternoon we spoke with several brethren and sisters who had not been home when we were in Pachgatgoch, such as Martin and Justina and Paulus, also our Susanna. Susanna has become very unfeeling. Paul[us] was agreeable. The enemy sought to discourage Martin and Justina by reminding them of their former sins. In the evening we had a very blessed hour on our watchword. The Lamb quite delighted us.

☽ [Monday], April 17

Yesterday evening Moses heard from Isaac Yanaram that their [the Indians'] land was now entirely gone and that they will have to leave it.[36] Thus they readied themselves and assessed their houses and [their] work, and [then] went to become reconciled with the man who purchased the land, and they sold everything.[37] I went to a blacksmith in Salisbury to retrieve something I had on order with him. I now have resolved to go to Bethlehem with the Indians, as it looked entirely so that the majority would turn that way. Our brethren and sisters from Pachgatgoch went home today, and this time, only Abraham and Joshua went to Wanachquaticok, in the name of the others, to confer there on this matter.

♂ [Tuesday], April 18

This morning I returned home and learned how all of them had sold their goods. The man dealt quite honestly with them and wanted to give them about 220 pounds New England money for their work. In the evening Br. Samuel came here from Pachgatgoch, and through him Br. Gideon sent word [that] those who did not have a mind to go to Bethlehem, he would rather see come to him [at Pachgatgoch] than go to Wanachquaticok, for he believed [that it] would be better for their souls at his place than at Wanachquaticok, and he wanted to receive them with love. Yesterday he did not want to say anything to them, for he saw [that] the majority was of such a mind as to very much want to go to Bethlehem, thus, he did not want to unsettle them in this regard. We had them assemble and I presented this [the situation] to them in these two ways. I told them [that] if they wanted to come to the congregation, the congregation would admit them and make them feel welcome. However, if they were not so inclined, Br. Gideon had made them a different *offert* [offer], and I, as one who loved them as well, wanted to advise them to that end rather than [to go] to Wanachquaticok. For they, no doubt, knew themselves that that was no place for someone who wanted to save his soul. They all tended to favor [going to] the congregation [at Bethlehem], but gave no positive reply. We let them be and [left it] to the Savior to guide the hearts as it best pleased Him.

☿ [Wednesday], April 19

This morning I let Br. Samuel go, not wanting to press for a further response, but asked the Savior to handle the entire matter. And now [that] he [Jonathan] was going to the congregation, Samuel, who had always loved Jonathan, was thus leaning that way as well. That afternoon I went to Salisbury to preach to the people [there], upon their repeated request, in a house on the [New] York line. Because I had told them that I would leave soon, they had persisted so much the harder. Not many people came, which pleased me in a way. Yet the Lamb let a gentle breeze of grace blow among us, and [had us] feel the power of His blood, so much so that I believe several hearts took something away from it. I stayed overnight with one whose name was Parks,[38] with whom I spoke a great deal. The Savior is setting him quite right. He is much removed from many of his peculiar fantasies.

♃ [Thursday], April 20

Today, when I came home, I again found Benjamin's father from Pachgatgoch here, because when he had seen how things were done with the land here, he went to New Milford of his own accord and informed the *governour*[39] about it, and complained about the people in Sharon. Hence the *governour* sent for the Indians, wanting to do right by them. This did not please me, for Moses was already not right in his heart, and I was very fearful of harm [being done] to the souls—and the other one was surely an instrument of Satan. However, before I grasped the matter fully, I went with Jonathan to Shekomeko to visit the Indians there; stayed there overnight.

♀ [Friday], April 20[40]

Spoke with Johannes and Deborah today, [also] with Martha and her mother. Martha is very bad, but the old woman truly longs for the Savior. However, we could not tell her[41] much and soon left. On arriving home, [we learned that] Moses had gone to New Milford to the *governour*, and Miriam was extremely confused. Yesterday's watchword was my consolation, and I asked the Savior to prevent harm. It was of great concern to me that he [Moses] would not do some harm in Pachgatgoch. At present, there was a great deal of confusion. But it was left up to the Lamb[d].

♄ [Saturday], April 22

Today I could not stray from the house, although I thought of Pachgatgoch a great deal and very much entreated the Savior to prevent harm there—that Moses would not say something there that could perhaps hurt some [people]. The brethren and sisters of this place who wanted to leave busily prepared themselves for the journey.

♄ [Saturday], April 22

Today I stayed home again and got our cart[42] ready for the journey.

☉ [Sunday], April 23

This forenoon we had our meeting. After that I stayed home and wrote until evening. We then had a blessed singing service in Moses's house.

☽ [Monday], April 24

This morning Ephraim Colver and Azariah Smith came from Salisbury to say their farewells, and at the same time, asked me warmly to remember them and [to] also ask the Brethren, on their behalf, to send them an English brother, when and where they thought it fit. Even if it could not be done for more than a limited time, they would be very pleased, for they and several of their neighbors very much wanted to have a brother from the congregation. And even if he [could] not [live] in New England, he could still be close to them, given that they lived on the border. They were very affectionate and truly wept on departing. Right after that I went to Pachgatgoch and met Moses on the way; he had carried out his business in New Milford. The dear hearts in Pachgatgoch were very glad that I came to them. I got to see our dear Christian there. I spoke with several about their hearts; the enemy pressed our dear Martin and Justina hard so as to throw them into confusion. I portrayed to them the heart of the Lamb[d] and His wounds, which revived them. The dear Lamb continues working here among the hearts. Brother Gideon and Joshua lamented that they too rarely had occasions among themselves, because now that there was ample work, they did not get together every evening as usual, and so they sensed they were missing something because of it. However, they thought, if a brother were to come some time and live among them, things would greatly improve. And owing to the friendliness of the *governour* toward them—or whoever is the main person at the *court* in New Milford—and his kind inquiry about the Brethren, they thought no brother would ever be hindered here again, and several [would] benefit from this. In the evening we had a meeting that was blessed and feeling. I did not detect that Moses had said anything bad here, but instead had conducted himself most agreeably.

♂ [Tuesday], April 25

Visited all the houses today and was given their [the Indians'] greetings to pass on to the brethren and sisters. Magdalena has acted in a somewhat unwarranted manner because she was not pleased that so many brethren and sisters, and in particular her friend[43] Johannes, wanted to go to the congregation; however, the Savior also let her feel it. Martha's son changed his mind about going to the congregation and stayed behind. I took a very heartfelt leave of them, at which time the poor hearts[d] expressed themselves in a very feeling manner. Today the first *columna* [Latin: column] left from Wechquadnach; [that is,] Jephthah, and old Cornelius, and his wife. On arriving home, we made some preparations for the others who wanted to leave tomorrow.

☿ [Wednesday], April 26

Today, Abraham and his 5 sons, Jacob and his wife and 3 children, Johannes and Lorellu's sister and his brother and her[44] little daughter[d] [all] departed; Joachim's wife also took her son with her.

♃ [Thursday], April 27

This morning we readied ourselves for our journey with our little cart. Jonathan had a mind to take it even as far as Bethlehem. We left at 9 o'clock, and all of Wechquadnach accompanied us for a distance, and when saying farewell, many tears were wept on both sides. My heart was overflowing, to be sure. Poor Abigail and Esther could not contain themselves and sobbed out loud. That there was indeed such true love in the hearts was very lovely to watch, but also very moving. We blessed them tenderly and recommended them [to] the side hole, and with that we departed. We took in the cart Jonathan and his Anna, and their little Nathanael, and Elenora's ill brother, [also] Judith and her son. We traveled blissfully and in good spirits and came through Filkintown this evening, even though driving with the cart had forced us to take an indirect route. We slept in the woods, blissfully and in a happy state of mind.

♀ [Friday], April 28

This morning a Negro who was looking for his ox visited us. We told him something of the Lamb[d], at which time he looked at us in a very timid way. Things proceeded very well throughout the entire day, and several times we heard from our other hearts[d] that they were not very far ahead of us. However, we spent about 2 hours with a blacksmith who made us something for our cart; hence we did not get to see them today. People took us into their house and were very friendly toward us, and also gladly provided for the horses[d]. We were happy, for it rained that night.

♄ [Saturday], April 29

This morning we made a new axletree for our cart, and after that, we drove to the [North] river. We only had one mile [to go] to the *ferrey*. The people [with whom we stayed] did not charge us anything for our food or horses; I thanked them very heartily, for they certainly were of much help to us. We soon arrived at the *ferrey*. There I went about collecting all of our *companie*, for they were not all there, and we rode across the water as soon as it was possible. Now, with everyone having crossed, their hearts jumped for joy. I then sang an Indian verse with several [of them], and we thanked the Lamb[d] with tears of joy that He has taken us this far. We did not get far before we encamped, [so] that our *companie* might get in order. In the evening a man from the nearest house came to us, along with several others. He very much requested that I deliver an exhortation or a sermon to them tomorrow, for they had no ministers in this area. I agreed to it, at which they showed themselves very grateful.

☉ [Sunday], April 30

Today the man returned and asked me to come for breakfast. He was acquainted with several of our brethren from previous times[45] and was called Hamilton. They announced it [the religious service] down along the [North] river as far as they could and as the shortness of time would permit. It was 2 o'clock [when] between 40 and 50 people came. I talked to them about the dear Savior's word. The Savior was manifest among us, and we felt a gentle breeze of grace. Afterward, there was the opportunity to speak separately with several [people], who in their way made their hearts known quite agreeably. In the evening, after having gotten rid of all the white people, I took the opportunity to speak with our dear Indians, and was rather earnest concerning a particular matter. We wept for the stigma in the side [of Christ], yet at the same time He was our Peace. After that we went to rest in His arms.

☽ [Monday], May 1

Very early today we readied ourselves for our journey in the order in which we had arranged it, so that the weak could advance, always riding on horseback for a bit, taking turns; thus things proceeded very well and orderly, and we advanced very well and without discord, which was exceedingly pleasing to me, and the Savior blessed us very much. Today we went a great distance with our large *companie*. In all, the children included, we were 30 persons and two pregnant sisters; [that is,] Sarah, David's wife, and Anna, Jonathan's wife. But the Lamb held His hand over us at all times so that no one suffered harm. And [with] all the people we met, it was as if the Savior made their hearts inclined to helping us along the way, so that on the entire journey not even one person looked askance at us. Tonight we encamped near a beautiful creek. Throughout the night 2 or 3 different companies of white people passed through, but they conducted themselves very modestly. We rested here [feeling] extremely blissful and comfortable in our hearts. Little Nathanael preached to all of us about the wounds that the Lamb[d] had suffered to His body, and seeing the sharp thorns that stood right by our beds, he asked his father if those were the thorns with which the Savior was crowned. He also wished the brethren all around a good [night] and said, *ni 'ndah wutzhămachak anapapăquaik pachtamăwas, ne wapochquan; Das ist mein hertz ist in Wunden Gottes verschloßen[,] auch in die Seite.*[46] Thereupon he fell asleep.

♂ [Tuesday], May 2

Early today we traveled on. Old Jephthah went ahead as soon as, or before, the sun was visible, as he had done every morning on the entire way, so that he always made way of one mile or 3 before the others were able to catch up with him. We soon came to a house; the man's name was John Simson. He was very kind and let us have flour and bread for the journey, and although we paid for it, it was nonetheless a great kindness to us. He also asked that, should a brother be able to come there to preach, he would be very glad, for they had no one there. And even if a brother was only passing through and came not more than 3 hours before nightfall, they could still arrange for it [the preaching] for the following forenoon, so that he may not even delay himself long. He also gave us milk, and appealed to us that no brother pass his house by. We continued on, but our dear old Cornelius and his wife began to grow very tired since they also could not endure the horseback riding, delaying us at least a good 2 hours. On arriving at Tidesworth's, Jonathan left the cart there, and because Cornelius saw [that] he could not continue this way, he too desired to be left. Hence we left him and his wife, and went another 3 miles to a large spring near the great meadows. There we encamped; we appealed to the Lamb[d] and His side hole to help us and them through [this]. We all were very glad that we were getting closer to the congregation.

☿ [Wednesday], the 3rd of May

This morning we traveled on and exited the woods at the plantation, which is about 15 miles long. It was about 1 o'clock when we reached the first house. Our watchword was especially weighty to me today, just as all of them had been very fitting throughout the entire journey, for today our provisions rapidly started to run out. However, the Savior has kept all of the hearts from resigning, so that every one remained in rather good spirits throughout. And I had steadily made haste along the way, as much as possible, for I was concerned about it, for it has been difficult to purchase any [provisions]. However, the Lamb blessed the little we had and brought us to young Samuel Green[47] this evening. They gave us nearly 3 pails of milk and one half bushel of Indian corn flour for our entire *kompanie*. That helped us out a great deal. We slept in the woods 1/4 mile from his house, near a beautiful creek, very blissfully, softly, and well.

♃ [Thursday], May 4

This morning Samuel Green and his wife visited us and brought us some milk. They greatly delighted in such a beautiful *kompanie* of Indians. We set out on our journey as soon as it was possible, that we may hopefully reach Nazareth today. We made it across the Delaware [River] safe and sound.[48] [At] 1 o'clock that afternoon it began to rain, but we reached Nazareth at 7 o'clock. Our dear brethren and sisters there were very glad to see us, and we were happy and very grateful that the Savior brought us this distance safely and in good health, for it rained very hard that night so that it would have been hardly possible for us to shelter ourselves or our belongings in the woods. Here we rested very blissfully and softly, with cheerful and grateful hearts that our dear Savior has preserved us with His side hole, and not only restored to health those who had left home ill, but then averted it [sickness] from those who on the way looked as if they would get ill, so that everyone was well.

♀ [Friday], May 5

Today at 10 o'clock it stopped raining; thus we all readied ourselves to go to Bethlehem. At the halfway point we laid over, and [I told] our dear hearts a little about the Savior—that they may gain hearts[d] that are warm, bloody, and in the spirit of the side hole at the place where we all arrived that afternoon, to our joy and that of our dear brethren.[49]

Abraham Büninger

29 March to 6 December 1750

♃ [Thursday], March 29, 1750[1]

I left Bethlehem again with the intention to return to Pachgatgoch, to the Indian congregation[d] there. I took the route by way of New York, where I arrived on March 31.

☉ [Sunday], April 1

I rested, for I was very tired and worn out from the journey.

☽ [Monday], April 2

The brethren and sisters advised me to go by water as far as Rhinebeck, which I did, saying farewell to the dear brethren and sisters in New York.

♂ [Tuesday], April 3

The *shallup* [shallop] left New York. We had a headwind nearly the entire day.

☿ [Wednesday], April 4

It was calm until about noon when we got a fair wind allowing us to still reach the Highlands.

♃ [Thursday], April 5

I came to Rhinebeck; stayed overnight with Jacob Maul.

♀ [Friday], the 6th

I continued my journey. Zacharias Haber helped me with my pack for a good way. Past noon I came to Joh[annes] Rauch[2] in Shekomeko.

♄ [Saturday], April 7

I came to Pachgatgoch. The Indian brethren and sisters were very glad, and so was I, that we saw one another again. They right away asked me about their sisters and brethren in Gnadenhütten. I told them everything edifying that I knew. In part, they seemed to be satisfied with it; yet I heard afterward that they would have liked it had I they [their sisters and brethren] written to them from Gnadenhütten. I found Br. Post and his Agnes, who were here [and] well.

☉ [Sunday], April 8

I held the meeting. After the meeting I read aloud Br. Cammerhoff's letter that he wrote to the Indian brethren and sisters. It stirred great joy in them, especially because they learned that soon a brother shall come again to celebrate Communion with them. After that I visited the brethren and sisters in their huts. They all exhibited much joy. However, I saw from various circumstances that something has crept in, which alarmed me greatly. Br. Post held the meeting in the evening.

☽ [Monday], April 9

I conferred with the brethren about how it would be possible to bring the wood for building a schoolhouse to this place. They said that they wanted to roll the wood (which was already cut) down the mountain.[3] I only needed to get a wagoner to haul it to this place. I right away went to the nearest neighbor, who refused me, however. When I came back home another one of the neighbors, who apparently had heard what I wanted, was here. He offered to haul it home; he started that same day. Br. Post held the meeting in the evening.

♂ [Tuesday], April 10

All the brethren were industrious, rolling the wood down the mountain. Br. Post and I laid the sills for the schoolhouse[d] that very evening.[4]

☿ [Wednesday], the 11th

The brethren again worked industriously; we laid up [the logs]. Several [brethren and sisters] had gone out.

♃ [Thursday], April 12

[Today] was a day of fasting and repentance, which I needed to celebrate. I did so alone, in quiet. Br. Post went to Wechquadnach; the Indian brethren into the woods to work on their canoes.[5]

♀ [Friday], April 13

Hauling the wood to this place was completed today. Most of the Indian brethren and sisters came home.

♄ [Saturday], April 14

Br. Post returned from Wechquadnach; I worked on the schoolhouse. In the evening meeting the Lamb^d manifested Himself very clearly and mercifully.

☉ [Sunday], April 15

Our Lamb^d of God was very much near us in all the meetings. I also visited all the huts; wrote to Bethlehem.

☽ [Monday], April 16

Brother Post with his Agnes went to Bethlehem. Most of the Indian brethren and sisters went out to work.[6] There was no meeting in the evening.

♂ [Tuesday], April 17

I worked on my house^d.[7] Brother Gottlieb and Samuel went to New Milford.

☿ [Wednesday], April 18

I again held school. The Lamb^d was most near me during the evening service. One could see in the brethren and sisters that the Lamb^d with the side hole^d was among us.

♃ [Thursday], April 19

Today the Lamb^d continued to let us feel some of the peace that He had bestowed upon us yesterday.

♀ [Friday], April 20

Old Br. Jephthah came from Stockbridge; told me that the Indians there would very much like a brother to visit them. Toward evening dear Br. John Wade came entirely unexpectedly. Right away we resolved to go to Stockbridge.[8]

♄ [Saturday], April 21

We set out on our journey. That day we visited several of the separatists,[9] such as *Esqr.* Hopkins,[10] who is a pleasant man, and his wife too is very modest.

Fig. 2. A Stockbridge Indian, 1778 (watercolor).
Courtesy of the Bloomsburg University Archives, Bloomsburg, Pennsylvania.

We visited Wechquadnach. The Indians were very friendly. Afterward, we visited Azariah Smith, and Culver, who had just come from Bethlehem; stayed with him overnight.

☉ [Sunday], April 22

Br. John Wade preached to several of the separatists in Culver's house, who had their meeting there. After the sermon we continued on, yet had to pass by the Presbyterian *mitting* [meeting] house, and because the people were assembled just then, we too went inside. When I returned, I heard that this had its positive *ef[f]ect*: The church people reportedly said, now one could tell that the Moravians were not satisfied with the separatists, for they [the separatists] did not go to church. We still went as far as Sheffield that day.

☽ [Monday], April 23

At 11 o'clock we reached Stockbridge. We first called on Br. Wilhelm,[11] who was very glad to see us; he showed us every kindness, and one can truly tell by looking at him that he is one of us. We visited almost every house, but first Captain Sankiwenecha,[12] who has been to Bethlehem before. We had ample opportunity to portray the Lamb[d] to them. We saw that they were very *attent* [attentive], and seized from our eyes, as it were, what we told them. We met old Ebenezer on the road, telling him at once something about how much the Savior loved him, and that He shed His blood for him. Right away tears ran down his cheeks. He said he clearly saw that he needed a Savior and that things could not go on this way with him, or with Stockbridge. He only wished that God may deliver them before long. He promised me he would visit Pachgatgoch some time soon. This Indian had once been the interpreter for the others. But they have deposed him, and now it appears [that] he is greatly despised. Because the Indians [at Stockbridge] were under the assumption that John Wade was a preacher, the headmen among them decided to charge him with [delivering] a sermon. However, they were very cautious that no harm may result from it. Thus, they directed their proper interpreter (who had not been in council) to charge Br. J. Wade with it, and to request this of him. Br. J. Wade was not immediately resolved. We told him [the interpreter] [that] circumstances might arise from this [Wade's preaching] which would not please them [the Indians], or us. Thus we went to the headmen ourselves, together with him [the interpreter], and put it before them. They said, however, that it was of no consequence that they would not have a regular preacher this time, and that all the Indians would be pleased to once hear a brother preach. Following their decision, Br. John Wade decided to preach to them, which was immediately announced, and although it was already totally night, a large number of Indians came together. Before the sermon we sang 2 v[erses] from our English hymn book, and the Indians sang 4 v[erses] from their books. The words on which Br. J. Wade spoke were: *Kündl groß ist das Keheimniß der Kottseligkeit, Kott offenbahret im Fleisch.*[13] One could well sense how the heart of the dear heart[d] was burning then; he was all life, and so were the Indians. They understood everything. After the sermon we sang again as before. When the meeting was over, all the Indian men, women, and children came and took their leave, shaking our hands and likewise thanking us.[14]

♂ [Tuesday], April 24

We again prepared ourselves again for travel, visited yet several houses, [and] got many greetings from those Indians who have friends[15] in Gnadenhütten, which we promised to pass on to them. Some told us that they wanted to visit Gnadenhütten this summer. There is already such familiarity between them that they would visit Gnadenhütten often if it were not so very far, for they are very much inclined that way. The news that some had moved to Osweko has no basis.[16] Only some young people, who intend to come back, went there. We felt very comfortable in Stockbridge, [so much so] that we even talked to each other about it on our return journey, delighting in it. One can tell that the Indians love us, and in part believe [that] we are a people distinct from all others. We also had the opportunity to see the house and the school built for the maintenance and *information* [of] 20 Indian boys, who shall be educated so that, in the future, they can be used as teachers and schoolmasters. The *rector* himself had invited us.[17] He also acted modestly toward us. We pointed out to him as well as to the other schoolmaster[18] the *Acte* [Act] *of Assembly*,[19] who was very surprised that we are recognized as an Episcopalian church,[20] and are to enjoy more rights and freedom than the Presbyterians. After we left Stockbridge, it began to rain very hard. We called on old Ebenezer who lives 1 mile from that town. We were quite well received at his [house]. That day we proceeded no farther than about 18 miles.

☿ [Wednesday], April 25

This morning we parted ways, and so we had to bid each other farewell, which happened with a kiss of peace and of love. At the same time we reminded ourselves that we were strangers and pilgrims who had to make their way straight through the wilderness, following the Lamb[d]. I thought I would reach Pachgatgoch that day, but had to lay over because my shoes were torn, and that caused me not to get any farther than Sharon.

♃ [Thursday], April 26

I came home in good time, finding all the Indian brethren and sisters in good spirits. While I was gone, they had worked diligently on their schoolhouse. I still visited them in their huts; found Sr. Sarah very ill. In the evening I passed on the greetings that I had for the brethren and sisters of this place from the Indians in Stockbridge, which stirred great joy.

♀ [Friday], April 27

Most of the brethren and sisters worked on the schoolhouse; the brethren built the roof and the sisters carried water and clay[21] to this place so that the firewall,[22] the roof, and also the exterior all around, were plastered that day.[23] During the meeting in the evening, the Lamb[d] could be felt near us with His side hole[d].

♄ [Saturday], April 28

The brethren wanted to set their canoes afloat. I too went with them, helped them, and spent the day with them. In the meeting the Lamb[d] was very much near us. I had a most blessed and sweet night's rest.

☉ [Sunday], April 29

I went visiting in all the huts. Most of the brethren and sisters bemoaned their poverty, into which they have repeatedly come as a result of peevishness. This pained me greatly, yet the Lamb[d] strengthened me so that in the meeting I was able to recommend Him, with His wounds and side hole[d], to all poor sinners. In closing the meeting, Br. Samuel asked that the brethren and sisters remember him, and appeal to the Savior on his behalf, for he felt so very poor.

☽ [Monday], April 30

I worked on my house[d]; also had 1 acre of land plowed, which I intend to plant with Indian corn.[24] I visited the ill Sr. Sarah; she said that she felt so well, she felt all warm inside her heart.

♂ [Tuesday], May 1

During the morning blessing I remembered the church festival that came to me during prayers, and I laid myself and the entire assembly into the side hole[d], asking the Lamb[d] to bless us along with all the other congregations[d], and to forever shield us against all the tumultuousness of the world, instead to keep and preserve us in the side hole[d], in one faith, and [in the] enjoyment of salvation. I said this afterward to several brethren and sisters, which was very weighty to them. After that I held school. Toward evening the brethren and sisters helped me plant my corn.[25]

☿ [Wednesday], May 2

I visited the ill Sr. Sarah, who is starting to grow weakly. Her heart rejoices each time she is told something of the Lamb[d]. In the morning and in the evening a warm breeze[d] from the side hole[d] could be felt. Nathan Gaylord of New Milford visited us, who told me that he felt a strong urge to tell the people to come to J. Christo, also gave me to understand that he would like to preach to the Indians. However, because he did not come straight out with it, I did not reflect on it. We parted from each other on friendly terms. He intends to visit Bethlehem sometime.

♃ [Thursday], May 3

I had a blissful day; I held school [and] visited several huts, finding the brethren and sisters lively and joyous. I prepared some more land for myself for planting.

♀ [Friday], the 4th

I had been very much indisposed for several days, but today in such a way that I thought I would get the ague,[26] yet held school nonetheless. I visited the huts toward evening; many are sickly.

♄ [Saturday], May 5

I was able to work again. The Lamb[d] was near us in the meeting. Afterward, Br. Joshua and several others spoke with me concerning the children. I told them that I alone could not correct the children if they completely let them have their own way at home, and that I would ruin the children if I treated them harshly. My business was merely to now and then tell the children something of the Lamb[d]. They all said it was true, it was their fault.[27]

☉ [Sunday], May 6

I went visiting in all the huts, finding all the brethren and sisters well; Sr. Justina is somewhat feverish. In the meeting the Lamb[d] could be felt near us. We had a small singing service in the evening, on which occasion we sang English verses[d]. We intend, henceforth, to conduct a small singing service in this manner every Sunday.

☽ [Monday], the 7th

I held school in my house[d] for the first time. It was very cozy for the children and me. I had a blissful talk with Br. Jeremias. He said that it made his heart feel so well every time someone told him something of the Savior and how he will be able to get to Him.

♂ [Tuesday], the 8th

I had a favorable opportunity to talk to Br. Johannes and to portray the Lamb[d] to him. He was very straight in telling me about his heart, and how he could say about the Savior's wounds, that they were for him as well.

☿ [Wednesday], May 9

Br. Joshua and Jeremias came from New Milford, where they had been fishing.[28] I visited the ill Sr. Sarah and her son, who is not yet baptized, but very ill. I was able to speak with him of the dear Savior and of His love for man. His heart looked all soft, and he listened quite eagerly. I planted beans for myself.[29]

♃ [Thursday], the 10th

I held school, worked on my house[d], [and] spoke with Br. Samuel, who is getting himself involved in difficulties, against which I advised him.

♀ [Friday], the 11th

The brethren and sisters helped one another with planting; I visited them at work. Old Sr. Maria went to New Milford in order to learn something about her son, who has been gone for nearly 2 months. She is worried about him. I finished planting.

♄ [Saturday], May 12

I wanted to move into my house[d] but was unable to finish it completely. I had a blissful day. In the evening the Lamb[d] was very much near us in the meeting. I had a very blissful night's rest; in my thoughts I was mostly in Bethlehem.

☉ [Sunday], the 13th

At the morning blessing, and also during the sermon, the Lamb[d] could be felt quite near us with His side hole[d]. The ill Sr. Sarah is starting to improve a bit. My heart was greatly comforted when visiting. Petrus said he now saw how the heart looked by nature; it was akin to a rock covered with moss that a person was unable to see until the Savior pointed it out to him. The other brethren and sisters also declared themselves very agreeably, in their own way.

☽ [Monday], May 14

The Lamb[d] was very much near us during the early service. The brethren and sisters readied themselves to go to the seaside. This was fairly difficult for me given the circumstances, for these are very dangerous trips for the poor brethren and sisters.[30]

♂ [Tuesday], the 15th

The brethren and sisters were again busy with [preparations for] their journey, for they have to carry the goods for a distance of 3 miles down along the water, since they cannot get over the falls with the canoes.[31] In the evening I asked the brethren and sisters to abide in the Savior with their hearts, and to look upon Him, and not lose their way, one from the other.

☿ [Wednesday], the 16th

At the morning blessing I entrusted to the heart of the faithful Lamb[d], in particular, the brethren and sisters who plan on departing, to look after and care for them. Soon after, they left; most of them to the seaside, the others to New Milford to fish. No one stayed home except for Petrus, Gottlieb, Jeremias, I, and the children, with whom I held school. I was in a rather happy state of mind today, and could wish the brethren and sisters peace.

♃ [Thursday], the 17th

I went about my work quietly and was blissful inside the side hole[d]; also visited the sick.

♀ [Friday], the 18th

Br. Gottlob, who had visited his brother, came back home. He had left here in February, but was ill for nearly 6 weeks. The brethren and sisters who stayed home complained that I have not held a meeting for them in 2 days on account of the others being away. I said that neither Br. Joshua nor Samuel was home; they said why, I knew English.[32] Hence I held a meeting for them this morning, and the Lamb[d] could be felt in our midst.

♄ [Saturday], May 19

Today I had some more wood hauled to this place for my house[d]. Br. Samuel too was home again. Simon and Hannah came that day as well. Also, Sr. Esther and her mother came from Wechquadnach to pay a visit.

☉ [Sunday], the 20th

After the morning blessing I visited all the huts, finding all the brethren and sisters in rather good spirits, which greatly comforted my poor heart[d], as it was just now a little difficult for me because I was so very much alone. But I had a blissful day with the brethren and sisters.

☽ [Monday], the 21st

Esther and her mother went back to Wechquadnach. Because there were not many brethren and sisters at home [at Pachgatgoch], I went to Johannes Rau to learn whether he still intended to go Bethlehem. He was unable to promise me this with certainty. He is very amicable in his manner.

♂ [Tuesday], May 22

I visited Wechquadnach, finding all the Indians warmhearted. Br. Timotheus said [that], upon being completely restored to health, he wanted to go for a visit to Bethlehem in three weeks' time. He also said that he wanted to take old Brother Jephthah with him. I returned to dear Pachgatgoch in the evening.

☿ [Wednesday], the 23rd

We had a blissful morning blessing about our Lamb[d]. I also held school. Assuming that the brethren and sisters would return home soon, I moved into my house[d]. Until then I had lived with Br. Gideon, also had to look after old father Jephthah, given that Gideon and Martha were also at the seaside. Petrus came home today.

♃ [Thursday], the 24th

I received word that the brethren and sisters had returned from the seaside to as far as New Milford. Also, the sick are starting to improve.

♀ [Friday], May 25

Br. Gideon and Martha, Joshua and Elisabeth, as well as Sr. Caritas, returned home today. In addition, Gottlieb's mother, who lives on the seaside, came for a visit. Br. Gideon told me that the journey went very well and that the brethren and sisters who were still behind are all well. We had a blissful evening service[d] during which the side hole[d] was very much near us.

♄ [Saturday], the 26th

I observed a blissful Sabbath; the brethren and sisters also were in rather good spirits. I was thus able to sense the work of the dear Mother and see how she was occupying herself with these souls.[33]

☉ [Sunday], the 27th

The Lamb[d] was especially near us at the morning blessing, enabling me to feel how He loves the Indians, and that gave me courage and joy. During visits, all the brethren and sisters were very lively. I had the opportunity to speak with old Seijakes about the Savior; he is an Indian who enjoys hearing it. He lives 3 miles from us, down the river.[34]

☽ [Monday], May 28

During the early service the bloody Lamb[d] with His side hole[d] was once again very much near us. Most of the brethren and sisters went out to work. I held school.

♂ [Tuesday], the 29th

The brethren who were home helped me split chestnut blocks for a floor in my house[d].[35] While at work, the Lamb[d] was very much near us. I visited the sick, and when the occasion arose, told them something about the Lamb[d] and His wounds.

☿ [Wednesday], the 30th

The last brethren and sisters who had been to the seaside came home, such as Priscilla's son and 2 daughters, also Martin and his wife and children. In the evening we had a blissful quarter-of-an-hour[d], which rendered my heart[d] much lighter.[36] Br. Gottlieb came as well and brought with him an Indian from Potatuck. He, however, avows not wanting to hear anything about the Savior. Perhaps he says no and comes after all.

♃ [Thursday], May 31

I visited all the brethren and sisters who came home yesterday. They have conducted themselves properly after all, but were complaining about themselves. In the evening I directed everyone to the Lamb[d], saying: He wanted to care for them anew.

♀ [Friday], Junius 1

During the early service it was important to my heart that the Lamb[d] preserve each one in the side hole[d] on this day. Afterward, I went into all the huts and asked that, with their hearts, they please abide in the Lamb[d] today. The brethren went hunting.[37] The Lamb[d] was once again very much near us in the evening.

♄ [Saturday], June 2

I recommended myself and everyone to the side hole[d]. The brethren went hunting again. They returned home in the evening. I talked with Br. Samuel about his mother, who is ill and will perhaps soon go to the Lamb[d]. I also talked with Sr. Hannah, Salome, Benigna, and with Esther, who came for a visit with her mother. We had no quarter-of-an-hour in the evening.

☉ [Sunday], June 3

I had a blissful day. The Lamb[d] was very much near me while visiting. We also could sense His presence during all of the occasions. Also, Br. Christian returned home again.

☽ [Monday], June 4

Most of the brethren went to New Milford once again to see whether there were any fish to be had, because so far they had gotten only very few. I asked them that, with their hearts, they please abide in the Lamb[d] and His wounds, that way nothing could do them any harm. I began laying the floor in my house[d]. Br. Jeremias helped me.

♂ [Tuesday], the 5th

Br. Gideon and Gottlob also went to New Milford; Br. Gottlieb went hunting. I visited the sick as usual, and whoever else was at home, portraying to them the Lamb[d].

☿ [Wednesday], June 6

Most of the brethren who had been fishing returned home. They were fairly lucky this time; they got 200 *scheed* [shad]. I had a rather blissful day.

♃ [Thursday], June 7

Br. Jeremias went to New Milford. I finished laying the floor. In the evening we had a blissful quarter-of-an-hour[d] during which the Lamb[d] was very much near us with His side hole[d].

♀ [Friday], June 8

The Lamb[d] again bestowed a new blessing upon the entire assembly, which quite invigorated my heart.

♄ [Saturday], June 9

Grube, the dear heart, came to us from Bethlehem and brought with him Br. Jonathan from Gnadenhütten. He was most heartily welcome to me and the entire brown assembly.

☉ [Sunday], June 10

Grube, the dear heart[d], did not want to undertake anything further; he wanted to rest. I conducted the hour at noon. In the evening Brother Grube passed on the affectionate greetings from Bethlehem and Gnadenhütten that he had for the assembly here. All of us were pleased to hear that everyone is well in Bethlehem and Gnadenhütten, for we had heard that a great illness had struck there and that many had died.

☽ [Monday], June 11

Grube, the dear heart[d], conducted the quarter-of-an-hour in the morning and in the evening. Today we spoke with the communicants, also with all those who are already baptized. We spoke with each one separately. Br. Jonathan interpreted. A number of issues transpired that caused us great pain. However, most expressed that their hearts were hungry and thirsty, and how long a time it seems to have been that they have not eaten of the flesh and drunk of the blood of the Lamb[d].

♂ [Tuesday], June 12

We went visiting in all the huts and rejoiced together with the brethren and sisters. We talked with brother and sister Jeremias and [the] Gottliebs regarding the baptism of their little children. They were thankful that the Lamb[d] wants to bestow this grace upon their children.

☿ [Wednesday], the 13th

Today was the day on which the Lamb[d] once again nourished us with His flesh and blood, that He made Himself known to us in a blissful manner as our Husband and Head.[38] Sarah, Leah, Salome, Benigna, and Anna came along for the first time; 34 in all. The Lamb[d] wanted to lay this blessing very deeply into their hearts to be sure.

[Part] 2.

♃ [Thursday], June 14/25, 1750

Grube, the dear heart[d], conducted the early service, in which he recommended this entire assembly to the bloody side hole[d]. I asked the brethren and sisters that they now let this great mercy (when the Lamb[d] gave to them His flesh to eat and His blood to drink) sink very deeply into their hearts, so that they will not be able to ever forget it again. At the same time he took his leave of them in order to return to Bethlehem. The brethren and sisters gave him many a heartfelt greeting for their brethren and sisters in Bethlehem and Gnadenhütten. They also asked that the brethren in Bethlehem not forget them—that they may not have to wait this long again until a brother came to hold Communion for them. At the same time they requested [through Grube] that the brethren send them an additional brother, so that 2 brethren would be here who could assist each other, so that, in case one [brother] went to Wechquadnach or Stockbridge or other places to visit, there would always be one brother staying here who could care for them. Br. Grube promised to bring it up to the brethren and at the *synodo*. The Indian brethren and sisters right away took their leave of Br. Grube. They all looked lively and very much full of light. Since none of the Indians from Wechquadnach had come here, Br. Grube thought it would be good if he went there himself and visited them. I went along and accompanied him to that place. We arrived there past noon, at 2 o'clock, finding the Indians all at home. Br. Jonathan inquired about their circumstances; they could not give him a positive reply. We resolved to stay there that day. Also, old Sister Erdmuth left Pachgatgoch for the seaside today, to bring one of her angels[d39] [from] there to this place.

♀ [Friday], June 15/26

We took an early leave of the Indians at Wechquadnach, traveling together to the southwest end of Gnadensee[40] where we kissed one another heartily and tenderly, and took leave of one another. Br. Grube and Jonathan went to Bethlehem. I returned to my dear Pachgatgoch, singing many a verse[d] along the way. I found all the brethren and sisters going about their work lively, joyously, and cheerfully. We had a rather blissful evening service[d] in the evening. The Lamb[d] could be sensed near us and revealed Himself to us. That night I had a very blissful and sweet rest.

♄ [Saturday], June 16/27

At the morning blessing our Lamb[d] could again be felt near us with His side hole[d], likewise at the evening meeting. Today I wanted to observe the Sabbath, thus I did not plan on doing anything other than to be blissful and to visit the brethren and sisters. Br. Amos and Petrus came home late in the evening.

☉ [Sunday], June 17/28

During the early service I talked some about the text and the words of the Savior. Afterward, I prayed to the Lamb[d] that He preserve all of us very blissfully in the side hole[d] and bless us on this day. I went visiting in all the huts, finding everyone lively and in good spirits. The Lamb[d] also was very much near us during the sermon. I spoke on the words: *Alle die Ihn anrührten wurden gesund. Item: So du Klauben hättest.*[41] The Savior especially impressed upon me to speak of these 2 matters. Moreover, I agreed with the brethren to hold a separate quarter-of-an-hour for the baptized ones and communicants each Sunday evening. I held it for the first time in the evening, at dusk. I asked the Lamb[d] to bless this occasion with His presence, and to always keep His bloody side hole[d] open, also, to flood us anew at all times with the blood and stream of water that flowed from Him, having washed and sanctified our souls[d] and bodies with it. Afterward, I talked somewhat about the great mercy—that the Savior has chosen us from among the world, selected us, and made us members of His body through baptism and the cleansing from all sins, and by imparting His flesh and blood during Holy Communion. We sang English and Indian verses[d], and the Lamb[d] could be felt being merciful toward the entire assembly. We kissed one another in closing. All the brethren and sisters looked lively and cheerful.

☽ [Monday], June 18/29

The early service took place in the schoolhouse[d] today. I talked about the words of the Savior. The Lamb[d] was quite near me and the assembly; some of the blessing that He had bestowed on us yesterday evening could still be felt. I held school again. Past noon I went on the mountain to get tree bark.[42] In the evening I spoke on the words: *Er ist Kott über alles gelobet in Ewigkeit.*[43] The Lamb[d] and the dear Mother could be felt there.

♂ [Tuesday], June 19/30

I again conducted the morning quarter-of-an-hour in the schoolhouse[d] and intend to proceed this way also in the future, because Br. Gideon's huts[44] [are] very uncomfortable and often there are strangers sleeping inside.[45] Moreover, the brethren and sisters prefer coming into the schoolhouse and do so more readily. I also visited the sick; several of the smallest children are indisposed. Today little Maria, Joshua's daughter[d], went to the Lamb[d], most blissfully and cheerfully. Several hours before her journey there, she, of her own accord, showed her father where the Lamb^d has His wounds. She was a child about whom one could always see and feel something special. She had been baptized by Br. Johannes [von Watteville], and is about 18 months old, according to her parents' calculation. In the evening I talked about the text and the words of the Savior.

For the [sake] of the texts and words of the dear Savior, I want to henceforth write [dates] in the New Style.⁴⁶

☿ [Wednesday], Julius 1, new stili [Latin: style]

The little heart^d Maria was buried toward evening. I spoke on the words *Was Er gegstorben ist das ist er der Sunde einmal gestorben, das wir durch seinen Todt das Leben haben sollen.*⁴⁷ I prayed at the grave side. The meeting took place in Gideon's huts. I visited several huts. Br. Simon too is becoming sickly.⁴⁸

♃ [Thursday], July 2

This morning the Lamb^d with His bloody side hole^d was near us. I spoke on the words of the day. Old Maria and Caritas and her 2 children went to Danbury. After school I went into the woods to cut wood for the upper floor of the schoolhouse^d.⁴⁹ All the brethren were busy surveying land, for they again sold (or gave away) a piece; they barely get 2 p. for the acre.⁵⁰ There was no meeting in the evening.

♀ [Friday], July 3

In the morning I spoke on the text and in the evening on the verse ~~Ihr blutigen Hände segnet uns etc.~~ [Blank] *Also hat Kott die Welt geliebet.*⁵¹ My heart^d was all warm on this occasion. I also spoke with Petrus and Thamar and several others.

♄ [Saturday], July 4

In the morning I spoke on the verse: *Ihr blutigen Hände segnet uns.*⁵² We also sing it often in English. On this occasion, I told the brethren and sisters what the actual purpose was of the meetings in the morning and in the evening. Tonight the blind Sr. Rachel was so weak that one thought she would go to the Savior. Also, Bartholomew and his wife and child arrived here for a visit, along with another Indian woman from Stockbridge. Sr. Esther and her mother also came here from Wechquadnach. I kept very quiet today, except that I went visiting. There was no meeting in the evening.

☉ [Sunday], July 5

All the meetings today took place in the schoolhouse^d. At 8 o'clock in the evening I spoke on the text and the words of the dear Savior. I spoke in accordance with the grace (and in keeping with the lowly status) that the Lamb^d bestowed on me. During the quarter-of-an-hour for the baptized ones, and for the communicants, the Lamb^d with His bloody side hole^d was inexpressibly near us, and the flames^d of His wounds glowed in all the Indian hearts^d. I spoke on the words: *Wer mich isset der wird um meinetwillen leben.*[53] All the brethren and sisters were quite heartily lively and joyous when visited. What the enjoyment of the body and of the blood does for the Indian brethren and sisters, and what effect it has on their hearts, is inexpressible. There was a terrible storm here this evening. I think that the wife of Timotheus was so anxious because she knew of no place to stay. She asked me, through Br. Samuel, to allow her and the others who were here for a visit to sleep in the schoolhouse^d, which I did.

☽ [Monday], July 6

At the morning blessing I recommended everyone to the care of the dear Mother and [to] the bloody blessing of our Husband. Afterward, the following brethren and sisters went out to work, for they are running a bit short since most people's provisions are exhausted[54]; Thamar, Gottliebe, [and] Leah; Gideon and Martha went as well, but returned home the same day. The brethren went bear hunting and got 2. Those who had been here for a visit went back home as well; they took leave most joyously. I went to visit old Seyäkes and his family, most of whom are ill. Yet the Savior provided me the opportunity to tell them something about His bloody wounds. In the evening I talked about the Lamb's text.

♂ [Tuesday], July 7

In the morning I talked somewhat about the text, [and] prayed to the Lamb^d for His merciful protection and preservation. The brethren again went hunting together and got 2 deer. I held school again and worked in my corn. There was no meeting in the evening as the brethren and sisters came home late. This evening we thought that old Sr. Rachel would go to the Savior. She had taken leave of her son Samuel already at noon.

☿ [Wednesday], July 8

This morning I held the meeting like yesterday. Toward evening our dear Sr. Rachel went to the Lamb[d]. She departed quite softly and blissfully, and so quickly that they were unable to tell me about it until her soul[d] had flown into the side hole[d]. She already had been weak and sickly last winter and throughout the entire spring, until now, when the Lamb[d] took her into His side. Yet she had persevered with much patience, and on many occasions made known her faith in, and attachment to, the Lamb[d]. She had also admonished her children to abide in the Savior. She had been blind for about 27 or 28 years. Her sons Jeremias and Samuel bear her witness that, except for the last 2 years, she had always still earned her own livelihood with broom and basket making.[55] She was also, otherwise, a woman of good sense, and was able to be of great assistance to her fellow sex (for she was a midwife), that even many white people availed themselves of her help and advice (when they no longer knew where else to turn). There was no meeting in the evening.

♃ [Thursday], July 9

The brethren sent Br. Lucas to New Milford to call home the brethren and sisters who are working thereabouts, and to inform them of the going home[56] and the burial of the late Sr. Rachel. Indeed, they all came at once; not one stayed away. I helped Br. Jeremias make the coffin.[57] Before we were done with it, 5 English people came who wanted to attend the burial. They said they wanted to pay Rachel their last [respects and] love and attend her burial. I told them that she was not to be buried until evening. I also told them the reason why it could not be done.[58] They said that they were sorry that they had not come at the right time, and neither did they have the time to wait this long. They were very cordial and kept quiet; 2 said they wanted to come back, but did not do so. We had the burial in the evening all by ourselves. Everybody who was in Pachgatgoch came. It seemed that everyone was looking forward to it. I myself was looking forward to it. I told the brethren and sisters about the state of blissfulness near the side hole[d] while alive, and about the state of blissfulness when one sees the Lamb[d] and is able to greet and kiss the visible [nail] marks in [His] hands and feet. It was a blissful occasion for all of us.

♀ [Friday], July 10

There was no meeting this morning. In the evening I spoke on the words of the Savior. A blissful breeze^d could be felt at the time. Moreover, the Savior imparted the matter to me plainly and clearly; all the brethren and sisters looked quite full of light. I again worked my corn.

♄ [Saturday], July 11

The Lamb^d was once again especially near us so that my heart^d became like wax as I presented Him with all our circumstances and appealed to Him. All the brethren and sisters and I had a blissful day. I washed my shirts, also held school, and finished getting my corn fully done. I visited the sick, most of who are well again. Br. Jephthah came from Wechquadnach in the evening.

☉ [Sunday], July 12

Our Husband and Lamb^d was again intimately near us at the morning blessing, and most of the brethren and sisters were present. The regular meeting took place at 10 o'clock, at which the Lamb^d revealed Himself. All of the brethren and sisters are quite joyous and blissful, and feel how much there is to appreciate about the Lamb^d. They can still feel the Communion in their hearts. During the quarter-of-an-hour for the baptized ones and for the communicants, our Husband and Chief Elder with His side hole^d was quite intimately near us. In addition, I spoke with the parents today about the children; I asked that each one please watch out for his own children. They should especially see to it that the children did not stray too far—that they always knew where they were and kept them in their huts at night. I asked that they please consider this point. Brother Gideon did his best in this regard. I also spoke with several brethren, such as Jeremias, Martin, and Christian—whether they would be willing to interpret at the services, particularly when Br. Joshua and Samuel were not at hand. For his part, Br. Jeremias said he would not be so bold as to do it [translate], but for the Savior he will risk it. The others expressed themselves in like fashion. Br. Joshua and Samuel gave them as much encouragement as they could, telling [them] how they had felt in the beginning, and how the Savior had stood by them and has helped them until now.

125

☽ [Monday], July 13

This morning Br. Jeremias began his interpreting. It went pretty well so far. I spoke on the Lamb's text. Br. Jere[mias] interpreted in the evening as well. Today I held school again and visited all the huts. Br. Lucas is once more ill; also Sr. Leah. Otherwise I found everyone blissful and in good spirits so that my heart rejoiced at that. Br. Jephthah went back to Wechquadnach. He is greatly distressed that there is no opportunity arising for him to [go to] Gnadenhütten.

♂ [Tuesday], July 14

During the early quarter-of-an-hour I spoke on the text. The Lamb^d revealed Himself to us. All the brethren and sisters were at home. I visited all the huts today; had a beautiful opportunity to speak with Jery's mother and to introduce the Lamb^d and His wounds to her. As I was talking to her about the Savior, her son joined us. He was so well pleased with it that he interpreted for his mother everything I said. There was no quarter-of-an-hour in the evening as there was a white man in our way.

☿ [Wednesday], July 15

In the morning I talked some about the text and the words of the dear Savior. I visited the sick. The brethren remembered that it was one year ago today that Brother Bruce went to the Savior.[59] I went into the woods to cut wood. In the evening I spoke on the words: *Er ist mit seinem eigenen Blute einmal eingegangen, in der Allerheiligste und hat eine ewige Erlösung gefunden.*[60]

♃ [Thursday], July 16

In the morning I prayed to the Lamb^d, [and] again spoke a bit about the text and the words of the Savior. After school I went back into the woods to cut wood. In the evening, as we were all assembled, 2 white men, who were arriving at the very moment, came in as well. They right away said they had not come here to disturb us, and should they hinder us in our duty, they would leave again. I told them if they were content with sitting on the floor like the Indians they may well stay. We sang several Indian verses^d. I prayed in German. The Lamb^d with His side hole^d was quite intimately near me. The men [I just] described only came to see whether they could get any Indians for work.

♀ [Friday], July 17

This morning we had the quarter-of-an-hour as usual. The Lamb[d] was especially near us. Afterward, I visited several huts; told them that I intended to go to Wechquadnach. I wanted to return tomorrow. They all gave me greetings for the Indians there. In Wechquadnach I found all of them in good health and in their previous state. There is again nothing more to be done at this time than maintain them in a state of friendship and acquaintance.[61]

♄ [Saturday], July 18

I came back to my dear Pachgatgoch; found all of them blissful and in good spirits. The disease that is circulating here is gaining ground among us as well, especially among the children. It is commonly a cold that settles in the chest and causes a violent cough. In the evening I spoke on the day's texts.

☉ [Sunday], July 19

In the morning I prayed to the Lamb[d] that He may reveal Himself to us this day and hide us all in His open side. At 10 o'clock the regular meeting took place. I could say very little, as almost everyone is suffering so from the cough that I was hardly able to hear myself speak. Afterward, I visited all the huts; found everyone well except for Br. Gideon. He said he has not felt well for two days. In the evening we could not have the quarter-of-an-hour for the communicants, for someone was in our way.

☽ [Monday], July 20

In the morning I spoke on the texts, and in the evening on the words: *Seid gleich denen Knechten die auf ihren Herren warten.*[62] The Lamb[d] could be felt quite powerfully on this occasion. I worked my corn today; held no school because many children are sickly.

♂ [Tuesday], July 21

In the morning I prayed to the Lamb[d]. I felt quite comfortable in my heart at the time. I again held no school. I worked my corn. We had a small meeting in the evening. Sister Justina, Martin's wife, was delivered of a young son tonight.

☿ [Wednesday], July 22

In the morning I talked a bit about the Lamb's text. The Lamb[d] revealed Himself to us very mercifully and was intimately near. As early as two days ago I too was overtaken by this illness that is circulating in the country (and which by now some of the brethren and sisters and their children have). It commonly starts with a cough and headache. But today I needed to take to my bed. I began to feel very light-headed; when coughing, I experienced heat inside the chest.

♃ [Thursday], July 23

I was laid up for most of the day, and because of the headache I was unable to be up for any length of time. In my heart the Lamb[d] and His bloody side hole[d] were very much near me. I also appealed to Him. Sr. Magdalena offered to assist me when I needed something. Br. Gottlieb, Samuel, and Petrus went out cutting, so did Br. Gideon.[63] Also, Sr. Caritas returned with her children. As for her [state of] mind, she looked very uneasy and confused. I could barely welcome her. My heart was greatly worried about her.

♀ [Friday], July 24

That day I had to settle in bed [and remain] very still. I could not keep my eyes open for the headaches. Sr. Magdalena was my nurse; in that, however, it proceeded entirely in the Indian fashion.[64] Yet the Lamb[d] gave me enough strength that I was able to help myself a little. The brethren and sisters who were out cutting yesterday returned home this evening with the news that the white people wanted to give one *buschel* of corn as a day's pay.

♄ [Saturday], July 25

Today everyone in Pachgatgoch who was able to pick up a sickle, so to speak, went cutting. Still and all, things proceeded fairly humanly, so that I heard of no disorder among the brethren and sisters. Yet they nonetheless complained about themselves. Today Br. Samuel fell ill, making it necessary for him to come home from work. My cough and headache were worse today than yesterday. In the evening I always get a fever and that lasts then until daybreak. I can hardly remember anything about this night. I asked my Lamb[d] to please stand by me and to protect me. I was hardly able to remember where I was or should be.

☉ [Sunday], July 26

The brethren and sisters came home today. I was so fatigued that day that I would not have been able to stay up for half an hour at a time. I very much wished for an opportunity to write to Bethlehem, however, none came about, at which I was very glad in the end. I would have frightened my dear brethren too much. That afternoon my nose started bleeding by itself, which soon gave me relief. Tonight I again became as weary and weak as the night before, yet I was better able to recollect where I was. Tonight a cold discharge started flowing from my right ear, which from this point forward caused me more pain than anything else. This, in combination with the violent cough, was very painful for me. Throughout everything, the Savior was very much near me today, and assisted me rather graciously. I was concerned I might perhaps receive a visit today from white people, but they all stayed home, which was most preferable to me indeed.

☽ [Monday], July 27

Br. Jeremias went cutting again. Br. Joshua and Elisabeth, Caritas and Priscilla, Thamar, Martin, and Samuel went to cut *rusches* [rushes] for their beds.[65] Simon came and brought his Hannah, who is sick, home with him. Paulus and his wife and Thamaseed went[66] to the seaside. The Savior also helped me through this day. I felt extremely weary, and since all my appetite was gone from the start, and I had, moreover, aside from a little butter and a piece of bread, not the least bit in the house, I could not even think of anything that would taste good to me, [even] if I had plenty of everything. Tonight I grew so weary and weak that it occurred to me that it was indeed possible that I was going to the Lamb[d]. This thought was the dearest to me: I told the Savior I would come right away, if it should please Him.[67]

♂ [Tuesday], July 28

Very early this morning, Br. Gideon came to me. He said he had thought of me many times that night. I was presently the sickest in Pachgatgoch, yet, nonetheless, always slept alone at night. I said I did not want to cause the brethren much *trubel* [trouble]. Gideon asked me if I wanted to take some of his medicine. I told him yes, most readily. He left at once and said he wanted to boil me something. In about one hour he returned, bringing a small kettleful[d]. Gideon said, Drink of this as much as you want, and right away gave me some of it to drink. I immediately felt in my body that it did me good. I drank of it frequently that day.[68] The Lamb[d] also added His merciful blessing to it so that I was able to get up again that afternoon and walk about out of doors a little bit, which was a true joy for me. I also had a more comfortable night than before. Today the brethren Samuel and Martin came home [from cutting rushes]. They said they were unable to stay there any longer because they were ill. They also told me that Sr. Priscilla was ill.

☿ [Wednesday], July 29

This morning at about 8 o'clock, little Abraham, Gottlieb and Magdalena's son[d], went to the Lamb[d]. He was born on April 20[/]9[69] of this year, and had been recently baptized by Br. Grube. Right from the beginning of his illness it looked like he was going to go to the Lamb[d]. Moreover, one could see in him his love affair for the side hole[d], which other Indian brethren and sisters had observed about him as well. Today the sick Priscilla came home, also Br. ~~and Sr.~~ Gottlob and his Juliana, who is still sickly. Br. Jeremias and Br. Gottlieb are ill as well. I had a fairly good day, being up most of the time, feeling very weak, however. Nonetheless, I was able to take a bit of a look around among the brethren and sisters, but I had to walk about with my head covered, for I am swollen on one side.[70] Today I cooked a bread soup for myself. It was apparently something rather rare in Pachgatgoch. Tonight I did not have much of a fever and also was not quite as sick.

♃ [Thursday], July 30

This morning we buried the little heart[d] Abraham. I would have liked to have said something to the brethren and sisters, but was unable to, for I felt so very weak. At the grave side I thanked the Lamb[d] that He took this soul[d] to Him. Today I was able to visit the sick again. Br. Gideon went to New Milford today. I was able to be up for almost the entire day. I wrote in the *diario*. Today I ate from the first fruits of my planting and working in Pachgatgoch. My heart was so glad and grateful to have experienced this moment, that I know not how to describe it. Until now I had mostly made do with the diet of the Indian brethren and sisters.[71]

♀ [Friday], July 31

Br. Gideon came back home. He told me that in New Milford there were a large
number of people laid up with this illness. Br. Joshua and his family returned as
well, as did Sr. Caritas. They told me that there are also many ill where they were.
However, one does not hear that many are dying. Sr. Hannah is very sick. In fact,
I was not quite as lively today as yesterday, for the discharge from my right ear is
still causing me much pain. I talked with Sr. Sarah—that she should consider
the Savior more with her heart, and hide herself deeper in His side hole[d].

[Part] 3.

♄ [Saturday], August 1, 1750

This morning I visited the ill Sister Hannah. She told me that things had improved with her somewhat; it also appeared to be a good deal better with her. Toward evening her illness changed so that it seems she will soon go to the Lamb[d].
The brethren went hunting today; returned home very late in the evening, yet
had not gotten anything. I again tried to work some. I had a rather blissful day
in the side hole[d]. The Indian brethren and sisters were otherwise all at home.
Several are still sickly, yet they are very affectionate and trustful.

☉ [Sunday], August 2

Today I once again held the meetings, which had remained suspended for nearly
14 days. In the morning I prayed to the Lamb[d] to take me and the entire flock
into His bloody side hole[d] and to preserve us therein. The regular meeting took
place at 10 o'clock. I spoke on the text; the Lamb[d] mercifully revealed Himself
to us; Br. Samuel interpreted. During the quarter-of-an-hour for the baptized
ones and the communicants, our Husband and Chief Elder was quite intimately
and feelingly near us. My heart was like wax as I looked upon the brown assembly and reflected upon their election by grace. They all were most joyous and
lively while being visited. This morning Br. Amos went from here to the seaside to let Br. Paulus and his wife, and another one of Br. Simon's sons, know
that their mother Hannah was [doing] very poorly and might go to the Savior
soon. She was laid up throughout the entire day, no longer knowing anyone.
In the evening, at about 9 o'clock, the Lamb[d] took her soul[d] from the tabernacle[d72] into His open side hole[d]. She had not been ill for more than 8 days, [yet]

it had affected her chest right away. During her illness a special inclination toward the Lamb^d could be observed about her. She was always joyous and cheerful when one visited her.

☽ [Monday], August 3

At the morning quarter-of-an-hour I talked a bit about the texts, and prayed to the Lamb^d to bless us today, as His assembly of sinners, and to hide us in His side hole^d. Next I went to work some. After a while Br. Jeremias came and brought me word that Br. Martin's youngest son had gone to the Savior. I went there right away; the child^d was not yet entirely gone, to be sure, but continued to live for about 1 more hour and [then] flew into the side hole^d. This child was born [on] the 21st day [of] July. It started having convulsions the night before and went to the Lamb^d at about 9 o'clock this morning.[73] Tonight we had the burial for Sr. Hannah and for Br. Martin's son^d. I talked a bit about the reason why the Lamb^d sometimes takes a soul^d swiftly into His side hole^d. I prayed at the graveside and thanked the Lamb^d that He has taken in these 2 souls^d. My heart was quite invigorated on this occasion. As for my body, I was fairly weak today, making me fear that I would become sick anew. My heart, however, was blissful.

♂ [Tuesday], August 4

At the early quarter-of-an-hour I prayed to the Lamb^d for His protection and blessing on this day. Br. Joshua, Christian, and Samuel and Gottlob went out to work. Martin, Lucas, and Salome went to New Milford but came back home that same day. Br. Petrus also went to work, so did Br. Gideon; Gottlieb and Magdalena went to cut *rusches*. I held school again and cut wood for my chimney. There was no meeting in the evening.

☿ [Wednesday], August 5

We had the regular quarter-of-an-hour in the morning. Later I visited the sick and those who were home; these were only a few, however. After school I went to Nicolaus Rauch[74] for some provisions but was unable to return home that day.

♃ [Thursday], August 6

I helped Nicolaus Rau do some work until noon. After noon I went back home; I found almost no one [there]. Paulus and his wife, as well as Br. Amos, and Thamaseed, had arrived from the seaside.

♀ [Friday], August 7

I conducted the early quarter-of-an-hour with about 6 or 7 brethren and sisters. I asked our beloved Lamb[d] to hide us and the others who are not at home in His bloody side hole[d]. I visited the sick. Sr. Sarah is once again ill, so are Br. Martin's children. Today Sr. Marth[a], Benigna, and Anna, who had been in New Milford, came back home as well. There was no school; I worked on my chimney. There was no meeting in the evening.

♄ [Saturday], August 8

I conducted the early quarter-of-an-hour like yesterday. I visited all the huts where there was someone at home. All the brethren and sisters were joyous. Br. Samuel came home too; he is once again ill.[75] I observed a blissful Sabbath. There was no meeting in the evening.

☉ [Sunday], August 9

We had the occasions as usual. Br. Martin interpreted for the first time. He did it without much difficulty, allowing me to rejoice at it with all my heart and express my gratitude to the Lamb[d]. I talked about the text. Br. Martin also interpreted during the quarter-of-an-hour for the communicants. The Lamb[d] revealed Himself to us rather near and mercifully. Br. Gideon, Petrus, Christian, and Gottlob came home. Although they complained about themselves, I could not see that they had gotten into anything. Br. Samuel and Sr. Sarah are very ill.

☽ [Monday], August 10

I could not conduct the early quarter-of-an-hour because it rained so hard. I held school again. It is still a sickly time in these parts. I was indisposed today and yesterday, and suffered from a great deal of cutting pains in the bowels. Other brethren and sisters complain about it as well. Sr. Agnes has had the ague for some time. Sr. Priscilla and Benigna are also ill. During the evening quarter-of-an-hour I spoke some about the words of the dear Savior; Br. Jeremias interpreted.

♂ [Tuesday], August 11

This morning we had a rather blissful quarter-of-an-hour[d]; Br. Martin interpreted. Today I went to Kent to see if I could get some boards to lay the upper floor in my house[d].[76] I can tell that the split planks will not work well. Moreover, I was hindered so that I will not be able to get them done in due time, because the wood lies in the woods a good way off. Four brethren helped me float the boards down the river. Also, the 2 brethren Simon and Friederich came from Gnadenhütten today. There was no quarter-of-an-hour in the evening.

☿ [Wednesday], August 12

At the early quarter-of-an-hour I talked about the texts. I portrayed to the brown hearts[d] the bloody Lamb[d] of God with all of His thirsting wounds. Moreover, Br. Martin interpreted it with a feeling heart. While being visited, Br. Martin, whose two children are very ill, told me that he would be very glad if his children, should they die, were first baptized with the Savior's blood and water. I told him this would be very good indeed, yet I believed his children would be restored to health. He also told me of his child[d] who went to the Savior—that it pained him greatly that it was not baptized. I told him not to worry about it; his child was with the Savior. Also, the 2 brethren Simon and Friederich left again for Wechquadnach from here. They want to return by Saturday and then go from here to Bethlehem. Br. Christian and Gottlob again went out to work. Petrus went to New Milford, and old Sister Erdmuth to the seaside with a little boy. I held school again. There was no quarter-of-an-hour in the evening; only a few were at home.

♃ [Thursday], August 13

At the early quarter-of-an-hour I prayed and asked the Lamb[d] to take this assembly, along with His other assemblies, deep into His side hole[d] on this day of blessing.[77] And the Lamb[d] was particularly near us. Also, I let the brethren and sisters know what the Lamb[d] had once done for His congregation on this day, and that every year on this day we expressly reminded ourselves of this grace, and that Communion was always celebrated in the congregation [on this day]. This made a great impression on them. They said they too wanted to remember it. Besides, they all stayed home that day. I had a blissful day. I did not hold school; visited all the brethren and sisters who are at home. Br. Gideon asked me whether we would soon hear something again of our brethren in Greenland.[78] Br. Petrus came back home. In the evening I talked about the words of the dear Savior for this day. I portrayed the Lamb^d in His crucified form, the way He so gently bled Himself to death to deliver us from our misery. The Lamb^d blessed me powerfully on that occasion.

♀ [Friday], August 14

At the early quarter-of-an-hour I talked a bit about the words of the dear Savior. The Lamb^d revealed Himself to His poor Indian assembly. I visited the sick. Brother Samuel is better. Sr. Sarah is still very ill; Benigna is also sick. Also, the 2 brethren Joshua and Gottlieb returned home with their families.

♄ [Saturday], August 15

At the early quarter-of-an-hour I spoke on the words of the dear Savior for this day, which were: *Ihr müsset von neuem keborhen werden.*[79] My dear Lamb^d assisted me rather mercifully with this theme; Br. Joshua interpreted. In the evening I spoke on the words: *Ich bin die Tür, und wer anklopfet dem sol aufgethan werden.*[80] The Savior gave me these words entirely unexpectedly. We had sung our Indian verses before; I did not know whether I should say something. With that, I opened the book^d of texts and received the words. Moreover, the Lamb^d revealed Himself there. Br. Martin interpreted. Most of the brethren and sisters are now at home. My heart felt quite blissful and revived at all the faithfulness that the Lamb^d shows to the brown assembly. Also, Br. Simon came back from Wechquadnach.

☉ [Sunday], August 16

Our merciful Lamb^d of God was near us during the early quarter-of-an-hour and blessed His Indian assembly. At the regular Sunday meeting I spoke on the day's texts. My heart was quite warm and invigorated from the bloody fullness of our Husband. I also had a beautiful theme; the words were: *Den Armen wird das Evangelium gepredigt.*[81] I told the brethren and sisters [that] because they had been so wretched and scorned, (not because they had been better than others, for they themselves knew well that they were as corrupted and prone to sin as all the other people) the Lamb^d had shown compassion and mercy to them, and had sent them His servants. They had been obliged to tell them about His death and wounds and side hole^d. I talked to them a great deal about this point. At the quarter-of-an-hour for the communicants a blissful breeze blew from the side hole[d]. How near the Lamb[d] revealed Himself to us, I cannot describe. I spoke on the verse *Wenn ich nur mit meinem Mann alleine.*[82] First we sang it in English. As they were being visited, the brethren and sisters were all quite heartily lively and joyous. There also came two Indians for a visit; one by the name of Jacob, who had lived here once. He furthermore has a boy who goes to school here. The 2nd is a young Indian from Peekskill. I asked him if he too had already heard that he had a Savior who died for him and shed His blood for him. He said he had never attended the *meetings*. He said, Perhaps if I attend the *meetings* once, I might like to hear something. His name is Wewunrunquan.

☽ [Monday], August 17

At the early quarter-of-an-hour I talked about the day's texts. The Lamb[d] could be felt especially close; Br. Martin interpreted. Br. Joshua, Samuel, and Lucas went to Wechquadnach to visit the Indians there. I worked on my chimney. Moreover, Br. Simon, who had come from Gnadenhütten, returned to Gnadenhütten from here. There was no quarter-of-an-hour in the evening. Br. Jeremias's and Christian's children are sick again.

♂ [Tuesday], August 18

This morning I talked a bit about the texts and prayed, and the Lamb[d] revealed Himself to us. Also, the brethren who had gone to Wechquadnach yesterday came back home. They said that Timoth[eus]'s wife was ill.

☿ [Wednesday], August 19

At the early quarter-of-an-hour I talked a bit about the day's texts. My heart felt very blissful at the time; Br. Joshua interpreted. Br. Martin, Anna, and Salome went to New Milford and returned that same day. In the evening I spoke on the verse: *Christi Blut und Kerechtigkeit.*[83] The Lamb[d] revealed Himself eminently on this occasion.

♃ [Thursday], August 20

At the early quarter-of-an-hour I talked a bit about the day's texts. I visited the sick who are starting to improve now. Also, Br. Paulus returned from Albany with his wife. Most of the brethren and sisters were home, going about their work. I had a blissful day. There was no quarter-of-an-hour in the evening; the brethren had gone into the sweat house.[84]

♀ [Friday], August 21

At the early quarter-of-an-hour I prayed to the Lamb[d] for His merciful protection and preservation in His side hole[d]. That day all the brethren who were home, also several sisters, helped me plaster my chimney.[85] This went on in an altogether loving and brotherly fashion. The schoolchildren carried the water here, and the sisters nearly all the clay, [from] what was certainly a good distance, and mostly uphill. Here I must praise the preparedness of the Indian brethren and sisters to serve others, for on all occasions when I am in need of their help, they are willing with all their heart. They have done many [things] for me without being asked, of [their own] free will, because they saw that it was needed. There was no quarter-of-an-hour in the evening.

~~♄ [Saturday], August 22~~

Late this evening Sister Erdmuth returned from the seashore, bringing with her 2 of her angels[d], a boy[d] and a girl.

♄ [Saturday], August 22

At the early quarter-of-an-hour I talked about the texts. The Lamb[d] especially blessed this occasion, and nearly all the brethren and sisters were present. The brethren went hunting, but did not get anything. I worked on my house[d] and threw clay onto the [walls] inside.[86] I had a very blissful day.

☉ [Sunday], August 23

During all of the occasions the Lamb[d] with His side hole[d] was quite intimately near us, and blessed us poor children. At the early quarter-of-an-hour I spoke some to the brethren and sisters and portrayed to them the Lamb with all of His wounds. During the regular Sunday meeting I talked about the day's words, and the Lamb[d] imparted the subject matter to me quite plainly and clearly. At the quarter-of-an-hour for the communicants, the Lamb[d] especially blessed His assembly of sinners. The Lamb[d] also delighted my heart when visiting; the brethren and sisters are indeed getting closer to the Savior's heart, and feel that the side hole^d is the best place^d for them. Br. Martin says, Everything that the brother tells us about the side hole^d is true. He said, before he had thought about whether all of this could really be true, but now he saw that everything was true. Also, I announced that I intended to go to Bethlehem this week.

☽ [Monday], August 24

At the morning quarter-of-an-hour I talked about the day's words; it was quite a blissful quarter-of-an-hour^d during which the Lamb^d with His side hole manifested Himself. Br. Joshua, Martin, and Lucas went hunting and intend to stay out this week. In addition, Br. Paulus and his wife went to Gnadenhütten from here. Br. Simon went out to work. Because I still wanted to see the Indians in Wechquadnach, I went there today; they all were at home. The wife of Timotheus is somewhat sickly. Toward evening Joshua and his hunting *compani* came to Wechquadnach as well. We stayed there that night.

♂ [Tuesday], August 25

I took my leave of Joshua and the other brethren early, likewise of those in Wechquadnach. They said to salute all the brethren in Bethlehem, Gnadenhütten, and everywhere I found any. I arrived back in Pachgatgoch at noon. I readied myself for the journey. In the evening there was no quarter-of-an-hour since almost no one was at home.

☿ [Wednesday], August 26

This morning during the quarter-of-an-hour I took leave of the brethren and sisters. I asked that they please not stray too far into and about the country, but to abide with their hearts in the Lamb^d. They all gave me many greetings for the brethren in Bethlehem, Nazareth, and Gnadenhütten. After I had taken leave of the brethren and sisters, someone came and told me that Christian's child would go to the Savior. I went there and looked at the child^d (he is a boy^d, about one year old). It still had some life in it. I said I had already prepared myself for the journey; they should bury it if it went to the Savior. The brethren said they wanted to do so. At about 11 o'clock I left my dear Pachgatgoch. Br. Gideon accompanied me for 6 miles to direct me onto the right path. Taking leave of me, he said I should salute all the brethren for him and come back as soon as possible, which I promised. After that I traveled my road cheerfully, blissfully, and in good spirits. The Lamb[d] brought me to my dear brethren in Bethlehem blissful and in good health on August 31.

[Part] 4.

Thursday, October 1, 1750

I traveled again to Pachgatgoch after having rested a while in Bethlehem, and having rejoiced and invigorated myself with my dear brethren. I took my route by way of New York, where I arrived on October 3. In New York I stayed with our dear Brother and Sister Rice and Hendrick van Vleck until I had an opportunity to get up the North River by water. This opportunity arose very slowly, and got delayed on account of the contrary wind until Wednesday, October 7, when the yacht sailed. Yet, [it] had to anchor again soon after as there was such a strong northeasterly wind. Around noon, Thursday, October 8, we got a south wind that lasted until about 12 o'clock at night. At that time we were already through the Highlands above the Fishkill, where I had intended to go ashore and then on foot to Pachgatgoch. Friday, October 9, the wind was once again very strong from the northeast, making it necessary for us to lie [at anchor]. Moreover, the crew was not able to put me ashore. The wind having subsided a little, and the tide being with us, we began to tack and reached Poughkeepsie by 9 o'clock in the evening, where the crew disembarked me. I was quite tired of this voyage, because there were 5 High German men aboard the yacht, 2 of whom had once been acquainted with the brethren in Shekomeko, and as they stated, had loved the brethren. They had the Dutch book that was printed in opposition to the congregation, as well as the High German one printed against us in Philadelphia.[87] They read in these 2 books, and spent their time with them all day long. What disdainful and disgraceful words these people uttered about the congregation cannot be described. They never started [anything] with me. [However,] one time they said to me that they believed there were, in fact, still some genuine souls among the brethren, and those were the wretched and the worst among them. I said I did not want to enter into a disput[e]. If they wanted to believe the things that were written in the books, they should do so.

Saturday, October 10

I journeyed from Poughkeepsie very early, recommending myself to the protection of my Lamb[d] and that of His angels. I thought I would reach Pachgatgoch that day, yet, with the way being unfamiliar to me, I had to frequently make inquiries, [and so] night overtook me when I was but 5 miles from my dear Pachgatgoch; thus I had to lay by.

Sunday, October 11

I came to the dear Indian hearts[d] in Pachgatgoch. The watchword read: *Der Kerechtigk Nutz, wird ewige Stille und Sicherheit seyn.* Isaiah 32., v. 17. *Laß uns gantz sicher Schlaffen.*[88]

The entire assembly rejoiced. They said that all throughout this week they had watched to see whether there was a brother coming. They were indeed all home, except for Br. Gottlob. They have not yet undertaken their journeys that they had planned.[89] I found the entire assembly quite well, so that my heart rejoiced and I was able to thank the Lamb[d] for His protection and preservation. Past noon I held a small conference with the workers. I told them that I had many greetings as well as several letters for them from the brethren in Bethlehem and Gnadenhütten, which I wanted to read to the brethren and sisters as soon as it was suitable. Br. Gideon said it would hardly be possible to do it today, for the sisters wanted to go sweating that evening. We decided that they should be read to the brethren and sisters tomorrow at the morning blessing. Br. Gideon also told me that he was satisfied with the brethren and sisters, as they had stayed mostly at home. Br. Gideon had been my housekeeper while I was gone, having taken care of all my affairs, so that my corn had been gathered and was in the house when I arrived here. In addition, the sisters had made some *akrithes*[90] for me. We had no meeting on this day.

Monday, October 12

Following the morning blessing I read aloud the letters that I had for the brethren and sisters, which greatly delighted them, especially that the brethren and sisters in Gnadenhütten are blissful and in good spirits and are thinking of them. When I read to them Br. Cammerhoff's letter, and they heard that he wanted to visit them soon, they rejoiced even more, especially on learning that he has never gone farther to visit the Indians.[91] I visited all the huts today and found all the brethren and sisters lively. In the evening I talked a little about the text. One was able to feel and enjoy the nearness of our Lamb[d]. In closing, I recommended everyone to the bloody side hole[d] and to the precious wounds of our Lamb[d].

Tuesday, October 13

At the morning blessing I talked a little about the text. The Lamb[d] revealed Himself to us and blessed every heart[d] who was present, so that I could feel it. Today most of the brethren and sisters went out to work in various places. In the evening I portrayed the Lamb[d] of God in His complete figure of suffering to the brethren and sisters.

Wednesday, October 14

At the early quarter-of-an-hour I spoke of the blessedness and the peace enjoyed by such a heart who remains near the wounds of the Lamb[d] and occupies himself only with Him. My heart felt very blissful on this occasion. Today the dear Br. Gottlieb was robbed of all his prime possessions by a disloyal Delaware Indian whom he had previously helped out of his difficulties and debts. The thief first got himself half drunk, or at least pretended to be, then snatched up everything that was at hand and ran away. Br. Gottlieb and Magdalena saw him run away with it; Gottlieb and Samuel chased after him, but did not lay eyes on him again.

Thursday, October 15

At the early quarter-of-an-hour I prayed with the entire Indian assembly to the Lamb[d], recommending us to His wounds and to the steadfast care of the dear Mother, the Holy Spirit. I visited all the huts that day; spoke with all the brethren and sisters who were at home. During these days I was still busy gathering my remaining harvest. In the evening we had quite a blissful quarter-of-an-hour[d]. I spoke of the redemption for the whole of our corruption through the wounds of Jesus and [through] His body having been slain for us.

Friday, October 16

At the early quarter-of-an-hour I spoke a bit on the words: *Er ist mit seinem Blut einmal ein gegangen, in das Allerheiligste, und hat eine ewige Erlössung gefunden.*[92] The

Lamb[d] bestowed upon me grace to talk with confidence about the the [sic] reconciliation He has brought about for the whole world with His own blood. I
spent the day by myself in blissful tranquility. I remembered my entering into
holy matrimony and what faithfulness the Lamb[d] has shown to me in this period of 4 years.[93] I completely gave myself to Him all over again, to have Him
do with me whatever pleased Him, and to take from me, my wife, and children, that which caused Him sorrow. In the evening we were unable to have
the quarter-of-an-hour, because 2 white people were in the way. Br. Martin
came back home.

Saturday, October 17

At the regular early quarter-of-an-hour I prayed to the Lamb[d]. Visited several huts,
but there was mostly no one at home. Past noon I went to call on old Seyakes,
but I did not find him home. Toward evening all the brethren and sisters who
had been out this week came home. Also, Bartholomew and Wampachonant
came from Wechquadnach. They brought with them a *string of wampom* [wam-
pum][94] and a written account of what the chi[e]fs of the Makwaschen [Mohawk]
nation[95] and the *chi[e]f heads* [headmen] of the Indians at Stockbridge have discussed and agreed upon with one another on the 4th.[96]

This conference is [was] actually nothing more than a renewal of the old relationship that the 2 nations have with each other. They also wiped away each
other's tears over the loss of the warriors, who they had lost in the course of
the last war.[97] Our Indian brethren do not really know yet why they were sent
this *string of wampom*.[98]

Sunday, October 18

At the early quarter-of-an-hour I spoke on the text and prayed to the Lamb[d] that
He may mercifully reveal Himself during all of our occasions and manifest Himself close to each heart[d]. In the general Sunday meeting I spoke on the words
of the dear Savior, Mt. 7.24: *So jeman[d] meine Rede höret und thut, den vergleiche
ich einem klugen Mann,*[99] and the Lamb[d] revealed Himself to us, mercifully and
near. Wampachonant from Wechquadnach, who, as he says, has not heard a
brother in 6 years, joined us as well. When he saw him in the *mitting* [meeting],
Br. Petrus said, it had seemed to him as if there were 20 more Indian strangers
with us. The Indians all love him and wish that he may convert. At the quarter-
of-an-hour for the baptized ones and communicants, our merciful Lamb[d] of

God was quite intimately and tenderly near us. I talked about the benefit for the brethren and sisters when they give their hearts fully to the Savior and occupy themselves only with Him. When visited, the brethren and sisters were quite affectionate; there were only a few who complained about themselves. The old women are the most cheerful. We also held a small conference about our winter lodging. The majority favors moving back into the old winter huts.

Monday, October 19

We were somewhat hindered in our early quarter-of-an-hour, for one of the neighbors came to us as we were already assembled. Almost all the brethren and sisters again went out to work. I, on the other hand, started holding school with the children. I was fairly anxious that day on account of the great number of departures on the part of the brethren and sisters. Br. Gideon also complained that he did not feel comfortable with it. There was no quarter-of-an-hour in the evening.

Tuesday, October 20

At the early quarter-of-an-hour I thanked the Lamb[d] for all His love and faithfulness that He manifests in us poor children. Asked Him further to show mercy on us and to have patience with us. I had a rather blissful day. The brethren who were still home went out to make canoes. There was no quarter-of-an-hour in the evening.

Wednesday, October 21

At the early quarter-of-an-hour I talked about the dear Savior's words of the day. Visited the brethren and sisters who were at home. Toward evening Br. Martin [and] Lucas came home, as did Joshua with his *companie*. I held school. That day I frequently thought of the brethren and sisters who are not at home.

Thursday, October 22

At the early quarter-of-an-hour I talked about the dear Savior's words of the day. Asked Him for a blessing from His bloody wounds. Moreover, we could feel and sense His presence among us. I again held school with the children. Visited the brethren and sisters who had come home yesterday. In the evening we had no opportunity to conduct the quarter-of-an-hour.

Friday, October 23

At the early quarter-of-an-hour I talked about the text. My most beloved Lamb[d] imparted this matter to me plainly, and invigorated me so that I once again took heart and was able to submit everything to Him and His steadfast care, and to have faith that He will preserve His own possessions well. Afterward, I visited all the brethren and sisters; also held school. In the evening I again talked about the blessedness that the poor sinners experience at the dear Savior's feet. Also, the 2 brothers, Paulus and Johannes, and their sister Benigna,[100] returned to this place from their visit to Bethlehem and Gnadenhütten. Brother Gottlieb traveled to Potatuck. Br. Martin went out as well to bring home his wife and children, as well as Sr. Priscilla ~~with~~ with her daughters, who last Monday had gone out to work.

Saturday, October 24

At the early quarter-of-an-hour I talked about the text. The Lamb[d] with His bloody wounds was again very much near us. I observed the Sabbath and reminded the Lamb[d] of all the souls and circumstances of His brown flock[d] in Pachgatgoch. Sr. Priscilla and her daughters came home, as did Sr. Caritas. There was no quarter-of-an-hour in the evening.

Sunday, October 25

At the early quarter-of-an-hour I talked about the words: *Das Blut Jesu Christi des Sohns Kottes, macht uns rein von allen Sünden!*[101] At the Sunday meeting I talked about the words: *Es kam das Er mit dem Tode rang, und seyn Schweiß war wie Blutstropfen, die fiellen auf die Erde.*[102] The bloody Lamb[d] of God was quite intimately and tenderly near us in these two meetings. Before noon all the brethren and sisters who had still been out came home. I visited most of them that same day. Also, I held a small conference with Br. Gideon and Martha, also [with] Joshua and Elisabeth; we had a great deal to discuss with one another. Together we agreed that, henceforward, we wanted to hold this conference on Sunday mornings, following the quarter-of-an-hour. Br. Samuel shall join us as well. At the quarter-of-an-hour for the baptized ones and for the communicants, I talked about the words: *Er ist seines Leibes Heiland.*[103] These words right away gave me the opportunity to say how closely we are related to the Savior and how He looks upon us, [and] how we need to look upon one another. Moreover, I told them why the

Savior looked upon us as members of His own body, and it was for this reason that we called ourselves brethren and sisters and kissed one another.

Monday, October 26

After our regular early quarter-of-an-hour, most of the brethren and sisters again went out to work. Br. Joshua and Jeremias went to Newtown. Nacban, Gottlieb's son, traveled to Potatuck to get his father, because Sister Magdalena is once again ill. Simon, along with his whole family, went to make brooms and other wares, as did Martin with his family. Priscilla went with her daughters [to a place] about 30 miles from here. Caritas, Gottliebe, and Leah also went as a *companie*. Old Maria and her son Christian went to visit a sick Indian who is one of their kindred. I did some work on my house[d]. There was no quarter-of-an-hour in the evening.

Tuesday, October 27

At the early quarter-of-an-hour I prayed to the Lamb[d], submitting myself and the entire assembly to the steadfast care of the dear Mother, that she may portray today for us much about the Lamb[d] and the side hole[d]. I visited all the brethren and sisters who were still at home. I made a few preparations for my winter lodging. There was no quarter-of-an-hour in the evening.

Wednesday, October 28

At the early quarter-of-an-hour I prayed to the Lamb[d], recommending the entire assembly (which is now fairly dispersed) to His merciful protection. It is now a dangerous time for the poor hearts[d] because they disperse so. I worked on my winter house[d]. I now have to build it twice as I had torn it down in the spring, taking of it what was usable for the summer house. The Indians had not wanted to move back into the old winter huts given that the land is not theirs and that they have lived in that location now for two winters. But with winter being just around the corner, and the winter huts already built, and with the owner of the land having given them liberty to move there again, they thus all have a mind to live there for yet another winter. And that is why I have to rebuild my house.

Thursday, October 29

We had no meetings since neither Br. Joshua nor Samuel was at home.[104] They did not come home until late at night, along with Br. Jeremias. I held school. Thought of the dear Bethlehem very much and wished myself there, for I felt disheartened on account of several matters.

Friday, October 30

Only 6 brethren and sisters attended the early quarter-of-an-hour. I prayed with them, and wished myself and them, and the entire assembly, deeply into the side hole[d]. Br. Gideon traveled to New Milford. I worked on my winter house[d]. There was no quarter-of-an-hour in the evening. Br. Joshua and Jeremias came home.

Saturday, October 31

At the early quarter-of-an-hour I prayed to our faithful Lamb[d], entrusting to His faithful loving heart all the circumstances such as they appeared to me. My heart was full of sorrow over some matters, causing me to be occupied with [them] all day long, and to breathe a sigh for Him on account of the[se] blemishes and faults. I wanted to visit the brethren and sisters but found no one excepting several children. Br. Gottlieb came back. There was no quarter-of-an-hour in the evening.

Sunday, November 1

During our meetings our faithful and merciful Lamb[d] of God was intimately and tenderly near us, so that one was able to tangibly feel how closely the side hole[d] is able to approach the brown hearts[d] and set their hearts afire, and that all their weak ideas and their shy dispositions are, by nature, not able to avert this. At the early quarter-of-an-hour I spoke on the watchword. The Lamb[d] invigorated me, and all at once freed me from me all the sorrow that I had felt, so that throughout the entire day I had a light, joyous, and confident heart toward everything that came before me. During the noon meeting I talked about the words: *Es ist kein ander Heil, es ist auch kein anderer Name gegeben, dadurch wir kunten selig werden, als allein der Name Jesu Christi.*[105] During our Sunday conference we remembered all the circumstances concerning this assembly. I told them that the Savior has bestowed joyousness upon me; they too should take heart and believe the Savior. We parted from one another with much love. We were not able to hold the quarter-of-an-hour for the communicants because the brethren had gone into the sweat house. Also, several brethren and sisters came home: Gideon, Lucas, Amos, Gottliebe, Leah, Benigna, and Salome. From these brethren and sisters we learned that Martin and Paulus are ill. Esther and Wampachonant's daughter came from Wechquadnach for a visit, likewise an Indian who lives 3 miles from here.

Monday, November 2

At the early quarter-of-an-hour I talked about the text. My dear Lamb[d] was very much near me, and I think also near each of the souls present. After the quarter-of-an-hour I talked with Br. Christian and Gottliebe on account of their poor housekeeping together thus far. Most of the brethren went hunting. Petrus, Thamar, and Elisabeth went to sell brooms and baskets. Benigna and Salom[e] went again to where they had been the previous week, where also Br. Simon, Paulus, Martin with his family, and Sr. Priscilla with her daughters are. I went to the mill in Sharon,[106] also at the same time to Satke[d],[107] and returned home in the evening.

Tuesday, November 3

Tonight I became very ill and got violent diarrhea, and at the same time, cold chills, so that it seemed I would come down with the ague. I had to stay in bed throughout most of the day. In the evening dear Br. Gideon brought me some of his medicine, which gave me immediate relief.[108] An unmarried person came to me who said that for about 2 or 3 years he has felt in his heart an urge to go to Bethlehem. He asked me what I thought about something like this. I told him I was unable to advise him in this matter. He should, however, weigh it carefully in his mind before he went. He is not a stupid person. That day old Erdmuth went with her family into the winter house.

Wednesday, November 4

My dear Lamb[d] helped me and soon restored me to health, making it possible for me to go to the winter huts again and work there a bit today. I had a rather blissful day. Br. Samuel returned from New Milford.

Thursday, November 5

I again went to work on my winter house[d]. The 2 sisters Sarah and Gottliebe also moved into the winter huts with their children. The past 3 days I did not hold the quarter-of-an-hour as there are very few home. I wished them all deeply into the side[d] [hole].

Friday, November 6

I conducted the early quarter-of-an-hour with the few who were still at home. I prayed to the Lamb[d] and laid myself and the assembly at His wounded feet, that He may render our hearts bloody and let His sweat and blood flow over our bodies and souls. I worked on my winter house[d], and at the same time visited the brethren and sisters who are living there [in the winter huts].

Saturday, November 7

At the early quarter-of-an-hour I prayed to the Lamb[d] along with the assembly that was present. Still and all, there were twenty attending the quarter-of-an-hour. I would not have thought that there were still that many at home. I, for the first time, went to my closest neighbor, as I was in need of some straw. Also, the brethren returned home from hunting. They had a fairly poor hunt. Br. Martin came as well, bringing word that all the other brethren and sisters intended to come tomorrow. Gottlieb's son arrived from the seaside. There was no quarter-of-an-hour in the evening.

Sunday, November 8

At the early quarter-of-an-hour I talked about yesterday's texts, on which occasion our gracious Lamb[d] of God mercifully revealed Himself. He let us feel what it is best founded on and with which doctrine one will make it through [life] most blissfully. At the regular Sunday meeting I talked about the day's texts, on which occasion the Lamb[d] put each one in touch with his heart. At the quarter-of-an-hour for the baptized ones and for the communicants, I talked about the words: *Lasset uns Ihn lieben, denn Er hat uns zuerst geliebet.*[109] On this occasion, the Lamb[d] put us in mind of His loving heart for us, and how He is so faithful toward us in every situation. I spoke for quite a while. After the early quarter-of-an-hour the brethren and sisters came home one by one. Sr. Johanna, who had visited Gnadenhütten, also came back, bringing her [daughter] and Sister

Juliana's daughter with her. They stayed in the winter huts, given that they are closer to Bethlehem than the summ[er] huts. When we received word that they were coming from Bethlehem, it was mentioned at the same time that Br. Cammerhoff had arrived, which touched off such a longing in the brethren and sisters that they looked for him probably 100 times that day.

Monday, November 9

We had a very blissful quarter-of-an-hour[d] this morning. I spoke on the words: *Er hat uns zuerst geliebet.*[110] I visited the brethren and sisters who had come home yesterday. They all complained about themselves. I told them that it pained me every time I saw them leave; they should submit themselves to the Lamb[d] all over again. He loved them and wanted to award them everything. In the evening I talked in the same manner with Br. Jeremias, who has been shy for some time. Br. Christian and Samuel went to New Milford; the former intends to work there this week. Several brethren and children helped me carry here the split wood that I had prepared for the winter house.

Tuesday, November 10

At the early quarter-of-an-hour I prayed with the brown assembly and thanked our bloody Lamb[d] for the faithfulness and love that He shows us daily. Most of the brethren and sisters were at the winter huts today. Br. Joshua and his family moved there to stay. Br. Jeremias helped me roof my house[d]. I had quite a blissful day. Br. Samuel came back home, and Br. Gottlieb returned from the seaside.

Wednesday, November 11

At the early quarter-of-an-hour I prayed again, and we recommended ourselves to the steadfast care of our Lamb[d] and to the unfailing care of our dear Mother, the Holy Spirit. Br. Martin and his wife traveled to the seashore. Br. Gideon, Petrus, Lucas, Simon, and Jeremias moved into the winter huts with their families. I worked there as well.

Thursday, November 12

I gathered my belongings that I wanted to take to the winter huts and moved there that day. Br. Gottlieb gave me his horse. In the evening we had our first quarter-of-an-hour in Br. Gideon's hut [at the winter huts]. The Lamb[d] was intimately near us and mercifully revealed Himself to us poor children. I visited all the huts, finding most of the brethren and sisters affectionate and in good spirits. Tonight I had to sleep in Br. Joshua's hut as mine was not yet in order.

Friday, November 13

We had quite a blissful quarter-of-an-hour[d] in the morning. I again visited several huts. Also made a bedstead for myself, and that night slept blissfully in my winter hut for the first time.

Saturday, November 14

At the early quarter-of-an-hour I portrayed to the brown assembly the Lamb[d] as a bloody figure with all of His wounds. In the evening our dear and faithful heart Cammerhoff arrived, whom we had long expected, and with him Br. Leonard Schnell. The brown assembly was heartily glad to see them.

Sunday, November 15

I conducted the early quarter-of-an-hour, Br. Cammerhoff the sermon and the quarter-of-an-hour for the communicants. The Lamb[d] was intimately and tenderly near us, and His bloody wounds sparkled very clear and bright for each heart. Moreover, Br. Cammerhoff and Schnell visited all the brethren and sisters in their huts and announced that they wanted to go to Stockbridge tomorrow.

Monday, November 16

Brother Schnell conducted the early quarter-of-an-hour. After that we traveled to Stockbridge, but took our road by way of Wechquadnach, visiting the Indians there.

Tuesday, the 17th

We reached Stockbridge, but found only a few Indians at home.

Wednesday, the 18th

We departed from Stockbridge and came as far as Sheffield that day.

Thursday, the 19th

We left early and came to Johannes Rau in the evening.

Friday, the 20th

We visited the *Hutberg*[111] in Shekomeko, and also went to Nicolaus Rau that day.

Saturday, November 21

We returned to our dear Indian brethren and sisters in Pachgatgoch. Br. Cammerhoff commenced the [act of] speaking that very day, and conducted the quarter-of-an-hour in the evening.

Sunday, November 22

Br. Cammerhoff conducted the early quarter-of-an-hour. He beseeched the Lamb[d], asking that He open wide his dear side hole[d] today, and especially flood this assembly, and to especially bleed His holy blood onto the heart of each soul[d]. Afterward, he also spoke with all the brethren and sisters [in preparation] for Communion, at which the Lamb[d] could be felt near. The sermon was after 10 o'clock, and past noon, at about 2 o'clock, all the baptized ones and communicants enjoyed a blissful love feast. Immediately after the love feast we had a very blissful baptism. Warop's wife was baptized and received the name Rebecca; her Indian name is Quarpem. Br. Samuel's daughter[d] also was baptized and received the name Christina. Shortly after the baptism, all of the communicants who were participating this time assembled. Before Communion the entire assembly knelt down, and Br. Cammerhoff beseeched our Chief Elder and Husband[112] that He wash away with His blood all faults and transgressions, and absolve each one anew. Directly afterward, Communion took place, at which time our Lamb[d] could be felt and enjoyed so inexpressibly powerful and blissful that I cannot recount it. Following Communion Br. Cammerhoff and Br. Schnell took leave of the brethren and sisters, who also gave them many heartfelt greetings to pass on to the brethren in Bethlehem and Gnadenhütten. Br. Cammerhoff and Schn[ell] proceeded yet for 3 miles that evening. I accompanied them and stayed with them that night.

Monday, November 23

We bade one another a heartfelt and tender farewell. Br. Cammerhoff and Schnell returned to Bethlehem by way of New York. I went back to my dear Indians, visiting all of them that day. Everyone is newly revived and invigorated,

[and] also so joyous and full of light that it seems to me I have never seen it like this for as long as I have been in Pachgatgoch. We had a very blissful quarter-of-an-hour[d] in the evening. Johannes went to New Milford.

Tuesday, November 24

We had another very blissful quarter-of-an-hour[d] in the morning. I talked about the words: *Wer an mich glaubet wird nicht zu schanden werden.*[113] Moreover, I announced that I intended to hold school again; the pupils all came, not one staying away. Br. Joshua and Samuel went to the mill and did not come [back] until late at night.

Wednesday, November 25

This morning we had another very blissful quarter-of-an-hour[d]. The Lamb[d] manifested Himself. I again held school and visited several huts; everyone was quite blissful and in good spirits. Several brethren made preparations to go hunting. We could not have a quarter-of-an-hour in the evening because the brethren went into the sweat house.

Thursday, November 26

Because most of the brethren were going hunting, I conducted a quarter-of-an-hour with the baptized ones and the communicants, asking them to please preserve in their hearts the grace that the Lamb[d] had bestowed on them. At the same time, I announced my journey to Bethlehem and promised them that I or another brother would come back to them soon. They said it was good that I told them, I should make sure to think of them often. Br. Joshua, Jeremias, Amos, Lucas, and several unbaptized ones went hunting. I visited all of them once more in their huts and bade them farewell. I also cut some wood suitable for a floor in my house[d].

Friday, November 27

We had another blissful quarter-of-an-hour[d]; Br. Samuel interpreted. He went today and joined the other brethren who are out hunting. I laid the floor in my house[d] and visited sick Br. Martin.

Saturday, November 28

At the early quarter-of-an-hour I prayed to the Lamb[d] and recommended myself and the entire assembly to the bloody side hole of our Lamb[d]. I observed a very blissful Sabbath; I read several homilies of the wounds. There was no quarter-of-an-hour in the evening.

Sunday, November 29

I prayed again at the early quarter-of-an-hour; the Lamb[d] was quite intimately and tenderly near me and the entire assembly. I was unable to hold the Sunday meeting as there is no brother here who can interpret.[114] Otherwise, the brethren and sisters are all heartily lively and in good spirits. One can no doubt tell by looking at their eyes and faces that they have been near the slaughtered body of our Lamb[d] and have enjoyed His flesh and blood. We could not hold the quarter-of-an-hour in the evening because the sisters were going into the sweat house. I prepared myself for the journey. Most of the brethren and sisters came to me and gave me many greetings for the brethren and sisters in Bethlehem and Gnadenhütten.

☽ Monday, November 30

Before I departed, I held another quarter-of-an-hour with the baptized ones and communicants and took leave of them at the same time. They were all quite lively and full of light. At 11 o'clock I departed, taking my road to Fishkill by way of Sharon.

[No entry for December 1]

Wednesday, December 2

Early in the morning I ~~traveled~~ ferried across the North River and went another 26 miles that day.

Thursday, December 3

I experienced very bad weather but nevertheless made it through the long meadows that day, as far as John Wilson.

Friday, December 4

I arrived at Br. Samuel Green's in due time, and unable to get across the terrible creeks during the day, I stayed there that night.

Saturday, December 5

I departed early from Samuel Green's. The Lamb[d] helped me safely across all the creeks, and also the Delaware, so that I arrived in Nazareth in the evening, and because they were in the process of celebrating the festival of our dear Husband, I even got my share[d] of it.

Sunday, December 6

I arrived back in my dear Bethlehem, the dear Lamb[d], who has preserved me so mercifully and blissfully, be praised.

Joachim Heinrich Sensemann

12 February to 16 June 1751

Pachgatgoch Diearium, from February 12, 1751[1]

I came to Pachgatgoch, to the dear brown hearts[d], on Friday the 12th. The watch-word of this day read: *Israel wird sicher alleine wohnen*, 5 Moses 33.28. *Dieß Kind soll unverletzet seyn.*[2]

I was very glad to see the dear brown hearts[d], and they [to see] me. I called on Br. Gideon. He received me with much joy, stepped outside the house, and [standing] in front of the door, called out that a brother from Bethlehem had arrived. Then everyone who was at home gathered in Gideon's house and wel-comed me with tender love. Joshua and Samuel right away made a fire in our house where I soon repaired. Gideon provided me with food. Had several vis-its from our dear brown hearts[d] that very evening. Jephthah expressed a great longing for Gnadenhütten; he had thought that one of his children would come for him, but so far no one had come. Yet his heart is in a quite agreeable state. He was sorry that Magdalena had come here.

The 13th

The watchword read: *Ich wiel sie miteinander in einen festen Stall thun*, Mic. 2.12. *Kein Übels wird begegnen dir des Herren Huth ist gut da für.*[3]

I went visiting in all the houses. They all received me kindly. I found Friederich, Abraham's son, in Simon's house. I spoke with him some; asked him whether he still loved me. He replied yes. I saluted him from his father and mother, like-wise from Br. Cammerhoff. Afterward, I summoned the conference brethren and sister[s],[4] Gideon, Martha, Joshua, Elisabeth, and Samuel, to my house; greeted them from the congregation[s] in Bethlehem and Gnadenhütten, es-pecially from our dear hearts Johannes [von Watteville], [the] Cammerhoffs,

[the] Hermans, [the] Grubes, Gottlieb, and Abraham Büninger. Informed them that the congregation had sent me to be with them in A. Büninger's stead for a while. Thus they were pleased at this. They had been looking for a brother daily. Also read aloud Gideon's daughter's letter.[5] I asked how things had gone in Pachgatgoch since Abraham had left for Bethlehem. They said, fairly badly, especially with the young people. They said that Anna Benigna is said to have gotten betrothed to an unbaptized Indian. I told them that not long ago several couples had been married in Gnadenhütten with the blessing of the congregation, and how cheerful and blissful they were together, and that the brethren also wanted to look after the people in Pachgatgoch who were in like circumstances, at which they rejoiced and wished that it may come to pass here in the same manner. They said, because there was such tumult at the place where they are living now [the winter huts], and given that the land did not belong to them, they had resolved to move back into the summer houses next week.[6] However, they first wanted to inform the rest of the brethren and sisters—whether they were satisfied with this. I told them that I had several letters to read to the brethren and sisters. What did they think would be the best time for this? They said, this Sunday; that way everybody would be home, and it was quite all right by me that way. Jeremias came home this evening; had gone threshing for a white man. He came to me and welcomed me, rejoicing that he found a brother from Bethlehem [here]; also brought me a piece of white bread that he had brought with him. Also, 2 Indians from Westenhook[7] arrived here today, [to wit,] Joseph, the brother of our late Jonas, and Jephthah's grandson, both of whom had attended school in Shekomeko.

Sunday, the 14th

The watchword read: *Kein Einwohner wird sagen Ich bin schwach denn das Volck, das drinne wohnet, wird Vergebung der Sünden haben, Is. 33.24. Gnade schien uns auf zu wecken, Gnade küste, Gnade schlief, ließ sich fühlen, ließ sich schmecken, Gnade brachte auch zu schief.*[8]

At 9 o'clock the baptized brethren and sisters gathered in Gideon's house. I saluted them from the congregation and from the brown congregation[d] in Gnadenhütten, and read to them Br. Cammerhoff's as well as the other letters. They were very *atent* [attentive] and very pleased that the congregation in

Bethlehem was still thinking of them. Afterward, Joshua came to me and reported that the brethren of Wechquadnach had requested to live here [in Pachgatgoch] with them, and that they had no objections. They wanted to give them some cleared land, and next year they would get back 10 acres from a white man; then they could have as much as they needed. The white people have taken from them — those in Wechquadnach — nearly all the land. Now they were daily awaiting a brother from there [Wechquadnach] who would bring them the[ir] full *resolucion* [resolution]. After that I conducted the service and passionately portrayed to them the Lamb[d] and His beautiful red wounds.

Monday, the 15th

The watchword read: *Gott weiß, ihr werdet befehlen euren Kindern und euren Hauße nach euch, daß sie meinen Weg halten.* 1 Mos. 18.19. *Und noch* 1000. *Herzen.*[9]

Given that Gottlieb had not come home yet, although he had left word that he would return home on Saturday, the brethren were thus concerned that he may have fallen ill in the woods. Accordingly, they sent Amos and his son to visit him and to tell him that a brother had come from Bethlehem. Also, I started school today. After school I cut wood, and after that I went visiting. Samuel told me that they had been very concerned because A. Büninger was staying away for so long. They had thought perhaps he had fallen ill along the way, even wanted to send someone to meet him, but they did not have anyone who was able to get away. Toward evening Amos came back home and Gottlieb with him. He came right away to visit me; he was very glad that he had received the message that a brother had arrived. In the evening he sent me a piece of a turkey,[10] and along with it, white bread.

Tuesday, the 16th

In the morning, we had [a] quarter-of-an-hour. After breakfast I had school with the boys. Old mother Erdmuth came to visit me. She was altogether full of light and in good spirits; inquired about several brethren whom she knew, also after Br. Martin, whether he had already a new wife.[11] In the evening we had a blessed quarter-of-an-hour; their hearts were warm from the wounds of our Lamb[d]. They stayed together yet for a good while, and Joshua spoke to them a great deal about the Savior.

Wednesday, the 17th

After the quarter-of-an-hour I had school with the girls. There were nearly 20 in school. Christian and Gottliebe went out with brooms and other items to sell. Beforehand I talked to them about their hearts. I went visiting in several houses, asking them [the Indians] whether they were in quite a happy state. Yet they all bemoaned their poverty. I then directed them to the wounds of our so beloved Savior, who would very much like to have them be blissful and in good spirits, if only they would go to Him and let this be granted to them. Juliana came toward evening. She was very warmhearted; spoke with me a great deal about her heart. Following the evening quarter-of-an-hour, the aforementioned Indian strangers from Westenhook came to take their leave of me. With them came 2 others. They told me that several Indians in Westenhook desired to see a brother there. They also said that there was a minister at the place for now, yet he intended to leave again in March; several people did not want him.[12] Joseph said, if he knew I was going to Bethlehem in the spring, he would go with me to visit his friends[13] in Gnadenhütten. He has felt a longing for that place for a long time now.

Thursday, the 18th

In the morning, several brethren and sisters came to take leave. Samuel went on horseback to Danbury to sell things. Priscilla, with 2 daughters, and A. Benigna went to New Milford to sell brooms and baskets. Jephthah came to visit me. Because it is still so cold, and the other brethren do not yet have a mind to move into the summer houses, it appears that we will continue living here for a while. Because they [the brethren] went into the sweat house today, we had no quarter-of-an-hour in the evening.

Friday, the 19th

Today Jeremias and his wife left to sell baskets and other items. I prepared wood for myself for burning, and afterward, I went out visiting. Many complained that they felt very poor. Paulus returned home from New Milford today. In the evening we had a blessed quarter-of-an-hour.

Saturday, the 20th

We had [a] quarter-of-an-hour in the morning. I thought of our dear Bethlehem, how the dear hearts [there] are presently preparing themselves for the

Sabbath. Old mother Erdmuth brought me several pan cakes[14] that she had baked for me. I then observed the Sabbath in my house[d] in quiet together with my most beloved Husband. Gideon went to Kent to fetch money for a man. Past noon the dear brown hearts[d] returned home in good spirits, [to wit], Jeremias and his wife, and Christian and his wife, [also] Priscilla with her daughters, and A. Benigna.

Sunday, the 21st

In the morning, after the quarter-of-an-hour, we had a passionate conference. They [the conference brethren and sisters] informed me how matters stood with the brethren and sisters. Gideon had spoken with Gihorn about his heart. He said he felt every day that he had a wicked heart. Abel was talked about as well, whether he should be visited sometime. They replied that this would be good indeed. Joshua volunteered to visit him. His wife, Caritas, should be talked to first. Afterward, I conducted the service; my heart felt very comfortable there. A. Benigna and Priscilla's daughter came to visit me; so did Thamar, who spoke with me about her heart. She is in a quite agreeable state. We had [a] quarter-of-an-hour in the evening.

Monday, the 22nd

The watchword read: *So spricht der Herr, der die verstoßenen in Israel zusammen gebracht hat, Ich will zu dem Haufen noch mehr bringen. Is.56.8. Ave herein ins Hauß.*[15]

After the quarter-of-an-hour I visited Christian and his wife; Sarah and the old mother Maria came there as well. I talked to them somewhat about their hearts. Christian is in a fairly bad state. He says, however, that he has wanted to pray to the Savior often, but could not do it. Since Abraham [Büninger] has been gone he has conducted himself badly, and his wife along with him. I showed him the way back; he should recover his senses, and the Savior would let him feel where he trespassed and acted contrary to the mind of the Savior, and he should ask the Savior to forgive him this, and [then] the Savior would wash it [his sin] away with His blood. Afterward, I held school. Past noon several single men came to visit me. I talked to them a little about the Savior, that He would like to render them blessed and wash them in His blood.

Tuesday, the 23rd

In the morning, after the quarter-of-an-hour, Joshua came and said that he, along with Gottlieb and Paulus and Amos, wanted to go into the woods to get tassels and other wood for baskets;[16] they would return home on Saturday. I spoke with all of them beforehand. Johanna and Magdalena also went.

Wednesday, the 24th

After the quarter-of-an-hour Gideon took leave of me to go to New Milford and to return home the next day. Petrus took leave as well. In the forenoon I had school with the girls. Simon came to visit me. He said that his children were doing great harm to his heart. Rebecca also came. Samuel went to an English man for threshing; so did Jeremias. Martin went to Dover. Thus, not many brethren remained at home.

Thursday, the 25th

After the quarter-of-an-hour I held school with the boys. Gideon returned home in good spirits today.

Friday, the 26th

I went visiting today. Everyone was very industrious. I talked with many about their hearts. Leah is very discontented that her husband is staying away so long while she is sitting here alone with her children.

Saturday, the 27th

We had [a] quarter-of-an-hour in the morning. I thought of our dear Bethlehem. Visited Gihorns and Warubs. They both are very friendly toward me; however, I have not had the opportunity yet to speak with them about their hearts. Talked also to Christian today. He was very affectionate. [I] said he should visit me sometime. Everyone returned home in the evening.

Sunday, the 28th

We had a blessed quarter-of-an-hour in the morning. However, because so many white people appeared, and owing to other circumstances, we had no occasion today until that evening.

Monday, *Mart[i]us* 1

Today's watchword read: *Gedencket nicht des Alten und achtet nicht auf das vorige, denn Siehe, ich will waß neues machen. Is. 43.18, 19. Weil noch zu keiner Kirchenzeit so blutig funckelte die Seit.*[17]

After the quarter-of-an-hour we had [a] conference. Gideon had spoken with Gihorn about his heart. Also concerning Joshua's going to Abel—we postponed it for now because his wife Caritas was not quite comfortable with it at this time. And, regarding my leaving for Wechquadnach—that I was not yet entirely resolved; perhaps I would not go this week. Afterward, I was visited by English people. The single women again left for the week to make brooms in the woods. Jephthah and Paulus also went along.

Tuesday, the 2nd

I had school after the quarter-of-an-hour. Samuel went to a white man 3 miles from here. He [the white man] sent me greetings and [said that] I should visit him sometime; he would like to talk with me a bit about the Savior.

Wednesday, the 3rd

Gideon came to visit me in the morning. Gihorn came as well. I took the opportunity to speak with him about his heart—that the Savior would like to render him blissful and cheerful. He said that his heart was being so greatly tormented by worldly matters. I said that nothing could calm his heart like the Savior's blood. The Savior is working on his heart, and I am hoping that he will become the Savior's. After that I had school. Gottlieb went to New Milford. In the evening we had [a] quarter-of-an-hour.

Thursday, the 4th

In the forenoon I held school with the boys. Past noon I went visiting in several houses and found them [the brethren and sisters] quite agreeable. Several are returning home from the woods today. That evening a good number attended the quarter-of-an-hour. I was able to portray to them the Savior and his loving heart for the poor Indians in quite a lovely manner. Had a visit from Gottlieb's son still that evening, who has a desire to be washed in the Savior's blood, as do Gihorn's son and several others.

Friday, March 5

We had [a] quarter-of-an-hour in the morning. Afterward, Gideon and I went to the summer houses to make [fire]wood. Gottlieb returned home. She [Gottlieb's

wife] came and brought me a piece of white bread and some apples that he [Got-
tlieb] had brought with him. Rebecca came to visit me. Her husband intends to
continue living here at this place. I asked whether she sometimes spoke with
her husband and son about the Savior, and did they not feel a desire to be baptized with the Savior's blood. She said yes, at times they felt a desire. The boy
is quite agreeable; he is a little shy.

Saturday, the 6th

The watchword read: *Es sollen manche Nationen erfahren, daß ich der Herr bin der
Israel heilig macht. Ezek. 37.28. Und Jesu Reich nicht pfantasey und lerer Traum gewesen
sey.*[18]

Following the quarter-of-an-hour Joshua came and said that he was moving
with his family into his summer house today. I said he should follow his heart
in that regard. I did not think, however, that he was moving away so quickly out
of anger, because he harbored something against somebody. He said that he
harbored nothing against anyone, [but] that his wife would like to go there.[19]
Martin and Samuel came to visit me. They are quite agreeable. After that, Timotheus and his wife, as well as Esther from Wechquadnach, arrived here. Also,
several brethren and sisters who had gone into the woods at the beginning of
the week returned home. In the evening we had a passionate quarter-of-an-
hour; it also was perfectly full. After the quarter-of-an-hour I spoke with Timotheus and Esther; I was quite pleased with them.

Sunday, the 7th

We had [a] quarter-of-an-hour in the morning. After that I spoke with Gideon
and Samuel about my going to Wechquadnach and the other places, and about
several other matters. Next, I conducted the occasion; I felt quite comfortable
there. Following the occasion I announced that the baptized brethren and sisters would have a separate occasion this afternoon; thus, they gathered at 2
o'clock, at which time I read to them the letter of our dear heart Johannes [von
Watteville]. It pleased them greatly and they expressed their deep gratitude,
especially [about] the greeting from Papa[20] and from the other brethren and
sisters. I then talked to them a little about the love of the brethren and sisters
for one another, and it was [*words crossed out*].[21] I informed them that I would

depart tomorrow; did not know how soon I would return home, yet would come
back as soon as possible. Thereupon we had the kiss of love, and with that,
we closed the occasion. Then Gideon talked to them a great deal more. In the
evening Gideon came and said that Joshua had sent his son in [to the winter
houses] — that Elisabeth was not well. Thus, 3 sisters went out. I told Gideon
he should let Joshua and Elisabeth know that, should the child be weakly when
she delivered it, I would baptize it. He sent Samuel out on Monday before daybreak; he brought word that she had [given birth to] a daughter and [that] she
was well and in good health.

Monday, the 8th

The watchword read: *Daß soll der Bund seyn. Mein Gesez will ich in ihr Herz geben, und
in ihren Sin schreiben. Jer. 31.33. Dein süßes Evangelium ist lauter Milch und Honig.*[22]

After the quarter-of-an-hour I took leave of all the brethren and sisters and
recommended them to the Lamb[d] and His side hole[d]. Gideon went with me for
a distance and showed me the most direct way to Filkintown through Dover.
That evening I came to Henry Filkin where Br. Büttner and I had been interro-
gated once.[23] He still remembers me. I stayed with them that night. I inquired
about Adolph; they let me know where I could find him.

Tuesday, the 9th

The watchword read: *Zu der Zeit wird man von Zion sagen, welche Wunder Gott thut.*
4 Mos. 23.23.[24]

I took leave and went to call on Adolph and his family. I came then to their
house; Tabea and her daughter were home. They were overjoyed at seeing me.
She right away sent word to let her husband know that a brother from Bethlehem was here; thus he came home at once. He rejoiced greatly when he saw
me, saying that he and his wife had been unable to sleep last night. They had
talked with each other, whether a brother was to come; had laid down, but
then had to get up repeatedly, and so they had to spend the night smoking tobacco. He reportedly had done damage to his heart by leaving Gnadenhütten.
He had lived thereabouts [i.e., in Dutchess County] for more than 20 years; it
had seemed to him that there was no better place in the world. Now he disliked
it so much; once he was gone, he would not come back for the rest of his life.

I asked whether he then intended to go back soon to Gnadenhütten with his family. He said he would go tomorrow if only he had paid his merchant, who he owed more than 4 # [£]. He daily feared to be taken to *prisson* [prison], and if he were to leave, they would bring him back. His wife was waiting for their[25] son and someone else from Wanachquaticok, and together they wanted to go to Gnadenhütten. However, he would then have to stay [behind] by himself and work that much longer. I advised them that I thought it would be better if they stayed together and paid half, and send the remainder from Gnadenhüt-ten when they had it. She was very sad, however. I asked whether they had heard anything [about] Johannes of Pachgatgoch. They said that he had stayed with them for a while, but now [he was] at a place called Pachqueick,[26] making canoes there, but without gaining much. I said, if he saw him again he should tell him to come home. He also told me about the 2 sons of Nimham's[27] daughter—that they had a longing for Gnadenhütten. They had been to Wanachquaticok, or Stockbridge,[28] but did not see that the Indians there lived any differently than other Indians in the woods; they too drank and carried on with all sorts of vice. They [the sons of Nimham's daughter] intended to travel with them [Adolph's family]. I then talked with them a great deal about the Savior and that things were proceeding so blissfully in Gnadenhütten. Thereupon we ate breakfast, and I then took leave of Tabea and her daughter. Adolph went with me for more than 3 miles and showed me the way through the woods; we still talked with each other about this and that. He said, he thought that, still and all, he would be back in Gnadenhütten in 6 weeks' time, and with that we bade each other farewell. That evening I came to H. Rau, who received me with much love. He asked about Br. Martin, whether he was married again, as well as about many brethren he knows. I then also went with him to our former house; I also vis-ited God's Acre.[29] His son wanted me to stay the night with them; he had not yet forgotten the brethren, but loved them still. But I went back home with H. Rau, and stayed that night with them. He told me that his 2nd daughter, also had died that winter, having left behind 8 small children.[30]

Wednesday, the 10th

I departed from H. Rau [and went] toward the North River to call on Corne-lius. Came to Jacob Maul's [house]. They acted very cordially, she [Maul's wife] in particular. He took me to Zacharias Haber. On the way I talked with him a little about his heart. He gave me to understand that something had crossed his path that had done him some harm. I said that would probably be Lischy's books.[31] But he did not want to take the blame—the books had fallen into his hands without his request. I stayed with him that night.

Thursday, the 11th

The watchword read: Er wird auf dießen Berg das Hüllen wegthun, damit alle Völcker verhüllet sind. Is. 25.7. Er leuchtet mitten in der Nacht.[32]

I went to Christian Führer. Jacob Maul and Haber went with me. He was overjoyed, saying he had thought the congregation had completely forgotten about them. We spent some time together, whereupon the two went back home and Fürer went with me to call on Cornelius. We then arrived at the house where he lived, but he was not there. Two other Indians [were there]: Wompecam and his wife and a girl; [i.e.] the father of our Johannes in Gnadenhütten, and Joseph's mother.[33] They were very pleased that I was visiting them. They said that Cornelius's wife had left him and gone to Canada, and he had gone to bring her back. I passed on to them greetings from their children and said that they were well. I asked where their son Ignatius was. They said that he had left yesterday, and had not come back home yet, and that they intended to come to Pachgatgoch in 3 weeks' time to live there. Next, I talked to them a little about their hearts. They said that they thought of the Savior often. I said they should salute their son; I was unable to wait any longer. I went home with Br. Führer and stayed with him that night. He has a great desire to be admitted to the congregation, like the people in Pennsylvania. He would not be able to profess allegiance to any other people but the Brethren, to be sure. In his heart he is otherwise in a quite agreeable state.

Friday, the 12th

Führer went with me to Jacob Maul. From there I went back toward H. Rau. Jacob Maul accompanied me for 2 miles in the woods. That night I stayed with H. Rau.

Saturday, the 13th

H. Rau had 2 horses saddled and took me as far as to his son Philip. From there I went to Wechquadnach. I came to a house; the people recognized me—that

I was from Bethlehem. They were glad to see a brother. They said that our late Br. Bruce had preached at their house a number of times, and that Br. Rice had been at their house. I was obliged to take the midday meal with them. Then I came to Wechquadnach; found Susanna at home. The others were in the woods to boil [sap to make] sugar. She immediately sent word there to let them know that I was here. Hence, Timotheus and his wife, Esther, and Ampiwochnant's 2 daughters, came home right away. Ampiwochnant, however, was hunting, and they did not know whether he would come home that evening. I then talked with all of them; I was quite pleased with them. The wife of Timotheus said that she had been ill and had felt a great longing for the Savior and His blood. However, feeling better, she did not find the same longing in her heart, and she was worried about that. I said she should simply give her heart to the Savior just like it was; only His blood could make it well. I told them that a brother would come from Bethlehem 8 days from this coming Wednesday. It would please me if they were in Pachgatgoch at the time. Susan said that she would probably not be able to get there given that she cannot walk well. They asked whether I had met with Cornelius and his wife. I told them that she had left him. They said that she had told him [Cornelius] already this winter that she did not want to stay with him because he had left Gnadenhütten—she wanted to go back to Canada. I stayed with them for some time, and they were very affectionate. Timotheus said that they had made up their minds to continue living there, if only the white people would not take the land that they still had. I then took leave of them and went to Nicolaus Rau; he had traveled to his father. She [Nicolaus's wife] wanted to keep me [there], but I went to Winegar and stayed with them overnight.

Sunday, the 14th

The watchword read: *Merk auf mich mein Volck. Is. 51.4. Hier lieg ich auf meinem Angesicht Befehl mich deiner Gnade.*[34]

I left Gerhard Winegar early; came to my dear brown hearts in Pachgatgoch toward noon. Found [the] Gideons, [the] Joshuas, [the] Samuels, [the] Martin[s], Petrus, [the] Lucases, [the] Gottliebs, and Jeremias in the summer houses. They were in good spirits and quite full of light. My heart rejoiced at finding them in such a happy state. Gideon had brought part of my belongings from the winter house to this place, and so I stayed here. In the evening we had a general meeting for which a fairly large number had gathered.

Monday, the 15th

We had [a] quarter-of-an-hour in the morning. After that I held school twice. Went to the winter houses and visited the brethren and sisters there. Gottliebe had been very ill, but was somewhat better now. I told Leah that I had heard from her husband; I believed he would come home soon. I found all of them in good spirits.

Tuesday, the 16th

I held school twice, and after that I went visiting in the houses. The mother of Schires is very friendly. He was not at home. At other times he attends the meetings regularly.

Our brethren hauled wood with the sleds. They also brought me 2 sleds full. I was very grateful to them for that. Also, I received word that Johannes had come home. All of the brethren were pleased by that, and so was I.

Wednesday, the 17th

In the morning, after the quarter-of-an-hour, Joshua said that he wanted to go out into the neighborhood to sell brooms and other items. I had him bring me one [loaf of] bread. Also, Petrus, Christian, Schiris, and several unbaptized ones went out to make *canuss* [canoes]. And Rebecca came from the winter house to visit me. She is an agreeable sister. Samuel came to visit me in the evening; he is very affectionate.

Thursday, the 18th

The watchword read: *Und sie sa[n]gen ihnen vor: Laßet uns dem Herren singen.* 2 Mos. [15.]21. *Bringet alle Sprachen zusammen in einen Glauben Amen.*[35]

I held school in the morning, after the quarter-of-an-hour. Gideon and Martha, and Samuel went to the mill, [and] I to the winter houses that afternoon to visit Johannes and to bring back with me some things from my house. Found Johannes quite full of light and lively. Most of the sisters had gone sweating. I visited Gihorn and his son, who had been in Bethlehem once, and who had been called a keeper of women.[36] His name is Winemo; today he is married and already has a daughter^d. I talked with him about the Savior. Was he not ready to give Him his heart? The Savior very much wanted to render him blessed. But he is very bold; he said no. I said, but the Savior loved him, he should reflect on it, and I felt in my heart that I could speak with him freely. I then went home. On the way I thought, if only the Savior could at some point break Winimo's pride and hardness. There was a separatist at my house. He said that many of their people would like to speak with me; why was I not coming to them as well? I said that I did not have the time; there were still many Indians who I had not been able to visit until now. I went into Warup's house; found the son alone. Spoke with him about the Savior and His blood; he was most affectionate, expressing the desire to be baptized with the Savior's blood. He is a right agreeable boy, this son of Rebecca.

Friday, the 19th

The watchword read: *Ich will sie unter die Völcker säen das sie mein gedencken in fernen Landen.* Zech. 10.9. *Daß man auch dort erfahre sein animum efflare.*[37]

After the quarter-of-an-hour I started collecting my dirty laundry and washed it. Went into several houses to visit and got some wood for myself. Gideon came and said that they were going into the *hat* [hot] house now, to sweat. Thus, we had no quarter-of-an-hour.

Saturday, the 20th

The watchword read: *Die Inseln harren auf mich.* Is. 52.5. *Man hat ihn, wo man um ihn weint.*[38]

In the morning we had [a] quarter-of-an-hour. Today came home: Joshua, Johanna with her daughter, as well as Priscilla's 2 daughters, Salome, and Benigna. Moreover, Johannes and Christian's son came from the winter houses to visit me. Friederich also came home from out of the woods.

Sunday, the 21st

The watchword read: *Dein Wille geschehe.* Mt. 6.10. *Durch des Lammes Herrden.*[39]

In the morning, after the quarter-of-an-hour, we met in conference. Gideon said that he had talked with Warop a bit about the Savior; he came to the meeting from time to time—was he not feeling something in his heart? Yes, he [Warop] certainly felt that he was in need of the Savior's blood. Then did he not feel that he wanted to be baptized with the Savior's blood? At that point he reportedly smiled and said nothing. In the same way, he [Gideon] had spoken with Schiris — did he not feel in his heart that he was living in a wicked way? He said yes. He would make up his mind not to do it, but was commanded to do it, regardless. He asked whether it had not yet occurred to him that he may be cleansed of it [sin] and freed from it with the Savior's blood. He said yes, from time to time he indeed thought about it, but now and then it likewise occurred to him [that] if he came into a bad way again, it would be even worse than now. Martha said that Caritas was ill. She reportedly said [that] if she died now it would not look good; she has done many bad things again since her baptism. Her father had sold her large kettle. About that she had thought a great deal and had not been able to feel satisfied. Now her heart reportedly told her, Why do I think so much of my kettle, why do I not think of the Savior? I surely stand in greater need of that, for my heart is in such a bad state. Thus, she let go of the kettle and longed to have the Savior and His wounds in her heart. Winemo, Gihor's son, was talked about as well, that he had been thrown onto a fire by a white man, and that his face was badly burned. On coming home he is said to have wept dearly, saying that if he had died now, [he] surely would have gone down to hell. Because it rained so hard today, and many brethren and sisters were indisposed, we postponed the occasion until the evening; also because no brethren and sisters from the winter houses were here. However, old Maria and 2 others came here that afternoon. In the evening we had a blessed service[d]. My heart felt quite warm to me.

Monday, the 22nd

After the quarter-of-an-hour I held school [and] visited Samuel, who is somewhat ill. Gideon and Martha went to visit the brethren and sisters in the winter houses; they found them fairly well and in good spirits. Gideon had spoken with Gihorn about the Savior. He had reportedly said all of it was true, but he did not open his heart. Johanna went to get her belongings from the winter house.

Tuesday, the 23rd

We had [a] quarter-of-an-hour in the morning. After that I held school with the boys. Priscilla's 2 daughters, along with Johanna, went into the woods about 3 miles from here to make brooms. Joshua and Samuel were somewhat sickly.

I went and got firewood for myself. Erdmuth came here to live in the summer houses. Christian's son made preparations for them to be able to move to this place.

Wednesday, the 24th

Gideon came and told me that he intended to go into the woods to the brethren and sisters to see what they were doing and in what state their hearts were, and whether they intended to come home this week. I paid a visit to several houses; found them [the Indians] quite agreeable. Joshua is a little better; he went out to a white man. Several sisters also went out, with brooms and baskets to sell. I also visited the brethren and sisters in the winter houses, finding all of them well. Further, an Indian stranger came here from Farmington to visit, the son of Schiri's brother. His father's name was Mameho;[40] he loved us. He died one year ago. He attended the meeting that evening.

Thursday, the 25th

After the quarter-of-an-hour I held school with the boys. Next I went to visit Schiris; also found the stranger there. Talked with him a little about the Savior. Schiris asked me whether a brother would come from Bethlehem this week; his heart felt a great desire to be baptized with the Savior's blood. I said I was glad that he felt a hunger and thirst in his heart. I was hoping that a brother would come, provided the high waters did not prevent it. Also, Gideon came back home. He said that not all of them were quite well in their hearts, and that Paulus was ill. Jephthah had come with him but grew tired and stayed in the winter houses. The others would all come home this week. In the evening the Indian stranger came to visit me.

Friday, the 26th

We had [a] quarter-of-an-hour in the morning. Jephthah came home. He visited me; complained about Magdalena, that she was behaving badly, the other unmarried people as well. He lodged with Gottlieb because there was no room in Gideon's house.

Saturday, the 27th

I longingly watched for a brother [*word crossed out*], as did all our brethren and sisters, for I had informed them beforehand that a brother is to come from

Bethlehem this week. Schiris and his cousin[41] came to visit me, as well as several other brethren. And I paid a visit to several houses. Lucas with his two sisters Salome and Benigna, also Simon's daughter Anna Benigna, and Johannes, Amos, and still others came home from the woods.

Sunday, the 28th

We had [a] quarter-of-an-hour in the morning. After that I summoned the conference. But because I was visited by other brethren and sisters, the conference was postponed. At 11 o'clock I conducted the service. It was perfectly full. However, given that Joshua was not quite well, Samuel had to interpret, and as he could not endure it because of weakness, I then had to take Martin in the end. Afterward, the sisters who arrived here today from the winter houses came to visit me. Joshua had been in the sweat house and felt a little better; he came and asked whether we should have an occasion before the brethren and sisters returned to the winter houses. I too felt like holding an occasion for them before they left. However, because several awakened ones were here as well, I held a general meeting, and I felt very comfortable thereat. Warup came to me and asked whether one or more brethren would come from Bethlehem this week. His heart greatly desired to be baptized with the Savior's blood. I told him that I was hoping so. In the meantime, he should make sure to frequently occupy himself with the Savior, so that his heart would be very hungry and thirsty, and allow the Savior to give much grace and blood into his heart. He said that he was thinking of the Savior and His wounds all the while. After that they went back home in good spirits. We then had a small quarter-of-an-hour that same evening.

Monday, the 29th

The watchword read: *Wir sind Knechte, und unser Gott hat uns nicht verlaßen, wie wohl wir Knechte sind. Ezra 9.9. Die nach den Regeln der Natur daheime wären versauret.*[42] We had [a] quarter-of-an-hour in the morning, and afterward, I held school. Our brethren set about making their fences.[43] Next I visited Samuel; he is rather weakly. I did not feel so well either; have gotten it in the chest, and a sore throat. I fell quite ill that night, so that I had little sleep that night. My chest felt very sore.

Tuesday, the 30th

I was unable to conduct a quarter-of-an-hour today. Many brethren came to visit me when they heard that I was ill. Gideon immediately boiled roots and gave me to drink of it. I felt some instant relief. Then they went back to making their *fens* [fences]. Next, several sisters came to visit me. Agnes brought me bread that she had baked from white flour. Schiris too came to visit me. I did not get out of bed much that day.

Wednesday, the 31st

The watchword read: *Zeige deinen Knechten deine Wercke. Ps. 90.16. So wollen wir auch fleißig seyn dich alle Stunden zu erfreuen.*[44]

Schiris came in the morning, telling me that he intended to go to Stockbridge now.[45] I said this did not please me; I thought that a brother was coming this week, and so it would be good if he was at home. He said that he had matters of necessity to attend to and was unable to postpone them any longer. He planned on leaving Stockbridge again next Monday. After that Gideon came, bringing me a kettle full of *besson* [medicine]. Past noon I went out again and visited Samuel and several other brethren. Samuel said that he had dreamed that night that a white and an Indian brother had arrived from Bethlehem, yet when he sat up, it was dark around him, and so it occurred to him that it had been a dream. This evening I conducted the quarter-of-an-hour again, and I felt very comfortable on that occasion.

Aprilis

Thursday, the 1st

The watchword read: *Der Herr baut Jerusalem und bringet zusammen die Verjagten in Israel. Ps. 147.2. Sein Werck kan niemand hindern.*[46]

I conducted the quarter-of-an-hour in the morning. Afterward, I held school with the boys. I still felt fairly weak.

Friday, the 2nd

After school I went visiting in the winter houses, but found few at home. They had gone into the woods to get wood for brooms and baskets. Jeremias and

Agnes and several other brethren and sisters went out to sell things. Samuel is quite ill.

Saturday, the 3rd

We had [a] quarter-of-an-hour in the morning. I thought of our beloved Bethlehem often and how was it possible that I was not seeing a brother from there yet. I left it to the Lamb for now, and to Him I entrusted myself and the affairs of my brown brethren and sisters. Thus, many came home today in hopes of finding a brother here.

Sunday, the 4th

The watchword read: *Breite deine Güte über die, die dich kennen. Ps. 36.11. Mache uns dir zur Gemeine.*[47]

In the morning, after the quarter-of-an-hour, we met in conference, wherein we conferred with one another about several matters. Something concerning Petrus came up as well—that he had reportedly conducted himself badly at the white people's [places]. With the brethren and sisters from the winter houses having arrived here, I conducted the service. It was perfectly full. The brethren and sisters who were here from the winter houses came to visit me. All of them were full of light and in good spirits. I also spoke with <u>Gihorn</u>. He <u>said that his heart desired to be washed with the Savior's blood</u>. Before they left I also conducted the quarter-of-an-hour, which is usually held in the [evening], and with that we closed that day blissfully and in a happy state.

Monday, the 5th

The watchword read: *Du siehest doch, daß dis Volck dein Volck ist. 2 Mos. 33.13. Du hast für uns bezahlet.*[48]

Following the quarter-of-an-hour I held school with the boys. Most of the brethren and sisters prepared themselves to go into the woods and to return Saturday. They then took a heartfelt leave of me; I reminded them to nicely watch out for their hearts, making sure that they will be full of feeling for the Savior and His wounds and blood. That way they also would return home nicely full of light, which they promised me. They went about 7 or 8 miles from here, all to one place. I had them salute Simon and Paulus, who had not come home.

Tuesday, the 6th

The watchword read: *Nicht für Volck alleine. Jn. 11.52. Sondern hohlt durchs Löße-Geld, die erschaffnen und erkauften Erstlinge aus aller Welt.*[49]

After the quarter-of-an-hour I held school. Erdmuth went to New Milford with her little boys. I visited those who were at home. They all were in good spirits.

Wednesday, the 7th

I held school—in the forenoon with the boys, and in the afternoon with the girls. I visited Samuel, who is still very weak; talked with him about his heart, finding him in quite a happy state. Gideon came to visit me; talked with him somewhat about Petrus, who had been taken away by a *kunstabel* [constable], whether a brother should go and see what they were doing with him. He said that Warop had gone [there], and that we would receive word through Jephthah, who had gone to the winter houses. Petrus came home in the evening. Priscilla and Caritas went to New Milford.

Thursday, the 8th

Because there were almost no brethren and sisters at home today, we had no quarter-of-an-hour. I held school with the boys. Schiris came back home. Samuel seemed to have improved somewhat. I went to the winter houses to visit the brethren and sisters; found them all in good spirits. Toward evening 2 friends from Seebruck,[50] Michel Hiell and Thomas Spencer, came to visit me and the [word crossed out] brethren and sisters. The one has been to Bethlehem twice. Their intention was to stay with me. I entertained them as well as I could. Michel Hill is a fine man.

Friday, the 9th

The watchword read: *Morgen ist der Sabath der heiligen Ruhe des Herrn Exodu[s.] Nun laß uns fröhlich singen das Consummatum est.*[51]

After breakfast I went with the 2 friends to visit the brown brethren and sisters, and after that they left. I accompanied them for probably one mile and then we bade one another a heartfelt farewell. Priscilla came home from New Milford. Gideon went to Dover. I thought about our dear Bethlehem often. Then Caritas came home from New Milford. Bartolomew arrived here from Wanachquaticok to visit me; said that Esther and his mother would come tomorrow as well. He was fairly full of light and lively. Gideon also came back home.

Saturday, the 10th

I observed the Sabbath in quiet. Jeremias went out to sell things that he had made. Bartolomew came to visit me, bringing word that Cornelius had died 10 days ago at [the house of] white people by the name of Cobes Decker on the Lolob Janssens Kil,[52] which made me a little sad for I had not spoken with him beforehand. He had not found his wife and had come back alone. In the evening several brethren and sisters came home, [to wit], Martin and she,[53] Paulus and his wife, Lucas and his 2 sisters, Amos, and Petrus's Anna. They all were full of light and in good spirits. Agnes, the wife of Jeremias, came home as well. In the evening, after the quarter-of-an-hour, I informed the brethren and sisters that Easter would be celebrated in our congregations tomorrow; that is when our brethren and sisters would go jointly to God's Acre early in the morning before sunrise, and remember our dear Savior's resurrection and the resurrection of our dear brethren and sisters who have gone home. Thus, we also wanted to have our quarter-of-an-hour a little earlier and remember our dear Savior's resurrection. They were quite pleased at this.

Sunday, the 11th

Before sunrise Gideon sounded [the horn][54] for the quarter-of-an-hour. Everyone assembled at once. I then talked a bit about the resurrection of our dear Savior, and that on that same morning many other bodies of those who are holy and had loved Him, and had waited and hoped for Him, yet went home before Him, had been resurrected. I felt especially comfortable in my heart during the quarter-of-an-hour and throughout the entire day. Toward noon the brethren and sisters from the winter houses arrived here. Thus we conducted the service at once, in the course of which I talked somewhat of how the Savior had revealed Himself to His apostles, and to His people who had loved Him, and had shown them His wounds, and so I wished that the Savior, in like manner, would reveal Himself with His wounds in their hearts. Rebecca and Sarah and several others visited me. We had [a] quarter-of-an-hour in the evening.

Monday, the 12th

After the quarter-of-an-hour I held school. Several brethren and sisters prepared themselves to go back into the woods. They came and took leave of me, [that is], Martin and his wife, Paulus and his wife, the wife of Jeremias, and several unmarried people. I visited the rest, and after that I got wood for myself.

Tuesday, the 13th

Having held school I went to Gaylords and brought back with me one bread and several other items. I visited Kihor and Warup; Rebecca had gone to Danbury. I found everyone at home quiet and in good spirits.

Wednesday, the 14th

Before noon I held school with the boys; there are few at home. Jephthah came to visit me. I called on Samuel and Lucia; they are a couple of agreeable brethren and sisters. Samuel is feeling better for the most part.

Thursday, the 15th

The watchword read: *Weide du dein Volck mit deinem Stabe.* Mic. 7.14. *Beij dem Grabe wieder funden.*[55]

I held school. Rebecca and the old m[other] Maria came home from New Milford. Erdmuth went to get her daughter. Samuel came for the first time again to visit me.

Friday, the 16th

After school I did my wash. Old Erdmuth came home with Juliana, and Petrus and Thamar from New Milford. I visited the brethren and sisters who are home, finding them altogether in good spirits.

Saturday, the 17th

Today the brethren and sisters who had gone into the woods that week came home. Several [came] even before noon in hopes of finding a brother from our dear Bethlehem, but did not find one: Martin with his wife, [the] Christians, Jeremias with his Agnes, Friederich and Amos, Lucas, Priscilla's daughters, and Benigna, [and] Magdalena. Joshua and his family were not able to come home all the way because of the bad weather. Also, Esther and Susanna came from Wechquadnach, having heard along the way that there were letters from Bethlehem for me in Sharon, yet by then they had gone several miles past it [Sharon]. I was overjoyed to hear something from our dear hearts[d].

Sunday, the 18th

We had [a] quarter-of-an-hour in the morning. Afterward, Joshua came home with his family. Next the brethren and sisters from the winter houses gathered here. Then we had our service. Several brethren and sisters from the winter houses visited me; they were very much full of light and in good spirits. Past noon we had a small conference wherein we conferred about several matters. Some of the brethren and sisters would have liked to have seen someone sent to get the letters this Sunday. Yet I intended to go myself this Monday. We had [a] quarter-of-an-hour in the evening.

Monday, the 19th

The watchword read: *Wir haben dier unßere Sache befollen. Jer. 11.20. Wir dinen deinen Willen.*[56]

A number of our brethren and sisters had resolved to stay at home and to hear what our dear hearts from Bethlehem had written. After the quarter-of-an-hour I set out to get the letters and arrived there before noon. Opening them at once, I found the sad news concerning our dear Mother Julia,[57] and about the dear heart Cammerhoff having been taken ill so severely. While [I was] in the process of reading, Timotheus from Wechquadnach entered the house; he was very much full of light and lively, telling me that <u>Benjamin and the younger Moses had arrived from Gnadenhütten</u> and had come to them this morning. Thus I right away resolved to go with him in order to hear in what state of mind they had left Gnadenhütten; secondly [because I] was hoping for further news, since the letters were one month old by now. We arrived there, and I found them altogether fairly full of light. They rejoiced when they saw me. I asked about our dear heart Cammerhoff, and they said that matters had improved with him to some extent, which was more than a small joy for me. Then they said further that they had no letters, but Nathanael and another brother [were coming] from

Bethlehem; they might arrive in Pachgatgoch this evening. They had the letters. Hence I wished to be in Pachgatgoch now. Talked with them and the others for a while and told them that I wished they would come to us in Pachgatgoch this Friday or Saturday, which several promised. Thereupon I took leave and got as far as Nicolaus Rau, with whom I stayed overnight.

Tuesday, the 20th

I set out early, for I had a feeling in my heart that I would meet [the] brethren. About 2 miles from Pachgatgoch I came upon Esther and Susan[n]a, who said that [the Indian] Nathanael and another brother from Bethlehem had arrived in Pachgatgoch yesterday evening, which was more than a small joy for me. On arriving there I found my dear heart Bezold [Pezold] and Nathanael in Gideon's house having breakfast with the brown hearts[d]. We then kissed each other affectionately and heartily. Our hearts rejoiced at seeing one another, and I especially. We went together to our house, and because I had not had breakfast yet, I made a little tea for both of us; Nathanael remained in Gideon's house where he had taken up lodgings. Gottlieb, the dear heart[d], brought me many a heartfelt affectionate letter[d], greeting[d], and kiss[d], telling me a number of things about Bethlehem and about the hearts[d] who are [working] at their plan in this country. After that we called the conference, and Br. Gottlieb passed on greetings to them from Br. Johann[es] [von Watteville], Cammerhoff, Herman, and from all of Bethlehem and Gnadenhütten. They were grateful, and it was very weighty to them. It was resolved, furthermore, that Br. Gottlieb, along with the Indian Nathanael, would have to stay here throughout this week since many of our Indian brethren and sisters had gone back into the woods. Afterward, Br. Gottlieb and Nathanel went into all the houses to visit, finding all of those who were at home full of light and in good spirits. In the evening the dear heart Gottlieb conducted the quarter-of-an-hour and passed on the greetings to all the brethren and sisters, at which they greatly rejoiced. Moreover, he informed them about the going home to the Lamb[d] of our dear and precious Mother Juliana, and about dear Brother Cammerhoff having been taken ill so severely, and that these 2 matters had prevented a brother from coming at the appointed time. After the quarter-of-an-hour Brother Gottlieb told me all sorts of delightful matters about our dear Bethlehem, at which I greatly rejoiced.

Wednesday, the 21st

The watchword read: *Er wird ihre Sache selber tractiren. Pr. 22.23. Er hält sein Wort mit Freuden.*[58]

Gottlieb, the dear heart, conducted a blessed quarter-of-an-hour. After that we had several difficult matters [to discuss]; we talked with Gideon and Joshua. Then we went to the winter houses to visit the brethren and sisters there. First, Gottlieb, I, and Nathanael visited Warup, who is presently not in a good state, however. Thereafter we visited Gihorn, who talked quite agreeably about his heart and desired to be baptized. He believed that, just as one could cleanse a bowl with water, the Savior's blood could cleanse his heart. The sisters of that place had gone to the summer houses. Thus we went back home. In the meantime, our brethren had prepared the benches in our house, and for the first time the quarter-of-an-hour was again conducted in our house. Everyone gathered and the house was filled to capacity. Then the dear heart Gottlieb spoke in a very hearty and fervent manner of the Savior's love for the poor sinners.

Thursday, the 22nd

We had [a] quarter-of-an-hour in the morning. Afterward, we spoke with Abraham's son, Friederich, who has been in a bad state for some time, which he did not deny, also with Lucas, who, with a broken heart, complained to us about his poverty of the heart. Also, a girl, Ertmuth's grendt scheid [grandchild], came, who tearfully requested to be baptized. Brother Gottlieb told her she should just occupy herself with the Savior and tell this to Him. We too wanted to remember her before the Savior. Nathanael visited Schiri, who [word crossed out] has gotten into fights because of others, and was presently unfit for baptism. Jeremias set out on horseback to buy bread for the love feast, yet returned home bringing none.

Friday, the 23rd

Sensemann held held the morning blessing and Joshua interpreted.[59] It was called to mind that this evening's quarter-of-an-hour was going to be for the communicants only. Then we began speaking with those brethren and sisters to whom things have happened during last Communion. Gideon and Martha and Nathaniel were also present, and Gottlieb's and Sensemann's hearts felt very comfortable on this occasion. Amos went out for bread and brought

6 [loaves of] bread. In the evening Br. Gottlieb conducted a blessed quarter-of-an-hour for the communicants, reminding ~~the brethren and sisters~~ them to examine themselves as to whether something had befallen them since last Communion, and [they] should go to the Savior with that and have everything forgiven them, because next <u>Sunday</u> the Savior <u>wanted to give them His flesh to eat and His blood to drink</u>, and that the Savior was willing to forgive them everything and to embrace them anew with His love.

Saturday, the 24th

The watchword read: *Er wird auß dem allen helfen.* Ps. 34.20. *Was sie drückt und bestrickt.*[60]

In the morning the heart[d] Gottlieb conducted a passionate quarter-of-an-hour. After that we again started to speak with the communicants, finding many quite abased and open so that our hearts rejoiced at it. Several, with whom some matters had come to pass, were very sincere and straight. We went to the winter houses to visit; found everyone well. Nathanael went to visit Gottlob. Thus we went back home and spoke yet with several brethren and sisters. Nathanael returned home; had not found Gottlob [and] had been unable to obtain any real word on him as to where he was. Br. Gottlieb conducted the quarter-of-an-hour in the evening; it was perfectly full. Moreover, from Wechquadnach came Esther, Timotheus and his wife, Ampwochnant and his wife, [and] Moses and Benjamin.

Sunday, the 25th

Nathanael, Gideon, and Martha came in the morning. Thus we soon we began speaking [in preparation for Communion]. Several candidates had applied for baptism. We only spoke with some, however. [We spoke with] <u>the wife of Timotius</u>, who had been ill that winter <u>and often desired to be baptized with the Savior's blood</u>, but no brother was there at the time, and [she] still felt [*words crossed out*] the same way in her heart. <u>We were not able to deny her</u> without doing harm <u>and told</u> her in the name of the Savior that ~~she~~ the Savior was going to fulfill her desire tonight at the love feast, and cleanse her from all the sins with His blood. <u>Joshua and Elisabeth desired</u> that <u>their child</u>, who is several weeks old, be <u>baptized</u> today with the Savior's blood. We could not but grant them their request and desire, and shortly thereafter, during the sermon that was attended by a fairly great number so that there was almost not enough room in the house for everyone, it [the child] was overflowed with the bloody stream from Jesus' side hole[d] and named <u>Anna</u>. Because there were many English people here who were waiting for a sermon, we were thus obliged to deliver a sermon so that they could get back home. After the sermon there was [a] love feast for all the baptized brethren and sisters; several candidates were taken along to join [in]. It was reported what the Savior was affecting in the brown hearts in various places these days. Then, the wife of Timotheus, who received the name Hannah, was overflowed with the stream from Jesus' side hole[d]. They all felt well on this occasion and we sensed a special feeling of grace. Following that, we had the quarter-of-an-hour for the communicants, with our Husband absolving us, and we felt that He was present. After that we parted for a while and made preparations for Communion. Then a signal was given and everyone reassembled at once, and our Husband spread out His body over each heart[d] in such a way that I cannot describe the feeling. Everyone was absorbed and melted to tears, and with that, each one retired to his house[d] blissfully and in a happy state. Nathanael came to us that very evening, having been sent by <u>an Indian stranger from Potatuck who requested to be baptized</u> by Brother Gottlieb [Pezold]. However, because he does not live here, we did not consider it any further, but if it was important to him to become the Savior's, he was welcome to move to this place, to our brethren. And so we closed this day with a heart melted to tears for our precious Husband for the grace that we enjoyed from Him during these days, and especially today.

Monday, April 26, 1751

Pachgatgoch *Diarium*

The watchword read: *Der Feind gedachte, ich will meinen Muth an ihnen kühlen. 2 Mos. 15.9. Gieb mir ein treue Liebe zu allen daß uns haß.*[61]

Br. Gottlieb held the quarter-of-an-hour in the morning. After breakfast Nathanael went to the winter houses to take leave of the brethren and sisters there. Br. Gottlieb spoke beforehand with those brethren and sisters who are going into the woods today to work, in particular with Joshua, who had not joined

Communion this time, telling him that he thought he had not acted properly. Sensemann wrote several letters to the dear hearts in Bethlehem. The brethren and sisters from Wechquadnach set out to travel home. They were full of light and in good spirits, especially our dear Sister Hannah and Esther. Nathanael returned home, and then Gottlieb and Nathanael took leave of all the brethren and sisters who were at home. Sensemann went along to accompany them; Gideon and Samuel escorted us one and 1/2 mile and then we bade one another a heartfelt farewell. Sensemann told them that he intended to be back with them in 2 days. They gave them many a heartfelt greeting and kiss to pass on to the congregation in Bethlehem and Gnadenhütten. We then recommended the brown assembly in Pachgatgoch to the steadfast charge and care of the Lamb[d]. We arrived in Wechquadnach late in the evening. The brethren and sisters received us with tender love. We were fairly wet from the rain. They gave us something to eat and prepared pleasant lodgings for us. We then went to sleep.

Tuesday, the 27th

The watchword read: *Der Herr hört es.* 4 Mos. 12.2.[62]

Gottlieb and Sensemann went with Timotheus to see the grave of our late Brother Bruce. His bones lie buried with many Indians; on his left they buried Lazara, Jephthah's daughter. We wished that his soul[d] may soon have the tabernacle[d] follow, if this has not already occurred. We went back home, and having taken breakfast with the brethren and sisters, we took a heartfelt leave of them. Came to Hannes Rau ~~toward evening~~ who kissed us heartily and led us into his house; he did for us what he could. Gottlieb passed on the greetings from Br. Martin and from several other brethren and sisters. He said that they have been looking for Br. Martin every day and would very much like to see him sometime. Because it seemed that the weather was going to be good, Gottlieb, the heart[d], and Nathanael set out to also go to Jacob Maul or Führer. Hans Rau and Sensemann accompanied them for a distance, and then we bade one another a heartfelt farewell. This hurt a little indeed, on the part of Sensemann. I stayed that night with Hannes Rau.

Wednesday, the 28th

I readied myself to get back to my brown assembly. Hannes Rau went [*number crossed out*] several miles with me on horseback, and then we took a heartfelt leave of each other. I came to a house to inquire about the way. The woman asked whether I was from Bethlehem. She was able to tell by looking at people's faces. I said yes. They were New Lights. She put food on the table and I ate a little, and then went on my way. In the evening I came to my brown people, who were glad to see me again. Petrus and Thamar made a fire for me and got water, and still others came to visit me. Gideon had gone to New Milford; Martha had the fever. Otherwise everyone was blissful and full of light, so that I was able to rejoice.

Thursday, the 29th

I held school in the morning. After that I visited the brethren and sisters who were at home. I found them still in such a state that I could see what our Husband had affected in them during Communion through His body[d] and blood.

Friday, the 30th

The watchword read: *Sein Rath ist wunderbarlich, und führts herlich hinaus. Is. 28.29. Ehe man gedenckt, ist mehr geschen, als man sich je zu ihm versehe.*[63]

Samuel set out on horseback; was arrested along the way because of some debt. However, under the circumstances, he conducted himself in such a manner that I can thank the Savior for it. I went to the winter houses to visit the brethren and sisters there; found them well and in good spirits, near the Savior and His wounds. Rebecca said that, at times, she had been sad on account of her husband, but now her heart was again full of light and happy. On returning home I sent Jeremias to see what the white people were doing with Samuel, who brought word that they had set out their claims [against him] and he would have to pay 5 # [£] in New England money in charges, and that Samuel had gone on horseback to Gaylords. Gideon returned home from New Milford in a happy state.

Saturday, May 1

I put in Welsh corn[64] today and thought of our dear Bethlehem a great deal. Jephthah came to me and said that he intended to have himself taken to Wechquadnach on Monday, and from there on to Gnadenhütten. Christian and Gottliebe came home from having been in the woods, as did Lucia and Priscilla['s] 2 daughters, and Petrus's Anna, as well as Caritas. They all were in good spirits and full of light.[65] We had a blessed quarter-of-an-hour in the evening.

Sunday, the 2nd

After the quarter-of-an-hour the brethren and sisters from the winter houses and several unbaptized ones, as well as Scheri, who has been working 4 miles from here, came to attend the sermon. It was fairly full for the sermon, and I felt very comfortable in my heart. I was able to portray with a warm heart the Lamb[d] and His wounds to them. The baptized brethren and sisters were told that when there was blowing [from the horn] there would be a separate occasion for them, which occurred at 2 o'clock, wherein several letters from Bethlehem were read aloud. And after that we had the kiss of love, and with that we parted blissfully and in a happy state. Toward evening we had our general quarter-of-an-hour. Afterward, several candidates came to visit me who appeared to have a hungry and thirsty heart for the watering place in Jesus' blood, which I wish for them soon.

Monday, the 3rd

In the morning, after the quarter-of-an-hour, several brethren and sisters made preparations to go into the woods: Agnes, Priscilla's and Petrus's daughters, Gideon's daughter Johanna, [the] Christians, and Petrus. I held school.

Tuesday, the 4th

The watchword read: *Ich schweige wol eine zeitlang, und bin stille. Is. 42.4. Und wird doch gemacht.*[66]

After the quarter-of-an-hour Gottlieb and Magdalena came and took leave to go to New Milford; asked that I keep an eye on their children. Thamar and Priscilla went with them. Thus, only a few remained at home. I held school in the forenoon. Past noon I wanted to go with Samuel to Gaylords, but we were unable to get across the river. I visited Gihorn's house; Sarah was in a happy state. Her daughter Maria was feeling somewhat sickly in her body. We had no occasion[67] today because there were almost no brethren and sisters at home.

Wednesday, the 5th

The watchword read: [word crossed out] *Um Zion willen so will ich nicht mehr inne halten, biß daß ihr Heil entbrenne wie eine Fackel. Is. 62.1. Wie Schön leuchtet der Wunden-Stern!*[68]

Br. Samuel and I left for Gaylords early. They welcomed us cordially; I also bought one bread and some meat; I ate and drank at their house, for which they wanted nothing. I visited his brother as well. In addition, there was a New Light with them who was glad to see me; he asked that I come and visit him someday. I did not promise him anything, however. Should I come that way, perhaps it would happen that I would visit him sometime. I went home. Gideon came to visit me in the evening. He was very affectionate. Agnes came home.

Thursday, the 6th

In the forenoon I held school with the boys. Gideon took leave to go 8 miles up the river to finish a canoe he had started. Samuel came to visit me; complained about feeling sickly again. Sister Thamar and Priscilla, [as well as] Gottlieb and Magdalena returned home from New Milford in quite a happy state. Petrus came home having hacked himself in the knee.

Friday, May 7

The watchword read: *Eß werden auch gebückt zu dir kommen die dich unterdrückt haben, und die dich gelästert haben. Is. 60.14. Die werden sehr erschrecken vor deiner Seligkeit.*[69]

In the morning I held school. I paid a visit to the houses, finding everyone full of light and in good spirits. Christian and Gottliebe came home from New Milford. He told me that the separatists had asked for me and that they loved the Brethren. In the evening we had a blessed quarter-of-an-hour.

Saturday, the 8th

Today I thought about our dear Bethlehem a great deal. Then the following brethren and sisters returned home from having been in the woods: Gideon, Simon with his entire family, Joshua with his wife and children, Lucas and his sisters, Johanna, Magdalena, [and] Petrus's Anna. Our Sister Hannah and Esther also came from Wechquadnach, being quite full of light and blissful in their hearts. Since last Communion the Lamb[d] has affected much in the brown hearts[d], here and in Wechquadnach. Bartolomew and another 3 Indian strangers from Wanachquaticok came here for a visit, as did Benjamin and Moses. In the evening we had a passionate quarter-of-an-hour.

Sunday, the 9th

I had several visitors in the morning. Around 10 o'clock Gideon came and said that the brethren and sisters from the winter houses had arrived, and so we prepared for the meeting. The house was fairly full. I was able to speak to them with a warm heart about the Savior's love for the poor sinners, and they all were attentive. The 3 strangers were present as well and appear to be agreeable people. One is the brother of Paulus's wife. Toward evening we had a blessed quarter-of-an-hour, and with that we closed the day with blessing.

Monday, the 10th

The watchword read: *Du elende, über die alle Wetter gehen, und die Trostlosen. Is. 54.11. Ey nun Tröst dich Gott!*[70]

We had [a] quarter-of-an-hour in the morning. Old mother Erdmuth came and took her leave to go down below New Milford. Thamar and Priscilla, along with her daughter Benigna, came as well, and said that they had readied themselves and now wanted to go with baskets to Danbury. They all were full of light and in good spirits. Christian went to New Milford. Gottliebe started to grow somewhat sickly today, but it passed again. Johannes went into the woods to make [a] *canuh*; brought word to Paulus and his wife that her brother was in Pachgatgoch and wanted to speak with her. In the forenoon I held school, and in the afternoon I went with Br. Samuel to an English man whom I hired to plow my Welsh corn field. Br. Martin came to visit me in the evening. Paulus and his wife came home.

Tuesday, the 11th

We had [a] quarter-of-an-hour in the morning. Jeremias went to work for white people. Samuel went to New Milford. I visited the 2 [sic] strangers; they were very friendly. I asked about Br. Wielm[71] and a few others I knew. They departed today, and Paulus and his wife went back into the swamp, as did Benigna. Gideon came and told me that he intended to go to New Milford now to buy nails. Joshua went into the woods to work.

Wednesday, the 12th

The watchword read: *Die Fürsten unter den Völckern sind versamlet zu einen Volck. Ps. 47.12. Die alte Unitas Fratrum.*[72]

I held school in the morning. Afterward, Gihorn came, who I had to bleed. Thamar and her company all returned home in a happy state. I got firewood for myself. In the evening Jeremias came back home, as did Gideon.

Thursday, the 13th

I held school in the forenoon. After school I went to the winter houses, finding the brethren and sisters who were at home well and in good spirits. Sarah asked me to bleed her, which I did. Joshua and Samuel returned home today, full of light and in a happy state. We had no quarter-of-an-hour this evening because they [the Indians] sweated.

Friday, the 14th

Soon after the quarter-of-an-hour several brethren and sisters who needed to bleed gathered, and I bled 5 this time. After that I began to wash my soiled things. Having finished with that, I went visiting; found all of them well. Gideon came to visit me; he is an old, affectionate man whom I love.

Saturday, the 15th

The watchword read: *Versiegelt die Knechte Gottes*. Rev. 7.3. *Blaße lippen, küßt Sie aufs Herz*.[73]

I went with Samuel across the river to an English man [to ask him] to plow my land, as the last one did not come. He promised me to plow it next Monday. Next the brethren and sisters who had spent the week in the woods came home in quite a happy state. We had a blessed quarter-of-an-hour in the evening.

Sunday, the 16th

We had a delightful conference in the morning. Various matters came up in the course of it. Because something had occurred between Gottlob and his wife, Elisabeth had to talk to her. She had wept because of it, and said that she had already shed many tears over this, thus, we forgave her for it and so did her husband. Given that Sr. Thamar also was not truly full of light, and [because] her husband Petrus was at the root of the matter, we resolved that Gideon and I, along with Joshua, would speak with both of them. We then had the general occasion, and I felt quite comfortable in my heart thereat. Afterward, we spoke with Petrus and Thamar. Petrus, however, did not want to admit his guilt, even though he was guilty. However, when I put his matters before him, he grew dissatisfied and walked away. Next, Warup and his wife Rebecca called on me, as did Sarah and Leah from the winter houses; they were well and full of light. Also, an English man came to visit me. He appears to be a simple, open-hearted man. He said that he had visited Büninger frequently, and he him. He asked that I visit him sometime as well, which I half promised him. Afterward, I conducted the last occasion and the man stayed for that as well. Everyone in Pachgatgoch was quiet and well.

Monday, the 17th

The watchword read: *Reumet den Weg, hebet die Anstöße aus den Wegen meines Volcks.* Is. 57.14. *Eine unverzaunte Bahn.*[74]

Gideon came in the morning and said that he intended to go to Dover today and return home in about 2 days. His business there was to show the line of a piece of land that had been sold 30 years ago.[75] Joshua and Jeremias went on horseback to Danbury to buy beans.[76] My man, who I had hired, came and plowed my land. We had [a] quarter-of-an-hour in the evening. Old Erdmuth came home as well.

Tuesday, the 18th

The watchword read: *Sie sind ja mein Volck Kinder die nicht falsch sind.* Is. 63.8.[77]

In the forenoon I held school, paid a visit to several houses, and thereafter, I went to visit the brethren and sisters in the winter houses. Found those who were home well and in good spirits. Also talked with Gihorn and Warup; they were very friendly. On returning home we had our quarter-of-an-hour. Several of the brethren stayed on with me.

Wednesday, the 19th

In the morning, Samuel, Martin, and Gottlieb,[78] and also several single sisters, came and helped me plant my Welsh corn. Then I held school. After school I went to a white man and bought a piece of bread and a little meat for myself. The people acted very friendly toward me. On returning home [I found that] Gideon had returned as well. He came right away to visit me. Gottlieb also called on me. Jeremias came home in a happy state, as did Joshua.

Thursday, the 20th

I held school in the forenoon; in the afternoon I worked in the field. Our brethren and sisters were busy with plowing and planting. In the evening I was paid
a visit by 2 neighbors who acted very friendly. In the evening we had a blessed
quarter-of-an-hour.

Friday, the 21st

After school Gideon came and asked me if there was not a brother from Bethlehem coming soon. I said I could not say anything for certain; I expected a letter from Bethlehem this week; that is when I would find out. I paid a visit to several houses; they [the Indians] all were full of light and in good spirits. Also,
Gottlob came home to plant and do other work.

Saturday, the 22nd

I thought of our dear Bethlehem a great deal and felt a deep longing to soon
find myself among the dear assembly. Several brethren and sisters came home
blissful and in good spirits.

Sunday, the 23rd

In the morning several brethren came to visit me, and at about 11 o'clock Gideon
came and said that they had all gathered, and so we commenced the service.
Everyone assembled, and the Lamb[d] was with us, and I felt very comfortable
while speaking. Afterward, Joshua came and asked me whether a brother was
going to come from Bethlehem soon. I said I could not say, but I assumed so.
Gideon needed to talk with Gottlob on account of several one issues. I spoke
with Thamar in regard to her husband.[79] She said that he had turned to his heart
and had said that he had not done things well. This lay heavy upon his heart;
he was very worried about this. Then I had a visit from an English man. Toward
evening we had the last occasion. Also, I informed Gideon that I intended to go
to Wanachquaticok tomorrow; would probably stay out this week. Magdalena,
Gottlieb's wife, remained seated after the occasion and wept dearly, saying
that she had not felt well in her heart this week. I said that I had noticed this
about her, but had not had any opportunity to speak with her. I asked her from
what it stemmed. She said that several brethren were treating her very harshly,
and that was the reason. I directed her to the Savior and to His wounds; that is

where she would rid herself of these things, and should not pay any attention to these matters, and with that she went home.

Monday, the 24th

The watchword read: *Gott sey Danck für seine unaussprechliche Gnade.* 2 Cor. 9.15. *Daß man nun einmal den Passat der Leichnamsluft gefunden hat.*[80]

In the forenoon I went with several sisters to plant my beans. After that Brother Joshua came and asked whether I still intended to leave today, and how long I thought I would stay out. He intended to go down to the seaside toward the end of the week; therefore, he would not be home this Sunday. Thus, I took leave of them and said he should just be sure to abide in the Savior and His wounds at all times. Several other brethren and sisters came to visit me. Our brown hearts[d] are quite full of light and in good spirits. They planted in common and did so nice and quietly, and with love. I then went to take leave of all the brethren and sisters, recommending them to the Lamb[d] and His wounds. They gave me many greetings to pass on to the brethren and sisters in Wechquadnach and Wanach-quaticok, and so I went on my way. Along the way I came to a man who said that the separatists had predicted that the day of judgment would come in 4 weeks. I arrived in Wechquadnach fairly late; several had already gone to sleep. Yet everyone grew lively, and they were glad when they saw me. They even wanted to make something to eat for me, but I soon went to bed, having passed on greetings to them from the brethren and sisters in Pachgatgoch.

Tuesday, the 25th

The watchword read: *Gott dein Weg ist heilig.* Ps. 77.14. *Unßer Fuß der gehet ihn schon manches Jahr, und daß Herz verstehet dich nun ziemlich gar.*[81]

Having spoken with the brethren and sisters in Wechquadnach a bit, and having found that they all were well and in a happy state, I set out on my journey toward Wanachquaticok. I came to several separatists who desired that I visit them. That evening I came to an inn; the people were very friendly, saying that 3 of our brethren had been there at the beginning of winter. One had looked like he was a *schentelman* [gentleman]. They asked me in a very modest fashion a few things about our congregation.

Wednesday, the 26th

The watchword read: *Wir fahren dahin der Gnade ergeben*. Acts 15.46. *Über Land und Ocean*.[82]

Early in the morning I set out and departed from there. I met P[83] *Captein* [Captain] Aaron's son. I asked where he was going. He said that his father was ill and that he wanted to go to the doctor to get medicine. When I had about one more mile to Wanachquaticok, an Indian came my way; it was Paulus, who had been in Bethlehem once, some years ago. He was very surprised ~~that~~ when he saw me, for he said he had heard that I was dead, and that was 2 years ago. He right away turned back with me and brought me to his house. His wife is Nathanael's sister, who together with her 2 daughters rejoiced at seeing a brother from Bethlehem. They right away gave me food and drink. After that he went with me to *Captein* Aaron, who was very ill. I saluted him [Aaron] from our congregation in Bethlehem and from Gnadenhütten, as well as from Pachgatgoch and Wechquadnach. He thanked me kindly [and] asked whether they all were in good health and well. Then I spoke with him a little about the Savior and His wounds and how He so loved the sinners. It pleased him to hear something about that. He was surprised that the brethren in Pachgatgoch had not sent a brother with me. I excused them, saying that because they were still planting I had not asked for it, otherwise they would have been pleased to send one with me. I talked with him for a while; told him I intended to visit him once more before I left, which pleased him very much. I visited our Br. Wilhelm, but he was not at home. His wife is ill as well. She immediately had [something to] drink prepared for me. After that we went inside the *Pforte*[84] wherein there are still other families living. We came to our Sr. Eva's sister and family. They were very glad to hear something about their sister and friends[85] in Gnadenhütten. Several [people] came from other houses to see me, and I should please come and visit them as well; and I visited all of them and talked to them about the Savior, that He had died on the cross and shed His blood so that they shall be saved and have feeling in their hearts. They all were very attentive. Eva's sister said that she wanted to go to Gnadenhü[tten] next fall to visit her sister and the congregation. After that I came to Ludwig Anton's sister and friends,[86] who asked me how he was. I said that he was in good health. I visited Bartolomew, but he was not at home. I talked some with his wife, and with Moses

Fig. 3. Johann (John) Martin Mack (1715–1784), missionary at Pachgatgoch (oil).
From the collections of the Moravian Archives, Bethlehem, Pennsylvania.

from Gnadenhütten, who is staying here, along with Benjamin. I visited still others who were glad that the congregation was still thinking of them, especially one, who said that he had actually been awakened in Shekomeko, by Br. Rauch. I should pass on his many regards to him [Rauch] and Martin [Mack]. His name is Nickolaus. Two old people called me into their house—Ruth's friends.[87] The man's name is Noah; dear, open-hearted people, who are not without feeling. They showed me all the kindness they could. It grieves me that the Indians came into the hands of the Presbyterians. They do not have another minister yet, but the minister[s] thereabouts go there and baptize anyone who allows himself to be baptized.[88] Jephthah's son came to me in the evening and said I should salute his father and tell him that he intended to come to Wechquadnach in 2 days time to hear if he his father wanted to go to Gnadenhütten or Wanachquaticok, and he would take him by horse to the place where he would like to be the most.

Thursday, the 27th

The watchword read: *Ich will euch tragen bis ins Alter.* Is. 46.4. *Mit der Kirch im heiligen Geist.*[89]

Early in the morning our Br. Wilhelm came to see me; he was very affectionate. I then spoke with him about his heart. He said that he was not quite blissful in his heart. I then talked to him a great deal about the Savior, and that the Savior wanted very much to render him blessed so that the others can tell by looking at him that he belonged to the Savior and the congregation. He said yes, that was true. I also spoke to Paulus and his wife and children about various matters regarding the Savior, how He so loved the sinners and wanted so much to let them feel His wounds in their hearts. She made me a present of about 2 # of sugar. After that I took leave of them and went with Wilm [Wilhelm] to his house. Paulus went with me. Next, we went to *Captein* Aaron, who I found fairly ill; I talked with him about various matters regarding the Savior, which he was pleased to hear. Then he said that I should pass on greetings from him to the congregation in Bethlehem and the other places. Perhaps he would not get to see them again, for it appeared that he shall die, and so it pleased him that he was able to have them greeted one more time. I said he should submit himself to the dear Savior's will, and then he replied that this would be best and that he wanted to do so. I also told him that I was going to go to my brethren in Bethlehem in about 3 or 4 weeks. If there was a message going to Pachgatgoch, I would be pleased to hear if he had improved. My brethren in Bethlehem loved him and they would be glad to hear when he was well again. He said yes, when he was better, he would let me know. And then I took a heartfelt leave of him and his wife. Paulus went with me to Bartolomew, where Benjamin and Moses were as well. However, there was a large *companie* of strangers with them, and so I took Bartolomew with me and talked some with him about his heart, but he could not tell me much. He said that he intended to go with his wife to Gnadenhütten soon. I searched for Tabea's son but was not able to lay eyes on him. After that we went to the schoolhouse, where 12 Indian children had been taken in, but there were none left, instead they all had gone back home. I asked what the reason for it was. Paulus said that they did not get enough to eat[90] and no clothing with which to keep themselves warm.[91] I also saw some of the Mackwash [Mohawk] Indians who had moved here this win-ter.[92] I also spoke with our Abraham's son—what should I tell his father? He said I should salute him and [that] he wanted to visit him soon. Several were not pleased that I was leaving again so soon. Paulus went with me for about 2 miles; he said if he was able, he wanted to visit the brethren in Bethlehem and Gnadenhütten this summer, and then I bade him farewell and thanked him for all his kindness. He said he loved us so much, he could come along to Beth-lehem just to please me.

Friday, the 28th

I arrived in Wechquadnach at about 10 o'clock; found the brethren and sis-ters well and in a happy state. I stayed with them for several hours; talked with them about their hearts. Timotheus said that his brother's wife and daughter would very much like to be baptized, but they were afraid of Ampiwochnant, who was very wicked. I also talked with the daughter about the Savior, that He would very much like to wash her with His blood. Sr. Hannah and Esther said that they wanted to come to Pachgatgoch tomorrow, and with that I took a heartfelt leave of them. In the evening I came to my dear brown hearts[d] in Pachgatgoch, but found only few at home. Most had gone to New Milford and to the seaside with *canuh* [canoes] and brooms to sell. Those who were home came to welcome me and rejoiced at seeing me again. Gideon and several oth-ers had greetings passed on to me and had me informed that they intended to be back home in 9 days.

Saturday, the 29th

I was fairly tired today from my journey. I nonetheless planted a few beans around my house and visited the brethren and sisters. Petrus had a bad foot—I should please bandage him, which I did. Past noon Hannah and Esther arrived here from Wechquadnach. Gottlob came home as well.

Sunday the 30th

Toward noon we had a meeting; Gottlob interpreted. ~~Afterward I went~~ also, Paulus's wife was delivered of a young son. Past noon I went to an English man who had asked me to visit him.

Monday, the 31st

The watchword read: *Der Herr hat uns geruffen.* 2 Mos. 3.18. *Da sind wir und noch taußend Bauren.*[93]

Hannah and Esther came and took leave of me. They were full of light and in good spirits. Simon, who wants to go with his children to New Milford, came as well, as did Priscilla. I reminded them not to forget the Savior and His wounds, and to salute the other brethren and sisters for me who are already there. Perhaps I would come down there as well. Next, I visited Paulus and his wife and little son; he was quite lively. Because they were about to eat, they asked that I stay on and eat with them. Gottlieb and his son came home from New Milford.

Tuesday, June 1

As almost all of the brown hearts[d] had gone to the falls below New Milford, and [because] an awakened woman by the name of Bostwick had frequently asked me, through others, to visit her sometime, I made up my mind and went to New Milford, and then to our brethren and sisters. I found a number of them there; others had gone farther down. Those who were there were overjoyed that I had come to visit them. Next, I went to the house of the aforementioned woman, but she had gone to the meeting of the separatists. Her daughter, who was home alone, acted very modestly toward me; she [the woman] came home late, bringing her preacher with her. They talked with each other a great deal until midnight and during that time he twice prayed so loudly that one could hear it 1/4 mile away. Finally, he asked me what, then, our ground[s] and doctrine were. I said our way was simple, and we did not make much noise, and that the Savior and His wounds and dying on the cross were our ground[s] and doctrine, [and also] to know Him, and the power of His suffering and Christ's resurrection. He said if we were in it so deeply, we were probably unable to commit any more sins. I said he was looking to start something. Yet we felt very well [about] what we were, and what [of] the Savior and grace were inside of us. Thus he went silent.

Wednesday, the 2nd

In the morning, after we had risen, the separatist preacher again delivered his prayers, and after breakfast he took his leave. *Mister* Bostwick also left to work in the field with his people. She stayed at home and talked with me about her heart, and that, through Sister Mack, she had enjoyed many blessings for her heart. I visited my Indian brethren and sisters, finding all of them well. Gideon, along with his Martha, Johanna, Joshua, Jeremias, Erdmuth, and several others, returned to this place from Potatuck. They rejoiced at finding me there [at New Milford]. Gideon asked [me] on what day I had returned home from Wanachquaticok, and how had I found things there, which I told him. In the evening I went back to the Bostwicks to stay with them that night. She said that if she were able to stay in connect[i]on with brethren and sisters from the congregation, it shall be more of a blessing for her heart than [being] with the separatists. But since she did not have any brethren and sisters, she, of course, would have to follow someone.

Thursday, the 3rd

The watchword read: *Schauet an den Fels, daraus ihr gehauen, und des Brunnen Gruft, darauß ihr gegraben seijd. Is. 51.1. Da gebahr Gottes Marterschaft.*[94]

In the morning I took leave of the Indian brethren and sisters, as well as of [the] Bostwicks, and went back to Pachgatgoch with Gideon and his family. I visited Sekes on the way, but found him alone. We talked some with him about the Savior, and [asked] when he intended to visit us in Pachgatgoch. He said it could perhaps happen next Sunday. I bought one bread for myself from Gaylord. Thus, we arrived at home toward evening. I found the brethren and sisters well.

Friday, the 4th

Today I started to hoe my Welsh corn. Paid a visit to all the houses where someone was at home. Petrus said that he had not done things well at the time when I, and Gideon, and Joshua had talked with him. As for himself, he believed that he does not know his heart well. I said he should just go to the Savior; He very much wants to give him [Petrus] everything that he was in need of, which he promised to do.

Saturday, the 5th

The watchword read: *Der Vater hat euch lieb. Jn. 16.27. Unßer lieber Vater du bist, weil Christus unßer Bruder ist.*[95]

I did my wash in the morning, and in the afternoon I went again into the field. Sister Thamar came and said 2 brethren from Rhinebeck were here; I needed to come home. And when I came home and saw them, it was Führer and Haber. We were happy to see one another. Also, they brought me a package^d of letters from our dear hearts^d in Bethlehem, at which I deeply rejoiced. But with that, I received the sad news of the going home to the Lamb^d of our dear heart Cammerhoff,[96] which in my heart I have probably sensed ever since I had heard about his illness, yet had nonetheless always thought differently. It saddened both of the brethren as well when I told them about it.

Sunday, the 6th

The watchword read: *Ich habe euch auch lieb. Mal. 1.2. Wangenpaar von Millionen Thränen der verliebten Kirche naß.*[97]

I informed Gideon that our dear heart Cammerhoff had gone to the Savior. He was very saddened by the news. I conducted the occasion toward noon. Gottlob interpreted because Joshua and Samuel had not come home. After the occasion I informed our brethren and sisters that I had received letters from Bethlehem and many greetings for them, but also word that the dear heart Cammerhoff has gone to the Lamb^d, at which they grew very sad ~~Indian brethren and sisters, finding them all well, and staying a short while with them, Br. Gideon arrived there from Potatuck. He rejoiced when he saw me, asking when I had returned home from Wanachquaticok and how I had found things there, which [I] told him~~ and wept many tears.[98] Some were so shocked that they remained sitting right where they were, not knowing what to make of it.

Monday, the 7th

The Indian brethren who were at home went out to an English man in the morning to hoe Welsh corn. The brethren from Rhinebeck also prepared themselves again for departure. Beforehand they visited the Indian brethren and sisters, taking leave of them at the same time. I accompanied them for 2 miles, and then we bade one another a heartfelt farewell. As soon as I had stepped into my house, Joshua from Gnadenhütten arrived. He was an unexpected guest, but I welcomed him with tender love. I asked whether he had not brought a letter for me; he at once gave me the letters and I saw the reason why the 3 brethren had come.[99] After we had eaten and readied ourselves, and had taken leave of our brethren and sisters, I went with him to Wechquadnach. We arrived there fairly late at night, greeted and kissed our brethren and sisters, and then we went to sleep.

Tuesday, the 8th

The watchword read: *Ihr solt heilige Leute vor [mir] seyn. Da habt ihr euer privilegium!*[100]

I first spoke with Jonathan and Joshua. Next we summoned Augustus; we asked him whether he had seen Sr. Esther and how he presently felt in his heart.[101] He said that he still felt the same way he had felt when the brethren in Gnadenhütten had put this before him. Thereupon we spoke with our Sr. Esther and presented the matter to her. She said that she had nothing against it; if her mother felt the same, then she should be glad. I felt very comfortable at her declaration. Thereupon we spoke with her mother, Hannah, who was somewhat more circumlocutory, yet had no objections. She deferred to Benjamin, however, [saying] that she was not able to completely settle this matter without his consent. Then Timotheus came home, who had gone out early. We also spoke with him about this matter, who said that it would please him if Esther would take Augustus for her husband; he had now opposed this matter 4 times,[102] [saying] that Esther should marry a brother, and in the end his wife Hannah had become so dissatisfied with him and said that the first one who came along asking for Esther's hand—she would no longer stop her. And he, Timotheus, had resolved not to have anything to do with this matter in the future. Besides, his wife apparently knew what sort of man Augustus was; he had often spoken to her about this. Given that it was almost evening, we were not able to do much more in regard to this matter. Also, 3 sisters and Samuel arrived here from Pachgatgoch.

~~Sunday~~ Wednesday, the 9th

Because the matter rested on Benjamin—and Sister Hannah told us that someone should go to Wanachquaticok today to get him—we thought that Timotheus would be the best messenger, who resolved to do it, going there on a horse with the agreement to be back home tomorrow evening. Samuel and ~~the~~ 2 sister[s] set out on their way back toward Pachgatgoch. I felt in my heart like going back to Pachgatgoch. I thought about it; it was difficult for me to leave. I talked with Jonathan and Joshua on that account. They thought that the matter was so far in good order. I stayed for another several hours, but I continued to feel I should leave. I gave the brethren yet several *instruckcion* [instructions] and entrusted this matter to the Savior. I took leave; the 3 brethren accompanied me for a distance and then we bade one another a heartfelt farewell. In the evening, fairly late, I arrived in Pachgatgoch. As soon as our brethren and sisters learned about it, a number of them still came to visit me. Also, there was an Indian stranger here by the name of M̈Segan.

Thursday, the 10th

Joshua, Jeremias, and Gideon, and several others, came to visit me in the morning.[103] Some had returned home in the meantime. I had Gideon and Joshua stay on with me; informed them that I intended to set out on my journey to Bethlehem next week. They said that they had thought a brother would come and hold Communion before my departure, also, that they had often thought that it would be good if 2 brethren were here, but they could not object to my journey. They both were very affectionate. Gideon said that he wanted to assemble the brethren tomorrow and have my Welsh corn fully hoed. I also spoke to them about a love feast before my departure, which pleased them very much. I sent Jeremias out to order bread and butter. Also, Lucas, Martin, and Jusstis [Justina?] returned home from the seaside. In the afternoon the little son^d of Br. Paulus fell ill. In the evening, after the quarter-of-an-hour, Br. Paulus approached me through Gideon about the baptism of his little son^d. However, because it was dark and very late, I went to take a look at the child, and we postponed it [the baptism] until the next morning.

Friday, the 11th

The watchword read: *Sorget nichts. Mt. 6.25. Gieb uns deinen Frieden o Jesu!*[104]

Gideon came in the morning and said that the child was quite bad, upon which I soon prepared for the quarter-of-an-hour. It being calm and warm, they thought that they could bring it into our house without doing harm. Paulus and his wife came with the child, and following the address, Sr. Martha took the child, and then it was buried into our Husband's death and His side hole^d, and received the name Joseph. A general feeling of grace was present. After the baptism it [the child] was consecrated by several brethren through the laying on of hands. Thereupon the mother took the child and carried it home. Afterward, Gideon called the brethren and sisters together and they hoed my corn. I had food cooked for them, and when they were done, they ate. I expected to see Joshua, Jonathan, and Augustus from Wechquadnach here today, but they did not come. Amos and several others came home from New Milford. Gottlob also came home to hoe his Welsh corn. Samuel went on horseback to Gaylords and got bread and butter for the love feast.

Saturday, the 12th

Several brethren and sisters came to me and said that they were afraid that they might stray from their hearts when I was gone. For if no brother was here, everyone would go his own way and fall into great disorder. I directed [*word crossed out*] them to the Savior and His wounds. There they could stay safe and blissful. Samuel sent on horseback to Wechquadnach today. I had the brethren saluted and inquired why they were staying away so long. He came home after the quarter-of-an-hour, bringing word that Timotheus had returned from Wanachquaticok, and that Benjamin had not been home, who they expected any time [now]. Also, that all the brethren and sisters in Wechquadnach were well and in good spirits. They, Jonathan and the 2 brethren, intended to be here in Pachgatgoch before the meeting tomorrow, if possible.

Sunday, the 13th

The watchword read: *An Dorfern gebrachs vor diesen bis ich auf kam eine Muter in Israel. Jg. 5.7.*[105]

In the morning we met in conference on various matters and made preparations for the love feast to take place following the service. After the conference I conducted the service. I felt very comfortable during the address and everyone was very attentive. Following the service the love feast was announced by blowing [the horn], at which point all the brethren and sisters congregated. I then told them various things, and the Savior was near me with His wounds and side hole[d]. Matters proceeded in a very orderly and agreeable fashion. We had slices of bread with butter and tea with milk. After the love feast some unbaptized ones came to visit me I visited. The dear hearts[d] Joshua, Jonathan, and Augustus also arrived here from Wechquadnach. Everyone gathered to welcome the brethren and rejoiced at seeing them in Pachgatgoch. We had a blessed quarter-of-an-hour in the evening. The brethren told me that Sr. Hannah, together with her sister, had gone to Wanachquaticok on horseback to speak with Benjamin, and, if possible, to bring him along and to be back home tomorrow, that is, on Monday evening, and at that point we shall have the whole word regarding her daughter.

Monday, the 14th

The watchword read: *Eß soll meinen Orten wieder wohl gehen. Zech. 1.17. Den lieben deinen zum Beschluß.*[106]

In the morning I conducted the quarter-of-an-hour and directed the dear brown hearts[d] to our Husband and His side hole[d], that they may be safe and in a happy state there, if only they cleaved to Him, and that He would care for them, likewise that His eyes would keep watch over them. They were indeed somewhat worried that they are to be left alone. After having had breakfast with the 3 brethren, and having readied ourselves, I took my leave in all the houses. Then everyone gathered at our house, and so we bade one another a heartfelt farewell. Several also accompanied us for a distance. I gave Gideon the key to the house.[107] They [the brethren and sisters] sent their very heartfelt greetings to the congregation, and with that, the 3 brethren and I went toward Wechquadnach. Toward evening we arrived in Wechquadnach, finding Esther and Susanna, as well as some unbaptized ones at home. Hannah and her sister came home late from Wanachquaticok, but did not bring Benjamin along.

Tuesday, the 15th

In the morning, I talked with Sister Hannah about what she had agreed to with Benjamin, concerning the marriage of our Br. Aug[ustus] and Esther. She was very sad, however, saying that Benjamin had said that he loved A[ugustus] and had nothing against the marriage on the part of A[ugustus]. He only feared one thing, however, and that was this: Because the Delawar Nacion [Delaware Nation] was a jealous nation, he thus feared that it [the Delaware Nation] would begrudge Esther [Brother] Augustus, and would soon seek to do away with her. To which we replied that she [Esther] was not going to live among *Wilde*,[108] but was going to live among brethren and sisters, and that I desired to hear from her [Hannah] only one of two words, which should be yes or no, for I could not hold up the 3 brethren any longer. Whereupon she [Hannah] replied that she was not yet able to say one word, but that we should please stay for one more day, because Benjamin was coming home this evening, and that is when we shall be given full *resolucion* [resolution] so that we would be able to go on our way tomorrow. Whereupon I asked the brethren if they wanted to wait another day. Thus, they agreed to stay for one more day. Augustus went out hunting and brought home a large buck. The evening came, we waited for Benjamin, but he did not come home.

Wednesday, the 16th

The watchword read: *Sie sollen nicht bauen daß ein anderer bewohne. Die Tage meines Volckes sollen seijn wie die Tage eines Baums. Is. 65.22. Ewige Wunden J[e]su! mein hauß zu wohnen. Ihr seijd in million aeonen noch immer neu.*[109]

In the morning, I arose and prepared myself for traveling. I woke the brethren as well and told them to get themselves ready now. I then told our most beloved Husband that He Himself would now have to settle our affair. On seeing that we were ready for travel, Sister Hannah, Esther's mother, got up and woke up Esther as well, left her house, went after Joshua and Jonathan, and said that she was now resolved to hand over her daughter, and [that] she shall travel with us now. Thus, she went into the woods at once and fetched her horse. Sr. Esther wept as she saw that we were ready for travel, not knowing at that point that she was to journey with us. Whereupon Joshua asked what she was weeping about. She said that up until now she had thought that she was going to travel with us to the congregation; now her hopes had vanished. To this Joshua replied that she should go ahead and rejoice, for she was traveling with us; her mother was already fetching her horse, at which she heartily rejoiced to hear such news. Our dear heart Augustus, who had been quiet so far and had submitted himself and this matter to the Savior, knew nothing other than what we had told him: that it was now only up to Benjamin. I had him called outside and told him how the matter stood, that Sr. Hannah had given her daughter to us to take her with us to the congregation now, and then to become A[ugustus's] wife. He should tell us now how he felt in his heart. He replied that he was grateful to the Savior that He had carried it to this point, and in his heart he still felt the same way he had felt at the time when the brethren had proposed this to him. Next, Hannah packed Esther's belongings and loaded them onto the horse, and then we took a heartfelt leave. Then everyone cried after Esther. Her mother accompanied her a little and then kissed her daughter and went home.

Abraham Büninger
27 June to 11 December 1751

Sunday, June 27, [17]51[1]

I took leave of my dear brethren in Bethlehem, who wished me much luck and the embrace and close feeling of the bloody side hole[d] for my journey to Pachgatgoch. Our dear heart[d] Sensemann accompanied me for 3 miles from Bethlehem. He also informed me of the present circumstances in Pachgatgoch and Wechquadnach. That day I traveled as far as Nazareth, where our faithful heart Johann Nitschmann spoke with me about the circumstances in Pachgatgoch.

Monday, June 28

After the morning blessing I continued the journey to Samuel Green's [place] by way of Friedensthal. That day I also had the opportunity to visit the Indians who are living on the land of old Samuel Green.

Tuesday, June 29

I traveled quite blissfully through the wilderness under the protection of our beloved Husband and His dear angels[d], and came to Isaac Dizort's [place] at about 3 o'clock. I intended to continue on for another good distance that day, but was unable to get any farther than about 4 m[iles] from I. D[izort]. Overtaken by a violent thunderstorm, I had to look for lodgings.

Wednesday, June 30

I set out early. The Lamb[d] helped me to the North R[iver] that day.

Thursday, *Julius* 1

I got across the North River between 8 and 9 o'clock. Was unable to advance any more than 20 miles that day as I needed to get my shoes soled; also was in need of several things that I had to buy at the river.

Friday, July 2

I had only 20 more miles to Pachgatgoch. Along the way I met Johannes, the Indian. He told me that they were well in Pachgatgoch, that they were working near the winter houses, and that he was journeying to Bethlehem and Gnaden-hütten. At noon I came to the winter huts and happily found all of the brethren there. (They were engaged in building a house for old Seyakes, who formerly lived 6 miles from here near Aaron Gaylord.) They were overjoyed that a brother was again coming to [stay with] them. Br. Gideon said that for the past 2 days he had felt that a brother was going to come today or tomorrow. There were several who said the same. Soon Br. Gideon went with me to the sum[m]er huts. I asked him how things have been since Br. Sensemann was gone. He said the brethren had not been out much. He believed that things were still the same as Br. Sensemann had left them. In the evening I conducted the quarter-of-an-hour, read Br. Sensemann's letter[d] to the brethren and sisters, and passed on to them the greetings that I had for them from our dear brethren in Bethlehem and Nazareth. I also informed them that a brother would come soon, at which they were very glad. I slept very blissfully in my house[d] that night.

Sabbath, July 3

In the morning, I conducted the quarter-of-an-hour on the texts. Paid a visit to all of the huts; many complained about their being poor and miserable. I also brought some wood home.

I conducted another quarter-of-an-hour in the evening.

Sunday, July 4

We had [a] quarter-of-an-hour in the morning [and] afterward, [a] conference with the workers. They told me of the circumstances concerning several breth-ren and sisters. Yet Br. Sensemann had told me everything beforehand. I pre-tended that I did not know anything about it, though. In addition, they related the circumstances surrounding Warrop's child, who had died last week and was buried here on God's Acre. This is how it had occurred with the child: Its father, Warrop, had been to New Milford with it. As he was walking in the open street, a Negro unexpectedly approached him from behind and pushed Warrop so that he fell hard on top of the child (who was on his [Warrop's] back), doing harm to it so that it died 11 or 12 days later. When it was dead, one of the neighbors here reported the matter to the *maggistrats* [magistrates] in New Milford, who right away called a *grand jury* and sent it to Pachgatgoch, where the child lay. The child was opened up by the doctors who were present, and it was recognized by the *grand jury* that the fall, brought on by the Negro, was the cause of its death. Afterward, the c[o]urt sat in judgment on it, but the Negro was able to present witnesses [who stated] that the child had eaten and drunk following the fall. Yet the child's parents, Warrop and Sr. Rebecca, knew nothing about that, but this did not help the matter, for the testimony of the witnesses was accepted as truth. Thereupon the c[o]urt advised Warrop to reach a settlement with the master of the Negro and take money for his child, which then happened. The master of the Negro paid Warrop 24 # [£] New England *corranzi* [currency], in addition to all expenses. The c[o]urt, however, acquitted the Negro so that not a hair on his head was harmed, so to speak. Br. Samuel acted as interpreter. He said: It had made him feel sick at heart that the poor Indians were so despised. The c[o]urt reportedly hardly cared about that. Soon after I conducted the regular Sunday service. I talked about the text. There was a general quarter-of-an-hour in the evening. The majority visited me in my house[d] today, also those who live at the winter huts.

Monday, July 5

We had [a] quarter-of-an-hour in the morning. Br. Jeremias went out working. The other brethren went hunting. I held school, also started hoeing some of my Welsh corn. There was [a] quarter-of-an-hour in the evening.

Tuesday, July 6

I conducted the quarter-of-an-hour in the morning. Martha, Johanna, Elisabeth, Juliana, and several others went to New Milford. Several went working elsewhere. The brethren went hunting again. Over these two days they got only 1 young *faen* [fawn]. I held school again and diligently went about hoeing the corn.

Wednesday, July 7

I conducted [a] quarter-of-an-hour in the morning. The brethren went to Rass[2] today to work. Joshua and Samuel returned today. I talked with Br. Gideon concerning Friederich, for I would like to have him gone from here because he is a tempter. Br. Gideon thought it best that we leave him until Martin [Mack?] comes. Gideon had once before bid him go. I also talked with Br. Martin, held school, and diligently went about the corn.

Thursday, July 8

I conducted [a] quarter-of-an-hour in the morning. The brethren started to jointly hoe their corn. I did not hold school because my corn is so grassy that I could hardly hoe it; hence I was quite diligent. I conducted [a] quarter-of-an-hour in the evening.

Friday, July 9

I conducted [a] quarter-of-an-hour in the morning. The brethren and sisters were again jointly working on their corn. I finished with my corn, also held school and the quarter-of-an-hour in the evening.

Saturday, July 10

[I] conducted the quarter-of-an-hour in the morning. Paid a visit to several huts, washed my clothing, also visited the winter huts, yet found no one [there] except for old Maria, and Leah, who cried hard over her heart and ruin. She is close to giving birth, and her husband Johannes has abandoned her, leaving her at home poor [and] with 3 small children. Also, Christian and Gottliebe came from New Milford.

~~Saturday~~ Sunday, July 11

There was [a] quarter-of-an-hour in the morning, afterward, [a] conference with the workers. I asked Joshua how things were going where the corn was being hoed. He said that the young folk were often light-minded. I told them how they had to act in that regard, namely, to be quiet and not to take pleasure in it. Furthermore, Gideon reminded us that some intended to go to the seaside. We rejoiced, hoping that next Sunday we will have our dear heart[d] Martin [Mack] with us. Our meeting place[d] was almost too small during our Sunday service, for everyone who belongs to Pachgatgoch is at home. I portrayed to them the Lamb of God as bloody figure, as their Savior and Redeemer of their sins. With a joyous and trustful heart I spoke on the words: *Bittet so wird Euch gegeben werden.*[3]

Next, I paid a visit to several huts, especially where the strangers were staying who also had attended the meeting. They all looked at me in a friendly manner. Also, I spoke with several about their hearts, in particular with Friederich. In the evening an Indian boy came to me, asking me whether I lived here; whether I taught the Indians and preached to them. I replied yes. I asked him where he lived. Answer: Here in Kent. I asked whether he had ever been here before. Answer: No. He had heard of us before; thus he had thought to come and see us one day. Then he asked me when we held meetings. I told him generally [on] Sunday at 10 o'clock. He said that he had a companion, and they had often said that they wanted to attend the meeting here as well. I asked of what nation he and his companion were. Answer: Of the Mohikan[der] nation.[4] I asked where they were born. Answer: Near Cape Cod, not far from Boston. I told him a little about the Savior and His wounds and that He died and shed His blood for him as well. I asked him, further, for how long he had been living here. Answer: Not for a very long time. He can speak English well, but no Indian, and is bound into service until he is 21 years old, as is his companion. He took a friendly leave and promised to return by Sunday. We did not have a quarter-of-an-hour in the evening because the brethren went into the sweat house.

Monday, July 12

I conducted the quarter-of-an-hour in the morning. I felt exceedingly comfortable and warm at heart. The brethren and sisters again jointly went about their work. I held school. After school I went to Wechquadnach to visit the Indians there, and to inform them that a brother would soon come from Bethlehem. Evening was falling just as I arrived there. Ampowachonat with his family, Anna [Hannah], Timotheus's wife, old Simon, and Susanna were at home. Old father Jephthah, Moses, and Benjamin had traveled to Wanachquaticok. I heard from them that the old King Aaron [Umpachenee] had died 7 days previous. I learned from the Indians that shortly before his end, Aaron had sent greetings to the Indians in Wechquadnach and Pachgatgoch. The greetings I had from Bethlehem and Gnadenhütten were well and cordially received. I am sorry that I was not able to speak with them much; never before have I felt so well in Wechquadnach as at this time.

Tuesday, July 13

In the morning, I set out from Wechquadnach to return to my dear Pachgatgoch; found that all of the brethren [there] were again working together in common. In the evening we had quite a blessed quarter-of-an-hour[d].

Wednesday, July 14

We had another blessed quarter-of-an-hour[d] in the morning. I talked about the text: *Er ist uns von Kott gemacht zur Kerchtigkeit, damit wollen wir vor K. bestehen.*[5] When we were assembled, one of the neighbors came, stood by the door, and asked whether he was permitted to enter. I said yes. He listened very thoughtfully. The brethren again worked in common. I held school and went visiting in several huts. Br. Joshua came to me and told me that Sr. Leah, the wife of Johannes, had been delivered of a young son. The poor sister is said to have had it so hard ~~hard~~ that both she and the child were nearly gone. They already had laid the child to the side, thinking that it had come dead from the mother. The child had lain like this for nearly half an hour before life could be felt in him. The mother had been the same—that no life could be seen in her. Sr. Elisabeth and Juliana were with her. We had [a] quarter-of-an-hour in the evening.

Thursday, July 15

I suspended the quarter-of-an-hour that morning because it rained very hard. I held school again; all of the children came. The brethren once more intended to work in common but had to hold off on it because of the bad weather. There was [a] quarter-of-an-hour in the evening.

Friday, July 16

There was [a] quarter-of-an-hour in the morning; Br. Samuel interpreted. The Lamb[d] was intimately near me. The brethren again worked in common. I held school; also visited all of the brethren and sisters. With most I talked about their hearts. We had [a] quarter-of-an-hour in the evening.

Saturday, July 17

In the morning, we had [a] quarter-of-an-hour. I brought in some wood for myself. Also went to Gaylords to buy some provisions. On returning to Pachgatgoch,

[and] to my unexpected joy and that of the entire assembly, I found our dear hearts Br. Gottlieb Pezold and Schwartz.[6] They brought for us many greetings of love and kisses from Bethlehem.

Sunday, July 18

There was no early quarter-of-an-hour. We held a small conference with the workers on various matters, in particular, that we had no wine for Communion. Br. Samuel was willing to go. Br. Gottlieb conducted the regular Sunday occasion. In addition, he conducted a blessed quarter-of-an-hour for the baptized ones in the evening.

Monday, July 19

Br. Gottlieb conducted the quarter-of-an-hour in the morning. Then, speaking with the brethren and sisters [in preparation] for Communion was begun. Br. Gideon and Martha interpreted.[7] I went to Aaron Gaylord to order bread for the love feast. I also talked with Sr. Leah. She said that as soon as she had laid eyes on her child, she thought that when a brother came, he should baptize it with the Savior's blood. I talked with Gihur as well. He asked me whether I thought that, with baptism, it was like with a soiled bowl—when it was washed, it became clean, inside and out. I did not give him an answer, though. Everything proceeded quite blissfully in Pachgatgoch today.

Tuesday, July 20

Brother Gottlieb conducted the early quarter-of-an-hour. There were still some brethren and sisters to be spoken with [before Communion]. This went on quite passionately and blessedly, and the Lamb[d] assisted us and was near us; all of the baptized ones were spoken with. Warrop, who is now called David, applied for baptism. He declared himself quite beautifully. The Lamb[d] too agreed that he shall be baptized. Jerry applied for baptism as well.

At 12 o'clock there was a general meeting for all the Indians. With a warm and feeling heart, Br. Gottlieb talked about the text: *Er ist der grosse Hirte der Schaffe.*[8] Our Br. David was baptized first; his heart was completely melted by the red flood from Jesus' side. This was also a blessing for everyone present, and a reminder of the grace granted them through baptism. Gihur was present as well, so was Jerry, and most of the unbaptized ones. They were very *attent* [attentive]. Also baptized in the course of this meeting were: the son[d] of Brother and Sister Gottlieb—he received the name Johannes; also the son[d] of Brother Johannes and Sister Leah, who received the name Joseph. And with that this blissful and blessed act was concluded. Immediately thereafter we made preparations for the love feast. We had bread and butter, and tea. All the baptized ones attended the love feast. It was a blissful love feast. Br. Gottlieb told us of the blissful days that the brethren in Bethlehem and Gnadenhütten enjoyed, and that the brethren bore us in loving remembrance at all times, which the Indian brethren and sisters were pleased and glad to learn. Soon after, we enjoyed the blissful absolution of our dear Husband and Chief Elder. He revealed Himself to us quite powerfully, and the hearts felt that they had experienced grace. We had Holy Communion in the dark. On eating His flesh and drinking His blood, body and soul entered into Him, and He embraced us as His souls and creatures[d] from His bloody side. The brethren and sisters all went home quite blissfully and with hearts full of light. We too retired blissfully, thanking Him for everything that He has affected in the brown assembly.

Wednesday, July 21

In the morning Br. Gottlieb conducted another passionate quarter-of-an-hour, wherein he also recommended to the brethren and sisters the enjoyment of the flesh and blood of which they had partaken and entreated them not to forget what the Lamb had affected in them. They shall now feel it in their hearts at all times, and not forget it. He then took leave of all of them in their huts, recommended them to the bloody side hole[d], and then set out from here with Br. Schw[artz] from Christiansbrunn. For their return journey they went from here through Rhinebeck. I went with them for several miles, bade the dear hearts[d] farewell, and returned to dear Pachgatgoch. Most of the brethren had gone out cutting [oats or wheat] at white people's [places]; the others hoed their corn, as they had started doing, and got done. On returning I found them all quite blissful. Sr. Thamar came to me, telling me about Caritas, who had not been present at Communion, that during Communion she had stood in front of the door, listening. She had cried hard when she came home because she had not been allowed to join. I told her that the Savior loved Caritas very much, and so did we, and if she abides in the Savior with her heart, the Savior will no doubt take her along again.

Thursday, July 22

I conducted the quarter-of-an-hour in the morning. All of the brethren were out working the harvest, except for Br. Gideon, and Br. Gottlieb, who is sickly. I held school again. I also began laying the floor for the loft in my house[d]. Also, I visited the brethren and sisters in the winter huts. They all said that they were well and blissful, especially Br. David and his wife Rebecca. The brethren had all gone out to work the harvest. Martin came home after all and interpreted during the quarter-of-an-hour. I thought much about the grace that that [sic] the Savior granted me on admission to the congregation 9 years ago today. I felt ashamed like a worm[d] for all the bad and worthless matters that cloud my heart so frequently. This verse frequently came to mind: *Werd ich nicht bald deine seyn, inig selig unverdrossen zu geschlossen, von etc.*[9]

Friday, July 23

This morning Pachgatgoch was as if emptied of brethren and sisters; thus, I was unable to conduct the quarter-of-an-hour. I held school again. Did some work on my house[d].[10] In the evening the dear Br. David and Petrus visited me. They started talking of the dear Savior of their own accord. Among other things, Petrus asked why the Savior was called Son of God. I I [sic] said, the Savior was God and has created us and everything. But because He assumed our flesh and blood and became like us, He was also called Son of God. I said that the Savior had very many names in the Holy Scripture; because He died for us and shed His blood for us, He was called Savior. Br. David inquired why then was He called Christ. I was afraid to give an explanation for that; he may not have understood it correctly. I told him, the Savior had sacrificed Himself for us, and had entered into the Holiest for us with His blood, and there He had made it known that He has shed His blood for us, and has redeemed us from sin, from the devil, and from the power of death. It was a blissful conversation [that we had] together. Br. Gideon, Samuel, Martin, [and] Amos came home late that night. They still came to me, wishing me a good night. Br. Gottlob had arrived yesterday already, ill with a toothache.

Saturday, July 24

I conducted [a] quarter-of-an-hour in the morning. There were only a few of us, but the Lamb^d was among us. The brethren went cutting again. They were cutting only for fare. Br. Petrus and Samuel came to me. Petrus said he had a favor to ask of me. I said he should tell me. He said, I feel like someone who was ill and has recovered a little; such a person fears above all to fall ill anew. He, Petrus, said [he] was now blissful in his heart, but he was afraid. Question: Of what? Answer: The brethren and sisters who are home all intend to go cutting for Mills today. He wants to give only food and drink [as payment]. "Hence I fear that many will drink too much rum," and he had come to me for this reason, to ask me to come along so that no pain may result among the brethren and sisters. I told him that if I knew the brethren and sisters wanted to be obedient, I would come. However, he persisted until I promised him to do so. First, I brought home some wood, hence I came to the cutters at about 11 o'clock, finding all of them lively, and fortunately, no stranger with them except for Mr. Mills. Things proceeded in an altogether orderly fashion. When the midday meal was ready, the brethren and sisters did not want to eat until Mr. Mills had prayed, by which he was amazed, saying [that] this [was] usually not *custum* [custom] among Indians. Everything went quite well until the evening when work had already stopped. At that point Mr. Mills still had about 1 *quart* or 3 *point* [pints] of *rum* that he gave to the Indians, making Samuel the servant—that he would distribute it—which happened. However, when I saw that the *bottel* went around too often, I said to Br. Gideon, he should now see to it that the brethren left. When Gideon heard this, he was the first to leave. Next, I went to Petrus and Gottlieb, telling them the same, who left at once. Poor Br. Samuel, who had gotten a little too much [rum] while performing his office of servant, in the end got into a quarrel with Gihur because he had passed over him once when distributing [the rum], at which Gihur took great offense. I went to Gihur and told him he should go into his house now, which he did. I took Samuel and led him home. The brethren who had been cutting elsewhere all came home as well.

Sunday, July 25

There was no quarter-of-an-hour in the morning; it was as if no one wanted to get up. Moreover, I felt uneasy about Samuel. I visited all the huts where there were brethren and sisters. With the exception of Samuel, I found everyone quite blissful and full of light, which in turn delighted me. The brethren and sisters having come from the winter huts, I held the general meeting. The house^d was perfectly full. Br. Joshua interpreted. I talked about the text. The Lamb^d was near us so that our hearts felt it. During the quarter-of-an-hour for the baptized ones and the communicants, I talked about the words: *Preiset Kott an Eüerem Leib, und an Eurem Geist.*[11] The precious Church Mother suggested this matter quite clearly to me, and I repeated it that way to the brethren and sisters. In closing we sang in German and Indian: *Tif nein, ins Seitelein.*[12] We also had the kiss of peace. In the evening Br. Gideon and Petrus visited me, saying that tomorrow they intended to go out cutting again.

Monday, July 26

I conducted the quarter-of-an-hour in the morning; Br. Martin interpreted. Nearly everyone went out. Martin with his family, [as well as] Lucas and Priscilla, went to the seaside, as did Sr. Erdmuth with 2 of her angels^d. Excepting Samuel, all of the brethren went out cutting. Martha, Johanna, and her daughter went to New Milford. I held school and worked on my house^d. Sr. Magdalena went to Dover with her children. I spoke beforehand with most of those who were leaving, asking that they abide in the Savior and His wounds, and not to forget what He has done for them. Also, I visited Samuel, but did not find him the way I would like it. The brethren and sisters who are off to the seaside promised to return in 14 days or 3 weeks. I thought of Bethlehem particularly often.

Tuesday, July 27

In the morning, I conducted a brief quarter-of-an-hour for the few who are still at home, recommending them and myself, and the entire assembly, to the wounds and side hole^d of our precious Husband, and to the steadfast charge and care of the faithful Church Mother. Br. Simon and his daughter Benigna also departed, who is [are] following those going to the seaside. Before departing, she came to me, took her leave, and said that I should think of her. The son of Martha's sister left as well. I was unable to hold school as all of the children are out. I put things about my house^d in order. Martha and Johanna came home.

Wednesday, July 28

There was almost no one at home, so that I was able to hold neither [a] quarter-of-an-hour nor school, and it was that way also the 29th. I was industrious, laying the floor in my house[d]. I frequently thought of the brethren and sisters who are working outside [of Pachgatgoch]. I appealed to the Lamb to protect them from all harm in His side hole[d].

[No entry for July 29]

Friday, July 30

I finished laying the floor in my house[d] and also did my wash. I thought quite often of the brethren and sisters who are outside [of Pachgatgoch]. My heart was greatly distressed on their account. Because almost no one was home, I held neither school nor [the] quarter-of-an-hours.

Saturday, July 31

I was indisposed with respect to my tabernacle, causing me to feel all weak and fatigued. I thought about what would be best for me. I resolved to go to Gaylords and to purchase something. I had lived off nothing else but Indian corn and blueberry bread[13] for more than 1 week, and this, I thought, was the cause of my weakness. When I came to Gaylords, they told me that Caritas had conducted herself very badly in New Milford and that they were very sorry for it. I bought some bread and butter for myself. Late at night Jeremias, Joshua with his family, Gottlieb with his family, and Paulus's wife came home. We again did not have any quarter-of-an-hours. Gottliebe also arrived with her children.

Sunday, August 1

There was no quarter-of-an-hour in the morning. The brethren were not all at home yet. Gideon, Petrus, Amos, and Paulus were still gone. However, in due time, all 4 of them came for the general meeting; all of the brethren and sisters from the winter huts ~~huts~~ came as well, along with the unbaptized ones. I talked about the text; Br. Joshua interpreted. Our dear Lamb[d] of God was near us and invigorated my poor heart so that I was able to portray to everyone His wounds and side hole[d]. This time I had no desire at all to hold the meeting. Yet the Lamb[d] let me feel that it was most necessary at present. I visited all of the brethren and sisters; they all lamented that they had strayed from their hearts. This pained me greatly; advised them to return to the Savior as poor sinners. He will forgive them everything. I also spoke with Christian['s] and David's sons about the Savior. Christian's son said it frequently occurred to him that he belonged to the Savior and would have to change. The brethren and sisters in the winter huts are currently the most blissful, especially Br. David and his wife. Br. Gottlob too was, in his own way, in a happy state. He declared himself quite agreeably. In the evening I had a quarter-of-an-hour with all of the baptized ones.

Monday, August 2

I conducted a quarter-of-an-hour in the morning. Some again went out to work. I held school, also went on the mountain to peel bark. Wanted to conduct [a] quarter-of-an-hour in the evening, but neither Br. Joshua nor Samuel was at home.[14]

Tuesday, August 3

There was [a] quarter-of-an-hour in the morning. I talked about the words of this day of Him who loves. Held school [and] again went on the mountain to peel bark. Br. Gideon returned home. The brethren went into the sweat house in the evening.

Wednesday, August 4

There was [a] quarter-of-an-hour in the morning. I held school. Again went on the mountain to peel bark. Br. Joshua went with his family to cut *rusches* [rushes]. Br. Samuel went to Wechquadnach. Br. Lucas returned from the seaside. In the evening Br. Gideon visited [me].[15]

Thursday, August 5

There was no quarter-of-an-hour in the morning. I visited those brethren and sisters who are still at home. Most were well and quite full of light. I also held school. Went with Br. Gideon on the mountain, showing him my bark that I peeled for a winter house.[16] He said he believed the brethren were all going to build winter houses. He too would prefer moving away in the winter rather than staying. In the evening Br. Jeremias told me that he intended to go and peel bark as well. Br. Samuel came from Wechquadnach. He brought us many greetings from there, also from Br. Jephthah and his son, who are coming from

Wanachquaticok. They brought word that old Aaron, whom we here had presumed to be with the Savior already for a long time, was still alive, but very weak. I came to think whether I should go to Wanachquaticok for a visit.

Friday, August 6

We had [a] quarter-of-an-hour in the morning. I talked somewhat about the text; Br. Samuel interpreted. I visited Petrus, and Thamar, who is sickly. As for her heart, she declared herself quite beautifully. She said her feelings about the Savior's wounds were such [that] she did not want to leave them; if she had to leave the wounds, she would view this akin to someone wanting to leave his house to sleep in the woods, where there is no house. The wounds were her house within which she dwelled with her heart. I was unable to hold school; all the children were out picking blueberries. Priscilla returned with her daughters from the seaside, as did Benigna, Simon's daughter. They all came home quite blissfully, visiting me at once. Also, Samuel's Christina is ill.

Saturday, August 7

We had [a] quarter-of-an-hour in the morning. I paid a visit to several huts where there were brethren and sisters. Thamar is doing better. I also visited the brethren and sisters in the winter huts, finding all of them blissful and in good spirits, especially Br. David. Sarah and Leah told me that they intended to go out next week. On returning home, one of our neighbors came to me. He did not enter into a dispute. He said he was visiting me this time as a neighbor. He left on most friendly terms. I still went on the mountain and gathered the bark that I had peeled for a winter house. Sr. Erdmuth returned from the seaside, also quite well. Joshua with his family likewise came. All of those who had been out hunting arrived as well.

Sunday, August 8

I conducted [a] quarter-of-an-hour in the morning; talked a bit about the text. I also met in conference with the brethren; I informed them that I intended to go to Wanachquaticok this week, for I had heard that old Aaron was still alive. Br. Gideon, who otherwise had intended to go to the seaside this week, at once decided to go too, for old Aaron is his *cussin* [cousin].[17] Br. Joshua had intended to go before this, because he has something to deliver there. Br. Joshua also talked about Paulus, that he was acting so badly, having brought rum into the winter huts yesterday evening, so that things had gone badly there that night. I paid a visit to several huts, asking them to abide in the Savior. I spoke with Lucas separately; he complains a great deal about himself. I visited Jery as well; his wife is now living with him again. In the general Sunday meeting I talked about the words: *Gott sante seinen Sohn in der Kestalt des sündlichen Fleisches, und verdammte die Sünd im Fleisch.*[18] The Lamb[d] invigorated me immensely, enabling me to talk freely and confidently about the deliverance from all sin through what He suffered with His own body as atonement for us. Moreover, that He has, by the grace of God, tasted death for us all. During the quarter-of-an-hour for the baptized ones and communicants, I talked about the watchword: *Ich glaube Eine heilige Christl. Kirche.*[19] It provided me a favorable opportunity to talk about baptism and Communion. I had quite a blissful day.

Monday, August 9

There was no quarter-of-an-hour in the morning as it rained so hard. We also were not able to proceed with our journey. I held school with the children. We had a blessed quarter-of-an-hour[d] in the evening.

Tuesday, August 10

We had [a] quarter-of-an-hour in the morning. I talked about the text and recommended myself and the entire brown assembly to the faithful care of the dear Mother. I readied myself for the journey. Br. Gideon went with me to Wanachquaticok. Br. Joshua, Amos, Lucas, and unmarried Magdalena went as another *companie*. Br. Gideon and I took the route by way of Wechquadnach and stayed there overnight. The others went through Sharon.

Wednesday, August 11

Br. Gideon and I set out early from Wechquadnach and reached Wanachquaticok that day. The other brethren were about 1 hour ahead of us, but they had horses. We right away visited the sick friend Aaron, who hardly knew us anymore, however. But Br. Gideon told him who we were and where we came from, whereupon he thanked us at once and said he was glad that we were visiting him one more time. He frequently thought of his *fr.* [friends] in Pachgatgoch, Bethlehem, and Gnadenhütten. Br. G[ideon] wanted to tell him something about the Savior, but it was as if the sick one wanted to beat him to it, and said, he thought of the Savior and His wounds all the time. He always thought about this, that He died for him and shed His blood for him. In the end, he also said we should salute all the friends in Pachgatgoch, Bethlehem, and Gnadenhütten for him, which I promised him. I did not say anything further to him, other than that he should abide in the Savior with his heart. Gideon and I were assigned a place in another house, where we were to sleep. The people there received us most kindly.

Thursday, August 12

Br. Gideon and I again visited old Aaron, but he was so weak that he was unable to talk. We did not tell him anything further while we were there. Br. G[ideon] and I paid a visit to all the houses where there were Indians. When the occasion arose, I told them about the Savior and His wounds; some were very *attent* [attentive]. Br. Gideon was my interpreter where they did not understand English. Br. Wilhelm was not at home, and his wife was ill. At present, there are very many sick in Wanachquaticok. On this day they had a day of fasting and prayer in Wanachquaticok on account of the impending installation of a new preacher.[20] I admonished all the brethren from Pachgatgoch to attend the sermon, which they did. I myself went as well. Toward evening I visited on my own several huts that are located one mile from the church. In the evening Br. Gideon and I took leave of our dear Aaron. I recommended him to the bloody wounds of the Lamb[d]. He was so weary and weak that he is no longer able to talk much. To all appearances, he will soon go to the Savior.

Friday, August 13

I and Br. Gideon I set out early, at daybreak. The other brethren followed us and caught up with us after we had gone 14 miles. Here Br. Gid[eon] continued on with the *comp[agnie]*. I had to stay behind to get my shoe mended. That day I got as far as 3 miles from Wechquadnach; stayed overnight with a friend who had been acquainted with our Br. Bruce. My heart frequently thought of Bethlehem and I wished myself there. I had quite a blissful day. The side hole[d] was right near me.

Saturday, August 14

I went by way of Wechquadnach, where I also saw the brethren. I intended to hold a meeting if it was fitting. However, everyone had left with the exception of Timotheus and Wampachonant. I did not stay very long at all and continued on alone as far as Pachgatgoch. All of the brethren then also returned home. Petrus and Thamar visited me at once, telling me that Sr. Salome had been bitten by a snake Thursday, during the night, [and] that she was still very ill, because no one was able to extract the venom as well as Br. Gideon. Furthermore, Petrus told me that the pigs had been in my corn and had done a great deal of damage. I visited Salome and checked on the corn, which was in a pitiful state on account of the pigs. I was quite glad and thanked the Lamb[d] that I was back in Pachgatgoch.

Sunday, August 15

We had the [a] quarter-of-an-hours in the morning. In the general Sunday meeting I talked about the words of the dear Savior for this day: *Ihr müsset von Neuem gebohren werden.*[21] The Lamb was near us with His side hole[d], and let us feel it. I felt quite comfortable and warm in my heart. Most of the Indian brethren and sisters attended the meeting. In the evening we could not have the quarter-of-an-hour for the communicants because the brethren went into the sweat house. I visited several brethren and sisters; thought of the congregation often, and of the blessing that the Lamb[d] will bestow especially on the married people's choir also on this day.

Monday, August 16

We had [a] quarter-of-an-hour in the morning. Br. Joshua went out with his family, but returned home in the evening. Wampachonant, who has been here for a visit, went back home, and with him, Br. Lucas. Petrus and Jeremias went to Gaylords to work. I held school. Visited Salome, Thamar, Caritas, and others, telling them all something about the Savior. In the evening 2 drunken Indians made a great deal of noise, so that the sisters who did not have their husbands at home had to flee into the woods. One of them chased after me especially. Yet I escaped him long enough to be able to get into my house. One time he got a hold of me, though. I asked him what he wanted with me. He said I had hit him once, now he wanted to see who was the stronger of us two. I told him he did not remember correctly; I could assure him that I loved him. As soon as I told him that I loved him, he walked away from me and wept. I made haste so as to get into my house[d]. I took Sr. Agnes, who was hiding in the woods, into my house[d], along with her children, as they were looking for her as well as for me. I told her the Savior would preserve us — she should just be quiet when the Indians came to the door, which she did. In the end, the drunken fellows got into a quarrel among themselves so that they both fought with each other. Then we had peace.

Tuesday, August 17

We had [a] quarter-of-an-hour in the morning. Br. Gideon went to New Milford. Paulus and his wife, Amos, Thamaseed, and Christian's son went to Stockbridge; the other brethren, excepting Samuel, went hunting. I held school. After school I went to Aaron Gaylord to see whether there was glass to be had in New Milford. He himself was not at home, and his wife was unable to tell me anything definite. I also wanted to visit the brethren and sisters in the winter huts but did not find them at home.

Wednesday, August 18

Given that almost everyone was out, I did not conduct [a] quarter-of-an-hour. It was hardly right, even for school; thus I only had the girls. I visited those who were still at home. Went into the woods to see if I was still able to peel bark, but it is already too late in the year.[22]

Thursday, August 19

There was again no quarter-of-an-hour in the morning; there was almost no one home. I held school with the few children who are at home, washed my soiled laundry, and carried some wood home.

Friday, August 20

I once again conducted [a] quarter-of-an-hour with the few brethren and sisters who are home; also held school. I visited the brethren and sisters, telling them, as the opportunity arose, something about the Savior and His bloody wounds. In the evening the sisters and children who had gone to pick blueberries came home. They had been out this week, having dried the berries as they collected them.[23]

Saturday, August 21

There was again [a] quarter-of-an-hour in the morning. I prayed to our Husband and Chief Elder for a bloody blessing of grace for this entire assembly. I talked particularly thoroughly with Br. Samuel, who has gotten into something and now does not know how to get himself back together. He said that he was very sorry for it and that it grieved him. I did not intend to do anything unusual, because it was the Sabbath. My heart thought of the congregation especially often. Also, the brethren returned from hunting.

Sunday, August 22

We had a blissful quarter-of-an-hour^d; I talked a bit about yesterday's ~~watch-word~~ texts. In the general meeting I talked about the watchword. I was greatly distressed on account of the present circumstances, yet I portrayed to them [the Indians] the Lamb^d with all of His wounds, along with the whole merit of His death. There were few brethren and sisters attending the meeting; from the winter huts, no one at all. During the quarter-of-an-hour for the baptized ones and the communicants, I warmly put the brethren and sisters in mind of the baptism and what the Lamb^d had granted them at the time, when He washed them with the blood and water from the side hole. I also visited all of the brethren and sisters who are at home. Except for Br. Gideon, they all complained about their poor circumstances.

Monday, August 23

I conducted [a] quarter-of-an-hour in the morning. Because no one from the winter huts was here yesterday, I went there right after the quarter-of-an-hour to visit them. Yet I found no one home other than Sr. Rebecca. I told her something about the Savior and reminded her of the grace that the Lamb^d had bestowed upon her. Br. David had left by then. I again held school with the children. I visited Petrus and Thamar, who were not home yesterday. In the evening we had quite a blissful quarter-of-an-hour^d.

Tuesday, August 24

We had [a] quarter-of-an-hour in the morning; I talked a bit about the text. I held school again. Br. Amos returned from Wanachquaticok along with 2 unbaptized

Indians. Paulus and his wife, who had promised to return today as well, have gone to Albany. Br. Amos also brought word that old Aaron, who had been ill for so very long, died last Saturday, on August 22.[24]

Wednesday, August 25

We had a blessed quarter-of-an-hour[d] in the morning. I went to Gaylords to see if there was still no glass to be had in New Milford. Gaylord told me that he had purchased glass, yet as it was night when he left New Milford, had been unable to bring it with him.

Thursday, August 26

We held [a] quarter-of-an-hour in the morning; I talked about the text. The Lamb[d] with His side hole was intimately near us. I held school again. Br. Joshua and Elisabeth went to New Milford.

Friday, August 27

We had [a] quarter-of-an-hour in the morning; our dear Lamb[d] of God was quite near us. I held school. Pachgatgoch was as if emptied of people. Most of the brethren and sisters and other Indians had gone out. I felt very blissful inside my Lamb[d] and His side hole[d].

Saturday, August 28

In the morning, I conducted the quarter-of-an-hour with 5 brethren and sisters, recommending myself and the entire assembly to the bloody wounds of our Husband. Afterward, I observed the Sabbath with Him. I frequently remembered the dear Bethlehem. I visited Petrus and his family. They are quite blissful; they expressed themselves right beautifully about how their hearts stood with the Savior. Simon also declared himself quite agreeably. In the evening all of the brethren and sisters, excepting Christian's family, came home, as did those who live in the winter huts.

Sunday, August 29

There was no quarter-of-an-hour in the morning. I had quite a blissful talk with the brethren and sisters who are members of the conference, at which time the

Lamb[d] was quite near us. He brought to the fore all of those matters that, for a long time, I had wished would be touched upon one day. Instead of inquiring [as] usual about the circumstances of the other brethren and sisters, I asked them plainly how they were doing, upon which Br. Gideon declared himself at once, saying how he felt. The general Sunday meeting was attended by almost everyone who lives in Pachgatgoch and the winter huts. I talked about the text. The Lamb[d] was quite intimately and tenderly near me and the entire assembly. The Lamb[d] was also quite intimately near us in the quarter-of-an-hour for the baptized ones and communicants. I also visited the brethren and sisters, finding most right blissful and in a happy state. Sr. Sarah was in especially good spirits, likewise Br. David. My heart was quite blissful at that which the Lamb[d] affects in the brown assembly. This time He has no doubt affected much in them. In the evening Br. Lucas came home from Wechquadnach, bringing word that old Simon was very ill there.

Monday, August 30

I conducted the quarter-of-an-hour in the morning. Br. Lucas told me that Timotheus and old father Jephthah intended to travel yet to Bethlehem this week. I right away wrote a letter to our dear Br. Johann Nitschmann, wherein I reported to him somewhat about the circumstances. Afterward, I went to Wechquadnach to deliver the letter to Timotheus, and to see how old Simon was doing. Br. Gideon, Samuel, and Jeremias went ahead. I found old Simon very ill, so that he may possibly go home. The Lamb[d] gave me a favorable opportunity to tell him something about His wounds and side hole[d]. Br. Gideon interpreted for me. After I had finished speaking, Br. Gideon continued to talk at length to all the Indians about the Savior in a way that one could feel that [it] was coming from his heart. Br. Timoth[eus] said that if old Simon was not so very ill, he would be on his journey to Gnadenhütten by now. Petrus and Thamar went to Danbury. Joshua left as well, to make backs.[25]

Tuesday, August 31

In the morning, I held a small quarter-of-an-hour for the Indians in Wechquadnach; the Lamb[d] was with us. My heart felt quite blissful. I soon set out on my return journey to Pachgatgoch. The brethren Gideon, Samuel, and Jeremias stayed behind for now. I found all of the brethren and sisters who were at home quite well. Br. Jeremias also came home.

Wednesday, September 1
We conducted a blissful quarter-of-an-hour[d] in the morning. I held school again. The brethren Gideon and Samuel came from Wechquadnach, saying that the sick person [Simon] had recovered somewhat. Salome and Benigna went to the seaside to fetch Br. Martin and his family from there.

Thursday, September 2
We had [a] quarter-of-an-hour in the morning. I held school. Visited the brethren and sisters in the winter huts. David and Leah were not at home. Sarah and Rebecca are quite blissful and in good spirits. Little Maria is sickly. Br. Samuel went to the seaside. Br. Joshua and Gottlieb returned home. I felt quite blissful inside the wounds of my Lamb[d].

Friday, September 3
We had a blissful quarter-of-an-hour in the morning. I set about making *acritches*, yet was prevented from doing so because of bad weather. Sr. Erdmuth came from Wechquadnach; old Simon has reportedly recovered somewhat. Br. Jephthah and Timotheus have not yet set out on their intended journey to Gnadenhütten. Petrus and Thamar came home as well; they had been out to sell baskets. Both came home in a quite happy state.

Saturday, September 4
I was unable to hold the quarter-of-an-hour in the morning, for I was very busy drying my corn, and it was lying about all over the house. Br. Lucas and Amos went hunting and will probably stay out for 3 weeks. Late in the evening, Christian and his family once again returned here. Also, Br. Samuel came from the seaside, bringing word that Br. Martin and his family were on their way to this place, [and] that an old Indian woman was with them, who wanted to visit Pachgatgoch once. She is old Maria's natural sister. Also with Br. Samuel came Gideon's son, Martin's brother, on a visit for a couple of days. He too had lived in Pachgatgoch in former times and had held school here.

Sunday, September 5

We had [a] quarter-of-an-hour in the morning. In the general meeting I talked about the words: *Wir haben einen Hohenprister auf dem Stuhl der Majestät, der ist der Pfleger der heiligen Kütter, und der wahrhaften Hütten.* Heb. 8.1, 2.[26] Our dear Lamb[d] of God was near us and invigorated me quite mercifully in my poverty. During the quarter-of-an-hour for the baptized ones and the communicants, our Lamb[d] manifested Himself quite intimately near us. Br. Joshua interpreted with all his heart. And the brethren and sisters were all right blissful and full of light. Immediately after the quarter-of-an-hour, Br. Martin and his family arrived back home from the seaside. It was a true joy for all the brethren and sisters to see them. The old Indian woman, Maria's sister, also came with Martin, as did Salome and Benigna, who had gone for them.

Monday, September 6

We had quite a blissful quarter-of-an-hour[d] in the morning. I went to Gaylords to collect my glass from there and to buy some provisions. Joshua, Elisabeth, Gottlieb, Magdalena, Jeremias, and Christian went to New Milford; the one mentioned last to work, the others to sell their baskets and backs. The Indian stranger left as well. He said he was now going hunting. On his return from hunting he intended to come here for a visit with his wife and children, and leave the children here so that they could go to school.

Tuesday, September 7

We had another blissful quarter-of-an-hour[d] in the morning. The brethren and sisters who were home started making *acritches*. I also made some more for myself, because I was not able to hold school in any case as all of the children were busy. Br. Jeremias and Agnes returned home. One of my neighbors visited me. He asked how was it that we were not better neighbors—I never even visited them and have been here now for such a long time. He did not think that any person would throw any obstacles my way. I replied that I did not have much time to spare, that my time was well used by holding school and whatever else I had to do. The man was most amiable, also did not ask any questions.

My heart felt blissful near the wounds of my Lamb[d]. I thought very much and frequently of my dear brethren and brethren and sisters in Bethlehem—what a beautiful day they will have.[27]

Wednesday, September 8

We had [a] quarter-of-an-hour in the morning; Br. Samuel interpreted. I was still busy drying my corn. The sisters and children were also diligently at work. I visited them; watched how they were doing it. I had quite a blissful day.

Thursday, September 9

We had [a] quarter-of-an-hour in the morning. I talked about the text; Br. Joshua interpreted. I visited several brethren and sisters, finding them quite blissful and in good spirits. They were again diligently drying corn. I told them that the drying of corn was a very old practice; that one could even read about it in the Bible.[28] They were very surprised that something like this also could be found in the Bible. I said the circumstances where such matters are mentioned were always pleasant. I carried home some clay to repair the chimney and house[d] [in preparation] for winter.

Friday, September 10

In the morning, we had quite a blissful quarter-of-an-hour[d] during which our Lamb[d] was intimately and tenderly near us. I had washday and washed my clothing. A white man came here to ask advice of Br. Gideon, for he has had pains in his joints for several years and no doctor is able to help him. Gideon advised him to build a sweat house near his house and to sweat frequently. The man is a Quaker.

I visited Justina. She said that she was so happy that the Savior had given her a young son. She has been in a constant state of bliss since he was born.

Saturday, September 11

We again had a blessed quarter-of-an-hour[d] in the morning. After the quarter-of-an-hour, Br. and Sr. Martin told me that, because the Lamb[d] has bestowed on them a little son[d], they felt in their hearts the desire to give a love feast for the brethren and sisters. They had felt this desire in their hearts on their journey home to Pachgatgoch, and they would like to give this love feast tomorrow.

I told them that this was good, and [that it] pleased me that the Savior had in-spired them to this end, yet they should make sure to speak also with Br. Gideon about it, which they promise to do. I visited the brethren and sisters in the win-ter huts and announced it [the love feast] to them. David and Rebecca were not at home. I also talked with Simon's Benigna, who came home yesterday evening; she had been as far as Albany and had left her brother Paulus there. An Indian came from the seaside to visit, and from Hartford, an Indian woman.

Sunday, September 12

We had [a] quarter-of-an-hour in the morning; I talked a bit about the words of the dear Savior. In the general Sunday meeting I talked about the watchword of the day; the Lamb[d] was near us and assisted me especially in pointing to His wounds. Our meeting place[d] was so full, ever so much as it could hold. The 2 strangers, who are here to visit their friends,[29] came as well. Past noon we had the love feast. Things proceeded in quite a delightful and blissful manner. Br. Samuel and I were servants. Martin and Justina declared themselves quite beautifully in front of the brethren and sisters, as did Gideon and Joshua. I re-minded the brethren and sisters of how it was in the beginning, and said that we had reason to sincerely thank the Savior, for we are now able to be together so peaceful and quiet; that no one was obstructing and disturbing us, [and] that the Savior has now made rum [room], making it possible for brethren to live here. I also mentioned the singing, that they had gotten into the habit of singing so very slowly, [and] that it would be much better and more blissful if the brethren and sisters remembered it [the song] better. After the love feast I also visited several brethren and sisters. The Indian woman who has come from Hartford visited me in my house[d]. I took the opportunity to tell her about the Savior and His wounds. Because she is able to read English, I presented her with an English song. I was unable to conduct the quarter-of-an-hour in the evening, for the brethren went into the sweat house.

Monday, September 13

We had [a] quarter-of-an-hour in the morning. I visited Christian but was un-able to talk to him as his house was full of strangers. Br. Joshua came to me, telling me that he, Br. Samuel, and Gottlieb intended to go hunting and would not return home until Saturday. I asked him how he had felt during the love feast yesterday, and how he had felt in his heart. He said he had not felt this way in a long time. It was as if he had rediscovered his heart. Before this he had felt nothing and had thought of nothing else but worldly things. However, when I mentioned what the Savior had told His apostles — [that] they would be recognized as His apostles if they loved one another — then his heart reawakened and told him, that is what you are lacking. Now he felt that he once again loved all of his brethren and sisters. Joshua also told me that Simon had told him that his heart awoke when I talked this way. Br. Petrus and Martin went out to work. Anna, Benigna, and Salome went out to make brooms. I worked in my corn, cutting off whatever is good for winter fodder.

Tuesday, September 14

We had [a] quarter-of-an-hour in the morning. I started making my window frames, also paid a visit to several huts; yet almost no one was home.

Wednesday, September 15

We had [a] quarter-of-an-hour in the morning. I talked a bit about the texts; Br. Martin interpreted. I continued working on the window frames. I visited the foreign Indian woman; she is staying with Jery. She was very friendly. Jery's wife presented me with 2 candles, which appear to be something rare. Br. Jeremias visited me in the evening. I mentioned to him the love feast, because he had not attended. He said that he had not understood Br. Gideon properly. That is why he came to me now, to tell me that he had not stayed away intentionally. He also was very affectionate and understanding concerning his affairs. Simon visited me as well; he is quite blissful now. Br. Gideon left to build a sweat house for the man who was here last week and had requested this of him. I had quite a blissful and sweet rest. The Lamb[d] was quite intimately near me in my sleep.

Thursday, September 16

We had no quarter-of-an-hour in the morning because it was raining. Moreover, there were hardly any brethren at home. I continued working on my window frames. The foreign Indian woman visited me again, as did Sr. Erdmuth, but they did not stay long. I had quite a blissful day. My heart remembered especially the Savior's office of Chief Elder. I fully gave myself up to Him anew, to His service, wherever He wants to use me, poor heart.

Friday, September 17
We had [a] quarter-of-an-hour in the morning; I talked about the words of the dear Savior. Br. Martin interpreted. I worked on my house diligently, also went and got some straw from one of our neighbors. Br. Gideon returned home, and several [Indians] came from hunting. Br. Amos brought word that Lucas had dislocated an arm, [and] that it was so bad that the doctor was unable to reset it; the arm was now very swollen. Lucas is reportedly in Wechquadnach at present. Amos also said that he had heard that Indians from Gnadenhütten were on their way to Wechquadnach.

Saturday, September 18
We had no quarter-of-an-hour in the morning. That night I started having the gripes and acute pains in my bowels, so that I was unable to get up in the morning. This persisted until about noon. I felt very fatigued the whole day. I received the word on Br. Lucas only today. I merely confused it in the process of writing. In the evening Br. Joshua, Gottlieb, and his son came from hunting, as did Br. Samuel. These 4 have been out this week and got only one deer.

Sunday, September 19
We had a blessed quarter-of-an-hour[d] in the morning. As we were singing our precious verse Ye bloody Hands with Blessings fild [filled], I looked to the watchword, which read: Ich bette zu Gott, meines Lebens; Seel der Seele, und des Leibes Töpfer.[30] I read it to the brethren and sisters, most of whom were present. Then I prayed and entrusted myself and the entire assembly to the faithful heart of the Lamb[d], our Chief Elder and Husband, with all of our circumstances, shortcomings, and failings. He was undoubtedly in our midst, bleeding onto our hearts. In the general meeting I talked about the words of the dear Savior and for this day: Das Himmelreich ist gleich einem Könige, der seinen Sohn Hochzeit machte.[31] And the Lamb[d] was near us with His open side, and had us feel how He was thirsting to embrace a soul. He was also near us in the quarter-of-an-hour for the baptized ones and communicants. Also, we met in conference; the winter huts

were discussed, and where the most suitable place would be for building. Br. Gideon said it is best to have a conference on this with all of the brethren and sisters. He wanted to summon all of them to his house this evening and then everyone could speak his mind. In the evening most of the brethren and sisters came into Gid[eon's] huts. The Lamb^d moved them to be all of one mind and to decide to build winter huts, and they wanted to choose the proper place for this purpose tomorrow. During this conference everything proceeded in quite a brotherly fashion; no one chose something before the other. I asked one brother after the other what his intention was; they all said they wanted to leave it up to their brethren and sisters. Each one said he wanted to go where his brethren and sisters went. I said, if the brethren were agreeable, we would go together tomorrow morning and choose the best spot. They all were of one mind in this. I visited most of the brethren and sisters and portrayed to them the Lamb^d in His bloody crucified form, and put them in mind of the grace that the Lamb^d has already bestowed on them.

Monday, September 20

We had [a] quarter-of-an-hour in the morning. Our dear Lamb^d of God was intimately near us. The brethren Joshua, Gideon, Gottlieb, and Samuel went out to look for a place where they could live this winter. I also went with them. Along the way they changed their minds and resolved to make a sledge-path to enable them to bring the wood down the mountain during the winter. The brethren right away started working on the sledge-path. I helped them as well. I went visiting in several huts and reminded them of what the Savior has affected in them. Several went out to make brooms. Priscilla went to Wechquadnach because her son Lucas is there and has dislocated an arm. In the evening Br. Martin received a message through an Indian stranger that his grandmother was very ill and had the desire to see him once more. Thus Br. Martin left from here with the messenger this very evening. His grandmother lives near the seaside.

Tuesday, September 21

We were prevented from holding the quarter-of-an-hour in the morning, so that I was unable to conduct it. I went to work on the sledge-path with the brethren. Our friend Culver visited me. He found me in the process of making the path

together with the brethren. Because he wants to leave tomorrow morning, I
went home with him and began to write to my dear brethren in Bethlehem. As
I was writing, Sr. Priscilla came from Wechquadnach, bringing me 2 precious
letters from Bethlehem, also bringing word that Br. Augustus and his Esther
had arrived. The dear Savior has timed this occasion well.

Wednesday, September 22

Culver left again in the morning. He took a very heartfelt leave. He said he did
not mean anything by not visiting me. Also, he had taken pleasure in the Indian
brethren and sisters. I held school again, also went to Gaylords to buy some
provisions. I visited the brethren and sisters in the winter huts. David was quite
lively; Rebecca was not at home. Sarah and Maria are both sickly. Leah went to
Woodbury. Old Kihur was exceedingly amiable. The brethren were not working on the path because the weather was bad.

Thursday, September 23

We had [a] quarter-of-an-hour in the morning. I worked with the brethren on
the path. So far things have proceeded rather well; the Savior has protected all
of us from harm. Often we had to move very large stones out of the way. Anyone who sees it will be amazed that the Indians ventured to make a path up
this rocky mountain.

Friday, September 24

We had [a] quarter-of-an-hour in the morning; I talked about the texts. The
brethren continued working on their path; I also went working with them.
We finished the worst part.

Saturday, September 25

Very early this morning the brethren left for the woods to get *splinters* [splints]
for making baskets so that I was unable to conduct the quarter-of-an-hour. I
did my wash and picked dry beans. Also, Br. Martin came back from Derby; his
grandmother has died. Martin said that he had prayed at the graveside. Several
white people had also joined them at the grave. This Indian woman was not
baptized, but she had had the desire to visit Pachgatgoch. Yet she had no longer
dared come here, for she was very old and sickly. With Martin came an Indian

woman with a boy for a visit at this place. She already has one child here who is staying with old Erdmuth. The Indian woman is friends with[32] Erdmuth. Erdmuth also came home, as did the brethren who had left in the morning.

Sunday, September 26

We had [a] quarter-of-an-hour in the morning; I talked about yesterday's text about the Lamb. Afterward, we met in conference; the Lamb[d] was intimately near us. Special mention was made of belonging wholly to the Savior, and cleaving to Him with body and soul, and that through this our tabernacles will become partakers of His nature and He can mold us as He wishes. And that the blood continues to act upon us until we grow to be in the spirit of Jesus, and that this occurs as often as we come near His body, more and ever more. In the general meeting I spoke about the watchword of the day. The house[d] was so filled to the brim that it occurred to me that I need to build a larger one. The Indian strangers who are here for a visit all attended the meeting. The Lamb was intimately near us. Br. Joshua interpreted with a warm and feeling heart. During the quarter-of-an-hour for the baptized ones and the communicants, I talked about tomorrow's text of the Lamb. The Lamb[d] right away put me on the path of speaking about the theme that we had dealt with at the conference. I felt quite comfortable when visiting. I portrayed the Lamb[d] with all of His wounds, and put the brethren and sisters in mind of the grace that the Savior has already bestowed on them.

Monday, September 27

We had a blissful quarter-of-an-hour[d] in the morning. I talked about the words: *Seyn Blut redet besser den Abels.*[33] The Lamb[d] was intimately near us; Br. Martin interpreted. I held school again, and snapped off dry beans.

Tuesday, September 28

We had [a] quarter-of-an-hour in the morning; I talked about the texts. The brethren Gideon, Joshua, Petrus, Gottlieb, and Jeremias worked on the [sledge] path. I helped them.

It was mustering day in Kent, when they elect new *offecirs* who, in accordance with their custom, give food and drink to the people. They had already announced beforehand that they would give enough to anyone who came, also to the Indians and Negroes. Hence, I asked the brethren to be on their guard, and to abide in the Savior with their hearts. None of the brethren went, excepting Samuel and Martin. Both of them returned home in a fairly good state. The unbaptized ones all came home drunk and created a great deal of noise. Priscilla had to flee with her daughters from her house. I gave myself up to my my [sic] Lamb[d] and was quiet in my house[d].

Wednesday, September 29

It rained fairly hard in the morning so that I suspended the quarter-of-an-hour, intending to conduct it in the evening, but was unable to do it then, for the sisters went into the sweat house. I visited Br. Samuel, Martin, and Christian. I also conducted school. The remaining time I spent with mending. Jery returned from Stockbridge. He brought with him a young Indian who is friends with him.[34] This young Indian lives in Farmington. Br. Petrus visited me in the evening. He said he felt as if he had found his heart; he loved all of his brethren. This morning his heart had felt hungry, thus, he thought, the brother will soon hold [a] quarter-of-an-hour. But after that time had passed, he thought, we will have [a] quarter-of-an-hour in the evening. And so he kept listening for when I would blow [the horn]. When that time had passed as well, he thought, now you must visit the brother. I told him how things had gone for me and the quarter-of-an-hour.

Thursday, September 30

We had [a] quarter-of-an-hour in the morning. I talked a bit about the texts. The young Indian from Farmington came to me and right away asked where Sensemann was; he knows Br. Sensemann. He told me he had visited him frequently this spring. In the evening he visited me again, and so did a couple of other Indian strangers. I read to them the hymn *Ein Lämmlein geht u. Trägt die Schuld*, etc., in English.[35] Also, the min[i]ster from Kent, Mr. Marsh, visited me. He was very cordial and assured me that he had nothing against the Brethren. What he had done against them previously, he did for want of reason. He was very young back then and had been installed to preach just at that time. Also, had not known anything about the Brethren aside from the terrible things he had heard and read in Tennent's book,[36] and so he undoubtedly had not acted the way he should have. He assured me that he now thought differently of the Brethren, [and] that he no longer wants to disturb them in their work among the Indians; instead, he wants to assist them when it is in his power. He asked me if if [sic] I thought that the brethren would take him in if he came to Bethlehem. He thinks they would still remember what he had done to them. I told him I believed the brethren no longer thought about it. He strongly urged me to visit him. But I did not make any promises to him; only if time would happen to bring it about. He said I shall be welcome in his house like his own brother any time. On bidding farewell he gave me his hand, wished me luck, and said he believed nothing else other than that our intention among the Indians was sincere. Old Maria and her sister returned from their visit among their friends.[37]

Friday, October 1

We had [a] quarter-of-an-hour in the morning. I visited Thamar; she has been sickly for some days. I administered balsam to her for sweating.[38] The brethren worked again on their sledge-path and finished it to the point that they now anticipate completing it in one day. I started working on a bedstead.

Saturday, October 2

We had [a] quarter-of-an-hour in the morning. I talked about the text. The Lamb[d] was intimately near us. I continued working on the bedstead. My heart felt quite blissful in the side hole[d]. I visited Jery; he is quite amicable. Thamar has recovered. Timotheus came from Wechquadnach. He told me that Susanna was ill, but old Simon [was] in good health. I took the opportunity to tell him something about the Savior.

Sunday, October 3

I suspended the quarter-of-an-hour in the morning because it was so very cold, and most of the brethren and sisters are still going barefoot. Timotheus visited me again, and just at the time when we were to meet in conference. In the general Sunday meeting I talked about the texts; the Lamb[d] was intimately near us. In the quarter-of-an-hour for the communicants I talked somewhat about the verse *Christi Blut u. Kerechtigkeit*,[39] and He was near us poor hearts[d] with His bloody wounds. Nothing new came up when visiting.

Monday, October 4

We had [a] quarter-of-an-hour in the morning; I talked about the texts. Afterward, I visited all the brethren and sisters who came home yesterday evening and who are leaving today to sell baskets: Martha, Johanna and her daughter, Priscilla and her daughter Benigna, as well as Petrus and Thamar. Paulus and his brother Amos, and Lucas, returned from hunting; his [Lucas's] arm has healed very poorly. Also, Timotheus went back to Wechquadnach. I worked on the bedstead and brought in wood.

Tuesday, October 5

We had [a] quarter-of-an-hour in the morning; I talked about the text. Several brethren went out to work. I visited those who were still at home. The foreign Indian woman who had been here for a visit left yesterday. She took her children with her. She said that she intended to return for the Christmas holidays. I worked on the bedstead. In the evening I visited Br. Gideon and Samuel.

Wednesday, October 6

We had [a] quarter-of-an-hour in the evening; I again talked about the texts. I visited Br. Martin; he said he was quite blissful. Old Sr. Erdmuth returned, and with her Johanna's and Juliana's girls. The wife of Lemuel Bostwick in New Milford sent me a piece of bread. I completed the bedstead and got some wood for myself. I visited Magdalena in the evening; Br. Gottlieb is not at home.

Thursday, October 7

I did not conduct a quarter-of-an-hour in the morning as there are hardly any brethren and sisters at home. Br. Joshua, Gottlieb, and Jeremias with his family, went out to sell baskets and backs. Martha and Johanna came home. I started gathering my corn, also visited those huts where there were brethren and sisters. The wife of Lemuel Bostwick sent me a dozen apples through Martha. Her husband wants to visit us soon.

Friday, October 8

We had [a] quarter-of-an-hour in the morning; our dear Lamb[d] of God was in our midst. I entrusted all the souls[d] and circumstances to His faithful and loving heart. Benigna, Simon's daughter, went to New Milford. I was hard at work gathering corn.

Saturday, October 9

We had [a] quarter-of-an-hour in the morning. I washed my soiled laundry. Also brought my corn home, so that all of it is now under the roof. I visited Br. Martin and Samuel in the evening. All of the brethren and sisters except for Petrus and Thamar came home. That day I thought of my dear brethren in Bethlehem very much; I was half hopeful that a brother would come for a visit.

Sunday, October 10

We had [a] quarter-of-an-hour in the morning. I presented our circumstances to the Lamb[d] and appealed to Him to bleed on us anew, and to forgive and cleanse where something has come about. Also, we met in conference, but nothing came up that was out of the ordinary. During the general meeting I talked about the words of the Savior during these days. My heart was greatly distressed about a number of matters so that I was not able to talk much. I felt the same way while visiting. We were hindered with the quarter-of-an-hour for the communicants, so that I was unable to conduct it.

Monday, October 11

We had a blessed quarter-of-an-hour[d] in the morning. Our dear Lamb[d] of God was intimately near us. I talked about the texts; Br. Martin interpreted. I held school again. After school I went to Gaylords, as I was in need of some provisions. However, I was unable to get anything other than butter, and for that I had to pay 10 *pens* [pence a] #. I also visited the winter huts. No one was home excepting Sarah and the old, as well as little Maria, who is ill. The brethren started gathering their corn.

Tuesday, October 12

We had [a] quarter-of-an-hour in the morning. I prayed and recommended all of us to the bloody side hole[d]. After the quarter-of-an-hour I visited all the brethren and sisters. Next, I held school again. I prepared clay for plastering the inside of my house[d]. A day of *exerccicium* [Latin: exercise] again occurred in Kent, hence everyone who went would receive presents like before. None of the brethren went there, regardless. In the evening Sr. Priscilla came home with her daughter Benigna. They had to leave Petrus and his family behind because Anna is sickly.

Wednesday, October 13

We had [a] quarter-of-an-hour in the morning. I talked about the words of the beloved Savior: *Suchet Euch die rechte Speise.*[40] The Lamb[d] revealed Himself to us; Br. Martin interpreted. I plastered my house[d]. The brethren were gathering their corn. Br. Gideon visited in the evening.

Thursday, October 14

We had [a] quarter-of-an-hour in the evening; I talked about the text. Br. Joshua interpreted. I held school, also gathered beans. I have got all of them [the beans] in the house now. Br. Joshua visited in the evening.

Friday, October 15

We had [a] quarter-of-an-hour in the evening; I talked about the texts. Br. Martin interpreted. I held school. I carried home still more clay and plastered my house[d]. The brethren had their corn hauled home. In the evening they went about husking their corn in common; I helped them.

Saturday, October 16

We had a blissful quarter-of-an-hour[d] in the morning; I talked about the text. Br. Martin interpreted. Then I went visiting in the winter huts, but met none of the baptized ones, other than Sarah and her daughter, little Maria, who is still sickly. Sarah was quite lively and full of light. Sarah's son's wife and her mother came from the seaside for a visit. On my welcoming the old woman she right away said, *I poor Wamem [woman] am come again to see you.* Her reply took me by surprise, so that I was unable to say anything in response. One year ago she had behaved very badly here, acting as if she wanted to tear everyone apart. However, after a short while she again started pouring out her heart and said she was the poorest creature in the world. I sat down with her and asked what was wrong. She said once more, *I am a wretched creature, I have lost everything.* She had lost God as well. Several years ago she too had feeling in her heart, and had seen Jesus Christ once. But she had lost Him and become a sinner. That

237

sum[m]er when her daughter died, her heart was reawakened. Now she saw that she was a poor creature. At times she felt some life. That is when she hoped that things would soon turn for the better. But soon after, she would once again succumb to sin, and she lived all sum[m]er in this way. Now she was here to visit her friends.[41] However, one year ago she had acted so badly that she was ashamed to go among them.

I told her about the Savior—that He was a friend of sinners. She should go before Him just the way she felt; He will wash her with His blood and forgive her everything so that she could remain forever blissful. I then took leave of her. After I had walked a distance from the house, she came running after me, making me a *praesent* of 6 apples. I had also spoken with Gihur; he was friendly, but appeared *indiferent* to me. I washed my soiled laundry and carried wood home. In the evening Timotheus and Ampawaechnant came from Wechquadnach. The wife of the latter had reportedly taken a very bad fall off a horse the week before. Timotheus had intended to go to Gnadenhütten with his Hannah this autumn. He said he was not able to go now that this fall had occurred.

Sunday, October 17

We had [a] quarter-of-an-hour in the morning. I talked a bit about the watchword; Br. M[artin] interpreted. Br. Joshua interpreted during the general meeting. I talked about the words: *Wenn Euere Sunde gleich Blut roth ist, etc. Wer in Jesu Wunde das Heil gefunden, der wird so h. als Jesu Wunden.*[42] The Lamb[d] was in our midst and let us feel how His loving heart embraces poor sinners. The foreign Indian woman also attended the meeting. In the quarter-of-an-hour for the communicants, I talked about yesterday's watchword: *Euch ist gegeben, das Ihr im Blut des Lammes liegt und in all Euere Kriegen siegt.*[43] The Lamb[d] was near us and gave me joy to speak and to portray the dear Lamb[d] of God with all His wounds to the hearts of the brethren and sisters. When visited, the brethren and sisters who had been home last week were affectionate and full of light. Br. Joshua and Samuel visited me, each one separately. I took the opportunity to talk with them about their hearts. I reminded Br. Joshua of his first grace, and how close the Savior had been to him. Br. Samuel was very candid and acknowledged what has kept him back until now. I would have liked to have held conference as well, but was unable to get the brethren together. Petrus, Paulus, Christian and his son, and Lucas came home. He [Lucas] has been to the doctor in New Milford with his dislocated arm, but that has not helped him any.

Monday, October 18

We had a blissful quarter-of-an-hour[d] in the morning; I talked about the texts. Br. Joshua interpreted. I held school again. Christian and his son went back to New Milford. All the young people went to one of our neighbors to strip[44] corn. On that occasion, the white people do not give a day's pay, but food and drink, and in that respect they often give more than necessary. Two of the unbaptized ones came home drunk. I locked myself in my house[d], for I did not trust them. Br. Gideon visited me and stayed with me until the tumult was over. The brethren and sisters helped Br. Samuel gather his corn. I cut wood for a pigsty. Br. Timotheus went back to Wechquadnach.

Tuesday, October 19

We had [a] quarter-of-an-hour in the morning. Yesterday and today I was prevented from holding school since everyone set about stripping corn. Also, they readied themselves to go to New Milford, because a large *general* muster is taking place [there]; nearly everyone went. Br. Gideon and Jeremias stayed at home. I visited all of the brethren and sisters before they left, asking them to please abide in the Savior, and to remember His wounds. They promised me this, to be sure, but my heart was full of sorrow for them. I brought home as much wood for the pigsty as I could.

Wednesday, October 20

I did not conduct a quarter-of-an-hour in the morning as there is almost no one at home. I visited the sick. Juliana is very ill, as is Br. Martin's oldest boy. Anna has got the ague. This is presently epidemic in New England, along with the bloody flux.[45] Br. Jeremias went to New Milford. I carried [in] wood for the pigsty.

Thursday, October 21

I again did not conduct a quarter-of-an-hour. It rained all day. I held school with the few children who were still at home. Visited the sick and mended a shirt for myself.

Friday, October 22

We did not have a quarter-of-an-hour in the morning. I visited the sick and whoever else was home. I also started laying up my pigsty. Past noon the brethren and sisters came home one by one. First, Br. Jeremias arrived, then Joshua and Elisabeth, Samuel and Lucia, Salome, Benigna, Simon and his Benigna, also Gottlieb's son Nacbar. I also visited Br. Samuel, for I had heard [that] he had drunk too much *syder* [cider].

Saturday, October 23

I conducted the quarter-of-an-hour again in the morning. Went visiting in all the huts; Joshua was most amiable. He had not gone to the *exercicium*. He went to Woodbury to sell baskets. The other brethren came home as well. With Martin came his brother; he has been here for a visit once before, not long ago. In addition, Paulus, Amos, Lucas, Gottlieb, and Magdalena came. It rained nearly all day. I washed and mended, and carried home wood. I had intended to pay a visit to the winter huts, but it was good that I did not go there, for I would not have found anyone home.

Sunday, October 24

We had a blessed quarter-of-an-hour[d] in the morning. I talked about yesterday's watchword: *Der Herr hat uns den Sabbath gegeben.*[46] I was glad that I now had the opportunity to tell the brethren and sisters something about the Sabbath. The verse[d] under the watchword inspired me with the theme. In the general meeting I talked about the words: *Shie [Sieh], das ist Kottes Lamm, das der Welt Sunde trägt.*[47] The Lamb[d], with His most beloved side hole[d], was near us especially intimately. My heart was all warm from the subject. I portrayed to the brown hearts[d] the Lamb[d] in the way He bore their sins and atoned for them. I also visited all of the brethren and sisters; they were amiable. They did complain about themselves, but my heart was nonetheless afforded comfort concerning them. I directed all of them to the Savior and His wounds. We were not able to have the quarter-of-an-hour for the communicants because the brethren went into the sweat house. Br. Martin had a doctor summoned to his sick child as it is vomiting violently. The doctor administered [something] to stop the vomiting, which happened. But the child started to get worse right away. In the evening he told his father he loved the Savior, and these were the last words that were heard from him.

Monday, October 25

We had [a] quarter-of-an-hour in the morning. After the quarter-of-an-hour I visited Martin's sick child. It appeared as if he would soon go to the Lamb[d]. I visited Juliana as well. She too had taken something administered by the doctor. Yet she felt worse than before. Br. Jeremias went to New Milford; he returned home in the evening. ~~I held sch~~ I worked on the pigsty and finished it, except for the roof. I frequently thought of the dear Bethlehem and wished that a brother would come soon.

Tuesday, October 26

We had quite a blissful quarter-of-an-hour in the morning. I talked about the texts; Br. Martin interpreted. I visited the sick child several times throughout the day. I held school and went on the mountain 3 times to get bark. In addition, I talked with Paulus about his heart and directed him to the Savior. I also visited Br. Joshua. I asked Martin if he was going to be pleased when his child went to the Savior. He said he would not hold [on to] it; if the Savior wanted to take it, it was His. Around midnight it [the child] fell asleep, blissfully and softly. His parents said that he had often talked about the Savior and His wounds, and said he loved the Savior. He had sung the verse[d], *Wanechk paquaik, Wanechk paquaik, p[p]., Seitenhöhlgen, Seitenhöhlgen,*[48] *p[p].,*[49] quite well. I remember that I had heard him sing it frequently in the woods when he was alone. I thought of my dear hearts in Bethlehem very much and believe that they have had quite a blissful day.

Wednesday, October 27

We again had a blissful quarter-of-an-hour in the morning; I talked about the text. The Lamb[d] was intimately near us. I talked with Br. Martin [about] when he wanted to have his child buried. He said, In the evening. I went to the winter huts and made it known to the brethren and sisters there. Leah, Rebecca, and old Maria were not at home. In the evening we had the burial. I conducted a small quarter-of-an-hour. I told them that if one occupied himself a great deal with the wounds and the side hole[d], and loved them, then one was also looking forward to seeing and kissing them one day, and that made going from the tabernacle to the Savior something that one could hardly wait for. My heart felt very blissful during this *meditation*. I prayed at the grave side. Br. Martin told me, he continued to feel this way—he wished that all of his children were baptized.

Thursday, October 28

We had [a] quarter-of-an-hour in the morning; I talked a bit about the texts. Br. Martin interpreted. I held school. I visited Br. Martin and Joshua. The brethren went hunting, returned home in the evening, and had not gotten anything. Two men came here from Woodbury to collect on debts from the Indians. First they came to me and told me that they have come here *a porpos* [à propos] to see me and to talk with me about my affairs. I was surprised, but I gave no answer. Then they asked me about many issues to which I answered them very curtly. In the end they told me the real reason why they had come here, and that was to collect on debts from the Indians. They were so bold so as to demand of me that I pay off the debts or at least be good for them. But I told them that this was not at all my business, to meddle in the Indians' external affairs. Moreover, the accounting appeared to be quite wrong, for they had put 8 # [£] 15 shillings to the account of John Jeremeia Cocksure. But since this was not the name of Br. Jeremias, they were not able to lay this charge to him. Moreover, Jeremias said that in all of his life he had not purchased anything from that man. They nonetheless sought to trick him in any way possible to get him to become entrapped by his [own] words. But Br. Jer[emias] insisted that he had never been in that man's house. They wanted to take Br. Amos away and make him a *serven* [servant] for what he owed. In the end, Br. Amos had acquiesced—that he would go with the men. However, the Savior made it happen that just at that moment one of our neighbors came along, who warranted for him, and so Amos stayed here.

Friday, October 29

We had [a] quarter-of-an-hour in the morning. The brethren worked again on their sledge-path. I also worked with them. In the evening our dear heart[d] Sensemann came to us, bringing us many heartfelt greetings and kisses from our dear Brother Johann Nitschmann and other dear hearts in Bethlehem,

Nazareth, and Gnadenhütten. I and the dear Indian hearts[d] rejoiced at seeing him among us once again.

Saturday, October 30

Because our dear heart Sensemann had to leave several things behind with Johannes Rau, I went today to retrieve them from there. Before leaving I conducted the quarter-of-an-hour; talked a bit about the watchword. Br. Martin interpreted. Br. Sensemann visited his dear Indian hearts[d]. I returned home late at night with the things that had been left behind.

Sunday, October 31

There was no quarter-of-an-hour in the morning. Several of the Indian brethren and sisters visited us, to whom our dear heart[d] Sensemann portrayed the faithful heart of our dear Lamb[d] of God. Br. Sensemann held the general Sunday meeting. He talked about the watchword and portrayed the bloody Lamb[d] of God with all of His wounds to the brethren and sisters. He did so in the quarter-of-an-hour for the communicants as well, saying at the same time how a heart felt who had given himself fully to the Lamb[d]. In the course of the day we were yet visited by several of the Indian hearts[d].

Monday, November 1

We had [a] quarter-of-an-hour in the morning. I talked a bit about the words: *Also hat Kott die Welt geliebet.*[50] Afterward, I held school. The dear heart[d] Sensemann visited the Indian brethren and sisters. He also paid a visit to Jerey, who he told about the Savior and His wounds. During the remaining time we worked and arranged things for ourselves. Br. Amos, Lucas, and Martin went hunting, the last of whom intends to return by Sunday; the others will most likely stay a little longer.

Tuesday, November 2

Br. Sensemann conducted a blessed quarter-of-an-hour in the morning. He also held school and visited several brethren and sisters. I worked with Br. Joshua and Petrus on the [sledge-] path. Br. Sensemann also helped once he was finished with school. The path is now completed so that one could drive on it if necessary. The brethren prepared themselves to go hunting.

Wednesday, November 3

I conducted the quarter-of-an-hour in the morning; talked a bit about the texts. We had Br. Gideon join us for breakfast; talked with him about a number of circumstances. Br. Sensemann held school. After school we took a *cannue* full of split planks from the winter huts up the river to the *sum[m]er* huts. The brethren went hunting. Those who went were Br. Joshua, Samuel, Jeremias, Martha's son, Gottlieb, and his son. We took leave of them beforehand, recommending them to the Lamb^d.

Thursday, November 4

There was no quarter-of-an-hour in the morning as most of the brethren are out hunting. Br. Sensemann held school. I ~~was~~ went into the woods; cut and carried wood home. We also went to one of our neighbors to sharpen our tools. Br. David and another Indian went to join the brethren who had left yesterday to go hunting.

Friday, November 5

Brother Sensemann held school. I cut firewood all day long.

~~Sunday~~ Saturday, November 6

In the morning, I went to one of our neighbors to see whether he could haul wood for us. I cut wood again; Br. Sensemann also helped. In the evening our dear Br. Post came from Bethlehem to visit the Indian hearts^d, and to bid them farewell at the same time, for he is going to Europe. He brought us many heartfelt greetings and kisses from our beloved hearts^d in Bethlehem. Also, Br. Gideon returned from New Milford.

Sunday, November 7

Given that there are almost no brethren at home, and no one who can interpret, we thought it best to conduct a small quarter-of-an-hour with the brethren and sisters who are here.[51] Br. Post conducted it; he talked about the words of the dear Savior of this day. Since arriving here, Br. Post has visited all of the Indian hearts^d, and as the opportunity arose, told them something about the Lamb^d and His wounds.

Monday, November 8

Brother Sensemann held school. Br. Post set about [making] a trunk. I cut firewood and went to a neighbor to order bread for a love feast.

Tuesday, November 9

Brother Post finished the trunk. Also, we had firewood hauled home for us. In the evening I went for bread and milk for the love feast. We had intended to hold it that evening but were hindered because the bread had not been baked in time. Br. Gideon summoned the brethren and sisters for tomorrow morning.

Wednesday, November 10

We had the love feast in the morning. Br. Sensemann talked about the blissful fellowship that we enjoy with one another when the brethren and sisters with their hearts abide in the Lamb[d] and His wounds. Also, Br. Post informed the brethren and sisters that he intended to go across the great water and visit the brethren and sisters there. The Indian brethren and sisters sent with him many greetings of love, in particular for our dear *ordinario*.[52] Those who knew him in the past were well able to remember him, and think of him often. After the love feast we talked with Br. Gideon. He gave us to understand that it would please him if he could see the brethren who are going to Europe and speak with them beforehand. He immediately resolved to go with Br. Sensemann and Post to New York.

Thursday, November 11

In the morning the dear hearts Sensemann, Post, and Gideon left from here for New York to see the brethren and sisters who are going to Europe, especially our dear Johann Nitschmann. I again set about the work that still needs to be done. I also went out to buy some provisions.

Friday, November 12

I wanted to hold school, but there were no children at home. I continued with my work.

Saturday, November 13

I frequently thought of my dear hearts in Bethlehem, and what a blissful day this had been there 3 years ago, and how everyone had tearfully paid homage to our beloved Chief Elder.[53] Our Br. Johannes, the Indian, returned here from his journey to Gnadenhütten. He is still very sickly. He has been traveling for 3 weeks from Gnadenhütten to this place. Along the way he laid over at [the house of] a *New Light* who cared for him well, not charging him anything. Christian and David returned from hunting; they get nothing.

Sunday, November 14

Brother Martin returned home from hunting that morning. He had been out for more than 14 days and did not get anything. I went visiting in the winter huts. Leah was back home; she had returned that Thursday. She greatly lamented her poverty. I directed her to the Lamb[d]. Christian and David were very affectionate and revived. I arranged for a quarter-of-an-hour with them for that evening. Br. Martin interpreted during the quarter-of-an-hour. The Lamb[d] was near us and revealed Himself to us. After the quarter-of-an-hour I visited Martin; he is very much indisposed as a result of his journey.

Monday, November 15

I was unable to conduct the quarter-of-an-hour in the morning. I went to the mill in Sharon and returned home in the evening.

Tuesday, November 16

I was again unable to conduct the quarter-of-an-hour as Martin is still indisposed on account of his feet. I had washday. Christian repaired his hut.

Wednesday, November 17

In the morning I had a quarter-of-an-hour with the few brethren and sisters who were still at home. I talked about the words of the dear Savior: *Wer an mich glaubet, der hat das ewige Leben.*[54] Martin and his wife, also Agnes and Lucia, went out to sell things. I worked diligently.

Thursday, November 18th

[Today] was the day of Thanksgiving in New England.[55] The brethren and sisters and almost everyone who was at home went out among the white people, because that day they will be presented with things everywhere. I visited the brethren and sisters before they left, asking them to abide with their hearts in the Savior and His wounds. I diligently went about the work that I have yet to do before leaving for Bethlehem.

Friday, November 19

Pachgatgoch was again as if emptied of people. There was no one home except for some children. I visited them several times throughout the day.

Saturday, November 20

Several brethren and sisters came back home: Magdalena, Lucia, Benigna, and Anna; from hunting returned Br. Gottlieb and his son, Paulus and his brother, as well as Lucas. I went visiting in the winter huts, yet found no one except Christian. He was very affectionate and amiable.

Sunday, November 21

Brother Martin came home. I resolved to still conduct a quarter-of-an-hour, thus announced it among the brethren and sisters. In the evening we had the quarter-of-an-hour. I felt very comfortable and the Lamb[d] was near us.

Monday, November 22

I conducted [a] quarter-of-an-hour in the morning. Several brethren and sisters went out to work. I visited Lucas. He complained that his heart was not in a proper state. I directed him to the Savior and His wounds. I worked diligently.

Tuesday, November 23

I visited the brethren and sisters who were at home, talking with several of their hearts, directing all of them to the bloody wounds of our Lamb[d] of God. Br. Gottlieb and his son Nacbar went hunting. I worked diligently.

Wednesday, November 24

That day almost all of the brethren and sisters returned home. First came Sr. Thamar, Caritas with her children, Elisabeth with her children, and Agnes with her children. Late in the evening Br. Joshua, Samuel, and Jeremias returned from hunting. They had a fairly successful hunt.

Thursday, November 25

I wanted to conduct [a] quarter-of-an-hour in the morning, but was hindered. I visited the brethren who had returned home late yesterday evening. They all were quite lively and cheerful. My heart felt very much comforted by them. Br. Petrus returned home as well. I worked diligently.

Friday, November 26

We conducted a blissful quarter-of-an-hour[d] in the morning. The Lamb[d] was intimately near us with His wounds. Two of the neighbors came here to haul wood. One cart hauled [wood] for me all day long, and the other for the Indian brethren.

Saturday, November 27

We again had a blissful quarter-of-an-hour[d] in the morning. Today the two neighbors came back with their carts; they hauled wood for the Indian brethren. I went visiting in the winter huts. David and Rebecca had returned home yesterday. They were most amiable. Leah greatly lamented about her poor circumstances. Br. Joshua visited in the evening.

Sunday, November 28

We had no quarter-of-an-hour in the morning. In the general Sunday meeting I talked about Heb. 10.24, 25. The Lamb[d] was near us and revealed Himself to us. The house[d] was fairly full of brethren and sisters. Most of the unbaptized ones attended the meeting. In the quarter-of-an-hour for the baptized ones and the communicants, I talked about the beautiful text on the large side hole. My heart felt quite blissful. I portrayed the Lamb[d] with all of His wounds to the Indian hearts[d]. I was hoping that our dear heart[d] Sensemann would arrive, but he continued to stay out.

Monday, November 29

We had a blissful quarter-of-an-hour in the morning. The brethren went hunting and returned home in the evening. I did some work on my house[d]. Br. Timotheus and Moses came from Wechquadnach for a visit. They intend to go to Gnadenhütten next week. I also went visiting in several huts.

Tuesday, November 30

We had [a] quarter-of-an-hour in the morning. Also, I resumed holding school. The brethren ~~came~~ went hunting and returned home in the evening. Br. Timotheus and Moses went back to Wechquadnach. In the evening I went out and bought candles. Br. Gottlieb and his son returned from hunting.

Wednesday, December 1

We had [a] quarter-of-an-hour in the morning. The Lamb[d] was intimately near us with His wounds. Br. Joshua interpreted. I held school. Also, I finished the work that I had intended to do before being able to go to Bethlehem.

Thursday, December 2

We had [a] quarter-of-an-hour in the morning. The Lamb[d] was intimately near us. I visited the brethren and sisters who were at home, reminding them of the Lamb[d] and His wounds. Held school with the children, and repaired the roof of my house[d]. In the evening the dear hearts Sensemann and Gideon came back from New York. They brought us many heartfelt and fervent greetings from our dear hearts who are going to Europe, especially from our precious Johann Nitschmann.[56] He [Nitschmann] also wrote a heartfelt letter[d] of farewell to the Indian brethren and sisters. My heart truly wept and I was very sorry that I had not been able to see our precious Johann one more time.

Friday, December 3

I arranged yet several necessary things in our house[d]. Br. Sensemann visited the brethren and sisters. Br. Gideon had enough to do recounting what he had experienced in New York and how the brethren [there] had received him.

Saturday, December 4

I readied myself early to go to the mill as it is fairly difficult for one brother alone if he has to leave Pachgatgoch. The Savior happily assisted me so that I returned home in good time. Br. Sensemann went visiting in the winter huts.

Sunday, December 5

I held the general meeting. The Lamb was intimately near me with His bloody wounds. Brother Joshua interpreted. Brother Sensemann conducted the quarter-of-an-hour for the baptized ones and the communicants. He also read to the Indian brethren and sisters the letters[d] that had been written to them. Moreover, Br. Sensemann announced to the brethren and sisters that I intended to leave from here for Bethlehem tomorrow. In the evening we also were visited by several brethren.

Monday, December 6

In the morning, by way of farewell, I once more conducted a quarter-of-an-hour for the brethren and sisters. They gave me many heartfelt greetings for the dear brethren and sisters in Bethlehem, Nazareth, and Gnadenhütten. Our dear heart[d] Sensemann accompanied me for 3 miles. He gave me many greetings and kisses of love for all of his dear hearts[d] in Bethlehem and Nazareth and Gnadenhütten. We took a heartfelt and tender leave of each other. The dear heart Sensemann turned around [to go] to his dear Indian assembly, and I took the most direct road to my dear brethren and sisters in Bethlehem. I had quite a blissful journey; the Lamb[d] was near me with His wounds.

[No diary entries until December 10]

Friday, December 10

I came to my dear hearts Michlers in Friedensthal.[57] They right away told me the joyous news that our dear heart Joseph [Spangenberg] had arrived from Europe and had been to their house.[58] I stayed with them that night.

Saturday, December 11

In the morning, I took my leave from the dear brethren and sisters in Friedensthal and went to Nazareth. [I] visited the children[d] and spent some time with

Br. Samuel and other brethren. Afterward, I went to Bethlehem. I immediately found my dear and precious heart Joseph, who welcomed me affectionately and lovingly, as did all of the dear hearts. What my poor heart felt at this time, I cannot describe, and I will not forget it. Now, my dear Lamb[d], my faithful Savior, be praised for all the precious faithfulness and patience that He has shown me, and in particular in Pachgatgoch, and that He has stood by me so steadfastly, and has helped me through.

Joachim Heinrich Sensemann
6 December 1751 to 15 April 1752

Pachgatgoch *Diarium*, the 6th of December, *Anno* 1751[1]

Added in *copia*[2] to the Bethlehem *diario* of January 1752[3]

Monday, December 6, 1751.

The watchword read: *Unter ihm wirds wachsen, und er wird bauen des Herren Tempel. Zech. 6.12. Die Kirch da er Ältster ist.*[4]

In the morning, the dear heart Abraham Büninger readied himself for his journey to our dear Bethlehem. Beforehand, he conducted the quarter-of-an-hour for the dear brown hearts[d]; almost everyone stayed on and bade him a heartfelt farewell, also sending many a greeting[d] to the dear hearts[d] in Bethlehem. I accompanied him for 3 miles from here, across the water, and then we embraced and kissed each other tenderly and dearly. I bade him salute the congregation in Bethlehem and Nazareth and the other places heartily, and not to forget me in my loneliness among the brown assembly. Thus I set out to return; found the Indian brethren digging out and lining their spring with stones. I too helped with it. Afterward, I went home and cooked food for myself, but it did not taste any good to me. That same evening I cried many a tear[d] before the pierced feet of the Lamb[d], for myself and the brown assembly.

Tuesday, the 7th.

I conducted [a] quarter-of-an-hour in the morning; entrusted the brown assembly to the pierced heart of the Lamb[d] by means of a heartfelt prayer. I felt very comfortable on this occasion. Before noon I held school with the boys, and after noon, [with the] girls. Afterward, I went visiting. [The] Joshuas and

[the] Samuels came, saying that they intended to go into the woods to hunt, and the sisters, to make brooms and baskets. They took a heartfelt leave of me. Benigna, Simon's daughter, took leave to go along with Caritas to Newtown to work there.

I went visiting in all the houses and talked with them about their hearts. Most were blissful and in good spirits. Some felt poor; I directed them to the Lamb[d] and His bloody wounds, wherein they can be quite blissful and cheerful. In the evening I held the quarter-of-an-hour on the Lamb's text: *Er fürete sein Volck wie eine Herde Schaafe.*[5]

Wednesday, the 8th.

I conducted the quarter-of-an-hour in the morning on the Lamb's text: *Freuet euch ihr Heiden mit seinen Volck.*[6] I felt comfortable on this occasion. Martin interpreted. In the forenoon I held school with the boys. Next, David came from the winter huts where we had lived the previous winter. I took him into my house and talked with him about various matters concerning our bloody Lamb[d] and His wounds. I believe it was a blessing for him.

Later, he [David], Gottlieb and his 2 sons, Martin, and an unbaptized one by the name of Weiti set [out] and went hunting. They came and took leave of me beforehand; they thought to return home next Saturday.

In the afternoon I held school with the girls. I gave each child a *biskit* [biscuit], which the New York brethren and sisters had sent with me. They were greatly pleased by it. I also went to several brethren and sisters to visit them, but only a few are at home.

Thus we suspended our quarter-of-an-hour. Late in the evening an English man, who had been hunting, came into my house. He lodged that night with Gideon.

Thursday, the 9th.

Before noon I held school with the boys, and past noon, with the girls. I visited old Maria, the mother of Petrus and Christian, who had been down in Danbury for 2 months. I talked with her about her heart. She was full of light and in good spirits; said she was grateful to the Savior that she was back at home.

I visited Christian, who also had returned home from hunting.

Friday, the 10th.

I held school again. Visited Gideon, Petrus, [and the] Priscillas. All of them were well and in a happy state.

Jeremias returned home from hunting, yet had not shot anything.

Saturday, the 11th.

I went visiting in the winter huts on this and the other side of the river, yet found no one at home other than the ill Maria, Sister Sarah's daughter, along with several other children. Also went to an English house to buy some white bread. On returning, I found our dear brethren and sisters, [the] Joshuas and [the] Samuels at home, having come back from hunting, blissful and full of light.

Toward evening [the] Gottliebs came home as well, together with the other brethren. They had shot only one buck, 1/2 of which Gottlieb presented to David, and 1/4 to Martin.

We had a blessed quarter-of-an-hour[d] in the evening. I talked about the watchword: *Ihr solt mir ein pristerlich Königreich sein.*[7]

Sunday, the 12th.

In the morning, Sr. Magdalena came and brought me a piece of the deer that her husband had shot. Also, old Erdmuth returned home with her daughter Martha, and [with] Johanna, Martha's daughter.

The brethren and sisters from the winter huts having arrived, I held the general meeting, and in the afternoon, I conducted a quarter-of-an-hour for the baptized ones. It was a blessing for all of them. I also talked with Brother David about his heart; he was well and full of light.

Monday, the 13th.

We had [a] quarter-of-an-hour in the morning; Joshua interpreted. After that I held school; in the forenoon with the boys, and in the afternoon with the girls. Paulus returned home from hunting.

We had a blessed quarter-of-an-hour in the evening. Gideon and Samuel stayed on with me for a while. His stay in New York has been a true blessing for Gideon. He intends to go to Bethlehem next spring to visit the congregation.

Tuesday, the 14th.

In the morning, after the quarter-of-an-hour, Br. Joshua went to Newtown to have his gun[8] worked on. I held school before and after noon. We had [a] quarter-of-an-hour in the evening; Martin interpreted. My heart felt quite warm on this occasion.

Wednesday, the 15th.

Following the early quarter-of-an-hour the Indian brethren made preparations to drive[9] the sleds. I gave them ropes for this purpose, which I had brought from New York. They were amazed [*words crossed out*] that I had ropes, for they had already been in a quandary on this account. Some drove and others ~~made~~ cut wood for themselves in the woods. We had a passionate quarter-of-an-hour in the evening; the Lamb[d] was near me. I talked about the Lamb's text: *Weißet meine Kinder und das Werck meiner Hende zu mir.*[10]

Thursday, the 16th.

Gideon stayed on after the quarter-of-an-hour and told me that he intended to go into the woods to search for his pigs. Now that there was snow on the ground, he would be better able to find them.

I held school twice. The Indian brethren cut wood. Things are proceeding quietly and agreeably among them. The Lamb[d] is with us. What is most difficult is that they live so dispersed. Gideon came home in the evening, but had not found his pigs. He said they have probably been stolen.

Friday, the 17th.

In the morning, following the quarter-of-an-hour, I went on the mountain to visit sick Juliana. Found her in a fairly poor state with respect to her tabernacle. I talked with her about her heart. She was joyful and well. She said she had given herself to the Savior. Her husband Gottlob had just left to go hunting in the woods when I came. Her mother, Erdmuth, was somewhat saddened on account of her daughter, for it appears that she will go home. I said that the dear Savior had died for ~~them~~ us, and that He had all the enemies under His feet, so that our soul[d] would simply fly from the tabernacle into His side hole[d]. Once the heart was inside, we need not worry about anything else. I also visited Martha and her daughter Johanna, Br. Gideon's wife and daughter, who live up there as well. Gideon had talked with Martha about her son's bad conduct, and had said that such people were not suited to be in Pachgatgoch; they could go to some other place. This had offended her and [so she] moved with Johanna and her daughter to her mother on the mountain. However, they are very uneasy about it. I was not able to talk much with them. We had a blessed quarter-of-an-hour in the evening. I talked about the Lamb's text: *Also hat Gott die Welt geliebt das er seinen eingebohren Sohn her gab.*[11] Martin interpreted. He stayed on after the quarter-of-an-hour and said he wished from the bottom of his heart that all the brethren and sisters may ~~had~~ have felt this in their hearts the way he had. He is a blissful heart[d]; may the Lamb[d] preserve him this way. The brethren were worried because Joshua was staying out so long; they had decided to send someone for him if he did not come home tomorrow.

Saturday, the 18th.
I conducted [a] quarter-of-an-hour in the morning. Afterward, I washed my laundry. It was very cold that day. Joshua came home in good spirits. The man where he had to carry out his business had not been home. Our Indian brethren hauled wood with 2 sleds. We had [a] quarter-of-an-hour in the evening; Joshua interpreted. Samuel and his wife stayed on with me.

Sunday, the 19th.
I conducted the general occasion in the forenoon. David and his wife and children, likewise Sarah and Leah, as well as several unbaptized ones from the winter huts were here, as was old Erdmuth. She came to me following the occasion and talked with me about her heart. Next, I conducted a quarter-of-an-hour for the baptized ones, wherein I felt most comfortable. Also talked with David about the Savior and His wounds. He was lively and full of light. Moreover, I informed the brethren and sisters that I intended to go to Wechquadnach on Monday or Tuesday, and with that we ended the day quite blissfully and in good spirits. Lucas and Johannes came home from the hunt late.

Monday, the 20th.
After the quarter-of-an-hour I summoned Gideon to have breakfast with me, which he did. I talked with him about his wife. He went to visit her. He also brought me a greeting from sick Juliana; had talked with her about her heart.

She had said that she thought of nothing else but of the Savior and His wounds. (Johannes and Paulus went to Danbury to sell skins[12] and to buy blankets in exchange.) I held school twice. We had [a] quarter-of-an-hour in the evening; I felt quite comfortable thereat.

Tuesday, the 21st.
I conducted the quarter-of-an-hour in the morning. After the quarter-of-an-hour I informed the brethren and sisters that I intended to go to Wechquad-nach to visit the brethren and sisters there. Thus they gave me many a greet-ing[d] to pass on to the brethren and sisters at that place. I gave Samuel the key to the house and set out on my journey. I arrived in Wechquadnach that after-noon, finding them [the Indians] in the winter houses. They were glad when they saw me. I saluted them from the brethren and sisters in Pachgatgoch and Bethlehem, at which they rejoiced. I talked with them about their hearts. Sr. Hannah was full of light and in good spirits. Susanna was somewhat sad. She said that her brother has died, which has been very difficult for her. I then talked with them about various matters concerning our wounded Husband and His wounds, and that He wanted for us to be blissful and cheerful hearts[d] inside His wounds. Timotheus had traveled to Gnadenhütten 4 weeks previ-ous. I also talked with the unbaptized ones about the Savior and His love for the poor Indians. They thought I would stay there that night and made arrange-ments for where I was to sleep. But I said that I was not able to stay this time; I would stay with them longer next time. I expected a brother from Bethlehem tomorrow—and that we would have Communion in Pachgatgoch next Satur-day. I wished to see them there that Friday. They were pleased to hear it. Han-nah said she intended to come unless her sickly tabernacle stopped her. I still set out, and on Wednesday, the 22nd, walked by moonlight 6 miles to the son of Hans [Johannes] Rau, where I stayed overnight. In the morning I set out from there for Pachgatgoch. I found all of the brethren and sisters well; they were glad to see me again. That evening I conducted the quarter-of-an-hour on the Lamb's text; Samuel interpreted.

Thursday, the 23rd.
Following the quarter-of-an-hour I felt very sickly inside my tabernacle. I made some tea for myself; thought about lying down in my bed. Unexpectedly, the

dear heart Grube stepped into the house. We embraced and kissed each other quite tenderly; my illness subsided for joy. He brought me many a letter[d], greeting[d], and kiss[d] from the dear hearts in Bethlehem and Nazareth, and especially from the dear and precious heart Joseph Spangenberg, at which I deeply rejoiced. It was no small joy to the dear brown hearts[d] that the congregation remembers them so faithfully. They all welcomed him warmly, baptized ones and unbaptized ones. Past noon we went together on the mountain, 2 miles from here, and visited sick Juliana and her mother Erdmuth. Brother Grube talked with the sick sister about her heart. She declared that she felt well and cheerful in her heart. He also talked with her about Communion. She said her heart hungered and thirsted for the Savior's flesh and blood. Erdmuth too was well and full of light. The others were not at home, except for 2 girls with whom we also talked about the Savior and His wounds with a feeling heart. Gideon came to us. With him we talked about a conference tomorrow morning, which he thought would be good. In the evening the dear heart Grube conducted a blessed quarter-of-an-hour, also passing on the greetings from the congregation in Bethlehem and Gnadenhütten, and that the congregation wished them deeply into the wounds and the side hole[d] of the Lamb[d], for which they were heartily grateful. In the evening the dear heart Grube read to me the heart-refreshing *Gemein-Nachrichten*,[13] as well as the speeches by dear, precious Papa,[14] and then we went to rest blissfully and with a happy heart in the soft bed[d] of our Husband's side hole[d].

Friday, the 24th.

Br. Grube conducted the quarter-of-an-hour in the morning. After the quarter-of-an-hour[15] we had the conference brethren and sisters stay on in our house; talked with them about Communion, and that we intended to have a love feast with all the baptized ones beforehand, and for that we needed someone to get bread, which Sensemann had already ordered baked. Samuel furnished his horse for this purpose, and Simon's son got it [the bread]. Then we began speaking with the brethren. They were fairly straight; they said how they stood with the Savior at this time. Samuel was not a sinner with respect to the circumstances that had come to pass with him that summer; [he] was looking to blame other brethren.[16] Hence, he was not able to join Communion this time. Afterward, we started speaking with the sisters. Joshua was present most of the time. We felt the close presence of the Lamb[d] in our hearts. Although there were various matters that, to be sure, caused us pain, the Lamb[d] nonetheless helped us through everything.[17] In the evening ~~conducted~~ the dear heart Grube conducted the quarter-of-an-hour.

Saturday, the 25th.

On the first Christmas morning the dear heart Grube conducted the quarter-of-an-hour, with blessing. He talked to the brown hearts[d] about the child[d] Jesus, who was born that night. Afterward, we also spoke with several brethren and sisters, especially with Gideon and Martha. She said that we would probably not take her along to Communion, for she was living on the mountain and far away from us. We said we did not want to start in on that, she should simply tell us about the state of her heart, and whether she loved her husband. As she [sic] we started speaking with her of her heart, she wept; ~~and~~ they both became sinners and forgave each other, and she went home with her husband and both were in good spirits and full of light. Next, Br. Grube translated with Br. Joshua 2 verses from German into the Womponaeksche tongue.[18] The first, *O wie weind mein Herz*; and the 2nd, *Drück unß an dein Hertze an deine Wunden*.[19] Joshua made it known in all of the houses [that] all the children shall come to the quarter-of-an-hour at the blowing of the horn. However, because there was not enough time, we were unable to have word sent to the other places. We also made preparations for the small love feast, and this we held with them with buttered slices of bread. Twenty-four came to the love feast. Br. Grube sang several verses[d] with them and told them about our little Jesus, that He too had become such a small child and that He loved them very much. We felt quite comfortable on this occasion. Br. Grube went into several houses to visit. He talked with old Maria's sister. She expressed the desire to become the Savior's. Br. Martin and his wife Justina came and applied for the baptism of their little son[d]. This was promised them and they were overjoyed about it. Several unmarried persons also came, requesting to be baptized. We promised to remember them. A quarter-of-an-hour was conducted with the communicants, during which a longing for the

Savior's flesh and blood was felt. At the same time, the brethren and sisters were informed that, at dark, a public occasion would take place, wherein the son[d] of our Br. and Sr. Martin is to be baptized. Also, that when there was now the blowing [of the horn], we would come together for the love feast. Then preparations were made for the love feast. We had slices of buttered bread and chocolate. Also, the 2 new verses were read and sung to the brethren and sisters. They were very pleased by this. Thus the general service took place at dark, during which our dear heart Grube talked about the bloody stream coming from Jesus' side. This was accompanied by a blissful feeling. Then the son[d] of our Br. and Sr. Martin was baptized into the side-holed [word crossed out] death of Jesus and named Jacob. A short while after this meeting, the communicants gathered for the absolution, at which time our beloved Husband looked most graciously upon His brown assembly of sinners and gave absolution. And immediately thereafter the blissful enjoyment of the flesh and blood of Jesus Christ took place. His brown assembly was revived entirely anew, and inside their dear patamaos[20] they felt very much in the spirit [of the Lord] entering them. And with that everyone retired blissfully to Jesus' wounds. This time 20 brown hearts were partakers. Some were not were not at at home, and some stayed away of their own accord because of their circumstances.

Sunday, the 26th.

After our breakfast we set out together with Br. Joshua, and went on the mountain to sick Juliana to take Communion to her. She was quite hungry and eager for it. We also talked once more with her daughter about the Savior and baptism, for which she had asked. Then we returned home. Gihorn and Schiri came to us and talked about their hearts—that they would like to be baptized. We reflected upon it before the Savior, but did not get assurance in this matter yet. They are two special men on whom the Savior has been working for a long time. Sr. Martha came and said her son Maramob talked to her at length about his heart last night. At the child's baptism yesterday he had thought, if only he could become as blissful as this child. He felt very wicked and corrupted in his heart and desired to be helped. At 12 o'clock the general sermon took place. Br. Grube talked about the text Jesus hing am Chreutze[21] and portrayed the bloody

Savior with His wounds to the brown hearts. Magdalena came and said that her oldest son Nakpan had a great longing to be baptized, and has not been able to sleep for several nights because of it. We summoned him and talked with him, and found that there was a sincere desire present in his heart. We also spoke with David's son, who also demonstrated a longing for the Savior and for baptism. Br. Grube visited the brethren and sisters in their huts, finding them quite blissful and full of light, also told them that now was a good opportunity if they wanted to write to Papa, Br. Johannes [von Watteville], and Mother Anna [Nitschmann], which pleased them greatly. Next, there was the quarter-of-an-hour for all the baptized ones, wherein we recommended ourselves anew to our bloody Husband and His wounds. In the evening Br. Sensemann conducted the service and talked about little Jesus, who became so poor for us, and so this day too was blissfully closed.

Monday, the 27th.
Brother Grube delivered the morning blessing. Next, the brethren and sisters came and dictated to Brother Grube [a] letter for dear Papa, Johannes, and Mother, greatly rejoicing at that, and that they had so many more brethren and sisters across the great water. Br. Grube and Joshua translated into the Wompanoa tongue the verse[d] _In unßers Hertzens Grunde p[p], erschein uns in den Bilde, p[p]_.[22] Thereupon we talked with the candidates for baptism, and the Savior gave us 2 to be baptized into His death. We consoled the others by holding out hopes for the future. There was a general meeting in the evening, and in the course of it, 2 hearts were baptized with the blood of Jesus. The first one was Gottlieb and Magdalena's son, about 18 years old. Br. Grube baptized him, naming him Philippus. The other one was Martha's son, about 20 years old, whom Brother Sensemann baptized and named Jonathan. The Savior was quite near all of us during this holy act. The brethren and sisters were exceedingly happy about these 2 new brethren. They all went into their huts in good spirits. I wrote in the _diearium_. Br. Grube went from hut to hut to visit one more time, and had a pleasant talk about the Savior at Schirry's, where there were several other unbaptized ones. I then wrote several letters to my dear hearts in Bethlehem, and with that we went to bed, blissful and in good spirits.

Diarium for Pachgatgoch, December 28, 1751.

Tuesday, December 28, 1751.

The watchword read: *Bleib beij uns.* Lk. 24.29. *Da hast du Herz, und Hände, daß wir bis an das Ende wolln deine treue Seelen seijn.*[23]

Following the quarter-of-an-hour the Indian brethren and sisters stayed on and took leave of Br. Grube, sending heartfelt greetings to the congregation[s] in Bethlehem, Nazareth, as well as to the brown congregation[d] in Gnadenhütten. Br. Grube then set out on his journey to Bethlehem by way of New York. ~~Sensemann~~ I accompanied him as far as Gaylords, where they[24] kissed and took a heartfelt leave of each other. I bought some bread for myself and set out to return to my dear brown brethren and sisters, all of whom I found well. In the evening I conducted the quarter-of-an-hour; Joshua interpreted.

Wednesday, the 29th.

After the morning blessing I held school with the boys, and then with the girls. I went into all the houses to visit, finding the brethren and sisters full of light and in a happy state. I conducted the quarter-of-an-hour in the evening on the watchword: *Sehet, jetz ist die angenehme Zeit.*[25] I was able to portray the bloody wounds of our God on the cross to the brown assembly passionately [and] with a feeling heart.

Thursday, the 30th.

After the quarter-of-an-hour I went with Br. Petrus on the mountain, visiting sick Sister Juliana and the other brethren and sisters there. They were lively and in good spirits. I also talked with Brother Jonathan, who is feeling well in his heart following his baptism. I told him to stay with his heart in the Savior and His wounds at all times. He was now like a small child who was born and constantly needed to enjoy his mother's milk; so too was he in need of nourishment from the wounds of the Savior. Petrus and I cut a piece of wood from which we made a trough for me to use. In the evening, following the quarter-of-an-hour, several brethren stayed on with me, to whom I had to sing the new verses[d] that Brother Grube had translated, so that they could learn the melody.

Friday, the 31st.

Sr. Priscilla came after the morning blessing and brought me 1/2 [loaf of] bread and a piece of cheese that Gaylord, a separatist from New Milford, was sending me, who requested that I please visit him sometime. In the forenoon I held school with the boys, and past noon with the girls. We had a blessed quarter-of-an-hour in the evening. I remembered the blessed time that our congregations will now have again. I also felt quite comfortable in my heart, and my spirit was with them, I could feel that.

Saturday, _Januari[us]_ 1, 1752, _n. st._

The dear Savior's words read: _Da ward sein Nahme genenet Jesus._[26] At the morning quarter-of-an-hour I informed the brown assembly that today was the first day of the new year. Entrusted myself and the brown hearts to the pierced heart of our Lamb and Chief Elder by means of a prayer of the heart, and that He may flood us anew with the stream from His bloody side and wash away all of the old. Gideon came from the mountain, bringing me word from the brethren and sisters there. Magdalena said her son Mackwa had told her with a sad heart, now that his brother also had been baptized with the Savior's blood, that he felt as if all the baptized ones had traveled to another town and he has been left behind alone. In the evening I talked about the Lamb's text.

Sunday, the 2nd.

Several brethren came to visit me. Thereupon the brethren and sisters from the winter huts came, and so I conducted the general service. Afterward, I talked with Jonathan, who is feeling blissful and full of light since his baptism. Next I talked with Johannes and his wife Leah. Something had come between them. I conducted a quarter-of-an-hour for the married people, at which they rejoiced. In the evening I was paid a visit by several unbaptized ones, with whom I talked about their hearts. I sensed the Savior's work on their hearts.

Monday, the 3rd.

I delivered the morning blessing at an early hour. Lucas and Johannes went hunting. Paulus and 2 unbaptized ones went to Wanachquaticok. Several sisters went out with baskets. The brethren were hard at work, hauling wood. After school I went visiting, finding everyone who was at home in a happy state. Sr. Thamar has been feeling sickly for several days, but she appears to be improving. She was desirous of joining the occasion again, but I could not advise her to that end. We had a blessed quarter-of-an-hour in the evening; I talked about the Lamb's text: *Simeon nahm ihm auf seine Arme p[p].*[27]

Tuesday, the 4th.

After the morning blessing I held school with the boys, and past noon with the girls. We had [a] quarter-of-an-hour in the evening. The Lamb was especially near me, and the bloody wounds were sparkling among us. The brown hearts have been especially full of light and in good spirits since last Communion. In the evening I visited Jeremias and Agnes; they were very affectionate. Joshua and Elisabeth were also there.

Wednesday, the 5th.

After the morning blessing I readied myself to visit the brethren and sisters in the winter huts; found Sr. Sarah and the other sisters well. Gihorn was happy that I came to visit him; took me to the other side [of the river], to David's hut, who had gone hunting with his son. Rebecca was in a happy state and full of light; she was glad that I came to visit her. I also found old Maria there, who is quite lively and full of light. On [my arrival] home, several brethren and sisters came and said that the soul of Sr. Priscilla's sick daughter[d] appeared to be flying away. I went to visit her together with Gideon. I indeed found her to be very ill and emaciated. Her mother said that a short while ago she had said to her, if only she could be baptized with the Savior's blood beforehand; she thought she was going to depart soon. And that her mother shall not grieve for her, for she was going to the Savior. I asked her if in her heart she felt a longing for the Savior's blood. She replied yes. Thereupon I consoled her [with the news] that the beloved Savior was willing to wash her with His blood and give her a new heart and life. However, we intended to baptize her tomorrow morning in the course of the morning blessing. Yet if she were to become worse, they should call me and several of the brethren and sisters.

Thursday, the 6th.

Gideon came and said that the little girl was becoming increasingly worse. Thus I had them make preparations in their house. Gideon informed the brethren and sisters that the morning blessing would be delivered in Priscilla's house, and that the sick child shall be baptized. After the blowing [of the horn], everyone assembled there. An Indian stranger from Potatuck was also present. I then said something, that the Savior had died on the cross and had shed His blood for the sins of the whole world, which those poor sinners experienced in their hearts who knew not how to help themselves and came to Him with their poverty and depravity. All of His merit and His righteousness would be given to them to own [words crossed out] and to wear—with which they could enter heaven,[28] p[p]. Having sung several verses, we stood up. Sr. Priscilla, who was seated behind the sick girl, sat her up and held her in her arms. Thereupon I stepped up and absolved her in the name of our Husband and Chief Elder, blessed the water with a heartfelt prayer, and [asked] that the Savior may let the stream that flowed from His side flow into this water.[29] And then she was flooded with the stream from Jesus' side and received the name Esther. The Savior's presence was palpable, to which the brown brethren and sisters also testified following the baptism. Some of the brethren went out hunting. I held school with the boys. We had a blessed quarter-of-an-hour[d] in the evening.

Friday, the 7th.

Gideon came to my door in the morning, at daybreak, saying that Esther appeared to be going home now. I went there, finding her fairly bad. I consecrated her through the laying on of hands during the singing of several verses[d]. She recovered, though. All of the sisters from the winter huts came to visit her. I held school. Lucas, Esther's brother, came home from hunting along with Johannes. Each brought a deer with him. In the evening, after the quarter-of-an-hour, the brethren held a conference in Gideon's house on account of outward circumstances. I visited sick Esther. She was having continuous convulsions. At about 11 o'clock Gideon came and told me that she had now gone home.

Saturday, the 8th.

After the quarter-of-an-hour the brethren asked when I thought the tabernacle[d] of little Esther should be put into the ground. We decided on Sunday,

265

at 1 or 2 o'clock. Johannes went to Wechquadnach. Beforehand, I spoke with him about his heart and still other circumstances related to his wife. I went 2 miles from here and bought some bread and salt for myself. Martin made the coffin. Several brethren made a fire on the spot where the grave is to be dug so that the ground would thaw, for it was frozen more than 1 and 1/2 feet deep.[30] Because our brethren wanted to go into the sweat house, we ~~held~~ had the quarter-of-an-hour a little earlier.

Sunday, the 9th.
The brethren and sisters from the winter huts having gathered, I conducted the general service. Schiry and his mother came from 4 miles away to attend the meeting. The bloody wounds of our God were near me, and everyone listened *aten* [attentively]. After the blowing [of the horn] at 2 o' clock, everyone gathered in our house. Following a brief address, the tabernacle[d] of Sr. Esther was taken to her place[d] of rest. It proceeded in a nice and orderly fashion. Because it was such rainy weather, everyone[31] stayed here. That evening I also conducted a quarter-of-an-hour. The house was fairly full. Several [brethren and sisters] stayed on with me after the quarter-of-an-hour, and with that the day was ended blissfully.

Monday, the 10th.
We had [a] quarter-of-an-hour in the morning. Afterward, I butchered a small pig[d] that I had fattened some. Petrus and Samuel helped me. A sister brought word to me that Sister Juliana was having convulsions.

Tuesday, the 11th.
After the quarter-of-an-hour Br. Martin came and took his leave, saying that he intended to go out on horseback with baskets [to sell]. Moreover, almost all of the brethren readied themselves to go hunting. I went on the mountain and visited sick Juliana; found her in a very bad state with respect to her tabernacle. I asked her how she felt in her heart when she thought that the Savior might perhaps call her to Him. She smiled and said she felt most comfortable with it; the Savior shall take her if He wanted to, her heart was feeling His wounds, p[p]. I rejoiced over her. I read and sang to her the verses[d] that Br. Grube and

Joshua had translated. She delighted in them. Her mother, Erdmuth, was also in a happy state and full of light, and so were the others. Johannes came home from Wechquadnach full of light and in good spirits. We did not have [a] quarter-of-an-hour as nearly everyone was out.

Wednesday, the 12th.

I held school twice. Br. Martin came home toward evening. I conducted the quarter-of-an-hour; Martin interpreted.

Thursday, the 13th.

In the forenoon I held school with the boys, and in the afternoon, with the girls. Martha came down from the mountain with her son Jonathan, who right away came to visit me. I asked him how he felt in his heart. He said that he felt well. Also, the brethren returned home from hunting, lively and full of light, yet had not shot anything. We had [a] quarter-of-an-hour in the evening; I talked about the Lamb's texts. I felt quite comfortable thereat.

Friday, the 14th.

After the quarter-of-an-hour I held school with the boys. There also came an English man to visit me. Our Indian brethren were hard at work splitting [fence] rails. I visited several brethren and sisters whom I found well and quite full of light. In the afternoon I held school with the girls.

Saturday, the 15th.

In the morning, following the quarter-of-an-hour, I had a small love feast with the 2 newly baptized single brethren. They were heartily full of light and well; I am happy about the grace that the Lamb[d] has bestowed on them. The brethren were busy hauling wood. I did some of my white wash. Br. Martin came to visit me; I spoke with him about his heart. He said that he felt well and blissful in his heart and knew of nothing that could disturb him in this. Christian returned home from New Milford, Schiris from his winter house. In the evening, following the quarter-of-an-hour, several brethren stayed with me for a good while.

Sunday, the 16th.

Because it was so very cold I thought that surely no one would come from the winter huts. Yet, soon after, Jonathan and several others came down from the mountain, and after a short while, Gideon came and said that all the brethren and sisters were here. Thereupon I right away made preparations and blew the horn. Thus everyone assembled in our house so that they hardly had room to sit. The Lamb[d] was near us. For the text I had Rom. 8.32, Ist Gott für uns wer mag wieder uns sein, p[p].[32] Past noon all of the baptized brethren and sisters came alone. I conducted a Bible lesson for them based on the 3rd and 4th chapter[s] in Matthew, because the Lamb's texts throughout this week had dealt with the Savior's temptation; Joshua interpreted. They all listened atent [attentively]. I talked with Sr. Leah. Joshua and her mother Sarah were present. Because her husband Johannes had stayed out several times for long periods, she had carpingly told him to leave, which he did. He had stayed for a while in Gnadenhütten last summer. Now he would like to set the matter right again, but it cannot be done yet. I also talked with Christian, who had stayed awhile in New Milford, pointing out to him that, [now that he was one of the] brethren, things could no longer go on in the same manner as with the unbaptized Indians, intent on following their old ways. He recognized this himself, with sadness. Petrus and his wife Thamar came to me, saying how they stood in their hearts. He said that he felt very poor. I directed him to the Savior and His bloody wounds; they were open for those who are poor. Thus this day too was ended with blessing.

Monday, the 17th.

After the morning blessing I visited Schirÿ. He is very amiable. He told me at length about the bad state into which he had brought himself. I said that the Savior was able to help him out of everything; he shall simply give himself up to Him. He expressed his longing to this end. I held school with the boys. Afterward, an unmarried person[33] came to me; said whether I had heard that he intended to marry Benigna, Simon's daughter, and what I thought of it. I said I had heard about this at some point, but she had not told me anything about it. I would have indeed preferred that he had given his heart to the Savior beforehand, and if he intended to live according to his mind and will, it would be better for both of them if he married an unbaptized Wildinn [Wilden].[34] But he said that he wanted to give his heart to the Savior. He only desired that a brother would come from Bethlehem. Did I not know at what time a brother was coming? I was unable to tell him a specific time, however. I told him, given that the two of them had so far agreed with each other on this matter, I had nothing more to say about it; I wanted to wish them mercy and blessings for it. She [Benigna] went to his house that same day, to the place where the winter houses are.[35] It hurt me a little, to be sure, for she had enjoyed many a blissful time in the single sisters' house in Bethlehem. We had a blessed quarter-of-an-hour in the evening.

Tuesday, the 18th.

I delivered the morning blessing at an early hour. In the forenoon I held school with the boys. The Indian brethren were hard at work making [fence] posts and rails. Word came from the mountain that Juliana was very ill. I held school with the girls. Gideon and several other brethren stayed on with me for a while after the quarter-of-an-hour.

Wednesday, the 19th.

I went on the mountain to visit sick Juliana and the other brethren and sisters there, finding all of them well. Sr. Juliana lay there like a sheep, greatly emaciated. She is merely waiting for the Savior to call her home. It delighted her when she heard that I was there. I then talked with her about the Savior and His wounds, at which she rejoiced. Jonathan went down with me. We had [a] quarter-of-an-hour in the evening; in my heart, I could feel the Savior near me with His bloody wounds. Jonathan and Philippus were with me for a while that evening. I also visited Martin and the stranger from Potatuck. That evening I very much felt like weeping, but did not know why.

Thursday, the 20th.

After the morning blessing the Indian brethren readied themselves to resume their work. They held a conference with one another because the hunt is now almost entirely over, ~~because~~ and the English, by [their] shooting, are taking away all of the deer from them. And when going to work among the white people, they suffered damage to their hearts. Hence, they intend to plant a lot of Welsh corn and work at home. (The Savior shall give His blessing for it; it surely will be better for their hearts.)[36] I went visiting in several houses, finding them [the brethren and sisters] quite well. We had no quarter-of-an-hour in the evening because the brethren were sweating. (I wrote in the *diearium*.)

Friday, the 21st.

Following [the] morning blessing I held school with the boys, and in the afternoon, with the girls. I called on Petrus and his wife Thamar. They both were well in their hearts and full of light. Sr. Priscilla and several others returned home from New Milford in good spirits. Toward evening there came word that Sister Juliana was very bad and that it appeared that her soul[d] was going to fly away. Gideon and her sister, Martha, set out at once and went to her. I too would have still liked to have gone there but was unable to being that it was so late. We had a blessed quarter-of-an-hour in the evening, and sang for Sister Juliana in Indian: *Seiten höhlgen[,] Seitenhöhl[,] Seiten höhlgen[,] sie ist dein.*[37]

Saturday, the 22nd.

Jonathan came down from the mountain in the morning, bringing word that Juliana had gone home yesterday evening. Joshua took several brethren with him to bring her down. I went 2 miles from here to buy some wheat bread as my stomach was very bad from the Indian bread, but was unable to get any since all the mills were frozen.[38] On returning home Gideon came and recounted how Juliana had been alert until breathing her last, and that up to that point he had spoken much with her about the Savior and His wounds. She reportedly replied that she thought of nothing else other than to mind the Savior and His wounds in her heart. At about 12 o'clock she is said to have gone home softly, without a stir. Everyone who until now had lived on top [of the mountain] came down. Joshua went and got board[s] for making the coffin. Preparations were made so that she could be buried tomorrow. We had the evening quarter-of-an-hour a little earlier, because the brethren wanted to sweat.

Sunday, the 23rd.

I had Gideon and several other brethren join me for breakfast. Because the sickly Maria, Sarah's daughter, desired so greatly to attend the meeting sometime, they brought her up from the winter huts on a sled. As soon as everyone was assembled, Joshua brought me word, and then the meeting was called by blowing [the horn]. A fair-sized assembly came together; my heart was burning for the brown assembly. I talked to them with a feeling and warm heart about the blessedness that a child of God experiences in fellowship with the beloved Savior and His wounds. After the meeting I spoke with Christian and his wife Gottliebe; he has put himself in a miserable situation as a result of his bad conduct. He had committed his son into servitude, and because he ran away, he had to take his place. I see this as divine providence on the part of the Savior, however. (Gideon said my wood was almost gone—should he not arrange for the brethren to cut wood for me? I had no objections, saying if they had the time at some point, it would be good.) Thereupon preparations were made for the burial of Sr. Juliana's tabernacle[d]. Following the blowing [of the horn], the brethren carried the body and set it in front of our door. Several verses were sung and a short address was delivered [about] how the Savior welcomed so lovingly into His bloody arms the poor sinners who came to Him with a broken heart, and showed them His bloody wounds that He had received for them, which we have observed about our Sister Juliana, p[p]. Next, the coffin was lifted up and German and Indian verses[d] were sung. The brethren and sisters walked in the same order as in our congregations;[39] it proceeded nicely and well. (Samuel came in the evening and said Gideon had arranged for the brethren to cut wood for me.)

Monday, the 24th.

Because there was such a fierce and cold wind blowing, I wanted to prevent the brethren from having wood cut for me. However, since they insisted, I gave Martha dried green corn, beans, and meat for her to cook for them. I went out with the brethren. Thus, before long, 3 sleds followed to haul the wood home. They brought home a fairly good amount indeed. Yet more than half [of the wood] stayed out [in the woods]. On returning home, Br. Gideon sent the food to our house and summoned the brethren. Joshua was the servant and distributed it. I sang one verse, *Mene nana hannemewe taquach*; in German, *Gieb unß unßer ewiges Brodt*,[40] p[p]. Then we ate. I said, the willingness of the brethren made me happier than as if someone had given me a big *present*, and I thanked them for their love. The stranger from Potatuck, who is staying here, joined us as well. We had a blessed quarter-of-an-hour[d] in the evening.

Tuesday, the 25th.

We had the morning blessing at an early hour; ~~and~~ before noon I held school with the boys. Afterward, I visited the brethren and sisters, all of whom I found well. Christian and the Indian stranger went to New Milford. Past noon I held school with the girls. Caritas came and talked with me about her heart. We had [a] quarter-of-an-hour in the evening. I talked about the Lamb's texts.

Wednesday, the 26th.

I delivered the morning blessing at an early hour. Jonathan and several other brethren went to New Milford to sell spoons[41] and other items. I held school twice. The other brethren were hard at work hauling wood. Sister Magdalena came to me and said that for several days she has not felt quite full of light in her heart. She has been holding something against her husband (he was supposed to have butchered a pig so that she would have some meat in the house, and he did not want to do it).

Thursday, the 27th.

Today, following the morning blessing, Gottlob came home and was very ill. He had been working for an English man. I visited him, but things had improved somewhat. In the forenoon I held school with the boys, and in the afternoon, with the girls. I went visiting in all the huts; the brethren and sisters were all in good spirits. Because our brethren were sweating, and several English men were lingering about here late, we had no quarter-of-an-hour in the evening. Philippus came home from New Milford.

Friday, the 28th.

I delivered the morning blessing at an early hour, entrusting the brown assembly to the pierced heart of our Husband and Chief Elder, p[p]., by means of a heartfelt prayer. Jonathan returned home from New Milford in good spirits. I went and visited the brethren and sisters in the winter huts. First I came to David, who was delighted to see me; he was well and full of light. He said he wanted to go with me across the ice to the other brethren and sisters to visit them now as well, and so we went together. I felt very comfortable about them; they all were affectionate and well. Joshua went out hunting. Returned home soon after, having shot a large buck. We had a blessed quarter-of-an-hour in the evening. My heart felt full of feeling and warmth from the blood and wounds of the Savior.

Saturday, the 29th.

After the morning blessing old Maria and Erdmuth stayed on with me; both are well and in a happy state. Erdmuth told me that she intended to go to her elderly brother in Potatuck next week; he is said to be 100 years old and no longer able to walk. Next, Gideon came and told me that last summer the old man had told him he wished he were in Pachgatgoch; his heart was longing to become the Savior's. There were several more like him at that place who have said they felt in their hearts that what they had heard from the brethren about the Savior was true. Today I was frequently with my heart in my dear Bethlehem, and felt a gentle quietude in my heart. I very much felt in the spirit of Communion and thought the congregation was perhaps enjoying the body of our Husband; thus, I went to sleep as if I had enjoyed it with them.

Sunday, the 30th.

In the forenoon I conducted the general service; had the text Jn. 20.19, 20. The Savior was near us with His bloody wounds. That afternoon I conducted a quarter-of-an-hour for all the baptized ones, and we enjoyed the kiss of love peace. Thamar came to me and lamented that she was not feeling well in her heart today. I asked what the cause of it was. She said that her husband Petrus had asked her for a long pipe,[42] and she had not wanted to give it to him, and so he became discontented with her. I said, when she got home she should right away give him a pipe and tell him that she had not done things nicely yesterday evening. She was pleased that I gave her this advice and said she wanted to do so at once. She said that her daughter Caritas told her that she felt a great hunger to eat the flesh and drink the blood of the Savior. Joshua sent me a piece of the deer that he had shot. The brethren went sweating.

Monday, the 31st.

We had the morning blessing at an early hour. The wounds of the Lamb sparkled among us. Several brethren stayed on with me for a while. Sr. Sarah (who had stayed here overnight) took leave of me and went to the winter huts where she lives. I went into several huts to visit. Afterward, I held school with the boys. Jonathan went to the winter huts to visit the brethren and sisters there. Two English men came and bought Welsh corn from several brethren. In the afternoon I held school with the girls. Visited [the] Gottliebs and several other brethren and sisters whom I found quite well and in good spirits. In the evening, following the quarter-of-an-hour, I had Petrus stay on with me and talked with him about his wife Thamar; I said he should tell her to come to me sometime tomorrow. However, she came that very evening and talked with me about her heart, as well as about the other circumstances related to her husband.

Tuesday, February 1.

I delivered the morning blessing at an early hour. Afterward, I went into several houses to visit. Gottlob went out again to work for an English man. Thereafter I held school with the boys, and after that, with the girls. I visited Brother Martin and Justina, asking them about their hearts. They both said that they felt well in their hearts. We had a blessed quarter-of-an-hour in the evening. The wounds of our Lamb^d of God were most sensible in my heart. Joshua and Elisabeth stayed on with me for a while; both are affectionate, full of light, and blissful. I reminded them to go visiting frequently this week and to talk with the brethren and sisters about their hearts. I intended to hold a conference on Sunday morning so that they could report to me on the brethren and sisters, which they promised to do.

Wednesday, the 2nd.

I delivered the morning blessing at an early hour. The Lamb^d was near us. The Indian brethren were hard at work hauling [fence] rails. Before noon I held school with the boys, and past noon with the girls. Toward evening Timotheus, who had returned home from Bethlehem 2 days before, came from Wechquadnach, bringing me a package of letters from our dear hearts in Bethlehem, from Br. Joseph [Spangenberg], [Matthew Godfrey] Hehl, Nathanael [Seidel], [Johann] Graff, and from my beloved wife and other hearts^d. This refreshed me anew and I delighted in the blissful news from Bethlehem and Gnadenhütten. Next, we had [a] quarter-of-an-hour. There was a special feeling of grace present. I told the Indian brethren and sisters that I had received letters from Bethlehem; I wanted ~~intended~~ to read from them next Sunday. They were happy about this.

Thursday, the 3rd.
After the morning blessing I had Timotheus join me for breakfast, who told me some things about Gnadenhütten, also, that his heart had been well. I spent the day cheerful and blissful with my precious letters[d] that I had received. Timotheus set out to return home, saying that he intended to come and visit us in about 14 days. I conducted the quarter-of-an-hour in the evening; Samuel interpreted.

Friday, the 4th.
Following the morning blessing I went to the winter huts, and from there to Aaron Gaylord to buy some provisions for myself. Because the weather was so bad, the people did not want to let me leave. Thus I stayed there. He [Gaylord] desired to hear something from me about the Savior, and so I told them about the Savior and His righteousness that He purchased for us on the cross with 1000 pains, p[p]. He fell on his knees and prayed most heartily.

Saturday, the 5th.
I set out again and came to my dear brown hearts[d]; found all of them in good order. I went into the house of Jeremias, finding Thamar there alone along with her 4 daughters. Because Agnes was lying down I asked whether she was ill. Thus, Thamar said she had a small child and showed me the little heart[d]; she had been delivered that morning. I wished her mercy and blessings for it [the newborn]. She thanked me most heartily. The brethren and sisters were all glad when they saw me back at home. We had [a] quarter-of-an-hour in the evening; the red wounds of Jesus were most feelingly near to me. Christian and Johannes returned home from New Milford.

Sunday, the 6th.
After breakfast, Joshua summoned the conference. Gideon, Joshua, and Elisabeth, and I first sang a verse in Indian, *Drück unß an dein Hertze*,[43] p[p]. They related to me some news about the brethren and sisters they had visited. Some had felt poor in their hearts. We were blissful together. As soon as the brethren

and sisters had assembled, Joshua came and informed me of it, and then the meeting was called by blowing [the horn]. I talked about the text from Psalm 64.9, 10; the wounds of Jesus were near me. Past noon, after the blowing [of the horn], all of the baptized ones came. Thus, I read to them from the letters that I had received from Bethlehem. They were delighted that the congregation thinks of them so much and that Br. Joseph ~~Spangenberg~~ himself would perhaps visit them. They openly gave thanks for it. Christian asked if I knew when a brother was going to come from Bethlehem so that he would not miss it, [for] he intended to go to Wanachquaticok. Beyond this I also talked with him about various matters concerning his heart.

Monday, the 7th.

I delivered the morning blessing at an early hour. The Lamb^d was near us. Old Erdmuth stayed with me for a while. I talked with her about her heart. She said that she felt well in her heart. I went visiting in nearly all the huts, with blessing. Next, I held school with the boys, and afterward, with the girls. Sr. Priscilla came and said that she intended to go to New Milford together with her daughter Benigna, expecting to stay out for 3 days. She was warm and full of feeling in her heart. We had [a] quarter-of-an-hour in the evening; Joshua interpreted. He is very lively and blissful. Jeremias sat with me for some hours and tearfully bemoaned his circumstances.

Tuesday, the 8th.

In the morning, I delivered the morning blessing at an early hour. Martin said that he intended to go to New Milford to sell spoons and other items. Gottlieb also took leave to go to the same place. I told them, if only their hearts felt the rosy red wounds of Jesus at all times, then they would have no worries. Erdmuth and her [grand]daughter Johanna went to Potatuck today. I held school.

Wednesday, the 9th.

I delivered the morning blessing at an early hour. Most of the Indian brethren went hunting. Gideon went to Kent. I went visiting in several huts. I held school; in the forenoon with the boys, and in the afternoon with the girls. In the evening the brethren returned home from hunting, but had not shot anything.

Thursday, the 10th.

Following the morning blessing, several brethren again went out hunting. I held school. Br. Martin returned home from New Milford in good spirits, as did Priscilla with her daughter Benigna. In the evening the brethren came home from hunting in a happy state. Petrus stayed with me for a while; he is lively and in good spirits.

Friday, the 11th.

After the morning blessing I washed my laundry. I visited Gottlieb, who has returned home from New Milford. Samuel and his wife Lucia went by sled to Kent to get boards. He intends to build a new house this spring. We had a blessed quarter-of-an-hour in the evening. Several brethren stayed on with me for a while. Martin told me how he had fared on his journey. He is a blissful heart^d.

Saturday, the 12th.

I delivered the morning blessing at an early hour, entrusting the brown assembly to the Lamb^d so that He may be feelingly near to each one with His bloody wounds. I felt quite comfortable on this occasion. I frequently thought of our dear Bethlehem. I visited several brethren and sisters and talked with them about their hearts. Christian came home from New Milford, Schiry from his winter house.

Sunday, the 13th.

Samuel came and said that all of the brethren and sisters were here. Thus I made preparations and called the meeting by blowing [the horn]. I talked about the text; the Savior was near us. That afternoon I held a meeting for all the baptized ones, wherein I felt quite comfortable. We also enjoyed the kiss of peace. Next, I visited Br. Martin, with whom a stranger is staying. I intended to talk somewhat with him about his heart, but he made off. The Savior is working on his heart, but he does not want to hear [anything]. On returning home I saw a man coming up in front of the Indian houses, thinking this person looked like a brother. That is when I heard him speaking English, and so, I thought, this is not a brother from Bethlehem. I went into the house and added wood to the fire, thinking that if this is a brother, he will be here soon. At that moment H. van Vleck flung his arms around my neck, embracing and kissing me. I did not know what to say for joy and surprise. Yet, I thought he had brought my wife with him—I asked whether my wife was here. He said no, but 4 more brethren were here, who were at the door by then, all of them flinging their arms around my neck. All the Indian brethren and sisters were already at our door, welcoming them with much love and surprise. They [the brethren] were Owen Rice, [John] Kingston, Van Teick, and Rieth.[44] Jeremias took their horses to an English man to have them fed. They brought many a heartfelt greeting[d] and kiss[d] for me and for the brown brethren and sisters in Pachgatgoch from the New York brethren and sisters. Thus, we were blissful in each other's company. That evening we resolved to hold a love feast for the baptized ones tomorrow. Joshua and Gideon brought Indian mats on which the brethren were to sleep, and so they laid down by the fire, in the Indian way.

Monday, the 14th.

In the morning I went to Gideon and said that we wanted to have a love feast, which pleased him greatly. He right away sent a brother to the brethren and sisters in the winter huts and had them informed. Soon after, baptized ones and unbaptized ones came up. After the blowing [of the horn], all of the brethren and sisters gathered in our house. Several verses having been sung, biskit [biscuits] and tea were passed round. The brown brethren and sisters delighted in the white ones, and the white ones even more so in the brown ones. Everyone felt quite well. Br. Rice related how matters were in New York, what the Savior was affecting with his red wounds in the hearts there. Moreover, that the beloved Savior now had also lit a fire here in Pachgatgoch, and that this shall burn stronger yet, so that many more [Indian] nations shall be kindled by it, at which they deeply rejoiced. Then we enjoyed the kiss of peace and parted quite cheerfully. Past noon Br. V. Vleck and Van Dyck took their leave of all the brethren and sisters in all of the huts and set out for New York by way of Esopus. I accompanied them. Brother Amos went with them to the man where the horses were. Br. Rice then told me much joyous news about Bethlehem and the synod, how blissful everything had been there. In the evening I called the quarter-of-an-hour by blowing [the horn], upon which everyone assembled. Br. Rice conducted it, talking about the text: *Ihr werdet mit Freuden Waßer schöpfen aus den Heill Brunen,*[45] p[p]. In the middle of his address, the brethren and sisters saw Gideon's house engulfed in flames. There was nothing to be saved. The wind was blowing so strongly that one could not help but think that all of them [the huts] would go up in flames. But the Savior allowed ~~it only~~ the fire only that one [hut]. That evening I gave Gideon a blenckete [blanket] off my bed as a present so that he could keep himself warm that night.

Tuesday, the 15th.

Brother Rice conducted the quarter-of-an-hour in the morning with blessing. Following the quarter-of-an-hour, all of the Indian brethren and Sisters remained seated. Then the New York brethren went round and took leave of each one [*words crossed out*]. An exceptional feeling of love was felt. The brown hearts felt shamed that the New York brethren and sisters have so much love for them. They sent heartfelt greetings to all the brethren and sisters in New York. After we had eaten breakfast, the brethren set out on their journey. I accompanied them almost as far as New Milford. The New York brethren could not express how comfortable they had felt among the brown brethren and sisters. They would not trade their having been here for anything. Having embraced and kissed one another, I set out to return. By the time I arrived home, the brown hearts[d] had almost finished building another house[d] for Gideon. I was not able to watch it without weeping, that is how much this delighted me. Gideon and Joshua had sent Jonathan to Potatuck to tell Martha and Erdmuth that their house and belongings had burned, so that they would not be frightened when they came up and suddenly heard about it.

Wednesday, the 16th.

I delivered the morning blessing. The bloody wounds of our God were feelingly among us. [The] Joshuas, Samuel, and Jeremias went to Woodbury. Lucia and several other sisters went to New Milford. Before noon I held school with the boys, and past noon with the girls. I visited several brethren and sisters. I conducted the quarter-of-an-hour in the evening; Martin interpreted.

Thursday, the 17th.

Following the morning blessing I went to visit the brethren and sisters in the winter huts. I talked with all of them about their hearts. They were full of feeling and well. When I came home, Sr. Priscilla and her daughter came to visit.

I conducted the quarter-of-an-hour in the evening; talked to the brown brethren and sisters with a feeling and warm heart. That evening Br. Martin and Justina came to visit. Several other brethren were there as well.

Friday, the 18th.

After the morning blessing I intended to go to [John] Mills to pay for the [feeding of the] horses. But I did not feel quite right about it; contemplated it for more than one hour. Because I had to go across the ice, it occurred to me that I might fall in. I took out the *commen prayer* [book], therefore, and opened it to a verse. I got the 4th verse from the prayerful hymn *Und ihr geliebten Brüder,*[46] p[p]. That made me even more hesitant, but I felt in my heart an eagerness to go. When I reached the *krick* [creek] from which Pachgatgoch derives its name, it was thawed in the center, though a rail had been laid over it, and I got safely across it and also across the river.[47] [When I arrived] at Mills's, the woman told me that, before this, she had experienced much from the Savior. When I asked her how matters stood now, she wept and said that she had strayed from the Savior's love and had fallen into disgrace. Thus, I directed her straight to the Savior and His wounds. She was very happy that she could talk with me about the Savior. Then I set out to return. When I reached the *krick*, the rail was still lying across it. Yet, no sooner had I stepped on the rail than all of the ice broke away from under me. Thus, I found myself standing in water up to under my arms. I had a bottle of milk and half a [loaf of] bread; the bottle was on the bottom and the bread floated on the water. However, I got out safely [and] fished my bread out. Because an Indian boy happened to approach just at that moment, he was able to retrieve the bottle. Then I went home, made a fire, and put on dry clothes. Sister Lucia and Anna came home from New Milford in good spirits, as did Erdmuth from Potatuck. I visited her that same evening. Jonathan had missed her; Joshua had told her about it, that her house had burned down. Yet she was very calm about it. In the evening I conducted the quarter-of-an-hour; Martin interpreted. We felt quite well on this occasion.

Saturday, the 19th.

Today I frequently thought of our dear Bethlehem. I held school with the boys before noon, and with the girls past noon. Samuel and several other brethren and sisters came home in good spirits. We had a blessed quarter-of-an-hour in the evening. I visited Brother Martin and his wife Justine. Martha and Johanna came home.

Sunday, the 20th.

Samuel came and told me that they had had a joyous journey together. Joshua, Elisabeth, [and] Jeremias came home at this time. Baptized ones and unbaptized ones came from the winter huts, and then the meeting was called by blowing [the horn]; Martin interpreted. After the meeting I talked with David about his heart; I was able to delight in him. Then [I talked] with Sarah and Rebecca. In the afternoon I conducted a quarter-of-an-hour for the baptized ones; there was a feeling of grace present. Following the quarter-of-an-hour Gideon invited all the brethren and sisters to his house for a love feast that his wife wanted to give. I too was invited. The brethren and sisters having assembled, they sent a servant and had me summoned. When I arrived there everything was in good order. I sang several verses and then the food was passed around. I had been worried all along that Martha and Johanna would come home greatly confused because of their house and belongings having burned. Thus, I asked Martha when she had made up her mind to give this love feast. She said when she moved down from the winter huts on the mountain, she had thought to give a love feast for the brethren and sisters once she returned from Potatuck. When she received word that her house and everything in it had burned, it had occurred to her: Now you can no longer hold a love feast. But then she thought that she would use whatever she had left. I asked her how she had felt when she heard that her house had burned. She said that she had not wanted to deal with it, yet had not been able to go to sleep at night because of this. That is when she thought, The Savior and His wounds are still here, and she began to feel them close to her and she felt well. Erdmuth said it [the fire] had confused her a little, but she had right away turned with her heart to the Savior again, and there she started to feel well once more. It was quite a blessed love feast; everyone who was there was happy. I said I truly believed that the Savior will feel great joy in his heart at seeing us sit here with such feelings of love for one another. You know in what way you used to come together before you knew the Savior and His wounds. Then they said, this is true. At that time we came together to drink, to dance, to fight, and for all sorts of indecent ways of life. They were grateful to the Savior that He has delivered them from this and brought them to His wounds. We then sang several v[erses] and thus parted in good spirits. David, Rebecca, and Sarah stayed here tonight.

Monday, the 21st.

We had the morning blessing at an early hour. The red wounds of Jesus were feelingly near to us. David and Rebecca took a heartfelt leave of me and went home. Christian went to New Milford. Lucas went to a merchant to pay a debt, and from there to Potatuck to visit Martin's brother. I held school twice. I conducted the quarter-of-an-hour in the evening; the wounds of our Husband were near me. Gideon complained that he was not feeling well in his body.

Tuesday, the 22nd.

Our Husband with His wounds was near us during the morning blessing. I went visiting in Petrus's hut; talked with the brethren and sisters [about] how they are to act when dealing with their children, particularly with those who are baptized. They shall be preserved and raised in grace. We did not baptize any children unless we had faith in the brethren and sisters that they would care for their children's souls as they cared for their own. This was a weighty matter to all of them. I visited Joshua and Elisabeth, who are both in a happy state and full of light. Gideon was feeling a little better. The air[48] in Gideon's house is now better than before. By means of the fire, the Savior has put Martha, and her mother [Erdmuth], and daughter [Johanna] back in touch with their hearts. Gottlieb brought home a deer, of which they immediately sent me a piece. I conducted the quarter-of-an-hour in the evening. Our particular text reads: *Der Herr Jesus Christus mit allen seinen rothen Wunden Beulen und Strimen, das tönet und hafft in die Hertzen.*[49] Samuel was with me in the evening; he is affectionate, lively, and full of light. I also visited Martin and Justina.

Wednesday, the 23rd.

After the morning blessing Erdmuth stayed on with me for a while; she is very weakly. Gideon drank several bowls[d] of tea at my house because he was not feeling quite right. Next, I held school with the boys. Chopped some wood into small pieces for myself. Afterward, I held school with the girls. I conducted the quarter-of-an-hour in the evening; I felt comfortable thereat. I asked Martin about his heart. He said that he felt well; he was feeling the wounds.

Thursday, the 24th.

Today I did not feel all too well inside my body, thus, I stayed home. We had a blessed quarter-of-an-hour[d] in the evening. Samuel stayed with me for a while in the evening. I talked with him about his heart. He said that once in a while his heart still wants to stray and turn away from the Savior, and [that] he had to constantly watch over that.

Friday, the 25th.

~~In the morning~~ I delivered the morning blessing, giving thanks to the Savior for all the mercy that He has shown ~~also~~ to the brown assembly here in Pachgatgoch, and that He may gather into His bloody arms everyone He has washed with His blood, p[p]. I felt especially well on this occasion. I went to the brethren and sisters in the winter huts. Several had gone out. I talked with Sr. Leah about her heart. She said that she often thought she was the most corrupted person, but when she looked to the Savior and His wounds, she felt well. I talked with David and Rebecca about various matters concerning the Savior and His wounds; her heart was eager to listen. I felt quite well on this occasion. Jonathan came home from Potatuck. I conducted the quarter-of-an-hour in the evening; the Savior was near us.

Saturday, the 26th.

Following the morning blessing I went into all the houses to visit. Several were [out] cutting wood, and those who were at home were busy making baskets. I thought much about the congregation in Bethlehem. Amos, who was working 4 miles from here, came home in good spirits. Several other brethren and sisters who live in the winter huts came with him.

Sunday, the 27th.

Schyri came home with his family. Also, the brethren and sisters from the winter huts and several other unbaptized ones came for the meeting. The Lamb[d] was near me so that I was able to passionately portray the ~~red~~ wounds and the entire martyred body of Jesus to them. David and Rebecca said that they intended to go to the seaside next week. I spoke with them about various matters concerning their heart[s]. Both were childlike and full of light. That afternoon I conducted a quarter-of-an-hour for the baptized ones, reminding the brethren and sisters that they had to do nothing else but abide with their hearts in the Savior's wounds. I felt comfortable on this occasion. Samuel came in the evening and said that he wanted to haul home my wood that was still out [in the woods].

Monday, the 28th.

I delivered the morning blessing at an early hour, thanking the Savior for the grace that He lets us feel here in Pachgatgoch. Also, I recommended myself and the brown brethren and sisters to His care and bloody arms. After breakfast Samuel came with the sled to get my wood. I rode with him. He brought all of it home, 6 sleds full. Joshua went on the mountain to work. I conducted the quarter-of-an-hour; Martin interpreted. The Savior was near us.

Tuesday, the 29th.

After the morning blessing Sister Thamar came to me; told me about her heart and how matters stood in her house with respect to the Savior. They are reportedly were all well in their hearts. Before noon I held school with the boys, and after noon with the girls. A foreign, unmarried person from Potatuck by the name of Kwànau Sawonet came to me, with whom I talked about the Savior and His love for the Indians. He said that he frequently thought of the Savior. He also attends the meetings regularly. Gottlob, who intended to go down to the seaside, stayed with me for a while in the evening. However, I did not approve of it [his going to the seaside], thus, he stayed home.

Wednesday, March 1.

I delivered the morning blessing at an early hour; the Savior was near us. I went visiting in the huts. Talked to Schyri's mother about the Savior, and His suffering and death out of love for poor mankind, so that they may be saved, and that she could partake of this as well, p[p]. She was quite pleased to hear this. Next, I went into Petrus's hut; asked old Maria's sister if she did not at times think of the Savior. She said yes, but her heart continued to want to see a different path. I told her that the Savior's blood needed to wash her and bestow upon her a fresh heart, p[p]. I bid Sr. Thamar to talk to her about the Savior in the meantime. I also talked with Caritas, who said that occasionally something would get in her way that rendered her unblessed. I directed her to the Savior; His blood was able to root out everything in our hearts if only we allowed the Savior to take it away. I went visiting in several more huts, finding them [the brethren and sisters] well and in good spirits. The Indian brethren and sisters greatly long to see a brother from Bethlehem. Martin said that he had not been able to sleep that night; he thought, A brother is coming tomorrow. Samuel said he had dreamed he saw brethren coming. Hence, he ran outside many times and looked about. Gideon came and said, Now it is certain, the brethren and sisters are departing from Bethlehem this very moment. We had a blessed quarter-of-an-hour in the evening. Samuel and Lucia came to visit me.

Thursday, the 2nd.

After the morning blessing Christian came from the winter huts, saying that his wife Gottliebe was very ill. During the night she told him to go to me as soon as day broke so that I would please visit her; she thought that she would go home. I soon set out and went with him. Nearly all the brethren and sisters followed. Once there, I asked what it was that she had to say to me, and how she was feeling in her heart. She said that her heart was quite well and that the wounds of Jesus were feelingly near to her. This pleased me, I told her, ~~if only~~ but this was not only in her mind, or was it? She said, No, no, I am feeling the wounds in my heart and my heart is well as a result, so much so that my pains are disappearing completely because of it. I told her to give herself up to the Savior, [to let Him] do with her as He pleased, and to simply abide in His wounds. She said yes, that is what she would do. I went visiting in the remaining huts. Talked with Gihorn about the Savior. He said he understood everything; it was true. I visited on the other side; David and Rebecca had gone out with baskets [to sell]. Old Maria was quite full of light and lively; her heart was full of feeling about the wounds of the Savior. I then visited Sr. Gottliebe again and took leave of her, promising to visit her the next day, if I was able to.

Friday, the 3rd.

Following the morning blessing Gideon came to me. I said I did not know what was wrong with Schyri, he did not behave as before. Gideon said that he [Schyri] was very dissatisfied that the brethren did not want to baptize him. He has been hopeful now 3 times, that when a brother from Bethlehem was here, he would be baptized, but it did not happen. It seemed that the brethren did not want to baptize him. I told Gideon to visit him and talk with him about his heart, so that he [would] look to himself for the cause, because the brethren loved him and have wished for a long time for Schyri to be baptized with the Savior's blood. I visited Martin and Justina. Gottlob had gone on the mountain to make wooden utensils. The brethren are all hard at work. Because the ice would no longer hold, and with the river not being clear, I was unable to get to the winter huts. We had a blessed quarter-of-an-hour in the evening. Joshua and Samuel stayed on with me for a while. We were quite blissful together, and they recounted many a matter concerning their first counseling, when the brethren came to them.

Mart[ius], 1752.

Saturday, the 4th.

After the morning blessing I visited the brethren and sisters; talked with several about their hearts, where I found the opportunity. In spirit I was frequently in Bethlehem. Word came from the winter huts that Gottliebe had improved somewhat. We felt comfortable during the quarter-of-an-hour in the evening.

Sunday, the 5th.

Several brethren and sisters came from the winter huts. Christian brought me word from his wife Gottliebe, that she had improved somewhat, but 2 children had fallen ill as well. Witlÿ, Benig[na's] husband, was also reportedly very ill. We had the meeting; the Savior was near us with His wounds. Following the meeting Christian and several other brethren and sisters set out to return home because of the sick. I felt especially comfortable during the quarter-of-an-hour for the baptized ones.

Monday, the 6th.

After the morning blessing I readied myself and went to the winter huts. Gottliebe told me that her illness had affected her head a number of times so that she did not know what she was saying. I asked her how her heart was. She said that she felt well. Occasionally, something would occur that wanted to render her unsaved, but she was looking to the wounds of the Savior with her heart. I found Witlÿ very ill. Asked him whether he had not thought of the Savior. He said yes, he had thought of Him frequently and had wished that he was washed with the Savior's blood. Because of his being so weak, I was not able to talk with him much; I directed him to the Savior. David and Rebecca came here to visit the sick. They were glad to find me here. Talked with the brethren and sisters about various matters—how good it would be if a person, in times of health, gave himself fully to the Savior and His wounds so that His blood would wash away all the old and wild manners, so that a person would grow to be very much in the spirit of Jesus and the wounds. That way one would be calm and peaceful even when ill. This was plain to them and rendered them full of good feeling. Then I set out to return home. Gideon came and asked how the sick were. I told him how I had found them and that it would please me if a brother visited them tomorrow. He said that he wanted to go. Ampiwochnant came here from Wechquadnach. I visited him and asked if the brethren and sisters [there] were in good health. He said yes. I also learned that Christina, the wife of Cornelius, was there.

Tuesday, the 7th.

Gideon went to visit the sick. Lucas came and told me that he wanted to go to Wechquadnach, and from there on the bear hunt. I had greetings passed on to the brethren and sisters and intended to visit them before long. I held school with the boys. Joshua went among the white people to sell wooden utensils. I conducted the quarter-of-an-hour in the evening; ~~Joshua~~ Samuel interpreted. The wounds of Jesus were near me. Gideon told me in what state he had found Gottliebe and the other sick persons, and what he had discussed with them concerning their hearts ~~with them~~. Also, she [Gottliebe] has reportedly improved somewhat. Joshua returned home in good spirits today.

Wednesday, the 8th.

I delivered the morning blessing at an early hour; the Lamb^d was near us. Afterward, I went to visit Schÿri. He is longing to be baptized. I also visited old Maria's sister, as well as several other brethren and sisters. Magdalena came and said she intended to go on horseback to Wechquadnach tomorrow to visit the sisters and the other Indians [there]. I had no objections. In the evening, following the quarter-of-an-hour, [the] Joshuas, [the] Samuels, [and] Jeremias stayed on with me. Joshua said he intended to visit the brethren and sisters in the winter huts tomorrow.

Thursday, the 9th.

Following the morning blessing I held school. Joshua told me that the brethren and sisters were in good spirits and [that] the sick had improved somewhat. I conducted the quarter-of-an-hour in the evening, with blessing.

Friday, the 10th.

After the morning blessing I held school with the boys, and in the afternoon, with the girls. I visited in several huts; the brethren and sisters were busy working, and in good spirits.

Saturday, the 11th.

(In the morning I delivered the morning blessing; the Savior was near me with His wounds. I washed my white linen.) An English man came to me who took several Indian brethren with him to work. I frequently thought of the dear Bethlehem. We had a blessed quarter-of-an-hour in the evening.

Sunday, the 12th.

I visited [the] Joshuas. Then, Samuel and Gideon came and said that the brethren and sisters from the winter huts were here. (Gideon lamented that the young people would get together in his house and often were very light-minded.) Next, I called the meeting by blowing [the horn]; the red wounds of Jesus were near me. Joshua interpreted with a warm and feeling heart. Everyone was *attent* [attentive] and quiet. Sarah and Leah stayed on after the meeting and reported how things were going in the winter huts. They further said that they intended to work in the woods next week; their corn was used up. Moreover, they were indebted to a merchant. In the afternoon I had a blessed quarter-of-an-hour[d] with the baptized ones. The brethren and sisters from the winter huts set out to return home. The brethren from here went sweating. I talked with Jonathan, who, in light-minded *compagni*, has again gotten himself into something. I pointed out to him that he should remember what the Savior has affected in him, p[p]. He was sad and said it was true; promised to cut himself off from this.

Monday, the 13th.

I delivered the morning blessing at an early hour, entrusting myself and the brown assembly to the Lamb[d], that the red wounds may sparkle quite bloody in the heart of each one. Christian came from the winter huts, saying that Gottliebe was again walking about and that the others also had improved somewhat. In the forenoon I held school with the boys, and in the afternoon with the girls. I went to Kent to buy a little bread for myself, but got none. Joshua told me that they had agreed that some brethren should go to Wanachquaticok to get the Indian Jhan. They want to tell him about their land in their language, and he shall write it down in English. This they want to take to the co[u]rt in order to keep [their] land.[50] I was not able say much by way of reply. I held the quarter-of-an-hour in the evening; I felt quite comfortable in my heart.

Tuesday, the 14th.

I delivered the morning blessing at an early hour. I visited Br. Martin, who had been out and had gotten among drunk people. They beat him, about which he has grown somewhat somber. However, there was no opportunity for me to talk with him about this. I held school; first with the boys, and afterward with the girls. Salome told me that, together with her sister, she intended to go out with baskets tomorrow.

Wednesday, the 15th.

Agnes and Magdalena, Salome, and several others went to Sharon with baskets and brooms to sell, intending to go from there to Wechquadnach. Gideon said that he had a mind to go to New Milford today. However, because it started to rain, he put it off. I went visiting in several huts; talked with some about their hearts. Sister Priscilla is somewhat sickly, but as for her heart, well. I spoke with

Jeremias. I felt quite comfortable about him. His heart was full of feeling and well. I visited Samuel and Lucia. Both are dear hearts; with him, things could go deeper into Jesus' wounds.

Thursday, the 16th.

After the morning blessing I held school with the boys. Next, I went to visit the brethren and sisters in the winter huts. Came to David's hut first. David and Rebecca had gone with baskets to Danbury. Old Maria, who was well and full of light, was home alone with the children. The son of Sekes was there, who said that his parents would move back here in 3 weeks time. He took me across the river by canoe, and there I spoke with the remaining brethren and sisters who all are well and in a happy state. Gottliebe has almost entirely recovered. Sarah and her daughter Leah intended to go to Woodbury tomorrow to work. The sisters returned from Sharon in the evening; they had been unable to get to Wechquadnach because it rained so hard. We had a blessed quarter-of-an-hour[d].

Friday, the 17th.

I delivered the morning blessing (with blessing). Gideon went to New Milford to visit some friends[51] who love the Savior, and also [to take care of] other matters. I held school twice. In the evening I conducted the quarter-of-an-hour on the text: *Er hat sein Kleid in Wein gewaschen, u. seinen Mantel in Weinbeern Blut.*[52] With a warm and feeling heart, I was able to portray to the brown hearts[d] the bloody Savior with all His wounds, welts, and bruises. Petrus and his wife Thamar stayed on with me for a while. He told me about his heart—that at times the former Indian ways wanted to re-enter his mind—and whenever he engaged in something in thought, ~~and~~ he would afterward, on approaching the Savior with his heart, feel as if he had been called upon to go up a very high mountain that he could climb only with great difficulty, p[p]. I told him that he need not engage in these thoughts, he should let himself be entirely freed from them through the Savior's blood, p[p].

Saturday, the 18th.

In my heart I very much felt in the spirit of the Sabbath today. I visited several brethren and sisters. Gideon returned home from New Milford in good spirits.

An unbaptized Indian from Wechquadnach came, bringing word that Simon from Gnadenhütten had arrived and intended to come here tomorrow. In the evening I conducted the quarter-of-an-hour with blessing.

Sunday, the 19th.

Several sisters arrived from the winter huts, and then the meeting was called by blowing [the horn]. Thus, everyone assembled. I talked about the text: *Eß wird den noch dazu kommen, das Jacob Wurtzeln wird, und Israel grünen u. blühen, p[p].*[53] It was pointed out that the Savior and His death, wounds, and blood were the fruit to which the text referred, which is spreading throughout the world. I felt quite comfortable on this occasion. In the afternoon I had a blessed quarter-of-an-hour with the baptized ones; talked about the love of the brethren and sisters for one another, p[p].

Monday, the 20th.

After the morning blessing the Indian brethren went to jointly build their *fens* [fence]. I held school with the boys. Afterward, I went to visit them [the brethren]. Everyone was industrious and matters proceeded in a very orderly fashion. In the afternoon I held school with the girls. Also, Moses and Simon from Gnadenhütten arrived here. In the evening I conducted a quarter-of-an-hour with blessing. Moses and Simon stayed on after the quarter-of-an-hour and I received them with love. They brought me heartfelt greetings from Hannah and the other brethren and sisters in Wechquadnach. Did they not have a letter for me, I asked. They said no. Did the brethren not know that they wanted to come here? They said they had not told anyone except their wives. I asked them about their hearts, if they were in a happy state and well. With deep sighs, they said no. Thus, I talked with them about various matters concerning the Savior, how blissful it was when our hearts felt the bloody wounds of Jesus. They were very sincere and straight. They told me some things about the brown assembly in Gnadenhütten, at which I was able to rejoice.

Tuesday, the 21st.

After the morning blessing Moses and Simon stayed on with me and joined me for breakfast. Then they went to visit the brethren and sisters. I held school twice. I conducted the quarter-of-an-hour in the evening. The Savior was near me. Several brethren stayed on with me for a while.

Wednesday, the 22nd.

Christian came from the winter huts, saying that Sister Leah's little girl was very ill because her mother Leah was not at home. Hence, I had Gideon go and visit the sick child and the brethren and sisters there. Petrus went with him. Moses and Simon told the brethren and sisters of this place much about Gnadenhüt-ten, which, in part, was not very edifying. I held school twice. Gideon brought me word that the child was fairly ill and that they had sent for her mother. Also, he had talked with the other brethren and sisters about their hearts, who all were well and in good spirits. I conducted the quarter-of-an-hour in the evening; Jesus' wounds were near me.

Thursday, the 23rd.

Following the morning blessing, Martin and Joshua went out with cans[54] and spoons to sell. Petrus came to me, lamenting that it grieved his heart that some of the young menfolk were so light-minded. I told him that, for the time being, we could not change that, as not all of the brethren and sisters were of one mind. Some of them still loved their children and friends too much.[55] We had to leave this to the Savior. He [Petrus] should merely look to his heart; the Savior would help us along. I went visiting in several huts; talked with Justina about her heart. She said her heart was again well and full of light. Joshua came home in good spirits. I conducted the quarter-of-an-hour in the evening; Joshua interpreted. I felt quite comfortable.

Friday, the 24th.

I delivered the morning blessing at an early hour. Went visiting in several huts; talked with Magdalena about her heart. Afterward, I went to Kent and brought back some milk for myself. David was taken to the *justus* [justice] on account of a small debt that he had guaranteed. We had a blessed quarter-of-an-hour in the evening.

Saturday, the 25th.

I delivered the morning blessing at an early hour. Next, I went visiting, spending awhile in Jeremias's house with Moses and Simon. Afterward, I washed some of my laundry. I got such a headache that I had to lie down ~~in bed~~. Because I was not able to conduct the quarter-of-an-hour, and there not being any blowing [of the horn], Gideon came to me. On seeing that I was lying down, he said he had thought right away that I must be ill. He went and told the brethren about it, whereupon most of them soon came to visit me. Samuel stayed with me for a while and gave me some assistance. After that I had him go home and take the key with him so that he would be able to get into the house in the morning. Sr. Hannah came here from Wechquadnach.

Sunday, the 26th.

With daybreak, Samuel came and asked how I was doing. My headache had eased somewhat. He made a fire. Several other brethren came to see me. After that I got up and prepared some tea for myself. Gideon and Hannah came to visit me. I talked with her at length about her heart. She is an agreeable sister; I delighted in her. Old Erdmuth and Priscilla also came to visit me. Several baptized and unbaptized ones arrived from the winter huts to attend the meeting. I was weak to be sure, but nonetheless readied myself to conduct the meeting. Samuel made preparations for it in the house, and this was followed by the blowing [of the horn]. The house became fairly full; the Savior was very feelingly near to me. I was able to feel that there were hungry and open hearts present. In the afternoon I conducted the quarter-of-an-hour for the baptized ones with blessing. I felt especially comfortable in my heart throughout the entire day.

Monday, the 27th.

I delivered the morning blessing at an early hour, recommending all of the brown brethren and sisters to His charge and deep into His wounds. Soon after, Hannah came and took leave to return to Wechquadnach. I then talked with her somewhat about her heart; had her salute the ~~other~~ baptized and unbaptized ones for me. I went visiting in several huts. Afterward, I held school. In the evening we had a blessed quarter-of-an-hour. Moses and Simon stayed with me for a while. The Indian brethren gathered to speak about their land, for the *justus* of New Milford is to mete out to them as much land as the *corth* [court] has agreed on.[56]

Tuesday, the 28th.

Following the morning blessing Moses and Simon came, taking leave of me to return to Wechquadnach. Joshua went hunting with his son. He expects to come back home on Thursday. Withly, Benigna's husband, came to me. I talked with him about his heart. He longs to be baptized. I conducted the quarter-of-an-hour in the evening; Samuel interpreted.

Wednesday, the 29th.

After the morning blessing I held school with the boys. Samuel came and told me that he intended to go to New Milford to sell wooden utensils. Joshua came home today because the weather was so very bad. Given that I did not have a brother there to interpret, I conducted the quarter-of-an-hour in English.

Thursday, the 30th.

I delivered the morning blessing at an early hour. Afterward, I held school twice. Next, I went to visit the brethren and sisters in the winter huts. First, I came to David's hut; talked with Rebecca. She was affectionate and full of light. Thereafter I went to David, who was working in the field with his son. I talked with him about his heart. He was well. His son had to take me across the river to the other brethren and sisters, all of whom I found affectionate and well. They were pleased that I came to visit them. I felt exceptionally comfortable among them. Gottliebe said that since her illness she had felt quite well in her heart. Samuel returned home from New Milford in good spirits. I made it known to the brethren and sisters that the dear Savior had begun His suffering tonight, sweating His bloody sweat for our sins, p[p].

Friday, the 31st.

After the morning blessing I held school with the boys. Thereupon I visited Jeremias; he was affectionate and well. Several brethren and sisters went to Kent with baskets and brooms to sell. This week I and the Indian brethren and sisters have been longingly on the lookout for a brother from Bethlehem. Also, I went visiting in several huts. Then I held school with the girls. I often thought of the dear Bethlehem and the time of grace that the brethren and sisters are presently enjoying there [*words crossed out*]. Br. Martin and Samuel came to me.

The former said that yesterday he had thought for sure that brethren from Bethlehem were going to come. He had been down the path, thinking that he wanted to welcome them there, but had to return home alone. Perhaps the waters were too high so that they were unable to cross them.

Saturday, ~~March~~ April 1.

I delivered the morning blessing at an early hour; the wounds of the Savior were near us. Jeremias went to New Milford with buckets and other wooden utensils to sell. The other brethren and sisters were hard at work at home. I observed the Sabbath. At times melancholies were intent on entering my head, but the Savior is near me, especially with His wounds. Moreover, things are going quite well with the brown brethren and sisters so that I can feel blissful and cheerful in my loneliness. In the evening I conducted the quarter-of-an-hour with blessing. I told the brethren and sisters that we were going to have tomorrow morning's quarter-of-an-hour a bit earlier than usual, for all of our congregations would go to God's Acre tomorrow morning and remember the Savior's resurrection, as well as the brethren and sisters who have gone to the Savior and the resurrection of their bodies; and we wanted to do that here in our house. This was very weighty to them. Jeremias returned home in good spirits.

Sunday, the 2nd.

At daybreak I made all the preparations and called the quarter-of-an-hour by blowing [the horn]. Soon after all of the brethren and sisters assembled. We sang several verses[d], and then I talked a bit about the Savior's resurrection and [that of the] many bodies of the saints after Him, p[p]. We felt quite well. Toward noon, as all of the brethren and sisters were gathered, I conducted the general service. My text was from Luke, ch. 24, v. 36, p[p]. The Savior was near me in my heart. I talked about the state of the apostles at the time, and in what state a heart was, even if it strayed from the Savior and into something else. On the other hand, [there was] the ~~more~~ more than motherly love of the Savior, and with what tenderness He seeks to set His apostles right again, as well as such hearts [that have strayed], p[p]. I conducted the quarter-of-an-hour for the baptized ones in the afternoon. We felt quite well. ~~Everyone~~ Jeremias came to me for a while. We had a heartfelt talk with each other. Today Christian and his family came up from the winter huts to live here.

Monday, the 3rd.

After the morning blessing I visited Christian and Gottliebe in their house. They were affectionate and full of light, and delighted that I came to visit them. I also went visiting in several [other] huts. The brethren readied themselves to jointly work on their *fenss* [fence]. In the forenoon I held school with the boys, and in the afternoon, with the girls. I went out to visit the brethren at their work. They were just then ready to go home. My heart rejoiced at finding them so quiet and childlike. Then they all went into Gideon's hut to eat. I went in as well and ate with them. In the evening I conducted the quarter-of-an-hour on the text: *Kom herein du Geseegneter des Herrn.*[57] The wounds of Jesus were feelingly near to me.

Tuesday, the 4th.

I delivered the morning blessing at an early hour. The Savior was near us. The brethren again readied themselves to work on the *fens* [fence]. Justina told me that she intended to go into the woods about 4 miles from here to work; expected to be back home on Saturday. An Indian from the Highlands passed through; he came to visit me. He stayed for the quarter-of-an-hour afterward.

Wednesday, the 5th.

Samuel and Joshua went to Kent to see whether the surveyors would come today to survey their land, but they did not meet them. The Indian from the Highlands went home. I sent along greetings to Abel, who lives at that place. I held school twice.

Thursday, the 6th.

I delivered the morning blessing at an early hour. Afterward, I announced school by blowing [the horn]. But because several of the boys were ill-behaved, I bade them go home. The Indian brethren went to make shingles for Joshua; however, they had to put it off because it started to rain hard. Gideon and Samuel came to me. I told them that the boys had been so ill-behaved in school that I was compelled to send them home. They were saddened by this. We had a blessed quarter-of-an-hour in the evening. Jeremias stayed with me for a while in the evening, inquiring whether his boy had been at fault. I related the matter to him.

Friday, the 7th.

I delivered the morning blessing at an early hour. I felt quite comfortable in my heart. I entrusted the brown assembly to the Savior's wounded heart. I intended to go to the winter huts, but I had to stay home because the weather was so bad. I went visiting in all the houses. The Indian brethren were making shingles for Joshua. Joshua came to me in the evening and told me about his heart. He said that his wife Elisabeth was not quite full of light, but he did not know at this time what was causing it. He also told me about several brethren who he thought were not quite feeling the Savior's wounds.

Saturday, the 8th.

I washed my laundry after the morning blessing. Afterward, I went visiting in several huts. The brethren and sisters were in good spirits and full of light. Martin went to bring his wife Justina back home. Salome and Anna, Petrus's daughter, came to visit me. I talked with them about their hearts. Both were full of light and in a happy state. In the evening, following the quarter-of-an-hour, Jeremias and Agnes, Samuel, and Joshua stayed with me for a while. Joshua asked Jeremias and Agnes what they were thinking regarding their small child. Had they not thought about baptism? They said yes, they had supposed that the child would be baptized on the first Sunday. He [Joshua] told them that they had not said so, however. Thereupon they said that they did not know this. They had thought that they would be told by me, and having heard that a brother would soon come from Bethlehem, they had thought I wanted to put it off until then.

April

Sunday, the 9th.

Toward noon the brethren and sisters arrived from the winter huts, and then the meeting was called by blowing [the horn]. I sang German and Indian verses[d]. Afterward, I talked about the text Jn. 20.24, p[p]. The Savior was near us with His wounds. Sarah and her daughter Leah came to me and complained that they have had a great deal of disturbance because of Wenemo's wife. Sarah asked me how she should behave; this woman wanted to hit her all the time, and fair words were not helping. I told her [Sarah] that when she came into her house to hit her, she should have her taken outside, and should let her talk or rail against her; she [Sarah] would not become worse as a result of being railed against and should continue to abide in her ♡. She [Wenemo's wife] was just not a converted woman. Furthermore, they said that they intended to go and work in the woods again tomorrow, and that they would stay out for a week. Next, I conducted the quarter-of-an-hour with the baptized ones with blessing. Afterward, the brethren went into their sweat house.

Monday, the 10th.

I delivered the morning blessing at an early hour. I felt quite comfortable on this occasion. After the morning blessing I informed the brethren and sisters that, at the first blowing [of the horn] for school, the older boys are to come, and the second time, the little ones. The Indian brethren helped Samuel make shingles; I visited them. They were in an altogether happy state going about it.[58]

After school I intended to visit Brother David in the winter huts, for I had not seen him or talked with him for some time. Having gone for about 1 mile, I saw Joshua and Bathsheba of Gnadenhütten coming toward me. I delighted in advance at hearing something from our dear brethren and sisters in Bethlehem [word crossed out], or to see someone [from there]. We then kissed one another affectionately. That I had met them was especially weighty to them. Thus, I went back with them. As ~~the~~ some of the Pachgatgoch brethren and sisters saw us coming up through the field, they announced it among the huts, whereupon everyone came out to see who of the brethren and sisters was coming, for they have been on the lookout for a brother from Bethlehem for a long time. Gideon came to meet us just outside of Pachgatgoch, welcoming Joshua and Sr. Bathsheba with tender love, and then everyone started toward us. A large number went with us into our house where Br. Joshua delivered to me a letter from our dear heart Joseph [Spangenberg], wherein, along with many heartfelt greetings and kisses for the dear brown hearts, he reminded us to receive Joshua and Bathsheba with tender love, like we would [receive] him, and that he, along with several brethren, was on his way to visit us. We lodged [the] Joshuas [from

Gnadenhütten] in the house of Brother Joshua, Gideon's son. In the evening, following the quarter-of-an-hour, I passed on to the brown ~~hearts~~ brethren and sisters the greetings from Br. Joseph, and that he was on his way to us, at which they deeply rejoiced. Joshua of Gnadenhütten did likewise.

♂ [Tuesday], the 11th.

Joshua and Bathsheba joined me for breakfast. Afterward, I went with Joshua to visit the brethren and sisters in their huts. We talked with several about their hearts. Some said that they were overjoyed when they saw Joshua and Sr. Bathsheba coming; they would not have been able to rejoice as much had they seen their parents approaching. Because several sisters had gone to Woodbury to work, [a] two-day journey from here, and intended to return no sooner than in 14 days, I sent Christian's son to inform them that we were expecting dear Brother Joseph any time. Gideon went to visit the brethren and sisters in the winter huts, yet did not find many at home. Bathsheba visited the sisters quite diligently. They were quite open with her and told her everything about how matters stood with them in their hearts. Joshua of Gnadenhütten interpreted ~~in the evening~~ during the evening quarter-of-an-hour.

☿ [Wednesday], the 12th.

After the morning blessing several sisters went out with baskets and brooms to sell. Sr. Caritas came home from New Milford. Poor Schiry also hurried here on hearing that brethren from Bethlehem were expected to arrive. Also, Ampiwochinant arrived here from Wechquadnach. The Indian brethren made new *fens* [fence] posts for me.

♃ [Thursday], the 13th.

I thought that the dear heart Joseph, along with the other brethren, would arrive here today. Hence, I went with Joshua of Gnadenhütten for one mile to meet them. However, because we did not meet them, we returned home. Joshua went to Ampawochnant to tell him that Br. Joseph and several other brethren from Bethlehem were going to come this week for certain [*words crossed out*] ~~wanted to come~~. He shall make this known to the brethren and sisters in Wechquadnach, which he promised to do. I sent Samuel to order bread for the love feast.

Christian's son came and brought word from Woodbury that Sister Sarah and the other sisters were already on their way to Pachgatgoch. I went visiting in several huts, finding the brethren and sisters in good spirits and full of light. In the evening, following the quarter-of-an-hour, several brown brethren and sisters stayed on with me. Travelers came to the door. We thought they were our dear brethren from Bethlehem. However, they were 5 English men who had surveyed land in this area, having been sent out by the *gofermente* [government]. One [was] a *captein*, and [one] an *advocate*, the surveyor, and 2 others. They requested to lodge with me that night as it was very dark and there was no house nearby; they would be satisfied with sleeping on the *flor* [floor]. I told them that if they wanted to make do with it, they were welcome. They were quite glad about this. I had several Indian mats brought here [and I] gave them as many of my blankets as I could spare. They conducted themselves in a rather *honet* [honest] fashion.

♀ [Friday], the 14th.

At daybreak the *shentel* [gentle] folk readied themselves to resume their land surveying. They were very grateful for the kindness that I had shown them and bade me a cordial farewell. They took Brother Samuel with them to show them the Indian line trees.[59] This morning we had no quarter-of-an-hour. Before noon I held school with the boys, and past noon with the girls. The Indian brethren helped Joshua make shingles for the new house. Br. Joshua and Bathsheba of Gnadenhütten ~~engaged a great deal in~~ visited diligently, talking with each and every person about his heart. Samuel had spoken with the advocate about their land—that they had too little. He [the advocate] had referred them to the *cord* [court].

♄ [Saturday], the 15th.

I was somewhat troubled that Brother Joseph failed to arrive for such a long time. The brown brethren and sisters, who have now been hungering for Communion for a good while, thought that they would eat the Savior's flesh and drink His blood tomorrow. We thought perhaps one of ~~them~~ the brethren had fallen ill. Because the brethren and sisters of the conference did not fully trust ~~it~~ Ampiwochnant to announce in Wechquadnach that dear Br. Joseph was coming, Br.

Amos was sent there early to make it known to the brethren and sisters. The Indian brethren worked on Joshua's house. In the forenoon I held school with the boys. Past noon I visited the brethren at their work. Sister Bathsheba came informed us that 3 men were approaching on the other side of the river—perhaps it would be Br. Joseph. When we looked closely, it was the dear heart Joseph [Spangenberg], Christian Fröhlich, and Carl Gottfried Rundt. I and several Indian brethren and sisters went to meet them at the river. We saluted one another across the water. But because we had no *conu* [canoe] on our side, I had to watch them until they came over to us, where I welcomed the dear heart Joseph, along with the other brethren, with tender love. The brown brethren and sisters did so as well.

Carl Gottfried Rundt

15 April to 22 May 1752

Diarium of Pachgatgoch from April 15 to 24, *n. st.* 1752[1]

Account of the events among the brown assembly in Pachgatgoch since Br.
Joseph's [Spangenberg] presence there in the month of April, 1752.

♄ [Saturday], [April] 15, *n. st.*

Br. Joseph, together with Br. Fröhlich and Rundt, arrived in Pachgatgoch around
noon.[2] Br. Sensemann and Gideon, along with Br. Joshua from Gnadenhütten
and his Bathsheba, welcomed us down at the water, which is called the Housatonic River, which we had crossed by *canoe*.[3]

As soon as we stepped into Br. Sensemann's room, all the brown brethren
and sisters, old and young, came to welcome most heartily Br. Joseph and the
two brethren arriving with him.[4]

Once the brethren and sisters had gone home, one after the other, and Br.
Joseph had enjoyed himself and conferred a bit with Br. Sensemann, thereafter directing Br. Gottfried (that is how the Indians now call Br. Rundt)[5] to
take charge of the *diarium* of this place, he [Br. Joseph] then[6] went out with Br.
Sensemann to visit and to salute ~~one after the other~~ the brethren and sisters
in their huts. Afterward, he also viewed the land that belongs to them. Meanwhile, the other two, Br. Christian [Fröhlich] and Gottfried [Rundt], prepared
something for the evening meal.[7]

~~After the meal~~ in the evening[8] the usual ~~evening service~~ occasion[9] for all
the brethren and sisters took place, which Br. Joseph conducted. Joshua from
Gnadenhütten interpreted.

After the occasion, those brethren and sisters of this place with whom the
regular conference had previously been held—yet which for certain reasons

had not taken place for a while—stayed on in Br. Sensemann's room, along with Br. Joshua from Gnadenhütten and his Bathsheba. Br. Joseph announced to them that a conference would be held tomorrow after breakfast, to which the now present brethren and sisters shall come.

Afterward, primarily because we were fatigued from our journey, we retired nice and early, making a fine fire in the fireplace, partially laying our *blanquets* on the ground, and partially covering ourselves with them, and ~~thus had~~ then we[10] [had] our first night's lodging here in Pachgatgoch, with quite a blissful and cheerful heart.

☉ [Sunday], [April] 16

~~Thus~~ there was right after 7 o'clock a[11] ~~the~~ conference ~~planned for yesterday.~~ ~~The persons who were present for it are~~ of the white brethren and sisters ~~the following~~ there were:[12] Br. Joseph, Sensemann, Christian Fröhlich, and Gottfried, this is what Br. Rundt is called by the Indians;[13] of brown ones ~~brethren and sisters there were~~, Br. Gideon and Martha, Joshua and Elisabeth, Joshua and Bathsheba from Gnadenhütten, and Br. Samuel [were] present.[14]

Br. Joseph began the conference in the following manner:

First, he wished the brethren and sisters a heartfelt good morning, and that the peace of the Savior may also manifest itself powerfully in this conference, and [that] His dear and precious wounds may bestow upon the hearts of all the brethren and sisters a light as bright as the sun now shining in the sky.

~~This following he~~ Br. Joseph[15] informed the brethren and sisters ~~that he would have liked to have brought~~ why[16] Sr. Sensemann ~~with him~~ had not come along this time,[17] but because Br. Sensemann was now going to the synod in Philadelph[ia], he himself would afterward bring her with him to this place from Bethlehem.

So that the brethren and sisters of this place would not be by themselves during Br. Sensemann's absence, he was thinking that ~~leave with them~~ Br. Christian and Gottfried would stay here for a period of time.[18] The brethren and sisters were overjoyed at this, especially since Br. Joseph added that these two brethren, above all, greatly loved the Indians. And the latter [Br. Rundt], who back in Europe had been with our children in the congregation for a full 3 years, and loved the children most specially, would hold school for their children here. And most of them already knew Br. Christian anyhow.

The reason for leaving these brethren, who we could not readily spare, to the brown brethren and sisters, was solely because of the great love that the congregation felt for the Indians.

Br. Joseph added that so far we have taken great joy in Gnadenhütten. The conference brethren and sisters of that place were of great assistance to the brethren there, partly by visiting their brethren and sisters, which they did daily, [and] partly by nicely keeping control of their own children. Thus, he also expected from them that they, as much as it is possible for them, keep proper control of their children and guide them with words and good examples.[19]

It would be of utmost joy to the congregation if the old and young here would truly prosper in the sight of the Savior and delight His heart.

Br. Joseph asked further what they were thinking regarding the upcoming *synodi*. Would it not be good if perhaps a couple of the brethren and sisters from among them came along to the *synod*?[20]

Br. Joshua replied, he was almost inclined to go to the *synod* in company with the brethren.

This point, however, was postponed for a later and more certain *resolution*. In the meantime, the brethren and sisters should reflect on it a bit, and later on inform Br. Sensemann of their thoughts on this.

Furthermore, Br. Joseph presented to them his thoughts in regards to their planting. He said he had viewed their land yesterday, and because the time for planting was soon approaching, this was his opinion: Could not and would not the brethren and sisters want to plant some more Welsh corn in the future? He had important reasons that prompted him to make this proposal to them.

First, the brethren and sisters could, if they did this, stay home more and better enjoy the occasions and all that is good at this place, and then [. . .][21]

Thus, they would not need to solicit here and there from other white people, who are opposed to the Savior's people, the one thing or other that they require solely to satisfy their external needs.[22]

Thereupon they declared that they[23] had had this intention already the previous year, [that is,] to plant more Welsh corn, for just this reason, which Br. Sensemann confirmed.

Further, Br. Joseph said [that,] in looking over their land yesterday, he had thought to himself whether it it [sic] would not be good and to their advantage if, instead of the many poor horses that they kept for themselves, they would buy a couple of good, strong horses with which they could break open their land and cultivate it properly.

They replied that they liked the proposition alright, but they were unable to make it happen at this time.

Br. Joseph also expressed his satisfaction at learning[24] that the brethren and sisters had not been out and about, here and there, during the past winter, but instead had stayed here at this place as much as possible.[25]

Then Br. Gideon noted that he had ~~already~~ proposed to his brethren ~~here~~ whether it would not be good if 3 brethren as one [group] went into the forest alone, without taking along their entire families, and made *canoes* there which they could afterward sell to the white people. Their women[26] should get wood from out of the forest and make brooms from it at home. But not all of his brethren were of his opinion. They argued that it was much easier for them if they went there with their entire families and made everything there where the wood stood.

Thereupon Br. Joseph said there was only one thing that he would not like to see, namely, that our brown brethren and sisters fall into the hands of ~~those white~~ certain wicked[27] people and ~~were~~ become[28] indebted to them; and ~~this the white~~ some[29] people would only too gladly have happen, because they always had their wicked intentions and their underlying deceitful advantage as a goal. It would be nice if our brethren and sisters (according to the Bible) were not in debt to anyone, with the exception that they loved all of mankind.

They were asked whether these proposed matters pleased them all. Brother Gideon and Samuel, in the name of the others, expressed that they were well pleased by this.

They also were spoken with about their school,[30] and the brethren and sisters were told that the very same would be considered at the next *synodo*. It would be looked into how their present German school could be changed into an English one, because it had been learned that the brethren and sisters would like it that way, and almost all of them knew English ~~themselves~~ (but not German),[31] and also [because they] always had dealings with such people who spoke English.[32]

Furthermore, Br. Joseph told them how Br. Grube was presently endeavoring

to teach both German and English to the dear brown ones in Meniolagomekah, and his joy was manifested there in the great pleasure that they take in it,
as well as in everyone's obedience.

Br. Grube, along with Br. Ant[on Seiffert] and his wife, and with Augustus,[33]
had been to the Easter celebration in Bethlehem.

Br. Petrus [Böhler] and Nathanael from Gnadenhütten also have now gone on
a journey to Wyoming to visit the Indians there—as several from among them
[here] long to do—and had left Bethlehem at the same time as we.

Br. Joseph also announced to them that he would celebrate a love feast tomorrow with all the baptized brethren and sisters, and relate to them beautiful
news from St. Thomas, as well as Nathan[ael] Seidel's journey through Pennsylvania and Maryland. Moreover, he would add some of the news that we had
received from our brethren and sisters across the great water.[34]

Likewise,[35] with regard to Communion, he [Br. Joseph] would yet further
speak with the brethren and sisters, and if it [Communion] could not be celebrated now, he would then make a proposal at the *synodo* to that end, so that
it would happen soon; but the exact time could not yet be determined at this
point. In the meantime, he would look upon all of the brethren and sisters here
to be sure, and speak with them, because this was indeed the main reason why a
visit by the brethren to the brethren and sisters was taking place; namely, that
it could be learned how much they loved the Savior and if their hearts nicely
lived and burned in His blood.

It was asked whether all their brethren and sisters who were supposed to
gather were already assembled at this place.

They replied [that] not many brethren had stayed away, other than Amos and
Johannes. Paulus has been out for a long time.

Hereupon, Br. Joseph read aloud a letter that the daughter of our Br. Gideon had
written to him, as her father.[36] It was written in German, thus, Br. Joshua from
Gnadenhütten interpreted it, and the letter was handed over to Br. Gideon.

The brethren and sisters also were promised that a couple more letters from
Br. Martin Mack and Abr[aham] Büninger shall be read to them at the love feast.
Br. Martin had very much wanted to visit them himself, but the approaching
time for planting had prevented him from doing so.

In regard to the conference with the brethren and sisters here, which had been suspended for some time: It was called to mind that it was most necessary and useful for a number of reasons, and it would be pleasing, therefore, if it got started again, now during the time when Br. Sensemann would be absent, but also especially when he returned again.

The brethren and sisters were asked for their view in consideration of this point.

Br. Gideon replied: the conference was very pleasing to him for his part, however, the other brethren needed to indicate for themselves whether they felt the same way.

Br. Joshua replied: he found it important for his heart, yet he does not, at this time, recognize the intentions and the purpose of it. Sisters Elisabeth and Martha said the same.

First, Br. Joseph explained it [the conference] to them by means of a couple of parables. Thereupon, he said one could express oneself in a conference more freely and securely about many subjects that not just anyone would understand right away if one talked to the whole, and which were not necessary for each and everyone to know.

Br. Samuel,[37] in the end, declared himself very beautifully ~~with respect to this point~~, to wit, that his heart was fully inclined that way, and [that] he would be pleased to see the conference being treated in the right manner; [that is,] if the conference brethren and sisters conducted themselves (as he expressed it) like a couple of children and natural brothers, were nicely reserved, and expressed themselves lovingly toward one another.

Br. Joseph replied: Yes, that way it would be beautiful, first, because the Savior was present at each and every conference. Second, that way He would delight in it when the affairs that concerned so many brethren and sisters were treated properly. And then, it was also true [that] we needed to adopt the manner of the children and enjoy learning.

Thereupon, he further related to them, with much circumlocution, an example of how, on occasion, harm as well as good could be effected by the conference brethren and sisters.

Br. Gideon was consulted regarding his daughter's marrying. He declared that he would be pleased to see the marriage happen, but he would like to know first what kind of person this was who his daughter was to receive in marriage.

His wife, Sr. Martha, also did not object to the marrying of her daughter, and was of the same mind as her husband.

In closing, Br. Joseph added that here they now had an example of how conference brethren and sisters could cause harm. Because if what was just now spoken about would be told to others, who indeed need not and should not know about it, then harm would certainly result from this.

However, because various matters continued to come up with respect to the aforementioned marriage, Br. Joseph concluded the following in regard to this point: When the Savior directed something, when something came from Him, He made it so in the hearts of those people who are affected by it; that they would be able to willingly acquiesce to it and submit to His will with all their hearts.

And because Br. Gideon and Sr. Martha, in the end, expressed themselves in a way as if they had heard from someone that their daughter Christina had already been promised to another person, Br. Joseph, therefore, showed them that not only was this an obvious lie, but he added that the brethren and sisters who had heard something of this nature should have properly inquired with the brethren about the truth of the matter.

And precisely from this [example,] the brethren and sisters could see the great good and advantage of the conference; for when falsehoods were spread, the brethren and sisters right away could be informed of the true circumstances regarding such a matter.

If the brethren and sisters had anything more to bring up, they could put it off until the next conference. And with that finally,[38] the conference, which had lasted over 9 quarter hours, was closed.

After one hour, around noon, all of the brethren and sisters gathered for the sermon, which Br. Joseph delivered, wherein he, in brief, entrusted to the brown hearts the entire content of the gospel with a great deal of emphasis and manifestation of the spirit. Br. Joshua of Gnadenhütten interpreted. The brethren and sisters were extraordinarily attent [attentive], and, in general, a very blissful feeling of grace could be felt on this occasion. There was a nice assembly gathered, and those who did not have room to sit on the benches sat on the ground, close together.

Past noon, in the 3rd hour, there was an occasion for the baptized ones.

At 5 o'clock there was a love feast with the brethren and sisters who are part of the conference. The opportunity presented itself that the brethren and sisters were spoken with about various beautiful and in part weighty [matters], as well as many a matter of the heart, and their open nature, heartfelt declarations, wise responses to the questions posed to them, and [other] such matters caused us to stay together until half past eight, although it seemed to us that we had not sat together for much more than one hour.

The cont[ents] of the subject matter [discussed], in short, were these:

1) Joshua, Elisabeth, and Sam[uel] ~~are~~ were,[39] up until now, employed as servants;[40] they have an aptitude for it, and also willingness, and the conference was in favor that they could be given this office, item that it would be good if they were introduced to the congregation.

2) So far Joshua has been employed as interp[reter], Samuel and Martin in his absence. It was called to mind that the 2 mentioned last could be employed more often, even when Joshua was home, and that with respect to this, not only should their aptitude be considered, but also whether their hearts were quite blissful in the Savior and His wounds.

3) As for Communion, the brethren and sisters declared that they hungered for it and would be very glad if it could be held. Joshua, of his own accord, admitted that he was presently not in a good state, and for that reason did not know if he would be able to join.

4) It was resolved that Br. Samuel is to go to Kent in the morning to get some wine from the diacono [Latin: deacon] there. At the same time he should bring something for the love feast for the brethren and sisters in Pachgatgoch.

5) Also, Jonathan is to go to Wechquadnach and announce our arrival there, and at the same time invite our brethren and sisters there to the love feast. To that end, he is to set out before daybreak.

6) Various candidates for baptism were talked about, and Br. Sam[uel] reported particularly on his little girl of 4 years, that she had certain hopes for it [baptism] and already would frequently lay herself on his knees and demonstrate with words and gestures how and in what way she will receive baptism. She reportedly often says:

Then her sins would be washed away and she would become dear and pleasing to the dear Savior. The candidates for baptism would still be spoken with separately.[41]

☽ [Monday], [April] 17

Br. Jonathan left here for Wechquadnach before daybreak to invite the brethren and sisters there for the love feast. At 7 o'clock the regular early service took place.[42]

At noon the brethren and sisters assembled again for the conference, wherein Br. Joseph first announced to them that we did not get any wine from Kent.

Initially we had intended to come here from N. Y. by water and bring wine with us, but because we had to go on foot later on, the wine too had to stay behind. However, their Communion would be remembered at the *synodo*, and if Br. Sensemann was not back at this place in 5 weeks time holding Communion for them, then a brother would be appointed in the meantime, who would come to them and hold it for them, so that ~~therefore~~ on the Sunday before Pentecost, or on May 23, new style, Communion ~~infallibly~~ shall be held. The brethren and sisters are to accommodate themselves accordingly so as to be home at such time.

Moreover, at the *syn[od]*, the attempt would be made to fix a certain time when, henceforth, their Communion is to be perpetually held at this place. It would not be necessary, it was added, that a brother came here from Bethlehem for this purpose every time; instead, Br. Sensemann, who was ordained a *diac[ono]* by the congregation, would administer their baptisms and Communions.

The question was posed whether there was someone among them who would like to come along to the *synod*.

They replied that because of several necessary matters that they intended to take up at just this time, this would not work very well.

Thereupon Br. Joseph promised them that he, along with Br. Sensemann — because they were both fully aware of their circumstances — would remember them there [at the synod] and look out for their best interests, with which they were most satisfied.

It was further asked, because they intend to go before the *court* for the purpose of purchasing a little more land, whether they perhaps had a good friend to whom they could turn with respect to this matter, and who had some knowledge of how their affair should be handled before the *court*.[43] Br. Joseph said he had heard that the *country* [possibly intending "colony"] was claiming the land all around this area, and that they had taken the land away from those people who had purchased land from Br. Gideon without paying them for it, for they assumed it to be theirs.[44]

Br. Joseph and Sensemann furthermore indicated that they [the Moravians] were in favor if they [the Indians] had someone from among the white people (who loved the Indians) who would take up their affair in *court*. They feared [that] the white people, little by little, were looking for ways to make themselves masters of their place and lords over their possessions.

In the end, Br. Joseph made them this proposal: Would it not suit them, if, while in New York, he called on a *lawyer* about this, and presented their plan to such a man who understood this kind of matter as well as the laws of this country, so that he could draw up for them a formal, proper *petition* to the *court*, upon which they could afterward, in the presence of two witnesses, write their names or set their marks, and then take it before the *court*.

They were most satisfied with this, and Br. Joseph thereupon took *notice* of the location and nature of their land, of the number of their families, of their usable and unusable land, and such associated, essential particulars, [then] put it on paper and promised to the brethren and sisters he would take care of this in New York, or in Philadelphia, and that the brother who would come here from Bethlehem the next time to hold Communion for them shall bring the prepared *petition* with him.

Afterward, the brethren and sisters were talked to about a certain piece of land on which Br. Christian [Fröhlich] intends to plant some ~~more~~ Welsh corn ~~than has happened thus far~~ this year.

Also discussed was the addition of a new room to Br. Sensem[ann's] house, in which, henceforth, the boys' school could be held, while Sr. Sensemann would hold the girls' school in the other [room]. The brethren right away offered to perform every possible kindness[45] in that regard, and to faithfully assist Br. Christian with this. Br. Christian would like to be finished with the construction before Sr. Sensemann came to Pachgatgoch.

The love feast would take place past noon; Br. Joseph would also still speak with the candidates for baptism. And with that, this conference drew to a close.

311

After the meal, while the brethren Christian and Gottfried prepared for the love feast, Br. Joseph spoke with the candidates for baptism outside, and the following transpired:

1) Old Maria's sister expressed [that] she longed to be washed with the blood of the Lamb.

2) Tscherry said, he has been waiting to be baptized for one year, and when brethren arrived here from Bethlehem, he had always thought it [the baptism] would happen.

3) Jeremias and his wife said about their child that they had submitted it to the Savior as soon as it was born, that it was His and should remain His forever, thinking, at the same time, that the brethren themselves would remember the baptism of their child. However, Br. Sensemann had been of the opinion that the parents should approach him about their child's baptism.

4) Joshua's son is a dear and obedient child and feels something of the work of the Holy Spirit on his heart.

5) Samuel's girl is an agreeable and lively child.

At 4 o'clock the love feast took place, for which also Timotheus and Sr. Hannah of Wechquadnach came today. At this time, the news and letters that had been promised were read to the brethren and sisters.

It was altogether a very delightful and blissful occasion, and because our most beloved Br. Joseph also revealed his extraordinary fondness and love for the brown brethren and sisters in the end, expressing his whole heart to them, the love feast lasted quite a long time.

After the love feast, several brethren and sisters stayed on with Br. Joseph, with whom he rejoiced a great deal, discussing one or another necessary and useful matter.

Thereupon we all retired, with hearts that are truly grateful to our most beloved Savior for the very special grace enjoyed on this day.

♂ [Tuesday], [April] 18

At 7 o'clock in the morning the baptism of our Br. Jeremias's little girl took place, who was named Catharina. It was a very respectable *actus*, on which occasion many an eye became moist from an innermost feeling of the heart and of grace. Having been baptized, the child was consecrated by Br. Joseph and the 3 sisters, Bathsheba from Gnadenhütten, Elisabeth, and Martha, by the laying on of hands.

After this the conference brethren and sisters stayed for breakfast in Br. Sensem[ann's] house, and on that occasion, Br. Joseph had the names of all the brethren and sisters and their children told to him, the baptized ones as well as the unbaptized ones, which he wrote down and took with him.

Hereupon he conducted the quarter-of-an-hour services:

First	7 sisters with their infants
afterward	12 little girls
	6 single sisters
	12 couples of married people
	4 unbaptized boys and
	3 baptized single brethren
	11 small boys and
	6 widows

Following all of these delightful and blissful events, our most beloved Br. Joseph as well as Br. Sensemann readied themselves for departure.

In bidding farewell to the dear Indian hearts, things proceeded with great feeling, and the moist eyes that could be seen on both sides said more than enough about the extraordinary fondness that our dear Br. Joseph feels for his Indians, and their hearts full of love for him.

The two brethren, Christian and Gottfried, had the pleasure of accompanying Br. Joseph and Sensemann for a distance. And after an equally exceedingly tender and childlike farewell, they returned to the place assigned and now so dear to them, wishing that the Savior may bless their being there with blessing and grace from His wounds.

Immediately upon first entering the room, Br. Gottfried entrusted himself and his dear Br. Christian to the care of the Savior by means of this simple verse[d]:

Mach alle unsere Thaten
hilf stets das beste rathen
segnet ihr blutgen Hände
den Anfang, Mittel u. Ende.[46]

Further continuation of the diarii of Pachgatgoch:

As soon as we had arrived home from having accompanied our dear Br. Joseph, we put a few odds and ends in our room in order.

Afterward, Br. Christian, for the first time, conducted the usual evening service for the brethren and sisters in English; Br. Joshua interpreted. In the end, he again passed on to them the tender hearts of Br. Joseph and Sensemann and their love for the Indians, along with their greetings.

After the evening meal Br. Gottfried wrote in the *diario, it.* a letter to Br. Hehl, and meanwhile, Br. Christian conferred with Br. Joshua in his house about the construction that we are planning. Joshua himself had pressed Br. Christian to that end.

[Wednesday, April] 19

The early service took place at 6 o'clock.

Afterward, the brethren Gideon, Joshua, and Samuel stayed in our house, and in keeping with the agreement reached yesterday evening, decided on when, and in what way, the construction was to be undertaken.

First, they declared themselves thusly, that it should be started at once, before the time for planting was here; there should be as many brethren as possible employed for it, and all those who are to work on it shall be spoken with beforehand.

These brethren, then, were at once summoned, and everything that was necessary was agreed upon with them. They all were filled with willingness.

Also on this occasion, Br. Christian sought to take precautions, that there may not be light-mindedness or the like arising, when in the future so many persons would be working closely together.

Hereupon Br. Christian, the Indian, offered to give up his own wood for this purpose, which he had arranged to have cut down some time ago. Previously, he had wanted to build a house for himself with it; however, he did not see himself being able to take on the construction at this time. The wood is reportedly still lying in the woods.

At this, Br. Christian Fröhlich made this suggestion: He thought it best if the wood was brought out of the woods to this place and was then appraised by the brethren Gideon, Joshua, and Samuel, so that the Indian brother Christian could be justly compensated. This was at once agreeable to everyone.

No sooner said than done. The work was begun right away. Several brethren from the winter huts were called for assistance, and with that, they marched into the woods.

We had Welsh corn and meat cooked by Sr. Elisabeth for the brethren who were going to work.

Toward noon a man from our neighborhood visited us and spoke with Br. Christian about various matters; however, because, in the end, his conversation turned to various subjects of religion (as is commonplace in these parts), Br. Christian broke [it] off as quickly as possible, dismissing him with humbleness and love.

In the afternoon an extraordinarily delightful procession of Indians could be seen. Our whole town (I should like to say)—young and old—had gone, without having been pressed by us, onto the high mountain behind our house, to carrying hither from the woods there the wood for our construction, which previously had been cut down and belongs to the Indian brother Christian, as well as the wood that was cut by the brethren today; and now they came marching down all at once. This was delightful to watch, as each one came trundling down with joy, carrying hither his large and small pieces on his back. Many a large beam needed to be carried by about 8 to 10 men. We would have wished for our dear Br. Joseph to have seen this with his [own] eyes.

At this, both of us white brethren, with a greatly moved heart, thought: Oh God, reward that man who once lay fainting at this mountain, working, and sweating blood, so that in doing so he would make the wild, obstinate, and lazy Indians into such willing people who immediately do everything with joy, as soon as they hear that it is to be done for the Savior.

Afterward, the brethren who had come from working in the woods ate in Gideon's new house what Sr. Elisabeth had prepared for them.

And thereupon the brethren and sisters went once more into the woods for wood.

By the time they returned home it was evening, and the usual evening service was conducted for them. At its conclusion, it was announced that from now on the brethren and sisters would be given two signals every morning by blowing [the horn], so that they could prepare themselves a bit at the first [blowing], and at the next, soon after, come directly to the meeting.

During the evening service Br. Gottfried sang the first Indian verse[d] to the congregation. In German it is called _Xti Blut u. Gerechtigkeit_.[47]

Because all of our people were so filled with willingness, late that same evening Br. Christian brought all of his meat that he had stored up and almost all of his Welsh corn to Sr. Elisabeth to cook for the workers tomorrow.

Hereupon we retired blissfully.

The 20th

Shortly after 5 o'clock the early service took place. From time to time it is conducted shortly after sunrise.

After breakfast Br. Christian went into our neighborhood, 2 miles from here, to Mst. [Master] Mills, to get some bread for us. He also had to arrange several other matters there besides.

In his absence, 4 sisters, [to wit,] Thamar, Caritas with her daughter, and Gideon's daughter, reported that they would go to New Milford and stay out for several days.

Br. Gideon, of his own accord, had reminded the brethren and sisters that they should always let the brethren know when and where they went, so that in the meantime they could be remembered before the Savior.

Soon after, the single Br. Lucas visited Br. Gottfried, who, owing to [his] lack of the English language, could not say anything more to the former than _Our Savior loves us very much. He has shed all his Blood for us, let us love Him[,] p[p]._

Hereafter Br. Gottfried held school, first for the older and then for the little boys. Of the latter, some came flying hither as swiftly as birds, so that the piece[d] of shirt that they still wore about their their [sic] bodies came flapping together above their heads, and when school was out and they got back outside, it went almost more swiftly yet. School will continue daily.

As soon as Br. Christian had returned home, we put things in order up in the loft of our house, and especially sought to carefully put aside, in a separate spot[d], the things left behind by Br. Sensemann. Br. Christian also created a *repositorium* [Latin: repository] in our room, as best as it could be done.

Toward 1 o'clock ~~the same~~ Br. Christian conducted a quarter-of-an-hour for the little girls; Joshua interpreted. It will be conducted every day at the same time.

Thereupon he [Br. Christian] went to the brethren in the woods and helped them some with their work.

In the meantime Br. Gottfried busied himself with cooking, washing, cutting wood, and the like.

Throughout the entire day the brethren and sisters were most industriously at work in the woods, and carrying to this place our wood for building. Sr. Bathsheba from Gnadenhütten also did her best thereat.

Both of us brethren did not have our midday meal until late in the afternoon, and took the evening meal along with it. Thus, we were done all at once.

Following the evening quarter-of-an-hour several brethren stayed on with us for a while, among them the single Br. Jonathan, until each one went to retire.

Afterward, Br. Gottfried still sat down and wrote some.

The 21st.

This forenoon Br. Christian visited all the brethren and sisters in their huts, and then busied himself with all sorts of domestic matters.

As we were unable to give the brethren who are helping with the construction any meat to go with the Welsh corn this noon, while they, on the one hand, are proving themselves so industrious and are working well, and on the other hand, some among them are so poor that they have nothing stored up at home to eat—and if they were to go to the white people to earn something there for themselves, our construction would necessarily have to come to a standstill—Br. Christian, therefore, went 2 miles from here to buy there a piece of meat for them (which is very expensive here). He afterward divided it so that it would last for 2 meals, and brought the first part, together with the Welsh corn that goes with it, again to Sr. Elisabeth to cook it for the brethren for the next day. Sr. Bathsheba from Gnadenhütten is helping her with it. There are 13 persons who are sharing in it [the food]. Yet there always comes (as one well knows) a child here and there to help, and then it goes according to the scripture _Daß ein jeglicher ein wenig nehme_,[48] also on this occasion.

All day long the brethren were hard at work making shingles for the roof of the new house. They were overjoyed that they, quite unexpectedly, had found in the woods beautiful wood for this purpose (which is generally simply called shingle-wood here).[49]

On that account it is to be noted [that] the brethren said the following to us at work today: Br. Gideon had previously looked very hard for precisely this sort of wood for his new house and was unable to find it; the white people in this area have walked about and put great effort into their search and had found nothing either. Now [that] we are building a house for the Savior, and are thinking of nothing else but the shingles, here, right away, there is a fine tree of this kind. The Savior has surely saved this tree for this purpose.

Toward evening Br. Gottfried had Br. Joshua join him in his house for a short hour, as he had done yesterday, singing with him through several of the Indian verses that we have got here so as to impress upon himself the Indians' way of pronunciation and their accent, for he has to sing them aloud during the regular occasions. It will henceforth continue this way every day.

After the evening quarter-of-an-hour, 2 white people from our neighborhood came here to this place and took away an Indian boy who, several days ago, had turned up and had stayed in Br. Jeremias's hut (who Br. Joseph also had seen and spoken with during his presence). They said they had ordre [orders] from the Mst. [master] from whom the boy had escaped to bring him back. Both of us brethren have neither interfered in the staying-here, nor in the taking-away of the Indian boy. Nonetheless, after both people had taken the Indian boy into their custody, they came to us into our room, sat down, and Br. Christian spoke with them a little and about something else. (Matters of religion usually are indeed the first discours with the New Englanders.)

♄ [Saturday], the 22nd.

The morning and evening occasions, item both of the boys' schools, took place as ordinair [ordinarily].

In the morning Br. Martin reported that he was going to leave, but he would return the same day.

Sr. Thamar came back home today.

Our brethren working on the construction labored industriously on the shingles today.

A man from the neighborhood, who had some business among the Indians, visited us in the afternoon.

We also learned through Sr. Thamar today, who came from New Milford, that our dear Br. Joseph had preached there in the house of the *justice* of that place on the festival day that was observed here in New England. It gave us and the Indian brethren and sisters special joy that a man who had formerly led the brethren to jail now offered his house for the preaching of the Brethren.[50]

Late in the evening Br. Gottfried heard Br. Martin singing the Indian verse[d] *Wanechk Paquaik* (in German: *Seitenhöhlgen, Seitenhöhlgen,*[51] p[p].) in his hut, which prompted him (especially because the moonlight was so beautiful) to sit down together with Br. Christian in front of the door to our house and play this as well as a number of other verses on his *flaut[o]-trav[erso]*.[52] He right away had ~~several Indian boys around him as~~ listeners.

Hereafter he [Rundt] also wrote in the *diario*.

☉ [Sunday], the 23rd

In the morning, at 7 o'clock, we held the regular conference with the brethren and sisters who are part of it.

First, we posed a question to them: whether they were satisfied with us two brethren and if the brethren and sisters at this place loved us for the sake of the Savior? They confirmed both with a unanimous yes.

Hereafter we assured them of our extraordinary love for them.

Further, they[53] were asked if they wanted to take advantage of the opportunity now, and send something in writing to the *synod* in Philadelph[ia] through Br. Joshua from Gnadenhütten. They were willing to do so, and Br. Gottfried put their statement on paper, in the English language.

Our building, which is presently being worked on, was also talked about, and we learned that the brethren were still filled with willingness to continue working.

(N.B. At other times the Indians have a way to approach a matter vigorously, but then also drop it readily when something else comes along.)

With respect to their school, the brethren and sisters made a request of great importance to them; that is to say, that the sooner their children start learning English, the better. They also had this point [*word crossed out*] included in their letter to the *synodum*.

(Incidentally, it is necessary to remark here that, when someone comes here to instruct the boys at this place in English, that person also has to bring along the necessary books for this purpose, because there is nothing at all of such things at hand here.)

The interpreting during the daily occasions was reflected upon, at which time the 2 brethren, Joshua ~~Martin~~ and Samuel, who are employed for interpreting, proposed this: They wanted to take turns interpreting, along with Br. Martin, and in the event that the one who was supposed to interpret just then does not feel quite warm in his heart to do so, he would indicate it, so that someone else could do it.

Br. Gideon issued a reminder that we, in due time, should arrange to get the necessary glass for the windows in our new house from New York.

The question was posed whether Br. Christian would get a horse from the brethren when he went to Joh[annes] Rau 14 days from tomorrow, and retrieve from there the items that we are expecting from New York. He was promised this, and it was added that an Indian brother shall go with him, which pleased Br. Christian very much.

Finally, Sr. Martha voiced a request that consisted of the following: Whether her daughter Christina in Bethlehem could come here with Sr. Sensemann for a visit, <u>if she herself wanted to</u>. At this, Br. Gideon added, it should be a visit just to see one another, afterward, she could go back again.

At 11 o'clock the regular sermon took place, for which several brethren and sisters from the winter huts, and also Tscherry, had come.

Toward 4 o'clock the quarter-of-an-hour for the baptized ones took place.

Today we also wrote a letter to the *synodum* ~~of the Unitas Frat[rum]~~ in Philadelphia.

In addition, Br. Gottfried wrote a letter to Br. Joseph and Br. Nathan[ael] Seidel, and, on the whole, sought to complete the *diarium* of this place so that when Br. Joshua from Gnadenhütten arrived here, who had departed 6 days ago to go to Westenhook, he would find everything ready and could take it with him to Bethlehem.

Br. Gottfried earnestly requests that for the sake of our congregation a book[d] in 8*tvo* [octavo], wherein white paper is bound, is sent with the first brother who comes here, to enable him to write the few Indian verses[d] nicely into it and preserve them. It is no doubt quite bad when one sheet [of paper] is here and the other there, the sheets themselves are torn, and are beginning to take on the color of our chimney.

Br. Christian also wrote to Br. Hehl, *item* to his wife in Bethlehem, and visited the brethren and sisters in the huts.

Moreover, ~~the same~~ Br. Christian had the 3 brethren who are to be employed for interpreting come to us in the evening, and he spoke with them about this subject. And because some pleasant discourses arose afterward, Br. Gottfried took out his Indian verses, read them to the brethren, and had himself corrected. The brethren parted from us very lively and in good spirits, and we noticed [then] that we had sat together for more than two and a half hours.

☽ [Monday], the 24th

Br. Samuel interpreted during the early service.

In the forenoon Br. Christian went into our neighborhood, 2 miles from here, on account of some business.

Br. Christian, the Indian, also left today, but returned in the evening.

We learned that yesterday afternoon our Br. Gideon had conferred with several brethren and sisters, among whom was also Sr. Bathsheba of Gnadenhütten, having pointed out to them that we 2 brethren could not feed those persons who are working on the building every day: first, because we were only here on their account, and that was already a lot; finally, the building was only for the benefit of the Indians to be sure. Thus, they should make arrangements among themselves to provide their own food, as best they could. And because several among them were very poor, he [Gideon], for his part, would do what he could [to help]. Indeed, tomorrow he right away wanted to send a *buschel* of corn to the mill so that it would be ground and then baked into bread for the workers.

Today the brethren continued working with a great deal of joy. Our old Gideon also is going about it very industriously.

Whereas our new building was at first supposed to be smaller than Br. Sensemann's, now it will be one shoe larger.[54] The reason for this is twofold: one, the cut wood, as we received it from the Indian brother Christian, was one shoe longer than the old house, and under those circumstances the brethren did not want to cut off each piece of wood by one shoe in length. Later, they were also pleased to see that the new house became somewhat roomier than the old, for they thought, if only one single person is to live in it, who does not take up much room, then we could in the future perhaps hold our meetings in it, and then it is more comfortable for us. Moreover, the house will also have a pretty appearance from the outside, once the roof is covered with nice shingles.

In the evening, at the 9th hour, as Br. Gottfried was about to close this *diarium*, we heard someone calling out loudly from the other side of the *river*, and when we listened for it outside, it was our Br. Joshua of Gnadenhütten, who arrived here very tired having walked some 40 miles today. We gave his wife some tea and sugar, [and] also bread, so that she could prepare tea for him and he could refresh himself.

Pachgatgoch *diarium* from April 25 until *May* 22, 1752. *n. st.*

♂ [Tuesday], the 25th

Br. Martin interpreted during the early service.

Br. Joshua from Gnadenhütten, along with his Bathsheba, joined us afterward for breakfast.

They subsequently readied themselves for departure, taking a heartfelt leave of us and the brethren and sisters in the huts, and departed for Bethlehem.

We gave Br. Joshua the *diarium* of this place, from the 15th to the 24th of this month, to take with him, along with a *paquet* [packet] of letters, for delivery to Br. Hehl in Bethlehem.

Sr. Erdmuth went to Wechquadnach early today and will stay there for several days.

The brethren's work on the building proceeded very nicely today. In the afternoon, when Br. Christian helped them with it, he asked them if they had also heard that our Savior had been a carpenter and had put up houses of just this kind. They replied: Yes, they knew this very well. They greatly delighted ~~that they~~ in <u>this</u> circumstance of the life of our Savior having been brought to mind.

Because the brethren wanted to go sweating after they were done working this evening, they asked that the evening occasion be conducted somewhat later than usual, which they were granted.

☿ [Wednesday], the 26th

Soon after the early service Br. Christian went to the winter huts to visit the brethren and sisters there. He found Br. David ill, [and] heard this and that about the great external poverty of the brethren and sisters, where especially Sr. Leah pointed out that she was in direst need. Her husband had left her, and her corn had been stolen from her the previous fall.

Today we again had meat and Welsh corn with beans cooked for our brethren doing the construction. The work progressed very well.

Because the limbs of our bodies had complained already for several nights that they were not bedded softly enough, we thus sought to come to their aid today. Br. Christian had tracked down a place where feathers can be gotten for free. That is where both of us went, namely, down toward the river, along the Indian field. There we found here and there on the uncultivated land some coarse, dried grass from the previous year. This we tore off with our hands and then made from it quite a soft under-bed for ourselves.[55]

All day long the woods on the mountain had been on fire, on the side where our huts stand, about 1 or 2 miles distant from where we are. Toward evening the fire on the mountain moved along behind our huts and grew very large. Thus, our brethren went to the fire to try to prevent it from getting to their fence. With time drawing near to when the evening occasion was supposed to be conducted, the brethren sent old Gideon to us to request that it may be suspended for today, which happened accordingly. At 9 o'clock they came home in good health, but very tired. At 10 o'clock the flames of the fire behind our huts became very large and it looked frightful. Therefore, Br. Christian went to the brethren, asking that they keep close watch, for the wind was now starting to blow harder than before. The good fortune in this regard was that the wind blew the fire <u>past</u> our huts.

♃ [Thursday], the 27th

When we got up in the morning the fire had ceased for the most part; only one small line of it had moved down to the *fence* of the brethren and sisters, which could not do any damage, though.

Following the early service everyone set about his work, and after the midday meal there occurred something of note: that the thus far prepared and joined wood was raised for the new house. Every one of the brethren and older boys who was home helped with it, and after 6 o'clock it was finished. Not only did it go without harm to anyone but also so quietly that one could also truly rejoice at that. The construction people were extraordinarily joyful on this occasion and said this was the Indians' first house that they were building this way in this area.[56]

Br. Christian and Gottfried were very much astonished that the Indian brethren, while working on the building, as long as it lasted, conducted themselves like children, and that every time a situation arose when one person as well as the next was able to arrange, say, or do something, [they came to an agreement]; therefore, no dislike for or discord against the other person was seen or heard.

In addition, it is to be noted here that the new house will be almost 2 shoes longer and higher and 1 shoe wider than the old one. Three windows out to 3 sides are to go in, if only the glass for them would get here soon. Had we the iron nails here that we are expecting from New York, then the work would be continued tomorrow, but now it must be suspended. Laths, shingles, and *clapboards* are lying here ready.

The evening occasion was conducted earlier than usual because the brethren very much wanted to sweat this evening.

After this everyone went to rest in good spirits.

♀ [Friday], [April] 28

We cleaned up our construction site a bit.

Afterward, Br. Christian went to Kent and bought from the saw mill there ~~317 foot~~ boards for 62 *sh.* [shillings], and also a type of *white-wood boards* for 9 *sh.*, and brought them down to the water, [a task] with which he occupied himself until evening, so that he came home quite tired.

Having held school, Br. Gottfried busied himself with all sorts of domestic matters, *item* with reading and writing in English.

In the afternoon he visited in their huts all the brethren and sisters who were home, finding them quite cheerful and going about their work most industriously, making buckets, troughs,[57] baskets, and brooms.

The external needs makes it necessary for some brethren to go daily to white people in the neighborhood and work <u>there</u>. Thus, they return home in the evening, some before, some after the occasion.

♄ [Saturday], the 29th

Nothing out of the ordinary occurred.

☉ [Sunday], the 30th

At the conference in the morning, Br. Christian presented Sr. Leah's needy circumstances to the brethren and sisters, and put to Br. Gideon the request whether he could sell him one 1/2 *buschel* of Welsh corn and to present Sr. Leah with such. He was willing to do so.

2)[58] It was learned that the brethren and sisters were not satisfied with Sr. Bathsheba [from] *Gnadenhütten*, and for this reason: Following the conference held here in the presence of Br. Joseph, she had talked to the single women and encouraged them to come along to Bethlehem, although their mothers had been completely against it.

3) The brethren and sisters also expressed their displeasure at the fact that, in all of Pachgatgoch, the content of this now intended conference was known, and because Sr. Martha was also seen as guilty in this regard, the two brethren, Gideon and Joshua, thus pointed out to her, in the presence of the conference, her wrong conduct. (Gideon is Sr. Martha's husband, and Jos[hua] her son.)

4) Our unmarried persons of both sexes were recommended to the heart and to the prayer of the brethren and sisters, adding to this that one still did not feel confident about them. At the same time, however, one did not quite know how to reach them presently.

5) The help of the brethren was requested in bringing to this place

tomorrow, via the *river*, the boards that had been purchased. A garden also was discussed, which we intend to lay out and fence in behind our [partially] old and new house.

The sermon took place at the usual time, to which several brethren and sisters from the winter huts had come.

In the afternoon, after the quarter-of-an-hour for the baptized ones, the Brethren Samuel, Jeremias, and Petrus stayed with us for a while, at which time a very beneficial *discours* took place with them.

The remaining part of this day was spent very quietly in the huts, especially since the weather was such that one did not like going outside.

In the evening, Br. Christian went visiting in all the huts. The occasion for this was mainly this: that he had not seen a couple of the brethren and sisters, who were at home, at the quarter-of-an-hour for the baptized ones.

☽ [Monday], May 1

Following the early service, [and] because the ground inside our new house stood in need of substantial filling-in, both of us brethren began to undertake this [task] until about 9 o'clock when school began, by first breaking out of the soil the very many stones in the area next to and behind the new house where we intend to lay out a small kitchen garden. With these [stones] the filling-in shall have its beginning, before we dig and use the necessary soil to that end.

Afterward, Br. Christian, along with several Indian brethren, went with 2 *canoes* on the *river* up to the place from where our *boards* were to be retrieved. The Indian brethren arrived with their loaded *canoes* shortly past noon. Br. Christian, however, who later came rafting swiftly down the *river* on some of the purchased boards, had difficulty landing them here.[59] As the water was quite high and the wind very strong from behind, he was carried farther with his boards than he wanted to [go]. Thus, he jumped into a *canoe* that was tied up near us, and in it chased after the boards that were floating away. But to control the *canoe* and also the boards with only one pole in hand, given such strong winds and the current, was truly hard and dangerous work. To a person who watched this from the place above where the huts are standing, it was frightful. Finally, it again got to the point that he was able to once more jump out of the *canoe* and onto the boards, with several brethren from the huts coming to his aid with the other *canoe*.

As soon as Br. Christian had partly washed [and] partly dried his clothes, we began to clear the area that is be used for the garden of the bushes that are standing on it, and to fence it in, for we need the *fence* right away, even before we plant any garden seeds. We busied ourselves with this work until the evening meeting.

Today the Indian brethren who were at home also worked industriously on their own new *fence* that they are building directly behind their huts.

During the evening quarter-of-an-hour Br. Christian portrayed to the brethren and sisters the patient Lamb and slaughtered sheep, Jesus Christ, plainly and emphatically. Br. Gottfried closed with a couple of ~~composed and~~ quite suitable English verses.

♂ [Tuesday], the 2nd

Several sisters who had gone out the previous week returned home this afternoon.

Today we progressed with our garden to the point that we were able to plant the seeds.

☿ [Wednesday], the 3rd

Br. Christian went back to the place where he had bought the boards earlier and got himself several more, which are to be used for the floor. Today his ride on the *river* was not as dangerous and difficult as the day before yesterday.

As for the rest, everything at our place here proceeded as usual.

Little by little we are learning that our Indian brethren, who have to leave our place to work for white people, are regarded by them as honest, believable people after all. An example thereof is this:

An Indian brother from our place worked for white people in the neighborhood. When someone there asked him about something, he gave the appropriate response to it. But because the man who had asked him doubted the correctness of the response, another New Englander being present turned the scale this way: You can believe the Indian; he is a *Moravian* and the *Moravians* do not lie.

♃ [Thursday], the 4th

An Indian stranger visited our Brother Samuel. He is one of his relatives.

So that our construction would not be at a complete standstill, we started preparing the floor today, which is to be continued tomorrow.

Also, this afternoon our construction people assessed the wood that we received from Br. Christian, the Indian, and used for the new construction. They found it to be worth 40 shillings of local money.

In the evening we remembered our precious brethren and sisters who have (as we believe) now assembled in Philadelphia for the syn[od].

♀ [Friday], the 5th

Our brethren were cheerfully at work. Having discovered how the laths could be fastened well to the rafters up above without iron nails, they were started to be affixed.

In the afternoon one brother left work to see whether he could catch some fish. One could tell, to be sure, that this did not entirely please the other brethren, who continued working, for each and every one of them could have done the same. But what happened? After awhile, he came home and brought with him nearly 2 buckets full of fish, had them cooked by his wife, and fed with them all of us who had been at work, and with that, no one had anything to say against the brother's leaving; instead, it pleased everyone that this way his evening meal was taken care of at no concern on his part.

During the evening occasion the Savior's diligence, while working during the days of His presence here, was entrusted to the brethren and sisters. And at the same time, it was pointed out what a blessed affair it was when, in the course of all the external work, when the hands and the mind are always used as much as it is necessary, the whole heart nevertheless cleaves to the Savior.

♄ [Saturday], the 6th

In concluding the usual early service, Br. Gottfried sang to his dear Indians the following verse[d]:

> Bleibet doch ihr blutgen Wunden
> und du großer Seiten-Riß
> Tag und Nacht und alle Stunden
> unsere Indianern süß
> Ja du Seiten-Höhlgen

blut auf jedes Seelgen
hier in diesem Gnaden-ort
immerfort.
Mach sie selig hier und dort.[60]

The Indian stranger who was mentioned the day before yesterday left today.

Because of the considerable heat yesterday and today, many a drop[d] of sweat was shed by the brethren at work.

Today we again had Welsh corn and meat cooked for our workers.

Br. Christian visited Br. Gideon today, as he had already done once this week. It happened mainly for this reason: that he could see his [Gideon's] wife, Sr. Martha, and salute her warmly, as it has been noticed that she has not been quite full of light since the last Sunday conference. For that reason she also has not attended any of the occasions.

At the evening meeting, almost all of our brethren, who are ordinarily accustomed to coming home on Sunday, were already assembled. Sr. Martha was present as well.

Afterward, Br. Martin stayed with us for another short hour, and Br. Christian had a delightful discours with him about the Savior's love for us and the love of the brethren for one another, as the marque [mark] by which the Savior's people are recognized.

Because our Sabbath has made us tired today, we now hurried with joy to our rest.

☉ [Sunday], the 7th

The sermon was delivered around noon, to which came not only the brethren and sisters from the winter huts, but also another Indian with his family, so far unknown to both of us.

In the afternoon, after the quarter-of-an-hour for the baptized ones was finished, Br. Christian announced to the brethren and sisters that he intended to go with Br. Gideon to the North-River tomorrow and return as soon as possible.

On leaving the occasion, the brethren and sisters who had come from the winter huts also took a look at our building, and greatly rejoiced in it.

Today Br. Christian visited all the brethren and sisters in their huts before his departure, and found them in good spirits.

Also, he twice had the opportunity today to apply his surgery, in that he bled Br. Gottfried in the forenoon, and pulled a bad tooth for Br. Philippus in the afternoon. Both went very well.

~~We presented~~ Sister Leah from the winter huts was presented with ~~the~~ a half buschel of corn ~~which we had bought for her from Br. Gideon~~.[61] She thanked us for it with tears.

Today there also came here for a visit 2 unmarried Indians from Potatuck.

Noteworthy as well is the great quiet that rules *in specie* [Latin: especially] on Sundays in the huts of our Indians and among the brethren and sisters. This can be observed as well each time in the evening when their occasion is over.

☽ [Monday], the 8th

Having conducted the early service, Br. Christian still had to bleed an Indian, [the one] who was here for a visit from Potatuck.

Thereupon he departed from here for the North River with Br. Gideon. As the Indians' horses are very poor, they took 2 horses with them. Br. Christian promised to be back home within 4 days, unless he unexpectedly had to wait for the items in question.

Today Br. Jeremias took down his hut, which is the closest to the front of our house, and set it up behind the *fence*, not far from Br. Samuel's hut. He probably did it mostly so that he can now lay out a small garden behind his hut, for which he did not have any room here; this our small laid-out garden has effected in him.

That way we are gaining a nice space in front of the old and [partially] new house. And once we are finished with the construction and have this place cleaned up, and have removed the woodpile and wood-cuttings away from the front of the house and moved it to the back of the old house, then, with time, it will become green and have a good appearance.

In the afternoon Br. Martin and Joshua also began to fence in for themselves an area for a garden. And so it appears that what Br. Samuel told us a couple of days ago truly seems to be the case; namely, that presently some new movement has come from among the brethren which has the effect that they arrange their external affairs a little bit better than has happened thus far, like planting a little more for themselves and such, so that in the future, little by little, they would not need to go to the white people and work there. This cannot but please both of us brethren a great deal.

The two sisters Hannah and Magdalana of Wechquadnach arrived here in the afternoon.

Having occupied himself with a number of domestic matters today, Br. Gottfried read some English, and afterward enjoyed himself by reading the 26th speech of our precious *Ordinarii*[62] from a[nn]o 1747, which caught his eye and fell into his hands by chance.

In other respects, he was put a bit on the spot by the departure of Br. Christian, in that he had to conduct the occasions now in the morning and in the evening in <u>English</u>. He was not lacking the depth of heart to be sure, but the volubility of speech. However, one cannot have a great deal of reservations when it comes to these matters. He recommended himself to his Husband and approached this [task] poor and willingly.

After the evening service, everyone who has found his eternal placed there retired to the bloody wounds of the Lamb in a happy state.

♂ [Tuesday], the 9th

Having conducted the early service, Br. Gottfried had Br. Joshua stay on to sing with him through some Indian verses.

This week our construction will be at a standstill until Br. Christian brings the needed iron nails with him, for they are now lacking. The floor is already cut to size and fitted in, and the laths are affixed.

Because there was still a space left under the floor that had to be filled in with soil, this then was Br. Gottfried's work, outside of school today.

Today in school ~~he~~ Br. Gottfried was missing Br. Simon's son, an older boy, and upon inquiring about him, he learned that the boy was so ill that he could not keep on his feet for weariness; he reportedly had severe head and backaches. ~~To Br. Gottfried~~ This boy moved him to pity, and at home he looked for some jars[d] containing medicine. However, as he himself is not knowledgeable about medicine, and as there were no *signa* [Latin: inscriptions, i.e., labels] to be found on the jars about what sort of *species* were contained therein, the choice was difficult for him to make. Finally, he took a taste from a jar[d], where not all of it, but most of it, was *bezoar*.[63] In his mind he deemed this to be good, and following the evening service, administered of this to the boy, distilling 50 or 70 [drops] with water, trusting that the spilled drops of the blood of Jesus could and would bless it.

Most of the brethren had gone out today. Those who stayed at home worked on their gardens, fences, and huts.

Several sisters also had left to get the particular wood that they require for making baskets. They returned in the evening.

☿ [Wednesday], the 10th

After the early service, Br. Gottfried inquired about the sick boy and learned that matters had improved with him to the point that he would perhaps come to school today, which happened later on. Br. Gottfried made him a jug^d full of tea in the afternoon.

Given that stones had to be wedged under the sills of the new house, which in some places are somewhat high off the ground, and soil needed to be thrown on afterward, Br. Gottfried busied himself with this today, aside from his usual daily occupation.

Several brethren left in the forenoon to catch fish, and they brought home a considerable quantity in the afternoon.

A man, a native of Albany,[64] residing 5 miles from Shekomeko, arrived here wanting to buy corn from our Indians. But he had come (as the saying goes) to the hospital for a roast.[65] Because he spoke High German,[66] Br. Gottfried talked with him some. He knew something about Bethlehem and at some point in time had intended to go there.

Late in the evening, shortly before the occasion was to begin, and while Br. Gottfried was still outside digging, having worked himself into quite a sweat, he suddenly experienced the onset of a violent headache, which compelled him to suspend the evening occasion and lie down at once. The evening air indeed is usually quite comfortable for doing such [work] outside, but perhaps it was too cold this time, if one has heated oneself in the process. He could not sleep probably for several hours afterward, though by and by the pain disappeared.

♃ [Thursday], the 11th

Br. Gottfried conducted the early service yet again.

Br. Samuel went out 5 miles from here and returned home in the evening.

Br. Martin has for some time been working for our neighbor Mst. Mills. Yet he is always present at the morning and evening occasion. That is also how some other brethren do it when they work nearby.

As per their promise, Br. Gottfried expected the two brethren Christian and Gideon in the evening. For that reason he had cooked Welsh corn. But they did not arrive yet.

♀ [Friday], the 12th

Because it rained all day today, all the brethren and sisters stayed in their huts.

An older boy, who had been out for 4 days, 24 miles from here, came back home in the afternoon and reported to Br. Gottfried.

Br. Gottfried was also visited by the unmarried Br. Lucas in the afternoon.

♄ [Saturday], the 13th

In the forenoon our old Sister Erdmuth visited Br. Gottfried, who spoke with her some about the beloved Savior and His precious wounds.

Because Br. Christian had also arranged with Mst. Mills, our neighbor, for his people to plow 2 fields[67] for us, this work was thus carried out this week during his [Br. Christian's] absence.

In the afternoon, already somewhat late, Br. Christian, to our joy, finally arrived here with his old Gideon. They had to lay by because of yesterday's steady rain.

At Joh. Rau's their two Indian horses had run away, which they had led into the field for grazing, and Joh. Rau had given them one of his best, strong horses to take with them, on which to bring our things here, on the condition that Br. Christian return it himself.

On the arrival of both brethren we immediately had our house completely filled with brethren and sisters, boys and children, in keeping with the Indian way. After they had dispersed somewhat, Br. Gottfried prepared the afternoon luncheon for the arrivals. And after the items that had been brought were moved a bit to the side, Br. Christian conducted the evening occasion, and in closing, passed on greetings to the brethren and sisters from the dear Br. Jos[eph] [Spangenberg] and Sam[uel] [Herr?].

Afterward, we sat down in quiet and read with considerable appetite the beautiful letters and extracted news from Bethlehem and Europe that our dear

Br. Joseph had sent us from New York. We truly marveled at the effort he had made to write to us so much in his own hand, and regarded this as a sign of his great love for us.

Thereupon we went to bed much rejoiced.

(N.B. The items that we received without [having submitted] a *specification* have all [arrived] in good order and undamaged, and we most heartily thank our brethren and sisters for their love and efforts in our name and in the name of all those who will benefit from it.)

☉ [Sunday], the 14th

During the conference [the following was related] to the brethren and sisters:

1) The English letter that Br. Joseph wrote to the conference was read aloud by Br. Gottfried; Br. Joshua interpreted. The brethren and sisters greatly delighted in the news and the information that was therein related to them by Br. Joseph.[68]

2) The brethren and sisters were informed that all the Indians were subject to the *law* of the Connecticut *goverment*, and thus had to conduct themselves nice and quietly on all occasions, and in accordance with the laws of this place, for the sake of [their] conscience, not for fear of punishment.

3) That the brethren should plant for themselves as much as is possible for them, so that afterward, they would not need to run about in the woods or near the white people.

4) We would arrange for a little bit of land to be plowed for old Sr. Erdmuth on account of her incapacity and because of her age.

5) Then Br. Christian requested for the coming week the faithful assistance of the Indian brethren for the construction, because he now had the required nails in considerable supply.

6) There was also an English letter from Br. Post that was brought here yesterday as well. But because it concerned all the brethren and sisters in Pachgatgoch, Br. Gottfried would therefore read it to the entire assembly after the sermon.

7) Because it appeared to want to become custom here—that sometimes, after the meeting is ended [and] before the brethren and sisters leave, [that] the brethren and sisters need to be reminded about
external matters, for example, concerning their animals, chick-
ens, eggs, fields, and such, and this having been addressed by an
Indian brother, generally the interp[reter], and we do not at all deem
this thing to be proper—we asked the brethren and sisters to suspend this henceforth. If it was absolutely necessary to point out
something to the brethren and sisters, then one would have them
assemble at a different time, when it could happen more suitably
and better, also when there was more time for it. With that the conference was closed.

Toward noon the regular sermon took place. This after the letter from Br.
Post mentioned earlier was read to the entire assembly. Br. Joshua interpreted
it sentence by sentence. The greetings from Br. Johannes [von Watteville], Pyrlaeus, and Joh. Wade were passed on as well.

In the afternoon a couple of unbaptized menfolk joined the quarter-of-an-
hour for the baptized ones, because they wished to know what special matter
was treated there. They were permitted to do so this time, but without future
continuation. One of them was Benigna's husband.

Toward evening Br. Christian went with Br. Gottfried to view the two pieces
of land that had been plowed for us; namely, the one piece, 3/4 acres that Br.
Sensemann had used before, and then the 5/4 acres that were added this year.
In the process, Br. Christian selected several places[d] where we want to plant
beans, cucumbers, and squash.

Having returned home, Br. Christian told Br. Gottfried further details about
his journey. For example, that along the way he was received rather well by the
friends with whom we are acquainted; that he had the opportunity to speak
with several persons about our Savior and about blissful themes; that a couple
of those friends spoken to on the way want to visit us here in Pachgatgoch for
Pentecost; that Joh. Rau especially showed himself very amiable toward him;
and [that] our old Br. Gideon had truly acted like a child of God on every occasion. About the one mentioned last, Br. Christian could not say enough.

At this point it is not unfitting to note that, since our brief stay here, both of us brethren have experienced our old Gideon and Br. Samuel as the 2 most childlike, simple, and at the same time, most affectionate brethren of this place, based on our perceptions, hearts, and feelings.

This evening we also learned that Br. Joshua did not want to plant anything this year. We will, however, investigate whether this matter is quite true, and what, then, the reason for this is.

Also, Br. Gideon summoned the brethren and sisters to confer with them about the partitioning of their land that they presently require for planting.

☽ [Monday], [May] 15

Immediately after the early service Br. Christian set out to return the borrowed horse home to Joh. Rau, and to see whether our 2 Indian horses had been recovered thereabouts.

Because the conferences of the Indians usually have to be long, those brethren and sisters who had been at Br. Gideon's yesterday evening went to him again right after the early service in order to arrive at a decision regarding their affair, which had not been possible yesterday.

Afterward, Br. Gottfried wrote a bit in the diary, then held school, and later helped the construction people a little, who were at work by this time, by lending a hand where he could. Because everything was already prepared and cut to fit, nailing the *clapboards* and shingles in place went rather quickly, and the brethren took great pleasure in their work.

A couple of Indian strangers turned up here in the afternoon, and for several hours watched the brethren go about their work.

One of them (to whom Br. Joseph had also spoken along the way, back when we went from New York to Pachgatgoch) attended the occasion in the evening; the other one went on his way.

Because the brethren were fatigued, they retired early.

♂ [Tuesday], [May] 16

Right after the early service, Br. Gottfried started to clean up some in front of our house, and having already yesterday evening gathered together in a circle pieces of small scrap wood, shavings, and dug-up brush, he thus set it on fire. This is usually the Indians' work in the evening, when, at the same time, their children warm themselves by the fire and also jump over it once, to be sure. However, it is unsafe toward night, and we have previously warned against it.

Today the brethren cheerfully continued their work on the building, and it proceeded to the point where, by evening, the house was faced with clapboards all around and the roof was finished.

In the evening, as the brethren and sisters were leaving the occasion, a drunken Indian, who is the son of Martha's sister and is here quite frequently, could be heard near the huts screaming and making some dreadful noise, which at once instilled fear in everyone. Br. Gideon and Petrus, for fear, did not even go home, and stayed with Br. Gottfried. Dear Br. Philippus also came here. After they had sat together like this for a while, Br. Christian arrived home, bringing one of the lost Indian horses with him; the other one came home on its own the next morning. He had found them in Dover, 5 miles from here. Thereupon Br. Christian began to report that he had lost his way, or should have lost it by all rights, and had neared the winter huts. There he reportedly came upon this previously mentioned drunken Indian, along with our Jonathan, the unmarried one, who also had gotten completely drunk. They both are said to have made a great deal of noise, threatened to destroy the huts of the sisters there, [and] indeed, even beat Sr. Leah. Br. Christian had reportedly spoken to Jonathan, who had listened to reason.

Thus, Br. Gideon and Petrus sat with us for part of the night, while the fellow made such a noise in the huts here, and afterward, they went home. However, Philippus stayed with us throughout the whole night, lying down.

☿ [Wednesday], the 17th
Inside of our new house everything that could possibly be done was done, with respect to nailing fast the floor, shutters, doors, p[p]., which afforded plenty of work.

Br. Christian asked Br. Gideon and Joshua to speak today with the Indian who was drunk yesterday, and make him understand that henceforth such noise and misconduct could not be tolerated here at this place, but that other measures would have to be resorted to. However, Br. Gideon's hands are tied, in that he cannot do as he wishes in this matter, or is able to, and this because of his own

337

wife.[69] He is in quite a spot, the poor brother. More mention shall be made of this in the future, on a more opportune occasion.

The occasions in the morning and in the evening took place as usual.

Late in the evening Br. Gottfried related to Br. Christian something about the circumstances in which he found himself on this day 10 years ago: that at the well-known *battallie* [French: battle] of Chotusice,[70] in Bohemia, a great many bullets had to fly past him for him to be able to sit here in Pachgatgoch among the Indians 10 years later; that back then he had already been to Herrnhut for a visit; that at that time, when the Austrian Hussars had plundered part of our [soldiers'] encampment, he too had lost his belongings[d], white linen and such, leaving him with nothing but the shirt on his back, yet that his little bible was left which the Hussars had picked out from among all of his belongings and thrown on the field into the dust; and more of the same.

Afterward, we went to rest inside the bloody wounds of our Lamb blissfully and in good spirits.

♃ [Thursday], the 18th

This morning, right after the occasion had been conducted, both of us brethren went into the field to plant Welsh corn and beans. And because we wanted to get all of the 5/4 acres done at once, we occupied ourselves with this until the 3rd hour in the afternoon, and afterward came home very hungry and tired so that we hardly had the desire and strength to cook a few beans for ourselves.

While in the field, we remembered our dear brethren and sisters in Bethlehem, and here and there, and that we should have had a special festival day today, because according to the old style, our Savior's Ascension Day falls on this day. It is not celebrated here, however. On this occasion Br. Gottfried mentioned that this was the first time in his life that he helped cultivate a field.

School was suspended today.

The Indian who was mentioned on the 15th is still staying here and attends the occasions once in a while.

In the evening we also busied ourselves somewhat in our new house.

♀ [Friday], the 19th

In the forenoon, after school, several surveyors entered our house in friendship. They had been sent by the *government*, yet they never expressed their intention in any way, but instead left on horseback right after having sat with us for a bit. While they were still with us, our dear Br. Sensemann arrived to our great joy. We surely had not expected him.

The letters from Br. Joseph, Hehl,[71] Nathanael, p[p]., item the news from Bethlehem, Philadelphia, and Europe, greatly delighted us.

No sooner had Br. Sensemann set foot in our house then the brethren and sisters all at once appeared in great numbers to welcome their dear Br. Sensemann, immediately inquiring whether he had brought along his wife, for they very much longed for her.

Next, Br. Sensemann viewed our new house, which is finished to the point that it can be used for the occasions. How Br. Sensemann found us, of what nature our new building is, and what we have done since his absence, he himself will be able to report to our dear brethren and sisters in Bethlehem by word of mouth, to which, for the sake of brevity, only [passing] reference is made at this point.

Br. Sensemann conducted the occasion in the evening, wherein he committed the inexpressibly tender, loving heart of our Savior to the care of our brethren and sisters.

Afterward, the conference brethren and sisters stayed on with us for a bit, and at that time our dear Br. Joseph's letter in English was read to them by Br. Gottfried, which was quite weighty to them, and joyous. They were told that there was also a letter from Br. Nathanael, which is to be communicated to them tomorrow; likewise, that the petition drawn up for the [Connecticut] assemblee had arrived as well, which also shall be read to them shortly.

Furthermore, it was then agreed that tomorrow, quite early, Br. Amos is to go to Wechquadnach to inform the brethren and sisters there of the presence of Br. Sensemann, and to announce that Communion would be held here on Sunday. Br. Sam[uel] is to do the same in the winter huts.

The love feast that we intend to hold was thought of, and several things that we require for it were procured.

♄ [Saturday], the 20th

The early service was delayed until the brethren and sisters from the winter huts were here. Only the baptized ones attended it, though. At this time dear

Br. Joseph's letter in English was read again, and then also Br. Nathanael's, and the greetings that Br. Sensemann has brought with him were passed on to the brethren and sisters.

Afterward, Br. Sensemann spoke [with the] brethren and sisters [in preparation] for Communion, and time was spent with this until the evening occasion. He felt quite comfortable in his heart at this time, and he rejoiced in it a great deal, in part [because of] the ardent longing of many of the brethren and sisters [and] their hunger and thirst for the sacrament, [and] in part [because of] the open confessions by others and [their] acknowledgment of the state of their hearts and what great respect they have for Holy Communion. The sisters Hannah and Magdalena from Wechquadnach also had arrived here today and were spoken with [in preparation for Communion].

Br. Sensemann conducted the evening occasion.

☉ [Sunday], the 21st

The speaking with all the baptized ones [in preparation for Communion] was continued by Br. Sensemann, from morning until after 12 o'clock noon. (As speaking with the Indian brethren and sisters proceeds very slowly.)

Immediately thereafter the regular sermon was delivered by Br. Sensemann, and for the first time in our new house at that.

On this occasion, there was first a German, and afterward a few Indian verses sung.

Next, the congregation rose and Br. Sensemann said a prayer that he delivered in the English language, wherein he most earnestly appealed, for himself and the dear Indians, for the close presence of the dear Savior today and henceforth, and for a rather blissful feeling of the wounds, as often as one would come together in this house for teaching and listening.

Thereupon the congregation seated itself again, and the sermon was delivered, during which a pleasant breeze of grace was felt.

In the end, "_Nun balsamire, Herz u. Haus mit Blut-Geschmiere_,"[72] p[p]., was sung.

Because of the many persons who were present—some 80 had been counted, not including the children—our room was barely large enough.

At 4 o'clock, all the baptized ones enjoyed quite a blissful, delightful love feast, wherein Br. Sensemann brought to mind that our dear brethren and sisters in Bethlehem probably were not able to imagine at this time that we were already sitting here together in a new roomy house, dedicating our new house by means of such delightful occasions. He further added that, given that the construction has by now proceeded to the point where it could be made use of during summertime, the two brethren, Christian and Gottfried, were now able to concern themselves so much the more with visiting and speaking with the brethren and sisters, as well as related matters.

Some 40 persons were present for the love feast, not including several children. Br. Joshua and his Elisab[eth] performed the duties of servants thereat.

At 7 o'clock, a quarter-of-an-hour and the absolution for the communicants were held.

Preceding the latter, with the brown assembly having knelt before the heart of the Friend of the sinners, Br. Gottfried sang some German verses (which are found in the enclosure),[73] and our bloody Husband of the souls absolved all of us with His pierced hand.

Having dispersed for half of a quarter-of-an-hour, the brethren and sisters were summoned for Communion by blowing [the horn]. The number of communicants from our brown assembly was 19 this time, and one sister was present as a candidate on this occasion. None of the unmarried persons attended Communion.

The consecration took place with the words that are spoken at the institution of the Eucharist, in English.

Because the words that can be said about the blissful enjoyment of His martyred body and His holy blood are indeed of little honor to our dear and most beloved Lord, it is better to keep silent. Enjoying, feeling, keeping, and loving forever surely continues to be the best. Offered by God, we have truly partaken of the Easter Lamb that, with ardent love, was roasted for us on the cross — and we have drunk from the blood of reconciliation — [and] that on the day of His coronation with the green crown of thorns smelled inexpressibly sweet on the Father's throne above.

Several German verses, which together with the Indian ones were recited solo by Br. Gottfried, partly before [and] partly after Communion, can be found in the previously mentioned enclosure.

The brethren and sisters having parted blissfully and extraordinarily cheerful, Br. Gottfried now was presented with something new and unexpected.

Der weiseste Regierer
Schickt her den Bruder Führer
u. läßt ihm sagen: <u>Komm zurück</u>
komm, u. erfahr ein neues Glück.[74]

Dear Br. Führer, who was sent here *express* from Bethlehem with letters from Br. Joseph and Nathanael, had hurried greatly to arrive here before Communion. However, he nonetheless came too late, not benefiting from it other than by hearing the very last verses recited while in front of the door of our house. We received him afterward with love, broke open the letters that he had brought for us, and learned from them[75] ~~each one in his own section, to his very own enjoyment, our particular instruction and ordre~~.

Having spoken with him for a while, we quite blissfully laid down to rest in the soft bed[d] of Jesus' side.

☽ [Monday], the 22nd

Br. Christian conducted the early service in the new house, which will continue in this way for now and is a great convenience for the brethren and sisters, given that here the air can flow through nicely in the summertime.

Next, the drafted *petition* of the Indian brethren and sisters of this place, sent here by Br. Joseph, with which they intend to go before the *Assembly of Connecticut* this month, was separately read and made quite plain to the Brethren Gideon, Joshua, and Samuel, and a clean copy was made of it by Br. Gottfried.[76]

Meanwhile, Br. Sensemann and Christian went to view the field that we have planted. They also had the opportunity to speak with some of our communicants, who were very much full of light and in good spirits.

The Indian brethren now went about planting Welsh corn, and did so quite industriously all day long.

At noon our brethren and [the] inhabitants of Pachgatgoch assembled in our new house for the signing of the *petition*, bringing with them 2 white people from our neighborhood to be present as witnesses. The *petition* was again read aloud to everyone, and afterward, 15 Indians signed it with their usual marks, around which Br. Gottfried wrote their names, roughly this way: *Gide + ons his Mark*. In the end the 2 witnesses also set their names on it and confirmed with a few words that they themselves had seen the Indians make their marks in person. A *cop[y]* was made of it, which is to be sent to Bethlehem. The brethren want to go with the *petit[ion]* before the *court* tomorrow.[77]

In the afternoon Br. Gottfried finished the *diarium* with the exception of today, and readied himself for his intended journey to Bethlehem tomorrow. He had thought, in order to first become quite acquainted here, he first wanted to begin living here [at Pachgatgoch]. And see, things already took a different turn. But the expression *Ey nun, so laß ihn ferner thun u. red ihm nichts darein* prompted [him] that he was ready to return [to Bethlehem] at once.[78]

Br. Christian wrote several letters to Bethlehem.

Then Br. Gottfried visited the brethren and sisters in all the huts; they did not yet know anything about his departure.

We see now that Br. Joshua goes about planting just as well as the other brethren. This is to be considered along with what was said about this brother on the 14th of this month.

The brethren who were in the process of planting Welsh corn sent Br. Joshua to us, inquiring through him whether they could do us a favor if they planted our field along with theirs. A great favor was rendered to us by this, because otherwise Br. Christian, who is now going to stay here alone, would have had to do this with much difficulty. Yet, when many of them get [together], then it is easily done.

Sisters Hannah and Magdalena took leave of us today and returned to Wechquadnach in quite a happy state.

Following the evening occasion, the baptized brethren and sisters were informed through Br. Sensemann that Br. Gottfried had received his *rappell* [French: recall] from Bethlehem, and [he] assured our dear brown hearts that the congregation would not forget them, but would assume every necessary motherly care for them, to the best of its ability. Moreover, the greetings from our dear hearts, Br. Joseph, Nathanael, p[p]. [and] indeed, from the entire precious congregation, were passed on to them.

Thereupon Br. Gottfried took a very hearty and tender leave of his dear Indian brethren and sisters, recommending them to the most lovely Lamb of God and His precious wounds.

He will take his route by way of Rhinebeck and Esopus to Bethlehem, because Br. Führer, at the same time, wants to visit his father at the first place.

Br. Sensemann, however, who also will leave from here for Bethlehem tomorrow, is going to travel by way of New York, owing to some business there.

[Page break]

[Enclosure]

Beilage zum 21sten May

Vor der Absolution

Da fällt dir nun um deinen Fuß
ein Häuflein brauner Herzen
die du durch deine schwere Buß
erlößt, in Blut u. Schmerzen.

2.
Du lieber Gott u. Menschen-Sohn,
der Armen ihr Berather,
Schenk ihnen Absolution,
Du höchster Erz-Beicht-Vater.

3.
Leg die durchbohrte Hand auf sie,
Laß sie Vergebung spüren,
und was du ihnen schenkst hie,
ja nimmermehr verlieren.

4.
Schmück sie schön mit Gerechtigkeit
mit der Schneeweißen Seite,

344

u. mach sie dir in künftiger Zeit
zu deiner ganzen Freude.

5.

Dein blutger Schweiß, der Klumpenweis
von deinem Leib gefallen
der mache ihre Herzen heiß,
o Schönster unter Allen!

Vor der Administ. des ges. Brodts

Die Braune Schaar ist wieder da,
Nun kann sie es nicht laßen.
Jzt kommt sie deinem Leichnam nach
jzt wird sie dich umfaßen.

2.

Ja was umfaßen Sie wird gar
von deinem Leichnam zehren
wie er am Holz verblutet war
Du kannst es ihr nicht wehren.

3.

Sie hungert ungemein nach dir;
Nach dir ist ihr Verlangen.
Komm, gib dich allen Seelen hier
wie du am Creuz gehangen.

Vor der Adm. des ges. Weins

Was schon gegeßen hat von dir
das will von dir auch trincken.
Es fühlen alle Seelen hier,
dein holdes freundliches Wincken.

2.

So arm u. sündig, schlecht u. klein
sie sich auch immer fühlen
sind sie doch Leute, die um dein
u. auf dein Creuz hinzielen.

3.

Sie laßen ihre Jährlein
vor dir, dem Lamm hinfließen.
Ihr durst geht ganz in dich hinein
Blut wollen sie genießen.

4.

Blut, das ihr Gott, der starke Held
ihr großer Heils-Erfinder
vergoßen vor dir ganze Welt
u. vor dir gläubgen Sünder.

5.

Das, das verlangen sie allein
in Specie nun Heute.
Gib ihnen von dem rothen Wein
aus deiner offnen Seite.

6.

Sie wollen gern als Würmelein
im Blute immer schweben,
u. in dein Herz begraben seyn
da ist ihr ewges Leben.

Nach dem AbMhl.

Das war einmal ein selger Tag
den uns das Lamm gegeben

das für uns auf der Schlachtbank
Nun wird sichs fröhlich leben.

2.

Und damit wäre heut geweiht
auch diese neue Hütte
dem Lamm, das unser Seligkeit,
am Creuz mit Blut erstritte.

3.

Lamm, fange nun aufs neue an
dein Pachgatgok zu segnen
Du lieber Herz-u. Schmerzens-Mann
Laß viel Blut darauf regnen.

4.

O Vater! Halt die Hut u. Wacht
durch deine starke Engel
nun immerfort, bey tag u. Nacht
auch über diese Sprengel.

5.

O Blut vom theuren Gottes-Lamm
u. o ihr heilgen Beulen
bringt jedes Herze hier in Flamm
Kommt segnen, stärken, heilen.

6.

Macht dir, o. Geist, Du Mutter-Herz,
du Land-und Leut-Bekehrer,
hier manche Seel noch täglich Schmerz,
Dein Mühen stündlich schwerer.

7.

Hör darum nicht auf von dem Lamm
und seinem Blut zu zeugen;
Es muß doch vor dem Creuzes Stamm
sich endlich alles beugen.

8.

Dem Gottes-Lamm sind doch schon
die Indianschen Heiden
bestimmt, vor seine Müh zum Lohn
und ihm zu ewgen Freuden.

9.

Ist denn das Fest[79] nun ganz vorbey?
Bewahr uns Gott! Wir halten
nun Feste alle tag aufs neu,
bis zum Kuß seiner Spalten.

(N.B. Der 5te vers muß nach dem 3ten folgen.)

Joachim Heinrich Sensemann

7 August 1752 to 18 February 1753

Pachgatgoch Diarium, From *anno* 1752, Month of August, the 7th until the 13th of October *a.c.*[1]

August 7, 1752

Brother Christian Fröhlich readied himself to travel ~~himself~~ back to our dear Bethlehem, beforehand taking leave in all of the huts. Br. Gideon went with him to Bethlehem. Br. Sensemann accompanied them for a few miles, and then they bade one another a heartfelt farewell. Meanwhile, Sister Sensemann had been paid a visit by the *minister* (Mr. [Cyrus] Marsh) and his wife from Kent, who acted very ~~modest~~ amiably. We had a blessed quarter-of-an-hour in the evening; Martin interpreted.

☽ [Monday], the 8th

~~In the morning~~ I delivered the morning blessing, entrusting ourselves and the brown assembly to the pierced heart of the Lamb[d] by means of a heartfelt prayer. Sister Priscilla, together with her daughter Salome, came home from having been in the woods. They were very glad to find us here. I presented them with several things that Brother Post had sent for them from London.[2] She was very glad and grateful for them. The sister[s] frequently come to visit my wife. I cleared a patch[d] of land for myself and sowed some turnip seeds.

☿ [Wednesday], the 9th

After the morning blessing several Indian brethren went into the neighborhood to work. My wife visited several Indian sisters. The *minister* from Kent called on us because it was raining hard. I presented a pipe of tobacco to him. Joshua and Elisabeth came home. They both came and welcomed us. I conducted the quarter-of-an-hour in the evening; Samuel interpreted. We thought of our dear Bethlehem much and we felt especially well.

♃ [Thursday], the 10th

I intended to visit the brethren and sisters in the winter huts today, together with my wife. I learned, however, that nearly all of them had gone working. We visited the brethren and sisters in the huts here; talked with them ~~the brethren and sisters~~ about their hearts. Lucia was very openhearted toward my wife and felt blissful and well in her heart. Lucas and Philippus came home from hunting, full of light and in good spirits. My wife was paid a visit by 2 unmarried English women. I conducted the quarter-of-an-hour in the evening, with blessing.

♀ [Friday], the 11th

Br. Gideon brought me a letter from Br. Christian Fröhlich, from which I learned that the white people had frightened Gideon with respect to the smallpox, and Br. Christian had therefore sent him back. I was pleased in a way. My wife and I went to the winter huts to visit the brethren and sisters there, yet found only Sr. Sarah and her daughter Leah at home, along with some unbaptized ones. My wife then occupied herself with the sisters, talking with them about their hearts. We went to see my old house where I had lived the first winter. When we returned, they [the Indians] had cooked us new Welsh corn. We ate and set out for home again. I still went to Kent and got some bread for myself. Meanwhile, my wife was visited by several Indian sisters.

♄ [Saturday], the 12th

We thought of our dear Bethlehem. The Indian brethren and sisters again gathered at home; Jeremias with his family, Christian from New Milford, Benigna with her husband, Sister Maria, and several more. They were affectionate and in a happy state. I conducted the quarter-of-an-hour in the evening; the Savior was near us.

☉ [Sunday], the 13th

Several English women came to attend the occasion. Afterward, the brethren and sisters arrived from the winter huts, and then we gathered for the sermon. The Savior was near us and everyone was *atent* [attentive] in listening. After the sermon I visited Martin. I talked with Gottlob about his heart. Next, I conducted the quarter-of-an-hour for the baptized ones, with blessing. In the end, we enjoyed the kiss of peace. My wife visited several sisters, and I was paid a visit by an unbaptized Indian, Sekes, on whose heart the Savior is working. In the evening we thought of our dear Bethlehem, and we felt especially well, and then we laid ourselves blissfully down to sleep.

☽ [Monday], the 14th

After the morning blessing I visited Christian and his wife Gottliebe, who wanted[3] to go to New Milford. Several brethren and sisters again set out in order to work for white people. My wife visited the remaining sisters.

♂ [Tuesday], the 15th

I went with Samuel to an English man on account of outward business. Martin and Lucas took leave to go to the seaside; Martin wanted to visit his brother. Joshua went to Newtown.

☿ [Wednesday], the 16th

We were paid a visit by 2 awakened English women from New Milford. They were most affectionate. My wife went with them to visit the Indian sisters. Because it became too late for them, they stayed here and went along to the quarter-of-an-hour in the evening. The Savior was near me with His wounds. I spoke about the watchword of that day. Joshua came home full of light and in good spirits.

♃ [Thursday], the 17th

After the morning blessing the 2 women readied themselves for their journey home. They had been quite pleased by everything, except that we did not pray as long and as much as they did in their meetings. I went into the woods to cut wood into clapboards.[4] I conducted the quarter-of-an-hour in the evening; Joshua interpreted.

♀ [Friday], the 18th

I went back to my work of making *klaborts* [clapboards]. My wife visited all the sisters who were at home, finding them all in good spirits and most affectionate.

♄ [Saturday], the 19th

Samuel went on horseback to Wechquadnach to visit the Indians at that place today, and old Erdmuth came home from there. The other brethren and sisters, who had been working for the English people that week, also came home. Schiry came to visit me along with an Indian stranger from Farmington. I talked with them about the Savior, and asked the stranger if he too felt in his heart a desire to become the Savior's. He answered yes.

☉ [Sunday], the 20th

[In the] morning I summoned the conference brethren and sisters, Gideon, Martha, Joshua, and Elisabeth. We began the conference with the verse^d *Seegne unß auß deinen Heiligen Wunden.*[5] I asked the brethren and sisters whether they felt well and cheerful in their hearts. One after the other, they began to say how they felt in their hearts. Afterward, we had to confer with one another on several subjects. We came to talk about Leah, that her heart was not in a good state, and that they had heard that Gottlob wanted to marry her. We said that we wanted to talk with her about this and hear whether there was anything to that matter. We felt right comfortable during the conference. After the brethren and sisters had assembled, I called the meeting by blowing [the horn]. Thus, everyone gathered. Three English people joined us as well. I spoke on John, chapter 6: *Das ist Gottes Werck das ihr an dem glaubt den er gesant hat.*[6] The Savior was near us, and everyone was very attentive. That afternoon I conducted a quarter-of-an-hour for the married people, and my wife, for the single sisters, both with blessing. We talked with ~~Sister~~ Leah. Her mother Sarah was present. We asked her [Leah] about her heart and how she stood with the Savior, but she was not able to say much by way of response. We inquired about the matter regarding Gottlob, and pointed out to her that she had been told enough when she sent away her husband Johannes—and if she took Gottlob to be her husband, she should know that she could no longer have any connection with us or with the Savior. Her mother Sarah was very sad. After that, 6 English people came in anticipation that there would still be a sermon. They came into our house for a while, and when the opportunity presented itself, I told them something about the Savior and His reward, which is ready for the poor sinners if only they came to Him just the way they were. One among them had been in Martin's house and had wondered whether the sinners were to come to the Savior. Martin had answered him that it surprised him [Martin] that this struck him [the questioner] as so strange; in his [Martin's] heart he felt it most plainly and weighty, and he had experienced it in this way. In like fashion, he [Martin] had spoken a good deal with them about the subject. They took a friendly leave of us, urging us to visit them.

☽ [Monday], the 21st

After the morning blessing I started working on our house, tearing off the old bast[7] and covering it[8] up with *klaport* [clapboard], which I had made the previous week. Gideon went to a white man on the other side of the winter huts. On returning, he brought word that Rebecca, the wife of David, had been delivered of a young daughter. Gideon announced this to the brethren and sisters after the quarter-of-an-hour.

♂ [Tuesday], the 22nd

We were paid a visit by Mr. Mills[9] and his wife. The wife has something of the Savior in her heart, thus, she came to speak with my wife about her heart. She lamented that she had allowed herself to get so deeply involved with worldly matters and had suffered damage to her heart. My wife directed [her] straight to the Savior, to give her heart to Him; that way, the [worldly] matters would surely fall away on their own. They both took their leave with great love, entreating us to please visit them, which we had to promise them.

☿ [Wednesday], the 23rd

We went to visit the brethren and sisters in the winter huts, finding Rebecca with her child well and in a happy state. David too was full of light and well, as were the other sisters. My wife took the little heart[d], and kissed it, and recommended it to the Lamb[d].

♃ [Thursday], the 24th

Old Sister Maria and Sarah came from the winter huts to visit us. Martin and Lucas came home in altogether good spirits. We had a blessed quarter-of-an-hour in the evening.

♀ [Friday], the 25th

In the morning, after the morning blessing, old Erdmuth came and joined us for breakfast, telling us something about her heart. She is blissful and in quite good spirits, and at 80 years of age such a good walker that, on hearing that we need something from 2 or 3 miles away, she is immediately ready to get it for us, and cannot be stopped from doing so.

♄ [Saturday], the 26th

Today I made preparations to see whether we could make a small oven so that we need not always go to the white people to buy bread whenever we want to hold a love feast; we talked with several brethren about this. Most of those who had been out came home. In the evening we conducted the quarter-of-an-hour; we felt comfortable in our hearts on this occasion.

☉ [Sunday], the 27th

We talked with Gottlob concerning Leah, whether he intended to take her to be his wife; Joshua was also present. He said no, he did not want to do that, yet he was not in a right happy state and full of light about it. We then pointed out to him the Savior's mind. Several English people came ~~with horses to attend~~ for the sermon. The brethren and sisters having assembled, the meeting was called by blowing [the horn]. We were disturbed in holding the quarter-of-an-hour as the white people stayed here in the Indian huts after the sermon, and some with us. Samuel came in the evening, saying that an English man wanted to have him arrested on account of an old debt of 3 #,[10] which Gideon had taken upon himself to pay, and for which he had received things in exchange. I said I would talk to Gideon about it.

☽ [Monday], the 28th

After the morning blessing Gideon had the brethren and sisters carry stones and clay for the baking oven. (Beforehand, we got Gideon, Joshua, and Jeremias together in our house, and talked about the debt to Doctor Sackett.[11] But Gideon did not want to agree to pay it.) Afterward, we set about building a small baking oven, so that we can bake bread ourselves when we want to have a love feast. [The] brethren and sisters were all industrious, and within a short time there were as many stones gathered as we needed for it. Jeremias and I started walling up [the oven]. Samuel and Lucas took leave to go out hunting.

♂ [Tuesday], the 29th

After the morning blessing Jeremias and I again went about our work. Gideon, [the] Joshuas, and [the] Martins came and said that they wanted to go into the woods this week to make *canuhs* and brooms so that they could buy blankets for the winter. Sister Priscilla went into the woods with her 2 daughters, along with some other sisters, to to get wood for baskets and brooms.

☿ [Wednesday], the 30th

We held no meeting as nearly everyone was out. I again went to work on the baking oven and it was entirely finished today.

♃ [Thursday], the 31st

Sister Priscilla came home in good spirits with her 2 daughters Salome and Benigna, and several other sisters. My wife visited the sisters. Sr. Magdalena had said that her son Mackwah very much longed to be baptized. He had been promised that he would be baptized when a brother came from Bethlehem.

♀ [Friday], September 1, 1752

I went to Sharon on account of outward business. Returned home in the evening, finding everyone who was home in good spirits.

♄ [Saturday], the 2nd

My wife and I went to visit the brethren and sisters in the winter huts. Most had gone out to work for English people [*words crossed out*]. The ones we found at home were full of light and in good spirits. On our way back home, we came upon Christian Führer from Rhinebeck. We learned that Henrich Martin was with him as well. They then gave me several letters among which was one from our dear Martin Mack, from which I learned that a great visit of the Nanticocs [Nanticokes] had occurred in Gnadenhütten and Bethlehem, and that the Brethren were welcome to them, which pleased us greatly. [The] Joshuas, [the] Martins, and Br. Gideon came home in good spirits and full of light. I

355

conducted the quarter-of-an-hour in the evening. The Savior was near us with His wounds.

☉ [Sunday], the 3rd

In the morning, several English people came to attend the sermon. However, being indisposed, I was unable to hold the meeting before noon, yet as matters improved somewhat, I held [the] sermon and quarter-of-an-hour in the afternoon.

☽ [Monday], the 4th

Because the 2 brethren from Rhinebeck wanted to visit the Indian brethren and sisters in their huts, I went with them. The Savior provided the opportunity in order that I could talk with several about their hearts, which was edifying and weighty to the 2 brethren. And because the weather was so rainy, they [the brethren from Rhinebeck] stayed with us today as well. We had a blessed quarter-of-an-hour in the evening.

♂ [Tuesday], the 5th

After the morning blessing both Führer and H. Martin set out on their journey home. I accompanied them to the first plantation. They expressed that they had felt well being with us. When I returned, my wife and I went about roasting green ~~dried~~ Welsh corn, which the English here call *schwit corn.*[12]

☿ [Wednesday], the 6th

Today nothing of note occurred. Samuel and Lucas came back home from hunting, not having shot anything more than one deer.

♃ [Thursday], the 7th

We again went into the field to make *schwit corn.* Sr. Priscilla and Magdalena came to help my wife. I conducted the quarter-of-an-hour in the evening. My wife and I talked about and thought of our dear Bethlehem a great deal. We felt especially well.

♀ [Friday], the 8th

After the morning blessing I went into the woods to cut wood [*words crossed out*]. My wife [*words crossed out*] was busy doing the wash. On returning home with a piece of wood, I found the dear heart Martin Mack in my house, together with his father-in-law Johannes Rau. I was surprised and delighted at the same time, for I ~~was~~ [*word crossed out*] had expected Brother Martin in about one month. We kissed and rejoiced most tenderly, being glad to see each other. Sensemann conducted the quarter-of-an-hour in the evening, with blessing.

♄ [Saturday], the 9th

Br. Martin Mack delivered the morning blessing, talking of the state of bliss that one is able to experience near the Savior and His wounds. We felt quite comfortable on this occasion. Hans Rau again set out on his journey. Martin and Sensemann accompanied him for a distance. Lucas went on horseback to the mill and got 2 *buschel[s]* of flour that Sensemann had ordered ground. Then Br. Martin Mack began to tell us about his journey, [about] how *mistisch*[13] it had looked at the Oneidern [Oneidas] in the beginning, and how the Savior had changed their hearts, that they not only let the brethren pass through their lands but were also helpful, such that the *chi[e]fs* from the other nations were summoned to Onondagon [Onondaga] by them, for which we could be grateful to the Savior.[14] ~~Sensemann conducted the quarter-of-an-hour in the evening.~~ Joshua, Gottlieb, and several other brethren returned home from hunting. On learning that Martin was here, they came and welcomed him with tender love. Br. Sensemann conducted the quarter-of-an-hour in the evening; Joshua interpreted.

☉ [Sunday], the 10th

Brother Mack held the meeting. Everyone who was present was very *atent* [attentive]. The Lamb[d] was feelingly near to us. That afternoon the baptized ones came alone, at which time Brother Mack told them about the visit that they were paid in Gnadenhütten from the Nanticocs [Nanticokes], which was very weighty to them. After the occasion the brethren and sisters were told that there would be a love feast tomorrow afternoon.

☽ [Monday], the 11th

After the morning blessing all of the Indian brethren and sisters readied themselves to build an Indian house for a family from the seaside that wants to move up here; some are already here. [*Lines crossed out*] ~~We found all of them industrious~~

~~in the field making Schwit corn. Almost all of them knew him, for they had seen~~
~~him at the seaside 9 years ago, and were glad to see him.~~[15] [The] Sensemanns
made preparations for the love feast, and after [the] blowing [of the horn], all
of the brethren and sisters assembled in the church.[16] Sensemann commenced
the love feast with a German verse[d], and then the female and male servants carried round the love feast's bread. Br. Sensemann said that he and his wife had
long desired to hold a love feast with the Indian brethren and sisters, but it had
not been possible sooner. Now that our dear Brother Mack was present, it was
more pleasing to us yet, and because he had undertaken a great journey among
the 6 Nations,[17] he would surely tell us something about it. Whereupon Brother
Mack began to tell them what the intention was of our travels among the 6 Nations, and then [about] the journey itself, and after that [he passed on to them]
a heartfelt greeting from Br. ~~Rund and~~ David ~~Zeisberger~~.[18] There was a feeling
of love and grace present. Everyone was joyous and full of light. Br. David and
Sister Rebecca came with their little daughter[d] and asked that she be washed
with the Savior's blood; it would be a blessing for them. We could not refuse
them. It was pointed out to them that children like this have to be preserved
and raised in the grace that they receive through baptism. There was a general
meeting in the evening, at which time everyone appeared here. Br. Mack delivered a blessed address. Afterward, it [the child] was flooded by Br. Mack with
the red stream from Jesus' wounds, receiving the name Anna Maria, and was
consecrated by 4 sisters, among whom were 2 at the age of 80, with the v[erse]
Die Seele Christi Heilige Dich.[19] And then everyone retired blissfully.

♂ [Tuesday], the 12th

Following the morning blessing, Br. Samuel was sent by Br. Mack to Johannes
Rau, for he intended to go straight to New York from here. Sensemann and
Mack visited the brethren at their house construction, and then they went to
the winter huts to visit the brethren and sisters there. They found everyone
busy roasting *schwit korn*. Br. Mack talked with some about their hearts. Br.
Mack conducted the quarter-of-an-hour this evening, portraying quite passionately to the brown assembly the Savior with His red wounds. The foreign
Indian woman attended the meeting regularly, and Br. Sensemann also spoke
with her about the Savior.[20]

☿ [Wednesday], the 13th

Brother Mack delivered the morning blessing by way of farewell, wishing that the brown brethren and sisters steadfastly abide in the wounds of the Savior with their hearts. After breakfast he, together with Sensemann, went visiting in all the huts, taking a heartfelt leave of all the brethren and sisters, and then set out on his journey toward New York. Sensemann accompanied him, and they had yet many a beneficial conversation with each other, and then they bade each other a heartfelt farewell. It surely hurts a little each time when one takes leave of one another. Sensemann set out to return [to Pachgatgoch]. He visited the brethren and sisters in the winter huts, finding them all affectionate and in good spirits. In the evening, after the quarter-of-an-hour, I passed on to them Br. Mack's greetings that he had sent back for them. It pleased them and they thanked him.

♃ [Thursday], the 14th

I delivered the morning blessing in the morning; the Savior was near me. I was able to present to the brown assembly the martyred Lamb^d quite in the spirit of the wounds. Sr. Sarah and Caritas went to the seaside to help bring up the Indians' belongings. My wife visited the sisters in all the huts; she had a heartfelt conversation with them, during which she felt most comfortable, delighting in the Indian sisters.

♀ [Friday], the 15th

My wife visited several sisters. Sr. Justina said that since the love feast and baptism she was feeling especially well. I visited several brethren, with blessing. In the evening, 2 unbaptized, unmarried fellows joined the meeting, seating themselves wrongly on the bench, who were told after the quarter-of-an-hour that, if they wanted to attend the meeting, they needed to be orderly, or they would be asked to leave.

♄ [Saturday], the 16th

Today nothing of note occurred, except that everyone went about his work industriously.

☉ [Sunday], the 17th

In the morning, we had the conference brethren and sisters assembled in order to learn from them whether anything had occurred among the brethren and sisters. We learned that everything proceeded along its path of grace.

After the brethren and sisters had assembled, the occasions were conducted as usual.

☽ [Monday], the 18th

I delivered the morning blessing at an early hour. The Savior was feelingly near to us. The Indian sisters were busy drying sweet corn,[21] for it had rained for several days and most of it had spoiled on them.

♂ [Tuesday], the 19th

Gideon, [the] Joshuas, and Martin went to the previous place,[22] about 9 miles from here, to make *canuhs*. I and my wife were busy gathering beans. My wife visited several sisters with whom she talked about their hearts.

☿ [Wednesday], the 20th

Jeremias and several sisters and boys rode with 4 horses to the seaside to get things for the Indians who want to move up here. Several brethren went bear hunting. Toward evening the brethren came home from hunting; they had shot a deer, of which they sent us a piece. We had the quarter-of-an-hour in the evening; Samuel interpreted. I felt quite well on that occasion.

♃ [Thursday], the 21st

The brethren and sisters were all going about their work industriously, and blissful at the same time.

♀ [Friday], the 22nd

Following many requests, I and my wife visited [the] Mills in Kent; [Mrs. Mills is] an awakened woman.

♄ [Saturday], the 23rd

After the morning blessing I visited the brethren and sisters in the winter huts, but found no one other than David's family, all of whom were full of light and in good spirits. Toward evening Gideon, and thereafter Jeremias and his *compani*, came home full of light and well, so that we rejoiced when we saw them.

☉ [Sunday], the 24th

A number of English people came, asking whether the meeting would begin soon. They were told, as soon as the Indians were assembled. Several Indian brethren came to visit me. Gottlob and several others came home. After the brethren and sisters from the winter huts had arrived, the meeting was called by blowing [the horn]. Everyone having assembled, we began the meeting with English and Indian verses[d], and then the text Jn. 57.15 was talked about; the Savior was near us and everyone listened quietly and *atent* [attentively]. Following the sermon I went with my wife to view God's Acre. Afterward, the quarter-of-an-hour for the baptized brethren and sisters was conducted with blessing. David and his wife Rebecca came to visit us; they both were affectionate. They took leave at the same time and went back home.

☽ [Monday], the 25th

I had intended to go to Wechquadnach today to visit the brethren and sisters and the other Indians there, but my chest had become so afflicted that I could hardly talk. Thus, I was unable to conduct the morning blessing. My wife also was not well. Almost all the brethren and sisters came to visit us. Gideon went with his Martha to visit the brethren and sisters in the winter huts. On coming home they brought us word that the brethren and sisters were well. Samuel and his wife Lucia both went 5 miles to get broom wood. Sensemann went to visit [the] Christians. They both were affectionate and hard at work making baskets. I delighted in them, which I also expressed to them. I conducted the quarter-of-an-hour in the evening, with blessing.

♂ [Tuesday], the 26th

My chest felt very poorly. Gideon boiled roots, of which I had to drink, but it was not having any effect. We felt comfortable during the evening quarter-of-an-hour; there was a tender feeling of grace present.

☿ [Wednesday], the 27th

All the brethren and sisters were going about their work industriously, making *canuh* [canoes] and baskets. Sister Susanna and Magdalena arrived here from Wechquadnach. Gottlieb had shot a bear, of which they sent us a piece as well.

♃ [Thursday], the 28th

I and Brother Samuel went several miles today, to an English man, on account of outward business. I also thought my sickness would subside in the process.

In the evening I conducted the quarter-of-an-hour with a warm and feeling heart.

♀ [Friday], the 29th

My wife and I went into the field to gather beans. Toward evening Brother Martin came down the river with a *canuh*. He was well and full of light, bringing us word that Joshua and his family were well and intended to come home tomorrow. Late in the evening Gideon came and said that he had just received word that Withly, Benigna's husband, who had been working for an English man 5 miles from here, had suffered a fall in the barn and lay like he was dead. I said they could send someone there as soon as possible, and if he wanted me, I would ~~come~~ go there the next day.

♄ [Saturday], the 30th

In the morning, Gideon and several other brethren and sisters went to visit the Indian who had fallen. Benigna and a number of other brethren and sisters came home. A neighbor brought the Indian who had fallen home on a horse. Timotheus, as well as 2 unbaptized ones, arrived here from Wechquadnach.

☉ [Sunday], October 1, [1752]

The general occasion was conducted around noon, afterward, [there were] several quarter-of-an-hour services by choir, wherein the brethren and sisters were full of light and in good spirits.

☽ [Monday], the 2nd

After the morning blessing Brother Gideon came to me, saying that the brethren wanted to go down to Gihorn and lay up a new house for him.[23] I visited them at their work, and things proceeded in an altogether orderly fashion. Because they came home very late in the evening, no quarter-of-an-hour was conducted this time.

♂ [Tuesday], [October] 3

Timotheus took leave and set out to return home along with his brother. Petrus went to the seaside with wooden utensils to sell. David and Rebecca came to visit us; they said that they wanted to go and work in the woods for several weeks. They were reminded never to lose sight of the Savior and His bloody wounds. Martin took leave to go and work in the woods along with his father and brother. In the evening, following the quarter-of-an-hour, [and] having eaten our evening meal, ~~came~~ we heard that a stranger was coming into Pachgatgoch. My wife said, Perhaps it is someone from Bethlehem. I replied, Who, then, will it be? Thereupon, to our amazement and delight, the 2 Indian brethren Nathanael and Anton from Gnadenhütten came through the door. We welcomed them with tender love. Nathanael soon handed us a package of letters and [passed on] many tender greetings[d] and kisses[d] from our dear hearts in Bethlehem, Nazareth, and Gnadenhütten, which was more than only a small joy for us. However, as I opened the letters, [the news] of our most beloved Christel's going home soon caught my eye, which cut my dear A. Catharine and me to the quick, causing that we almost could not read any further on account of our tears ~~and quite robbed me of my sleep that night~~. Gideon's house being too crowded, the 2 brethren slept in our house. Our most beloved Christel's going home quite robbed us of our sleep that night.[24]

☿ [Wednesday], the 4th

In the morning, Jonathan was sent to tell Gideon, Joshua, and Martin that 2 brethren, Nathanael and Anton from Gnadenhütten, were here [and] that they shall please come home. I then enjoyed myself with my dear letters[d] and rejoiced at the tender love of the dear brethren and sisters for us. Nathanael and Anton visited the brethren and sisters in their huts. At noon, the brethren Gideon, Joshua, and Martin came home. Nathanael talked with Br. Gideon [about] what his business here was, namely, to make known here and in Wanachquaticok the covenant that has been made between the Nanticoks [Nanticokes] and the Brethren in Gnadenhütten and Bethlehem. Gideon at once summoned all the Indians, great and small, and asked me whether this [*word crossed out*] could be announced in our church, which I allowed them. Beforehand, Nathanael opened the *belte* [belts] and *strings of wampon* [wampum], and I read to him what each said.[25] Everyone having assembled, we went into the church, and Nathanael made known to them one matter after the other. This was very dear and weighty to them, especially that they [the Nanticokes] wanted to hear words of our God and Lord. In the evening I conducted the quarter-of-an-hour, with blessing.

♃ [Thursday], the 5th

In the morning, during the morning blessing, our Husband was feelingly near to us. Nathanael and Anton set out on their journey to Wanachquaticok. (Gideon and Joshua [and] Martin again went into the woods to work on their *canuh*). I visited several brethren and sisters. In the evening, during the quarter-of-an-hour, 2 English attended the meeting; Samuel interpreted.

♀ [Friday], the 6th

I went into the woods today to cut wood for the winter. Meanwhile, my wife was visited by several Indian sisters. Gideon came home along with the 2 brethren Joshua and Martin. He came to visit us; said he was now finished to working in the woods.

♄ [Saturday], the 7th

During the morning blessing I entrusted the brown assembly to the care of the bloody wounds of our precious Lamb and Chief Elder. I felt quite comfortable on this occasion. Today we also thought of our dear Bethlehem a great deal and observed the Sabbath with them in our hearts. I wrote in the *diarium*. I am still somewhat sickly. I visited Brother Martin; he was affectionate and well. Several brethren came home in the evening.

☉ [Sunday], the 8th

In the morning, Samuel summoned the conference brethren and sisters to our house. Many a matter was conferred through about with them, especially about Communion. They expressed a great longing for it, and gave us to understand that they have been awaiting it for a long time. However, as the issues that had prevented it were pointed out to them, some became sinners and admitted that they were to blame for this [the delay]. Then it was agreed that it [Communion] should take place next Sunday. A true feeling of love could be felt. We kissed one another with heartfelt love, and then the meeting was called by blowing [the horn]. Owing to the bad weather, there were not as many present as usual; still, the Savior was near us. Past noon the quarter-of-an-hour was conducted for the baptized ones, and the heartfelt greetings from the dear hearts in Bethlehem and the other places were passed on, likewise [the news of] the going home of the most beloved Christel, which deeply grieved them. It was also announced that Communion shall be next Sunday; it was a great matter when the Savior gave us His flesh to eat and His blood to drink. During the coming days the brethren and sisters should discuss this with the Savior. We wished this for all of them, and [it] would be a great joy for us if they all would be able to enjoy this. Thereupon we had the Kiss of Peace and parted cheerfully.

☽ [Monday], the 9th

After the morning blessing I went visiting in several huts; found [there] Petrus, who along with Amos had just come home from the seaside. Gideon came and said he wanted to go with wooden utensils to Quaker Hill; perhaps he would not return home today.[26] Samuel also departed for several days. Sr. Justina visited my wife and told her that she felt so well near the bloody wounds of the dear Savior that she was not *capabel* [capable] of expressing it. We felt especially well during the quarter-of-an-hour in the evening and full of feeling.

♂ [Tuesday], the 10th

Following the quarter-of-an-hour it was announced that school would be commenced today. Before noon the boys' [school] would be held, and in the afternoon, the girls', which indeed had its rather nice beginning. The boys all have resolved to learn English; among the girls there is perhaps still one left who is learning German. Old Erdmuth was sent to Kent to order something for our upcoming love feast. The Indian brethren helped Joshua work on his new house.

☿ [Wednesday], the 11th

My wife visited several sisters in the forenoon, as I was holding school with the boys, and in the afternoon I visited the winter huts but did not find many [Indians] at home. In the evening some Indian strangers were present. The Savior was near us.

♃ [Thursday], the 12th

I talked with Brother Gideon about some Indian brethren and sisters who were working in the woods, whether someone should be sent to them. Br. Amos was charged with informing them that Communion would take place this Sunday, and that they had to be home this Friday. Toward evening our dear brethren Nathanael and Anton returned to this place from Wanachquaticok. The Indian brethren and sisters and we welcomed them with tender love. Gideon and Nathanael talked with each other. After the evening quarter-of-an-hour, Gideon summoned all the Indians to his house, where Nathanael then presented the *pelt* [belt] from Wanachquaticok, and the words that Abraham[27] ~~shall be Captein in Gnadenhütten shall~~, which pleased them well, and they too sent their word and a *pelt* [belt].

♀ [Friday], the 13th of October

I delivered the morning blessing at an early hour; Nathanael interpreted. During it I felt in my heart quite in the spirit of the wounds. Afterward, I also wrote several letters to my dear hearts in Bethlehem. Given that the Indian brethren had work to do several miles from here, they took a heartfelt leave of Br. Nathanael before [departing], sending warm greetings to the congregation[s] in Bethlehem and Gnadenhütten; the sisters did the same. Old Erdmuth sent greetings to her son Martin. He had always called her his mother, and therefore she wanted him to be saluted as her son, and she wished that when she died she could be buried in Bethlehem.

[PART 2]

Br. Joach[im] Sensemann's Pachgatgoch *Diearium*, from October 13, 1752, to January 17, 1753[28]

♀ [Friday], October 13, 1752

Brothers[29] Nathanael and Anton took leave of the Indian brethren and sisters and set out on their return journey to Bethlehem and [*word crossed out*] to Gnadenhütten. I accompanied them as far as through the Indian field, where we then kissed one another affectionately. They [*word crossed out*] asked me to give their heartfelt greetings to the Indian brethren and sisters following the quarter-of-an-hour in the evening, which I promised to do. On returning, we began speaking with the brethren and sisters [in preparation] for Communion. They were straight and openhearted. During the evening quarter-of-an-hour our Husband was right intimately near us.

♄ [Saturday], the 14th

After the morning blessing Br. Gideon came, asking whether he and several other brethren could leave for a little while and take their *canuh* [canoes] over the falls. We let them go. Meanwhile, we spoke with those brethren and sisters who could speak and understand English well. That afternoon Gideon and Joshua were present, the latter as *interpreter*. We sensed the continuous work of the dear Mother on the brown hearts. They were like sinners; some, who we, in part, would have taken along without hesitation, shed many tears and said, We feel too miserable in our hearts and cannot join Communion this time. In the evening I and my wife were busy baking for the love feast.

☉ [Sunday], the 15th

In the morning we spoke yet with some brethren and sisters. After that some awakened English people attended the sermon. I spoke on the text Matthew, ch. 5, *Selig sind die geistlich arm sind, denn das Himelreich ist ihr.*[30] The Savior was near us, making the word active in the hearts of the hearers. After the English people were gone, preparations were made for the love feast, and [after the] blowing [of the horn] all of the baptized ones came to the love feast. Several who were not in a good state at this time stayed away of their own accord. There was something said about love, [about] how blissful one was, being able to love, and there was such a feeling of love to be sensed. At the end of the love feast, the brethren and sisters who were to participate in Communion this time were let go (and that they are to assemble for the quarter-of-an-hour when there was another blowing [of the horn]). After some darkness had fallen, the quarter-of-an-hour was called by blowing [the horn], and when the communicants had assembled there was something said [to the effect] that all of us gathered here knew that we were sinners and needed for the Savior to wash each one [of us] with the ~~stream~~ water from His side, and to give absolution with His pierced hand. Whereupon we fell down [on our knees] and with a heartfelt prayer I ~~asked~~ entreated the Savior for this in English. We felt the absolution and a blessed feeling of peace and love passing through our hearts. Afterward, we enjoyed the kiss of peace. Brother Amos—who during the [act of] speaking himself had not felt confident about joining [Communion], and given that we [*word crossed out*] were

unable to reflect on him owing to the fact that he had been among white people for some time—joined us for the absolution. The the servant came and said
that Amos was present as well, whereupon I asked him [Amos] to come outside
and to me. I told him he was not joining Communion this time. He said, he had
talked with the Savior and was feeling a great desire to join; he would not allow himself be turned away, standing there like a poor sinner. I could not find
it in my heart to turn him away forcibly, and allowed him to go back inside. We
then came together for the enjoyment [*word crossed out*] of our Husband's flesh
and blood, and His martyred body and the exhalations from the grave passed
through our tabernacle and soul. In the end, "*In das weiche betlein deiner Seite*"[31]
was sung, and then we had the kiss of love, and then everyone retired blissfully.
This time there were 22 brown brethren and sisters present for the enjoyment
of Communion, and one candidate, Sarah's daughter Maria.

☽ [Monday], the 16th

We felt most comfortable during the morning blessing. Everyone still felt so
well and blissful on account of last evening. A great many sisters came into
our house after the morning blessing and embraced and kissed my wife, saying that they felt so well, they could hardly express it. Amos came to me and
said, Brother, my heart feels quite well; one could also see this in his eyes. Because some families are very poor and do not have any blenet[32] they said that they
needed to go down to the seaside with their canoes[33] and baskets to sell them.
Thus, the brethren and sisters agreed to go together, because some had otherwise wanted to go only in 3 weeks. We made preparations for a small love feast
with some of those who wanted to go down there; reminded them of the grace
they had enjoyed and that they should remember it during their absence, p[p],
which they promised to do. Then they all took a heartfelt leave and set out on
their journey. There were few who stayed home.

♂ [Tuesday], the 17th

My wife and I went about breaking off the Welsh corn, and because there were
almost no Indians at home, except only children, the meetings were suspended
for that time.

☿ [Wednesday], the 18th

Minister Marsh from Kent came to visit us. [*Words crossed out*] he said he had heard that his old friend Martin Mack had been with us and had not even visited him once. He was very sorry that he had not seen him. He remembered that he had not done things ~~better~~ nicely with the brethren, p[p]. He had heard that Br. Spangenberg had been here. He very much would have liked to have spoken with him. He said he might not be our neighbor much longer. We asked what the reason for this was; this [his leaving] would not please us. He said that, in part, he could no longer deal with his congregation. He could no longer make ends meet with his *salerius* [Latin: salary], and in addition, they were simply too ungodly. (He reported that when a short while ago he wanted to celebrate Communion, one [from among his congregation], of whom he had heard had cursed and sworn in the presence of more than 30 of his people, and had conducted himself *horübel* [horribly], now intended to join Communion. He had questioned him on that account [his cursing and swearing], yet he had denied it, and when he [the minister] asked for 2 witnesses among the 30, not one of them had either seen or heard it. And he believed that the way one [person] was, so were all the others).[34] I said that things were indeed easier for me in that regard among my Indians than for him among his Christians, for when I questioned the worst one among them on returning home from a journey, thinking that something might have occurred with him, he himself would tell me everything. I did not need any witnesses with them. He said, No doubt, I must put my people in mind of this matter. And then he took his leave, inviting us sincerely to visit him. We were not able to promise him this with certainty.

♃ [Thursday], the 19th

I and my wife went into the field to break off Welsh corn. Br. Petrus and Thamar came to help us. School had continued this week in due order.

♀ [Friday], the 20th

One of our neighbors came, bringing home our Welsh corn and some wood.

♄ [Saturday], the 21st

The sisters and children came and ~~peeled~~ helped us strip our W[elsh] corn and bring it up into the loft.

☉ [Sunday], the 22nd

We observed this Sunday in quiet today, thinking frequently of our dear Bethlehem.

☽ [Monday], the 23rd

We started holding school again. I went into the winter huts and from there to English people where I had to attend to something.

♂ [Tuesday], the 24th

We continued with our school.

☿ [Wednesday], the 25th

The first brethren, Samuel and Martin, came home from the seaside.

♃ [Thursday], the 26th

Br. Gideon and his family came home. Gideon came to us; we asked him how things had gone and where they were last Sunday. He said, in Derby. They had also gone to church there. I asked if they had met anyone who loved the Savior. He said, No, he had heard of nothing else there but of the great, almighty God. We resumed our quarter-of-an-hour that evening; Samuel interpreted.

♀ [Friday], the 27th

Several more families came home, bringing word that Benigna, Simon's daughter, was delivered of a son[d] [blank] on October 20. In the evening, during our quarter-of-an-hour, the red wounds of our Husband were right feelingly near to us.

♄ [Saturday], the 28th

Today I went into the winter huts and visited the brethren and sisters there. Joshua, along with Elisabeth, came home in good spirits.

☉ [Sunday], the 29th

We conducted the general meeting when the brethren and sisters from the winter huts were here; the baptized ones had their quarter-of-an-hour in the afternoon. Both [took place] with blessing.

☽ [Monday], the 30th

After the morning blessing I started holding school with the boys. Meanwhile my wife visited the sisters who were home. Jeremias and Samuel went hunting.

♂ [Tuesday], the 31st

The Indian brethren and sisters started breaking off and bringing home their Welsh corn. Samuel had shot a bear, which they brought home. We felt right comfortable during the quarter-of-an-hour in the evening.

☿ [Wednesday], November 1, [1752]

Nothing of note occurred.

♃ [Thursday], the 2nd

We continued with school and visited the brethren and sisters, who were full of light and in good spirits, going about their work industriously. We also remembered that the brethren and sisters were gathered in Oley this evening for the *synod* and were rejoicing together.

♀ [Friday], the 3rd

We often thought of our dear brethren and sisters at the *synodus* in Oley; our spirit too was with them. We were confident that they would not forget us or the brown assembly, for we do belong with them, and that heartened us in our absence. I went on the mountain to search for Sr. Priscilla's horse, and to take 2 *buschel* [bushels] of Welsh corn to the mill as the pounding is very toilsome, but was unable to find it [the horse]. In the evening I conducted the quarter-of-an-hour; the Lamb^d with His wounds could be felt by us.

♄ [Saturday], the 4th

I went out to buy some bread, but got none. Meanwhile my wife was busy with her wash. Brother and Sister Gottlieb came home from Old Milford. He brought his old mother from there, who wants to live with them.

☉ [Sunday], the 5th

We summoned the conference brethren and sisters for the conference in the morning. They reported on how things had gone on their journey to the seaside.

They all came home without harm done to their hearts, except for Martin, who had had a quarrel with an unbaptized person, ~~because~~ who[35] he was supposed to lead ~~him~~ out of a merchant's house as the unbaptized person was drunk. Thereafter we had the sermon; the Savior was near me. Following the quarter-of-an-hour Sister Sarah came to us; my wife talked with her about her heart. She said ~~that~~ she was quite well,[36] ~~except~~ however, that[37] she was somewhat concerned because her husband ~~wanted~~ wanted to go to Woodbury next week to work, and she had to come along. She was afraid of herself, because in former times she had loved the *seiter* [cider] so very much; we should think of her often. We said she should simply abide with her heart in the Savior and His wounds, then ~~it would not mean anything~~ there would be no danger that she would get involved in something. One of our neighbors came in the evening, requesting that Gideon please talk to the Indian brethren and sisters if they, big and small, could help him work the next day, which he promised them [sic] to do. He [the neighbor] also came to us and asked if we too were agreeable. We need not worry that he would throw them into disorder with strong drinks. We told him that we had no objections that they[38] ~~to~~ work at his [place].

☽ [Monday], the 6th

After the morning blessing almost everyone, big and small, went to Mr. Mills to work. I and my wife went to visit the brethren and sisters at the lowermost place[39] and found some at home, who were glad that we were coming to visit them. We talked with them about their hearts. They were well and in good spirits. We also visited some unbaptized ones.

♂ [Tuesday], the 7th

After the morning blessing I started school with the boys. Some are learning to read English quite nicely. Petrus and Sr. Thamar came to us, complaining about their daughter Anna, who was not minding them—what they should do with her. My wife talked with her about it. She found that there was a misunderstanding concerning the matter, yet admonished her in earnest to be submissive and obedient to her parents, which she promised. In the evening quarter-of-an-hour the Lamb[d] was near us with His red wounds, so that I wonder about it and feel ashamed.

☿ [Wednesday], the 8th

Here in the Connecticut *governument* [government] it is custom to celebrate a day of thanksgiving after all the crop has been harvested. On this day there is butchering and a great deal of preparation done as all the friends and acquaintances invite one another for a meal. Since it is also an old custom of the Indians to visit those white people, where they have good friends — [as a result of] which a disorder has come about at times, as I have heard — we let our brethren and sisters know, on a private occasion, that we would be pleased if they stayed nicely at home. We too were invited by ~~Leftenert~~ [John] Mills[40] for that same day, the 9th of November. But we declined with thanks, saying that we were not here for our own sake, but for [the sake of] the Indians, to set a good example for them, which he was able to understand. Joshua, Samuel, Gottlieb, and several others went hunting in the woods. They came beforehand and took leave of us; they said they intended to return home on Saturday. At most of the sisters' [houses] cooking continued — should they not, according to old custom, visit their old acquaintances and observe thanksgiving with them? Only few attended the meeting in the evening.

♃ [Thursday], the 9th

Most of the Indian sisters had decided to stay at home, yet some of them made off. One of our neighbors sent 2 of his daughters to invite us for the evening meal, but we had ourselves excused, politely and with thanks. My wife and I celebrated that day by ourselves; we visited the brethren and sisters who were at home.

♀ [Friday], the 10th

After school I went on the mountain to cut firewood.

♄ [Saturday], the 11th

The sister[s] who had been to the thanksgiving [celebration] came back home ashamed and broken [in spirit], so that they were nowhere to be seen. (Justina sent us baked goods that she had brought back. We would have liked to have returned [the gift], but we felt in our hearts so to accept it.) Then the brethren who had been hunting also came[41] back home. Christian too, and also an unbaptized one, came home from New Milford. I conducted the quarter-of-an-hour in the evening, with blessing. One could feel that there were sinnerlike hearts standing before oneself. We often have to become sinners by judging a matter more harshly than the Savior. He has an extraordinary patience with the Indian brethren and sisters. Even when they get involved in something, and then turn again to the Savior, He does not look upon them sourly because of it, but forgives and embraces them with loving arms.

☉ [Sunday], the 12th

My wife went to visit Justina. She said she was glad that we had not sent back the *pay* [pie]; otherwise she would have thought that we were dissatisfied with her. She had felt altogether well in her heart, and did so now as well; she had not had anything to eat at home and that had forced her out. Afterward, we had the meeting, and in the afternoon, the quarter-of-an-hour for the baptized ones, during which we felt especially comfortable.

☽ [Monday], the 13th

After the morning blessing Br. Joshua came to me and said he intended to hold a love feast for the brethren and sisters. I did not have any objections, or did I? The brethren and sisters rarely came to his house to visit him, thus he had thought of inviting them for a love feast. I said I should be glad; he should go ahead. I then started school with the boys. After school, Brother Gideon came and said that the brethren and sisters were gathered in Joshua's house; did I and my wife want to come. We then soon followed him, and found the hut completely filled; the brothers on one side and the sisters on the other, quite orderly. We then began the love feast with an Indian verse[d]: *Menenana hana mewe tachquoch*, or, in German, *Gib unß unßer Ewiges Brodt*.[42] I asked Joshua what the purpose of the love feast was. He said that he loved the brethren and sisters, however, not yet as much as he wished; thus he had thought that this love feast also shall be a a [*sic*] renewal of love. Gottlieb was the servant and passed round the food, *schwit*[43] corn and meat. We felt quite well thereat. After the love feast we went home. The brethren and sisters stayed together to talk about some issues of an outward nature. My wife commenced school with the girls.

♂ [Tuesday], the 14th
Nothing of note occurred.

☿ [Wednesday], the 15th
The Indian brethren agreed with one another that each household is to cut wood, which they wanted to carry home jointly, so that they could go hunting the coming week.

♃ [Thursday], the 16th
After the morning blessing everyone went to cut wood. Also, Ignatius, who had been in Gnadenhütten, arrived here. Sister Thamar fell ill; my wife visited her. She had said, her body was no doubt ill, but her heart was well, and this eased her ~~illness~~ pains. During our evening occasion the Savior was near us with His wounds.

♀ [Friday], the 17th
After the morning blessing Br. Gideon bid everyone come and carry wood. I readied myself to go on horseback to Wechquadnach. Jeremias loaned me his horse. On arriving there, I found Esther, Augustus's wife, with her little daughter[d] Hannah, and Jonathan's son Nathanael. They were glad to see me. She right away busied herself to prepare food for me. Next, Sister Hannah, Esther's mother, came home. I talked to them about their hearts but was not able to get much out of them. They said that they thought of the Savior often, and that they wanted to visit us in Pachgatgoch as soon as they were able to do so. I stayed with them for several hours. Sister Susanna, who was also there, said that she intended to come to Pachgatgoch next week and wanted to live there this winter. Timotheus and young Moses had traveled to Wanachquaticok. I came home very late that evening.

♄ [Saturday], the 18th
Everyone was well and busy carrying wood.

☉ [Sunday], the 19th
Samuel summoned the conference brethren and sisters in the morning. (I asked about Ignatius, whether he wanted to live here. But they did not know. They said

that he had said he wanted to leave again; the brethren had right away taken him along to carry wood. I told them that he had conducted himself badly in Gnadenhütten, and for that reason the brethren should watch him. I intended to talk with him today and ask him why he had come here). Meanwhile, 5 English men came to attend the meeting, thus I had to have the conference brethren and sisters depart. The brethren and sisters having assembled, the meeting was called by blowing [the horn]. The Savior was near us with His bloody wounds. That afternoon, after the quarter-of-an-hour for the baptized ones, I summoned Ignatius; Br. Joshua was present as well. I asked how and when he had left Gnadenhütten, and whether he intended to live here. He was very straight. He also said he intended to stay here this winter; he did not know where else to go. I told him I had nothing against it as long as he conducted himself here better than he had in Gnadenhütten. He said that from now on he was resolved to surrender his heart to the Savior anew.

☽ [Monday], the 20th

Brother Joshua came, asking how much longer it was until Christmas. I when he heard that it was but a few weeks, he talked to the other brethren and they all readied themselves to go hunting tomorrow, 40 miles from here. I held school that forenoon, and my wife that afternoon. I conducted the quarter-of-an-hour in the evening, with blessing.

♂ [Tuesday], the 21st

After the morning blessing Br. David came from the winter huts, and then the brethren left. They, the brethren, came and took leave, saying that they would come back home 4 days before Christmas. Gideon, Simon, Petrus, and Martin stayed home. In the evening, Sr. Magdalena came to our house and said that Gottliebe had been delivered of a son, but the child was dead. My wife went right away to visit her to see what the situation was. We thought perhaps it the child had become unconscious, but it had been dead for several weeks.[44]

☿ [Wednesday], the 22nd

After the morning blessing 2 joiners came bringing the window frames for the church. Br. Martin made the coffin for Christian and Gottliebe's child. The brethren who were at home buried it toward evening.

♃ [Thursday], the 23rd

My wife visited Sister Thamar and brought her a little tea, which quite revived her. Brother Gideon returned home from New Milford. Some of the awakened people had given him some meat for us, which pleased us greatly.

♀ [Friday], the 24th

After the morning blessing I started working on the church windows and puttied the glass. My wife visited the sisters, finding them all full of light and in good spirits. Thamar had improved somewhat. Sr. Susanna arrived here from Wechquadna[ch].

♄ [Saturday], the 25th

The sisters were busy carrying wood.

☉ [Sunday], the 26th

I held the meeting; Martin interpreted.

☽ [Monday], the 27th

After the morning blessing I went on the mountain to cut wood. Those of the Indian brethren and sisters who were home were blissful and in good spirits. Sr. Erdmuth went to Wechquadnach.

♂ [Tuesday], the 28th

After the boys' school I again went about cutting wood. Meanwhile my wife held school with the girls.

☿ [Wednesday], the 29th

In the morning, during the morning blessing, the red wounds of our Husband were feelingly near to us. Afterward, we held school.

♃ [Thursday], the 30th

We held school.

♀ [Friday], December 1, [1752]

We held school and visited those brethren and sisters who were at home. Two unbaptized ones came home from hunting, bringing word that the brethren were well and had shot 7 deer and 2 bears.

♄ [Saturday], the 2nd

Today we often thought of our brethren and sisters in Bethlehem, wishing to be near them for a few hours. Old Sister Erdmuth came home from Wechquadnach bearing a heartfelt greeting from Esther and her mother.

☉ [Sunday], the 3rd

An English woman came to attend the meeting. She said that her husband apparently would not be satisfied when he heard that she had come to our meeting, because he believed that we had a picture, and whoever saw it once would be immediately infected. She said that if this were true, she would like to see it once. She thought it surely could not do her any harm. I said [we have] nothing different from what Paul and the Apostles ~~from~~ had preached about, and this the Holy Spirit would have to paint into her heart; we had no external picture. Then we held the meeting. She listened very *atent* [attentively]. After the meeting my wife still spoke with her a great deal; she cried hard. After the quarter-of-an-hour for the baptized ones, Gideon went to visit Christian and asked him about his heart, if it was ill, for he had not seen him at the meeting for several days. He had replied, his heart was not ill, he had merely been hindered.

☽ [Monday], the 4th

Brother Petrus and Lucas went hunting. I started school with the boys; meanwhile, my wife visited the sisters in the huts. I visited Brother Gideon in the afternoon. He was hard at work currying hides. He said he thought the brethren would soon come home from hunting as the snow was too deep—they could not hunt. I conducted the quarter-of-an-hour in the evening; Martin interpreted.

♂ [Tuesday], the 5th

Martin, along with an unbaptized [Indian], went to New Milford. Because our firewood was almost all used up, an Indian sister had secretly carried several loads of wood to the front of our house. In the evening, after we had already gone to bed, the brethren arrived from hunting. On coming to the river, several fired shots so that they [in Pachgatgoch] would take them across by *canuh*.

☿ [Wednesday], the 6th

Joshua came and said that they had shot 20 deer and 2 bears. I asked how things had gone during that time, if they had been in good spirits and ~~had been~~ loving toward one another during that time. Yes, things had gone quite nicely, and they were grateful to the Savior for what He had bestowed on them; there were some unbaptized ones who had not shot anything.

♃ [Thursday], the 7th

Lucas and Petrus came home from hunting. They brought 2 deer that they had shot. We had a blessed quarter-of-an-hour in the evening.

♀ [Friday], the 8th

After the morning blessing 2 Englishmen came with 2 sleds to haul wood for us; several of the Indian brethren helped load them.

♄ [Saturday], the 9th

We went visiting in several huts; the brethren and sisters were full of light and in good spirits. Because I had intended to go[45] to the North River some weeks ago to see whether there were any letters from our dear brethren and sisters from Bethlehem and New York, I decided to go there on horseback next Monday.

☉ [Sunday], the 10th

In the morning we met in conference with our laborers. Gideon's thoughts were [that] the brethren should shoot 1 or 2 deer this week, and this way have a love feast for all the baptized and unbaptized ones. However, the remaining brethren and sisters did not view this favorably, because when this had occurred in the past [it] ~~was~~ had never been a blessing. I told them that I intended to go to Rhinebeck next Monday to visit the brethren and sisters and to see whether there were any letters from Bethlehem. After the brethren and sisters from the winter huts had arrived here, the meeting was called by blowing [the horn]. Thus everyone was gathered, and the church was quite full. Also, the Savior was also near us with His wounds. [In the] afternoon the baptized ones had their quarter-of-an-hour, with blessing. Several sisters, who had not been home for some weeks, visited us. They were affectionate and in good spirits.

☽ [Monday], the 11th

At the morning blessing I announced to the brethren and sisters that I intended to go to the North River today; thus, they gave me heartfelt greetings for the awakened people there. Old Sister Erdmuth stayed with my wife in the meantime. That evening I came as far as to Hans Rau, who was very glad to see me.

♂ [Tuesday], the 12th

I departed on horseback from H. Rau and came to Christian Führer toward evening, who heartily rejoiced when he saw me and welcomed me with tender love. He also showed me a small package[d] that the brethren and sisters from New York had sent for us, as well as a package of letters and the *Gemeinschriften*[46] from Bethlehem, which pleased me greatly—to see and to hear something from our dear hearts in Bethlehem. We went to Jacob Maul in the evening. Both he and she [his wife] were glad to see me. They said that they had thought of us often, and would have soon thought that we must be ill as I had stayed away for so long.

☿ [Wednesday], the 13th

I stayed with Führer; visited yet some awakened people. In the evening there came to us Jacob Maul with his wife [and] Henrich Martin with his wife. We had a blissful conversation with one another; they mostly lamented not having a brother[47] among them. They believed [that] if it were so, it would be a great blessing for them.

♃ [Thursday], the 14th

I took leave of them. Führer accompanied me for several miles and then we kissed each other and he returned home. In the evening I again came to Hans Rau, where I stayed overnight.

♀ [Friday], the 15th

I set out on my journey. It was very cold. I had to go mostly on foot because I could not bear it on the horse. Fairly late in the evening I came to my dear brethren and sisters in Pachgatgoch, some of whom had been on the lookout to welcome me. My wife and old Erdmuth had already said I was probably not going to come any more. I found my wife and everyone quite well and in good spirits. In the meantime, my wife had been paid visits by all of the Indian sisters. Nearly all of them would have liked to have stayed with her during that time. Paulus, who has not been here this winter, had come home in the meantime. A stranger had arrived as well.

♄ [Saturday], the 16th

I and my wife observed the Sabbath and visited the brethren and sisters in the huts.

☉ [Sunday], the 17th

The occasions proceeded in due order, as usual.

☽ [Monday], the 18th

We started our school. Most of the Indian brethren went hunting.

♂ [Tuesday], the 19th

Nothing of note occurred.

☿ [Wednesday], the 20th

Our Husband was especially near us in the morning during the quarter-of-an-hour. My wife visited the sisters, finding them all full of light and in good spirits.

♃ [Thursday], the 21st

The brethren came home from hunting. Joshua and Christian had each shot a deer. Until then school had proceeded in due order.

♀ [Friday], the 22nd

Everyone was in good spirits and hard at work carrying wood. We had a blessed quarter-of-an-hour in the evening.

♄ [Saturday], the 23rd

We baked bread for the love feast. Toward evening Sister Hannah, along with Moses and his wife Miriam, arrived here from Wechquadnach. In the evening, after the quarter-of-an-hour, Sister Miriam stayed here, embraced and kissed my wife, being happy to have found us here. ~~During the quarter-of-an-hour the brethren and sisters were also reminded that our dear Savior was born to-night, and that all of our congregations were keeping watch tonight and gave thanks to Him, appealing to Him at His bleeding feet that He leave His throne~~ [words crossed out]. ~~This was very weighty to them and a blessing. In spirit, my wife and I were with our dear hearts in Bethlehem. We had a small love feast with one another and were quite blissful.~~

☉ [Sunday], the 24th

When the brethren and sisters had arrived from the winter huts, the meeting was called by blowing [the horn]. In the evening, during the quarter-of-an-hour, it was made known that this was the night when the dear Savior was ~~begotten~~ born, p[p]. All of our congregations were keeping watch tonight and reminded themselves of the great mercy that had been brought upon us and mankind by this. My wife and I also remembered our dear Bethlehem. In spirit we were with them; we felt quite well.

☽ [Monday], the 25th

We had the sermon in the forenoon. The Savior was near us. After the sermon, preparations for the love feast were made. When everything was[48] ready, [the horn] was blown, at which point all of the baptized ones gathered in the church. There were 39 brethren and sisters, not counting the baptized children. We had slices of buttered bread and chocolate. They all felt quite well on this occasion. Among other things, the brethren and sisters were reminded that we had intended to hold Communion this evening, but that it could not quite be done. Then the dear Savior's incarnation was talked about and [it] was a blessing for all of us. After the love feast Hannah and Miriam came into our house, along with Moses and still other brethren. We talked with them about their hearts. Miriam said that her heart was not quite well — her husband had not conducted himself agreeably on the journey. He was reminded how blissful he had been before this; how was it that he has been in such a bad state now for such a long time. He admitted to it, to be sure; he said he did not know how it was happening. Whenever he had done something in the past, he had felt punishment for it right away. Now he did not feel quite the same way in his heart; he was very sad about this. We directed him to the Savior; His blood could soften and warm his hard and cold heart, p[p]. He thought about going back to Gnaden-hütten at the first opportunity, yet wanted to visit us beforehand. Hannah was also in fairly good spirits. We asked her about Esther, the wife of Augustus, if she intended to travel back to her husband soon. They said they thought [Esther would do so] when it was a little warmer; it was too cold for the child, otherwise she too would have come here together with them.

♂ [Tuesday], the 26th
After the morning blessing the brethren and sisters of Wechquadnach came and took leave. Miriam said that she felt well in her heart again. Our Pachgatgoch brethren were busy cutting and carrying wood. We started our school again.

☿ [Wednesday], the 27th
Nothing of note occurred.

♃ [Thursday], the 28th
After the morning blessing I held school with the boys. Meanwhile, my wife visited the sisters. Justina had told her, among other things, about her awakening and baptism. The awakening had occurred 2 days before her baptism, when that night she was unable to sleep because of her grief and appealed to the dear Savior to move the brethren so that they would inquire about her heart, which then happened, and that she could not express how she had felt at the time of the baptism. And until now she has always been blissful and in good spirits.

♀ [Friday], the 29th
Early, during the morning blessing, the red wounds of our Lamb[d] of God were near us. The Indian brethren and sisters all were in good spirits and working industriously.

♄ [Saturday], the 30th
We remembered our dear brethren and sisters in Bethlehem, wishing to be near them for only a few hours. I visited Lucas, who felt somewhat ill, and Jeremias, who also is feeling a little ill.

☉ [Sunday], the 31st

The meeting took place toward noon, wherein we felt well. That afternoon we had a passionate quarter-of-an-hour with the baptized brethren and sisters. It was also announced that tomorrow was New Year's Day,[49] that the sermon would take place in the forenoon, and [that we] wanted to hold a small love feast with the baptized children that afternoon. After the quarter-of-an-hour the old year was closed by means of a heartfelt prayer and thanksgiving.

☽ [Monday], January 1, 1753

When the brethren and sisters from the winter huts were here, the meeting was called by blowing [the horn]. The Savior bestowed on me grace and themes [to discuss] about the beginning, ~~of His~~ [when He] gave Himself up for us into [our] suffering; the listeners were very *atent* [attentive]. In the afternoon, [after the] blowing [of the horn], the sisters whose children are baptized came and brought the children to the love feast. The children were so still that not only were we amazed but also the Indian sisters themselves. My wife and I sang them delightful verses[d], at which time the children pointed to where the Savior had the wounds. The sisters were told that from now on there would be a quarter-of-an-hour for the children every Sunday. Sister Rebecca stayed on in our house for a while. She said that she felt quite well and blissful in her heart, which we could believe.

♂ [Tuesday], the 2nd

After the morning blessing Br. Gideon said he intended to go to New Milford today. We started school.

[No entry for the 3rd]

♃ [Thursday], the 4th

I went to visit the brethren. They were well and in good spirits. Br. Gideon said brethren from Bethlehem were coming next week. I asked who had told him this. He said, his heart.

♀ Friday, the 5th

After the morning blessing I and my wife went to the winter huts to visit the brethren and sisters there. They rejoiced when they saw us. We talked with them about their hearts. They all were well in their hearts. We found little Maria,

Sarah's daughter, ill with respect to her tabernacle, as a result of which she will probably go home. Otherwise she was well. While we were visiting the brethren and sisters, 10 unmarried English women had been [here] to visit us. They had been very sorry not to have found us at home.

♄ [Saturday], the 6th
I and my wife observed the Sabbath; we thought of our dear Bethlehem often.

☉ [Sunday], the 7th
The general meeting took place in the forenoon. Next, there was the children's quarter-of-an-hour, during which we felt quite well. Thereafter my wife conducted the quarter-of-an-hour for the single sisters. In the evening we also had a small occasion with the baptized ones, during which the Savior was near us with His wounds.

☽ [Monday], the 8th
After the morning blessing several brethren went hunting. Christian and his wife went several miles from here to work this week. Several of our brethren and sisters were longing for a brother from Bethlehem. In their dreams they also had seen 2 brethren coming, and believed that someone would come soon.

[No entries for the 9th and 10th]

♃ [Thursday], the 11th
I visited several brethren after school; talked with them about their hearts. Past noon, as I was just about to leave the house on account of outward business, I heard someone calling out from across the water. Turning that way, I saw 2 persons standing [there] who looked to me like brethren. Just as I was looking at them, they called out "Sensemann." I quickly ran outside and told my wife that there were 2 brethren across the water [and] along with me, [she] was overjoyed. I quickly went to bring them across. On reaching them, I saw that our dear and precious heart Nathanael [Seidel], together with David Zeisberger, was here.[50] We kissed and rejoiced with one another. I then led them to our house; my wife welcomed both brethren like angels[d] having come out of heaven. The Indian brethren and sisters were at once also there, and welcomed them with great

love, deeply rejoicing. ~~Our~~ the dear heart Nathanael conducted the quarter-of-an-hour that evening, bringing many a heartfelt greeting[d] to the dear brown hearts from the dear hearts in Bethlehem, ~~and~~ Nazareth, and Gnadenhütten, especially from the dear hearts [the] Hehls and [the] Lawatsches, about which the brown hearts were exceedingly happy. That evening I and my wife ~~could~~ could hardly finish reading our dear letters[d] for joy.

♀ [Friday], the 12th

The dear heart delivered the morning blessing; portrayed to the brown hearts the Lamb[d] with His wounds quite passionately and with fervor. Afterward, the conference brethren and sisters, Gideon, Martha, Joshua, Elisabeth, and Samuel, were summoned for the conference. Br. Nathanael then passed on, especially to them, heartfelt greetings from the congregation. He said that they had been sent by the congregation to see how matters stood with [the] Sensemanns and the brethren and sisters—whether they were in quite a happy state—and should[51] they find that the brethren and sisters longed for Communion, then he is to celebrate Communion with them. Gideon said his heart had longed for it for a long time. This they all said, and there were reportedly others who were longing for it as well, p[p]. [word crossed out]. For this reason a brother was sent to Wechquadnach to inform the brethren and sisters there that 2 [word crossed out] brethren from Bethlehem were here. Afterward, I went with Nathanael and David to the winter huts. The brethren and sisters who we found at home said that their hearts had greatly rejoiced at hearing that the brethren had arrived. Having spent some time with them, we returned home. Sensemann conducted the quarter-of-an-hour in the evening. All of us felt quite well thereat.

♄ [Saturday], the 13th

After the morning blessing the communicants stayed in church, where the dear heart Nathanael then announced to them that we intended to have Communion tomorrow, and that we therefore wanted to speak with the brethren and sisters today. They should stay nicely at home so that we could get a hold of them. The speaking [of the brethren and sisters] was thus soon begun, at which point the dear heart Nathanael asked them about their hearts. They were sincere and straight. We all felt quite comfortable on this occasion. Sr. Sensemann was hard at work baking bread for the love feast. Toward evening 5 brethren and sisters arrived here from Wechquadnach. Sister Miriam was spoken with that very evening. Yet her present circumstances were such that she was not able to join Communion this time. In the evening Br. David Zeisberger conducted the quarter-of-an-hour in English, quite passionately and with fervor.

☉ [Sunday], the 14th

Some other brethren and sisters were yet spoken with in the morning. Next, the dear heart Nathanael held the meeting, with blessing; there were some English men present who were very *atent* [attentive] ~~to listen~~. The servants, Joshua and Samuel, helped ~~to~~ prepare for the love feast. Everything being ready, the brethren and sisters were called by the servants, at which time the dear heart Nathanael told them some things about Bethlehem and Gnadenhütten, how blissful matters were proceeding among the brethren and sisters there. He also read to them a letter from the dear heart Mattheus [Hehl], which gave them joy—that the congregation thought of them so much. It was a blessing to everyone. Following the love feast, Esther from Meniolagomeka was spoken with. Yet her heart and circumstances were such that she could not join us for Communion. After the blowing [of the horn], the communicants assembled in church. Brother Nathanael delivered a brief address and said that now was the blissful time during which the dear Savior wanted to give us His flesh to eat and blood to drink, p[p]., before which we wanted to throw ourselves at His pierced feet and ask Him for the absolution that He Himself may perform for each one of us with His pierced hand. Thereafter we knelt before our Husband at His pierced feet and Nathanael said a heartfelt prayer for the absolution, and we felt in our hearts that the dear Savior was present and was absolving us. After that some verses[d] were sung in Indian and German, and Nathanael ~~blessed the bread~~ consecrated[52] [the bread, and] with the words of the institution [of the Eucharist,] ~~Thereupon~~ the brown assembly received[53] our Husband's martyred body and His blood. Passing through our hearts, souls, and bodies, a blissful and penetrating feeling of grace could be felt, which, even being in the dust, bowed us to His bored-through feet. Thereafter was the kiss of love. Br. Nathanael reminded the brown brethren and sisters that they should retire nice and quietly. Thereupon everyone retired to his hut[d], quietly and blissfully. Indeed, it was so quiet in Pachgatgoch, ~~that one did not~~ as if no one was there. There were 22 Indian brethren and sisters who partook of the body and of the blood this time.

☽ [Monday], the 15th

Br. D. Zeisberger delivered the morning blessing. All of us were still in the spirit of the body. The Indian brethren and sisters appeared well and quite full of light. After the morning blessing it was announced that the 2 brethren, Nathanael and Zeisberger, along with Sensemann, intended to travel to Salisbury[54] this morning and ~~thought~~ to return in 2 days. They soon set out on their journey. Sister Sensemann visited the Indian sisters, who could not express to her enough how well they were and what they had felt during Communion. That evening we came to the people who, in a letter to the congregation, had asked for a brother to preach among them about the Savior ~~and~~ and His wounds; they were very pleased when they learned that the congregation was remembering them, and that the brethren were coming to them.[55] That very evening they summoned the people who had signed their names to the letter.[56]

♂ [Tuesday], the 16th

In the morning the people assembled, at which time the dear heart Nathanael listened to their thoughts and promised them to communicate them to the congregation. We then set out on our way back to Pachgatgoch. My wife and the Indian brethren and sisters welcomed us with much love.

☿ [Wednesday], the 17th

Brother Nathanael had resolved to set out on his journey today, but because Brother and Sister Sensemann entreated [him] to stay on today, he, while the morning blessing was underway, came to feel that he should stay on with them and the brown assembly today. As there were also some matters to consider with the conference brethren and sisters, it was announced to them that the brethren were staying here today as well. We soon went visiting in the winter huts with Br. Joshua and Elisabeth; we spoke with an almost 80-year-old Indian woman who has been longing to be baptized for a long time, and after her renewed application, she was promised that she shall be baptized this very day. Having visited the huts, we went home and soon met in conference with the Indian workers. The entire conference was very pleased that this old Indian woman shall be baptized today. It was also resolved that Brother Joshua shall travel with Nathanael and D. Zeisberger part of the way, for they wanted to call on Brother Abel, who for several years now has been running about lost, and is shy and timid. The conference brethren and sisters, particularly Gideon, Joshua, [and] Samuel, sent their love and affection to the congregation[s] in Bethlehem, Nazareth, and Gnadenhütten, especially to the dear brethren and sisters across the great water, to the dear Jünger, the Mother,[57] Johannes [von Watteville], [and] Johann Nitschmann, p[p]. During the conference we felt quite well in the company of each other. The meeting in the evening took place at the usual time. There the candidate was ~~first~~ beforehand briefly spoken with about the importance of the matter that the Savior wanted to let befall her. Then she was clad in white by Sr. Sensemann, [and] ~~and~~ led into the church, [and] Brother Nathanael delivered a brief address about the love of the Savior for sinners.[58] Thereupon the baptismal water was brought in and the candidate knelt before the water, and so she was absolved by the laying on of hands, [and] then, right away baptized by Br. Nathanael into the death of Jesus by means of a threefold flooding, receiving the name Theodora. She was consecrated by her sponsors, namely by 7 sisters, by means of ~~the~~ a[59] verse and the laying on of hands. It was a blessed and feeling act. In closing, Br. Nathanael and David Zeisberger took leave of all the Indian brethren and sisters, and they sent their greetings to the congregation in Bethlehem and Gnadenhütten, and everyone was quite glad and in good spirits. This evening I and my wife wrote some letters and news to the dear congregation and to various brethren and sisters in Bethlehem, and we continued to be in rather good spirits together with the 2 dear brethren who had been with us now for several days, together with whom we have enjoyed ourselves a great deal.

Diearium for Pachgatgoch, from
January 18, 1753, to February 19 *ejd. ai.*[60]

♃ [Thursday], January 18, 1753

In the morning, the brothers Nathanael and D. Zeisberger readied themselves for their journey to Bethlehem by way of New York. Many Indian brethren and sisters came to see them once more, and to once again take leave of them.

Joshua went with them with the intention to call on Abel. Br. Sensemann accompanied them for several miles, when they still kissed one another heartily, and cheerfully went their way. Sensemann went back to his brown assembly. (Gideon came to Sr. Sensemann, telling her that he wanted to go out several miles [from here] on account of outward business.) Sr. Theodora went to the winter huts. In the evening Br. Sensemann conducted the quarter-of-an-hour with blessing, and passed on to the brown assembly the greetings that had been sent back with him by the brethren Nathanael and Zeisberger.

♀ [Friday], the 19th
Everyone was in good spirits and blissful. We were visited by several brethren. Sister Theodora was no longer able to like it at the winter huts; she came back here so that she could enjoy the meeting[s].

♄ [Saturday], the 20th
Sr. Sensemann went to visit old Theodora after the morning blessing. She asked her how she felt in her heart after her baptism. She replied she was feeling quite well in her heart. Before, she had been fearful of us, but now she loved us very much. Soon after, she also came to visit us. Br. Joshua returned bringing a little note[d] from dear Brother Nathanael, that they had been unable to find any [word crossed out] traces of Abel. Sensemann conducted the quarter-of-an-hour in the evening; Joshua interpreted. The peace of the Sabbath that a person experiences inside the wounds of the Lamb[d] was talked about, and we indeed felt that way in our hearts.

☉ [Sunday], the 21st
The sermon took place before noon, after that, the children's quarter-of-an-hour, which is a blessing for the children and mothers, [and] toward evening there was the quarter-of-an-hour for the baptized brethren and sisters; the Savior was near us. At the end we enjoyed the kiss of peace. Samuel stayed on with us for a while that evening; he recounted how he and his wife had been especially blissful and in a happy state since Communion.

☽ [Monday], the 22nd
Today we started holding school again. My wife visited several sisters; talked with them about their hearts. They were full of light and in good spirits, especially

Lucia and Theodora. I conducted the quarter-of-an-hour in the evening; Joshua interpreted.

♂ [Tuesday], the 23rd

After the boys' school I visited some of the brethren, who I found blissful and in good spirits. My wife and several Indian sisters visited Lucia, who was growing somewhat sickly. In the evening I conducted the quarter-of-an-hour with blessing.

☿ [Wednesday], the 24th

In the morning, before the morning blessing, Br. Samuel came and told us that the Lord had delighted him with a little son[d], and that mother and child were both well.[61] We wished him grace and blessing for this. Br. Samuel came to us past noon; said that his wife and he had talked with each other ~~about~~ on account of the baptism of their little son[d]. He said that throughout the entire time that his wife had carried him [the son], they had surrendered it [the child] to the Savior, thinking all that time that it would have to be baptized as soon as it was born. We said that we had no objections. Br. Gideon and Joshua were summoned to our house, to whom it was announced that Samuel's son[d] shall be baptized this evening during the quarter-of-an-hour; they were quite pleased to hear this. In the evening, the meeting having been called by blowing [by horn], and everyone having assembled, the grace of baptism and the covenant that the dear Savior made with the child to be baptized through this sacrament was talked about a little. Following the address, several verses[d] were sung. Then the water was blessed by means of a heartfelt prayer, and the dear Savior was appealed to, that He may mix it with the blood and water that flowed from His side. Then it [the child] was flooded with the stream from Jesus' side and received the name Timotheus, and was consecrated by Gideon, Joshua, and Jeremias by means of the v[erse] *Die Seele Christi Heilige unß*,[62] p[p]. There was an all-pervading feeling of grace present.

♃ [Thursday], the 25th

I visited Br. Martin; asked him about his heart. He said he felt well in his heart, yet his body was not quite well. Several Indian sisters visited my wife. Toward evening 2 Indian strangers arrived from Derby: Sr. Maria and Theodora's brother, and the daughter of Br. Philippus in Gnadenhütten by his first wife. The latter attended the meeting in the evening.

♀ [Friday], the 26th

After the morning blessing, old Maria came here from the winter huts.

[No entry for the 27th]

☉ [Sunday], the 28th

We met in conference in the morning. Br. Joshua reminded the other Indian conference brethren and sisters that they should show more loyalty toward the other brethren and sisters than has been the case thus far, which they all believed, and they are promising to exercise more loyalty than they had done so far. Following the conference the meeting was held, wherein the Savior was feelingly near to us with His wounds. In the afternoon there was first the quarter-of-an-hour for the children [and] afterward, the one for the widows, conducted by my wife, both blissful and with passion. Finally, the married people had their quarter-of-an-hour, wherein we felt quite comfortable.

☽ [Monday], the 29th

After the morning blessing several brethren and sisters left with baskets and brooms and other items to sell. We started school. After school I went to Kent on account of outward business. My wife visited several sisters, with blessing.

♂ [Tuesday], the 30th

I visited several brethren; talked with them about their hearts. They said that they have been in a quite happy state since last Communion. The brethren and sisters who had left with baskets yesterday came home in good spirits. Two Indian strangers came to stay here for a while.

☿ [Wednesday], the 31st

Br. Joshua came in the morning, asking me for advice about their land, which they want to fence into two parts so that they could use one for winter and the other for summer crops.[63] I told them that I would be pleased if they set up their affair properly. In the evening they met with one another in conference about this.

♃ [Thursday], February 1, [1753]

After the morning blessing Br. Gideon summoned the brethren, and then they went to split rails. Following the boys' school I went out to visit the brethren at their work. They were hard at work making rails, and things proceeded nice and orderly. We had a pleasant quarter-of-an-hour in the evening.

♀ [Friday], the 2nd
After the morning blessing the brethren again went about their work. Two awakened English men came to visit us. After they [were] gone I went on horseback to the mill in Sharon with Welsh corn. Returned home in the evening. Meanwhile, my dear wife had received visits from many Indian sisters.

[No entry for the 3rd]
☉ [Sunday], the 4th
When the brethren and sisters had assembled in the forenoon, the meeting was held. The Savior with His red wounds was among us. Past noon the quarter-of-an-hour for the baptized children took place, and thereafter the one for all the baptized ones, both with blessing. Several of the brethren and sisters from the winter huts visited us.

☽ [Monday], the 5th
My wife visited the sisters in several huts. In the meantime I held school with the boys. Past noon my wife was paid a visit by 4 English women. Toward evening one of our neighbors came to us. He said that previously he had thought that there could not be much good about us, because we went to live among the Indians, but now he knew us better and knew what our intention was among them. The Indian brethren went into their steam bath[64] to sweat. Thus we did not have an evening quarter-of-an-hour.

♂ [Tuesday], the 6th
After the morning blessing the brethren went to build a bridge. Our quarter-of-an-hour in the evening took place with blessing.

☿ [Wednesday], the 7th
After the morning blessing Joshua said that he intended to go to Wechquadnach with his wife today. Thus they soon came and took leave of us. We sent greetings to the brethren and sisters there. Later I went visiting in several huts;

talked especially with Br. Petrus about his heart, and that it would be good if he stayed home nicely and did not go among the white people much. He said that his heart was telling him the same and [that he] would therefore stay home.

♃ [Thursday], the 8th

Jonathan, Abraham's son, arrived here from Gnadenhütten together with his wife and 2 children.[65] He acted very amiably, but he did not bring me a letter from the brethren, from which we concluded right away that he must be in a bad state.

♀ [Friday], the 9th

My wife felt somewhat sickly. That afternoon I went to visit the brethren and sisters in the winter huts and found all of them at home. They were full of light and in good spirits; they were glad that I came to visit them. Br. Gideon went to New Milford. [Words crossed out] Anna, Jonathan's wife, came to visit my wife. She was affectionate and in a happy state.

♄ [Saturday], the 10th

We sat in our house[d], thinking much of our dear Bethlehem. Our Husband was near us with His dear, unctuous [i.e., anointing] wounds. [The] Joshuas came home from Wechquadnach, bringing us heartfelt greetings from the brethren and sisters there. [Joshua] said that the Wanachquaticok Indians had sent to those of Wechquadnach a *stren of wampen* [string of wampum], accompanied by the message that their gate was open to them[66] should they want to move to them. However, they had not yet informed them of a decision. Br. Gideon came home from New Milford. Some of the awakened people there sent greetings to us and word that we should please come and visit them, which they believed would be a blessing for them, because they felt very corrupted sometimes. We had a blessed quarter-of-an-hour in the evening. Jonathan and his wife stayed with us for yet a good while.

☉ [Sunday], the 11th

In the morning, Moses with his wife and son, along with an unbaptized [Indian], arrived here from Wechquadnach. They had to sleep in the woods that night. When the brethren and sisters from the winter huts were here, the meeting was held; the Savior was near us with His wounds. Thereafter the quarter-of-an-hour for the baptized children was conducted with blessing. Toward evening there was also a general meeting.

☽ [Monday], the 12th

After the morning blessing, I learned that Moses and Jonathan, the renegades from Gnadenhütten, had tried to confuse the brethren in Pachgatgoch about the congregation with all sorts of lies and recent news from Gnadenhütten that has arrived, which had some *afect* [effect] on Samuel.[67] I summoned Jonathan in Samuel's presence, and talked with him about it fairly harshly. Yet he wants to remain on friendly and good terms. They soon left from here for Wechquadnach. Samuel and an unbaptized [Indian] went with them.

♂ [Tuesday], the 13th

Gideon and Joshua came to visit us. We thought they had been made doubtful by Jonathan and Moses, but they were full of light and in a happy state, which pleased us greatly. We had a blessed quarter-of-an-hour in the evening.

[No entry for the 14th]
♃ [Thursday], the 15th

We held school after the morning blessing. Next, we went visiting in the huts, finding the brethren and sisters well and in good spirits.

♀ [Friday], the 16th

Our dear Brother Christian Fröhlich arrived from the precious brethren and sisters in Bethlehem with several affectionate letters[d] for the brown assembly, as well as for us, from which we learned that C. Fröhlich is to stay with the brown assembly in our stead for a while; and I and my wife could travel to New York a for a short time, to see and speak there with the dear Brother and Sister A. Johanna and Telk[remainder illegible] before their departure for Europe, which was more than a small joy for us.

He, C. Fröhlich, was welcomed most tenderly by the brown brethren and sisters; we conducted a passionate quarter-of-an-hour for them in the evening.

♄ [Saturday], the 17th

Sensemann and Fröhlich went to one of our neighbors to hire a horse for Sister Sensemann, to [go to] New York, which we obtained. In the evening Br. Sensemann conducted the ~~evening~~ quarter-of-an-hour with blessing.

☉ [Sunday], the 18th

In the morning the conference met, wherein several letters that we had received through Brother Fröhlich from Bethlehem were communicated to the conference brethren and sisters. Afterward, ~~there was the~~ the sermon was delivered by C. Fröhlich. Next, Sister Sensemann conducted the quarter-of-an-hour for the baptized children, at which time a blissful feeling could be sensed. Past noon, the quarter-of-an-hour for all the baptized ones was conducted, during which several letters from our dear Bethlehem were communicated through which the journey of Brother and Sister Sensemann ~~was made true~~ became known to the brown brethren and sisters. Following the quarter-of-an-hour, several brethren and sisters came to our house, some of whom were half doubtful whether we would return. But because we knew nothing beyond New York, we could assure them that we would come back.

Joachim Heinrich Sensemann

19 February 1753 to 27 February 1754

Chr. Fröhlich's Pachgatgoch *diar[ium]*, from February 19–April 11, [17]53[1]

February, the 19[th][2]

Brother and Sister Sensemann readied themselves for their journey to New York to welcome our dear and precious brethren and sisters, and also to take leave of them. I went with them for one mile, and then we bade one another a tender farewell for a short while. On my way back I went visiting in the winter huts, passing on greetings from [the] Sensemanns to the brethren and sisters. The brethren and sisters were right glad that I intended to stay with them again for this length of time. And then the evening service took place. I told them that I would preach to them again the old word, yet the old that was always new in our hearts. I appealed to the Lamb[d] to please let the blood from all of His wounds flow plentifully over our hearts. There was a sweet feeling present at the meeting, and then everyone retired quietly.

The 20th

First there was the morning blessing. I delivered it in the house because it was too cold in the church;[3] we felt well in each other's company. And then I visited nearly all of them [the Indian brethren and sisters] in their huts. Also went yet to the winter huts; had a heartfelt talk with Brother and Sister David.[4] And then I conducted the evening service. My heart delights in the brown flock, that the Lamb[d] is working on them, and will receive them as reward for His pain after all.

The 21st

The morning blessing took place with a heartfelt prayer to the bloody[5] Lamb[d], and then I cut some wood for myself so as not to burn up Br. Sensemann's supply.

One of the neighbors came asking me to please doctor his daughter. I said I had not come here for that; he should go to the doctors who lived here. I was not able to rid myself of him, however. He said he would not leave the house until I went with him. I went with him and gave her something, and the dear Savior blessed it. The evening service was blessed by the Lamb[d].

The 22nd
We felt well during the morning service. We entrusted all of the brown hearts to the care of the beloved Lamb[d], also those who have lost their way, so that He might bring them back and put them in His barn. Today no evening service took place as the brethren had gone sweating. I visited them at their sweat chamber [sweat house]. And then I retired blissfully to my room[d].

The 23rd
First there was the morning blessing, and then I visited the winter huts, for I knew that the wicked enemy [Satan] had [his] instruments there again. They were white people, who were felling trees there; they had brought rom [rum] with them that they wanted to give to the Indians. They were supposed to be good and work for them. This failed, however; they had drunk their rom and also cut their wood themselves. The Lamb[d] was near us during the evening service.

The 24th
I said we wanted to spend the entire day with the Lamb[d]; we felt especially well. Then I did my housework, baking and washing; visited in all of the huts. Also, Moses and his wife arrived here, as did Jonathan.

The 25th
First there was the sermon. Everyone from the winter huts [had come]; many white people were there as well. I said the meeting was not for white people but for the Indians, and [that] everyone should go to the church to which he belonged. However, since they were already here, they may go in this time. And then there was the quarter-of-an-hour for the small children. This is quite a delightful occasion. The dear Lamb[d] is especially near them, and they sit as still

as lambs^d, ~~opening~~ raising their little mouths up high wanting to be kissed. And then the quarter-of-an-hour for the baptized ones took place. I still paid a visit to some of the huts, and then everyone retired quietly.

The 26th

We felt well. I also went visiting in the winter huts; I was kind toward all of those who are timid, and encouraged them.

[The] 27th

We felt well during the morning blessing. One can feel that the Lord is near; He is in our midst. I also heard the Lamb^d being praised in the Indian language. [It] just sounds so very beautiful to hear the dear hearts sing following the evening service. How must the Lamb^d delight in them.

[The] 28th

I felt especially well during the morning blessing. My heart delights in the brown hearts and I love them very much. Moses and his wife, as well as Jonathan, came to take leave of me and return to Wechquadnach. They said they had felt well here; they intend to come back soon. I told them not to forget what the Lamb^d has affected in them, and then there was the evening service, and with that the day was blissfully brought to a close.

Martij the 1st

The Lamb^d can be felt during all of the occasions. His precious blood is flowing plentifully among the brown hearts in the face of all of their failings and shortcomings, which continue to frequently bar their way. Yet when [one talks] to them about blood and wounds, their hearts are nonetheless soft; that encourages one every time. I⁶ also went visiting in the winter huts. After the evening service, I paid a visit to several more huts, and then I went to rest in the protection of the Lamb^d.

The 2nd

After the morning blessing I went to [New] Milford to get something for my nourishment. I also visited *Justes* [Justice] Canfield. He was very kind, also asked about Br. Spangenberg, if he was well, sending him his heartfelt greetings.

The 3rd

I returned to the dear brown hearts; visited them in ~~their~~ their huts. They were glad to see me again. Also, Martin and she [his wife], and Lucas returned home from the seaside. They visited me shortly after their arrival, looking full of light. We felt well during the evening service. I still went visiting in some huts. Afterward, I retired blissfully, locking myself into my room[d].

The 4th

First there was the sermon about Domas [Thomas], how he had lifted his fingers and his hand into the dear Savior's nail marks, and what power the dear Savior's blood holds.[7] And then the meeting for the small children took place, a meeting[8] blessed by the dear Lamb[d], and then followed the quarter-of-an-hour for the baptized ones. I still went visiting in the winter huts since not many of them [the Indian brethren and sisters] had attended the meeting, and with that the day was brought to a close with blessing.

The 5th

The morning blessing was blessed by the Lamb[d], and then I cut wood for myself. Went visiting in some huts. We felt well during the evening service.

The 6th

It was sincerely requested of me to visit one of my neighbors, who is very ill. I had the opportunity to portray to him the Lamb[d] with all of His wounds, and it pleased him and all those around him. And then there was the evening service and everyone retired quietly. It delights me greatly that everyone is so quiet after the evening service, as if no one lived at this place.

The 7th

There was a sweet feeling present during the early service. I spent most of the day visiting. Simon, Jeremias, Martin, and Samuel stayed on after the evening service. We had [a] blissful conversation about the Lamb[d] and His blood—how good this tastes to us poor sinners, and then we retired blissfully.

The 8th

During the early service the Lamb[d] was prayed to heartily for our common well-being, that we may feel the precious blood in our hearts as warmly as it flowed from the dear Savior's side. An Indian from Farmington visited me. He said he could read and write. I asked him if he knew the dear Savior. He said no. He said he knew He was taking an interest in him. I said that was the most important thing for him to learn, how He had hung upon the cross for us, and how His body had been opened by a spear. Next, I went visiting in some huts. After the evening service I went visiting in the others.

The 9th

We felt well during the morning blessing. I also went visiting in the winter huts. Fieliebus,[9] ~~and~~ Jeremias, and Martin stayed after the evening service. We talked about the Lamb[d] and His love. They also recounted how much noise there used to be here in the evenings, and how everything is now so quiet. This the Lamb had accomplished, no doubt. Surely no man could have brought this about.

The 10th

I observed the Sabbath; felt blissful with my dear assembly.

The 11th

First there was the sermon; the beloved Lamb[d] was feelingly near, and then there was the quarter-of-an-hour for the baptized ones. I still paid a visit to some huts and then I quietly retired to my room[d].

The 12th

I went visiting in the winter huts, but there were not many at home. We felt well during the evening service.

The 13th

The morning blessing took place with a heartfelt prayer to the Lamb[d]. We remembered all of the congregations of heathens, and then one of our neighbors came asking me to please come with him; his child was very ill. I gave it something and things improved.

The 14th

I went visiting in the winter huts, finding them [the brethren and sisters] well. Had a blissful conversation with old Maria; she is so happy that she has found the Lamb^d even in her old age. There was a sweet feeling present during the evening service.

The 15th

I paid a visit to nearly all of the huts; it was a blessing for them and me. We felt especially well during the evening service.

The 16th

After the morning blessing I did my housework, also went visiting in some huts.

The 17th

I observed a blissful Sabbath. My heart was frequently with you in Bethlehem. There was a sweet feeling present during the evening service. The discourse was about the bloody Lamb. We appealed to Him for His blood to keep our hearts warm and pure at all times.

The 18th

First there was the sermon on the Lamb of God who has taken upon Himself the sins of the world, and then the meeting for the small children; thereafter the quarter-of-an-hour for the baptized ones, and then I still went visiting in some huts. And with that, the day was blissfully brought to a close.

The 19th

Most of the brethren and sisters came and said that their *Korn* would soon be used up; they needed to go out and earn something. The brethren intended to make canoe[s] and the sisters brooms. As nearly all of them left, there was no meeting. The minister of Kent [Cyrus Marsh] came to visit me. He was very cordial, saying he regretted not having stood by the brethren when they were led away from here, but he did not know us [then].[10] He did not want to put even the smallest obstacle in our way. He thought that since we have lived among them, the Indians were much better than they had been before. He asked that I come and visit him, and said we should not be *schei* [shy] with each other.

The 20th

I made some [fence] posts to make my garden a little larger. Also, I visited the brethren and sisters who had stayed here. My heart and my mind[11] were with you in Bethlehem nearly all day long.

The 21st

I went to [New] Milford to get something for my refreshment.

The 22nd

I went visiting in the winter huts; there were not many [brethren and sisters] at home.

The 23rd

I was hard at work in my garden, still visited the brethren and sisters who had stayed here, and then I retired blissfully, locking myself into my room[d].

The 24th

I observed quite a blissful Sabbath, all alone with my Lamb[d]. My heart was more in Bethlehem than here as there were not many brethren and sisters at home. They turned up one by one for the Sunday sermon.

The 25th

First there was the sermon. The dear Lamb[d] could be felt in our midst. That alone gives one courage, for the Lamb dispenses a sweet feeling at all of the meetings; and then the other occasions took place, and with that the day was closed with blessing.

The 26th

Almost all of the brethren and sisters went out to work. Some of the brethren and sisters told me [that] when they were alone in the woods like this, they could indeed talk with the Savior a great deal, yet they preferred being able to attend the meeting twice a day. I said I too preferred being able to see them every day and tell them something about the Lamb[d].

The 27th

I went visiting in the winter huts but did not find many [brethren and sisters] at home.

The 28th

I worked hard in my garden, also visited the brethren and sisters who had stayed here. The minister of New Fairfield visited me; I acted cordially toward him, and he toward me. He wanted to start a debate. I told him that I could not and did not want to do this; this [sort of discussion] has put an end to many a friendship—we wanted to remain friends. And so we continued to be such.

The 29th

I went to the sawmill to get boards for the church and was able to get them home on the water.[12]

The 30th

I visited the brethren and sisters in their huts; had a joyous conversation with our dear Brother Gitieon[13] about the dear Savior's love for us poor human beings.

The 31st

I observed another joyous Sabbath. I delighted in all of my dear brethren and sisters who are scattered all over the world to preach Jesus' martyrdom.

April 1, [1753]

First there was the sermon on Jesus' suffering and dying. I had no interpreters. We felt well in each other's company, and afterward, there was the quarter-of-an-hour for the baptized ones, and then I still visited them in their huts. And with that the day was closed with blessing.

The 2nd

The brethren and sisters returned to the woods to work. I worked hard in my garden.

The 3rd

I was again industrious going about the same work. Also visited the brethren and sisters who had stayed here. Then I still had a blissful conversation with our dear old Brother Simon about the blood of the Lamb, and both of us felt quite blissful.

The 4th

I went to [New] Milford for some provisions.

The 5th

Much to my joy, dear Brother and Sister Sensemann arrived back in Pachgatgoch, but not many brethren and sisters were at home. He also brought word that 3 more brethren were coming, Nathanael Seidel, Gottlieb Petzold, and [Mattheus][14] Kremser. We informed the brethren and sisters that the brethren and sisters would come.

The 6th

The dear hearts arrived here well and in good spirits. It was no small joy that there were so many of us here. The dear brethren and sisters brought for me many beautiful tidings from the congregation.

The 7th

We observed a joyous Sabbath, and the brethren and sisters came home one by one. We still held a conference with the workers, and with that the day was brought to a close with blessing.

The 8th

First there was the morning blessing, and then we began speaking with the brethren and sisters [in preparation for Communion], finding all of them blissful and in quite a happy state, and then there was the love feast during which our dear Br. Nathanael reported a great deal about the congregation. Our dear Br. Gideon also addressed his people in his language—that the brethren were taking great pains to bring the heathens and them to the beloved Savior; and [that] the beloved Savior has affected so much in them, yet they were still frequently committing such wrong. They should please no longer do this, [that is, cause] the beloved Savior and the brethren to grieve; he said it with a feeling heart. Afterward, we enjoyed quite a blessed Communion at which the Lamb[d] visited us with a sweet feeling. Everyone was very quiet and retired blissfully.

The 9th

First there was the early service, and and [sic] Br. Nathanael informed the brethren and sisters about the visit of the Nantegock [Nanticokes] in Bethlehem, and then we readied ourselves for our journey to New York. Br. Sensemann went with us for 2 miles and then we took a cordial leave.[15]

The 11[th][16]

At 8 o'clock we arrived in New York, where we were received with much love by our dear brethren and sisters.

[The following entries are by Sensemann]

Diarium of the brown assembly in Pachgatgoch, from April 9, 1753

☽ [Monday], the 9th

Br. Nathanael Seidel conducted the morning occasions, at the same time informing the entire brown assembly of the visit of the Nanticocks [Nanticokes] and Schawonos [Shawnees] to Bethlehem, which occurred in the month of March 1753, and the meaning thereof.[17] They all were glad to hear about it. Afterward, the Brothers Nathanael, Gottlieb Pezold, Fröhlich, [and] Kremser bade the Indian brethren and sisters a heartfelt farewell. Upon their request, Br. Samuel and his wife Lucia were granted permission by Br. Nathanael, [who was] in the process of leaving, to move to Gnadenhütten yet this spring. Br. Sensemann accompanied the brethren for several miles, and then we took leave of one another with many tender kisses[d]. I then set out to return to my brown assembly. [The] Joshuas, [the] Martins, and several other Indian brethren and sisters went into the woods some miles from here to finish making the *canuhs* [canoes] that they had started. I visited the brethren and sisters who were at home, finding all of them full of light and in good spirits.

♂ [Tuesday], the 10th

After the early service Sr. Erdmuth went to the winter huts to visit Sr. Theodora, who is ill. Sister Maria came from there to visit my wife, saying about Theodora that she was very ill with respect to her body. We sent her word that we intended to visit her soon.

☿ [Wednesday], the 11th

We resumed holding school with the children today. I went visiting in several huts. Gideon went to Dover on account of outward business. We also were visited by several Indian brethren and sisters.

♃ [Thursday], the 12th

We felt quite well during the early quarter-of-an-hour. Next, I held school with the boys; meanwhile my wife visited the sisters who were at home, finding them well and in a happy state. Jeremias came to visit us. I spoke with him; he was affectionate and abased.

♀ [Friday], the 13th

During the meeting the Savior was particularly intimately near to us with His wounds.

♄ [Saturday], the 14th

We went to the winter huts to visit ill Sr. Theodora. She was somewhat better than she has been. My wife asked her about her heart. She said her heart felt quite well to her; what was in her heart also was shining in her eyes. Several brethren and sisters returned home from the woods in a happy state. During the evening meeting the Savior with His wounds could be felt among us.

☉ [Sunday], the 15th

Toward noon there was the general meeting, afterward, the quarter-of-an-hour for the children, and toward evening the occasion for all of the baptized ones, with blessing.

☽ [Monday], the 16th

Today several families set out to return to the woods to finish the work they had started. Gideon went to Dover on account of outward business. I conducted school with the boys in the forenoon, and my wife with the girls in the afternoon. Several brethren and sisters went to the winter huts to visit the brethren and sisters there.

[No entry for the 17th]

☿ [Wednesday], the 18th

After school we visited the brethren and sisters who were at home. My wife had an edifying discourse with Sr. Justina about the Savior's suffering. Justina said that for several days she had not felt well with respect to her body, assuming she had a severe illness. But it had occurred to her that her illness and pains were nothing compared to the pains that the dear Savior had suffered for her. With that she had given herself up to the Savior, for Him to do with her as He pleased. Br. Lucas returned home from hunting; he was glad to find us here again. He brought word to the Indians that an English man had struck dead a Wanachquaticok Indian.[18]

♃ [Thursday], the 19th

Today Joshua returned home with his family, bringing a new *canuh* [canoe] laden with wood for baskets and brooms, which they intend to process at home. Several brethren went into the woods to work. Joshua interpreted at the meeting in the evening. During the meeting, the Savior's sufferings and martyrdom into which He entered mainly during this night, and what was purchased with it for us, p[p]., was demonstrated.

♀ [Friday], the 20th

We felt well during the early service. Today we frequently remembered our congregations, being among ~~them~~ and with them in our hearts and minds. We very much felt in the spirit of Good Friday, and several of the Indian brethren and sisters expressed themselves in like manner.

♄ [Saturday], the 21st

Today I and my A[nna] Catharine observed the Sabbath in quietude. Several Indian brethren and sisters returned home from the woods in good spirits. Toward evening we had visitors from Rhinebeck, Br. Führer and Henrich Martin, to [*word crossed out*] observe Easter with us. They brought us heartfelt greetings from the other brethren there. Our evening meeting took place with blessing. There were still Indian brethren from Wechquadnach arriving here late.

☉ [Sunday], the 22nd

On the 1st day of Easter not many brethren and sisters came from the winter huts. We did not know what the reason for this was, but soon learned that Sr. Theodora, as well as Sara's daughter Maria, were very ill, [and] for their sake several [brethren and sisters] needed to stay home. Toward noon the general meeting took place. Today's watchword was talked about; the Savior was feelingly near us. During the quarter-of-an-hour for the baptized ones, it was announced that a love feast for all of the baptized brethren and sisters would be held tomorrow, so that the brethren and sisters would stay home given that no one here in New England knows about some of the holidays throughout the year.

☽ [Monday], the 23rd

Toward 10 o'clock a signal was given, at which time all of the brethren and sisters who were at home gathered for the love feast. Before the love feast, however, Br. Amos was spoken with about his heart. He was like a sinner; said he felt his heart to be poor. Thus, he was given permission to join the love feast. The love feast was begun with German and Indian verses, and then the male and female servants brought in what had been prepared. At the love feast it was pointed out that the Savior and His sufferings were the only reason that we were together at this place, to which the 2 Rhinebeck brethren attested as well; otherwise, they would surely not be here among the Indians. There was a feeling of love and grace felt throughout. The 2 aforementioned brethren could not say enough [about how] well they felt during the love feast. Following the love feast, Mosses went back to Wechquadnach, [and] Joshua and Lucas to Wanachquaticok to learn how matters stood in regard to the Indian who had been struck dead. With the 2 Brothers Führer and Henrich Martin, I went visiting in the winter huts, finding Theodora and Maria very ill as for their bodies. After the evening meeting everyone joyfully retired.

♂ [Tuesday], the 24th

Following the morning quarter-of-an-hour the 2 brethren took to their road [to return] to their own [people]. I accompanied them and then we took leave of one another. Most of the brethren and sisters again went into the woods in pursuit of food. Not many stayed at home.

☿ [Wednesday], the 25th

Today we resumed holding school with the children. Afterward, we visited the brethren and sisters who were at home; they were full of light and in a happy state. During the evening meeting Br. Martin interpreted quite nicely. I and my wife remembered yet our dear Bethlehem.

♃ [Thursday], the 26th

Following the morning occasion we held school and visited the brethren and sisters who were at home.

♀ [Friday], the 27th

The brethren and sisters were hard at work making brooms and baskets.

♄ [Saturday], the 28th

After the early service several brethren and sisters readied themselves to bring their canoes down over the falls. I went into the winter huts to visit the brethren and sisters there. On my way back I came upon Gottlob, who had been at the seaside for a while to visit his friends.[19] I asked him about his heart and how things had gone with him in the meantime. He said that he had thought of us frequently and had felt a deep longing in his heart to be with us again.

☉ [Sunday], the 29th

The 2 Moses[es], [and] Joshua and Lucas with them, came down the river with 2 canoes. With the Indians having arrived from the winter huts — several Negroes came as well, likewise some Dutch and English — the signal for the meeting was given. The Lamb[d] with His wounds was passionately portrayed to them. Past noon the quarter-of-an-hours were conducted in due order.

☽ [Monday], the 30th

Following the morning quarter-of-an-hour several brethren and sisters came to us, saying that they intended to ride down to the seaside now [by canoe]. We reminded them to guard their hearts well, and not to get involved in anything ~~else~~ that could lead their hearts to stray from the Savior, which they promised us to do. Gideon went along as far as New Milford. Samuel intended to go to Woodbury to sell the land that they have in Potatuck, and then move with his family to Gnadenhütten.[20] Several old brethren and sisters and the children stayed home.

♂ [Tuesday], May 1 [1753]

Today I had my land plowed by one of our neighbors in order to plant it with Welsh corn. I visited the brethren and sisters in the winter huts, finding all of them well and in good spirits.

☿ [Wednesday], the 2nd

We held school. Br. Gideon came home from New Milford in a happy state. The brethren and sisters who had stayed home visited us frequently, especially old Sr. Erdmuth. Old Brother Simon and Petrus went to New Milford to sell wooden utensils.

♃ [Thursday], the 3rd

We continued holding school and visited the brethren and sisters who ~~are~~ were at home.

[No entries for the 4th and 5th]

☉ [Sunday], the 6th

Today several English people came to attend the sermon. I had no interpiter [interpreter]. The Indian brethren and sisters said they had understood me quite well. Samuel and Lucas came home. Samuel did not sell the land. One Indian family had not been agreeable to it.[21] He felt somewhat sickly. Sr. Sarah came to visit my wife.

☽ [Monday], the 7th

We resumed holding school. Jeremias and his wife Agnes returned home from the seaside in good spirits, bringing word that the other brethren and sisters were still back at the river catching fish. A man from Dover wanted to have me come to [see] a sick person. I said that I was not a doctor. He said a doctor who had tried everything and did not know what else to do had said that if there was one person in the world who could help him, it would have to be one of the Moravians, and for that reason he had come here. I should please go with him by horse. Because I was not able to rid myself of him, I sent ~~him~~ some of our medicine that we had brought for our own use from Bethlehem.

♂ [Tuesday], the 8th

Today several more families returned home from the seaside. They were very tired from their journey. I and my wife worked in the field; also remembered our dear brethren and sisters in Bethlehem, p[p].

[No entry for the 9th]

♃ [Thursday], the 10th

Samuel and the 2 Moses[es] went to Wechquadnach. A special feeling of grace could be felt during the evening meeting.

♀ [Friday], the 11th

I visited several brethren; talked with them about their stay down by the sea-side. They themselves admitted that they felt most blissful when they were able to stay at home. The father of the aforementioned sick person sent a manservant, and through him asked me to please come to him; his son was nearly recovered. As soon as he had taken the medicine he had improved. I went with him on horseback, but encountered many crowds on the way. The people waited for me along the way, wanting to ask me for advice about their situations. I had enough to do to rid myself of them.

[No entry for the 12th]

☉ [Sunday], the 13th

The occasions were conducted in due order. Toward evening Jonathan and Samuel came from Wechquadnach, bringing me word that the brethren and sisters there have decided jointly, also all the baptized ones, to move to Gnadenhütten or Wyoming, and that Jonathan is to go down to Gnadenhütten to inform the brethren there about it. Given this opportunity, I wrote a letter to Br. Martin [Mack] and [Johann] Schmick.

☽ [Monday], the 14th

After the morning quarter-of-an-hour Jonathan set out on his journey to Gnadenhütten. During the meeting this evening the Savior was near to us with His red wounds.

♂ [Tuesday], the 15th

Following the early service I held school with the boys. The Indian brethren and sisters were busy planting Welsh corn. I went visiting in several huts, finding them industrious and in good spirits.

☿ [Wednesday], the 16th

After the morning occasion I went to New Fairfield on account of outward business. Meanwhile, my wife was visited by many sisters; spoke with them about various matters concerning the Savior and His love for poor sinners.

[No entry for the 17th]

♀ [Friday], the 18th[22]

Everyone was busy with plowing and planting. We felt especially well during the evening service.

♄ [Saturday], the 19th

Several brethren and sisters who had been out this week in pursuit of food gathered at home. The 2 Moses[es] from Wechquadnach came here.

☉ [Sunday], the 20th

The Sunday occasions were conducted as usual.

☽ [Monday], the 21st

Several brethren and sisters came, telling us that they intended to go down to the falls at New Milford to catch fish, which every year around this time come moving up from the sea. Those who stayed home were busy planting. It proceeded quite pleasantly and orderly. The 2 Moses[es] too helped diligently.

[No entry for the 22nd]

☿ [Wednesday], the 23rd

I visited several brethren. The 2 Moses[es] took leave to return to their own. Several more brethren and sisters went down to the falls to catch fish. Thus, only a few remained at home.

[No entry for the 24th]

♀ [Friday], the 25th

After the morning meeting I went to Dutchess County to pass on to the awakened people there the message that had been given to me by Br. Nathanael, namely, that a brother from Bethlehem would soon come to them. When I announced this to them they were overjoyed at it, for they had already planned on writing to the congregation one more time. I felt very well there.[23] I set out to return, but was not able to make it home that day. Stayed that night with Nicolaus Rau, the brother of late Sr. Mack.[24]

♄ [Saturday], the 26th

I set out early for Pachgatgoch. Found my dear Catharine and the brown brethren and sisters, who were home, well and in good spirits. Old Sister Erdmuth had kept my wife company in the meantime.

☉ [Sunday], the 27th

Around noon the general meeting was held; Martin interpreted. Toward evening the quarter-of-an-hour for all of the baptized ones took place. Both with blessing.

☽ [Monday], the 28th

Following the morning quarter-of-an-hour I commenced school with the boys. However, presently there are only few at home. I went visiting in the huts. Gideon told us that he intended to go to the falls to see if he could catch some fish. We had him pass on greetings to the brethren and sisters for us. We told Gideon to see how things were going with them, if they all were in touch with their hearts.

[No entry for the 29th]

☿ [Wednesday], the 30th

Gideon returned home from New Milford, bringing a considerable amount of fish with him, of which he sent us some as well. He let us know that he had found the brethren and sisters in good spirits.

♃ [Thursday], the 31st

We remembered and spoke a good deal about our dear Bethlehem. In our hearts and minds we were frequently with them, wishing to see and hear something from the congregation sometime soon. At the meeting in the evening the dear Savior's ascension and His return were talked about, and that since that time His people have been awaiting His appearance and have been looking forward to it. A feeling of grace could be sensed.

♀ [Friday], June 1 [1753]

Several brethren went with baskets and other items to Filkintown to sell them. My wife visited the sisters; spoke especially with Elisabeth about her heart as she has not been quite full of light for a while. She said that the Savior has put her back in touch with her heart. She had seen that the heart of her husband

Joshua was not quite in a proper state. That was when she reportedly thought, it cannot be that both of us are becoming unsaved, and thus, she soon went to the Savior and begged His pardon. The dear Savior reportedly did forgive her, and once again made her heart well.

♄ [Saturday], the 2nd

Everyone who had been out during the week again gathered at home. The Savior was near to us during the evening service.

☉ [Sunday], the 3rd

The Sunday occasion was conducted as usual.

☽ [Monday], the 4th

After the morning quarter-of-an-hour Br. Gideon directed the brethren to help hoe our Welsh corn. And everyone who was at home came [to help], baptized as well as unbaptized. Thus we were done in half a day. They all went about it most joyfully. In the meantime my wife had prepared food, and so we gave them a meal to eat.

♂ [Tuesday], the 5th and ☿ [Wednesday], the 6th

Several of the brethren and sisters were busy hoeing corn. The occasions were conducted as usual.

♃ [Thursday], the 7th

Gideon and Joshua were spoken with about some of the brethren and sisters and their hoeing of the Welsh corn—to remind them regularly that they work their corn properly, so that they each family will have enough to eat next year, and need not go among the white people as much. This they promised to do.

♀ [Friday], the 8th

I was out on account of outward business. Meanwhile Br. Martin Mack and Nathanael arrived from Gnadenhütten. I learned about it along the way and hurried so much the more to get home. Found both of them [at home] and was delighted to see someone of our dear hearts from Bethlehem. Received many a delightful letter[d], which gladdened and refreshed us. In the evening Brother

Martin conducted a heartfelt and passionate meeting on the blissfulness [to be found] inside Jesus' wounds.

♄ [Saturday], the 9th

Br. Sensemann delivered the morning blessing entrusting the brown assembly to the care of the Savior's pierced heart by means of a heartfelt prayer. Br. Martin related to us some things about Bethlehem and Gnadenhütten and the other places, as well as about the dear Savior's work of grace there, for which we gave thanks to the Savior. Toward evening Christian Führer, H. Martin, Zacharias Haber, and Jacob Maul came from Rhinebeck to observe Pentecost with the Indian brethren and sisters [and] us. They rejoiced at finding Br. Martin Mack here. Br. Martin conducted the evening service with blessing.

☉ [Sunday], the 10th

On the 1st day of Pentecost, Br. Martin held the general meeting in German; Br. Nathanael interpreted. Everyone listened atent [attentively]. Afterward, he spoke with Br. Samuel about his moving to Gnadenhütten, which, for the time being, is not going to happen after all. Past noon the usual quarter-of-an-hour was conducted separately with the baptized Indian brethren and sisters, wherein Brother Martin informed the brethren and sisters of the congregation's mind, chiefly with respect to Communion—that we would have to suspend it for the time being because it cannot go on like this, with the excesses [committed] by some of the brethren and sisters.[25] For that same reason it was likewise suspended in Gnadenhütten at present. The brethren and sisters must not think that this was a small matter, p[p]. Some became very sad as they had assumed he [Brother Martin] had come to hold Communion, and now they were hearing the opposite. Also, many had been looking forward to it with all their hearts. Br. Martin talked then with Joshua, but he appeared to be somewhat indifferent. Br. Martin delivered yet a brief evening blessing in our house, in the presence of the 4 Rb. [Rhinebeck] brethren.

☽ [Monday], the 11th

Following the morning meeting, Br. Martin and Nathanael readied themselves for their journey, [in order to] first call on the Wechquadnach Indian brethren and sisters and to pass on to them the congregation's message. Sensemann ~~readied himself~~ went with them. The 4 Rhinebeck brethren set out to return home. We came to the place where they [the Wechquadnach Indians] live, but did not find any brother at home.[26] Having carried out our task, we continued on and stayed that night with Joha[nnes] Rau, Martin's father-in-law.

♂ [Tuesday], the 12th

We arrived in Rhinebeck at Christian Führer's [house], who welcomed us with much love.

☿ [Wednesday], the 13th

Having visited the brethren there, Br. Martin took leave and set out on his journey together with his dear Nathanael. Sensemann and also some Rb. [Rhinebeck] brethren accompanied them ~~for several miles~~ and then we bade one another farewell. Sensemann also inquired with Matth[eus] Hoffman about a package of letters that he was to receive there. But they had not yet arrived.

♃ [Thursday], the 14th

I set out to return. Arrived in Pachgatgoch late in the evening. Everyone had already retired. My wife had old Sister Erdmuth with her for company.

♀ [Friday], the 15th

Sister Sarah from the winter huts came to visit us. The Indian brethren and several sisters went to get barck [bark] for Gideon's new house. Br. Martin, the Indian, interpreted during the quarter-of-an-hour in the evening.

♄ [Saturday], the 16th

Joshua left on horseback to sell things to the white people. In the meantime his wife Elisabeth was delivered of a daughter[d]. My wife visited her. She had given birth to the child in the woods; was quite well, along with the child. Joshua came home. Came and visited us several more times today, yet said nothing about the child's baptism. This was, however, the reason why he came to us. We did not say anything about it either. In the evening he came once again; said the child was ill. Thus, my wife had to go there to see it, but it was not in any danger.

☉ [Sunday], the 17th

Joshua came in the morning, applying for his child's baptism. However, because he had been prejudiced against the workers in Gnadenhütten by some confused brethren from Gnadenhütten, and would rather see the Wechquadnach [brethren and sisters] at this place than in Gnadenhütten, and for that reason had not long ago expressed himself harshly against us on that account, I asked him about his heart—how it presently stood with the Savior. He surely could remember in what state he has been for some time. He said curtly that his heart felt somewhat better and more comfortable. I ~~explained to him~~ told him [that] when we baptized children, we first had to know that the parents themselves were on proper terms with the Savior. If they themselves were not on proper terms with the dear Savior, and were unable to deal faithfully with the grace that the Savior has bestowed on them, how could they preserve their children p[p].? He said nothing further and went home. Several English people came to attend the meeting. With the Indians from the winter huts having arrived here, the signal for the general meeting was given. Martin was unable to get on with the translating today, and so I preached to everyone in English. The Savior was near us. The occasions for the baptized children and for all of the baptized ones took place with blessing.

☽ [Monday], the 18th

I went visiting in the winter huts. Spoke with Br. David and Rebecca, and because they inquired about the baptism of Joshua's child, I told them the congregation's mind as it concerned the baptism of the children of the brethren and sisters. They grew very quiet. I also talked with the other brethren and sisters about their hearts, and that with their hearts they should abide in the Savior's wounds. They were quite well and in good spirits.

♂ [Tuesday], the 19th and ☿ [Wednesday], the 20th

The brethren were hard at work building a new hut for Gideon. We held school. The sisters were busy making baskets and brooms.

♃ [Thursday], the 21st and [Friday], the 22nd

We continued holding school; the brethren worked away at the huts. The occasions took place in due order.

♄ [Saturday], the 23rd

I and my wife visited the brethren and sisters in the winter huts. My wife talked with several of the sisters about their hearts. Theodora said that her heart was with the dear Savior day and night. If only she could again have enough strength to come up again and attend the meeting; her heart greatly longed for it. They were thankful that we had visited them. Jeremias and several sisters went to bid the Wechquadnach Indians farewell.

☉ [Sunday], the 24th

During the general meeting today's watchword, *O wie wiel ich noch reden daß er mir wird halten seinen theuren Eid*, Is. 38.15., was talked about.[27] Our heart rejoiced and was grateful for all the grace and blissfulness that the Savior has let flow our way from His precious wounds, p[p]. That day we felt especially well. Thamar came to visit us. My wife asked her about her heart. She said her heart felt quite well to her; also said that she intended to go to the seaside tomorrow along with her daughter Anna and an unbaptized Indian woman.

☽ [Monday], the 25th

Following the early service everyone went about his work. We visited those brethren and sisters in the huts who were at home. Jeremias and the other brethren and sisters returned home in good spirits from their visit with the Wechquadnach brethren and sisters.

♂ [Tuesday], the 26th and ☿ [Wednesday], the 27th

Nothing of note occurred. We felt well during the occasions.

♃ [Thursday], the 28th

After the morning quarter-of-an-hour we went into the field to work. Afterward, we visited several brethren and sisters.

♀ [Friday], the 29th and [Saturday], the 30th

The brethren and sisters who had been out this week in pursuit of food gathered at home.

☉ [Sunday], July 1 [1753]

Brother Martin came to our house; I was just then reading the Bible. I read something to him. He listened diligently; I asked if he would be able to translate everything. He said several passages were very difficult to translate into their language. I sent him to see whether the brethren and sisters had arrived from the winter huts, and when he brought word the signal for the general meeting was given. Today's watchword was talked about: *Hebe deine Augen auf, dieße alle kommen zu dir.* Is. 60.4.[28] It was stated that there was yet a great multitude that would have to be brought to the Savior and His wounds, and that the beginning to this was being made among several nations at this time, of which they at this place were also a part[d]. Brotherly love was talked about during the quarter-of-an-hour for the baptized ones; where this was not present, the brethren and sisters were not on [proper] terms with the dear Savior, p[p]. My wife visited several sisters; spoke with Priscilla about her heart. She said that at times she strayed from her heart because of her children—that they did not want to abide by the Savior. My wife said, that is why she [Priscilla] should stay that much closer to the Savior; that way she could set a positive example for her children, and also [would be able to] put in a good word for them with the dear Savior from time to time. I visited Schery, who had returned home yesterday from his visit with the Wechquadnach Indians. He said that several days ago some of them had set out on their journey to Gnadenhütten, and [that] the remaining ones would start out tomorrow. He was thinking of visiting them after the harvest. I met ManSchiro from Potatuck in Petrus's house. He is the cousin[29] of our late Johannes and looks just like Johannes. He acted most amiably toward me, and I likewise toward him.

☽ [Monday], the 2nd

After the quarter-of-an-hour old Br. Simon summoned the brethren to build a new hut for Sr. Priscilla. Everyone gathered; they went for several miles to get bast [bark] as they are building it entirely from bast. I and my wife went into the field to work. Old Sr. Erdmuth went to New Milford to get Welsh corn.

♂ [Tuesday], the 3rd

After the morning quarter-of-an-hour the Indian brethren returned to their hut-building. I visited them. Things proceeded quite agreeably among them. The evening occasion took place with blessing.

☿ [Wednesday], the 4th

My wife was paid a visit by Mrs. Mills and her daughter,[30] and when she wished to visit the Indian sisters, my wife went with them. She is an awakened woman who feels troubled at heart. My wife spoke with her a great deal about the Savior. Old Erdmuth returned home from New Milford in a happy state. Sr. Thamar, who came home with her daughter Anna today, visited us. We inquired how things had gone on her journey, whether she had been blissful and in good spirits. She said yes. She was reportedly very glad when she laid eyes on Pachgatgoch again. The people had asked her many things, also what her minister was preaching. She had said it would be better if they came here themselves and heard it, then they would know.

♃ [Thursday], the 5th

After the morning blessing we again went to work in the field. The brethren were still busy repairing their huts. Old Br. Simon worked not far from us. I went there to visit him, finding him engaged in a heartfelt prayer to the dear Savior. I stayed back until he was finished praying, and then I went to him; had an affectionate conversation with him. Toward evening I visited the brethren at their hut-building; they were helping one another in quite a brotherly manner.

[No entry for the 6th]

♄ [Saturday], the 7th

The Indian brethren began laying up stones for a chimney in Joshua's house. My ~~sister~~ wife called on Sister Justina. We were concerned about her, that her heart may not be in a proper state as she had gone out without saying anything. But she said that her heart was quite well. She had been driven out by necessity, for she did not have anything to eat in the house, and had intended to return home right away, [but] had not been able to sell her things. Thus she had been forced to stay out that night. Gottlieb, who also had been out with wooden utensils, returned home in a happy state.

421

☉ [Sunday], the 8th

Toward noon the general meeting took place, which some English people attended. The Savior granted me a warm heart [to speak] about His love for the poor sinners who do not know what to do, and [who] come to the Savior just the way they feel. We felt quite well on this occasion. After the sermon 2 of the English people came into our house. I talked with them about some matters regarding the Savior, in particular about His sufferings and martyrdom. During the quarter-of-an-hour for the baptized ones, today's text was talked about, p[p]. Following the quarter-of-an-hour I spoke with Christian about his heart. He said that he felt most comfortable when he was able to be home and hear about the Savior. In the evening Sr. Thamar told us about an old Indian woman who attended the meeting today for the first time. What was the meaning of this, [that] she could not help but shiver severely during the meeting[, the Indian woman asked]. She had thought to herself, she must have a wicked heart. Thamar had replied, Of course your heart is wicked; it is afraid of the Savior. My wife and I remembered our dear Bethlehem; we longed to see a brother from there soon, and then we retired blissfully.

☽ [Monday], the 9th

We held a small conference with Br. Gideon; we sent him to the winter huts to visit the brethren and sisters there. He had spoken with those who were at home about their hearts — how they stood with the Savior. He then brought us word from them.

[No entry for the 10th]

☿ [Wednesday], the 11th

Most of the brethren went to work the harvest at the white people's — cutting. Some worked their own Welsh corn. Two English people came, inquiring after an Indian who had committed himself into servitude with a man in New Milford, and has run away. They had heard that he had gone to Gnadenhütten. We told them that we had not heard anything about this and knew nothing about it, and had not seen him in several weeks. Besides, those people who planned matters of this sort would not inform us as we are opposed to such things. They believed us and went away. Indeed, none of the brethren knew anything about it. The Savior was near us during the evening occasion.

♃ [Thursday], the 12th

Most of the brethren again went out to work. The sisters [were] busy at home with their usual work of making baskets and brooms.

♀ [Friday], the 13th

I went visiting in all of the huts. After that I went with my wife to the winter huts to visit the brethren and sisters. We found several sisters at home, with whom my wife talked; she asked them about their hearts — on what terms they were with the Savior and His wounds. Theodora testified that her heart had fellowship with the Savior day and night.

♄ [Saturday], the 14th

The Indian brethren came home in good spirits. During the evening meeting it was explained that nothing had forced or driven the dear Savior to suffer for us other than His love for poor mankind, to set [them] free from [word crossed out] Satan's clutch, and to deliver them to His heavenly being along with Himself. We felt well on this occasion.

☉ [Sunday], the 15th

(In the morning, at daybreak, someone came and woke us up. When I opened the door, it was a man inquiring after the runaway Indian, and when I told him that he had been searched for at this place previously, he said that he was well aware of it. They had heard he was staying here, and they had orders to look for him at this place. I said that to my knowledge he was not here. But it was possible that I did not know it [for sure]; he should look for him. Thus, he took leave of me. There also were 3 men with him who stood guard at the ends [of the settlement], and so they searched all of the huts, but did not find him. They right away set out for the winter huts and did the same there as here. But [he] was not to be found there either.)[31] With the brethren and sisters having come up from the winter huts, the general meeting was held, wherein the Savior was near us. The quarter-of-an-hour for the baptized children is taking place with blessing. The little hearts are so quiet and one feels especially well on this occasion. Several foreign Indian women, who had attended the sermon today, came to talk with us about their hearts; one had been baptized by the Presbyterians and was feeling troubled at heart. She said that she has been unable to sleep some nights; had not found anyone among the English people with whom she could talk about her heart. We spoke with her affectionately, directing her to the Savior—that He most gladly took in all those poor sinners who did not know what to do and came to Him, letting them partake of every blessedness. She was very glad to hear this. She said that once she had told a minister that she felt so troubled at heart [word crossed out]. He had prayed over her, but that had not helped any. We told her to simply give herself up to the dear Savior; that way she would become blissful. Old Sr. Erdmuth, being present, told her how blissful her heart felt near the Savior and His wounds. Then there was the service for the baptized ones, with blessing. During visits, Petrus said that one time several weeks ago I had spoken with him and had admonished him, which he had not taken lovingly. He has felt troubled at heart on that account ever since. I said that I no longer held anything against him, [that] I had long forgiven him for that; he should simply ask the dear Savior for forgiveness for having so trifled away his time. That day we felt especially well and we observed the same with the Indian brethren and sisters.

☽ [Monday], the 16th
Because one of our neighbors intended to travel to New York, I wrote several letters to the brethren there and brought them to him. Meanwhile my wife visited the sisters. Elisabeth was sad that her little daughter[d] was not being baptized, and that her husband Joshua has often been irritable [?][32] for some time now. Apparently, she was not staying with her husband, but her heart grew sad when she thought about the child. My wife said that she [Elisabeth] knew only too well the circumstances concerning the child's baptism, because in his heart Joshua was not on proper terms with the Savior. She [Elisabeth] said that she was certainly well aware of this, and had often reminded him and had directed him to his heart. She wished that Br. Sensemann would please talk with him sometime. Perhaps that would help. My wife said she should abide by the Savior and leave all matters to Him; He would take care of it all right. This she

promised to do. Brother Martin said he believed that a brother from Bethlehem would come soon; he has been repeatedly on the lookout for him. When asked how he would know this, he said he felt his heart believing [it], and his ♡ was looking forward to it.

♂ [Tuesday], the 17th

Our Husband was near us with His wounds during the morning blessing. Our Indian brethren and sisters are very poor. Old Sr. Erdmuth told us that they had no food in their house. She needed to go out and see where there was some Welsh corn to be had. We gathered some dried green Welsh corn and beans and distributed them among those in need. They were very glad and thankful for this.

☿ [Wednesday], the 18th

Most of the Indian brethren went out to work in order to earn some corn. Fairly late in the evening our dear Brother [Abraham] Reincke arrived, having been accompanied here by Br. Führer. We were happy about their arrival, especially about our dear heart Abraham, and the heartfelt letters[d] and greetings[d] from our dear and precious brethren and sisters in Bethlehem. Several Indian brethren and sisters had learned about it [their arrival] also, and welcomed them.

♃ [Thursday], the 19th

In the morning all of the brethren and sisters who were at home came and welcomed Brother A. Reincke, happy to see a brother from Bethlehem. Afterward, I went with Br. Abraham and Führer to the winter huts but found few brethren and sisters at home. The majority had gone into the woods to work. In the evening Br. Abraham conducted an anointed and blessed meeting on the bloody wounds of our martyred Lamb[d]. Because Br. Führer [needed to] return home tomorrow, and also had business at the river, we wrote several letters to our dear brethren and sisters in New York and Bethlehem. In addition, Brother Abraham resolved to leave tomorrow for Salisbury to attend to his plan,[33] and because he is unfamiliar with this area, Br. Sensemann will accompany him there. We indeed would have very much liked to have him stay with us for a few days, but we could not very well keep him since the people [there] have been waiting for a brother for a long time.

♀ [Friday], the 20th

Brother Abraham conducted the morning occasion, wherein he informed the brown brethren and sisters that he intended to leave for Salisbury today. Besides, few Indian brethren were at home. However, he intended to visit them again soon when he expected to find all the brethren and sisters together. Brother Sensemann would accompany him there. They became a little sad that he was leaving so soon. Old Erdmuth said [that] for the sake of the brethren he could not leave so soon. They all would come home tomorrow to be sure. We took leave of the brown brethren and sisters. Sensemann promised them to return home tomorrow. We went together for several miles, and then Führer took leave and went toward home on horseback. He is a serviceable heart and he considers it a favor to serve the brethren. We then came to the area where the Wechquadnach brethren and sisters had lived.[34] We also looked at the house in which our dear heart Johannes [von Watteville] and Cammerhoff baptized many a brown heart into the death of Jesus, and in which our dear late Brother Bruce went to the Savior.[35] Br. Abraham was glad that this way he had the opportunity to see this area. Next, we came to the people[d] in Salisbury. I stayed there overnight.

♄ [Saturday], the 21st

I bade dear Brother Abraham farewell and set out to return to my hearts in Pachgatgoch. Arrived home fairly late in the evening.

☉ [Sunday], the 22nd

The occasions were conducted as usual, like before. The Savior was near us during all of the occasions that day.

☽ [Monday], the 23rd

Following the morning meeting Br. Gideon came; said that he intended to go out to work. If he found none, he would return home today. We yet talked a bit with him regarding a number of brethren about whom he was of one mind with us. Several other brethren went with him. Br. Martin interpreted during the evening meeting.

♂ [Tuesday], the 24th

Almost all of the Indian sisters went into the woods to get blueberries. The bloody wounds of our Husband were near us during the evening meeting.

[No entry for the 25th]

♃ [Thursday], the 26th

I visited several brethren. Toward evening the minister [Cyrus Marsh] from Kent called on us, as it appeared to be raining hard. We discussed various matters. Among other things, he said [something] about some of the awakened preachers, that from their pulpits they were running down the other preachers so horübel [horribly]. I told him that this was not the way we did things; instead, we preached the Savior crucified to the people. At the same time, I had a favorable opportunity to portray to him most passionately the Savior with all of His merit and wounds. My heart felt very warm to me on this occasion.

♀ [Friday], the 27th

Sr. Erdmuth told us that she intended to go out with other Indians to sell baskets and brooms. I went to the winter huts, but there were not many at home. Sarah and her daughter Maria were in good spirits.

♄ [Saturday], the 28th

My wife and I remembered the dear Bethlehem. Several Indian brethren and sisters who had been working away from home gathered at home. The peace that a poor sinner experiences inside Jesus' wounds was talked about during the evening meeting.

☉ [Sunday], the 29th

The righteousness of God, p[p]., was talked about during the general meeting. There were two English men present; to one of them this was most edifying. After the sermon he spoke further to me about his heart, at which time he wept. Next, there was the quarter-of-an-hour for the children, and then that for all of the baptized ones.

☽ [Monday], the 30th

Following the morning occasion several brethren and sisters went out to work on account of their food situation. Some went out with baskets and brooms to sell.

♂ [Tuesday], the 31st

Two joiners came to cover the interior of our meeting house with boards. I entrusted this work also to the care of our Savior, as well as to the whole of our circumstances. I remembered today's watchword, which reads, *So wird der Gott des Friedens mit euch sein.*[36] We were unable to conduct an occasion until the work was finished. Doctor Chase came, wanting to have me go to a sick person. He reportedly had tried everything, but was unable to help him. I told him that I was not here for that, and that I was not a doctor, p[p].

[*No entry for August 1*]
♃ [Thursday], August 2 [1753]
The work on our meeting house proceeded in a nice and orderly fashion.

♀ [Friday], the 3rd and ~~[Saturday], the 4th~~
The joiners continued. I visited several brethren. A number of brethren and sisters who had gone out at the beginning of the week returned home.

♄ [Saturday], the 4th[37]
Our meeting house was finished. I was grateful to the Savior that the work was completed. The joiners were very *content* and *plist* [pleased], and the Indian brethren and sisters [were] glad that it was nice and strong now, and warm in the meeting place. We conducted our meeting in the evening; the Savior was near us.

☉ [Sunday], the 5th
Today we remembered the days of grace that we enjoyed among the precious congregation in Marienborn 12 years ago.[38] The grace was fresh in our hearts; we gave thanks to the Savior in a childlike manner. We further entreated Him for His merciful guidance, p[p]. The occasions were conducted as usual, with blessing. Also, several of the brethren and sisters were spoken with about their hearts. Sr. Sarah told us about her sick daughter Maria, that she, her daughter, desired that the Savior take her to Him.

☽ [Monday], the 6th
Following the morning occasion, several brethren and sisters went out to work. I went visiting in a number of huts, finding the brethren and sisters in good spirits and full of light. We received a letter from New York, wherein we received news about St. Thomas and Bethlehem, as well as the *Irin*[39] (the *Irin*—that she

was to be expected with 30 brethren any day, which stirred in us a longing to hear [and to see] who might be coming with it).⁴⁰

[No entry for the 7th]

☿ [Wednesday], the 8th
I went to visit an Indian family 6 miles from here; found the daughter very ill.⁴¹ I asked her whether she was thinking of the Savior—she had attended the meeting frequently and had heard about Him that He loved the poor sinners so. She said that she thought of Him often. However, she was so ill that she was unable to say much about her heart because of the pain. I also spoke with Magdalena, who in former times had lived in the Sisters' house in Bethlehem. On the way back I went to the winter huts, to which Br. Gideon came as well. Sr. Sarah along with her sick daughter Maria was lively and in good spirits.

♃ [Thursday], the 9th
Gideon told us that he intended to go to New Milford, and wanted to visit Sekes's sick daughter along the way. Sr. Erdmuth came, having been sent by Sr. Priscilla to inform us that it was agreed among them that her daughter, Salome, was betrothed to Br. Jonathan, and that the parents on both sides were agreeable, and that they would be pleased if I married them. Sr. Priscilla felt ashamed that we had not been informed about the marriage of her daughter Benigna to Philippus. Magdalena, Philippus's mother, said that she had in fact told us about it, which had indeed happened one time, about 3/4 of a year ago. We sent word to her that we had nothing against the marriage. It was merely our desire that it occurred in an orderly fashion and with the consent of the parents. The evening meeting took place with blessing.

♀ [Friday], the 10th and ♄ [Saturday], the 11th
The brethren who had been out this week, some to hunt and some on account of other affairs, again gathered at home.

☉ [Sunday], the 12th
Joshua came to me. On that occasion I began to ask him about his heart. He said that he was thinking of the Savior all day long and that he felt well in his heart.

Yet he thought that he was still lacking in one respect, in that he was not truly a poor sinner. I told him that I too believed that about him, p[p]. I had him interpret during the general meeting. He is the best interpiter. Past noon the quarter-of-an-hour for the baptized children took place, and thereafter that for all of the baptized ones, wherein we felt quite well.

☽ [Monday], the 13th

Following the morning occasion, several brethren informed us that they intended to go with their families into the woods to work, to make canoe[s] and brooms. Some went hunting again. I went with my wife to one of our neighbors to buy some provisions. However, they were as rich as we. On returning home we found dear Brother A. Reincke with 3 additional brethren from Rhinebeck [there], who were most welcome to us.

♂ [Tuesday], the 14th

Br. Abraham R[eincke] conducted a passionate quarter-of-an-hour in the morning. Afterward, it was pondered whether we should hold a love feast today with those brethren and sisters who were at home, because the Rhinebeck brethren had brought with them things for it, and given that it had been a blessing for them when they [the Rhinebeck brethren] joined the love feast in the past. Br. Gideon was charged with informing the brethren and sisters about it so that they would make sure to stay nicely at home, who soon passed it on to be sure. Br. Abraham held the meeting in the evening, portraying the bloody Savior quite passionately.

☿ [Wednesday], the 15th

In the morning preparations were made for the love feast because the Rhinebeck brethren intended to be home still today, and when the signal was given, the brethren and sisters who were [at home] gathered, 24 in number, plus 10 baptized children. The letters[d] from the dear Jünger Johannan[42] to some of the Indian brethren and sisters were read aloud, which was more than only a small joy for them. Br. Abraham told them about his people in Salisbury—how hungry they were for the gospel, p[p].; all of us were quite pleased to hear this. We all felt quite well during the love feast. The 3 brethren from Rhinebeck took a tender leave of us as well as of the brown ones. During the meeting in the evening the Savior was near us with His wounds.

♃ [Thursday], the 16th

Brother Abraham Reincke and Sensemann visited the brethren and sisters in the huts. The occasion in the evening was conducted with those who were at home.

♀ [Friday], the 17th

During the early service it was announced that Brother Abraham Reincke would return to his people in Dutchess County today, and that Br. Sensemann would accompany him. In passing through, *Doctor* Chase and the *minister* of that same place came to our house. The *doctor* would very much like to have some medicine from Bethlehem. Br. Sensemann advised him to write a letter to our *Doctor* Otto on that account, yet he thought to travel there perhaps himself. They both were very cordial, and then they took their leave. We then set out on our journey, reaching Azariah Smith's house in the evening, where we found a ready welcome.

♄ [Saturday], the 18th

I took leave of dear Brother Abraham and set out to return [to Pachgatgoch]. I found my dear wife along with the Indian brethren and sisters well and in good spirits. The brethren and sisters who had been out this week in pursuit of food gathered at home as well.

☉ [Sunday], the 19th

Br. Samuel came home in the morning to attend the meeting, bringing us word from Martin and his wife that they all were well and blissful, also heartfelt greetings from them. They are working about 8 miles from here up the river, making *canoe*[s] and brooms. I also talked with Br. Samuel about his heart. Br. Samuel interpreted during the general meeting; the dear Savior was near us. The quarter-of-an-hours that afternoon took place with blessing.

☽ [Monday], the 20th

Following the morning occasion several sisters went out to sell things; those at home were busily going about their work, making brooms and baskets.

♂ [Tuesday], the 21st
Br. Gideon told us that he intended to go to the seaside with his wife Martha to visit his son who lived that way.[43] He also had to attend to other matters there. Martha took brooms and baskets with her to sell. The meeting was conducted with those brethren and sisters who were staying home.

☿ [Wednesday], the 22nd
Today I made some hay. Joshua and Jeremias returned home from hunting in good spirits, but had not shot anything. Joshua interpreted during the evening meeting.

♃ [Thursday], the 23rd
I went visiting in the winter huts. Everyone was very cordial toward me, baptized ones as well as unbaptized ones. Sr. Sarah also was quite revived and well.

♀ [Friday], the 24th
Old Sr. Theodora came to our house telling my wife about her heart—how well she was feeling near the Savior. Brother and sister Martin and [the] Samuels came home in good spirits.

[No entry for the 25th]
☉ [Sunday], the 26th
The occasions took place in their usual order.

☽ [Monday], the 27th
Following the morning blessing, several sisters went into the field to roast and dry green Welsh corn. Gideon and Martha returned home in good spirits from their visit to the seaside.

♂ [Tuesday], the 28th
Br. Martin told us that he intended to go to New Milford to sell cans[44] and other such items.

[No entry for the 29th]
♃ [Thursday], the 30th
My wife visited the sisters, finding them affectionate and in a happy state. She

also was paid a visit by an English woman. At the evening meeting I was able to passionately portray the bloody wounds of Jesus to the brown assembly.

♀ [Friday], the 31st

All of the Indian brethren and sisters were in good spirits. Outwardly, they were busy in the field, drying their green corn. Old Sr. Erdmuth came[45] home from New Milford in good spirits. Sr. Thamar visited us in the evening.

♄ [Saturday], September 1

I and my A. Catharine observed the Sabbath in quietude today. Our hearts were frequently in Bethlehem among our dear brethren and sisters. We also felt the nearness of our bloody Husband and we felt especially well. In the afternoon we visited several brethren and sisters.

♄ [Saturday], September 1, 1753[46]

I and my wife observed the Sabbath in quietude. Our hearts were frequently in Bethlehem among our dear brethren and sisters. We also felt the presence of our Husband and we felt especially well. Past noon we went visiting in several huts.

☉ [Sunday], the 2nd

The occasions today were conducted as usual. Everyone was calm and quiet in his hut. Erdmuth and Thamar came to visit us; we had an edifying discourse with them.

☽ [Monday], the 3rd

We felt quite well in the morning during the morning quarter-of-an-hour. The Indian brethren and sisters went about their work. Past noon Brother Gideon came, telling us that Abraham [the Indian] had arrived from Gnadenhütten. (I asked if he knew whether [he] had a letter for me; he should please ask him.) In the evening meeting the words of the Savior were talked about: *Fürsten und Herren regieren, von dießer großen Zeit Verseumniße sind seine Jünger dispensirt.*[47] It was pointed out that the Savior's kingdom was not from this world, and he who and he who thought to be someone among his people shall be everyone's servant. Nothing would be more comforting to my poor sinners than to rest eternally inside Jesus' wounds, p[p].

♂ [Tuesday], the 4th

Abraham had all of the brethren summoned to Gideon's house, where he informed them about the covenant between the Mahikander [Mahicans] and Delawar [Delawares].[48] Br. Gideon came saying that Abraham had not brought a letter. He was not coming [directly] from Gnadenhütten at present; besides, Martin [Mack] reportedly had not been at home. Moreover, he [Abraham] is said to have been expelled by Br. Martin. Brother Gideon said he thought that Abraham's heart was in a very bad state; he had talked to him on that account and directed him to the Savior.

☿ [Wednesday], the 5th

After the morning quarter-of-an-hour Abraham went to Wanachquaticok. I visited several brethren in their huts; I found them to be well. Several appeared to be somewhat concerned about Abraham.

[No entry for the 6th]

♀ [Friday], the 7th

Several brethren went out hunting. I wrote in the *diarium*.

♄ [Saturday], the 8th

The brethren and sisters who had been out in pursuit of food gathered at home again. During the evening quarter-of-an-hour the peace [felt] inside Jesus' wounds was talked about.

☉ [Sunday], the 9th

After the general meeting several brethren and sisters went to the winter huts to visit Br. David, who returned from the seaside with his family yesterday. Toward evening the quarter-of-an-hour for the baptized ones took place with blessing.

☽ [Monday], the 10th

Following the morning quarter-of-an-hour everyone stayed at home to welcome Brother Abraham Reincke, for he had given notice that he would come here again today. Toward evening Br. Abraham Reincke arrived, having been accompanied here by Azariah Smith. We, along with the Indian brethren and sisters, welcomed them with tender love. Br. Abraham conducted the evening occasion with blessing.

♂ [Tuesday], the 11th

After the morning quarter-of-an-hour Azariah Smith readied himself to return home on horseback. He said that he had felt particularly well here with the Indian brethren and sisters and during the meeting.

☿ [Wednesday], the 12th

During the morning blessing Br. Abraham Reincke announced to the brethren and sisters that he now intended to set out on his journey to Bethlehem. He was pleased that he has had the opportunity to see the Indian brethren and sisters. His actual *plan*, however, was in Salisbury. Perhaps a brother from Bethlehem would soon be sent come to them; Br. Sensemann would take him as far as Rhinebeck. Thus, they sent many a heartfelt greeting to Bethlehem, [New] York, and Rhinebeck, and with that we took leave of them. Meanwhile, my wife took old Sr. Erdmuth into her house for company. That evening we arrived at Br. Führer's [house], who received us with much kindness.

♃ [Thursday], the 13th and ♀ [Friday], the 14th

Several Indian families went out into the woods to work; those at home were in a happy state.

♄ [Saturday], the 15th

My wife was visited by several Indian sisters today. Sr. Johanna, and Jonathan with his wife Salome came home from their work in the woods in good spirits.

☉ [Sunday], the 16th

Several English men came to attend the meeting. One of them had spoken much about Abraham Reincke, that he had liked his sermon so well. My wife spent this Sunday visiting the Indian sisters.

☽ [Monday], the 17th

I took leave of dear Brother Abraham Reincke and the other brethren and sisters in Rhinebeck. I arrived at Azariah Smith['s house] in the evening and delivered the horse that Br. Abraham had taken with him; stayed there overnight. [Word crossed out]

♂ [Tuesday], the 18th

I came home finding my dear A. Catharine, along with the Indian brethren and sisters, well and in good spirits. They all welcomed me and were glad to see me back at home. Sr. Erdmuth said that this time, when Abraham Reincke came, she had thought for sure that Communion would be held; her heart had been looking forward to it for a long time.

☿ [Wednesday], the 19th

In the evening meeting it was pointed out that a child of God would not find any peace in the world, even if it could have ever glory. Instead, our peace was inside the wounds of Jesus; therein all the blissfulness can be obtained, p[p]., and the Savior was near us, and we felt His presence among us.

♃ [Thursday], the 20th

Most of the sisters went out to sell the things that they had made. Hence, we did not have any occasions.

♀ [Friday], the 21st

I went visiting in all of the huts. My wife did likewise; talked with Sr. Justina and communed with her from the heart.

♄ [Saturday], the 22nd

An Indian stranger from Farmington, Witly's brother, came here for a visit. Johanna, as well as Jonathan and his wife, came home from their work in the woods in good spirits; so did several sisters, from New Milford.

☉ [Sunday], the 23rd

At the general meeting several English women and adult men were present. The text *Ich bin die Tür*[49] was spoken about. The Savior was near me, and all the brown and white ones were attentive. Afterward, some English women stayed on with us for a while. Toward evening the quarter-of-an-hour for the baptized ones took place with blessing. Br. Martin and Justina were also spoken with.

☽ [Monday], the 24th

Several brethren and sisters returned to their work in the woods; some went hunting. Only a few stayed at home.

♂ [Tuesday], the 25th

Following the morning quarter-of-an-hour Br. Gideon came, telling us he intended to go to New Milford to sell [wooden] troughs. Thamar told us that an unbaptized Indian had asked for their[50] daughter Anna in marriage. The answer Sr. Thamar had given to his father was, how could he [the son] possibly think of marrying her daughter. After all, he was not a brother and did not even attend the meetings, nor did he so much as think of converting. We said that we were not able to advise her in this matter. She [Anna] was still young, and if she gave herself up to the Savior, He would care for her. I went visiting in several huts. Martin and several others went on the mountain to make troughs.

☿ [Wednesday], the 26th

After the morning blessing everyone who was at home went about his work.

♃ [Thursday], the 27th

Br. Gideon returned home from New Milford in a happy state. Martin and the other brethren came down the mountain with their work. Br. Martin interpreted during the evening occasion.

[No entry for the 28th]

♄ [Saturday], the 29th

I visited the winter huts, calling on the baptized ones and unbaptized ones who were at home. David returned home from the woods with his family.

☉ [Sunday], the 30th

With the brethren and sisters having come up from the winter huts, the signal for the general meeting was given. The Savior was near me so that I was able to portray with passion to the brown assembly Jesus' loving heart for the poor sinners. Many a tear[d] was shed by several Indians. Following the children's quarter-of-an-hour, Sr. Rebecca, who had strayed from her heart some time ago, was spoken with through my wife. She regretted that she had trifled away her time, and said that from now on she intended to stay at home; her heart was well again. A number of the huts were visited as well. Next, there was the quarter-of-an-hour for all of the baptized ones, with blessing.

☽ [Monday], October 1

Following the morning meeting Br. Martin and Justina took leave to go to the seaside with *canuoe* [canoes] and other things. Several others also went with them. We reminded them to make sure to abide in their hearts, which they promised us to do. I and my wife went into the field to break off Welsh corn.

♂ [Tuesday], the 2nd

After the early quarter-of-an-hour we returned to our work in the field. Sr. Erdmuth went to New Milford to visit from there Sr. Johanna, Jonathan, and the others who are working with her [Johanna] in the woods.

☿ [Wednesday], the 3rd

Following the morning quarter-of-an-hour we had one of our neighbors haul our Welsh corn home. Br. Jeremias helped us, and later several sisters and most of the children came to help us strip it. We spent several days with this work. Those Indian brethren and sisters who were at home were well and in good spirits.

[No entries for the 4th and 5th]

♄ [Saturday], the 6th

Sr. Erdmuth, along with ~~the~~ [the] Jonathans, came home from the woods in a happy state. Several others came together as well, namely, Elisabeth with her children, [as well as] Anna, her sister, having bought blankets with their [handi]work. They all were in good spirits and full of light. The beloved Savior was feelingly near to us at the evening meeting.

☉ [Sunday], the 7th

Toward noon, when everyone who wanted to attend the meeting had arrived from the winter huts, the signal for the general meeting was given. We felt quite well during the sermon. The Indians were *atent* [attentive] in listening. Then there was the children's quarter-of-an-hour[d]. The little hearts[d] are quite glad when their occasion is being held for them, and listen so diligently as if they understood it well. We were visited in our house by the brethren and sisters from the winter huts. My wife called on Sr. Magdalena, who is somewhat sickly. Several huts were also visited; everyone was in good spirits and full of light. Next, there was the quarter-of-an-hour for all the baptized ones.

☽ [Monday], the 8th

We went and visited the brethren and sisters in the winter huts. They all welcomed us with tender love, especially David and Rebecca; they both were very affectionate. Sarah was well; her daughter Maria is still ill, yet at the same time quite full of light and in a happy state. We also met an Indian stranger here who promised us to come and visit Pachgatgoch.

[*No entry for the 9th*]

☿ [Wednesday], the 10th

During the morning occasion the watchword, *Ihr seid alzu mal Kinder des lichts[,] dennes lammes Blut hält die Kleider rein,*[51] was talked about. Nothing feels more refreshing to us in our meetings than when there is a resonance for [the] blood and wounds. Sr. Gottliebe returned home from the seaside.

♃ [Thursday], the 11th and ♀ [Friday], the 12th

The occasions were conducted with those brethren and sisters who were at home.

♄ [Saturday], the 13th

Azariah Smith came from Salisbury with several letters from Br. A. Reincke in New York, as well as from Br. Führer in Rhinebeck, containing joyous tidings regarding the safe arrival of the *Irine*, and especially that of the 30 dear brethren and sisters of whom, however, no one was named other than our dear hearts [the] Böhlers; and [also] special news, which gladdened us very much. Owing to a hard rain we did not have a meeting in the evening.

☉ [Sunday], the 14th

In the morning we received through Br. Joshua, who had arrived from Sharon

439

late at night, a package of letters and *Gemeinnachrichten* from dear Brother Hehl, which refreshed our hearts in our loneliness. Afterward, the general meeting was held. During the quarter-of-an-hour for the baptized ones, the greetings from A. Reincke, the brethren from New York, [and] from Bethlehem, p[p]., were passed on to the Indian brethren and sisters, as well as [the news of] the arrival of the 30 brethren and sisters in [New] York, and *in species* [Latin: especially], dear Brother and Sister Böhler's [arrival], at which they exclaimed Hó Hò[52] and rejoiced, saying, We saw him [Böhler] in Shekomeko. They also were given hope that they would see a brother from Bethlehem at this place soon, at which they became hopeful that Communion, after which the majority greatly hungers, would once again be held then. Azariah Smith, who has been with us since yesterday, set out for home.

☽ [Monday], the 15th

After the early meeting school with the children was resumed. They assembled nicely, and also were quite agreeable. Old Sr. Maria, Theodora, and Caritas went into the woods to make brooms and baskets so as to be able to buy blankets and other items that they need for winter.[53]

♂ [Tuesday], the 16th

My wife visited the sisters while I was holding school. The best time to visit [them] is when the children are in school. The brethren and sisters are still busy breaking [off] and bringing in Welsh corn.

☿ [Wednesday], the 17th and [Thursday], the 18th

The occasions were held in due order. School was continued. This evening, all of the young people as well as several brethren had come together to strip off Welsh corn. I heard that it was proceeding with some levity, went to them, and greeted them, and looked at them. Then everyone immediately fell silent, and even afterward, no one could be heard talking.

♀ [Friday], the 19th

After the morning blessing I commenced school with the boys. Meanwhile my wife went visiting, and I went visiting afterward. For our noon meal we roasted

[a] turnip in ashes, for we had nothing with which we could cook it. In the afternoon a hare[54] appeared in front of the door and we caught it. We accepted it as if it had been given to us by our dear Father, and cooked a fine evening meal from it. As we were eating, we were reminded of the quail[s] that the people of Israel ate in the wilderness [words crossed out].[55] We refreshed ourselves with that and were grateful for it.

♄ [Saturday], the 20th

I went on horseback to the mill with Welsh corn. I received an affectionate letter[d] from our dear Brother Frederic Otto, with news about several brethren and sisters who have left Bethlehem for their posts with blessing, [mentioning] especially the time of bliss in our dear Bethlehem, p[p]., in which we rejoice and partake. My wife was visited by several English women. In the evening the meeting took place as usual.

☉ [Sunday], the 21st

During the general meeting the heart felt warm; the Savior was near us with His wounds. An English man was present. Everyone was *atent* [attentive], [the] brown [ones] and the English man. Afterward, there was the quarter-of-an-hour for the children, and then the one for the baptized ones.

☽ [Monday], the 22nd

After the morning occasion I commenced school with the boys; my wife called on the sisters. I went visiting that afternoon. The brethren and sisters are longing greatly to see a brother from Bethlehem. They have stayed home from the hunt for 14 days so as not to miss it [the arrival of a brother]. Jonathan had built 2 *conue* [canoes] in the woods; a white man took both from him, saying it was wood from his land. Now they have to carry their brooms and things down to the seaside on their backs.

♂ [Tuesday], the 23rd

After the morning quarter-of-an-hour Joshua and Jeremias, and several others with them, went on horseback to New Milford to buy [gun] powder and other things. Those who stayed at home were busy working in their huts.

441

☿ [Wednesday], the 24th

Brother Gideon said that he intended to go to New Milford today, and his wife and daughter Johanna to the seaside with brooms to buy blankets for themselves. Brother Martin came home with his wife Justina and [their] child. His child had been ill and that had prevented him from coming home sooner.

[No entry for the 25th]

♀ [Friday] 26th

Following the morning quarter-of-an-hour I went with my wife to the winter huts. We talked with the brethren and sisters and asked them about their hearts. They were[56] quite lively and very pleased that we were coming to visit them. We also talked with several unbaptized ones about whom we entertain fair hopes.

♄ [Saturday], the 27th

We sat in our house[d] and thought of our Sabbath's hearts in Bethlehem a great deal. [We] also were at times on the lookout for a brother. The brown brethren and sisters were industrious and in good spirits; several who had been out in pursuit of food gathered at home.

☉ [Sunday], the 28th

Baptized ones and unbaptized ones from the winter huts gathered. In addition, quite a number of English people came to attend the meeting as their minister is ill and unable to preach. Then the signal for the general meeting was given.

☽ [Monday], the 29th

After the morning meeting we commenced school with the children. Several brethren went hunting nearby. We visited old Sister Erdmuth, who is feeling somewhat sickly, but is in quite a happy state at the same time.

♂ [Tuesday], the 30th and [Wednesday], the 31st

The Indian brethren were on the lookout for a brother from Bethlehem. We continued holding school and visiting the brethren and sisters.

♃ [Thursday], November 1

Samuel and David, and others with them, went out hunting for several [*word crossed out*] weeks, about 40 miles [from here]. While bidding them farewell, we wished for them the close presence of our dear Savior and His wounds. Sr. Priscilla took 2 horse loads of brooms to Newtown.

♀ [Friday], the 2nd

I rode on horseback to the mill, about 10 miles from here. On my way back I visited sick Maria, Sarah's daughter. She told me that she thought of the beloved Savior continually and was near Him with her heart.

[*No entry for the 3rd*]

☉ [Sunday], the 4th

In the morning, the Sisters Martha and her daughter Johanna, along with Sister Priscilla, came home in good spirits and full of light. Owing to yesterday's rain and storm they had not been able to come home [sooner]. The meeting as well as the quarter-of-an-hours were conducted as usual. Sister Sarah petitioned us about the marriage of her son to Thamar and Petrus and Thamar's daughter Anna. In response we told her we wished her son would give his heart to the Savior; that would be better for him. Otherwise she was in quite a happy state. In the evening Sister Thamar also came to us about the same matter.

☽ [Monday], the 5th

After the morning blessing Sr. Thamar came, saying that Sr. Sarah had brought a packet for her daughter, (and that were fine blankets), and now she had informed her daughter about it.[57] She [Anna] had sent her [Thamar] to us; she [Anna] would do whatever we advised in this matter, and whatever pleased the Savior. We said that they should send the things back, and put it off [the decision] until a brother came from Bethlehem. Then we would inform her of the Savior's and our mind concerning this matter. Br. Joshua and Jeremias took leave of us to go hunting, possibly for 2 months. It was now their best time for hunting; they could no longer wait for a brother. However, Joshua said that should a brother come in the meantime, and we were able to let him know, he would come home at once. Also, he intended to send his son home on the 2nd Saturday. Everyone able to hunt left today. Of the brethren, Gideon, Simon, Martin, and Gottlieb, who is sickly, stayed home.

♂ [Tuesday], the 6th

In the morning, we held our meeting with the brethren and sisters who are home, and continued with holding school and visiting.

☿ [Wednesday], the 7th

After the early quarter-of-an-hour Thamar and several other sisters went into the woods to work [in order] to buy some more blankets. We visited old Erdmuth. Her heart is well, but she is very weak with respect to her body. It could well be that she will fly home soon.

♃ [Thursday], the 8th; ♀ [Friday], the 9th

The Savior manifested Himself during our meeting. [Lines crossed out] Minister Marsh of Kent came from New Milford and called on us as he was passing through. He said, Why had I not visited him even once while he was ill? He stayed with us for a good while and then he took a cordial leave. We had to promise him that we would visit him. Gideon had been his companion from New Milford.

♄ [Saturday], the 10th

In our minds we were frequently in Bethlehem, [and] were on the lookout for a brother again and again.

☉ [Sunday], the 11th

Toward noon the general meeting was held with blessing, afterward, the one for the baptized children. But because there were few brethren and sisters at home, no quarter-of-an-hour was conducted.

☽ [Monday], the 12th

Following the morning blessing we held school and went visiting.

♂ [Tuesday], the 13th

Several of the sisters readied themselves to go among the English people, for

444

they, the English, are holding their festival of thanksgiving this week. Yet, it was as if the Savior was against them, and in the end they were not able to get across the river and therefore returned home. Also, Mr. Mills, one of our neighbors, came wanting to invite us for ~~giving thanks~~ Thanksgiving. We declined with thanks, however.

☿ [Wednesday], the 14th

There are only a few brethren and sisters at home, thus there is just a meeting held in the mornings. But during these we feel particularly well. Today Br. Martin left on horseback with cans and other wooden utensils to sell.

♃ [Thursday], the 15th

During the meeting in the morning the gratitude of mankind toward God was talked about, especially that of God's children, and that they, in everything that they enjoyed, always returned to the *Pünctgen*,[58] [namely,] that the beloved Savior, their Creator, had ransomed them with His blood. Afterward, a man from Kent, having dispatched his son to us, sent us friendly salutations and invited us to their thanksgiving. However, we had our thanks passed on and let them know [that] we were not going out today; indeed, we were quiet and sat in our house[d]. We visited our brethren and sisters who were at home and made them a present of a bit of cabbage, for which they were most grateful. That afternoon Gideon went to New Milford to take there hides that he had curried.

♀ [Friday], the 16th

I along with my wife went to the winter huts to visit sick Maria, Sr. Sarah's daughter, and continued on ~~some~~ from there to buy some provisions.

♄ [Saturday], the 17th

We frequently remembered our brethren and sisters in Bethlehem; we observed the Sabbath in quietude. Gideon and Martin came home in good spirits. Jonathan and several unbaptized ones came home from hunting, bringing word that all of the brethren were well ~~and~~, having shot one bear and 5 deer.

☉ [Sunday], the 18th

There was the meeting toward noon, and after that the quarter-of-an-hour for the baptized ones. In addition, several brethren and sisters were visited.

☽ [Monday], the 19th

During the morning blessing the brown assembly, those absent as well as those present, was entrusted to the Savior's care by means of a heartfelt prayer. After the boys' school I left on horseback on account of outward business. On my way back I went visiting in the winter huts. Sick Maria told me that her heart felt quite well.

♂ [Tuesday], the 20th

Today old Sister Erdmuth again attended the meeting, the first time [since her illness]. After the meeting she came to our house to visit us. We continued to hold school and to visit the brethren and sisters.

☿ [Wednesday], the 21st

Martin, Gottlieb, and those who had returned home the previous Saturday went hunting. Hence, of the brethren, only Gideon and Brother Simon stayed at home. The older boys who usually attend school went with them [the hunters] as well.

♃ [Thursday], the 22nd

We felt quite well during the quarter-of-an-hour in the morning. Afterward, we held school. I visited old Brother Simon; asked him about his heart. He said that his heart felt well, and in my presence prayed to the dear Savior aloud. Told me that he was sometimes worried on account of his children.

♀ [Friday], the 23rd and [Saturday], the 24th

I spent my time making [fire]wood. I and my wife, as well as the Indian brethren and sisters who were at home, felt blissful inside Jesus' wounds. [*Words crossed out*]

☉ [Sunday], the 25th

Toward noon, when the signal was given, everyone who was at home gathered for the general meeting. After that we were paid a visit by several unbaptized Indians. Past noon the quarter-of-an-hours were conducted with blessing.

☽ [Monday], the 26th

Following the morning blessing I commenced school with the boys. Sister Erdmuth told my wife that her heart felt especially well and joyous today. She thought that someone from Bethlehem ~~was~~ must be on his way here.

♂ [Tuesday], the 27th

The sisters and brethren who were at home attended the meeting[s] regularly. We visited Anna, Thamar and Petrus's daughter, of whom we had heard that she was ill. We continued holding school.

☿ [Wednesday], the 28th and ♃ [Thursday] the 29th

Nothing of note occurred.

[The following entries are by Carl Gottfried Rundt]

♀ [Friday], the 30th

We felt quite well during the morning quarter-of-an-hour. Today we prepared some Welsh corn to take to the mill. After a long and eager wait, our two dear brothers Abraham Büninger and Gottfried Rundt arrived here in the evening to our great joy and that of the Indian brethren and sisters. They brought us many heartfelt greetings from our dear and precious brethren and sisters in Bethlehem, likewise much joyous news. The Indian brethren and sisters who were at home came very shortly to welcome them most heartily. Soon after, several Indian brethren who had been hunting came home as well. They were well, and had shot 15 deer and 2 bears.

♄ [Saturday], December 1

Br. Büninger conducted the early service, wherein he passed on to the Indian brethren and sisters of this place the greetings from the brethren and sisters in Bethlehem. Br. Sensemann took Welsh corn to the mill in Kent, and Br. Abraham Büninger and Rundt went to visit the brethren and sisters in the winter huts, who were overjoyed to see once again brethren from Bethlehem at their place. Shortly before evening they did the same in Pachgatgoch, where the Indian brethren and sisters also were very glad about their visit. Br. Gideon and his Martha delighted in the letter that their daughter had written them, as well as in her being well in Bethlehem.

Very late in the evening Br. Führer arrived here from Rhinebeck for a visit.

☉ [Sunday], the 2nd

Br. Büninger delivered the sermon. Soon after we summoned old Br. Gideon, and agreed with him to send Br. Samuel into the woods to the brethren who are still absent, who is to report to them that 2 brethren from Bethlehem are here, and that Communion will be held in Pachgatgoch next Sunday. Because we also learned that Sr. Theodora—who some weeks ago had gone into the woods several miles from here together with her own sister Maria—was very ill, it was agreed that Br. Christian, the son of Maria, is to visit them[59] and leave from here tomorrow. Past noon, first the quarter-of-an-hour for the baptized children was held, and afterward, the one for the baptized brethren and sisters. In the evening Br. Rundt read from the *Nachrichten* [*Gemeinnachrichten*] that he had brought from Bethlehem, and which give us so much joy. He will continue with this every evening throughout this week.

☽ [Monday], the 3rd

The early service having been held, Br. Sensemann went to the mill in Kent to bring his flour home. At the same time he visited *Minister* Marsh of that place, who for a long time, and on various occasions, had invited him to his [house]. He received him very cordially and courteously, yet Br. Sensemann did not stay with him long. In keeping with what was agreed upon yesterday, Br. Samuel went into the woods to the still absent Indian brethren, and Br. Christian to visit sick Sr. Theodora. Anna went into the woods with a horse to bring home her father, who had developed a bad foot on the way. Today Br. Büninger began making a sled for Br. Sensemann, to enable him to haul with it the firewood that he needed. Br. Führer helped him with it.

♂ [Tuesday], the 4th

Br. Petrus came home. We spent the day together most joyfully, each one going about his business. Late in the evening all of the Indian brethren returned home from hunting.

☿ [Wednesday], the 5th

Br. Büninger conducted the early service, and afterward, together with Br. Rundt, welcomed the brethren who had come home. Br. Führer took a very affectionate leave of us and went back home.

♃ [Thursday], the 6th

Shortly after the early service, which Br. Büninger conducted, the conference brethren and sisters came together, to whom dear Br. Mattheus's [Hehl] letter in English was read. At the same time, they were informed that tomorrow and the day after tomorrow the communicants would be spoken with [in preparation for Communion]. Not long after, all of Pachgatgoch was greatly unsettled by a *merchant* from Woodbury, who appeared here along with several of our neighbors, ~~and because he had several~~ [and] on account of debt claims against several Indians, he went into their huts during the absence of the Indians, seizing their deer skins and paying himself with them. Indeed, he paid himself with Johannes and Leah's 2 children for a debt that Johannes owed him, and immediately turned around and sold these 2 children to one of our neighbors.[60] Because Leah did not want to yield her children right away, this affair produced here, for a full 3 days, indeed, well into the nights, a mob of people and many a disturbance.

♀ [Friday], the 7th and ♄ [Saturday], the 8th

The speaking of the communicants [in preparation of Communion] proceeded thoroughly and with blessing. Those who were admitted to Communion this time felt quite poor in their hearts, and were very hungry and thirsty for Jesus' body and blood. And the Holy Spirit reaffirmed His work and manifold motherly faithfulness even in those who stayed away this time.

☉ [Sunday], the 9th

Br. Abrah[am] Büninger, with grace and blessing, preached on Jn. 15.16, *Ihr habt mich nicht erwählet, sondern ich habe euch erwählet.*[61] One of our neighbors also attended the meeting, along with his wife. Past noon, around 4 o'clock, there was a love feast for all of the baptized brethren and sisters and children; of the brethren and sisters there were 30 in number, and of the children 10. It was very weighty to them, for no love feast had been held here in a long time. In the course of it, the letter in English from Br. Mattheus [Hehl], that he had written to the brethren and sisters in Pachgatgoch, was read by Br. Rundt to the

449

joy and satisfaction of all of the brethren and sisters. At 7 o'clock the communicants admitted this time gathered for the absolution. Immediately thereafter, we, together with 13 Indian brethren and sisters, had the inexpressibly blissful enjoyment of the holy body and blood of our dear Lord in the sacrament, and then we went to rest blissfully inside the wounds of our dear Savior.

☽ [Monday], the 10th

During the early service we felt the close presence of our bloody martyred Lamb most powerfully.

♂ [Tuesday], the 11th

Br. Sensemann wrote several letters to the dear brethren and sisters in Bethlehem. Because a considerable amount of snow began falling toward evening, Br. Büninger and Rundt scheduled their departure from here for tomorrow morning. Beforehand, they visited the brethren and sisters in the winter huts and took a most affectionate leave of them.

[The following entries are by Sensemann]

☿ [Wednesday], December 12, 1753

Brother Büninger delivered the morning blessing and took leave of the Indian brethren and sisters. He also visited Br. Joshua, directing him to the Savior as a sinner, which he accepted with love. Sensemann accompanied the 2 brethren across the field and then they bade one another an affectionate farewell. I also hauled some wood to the house with my horse.

♃ [Thursday], the 13th

Brother Gideon came home from New Milford. The people had told him that the above-mentioned English man had not been able, by fair means, to get the Indian [Johannes] to sell his children, hence he had tried it with romm [rum], and thus overcame him. The occasions were conducted in due order.

♀ [Friday], the 14th

During the boys' school my wife visited several sisters. Our communicants look quite full of light and revived, and we are gladdened by this.

♄ [Saturday], the 15th

My wife and I were with the congregation in spirit. We felt a quiet Sabbath's peace in our hearts. The Indian brethren and sisters were in their huts, blissful and in good spirits.

☉ [Sunday], the 16th

We felt well during the general meeting. Sr. Sarah told us about her husband Kihor, that he felt a great desire to be baptized; had been on his way to tell us this, but had grown timid and returned home without having achieved his objective. Now he was sad about it. There was a pleasant feeling of grace felt during the quarter-of-an-hour for the baptized ones.

☽ [Monday], the 17th

During the morning blessing I was able to portray most feelingly Jesus' loving heart to the brethren and sisters. Everyone was attentive and eager. Old Brother Simon told us that his ill son had sent him word requesting that he please come to him; he had something to discuss with him. The Indian brethren readied themselves to go hunting again. We reminded them to be sure not to forget the beloved Savior and the grace that they had enjoyed, but to continuously refresh and strengthen themselves with the wounds of the Savior.

♂ [Tuesday], the 18th

After the early quarter-of-an-hour old Br. Simeon set out on his journey toward the seaside. We went visiting in several huts, finding the brethren and sisters well.

☿ [Wednesday], the 19th and [Thursday], the 20th

We visited the brethren and sisters in their huts.

♀ [Friday], the 21st

After the morning quarter-of-an-hour, Br. Gideon said that he intended to go to New Fairfield on account of outward business.

♄ [Saturday], the 22nd

Sr. Erdmuth came and said that a little daughter[d] had been born to Jonathan and Salome that night. I went visiting in the winter huts, yet some of the brethren and sisters had left on account of outward business. Br. Gideon came home in a happy state, visiting us yet before evening. Br. Lucas returned home from hunting, having shot 2 deer.

☉ [Sunday], the 23rd

At the general meeting there were English people and Germans present, along with the Indians. Sr. Sarah brought us word that Christian had returned home yesterday evening, having said that Sister Theodora had improved somewhat and that she wished that a couple of sisters would come and get her. Afterward, the quarter-of-an-hours took place in due order, wherein it was announced that holy Christmas was next Tuesday, given that it is neither known nor celebrated in this Jovernoman.[62]

☽ [Monday], the 24th

Following the morning quarter-of-an-hour several sisters went into the woods to get wood for brooms, who also returned home today. Christian again went to Danbury to fetch his mother Maria and Theodora. In the evening we put ourselves in mind of the birth of our dear and precious Savior. I would have very much liked to have celebrated a small love feast with the brown brethren and sisters, but had nothing for it. My wife and I were frequently with the congregations in spirit, especially in Bethlehem, and felt the presence of our dear Jesus[d] in our midst.

♂ [Tuesday], the 25th

On the 1st day of Christmas the general meeting was held around noon. Today's gospel was talked about and we felt a remarkable closeness of the Lamb[d]. Afterward, a small love feast was held with the baptized children, and in the course of it, it was pointed out how our children in the congregation rejoiced at ~~congregation~~ the birth of the beloved Savior at this time. We also felt quite well during the quarter-of-an-hour for the baptized ones; indeed everyone was full of light and ~~well~~ in good spirits.

☿ [Wednesday], the 26th

~~We~~ I visited the brethren and sisters in their huts. Rebecca and Caritas went to get sick Theodora and old Maria.

♃ [Thursday], the 27th

Following the morning blessing my wife commenced school with the girls. Old Br. Simon came home in a happy state, yet had not met his son.

♀ [Friday], the 28th

I visited several brethren. Gottlieb told me how in his heart he had felt so very much like a poor sinner last night, and that he had felt so well at the same time; he had never before quite felt it that way.

♄ [Saturday], the 29th

The Indian brethren came home from hunting in good spirits.

☉ [Sunday], the 30th

Br. Gideon came in the morning, saying that Sr. Priscilla and her daughter Salome, as well as Jonathan, had sent him to request baptism for their child. They had thought about it a great deal from the time it was born, and now it [the child] was ill and it seemed like it would go home. My wife visited it and found that it was fairly near its end. Thus the reply was sent to him [Jonathan] that it shall be baptized yet before the sermon. Brother Gideon right away summoned the sponsors and several brethren and sisters for this. We soon set out for Sr. Priscilla's hut, and then the little sick heart was flooded with the blood from Jesus' wounds and was named Priscilla. Afterward, several [brethren and sisters] came from the winter huts, at which time the general meeting was held, and in the afternoon, the quarter-of-an-hours.

☽ [Monday], the 31st

After the early quarter-of-an-hour the soul^d of little Priscilla, who was baptized yesterday, went to the Lamb^d. Hence preparations were made today for it [the child] to be buried tomorrow. During the meeting in the evening the brethren and sisters were reminded that today had been the last day of this year. Thus, each one shall examine his heart and beg the beloved Savior's pardon for all of his trespasses this very evening, and let absolution be granted him, so that the new year could be begun with new grace and new blessing, p[p]. We felt quite well thereat.

♂ [Tuesday], January 1, 1754

The brethren and sisters having assembled, the meeting was conducted. Right after the meeting there was the burial of little Priscilla's tabernacle[d].

☿ [Wednesday], the 2nd

Rebecca and Caritas came home. But because the snow that had fallen was so deep, they had been unable to get Theodora and her sister Maria through. Rebecca's little A. Maria had fallen ill on the journey. I went on horseback to the mill in Sharon. Gideon and several Indian sisters also went that way with brooms and baskets to sell. I returned home fairly late in the evening.

Thursday, the 3rd

Br. David came and said that his Anna Maria would probably go home soon. Sister Martha, Thamar, and still others went with him to visit the sick child. The sisters who had gone out yesterday in pursuit of food returned home today in good spirits.

♀ [Friday], the 4th

Following the early quarter-of-an-hour I went to the winter huts to visit the sick child and the brethren and sisters. Learned even before reaching the huts that the soul[d] of little A. Maria had already flown into the side ~~wound~~ hole of the Lamb[d]. It had been one the children most dear to us. On Christmas Day, when the children had a small love feast, and my wife was holding her, she did not want to go from her, and that was the last time that she had been at it.[63] I also took the opportunity to speak with David and Rebecca about some things.

♄ [Saturday], the 5th

We frequently remembered our Sabbath's hearts in Bethlehem; were among them in spirit.

☉ [Sunday], the 6th

In the morning, Br. Gideon and Samuel came; we talked about the burial of little A. Maria's tabernacle[d]. Jeremias was sent down to help bring the body up.[64] Everyone who was at home was present for the general meeting. The state of man before his conversion and following his conversion was talked about; the Savior was near us. Everyone was *atent* [attentive] in listening. Right after the sermon the tabernacle^d of little A. Maria was taken to its chamber^d. Things proceeded very orderly. Lucas and Philippus carried it [the body], and then everyone followed in pairs. German and Indian verses^d were sung. Later on we were visited by several brethren and sisters, and then there was the quarter-of-an-hour for the baptized ones, with blessing.

☽ [Monday], the 7th

When visited, Br. Martin related how well he often felt while interpreting, and how vivid these matters were in his heart. He frequently appealed to the Savior that He may please make it this plain to all of the brethren and sisters, so that it is felt by them. He often went and visited the other brethren and sisters to see and hear whether they too felt so well in their hearts.

♂ [Tuesday], the 8th

After school I visited several brethren in their huts. Sarah, David, and the whole family went to the *justes* [justice] in New Milford on account of Leah's children, because the *martschen* [merchant] is attempting to get the other 2 [children] as well. We are just sorry for little Joseph, for if he falls into the white people's hands, he too will be corrupted for life. Gideon also went to New Milford to see if he could effect something in regard to this matter.

☿ [Wednesday], the 9th

After the early quarter-of-an-hour most of the Indian brethren set out to go hunting again. Samuel stayed at home because his little Timotheus was very ill. I went visiting in several huts. Everyone who was at home was in good spirits and full of light.

♃ [Thursday], the 10th

I visited Brother Martin. We carried on a blessed discourse with each other. He wanted me to tell him about something from the Bible, which I did.

♀ [Friday], the 11th and [Saturday], the 12th

The meetings were held in due order. Each one of the brethren and sisters was blissful and in good spirits, going about his [or her] business. Old Sister Erdmuth is again somewhat sickly. Nonetheless, she had set out to come and visit us; said she had very much longed to see us.

☉ [Sunday], the 13th

No one from the winter huts came for the meeting. The Indian brethren and sisters suspected that sick Maria was in a very bad state, which indeed turned out to be so. After the children's quarter-of-an-hour Sr. Sarah sent us word that her daughter was very ill and that it appeared that she would ~~not [make] it much longer~~ soon go home. Thus I set out at once, and nearly all of the Indian brethren and sisters with me. On arriving there I found her no longer able to talk, but she nonetheless was quite intelligible. When I asked her if her heart was with the Savior, she expressed it [the answer] through facial expression. I sang several verses[d], and by means of a heartfelt prayer, entrusted her to the care of the beloved Savior's pierced heart, and surrendered her into His bloody arms. All the while she never ceased looking at me. Afterward, I set out to return home along with several brethren and sisters; some stayed there that night.

☽ [Monday], the 14th

In the morning there was the quarter-of-an-hour. Afterward, we held school. Gideon and several brethren and sisters visited us in our house.

♂ [Tuesday], the 15th

In the morning, following the morning blessing, they sent us word that Sarah's daughter Maria had gone home. Br. Martin and Samuel went there and [*word crossed out*] made the coffin. Gideon was sent there by us to communicate that she shall be buried tomorrow.

☿ [Wednesday], the 16th

Toward noon the body was carried up from the winter huts. Thus, there was a signal given soon after, and everyone gathered in the church. Following a brief address the tabernacle[d] of Sr. Maria was carried into her resting chamber[d]. Her father Kihor and mother Sarah came into our house for a while. As his daughter was going home, he had said he believed his sins were the reason that his daughter had lain ill for so long, and now had to die. He had long felt that he should give his heart to the Savior, but he did not do so, and this, he believed, was the reason [for her death].

456

[No entry for the 17th]

♀ [Friday], the 18th

I went to New Fairfield on account of our business. At the same time I visited the brethren and sisters in the winter huts. Several brethren are coming home from hunting, but had not shot anything.

♄ [Saturday], the 19th

Everyone who had been out in pursuit of food gathered [at home] without exception. We put ourselves in mind of the Sabbath's peace and blessing in the congregation, and partook of it.

☉ [Sunday], the 20th

The meetings were held as usual. We felt the nearness of the dear Savior. [*Word crossed out*] were visited in our house by several brethren and sisters, at which time we took the opportunity to talk with them about the state of their hearts.

☽ [Monday], the 21st [and] [Tuesday], the 22nd

The meetings were held as usual. The brethren and sisters were busy working at home.

☿ [Wednesday], the 23rd

Four brethren set out on their journey to Danbury to carry sick Theodora to this place, for she greatly longs to be here with the brethren and sisters.

♃ [Thursday], the 24th

We visited the brethren and sisters at their work in their huts.

♀ [Friday], the 25th

The 4 brethren brought Theodora, carried on 2 poles. They had a horse in front [and] they took turns carrying the ends. Her sister Maria and her brother, an unbaptized one, also came along. They were taken to Br. David's [house] at the winter huts.

♄ [Saturday], the 26th

Old Maria came here, Rebecca along with her. My wife spoke with Sr. Rebecca; she felt quite well in her heart.

☉ [Sunday], the 27th

After the general meeting Br. Gideon came and called us for the love feast that old Sr. Maria had prepared for all of the brethren and sisters in the house of her son Petrus. She said she was glad to be back among brethren and sisters, and out of gratitude to the brethren and sisters for bringing her and her sister here, she had prepared this love feast. Although she had no doubt been far away, her heart had nonetheless been here frequently. We sang German and Indian verses. Afterward, the quarter-of-an-hours were conducted with blessing.

☽ [Monday], the 28th

After the morning blessing Joshua set out with his family to work in the woods, and several others with them. We ~~commenced~~ held school with the children.

♂ [Tuesday], the 29th

Several others set out for the same place where Joshua is, to work, to make brooms and baskets, for such wood is not readily available hereabouts.

☿ [Wednesday], the 30th

After the early service Br. Martin told us that he intended to go out on horseback among the white people with wooden utensils to sell. We reminded him to diligently guard his heart so as not to suffer any harm among them, which he promised us.

♃ [Thursday], the 31st

The occasion and [the] visit were [conducted] in their usual order with the brethren and sisters who were at home. My wife visited Sr. Priscilla in her hut, asking [her] how her heart stood with the dear Savior. She said [that] she very much felt that she had a poor heart, but when she stayed near the Savior, her heart felt well. My wife reminded her that she was a widow, yet [that] the dear Savior intended to be her husband, p[p].

♀ [Friday], February 1, [1754]

Brothers Martin and Lucas came home in good spirits. We were paid a visit in our house by Br. Samuel and other brethren and sisters. Also, everyone at home was full of light and in a happy state.

♄ [Saturday], the 2nd

We remembered the Sabbath's hearts[d] in our beloved Bethlehem, while feeling blissful and cheerful being among our brown assembly. Jeremias went with wooden items to New Milford and [returned] home in good spirits.

☉ [Sunday], the 3rd

[It] was a very rainy day, yet old Sister Maria, 90 years of age, came up 3 miles in this heavy rain for the occasions. Old Sr. Erdmuth came to us; said her old tabernacle was very frail, but her heart was nonetheless well and in a happy state.

☽ [Monday], the 4th

Following the morning blessing I brought some wood to this place with my horse. Afterward, I held school with the boys. I went visiting in several huts.

[No entry for the 5th]

☿ [Wednesday], the 6th

I and several Indian brethren took advantage of the snow that had fallen during the night and hauled wood down from the mountain for ourselves. My wife visited the sisters in their huts.

♃ [Thursday], the 7th and [Friday], the 8th

School, as well as the occasions, took place in due order. The brethren and sisters all were in good spirits.

♄ [Saturday], the 9th

Everyone who had gone out in pursuit of food this week gathered at home.

☉ [Sunday], the 10th

The brethren and sisters from the winter huts having assembled here, the signal for the general meeting was given. Thus, everyone who was at home gathered for the meeting. Following the sermon, we were paid a visit by several sisters from the winter huts. We delighted in their well-being. Also, they said that they intended to go working in the woods for several weeks. The quarter-of-an-hours afterward were conducted with grace and blessing. We felt exceptionally well today; we saw the same in the Indian brethren and sisters.

☽ [Monday], the 11th

Following the morning blessing I had Samuel and Martin [come with me], who assisted me somewhat with matters outside. Next, I saw a brother approach the river. As I approached him, [I saw that] it was our dear Brother Rundt, who I brought across at once, welcoming him with tender love. Not only did the Indian brethren and sisters do the same, but all of the children rejoiced at his arrival. It was [due to] Br. Rundt's heart being filled with love for them. He gave the children small presents, [and] embraced and kissed them. Sr. Sensemann was visited by an English woman.

♂ [Tuesday], the 12th

[Word crossed out] we informed Brothers Gideon and Samuel that A. Büninger, together with his wife, would come to us in a few weeks, and then [the] Sensemanns would go to Bethlehem. Br. Gideon requested that we please take him with us, for he very much would like to see the brethren in Bethlehem and Gnadenhütten. In the evening Br. Sensemann conducted the evening occasion, passing on to the Indian brethren and sisters the greetings from Bethlehem, which pleased them greatly.

☿ [Wednesday], the 13th

Several brethren and sisters came from the winter huts to welcome Brother Gottfried Rundt. They were very glad, and because they heard that [the] Büningers would arrive soon, and [that the] Sensemanns would return to Bethlehem, they wanted to wait another 2 weeks. Br. Rundt commenced school with the boys today. The children quite love him. It is a pleasure for them to go to school.

♃ [Thursday], the 14th and [Friday], the 15th

The occasions were conducted with blessing; the other time was spent visiting the brethren and sisters and with outside work.

♄ [Saturday], the 16th

We remembered the Sabbath in our dear Bethlehem. Were paid a visit in our house by several brethren. In the evening Br. Sensemann held the evening meeting. The Lamb[d] was near us with His bloody wounds.

☉ [Sunday], the 17th

In the morning, Br. Joshua came from out of the woods to attend the meeting. He rejoiced at Br. Rundt's arrival; received him most cordially. The occasions were conducted amid a close feeling of the wounds of the dear Savior.

☽ [Monday], the 18th

Br. Joshua set out to return to his people in the woods. There having been some snow, Sensemann and Rundt were industrious hauling wood.

♂ [Tuesday], the 19th

Br. Sensemann visited the brethren who were at home, asking some about their hearts, how they stood with the Savior.

☿ [Wednesday], the 20th

Br. Sensemann visited the families that are working in the woods; found all of them full of light and in good spirits. They were happy about his visit [*word crossed out*]; said that they intended to come home Friday. The white people [there] bore them witness that they had conducted themselves agreeably. In the evening Br. Rundt conducted the occasion with blessing. Br. Sensemann came home late in the evening. Br. Rundt did not feel so well in his body, for which reason he took some medicine.

♃ [Thursday], the 21st

Br. Rundt delivered the morning blessing; read some verses from John the Evangelist, which were translated into Indian by Br. Samuel. Br. Rundt was bled by Sensemann. Past noon ☦ the 2 went together to visit the brethren and sisters in the winter huts; talked with baptized ones and unbaptized ones about the

461

state of their hearts. One unbaptized person said [that,] when I went to Bethlehem, I should assure the single sisters, among whom she had formerly lived for some time, that she intended to give her heart to the Savior. Her husband, who had applied for baptism several years ago, said the same—that it was still his intention to become the Savior's.

♀ [Friday], the 22nd

Following the morning blessing, Br. Gottlieb and Jeremias told us that they intended to go to New Milford to sell wooden items. Sister Johanna, and other brethren and sisters along with her, came home from out of the woods in good spirits.

♄ [Saturday], the 23rd

It was very quiet, as if everyone was observing the Sabbath. Joshua came home with his family toward evening, as did Jeremias from New Milford. After the evening occasion, Sister Elisabeth and several other sisters came to our house to visit us. School proceeded nicely in order this week, so that we delighted in it. The children also attend the meeting frequently.

☉ [Sunday], the 24th

Br. Sensemann held the general meeting. We felt quite well thereat. Br. Rundt [conducted] the children's quarter-of-an-hour, entrusting the little hearts[d] to the care of the pierced heart of the Lamb[d] by means of a heartfelt prayer. We were paid a visit in our house by several brethren and sisters. Toward evening the quarter-of-an-hour for the baptized ones took place with blessing.

☽ [Monday], the 25th

Brother Petrus and Sr. Thamar told us that they intended to go working in the woods for several weeks, as it was too difficult for them to carry the wood to this place from so far away.

♂ [Tuesday], the 26th

Because there was such fierce weather, everyone remained quietly in his hut[d]. The occasions were conducted as usual.

☿ [Wednesday], February[65] 27

The before-mentioned brethren and sisters set out for the woods; Jeremias [went] with them for several days. The remaining ones were visited by us in their huts. Br. Sensemann held the evening meeting; Br. Joshua interpreted.

Carl Gottfried Rundt
2 March to 14 May 1754

♄ [Saturday], *Marti[us]* 2, 1754[1]

Right after having delivered the morning blessing, we made use of the snow that was falling so abundantly throughout the entire day, hauling home from the mountain the wood that we had prepared this week, continuing with this until toward evening.

While we were still busy with this work, our dear Brother and Sister Abrah[am] Büninger arrived at our place, bringing us, to our great joy, many pleasant letters from our dear brethren and sisters in Bethlehem. They [the Büningers] were welcomed kindly and received with much love, first by us, and right afterward, by our Indian brethren and sisters, [and] likewise by all of the children.

We spent this evening with a very joyous *discours* [discourse] and [with the] reading of our letters.

☉ [Sunday], the 3rd

We had the conference brethren and sisters assemble in the morning and passed on to them the greetings from the brethren and sisters in Bethlehem, Gnadenhütten, and Meniolagomeka. Next, Br. Büninger reported somewhat on the blissful way of grace among our brethren and sisters, particularly at the last two places. Afterward, the letter of apology by Br. Jonathan of Gnadenhütten to the congregation was read to them.[2] This impressed the brethren and sisters deeply, as one was able to tell. Lastly, Br. Sensemann announced the upcoming Holy Communion for next Sunday.

Br. Abraham Büninger delivered the sermon on 1 Jn. 4.9. at the usual time, with blessing. An English man from our neighborhood was present for it.

The baptized children's quarter-of-an-hour took place in the afternoon, and immediately afterward, the meeting for the baptized brethren and sisters, wherein Br. Sensemann announced to them the heartfelt greetings from

the brethren and sisters in Bethlehem, and their keeping of them in loving remembrance; [also] informed [them] of Brother and Sister Büninger's staying
here and Brother and Sister Sensemann's replacement by them, and then made
known [to them] the upcoming great day, or the Holy Communion to be held
next Sunday.

We were yet paid a brief visit by several Indian brethren and sisters.

☽ [Monday], the 4th

Br. Büninger conducted the early service, and therein talked about the blissfulness and safe preservation that each poor sinner could experience each and
every day, if he allowed himself to be led, step by step, by the pierced hand of
the Savior.

Immediately thereafter, Br. Büninger left on horseback to buy a couple of
bushel[s] of flour for the upcoming love feast.

While school for the boys was held, Br. Sensemann went visiting in several
huts; after it [school] Br. Rundt did likewise.

Old Sr. Maria reported that she intended to go to her sister Theodora for a
couple of days. Br. Joshua did the same, who also went to Danbury for 2 days to
sell some handiwork there. Br. Büninger returned home in the evening.

Br. Sensemann conducted the evening occasion.

♂ [Tuesday], the 5th

The morning blessing having been delivered, Br. Sensemann and Büninger
went to the winter huts to visit. There they found only 3 sisters at home. The
brethren and sisters from the winter huts had sent a messenger to the brethren and sisters who are working in the woods, to call them home because of
the upcoming Communion.

Sr. Sensemann's school had to be suspended today because all of the girls
had gone out in today's warm weather to collect birch sap.[3]

Old Sr. Erdmuth and Magdalena visited the Sr. Sensemann and Büninger.

☿ [Wednesday], the 6th

During the morning blessing Br. Sensemann entrusted all of our Indian brethren and sisters, present and absent, to the care of the loving and pierced heart
of the dear Savior by means of a heartfelt and childlike prayer.

Afterward, Br. Büninger went to the mill in Kent with some Welsh corn for our use.

For some time now our Indian children have been attending the meeting[s] more frequently than before, and school is becoming more and more pleasant and important to them.

Sr. Sensemann, whose habit it is to visit one of the Indian sisters almost every day during the boys' school, was told during today's visit with Sr. Elisabeth, Joshua's wife, that an old Indian woman by the name of Maquaenwish, who has been living here for almost one year, had spoken with her about the state of her heart and had asked, among other things, whether a brother from Bethlehem would soon come here and baptize [Indians].

Br. Joshua returned home past noon, as did Br. Büninger soon after.

During the evening meeting Br. Büninger spoke about the blissfulness of those who are poor in spirit.

♃ [Thursday], the 7th

The snow that had fallen last night was of great service to us, as Br. Sensemann and Büninger were able to bring several sleds full of wood down from the mountain during schooltime.

In the afternoon, Sr. Sensemann and Büninger went to visit the Indian sisters, who were overjoyed to also see the latter in their huts.

♀ [Friday], the 8th and [Saturday], the 9th

Were in great part spent speaking with the brethren and sisters [in preparation for Communion], along with several preparations for the occasions that were to be held Sundays.

Br. Joshua and his Elisabeth were spoken with thoroughly and in detail about the state of their hearts thus far. They recognized themselves to be sinnerlike. He, in particular, declared that he had been proud, and because of that had been led into all the rest. As it concerned the baptism of his child, they, and truly we as well, were in a dilemma. However, in the end it resulted in the Savior's permitting the child's baptism.[4]

466

☉ [Sunday], the 10th

Br. Sensemann delivered the regular sermon, upon the conclusion of which the child of Brother and Sister Joshua was baptized by him into the death of Jesus and named Rosina. All of the children were present for this and sat on the benches in the front.

Soon after, the quarter-of-an-hour for the baptized children took place.

Around 4 o'clock there was the love feast for all of the baptized ones, 25 adults and 9 children. All of the brethren and sisters were very much in good spirits thereat, and Br. Sensemann and Büninger gave them many a beautiful account of our dear Indian brethren and sisters in Gnadenhütten and Meniolagomeka. In addition, Br. Sensemann announced his departure from here tomorrow.

At 7 o'clock, following absolution, we, together with 17 Indian brethren and sisters, had the blissful enjoyment of the holy body and blood of Jesus Christ in the sacrament, and then everyone went to rest most blissfully in the soft bed^d of our Lord's holy side.

On the whole, we enjoyed a very blessed day for our hearts today.

☽ [Monday], the 11th

Br. Rundt delivered the morning blessing. Thereupon Brother and Sister Sensemann readied themselves for their departure, and many Indian brethren and sisters came to take leave of them once more.

Pachgatgoch Diarium, from Mart[ius] 11 to May 14, 1754

☽ [Monday], the 11th[5]

Having bade Brother and Sister Sensemann a heartfelt farewell, we wished them a safe journey and had them set out on their road to Bethlehem in peace and with our love. Br. Büninger escorted them for several miles. We gave them various letters to take with them for our brethren and sisters in Bethlehem and Gnadenhütten.

Br. Gideon reported that he intended to go to New Milford for a couple of days; Br. Martin went out as well.

♂ [Tuesday], the 12th

While school for the boys was held, Br. Büninger went with his [wife] Martha to visit the brethren and sisters in all of the huts, finding them in good spirits. Our communicants of the day before yesterday especially had a way about them that was blissful and full of light.

The old Indian woman Maquaenwish had complained to an Indian sister about Br. Sensemann's departure, for she believed she needed to be baptized soon. She had been present the day before yesterday at the baptism of little Rosina, the daughter[d] of Brother and Sister Joshua.

☿ [Wednesday], the 13th

During the morning blessing Br. Büninger recommended, in a childlike prayer, all of our Indian brethren and sisters, present and absent, to the faithful and wounded heart of our Savior, for Him to bless, preserve, and care.

Because we intend to put another roof on our house, Br. Büninger, during school time today, went into the woods on the mountain to choose and fell a couple of large trees from which the necessary shingles can be made.

Past noon, Br. Gideon came home in good spirits, it. Br. Martin and Lucas.

Sr. Büninger visited several sisters in the huts, and in turn was visited by a number of others.

Following the evening occasion Br. Büninger requested the help of our Indian brethren in making the shingles tomorrow. They were very willing to do so.

♃ [Thursday], the 14th

Shortly after breakfast the brethren went about the aforesaid work and continued with it until the 6th hour in the afternoon. Meanwhile, food was prepared for them and the schools were held. The older boys and girls, along with several sisters, were industrious carrying the shingles to this place in the afternoon.

The meal was eaten together in our meetinghouse in the evening. There were 36 persons in number, young and old. It was a delightful sight, and everyone was very much in good spirits thereat.

During the meeting shortly thereafter, Br. Büninger spoke on Jn. 6.67, 68, Herr! Wo sollen wir hingehen[6] p[p]., and then everyone retired blissfully.

♀ [Friday], the 15th

Yesterday's work was continued by the above-mentioned company, and we entertained them like we had yesterday, with Welsh corn, meat, and bread.

During the evening meeting it was demonstrated [to the brethren and sisters] that God's children were not known to the world and would remain so, and that it has not yet been revealed what we shall be when Christ, our life, manifests Himself. 1 Jn. 3.2, Col. 3.4.

♄ [Saturday], the 16th

Irrespective of all our external occupations, we observed with our hearts quite a joyous Sabbath near the wounds and grave of our precious Lamb[d].

A separatist preacher from this area visited us and appeared to be very much inclined to discuss matters of religion with us, and to learn a great deal about the state of our Indian brethren and sisters here. However, he was dismissed as curtly and as well as it could be done, and [we] had him set out on his road.

☉ [Sunday], the 17th

During the sermon our Indian brethren and sisters were told about all of the stations of Jesus' suffering, from the Mount of Olives to His death, and this wonderfully weighty matter was recommended to their hearts for their continuous *meditation*.

The occasions for the baptized children and baptized brethren and sisters took place in the afternoon, as usual.

Monday, the 18th

After Br. Joshua had first inquired with us how soon a visit from Bethlehem could be expected here in Schaghticoke, he went with his entire family into the woods for several weeks, about 20 miles from here, to make *canoes* there. He and his wife have been in right good spirits and full of light since the last Communion and the baptism of their child. Br. Gideon went to the same area, *item* Petrus, ~~Jonathan and his wife~~ and Philippus with his wife. To commune with the Man of Suffering, and to stay close to His holy wounds, was much recommended to these brethren and sisters; Br. Joshua could occasionally hold a singing service[d] for the brethren and sisters in the woods.

♂ [Tuesday], the 19th

Br. Martin went out beyond Kent today, to work there; Jonathan and his wife went with him. The remaining brethren and sisters, who are still at home, were visited today.

☿ [Wednesday], the 20th

During our early occasion it was our passionate desire, as always, therefore, also especially today, to have the picture of our precious Savior's martyrdom before our hearts and eyes.

Sr. Thamar visited Sr. Büninger and testified to her how blissful and joyous at heart she felt near our Savior's wounds, particularly since the last Communion.

Following school hours Br. Büninger went with his Martha to visit the brethren and sisters in the winter huts. There they spoke especially with Leah, who henceforth intends to resume coming to the general occasions, which she has not attended for some time.

Benigna with her husband, as well as David's son with his wife, came home.

At 4 o'clock in the afternoon, Sr. Magdalena was delivered of a daughter[d]. On learning about it, Sr. Büninger visited her and brought her something for her refreshment.

♃ [Thursday], the 21st

After the morning blessing, Sr. Magdalena was once again visited by Brother and Sister Büninger, and it was recommended to her to surrender and dedicate her newborn child[d] to the Savior, beginning with the first minutes of its life. In regard to her child's baptism, she was put off until the arrival of a brother from Bethlehem.

♀ [Friday], the 22nd

Because of the snow that had fallen so abundantly, the early service was suspended, as had occurred with yesterday's evening occasion.

During the boys' school, Brother and Sister Büninger went visiting in several huts.

Sr. Priscilla went with some of her handiwork to [New] Milford to sell it there.

Very late in the evening the minister of Kent, Mr. Marsh, visited us. He was most amiable and courteous in his manner and very modest in his *discours*; asked about Br. Sensemann, and in the end, invited us to visit him in turn.

♄ [Saturday], the 23rd

Given the beautiful weather today, Br. Büninger was busy choosing and felling the necessary building wood for our roof.

As so many brethren and sisters had gone out, and several sisters here are feeling sickly, not many of our morning and evening meetings took place this week, but all the same with blessing.

☉ [Sunday], the 24th

An Indian by birth, who understands English and is bound to someone in our neighborhood as *serve* [servant], was present during the sermon and listened eagerly. Afterward, he conferred with Br. Samuel and then with Br. Büninger. He desired to read something in English for his edification, and because there was nothing else, he received as a present from us the noted *Pilgerbrief*.[7] He accepted it with pleasure and right away read in it for a while.

Before long, toward evening, the unmarried Br. Lucas was spoken with and reminded to let his former grace and the cleansing from sin in the blood of Jesus that he had attained be weighty and great to him, and to stay very close to the Savior and His wounds every day so as to remain protected from evil.

☽ [Monday], the 25th

The early service having been conducted, Br. Büninger went out about 10 miles from here to buy some provisions for us, but returned home in due time. Br. Lucas went out as well, to make [a] *canoe*.

Sr. Erdmuth and Caritas visited Sr. Büninger. The first one testified to the great desire she felt in her heart to taste and experience ever more of the power of the Savior's blood and wounds.

During the evening meeting the wonderfully great matter—that the maker of all creatures became one with our physical being inside the womb of a virgin—was recalled and entrusted to the care of the brethren and sisters.

[No entry for the 26th]

☿ [Wednesday], the 27th

During the early service we appealed to our beloved Savior for the intimate nearness of His blessed wounds also on this day. Upon its conclusion, Br. Büninger announced to the Indian brethren and sisters that there would be a meeting held in the winter huts this afternoon.

During the boys' school, Sr. Büninger went to visit the Indian sisters and found the few who are still at home all in right good spirits and well.

Past noon, Br. Büninger at once went with his Martha to the winter huts, and there held the aforementioned meeting with much grace and to the joy of the Indian brethren and sisters. He took Br. Samuel with him to interpret. Yet all of the sisters from here who could possibly get away went to attend the meeting there as well.

Br. Gottlieb went out with his son for a couple of days to build a *canoe*, and Lucas returned home.

During the evening occasion witness was borne to our Savior's faithful and merciful heart for poor sinners.

♃ [Thursday], the 28th

During the morning quarter-of-an-hour today's watchword was spoken about some.

Immediately thereafter Br. Rundt departed for Rhinebeck to visit our friends there. We sent with him many heartfelt greetings and a couple of letters for them; at the same time, we wrote to our dear brethren and sisters in Bethlehem.

Br. Jeremias went into the woods to choose several trees for [making] *canoes*.

Sr. Büninger visited Sr. Priscilla, who told her that her heart felt quite blissful and well to her, being near the Savior, yet she worried about her children.

Br. Büninger communed with Br. Samuel in a heartfelt manner. The latter said that, since he was baptized, he has never felt in his heart as blissful as now. In the evening the words *Ihr heißet mich Meister u. Herr, u. saget recht daran*[8] were talked about.

♀ [Friday], the 29th

Sr. Büninger was paid a visit by several Indian sisters. Lucia told her: Her heart was completely open toward the Savior, and toward her sisters just the same; she quite loved all of them.

Br. Gottlieb returned home with his son.

In the evening, during the quarter-of-an-hour, today's watchword was talked about. Our Lamb of God was in our midst.

♄ [Saturday], the 30th

We observed a rather quiet [and] blissful Sabbath together. We visited all of the brethren and sisters who were at home.

A traveling English man, a *separatiste* [separatist] who lives 50 miles from here, happened to call on us, inquiring about the way. He was very much surprised that we are able to live among the Indians, and he asked us where we came from. And when he was given the proper information, he acted as if confounded and said he had for many years felt the desire to see the Brethren and for that reason had often intended to go to Bethlehem. However, until *dato* [Latin: this date], he had never seen a brother. Now he was glad at this.

Today's text for our evening occasion read, *Die Gnade unsers Hn. Jesu Xsti sey mit euch allen.*[9]

☉ [Sunday], the 31st

The Sunday occasions proceeded in their usual order. During the general meeting Heb. 10.14 was talked about. Sr. Magdalena was present as well.

Because the minister of Kent was not home, up to 16 of his parishioners attended our meeting today. The Lamb[d] was especially near us with His bloody wounds. The strangers also appeared to be content.

☽ [Monday], April 1

During the early service today's watchword was talked about.

After school Sr. Büninger visited the Indian sisters. She found them well and going about their work industriously. Martha, Gideon's wife, had learned that we did not have many provisions left, thus, she made us a present of beans.

♂ [Tuesday], the 2nd

During the morning blessing we recommended ourselves, and all of our brethren and sisters who are presently in the woods, to the providence, care, and preservation of our faithful shepherd.

Br. Jeremias went into the woods to make a *canoe*. He was in quite a happy state.

Several Indian sisters who visited us testified that their hearts felt blissful and in right good spirits near the wounds of the Lamb.

Mr. Marsh, the minist[er] of Kent, who with his wife traveled past our house, called on us. They both were amiable and offered to assist us in every way possible; also requested our visit most earnestly. When he was told that many of his parishioners had joined our meeting the previous Sunday, and that we did not approve of such [behavior] to be sure, he replied: as far as he was concerned, they could go ahead, he was not opposed to it. After all, everyone could go wherever he liked it best.

☿ [Wednesday], the 3rd

During the early quarter-of-an-hour, today's watchword was entrusted to the care of the Indian brethren and sisters.

Past noon, Br. Büninger went with his Martha to the winter huts. There he conducted a quarter-of-an-hour for the few persons who were still at home, and then they all were thoroughly spoken with about the state of their hearts.

Our hearts felt very well during the evening occasion.

♃ [Thursday], the 4th

Toward noon Br. Büninger went out to buy flour for us, and returned home in the evening.

Br. Rundt came back from his visit to Rhinebeck. He had found our friends there well and in good health, and full of warm feelings for the Brethren. Before his departure he had conducted an occasion for them, and had entrusted to their care the surpassing worth of knowing Jesus Christ our Lord, the God on the cross.

♀ [Friday], the 5th

The schools proceed in good order every day, and the children show great desire to attend them. Several among them are very studious, joyfully learning their lessons when at home with their parents.

Aside from the school lessons and the usual visits to the Indian brethren and sisters, we kept ourselves busy with garden work this week.

474

The 6th

Am Sabbath waren wir stille,
und thaten aus der Fülle
des Lamms uns was zu gut:
Es schmecken doch die Gaben
die man sonst stets muß haben,
am Sabbath sonderlich sehr gut.[10]

In the afternoon, all of our brethren and sisters who had been in the woods working together until now came home on the river all at once, with 11 new canoes, bringing with them a good deal of wood that they need for [making] brooms, p[p]. We went to meet them and welcomed them at the river.

During the evening occasion we rejoiced with them at the merciful charge, care, and preservation of our faithful Savior, which we experience from Him every day or every hour.

☉ [Sunday], the 7th

In the morning we had the conference brethren and sisters assemble, and inquired with them about how things had gone among them and the remaining brethren and sisters since their absence. Thus, we learned to our great joy that our communicants had cheerfully lived side by side in peace, and had worked very diligently. At the same time we mentioned that this coming week was our Savior's so-called Holy or Passion Week, and reminded our brethren and sisters to stay especially close to the Lord and to the wounds of our Lamb of God in hopes of partaking of a special bloody blessing from Him.

The regular sermon was preached on Phil. 2.5–9. We were delighted to once again see before us all of our Indian brethren and sisters together.

The other Sunday occasions took place as usual. Following those, Sr. Büninger still visited several Indian sisters.

☽ [Monday], the 8th

The Indian brethren and sisters were industriously at work. Br. Samuel with his wife, it. Br. Martin with his wife, went out today to look for work.

During the evening meeting I started reading the Passion story of our Lord to the brethren and sisters, which is to be continued during this week's evening occasions.

♂ [Tuesday], the 9th

Br. Gottlieb went out with his son to work for several days.

☿ [Wednesday], the 10th

Br. Büninger and Rundt went to the winter huts. There a quarter-of-an-hour was conducted for the Indian brethren and sisters who were present. Old Theodora continues to be very ill. She was reminded to stay very close to the Savior's bloody wounds in her miserable outward circumstances.

[No entry for the 11th]

♀ [Friday], the 12th

Br. Gottlieb came home with his son, bringing a new canoe for himself. In the evening Br. Samuel and Martha came home as well. In the course of the week Br. Büninger broke some new land next to our house, for our use.

During the evening meeting we enjoyed quite a blissful service[d] in consideration of today's day of death of our Lamb of God. We celebrated His death and wounds in song, and in the end made a wish for us to be deep in the shrine that is His side.

♄ [Saturday], the 13th

During the early quarter-of-an-hour we especially remembered our Lord's divine peace in His grave, imparting from Him to our hearts a special blessing for today's great Sabbath.

Our Indian brethren and sisters were visited regularly by us throughout the entire week. Thus there have been frequent opportunities to point out and praise to them our Savior's loving heart.

The schools proceeded as usual.

During the evening meeting we quite exceptionally felt the nearness of our Love who had paled on the cross, and thereupon our limbs joyfully went [to] sleep in the earth with the Lamb[d].

☉ [Sunday], the 14th

On Easter Day all of the baptized brethren and sisters gathered before sunrise.

The story of our Lord's resurrection was read to them from Jn. 20, and then the opportunity was seized to speak, after the story of Thoma[s], about the blissfulness of those who believe in the Savior and love Him, although they do not see Him in person.

Br. Büninger and Rundt afterward went to our burying place and there, at the graves of our Indian brethren and sisters who have died in our Savior, they appealed to our Lord for eternal fellowship with Him. We also thought very often of our beloved Bethlehem and our dear brethren and sisters there.

The regular sermon was blessed, and attended by many. Thereupon an English man from our neighborhood, who had come to the sermon, asked for the well-known Pilgerbrief, because he liked it so much, and [because it] was useful.

Upon the whole, we enjoyed a very blessed day for our hearts today.

☽ [Monday], the 15th

During the morning blessing it was our heartfelt desire to have our bloody God and Lord very close for the sake of our hearts, like Thomas. At the same time, part of the litany was read aloud and prayers were prayed.

Br. Joshua and his wife went out, and Christian with his family arrived here in the evening. Br. Büninger right away had the opportunity to speak thoroughly with Christian. He admitted his transgressions, but nonetheless declared his loyalty for the brethren and sisters. Sr. Thamar also went out for several days.

[No entry for the 16th]

☿ [Wednesday], the 17th

Br. Büninger visited the brethren and sisters in the winter huts with his Martha, and spoke with them about the state of their hearts.

During the evening meeting the joyful approach to the throne of grace in time of distress was discussed, and then we went to retire inside the wounds of the Lamb.

[No entry for the 18th]

♀ [Friday], the 19th

Br. Joshua returned home well and in a happy state. During the evening occasion, abiding in the Savior, after Jn. 15.7. — as the surest means to remain preserved from sin, [the] world, and from all of earth's distress—was sincerely recommended to the Indian brethren and sisters.

♄ [Saturday], the 20th

At the morning blessing all of our Indian brethren and sisters, present and absent, were entrusted to the care of the loving shepherd's heart of the faithful Savior by means of a heartfelt prayer.

As often as they were visited this week, the brethren and sisters were found altogether quiet, in good spirits, [and] going about their work most industriously. And we fenced in the newly broken piece^d of land next to our house this week.

When visiting the brethren and sisters toward evening, several of them were found sickly, especially Br. Gideon. We also learned that old Sr. Theodora in the winter huts was very weak. Tsherri, who had been absent from here for a while, came back home.

☉ [Sunday], the 21st

The sermon took place at the usual time. Soon after, Br. Büninger went to the winter huts with his Martha to visit old Theodora. They found her exceedingly weak, though she still recognized Brother and Sister Büninger. When asked if, in her heart, she presently felt well and blessed, she made it known with a clear yes. Afterward, several verses were sung to her, and her soul was recommended to the bloody hands of our Savior, for them to lead her home blissfully.

While Brother and Sister Büninger had gone to the winter huts, the quarter-of-an-hour service[s] for the baptized brethren and sisters and the children were held. Right afterward, several Indian brethren and sisters also went to the winter huts to see old Theodora once more.

Br. Gideon and several of the other brethren and sisters were visited by us before evening.

☽ [Monday], the 22nd

In the forenoon Br. Büninger again went to the winter huts, as he had business in that area anyway. On returning, he found that Sr. Theodora had already gone home. Thus, he at once made the necessary preparations for her burial tomorrow, and in an orderly fashion charged the Indian brethren with what the one or the other needed to do for this.

♂ [Tuesday], the 23rd

Around noon the dead body was brought up from the winter huts. In the afternoon all of the Indian brethren and sisters gathered for the burial. First an address was given on Rev. 14.13, *Selig sind die Todten, die in dem Herrn sterben*.[11] And then they all followed [the body] to the grave in their order.[12] The body was lowered down accompanied by the words: *O ihr Wunden Jesu! wo wir drinn begraben, wollt dis braune Hüttlein haben*[13] p[p].

Sr. Theodora, who has gone home, was a widow of 70 some years of age, having been baptized here in Pachgatgoch by Br. Nathanael [Seidel] a little more than a year ago. Since her baptism she has been a quiet and cheerful heart, though she has been sickly for some years, and has not attended the meeting for several months. Now she is in peace.

Today Br. Gideon went out again today, and was likewise present for the burial.

[No entry for the 24th]

♃ [Thursday], the 25th

During the morning blessing we, for the benefit of our hearts, availed ourselves of the question our Savior asked Petrum [Peter] 3 times, *Hastu mich lieb?*[14]

Br. Joshua and Samuel went out today to do work for themselves.

♀ [Friday], the 26th

Sr. Thamar returned home and was right away visited by Sr. Büninger, who found her in a happy state and blissful at heart. Br. Joshua and Samuel came home as well. These days we frequently thought of Bethlehem and of our dear brethren and sisters there, and were expecting a visit from there.

♄ [Saturday], the 27th

During the morning blessing our dear Lord was entreated, by means of a childlike prayer, to pour the blessings from all of His holy wounds over all of our Indian brethren and sisters in general, and our brown assembly here in particular, and to grant them new powers of grace.

When visiting the Indian brethren and sisters this week, they, at all times, were found most industrious and busy going about their outward work, so that one delighted in it, and in their hearts they felt blissful and well.

At the evening meeting the love with which He loved us until His death was pointed out to the brethren and sisters.

☉ [Sunday], the 28th

The sermon was delivered with blessing on Jn. 10.14–16, on the one good shepherd who laid down his life for the sheep and now must, can, and will gather them from among all the nations. The meeting was attended by many.

After the other occasions, Br. Büninger went with his Martha to visit the brethren and sisters in all of the huts.

☽ [Monday], the 29th

Following the morning blessing, old Sr. Maria visited Sr. Büninger and informed her that she intended to move up from the winter huts this week to live here now, chiefly so that she would be able to attend the occasions every day. We were quite pleased to hear this.

On many occasions the Indian brethren and sisters express their desire to soon see a brother from Bethlehem at their place.

♂ [Tuesday], the 30th

In the morning Br. Büninger left on horseback to buy flour and some other necessary provisions for us; he returned home in the evening in good time, and at the evening meeting spoke somewhat about our commonwealth and the homeland, which is above, and about how blissful and happy a person was once he sent his heart ahead to where he wishes to be for ever and ever.

☿ [Wednesday], May 1

After the morning blessing Sr. Thamar reported that she and her husband would go out for several days with some handiwork [to sell].

Br. Büninger visited the Indian brethren and sisters in the winter huts in the afternoon, and his Martha all of the sisters at this place.

During the evening meeting we reflected upon the Savior as the friend of the poor sinners, once they appear before Him in their misery and bow before His cross.

♃ [Thursday], the 2nd

Shortly after the early service nearly all of the brethren went into the woods nearby to work, returning home with their finished work before the evening meeting.

[No entry for the 3rd]

♄ [Saturday], the 4th

During the morning blessing, the Savior was reflected upon as He who examines the thoughts of the heart and who brings to light that which occurs in obscurity.

Throughout this week the visiting of the brethren and sisters, as well as the schools, were attended to as usual. And we have been industrious with our garden work.

The Indian brethren and sisters have been working away most industriously throughout this week as well, especially since they intend to leave soon for the seaside with what they have made so as to sell it there.

At midnight we were very much gladdened by the visit of our dear Br. Sensemann coming from Bethlehem. It afforded us some extraordinary joy to be entertained by him for sometime into the night with an account of a number of good tidings from the congregation and especially about the arrival in America of our precious Brothers Joseph [Spangenberg] and Nitschmann, and of so many other dear brethren and sisters. And then we again retired blissfully.

☉ [Sunday], the 5th

All of the Indian brethren and sisters and children, little by little, arrived here early to welcome Br. Sensemann, each one rejoicing at seeing him back here so soon.

Then Br. Sensemann delighted us anew by handing out many a letter from our dear brethren and sisters in Bethlehem, Nazareth, etc. With these Brother and Sister Büninger received a quite painful message, of the blissful going home of their youngest child.

Br. Sensemann later delivered the sermon at the usual time, and in the afternoon, following the quarter-of-an-hour for the baptized children, he also conducted that for the baptized brethren and sisters wherein he reported the joyous news about the arrival of our dear brethren and sisters from Europe; the pleasant greetings from our precious Brothers Joseph and Nitschmann, as well as those from many other brethren and sisters; and, in general, the love of the congregation for them. They were overjoyed at this.

Br. Gottlieb and his Magdalena came forward and applied for the baptism of their child, who is already more than 6 weeks old. Br. Sensemann promised this to them, yet the *actus* itself was postponed until next Sunday.

☽ [Monday], the 6th

After the morning blessing, Br. Gideon informed us that he intended to go and visit the old Indian Sekes today, who is lying sick several miles from here.

In the afternoon Br. Sensemann went with Br. Rundt to visit the few brethren and sisters who are still staying in the winter huts.

During the evening meeting, which Br. Büninger conducted, the joy which the Savior imparts to His peoples' hearts, and the resulting soft wind of love that blows there, was talked about somewhat, based on today's text.

♂ [Tuesday], the 7th

Br. Büninger departed from here for Rhinebeck even before daybreak, to bring up from there the one or other necessary item from those things that had been sent to us from New York.

Also, Sr. Martha and old Erdmuth went to visit old Sekes, their kin. Several brethren went out, to [New] Milford.

We had our land plowed today, and Br. Sensemann visited those brethren and sisters who were at home. During the evening meeting, which was conducted by Br. Rundt, we availed ourselves of the declaration of the apostle for the benefit of our heart: *Ich hielte mich nicht dafür, daß ich etwas wuste unter euch als Jesum Xtum, u. zwar als gecreuzigt.*[15]

☿ [Wednesday], the 8th

Br. Sensemann delivered the morning blessing, recommending with a child-like prayer our brown assembly of this place to the beloved wounds of our Lamb of God—to bless, bleed on, keep holy, and to preserve until the blissful accompaniment home. During the evening meeting he spoke on today's beautiful text: *Ihr seyd alle Brüder*,[16] p[p].

Br. Gideon returned home in the evening, and after him, also Br. Büninger from Rhinebeck.

♃ [Thursday], the 9th

Shortly after the morning blessing Br. Sensemann had the conference brethren and sisters assemble and announced to them that he had been sent here by the congregation primarily for that purpose, to see and learn whether the hearts of the brethren and sisters felt quite hungry and thirsty for the flesh and blood of our Savior, so that he could then hold holy Communion with them. They expressed a heartfelt and sinnerlike desire for it and right away named several other brethren and sisters who came to mind, and of whom they knew longed for it deeply.

In the afternoon Br. Sensemann went with Br. Rundt to the winter huts, and at the meeting in the evening, Br. Büninger spoke on today's text: *Einer ist euer Vater*,[17] p[p].

♀ [Friday], the 10th

Only the communicants gathered for the morning blessing. Br. Sensemann informed them that the speaking with the brethren and sisters [in preparation] for holy Communion was going to take place, and he conducted a most blessed quarter-of-an-hour to that end. During the speaking itself, the brethren and sisters were found to be open-hearted and straight, and several among them expressed themselves in such an exceptional manner, and so full of feeling about the state of their hearts, their fellowship with the Savior, and [about] the love that they felt for Him and His wounds, that we delighted in it.

♄ [Saturday], the 11th

Toward evening a couple of our dear friends from Rhinebeck came to pay us a visit, namely Christ[ian] Führer and Jacob Maul. We received them with much affection, and the Indian brethren and sisters and children also were immediately present to welcome them.

☉ [Sunday], the 12th

Br. Sensemann preached on Tit. 2.11, 12, *Es ist erschienen die heilsame Gnade Gottes allen Menschen*,[18] p[p]. to a large gathering, with blessing, and right afterward,

Brother Gottlieb and Sister Magdalena's daughter[d] was baptized into His death in the palpable presence of our martyred Lamb[d] and named Martha.

In the afternoon the love feast for all of the baptized brethren and sisters and children took place; of the former there were 32 in number, and of the latter 11. Everyone was in a most happy state thereat.

At dusk our communicants assembled for the absolution. Blushing with shame like sinners, we knelt before our dear Lord and let ourselves be consecrated and absolved anew by His pierced, bloody hands.

Shortly thereafter we, along with 18 brown brethren and sisters, partook of the blissful enjoyment of the body and blood of our Lord in the holy sacrament, at which time we tasted and felt more of the power of the dead body of our martyred Lamb and of His wounds' juices than can be expressed. Our dear Führer and Jac[ob] Maul looked on. Then everyone retired blissfully inside Jesus' wounds.

☽ [Monday], the 13th

After the morning blessing, our aforementioned two friends traveled back home to Rhinebeck with right cheerful hearts, although yesterday evening our dear Führer had tearfully expressed his desire to share in more community graces in communion with the Savior's people. During school time Br. Sensemann bled many of our Indian brethren and sisters, and afterward, he went with Br. Rundt to the winter huts, where both took a heartfelt leave of the brethren and sisters there.

Br. Rundt conducted the evening occasion. In the end he recommended himself to the heart and love of each of our Indian brethren and sisters, for he will depart with Br. Sensemann from here for Bethlehem early tomorrow.

♂ [Tuesday], the 14th

Br. Sensemann still delivered the morning blessing, and then he, along with Br. Rundt, bade Brother and Sister Büninger, as well as all of our dear Indian brethren and sisters, a heartfelt and tender farewell, and with that, both departed from here in good spirits with the watchword: *Sie gürtet ihre Lenden. Und so durch die Welt gerannt.*[19]

No. A. Appendix to the Bethlehem Diario, 1747

**No. A. Appendix to the Bethlehem *Diario*,
from the month of June, 1747[1]**

[Item 1][2]

Indian families who arrived in Bethlehem from Pachgatgoch on June 20/July 1, 1747

---

1. Lucas, *Quawatschonit*, (to lead a child by the hand)

2. Priscilla, Lucas's wife, *Amanariochqua* or *Apénmaù*[,] means to unravel something, a loop or stocking.

3. *Gantaachquà*, Lucas's daughter, about 14 years [old], means she passes through the house diagonally.

4. *Papachgenōch* (it is dark), Lucas's son, 15 years old.

5. *Quiminsquà* (nearly red Welsh corn)[,] Lucas's daughter, 11 years old.

6. *Ajamōsqua*, it is shooting into ears [of corn], ears are developing, Lucas's daughter, 7 years old in August.

7. *Atechtanoàh*, Priscilla's mother, 70 years old, soon ripe.

---

8. Andreas, *As ha*, to cut [pierce or stab], about 30 years old.

9. Lea, his wife (*Uranẽsqua*, hen's tail) [Sherman's daughter].

10. *Utaramaüschà*, (he walks), Andreas's son, 7 years old.

11. Kahatsch, Andreas's son[d], 3 months old.

---

12. *Nangumáüch*, he walks straight, Schermann.

13. Thamar, *Ganapechtaù*, his wife, they came together.

14. *Mēhsqua, T'quáhiü*, insensible, as in a drunken state or illness, Shermann's daughter, almost 11 years [old].

15. *Pechtaüsquà*, daughter[d] of Josua in Pachgatgoch, 3 years old, to fold twice [Sherman's granddaughter].

16. <u>Abel</u>, *Unimachséchgamen*, he stands, (from the Highlands).

17. *Gewastásqua*, his wife, Sherman's daughter. The heart thinks of many things, is distracted [Caritas].

18. *Gahatsch*, his [Abel's] boy, 5 years old [Gabriel].

19. *Quatschel*, his girl, nearly 2 years old.

20. <u>Martha</u>, *Tatapenóa*, I can reach it with the hand, Gideon's wife.

21. *M'tachsansquà*, nestling, last child, 20 years old, daughter of Martha.

22. *Meschensquà*, (feel ashamed), Gideon's daughter, a widow, 26 years old [Johanna].

23. *Gunahapesquà* (an ornament of white *Seewand* [*sewant*: wampum] to hang from the ear), the daughter[d] of the previous one, 8 years [old].

24. *Uttagghem*, (soft), Simeon's daughter, unmarried, 18 years old.

25. *Maramap*, Martha's son, 14 years old, not ripe.

26. *Wenemüà*, the brother of Peneh's wife, 14 years [old], he made him angry [*böse*].

[*Page break*]
[Item 2][3]

Simon's daughter, *wutakem*, juicy Welsh corn, or milky corn — Benningna.
and his son *wanspachek*, a glow by the water when it is dark — Paulus
nasskaschak, black iron — Gottlieb
massahaampéochquah, a sckunck[?],[4] or blowing *schell* [shell] — Magdalena
Gidion's son, *wanawahek*, a deer with beautiful hair — Martin
his wife *quachscháwap*, one who walks in and sits down at once — Justina

Gidion's daughter, *meschanschquah*, a modest woman—Johanna

the mother of Petrus and Christ[ian], *apatanõme*, one who tramples the corn, and it straightens itself right away—Maria

nanakumãwocha, one who walks on and does not stop—Petrus

pentawãm, one who walks in the elbow of a *kreek* [creek]—Christian

Daughter of Petr[us] and Thamar—one who is nowhere at home, daughter *kiwaaschãschquah*—Caritas and her son Gabriel.

wawãpam, an acquaintance, or, I know him—Gottlob

nahpatschun, the mother of Jerem[ias] [and] Samuel, one who is poor and needs to be helped by others—Rachel.

nooskælekah, one who steps twice on one spot, Samuel's wife and the daughter of Petr[us] and Thamar—Lucia.

tschanãtamsquah, that is, unknowing, or an ignorant person, Martha's mother—Erdemuth.

papachkenõcha, now dark—Lucas.

The Wechquadnachs

wanequakseet, very good Welsh corn—Elenora.

Schauwabéam, one who is as weak as a small plant—Katherina.

wonakawechk, sand—Lazara.

Christian Heinrich Rauch

17 June to 27 July 1754

Christian Heinrich [Rauch]'s *Diarium* of his visit to Pachgatgoch, 1754.[1]

☽ [Monday], June 17

I departed from Bethlehem for Pachgatgoch with my dear Anna [and] with the blessing of my beloved brethren and sisters. On taking leave, genuine pains of love passed through me. Today I traveled as far as Rockhill's Mill.[2] Along the way, at the Delaware [River], [I] met Br. David Nitschmann[3] together with another brother whom I did not know.

♂ [Tuesday], June 18

Today I had a rather blessed journey with my Anna. I frequently thought of my beloved and dear brethren and sisters in Bethlehem. Past noon [I] came to Brunswick. I had planned on visiting my old K. Scheiler [Schuyler], but I found neither him nor her [Schuyler's wife] at home. In their stead, however, I found Brother and Sister Reincke, from whom I learned so much as to decide to go another few miles today. Beforehand, however, I assisted Brother and Sister Reincke in expediting their departure from Brunswick to New York, and afterward, I still continued my journey and advanced for several more miles.

☿ [Wednesday], June 19

We had a good and safe journey as far as Jackiss Cattelgaw,[4] by whom we were received with much love, staying with them overnight. We felt comfortable at his house.

♃ [Thursday], June 20

We departed from Jakes's [house]. He accompanied us for several miles. At noon I and my Anna came to New York, having traveled quite happily and blessedly.

Our brethren and sisters received us with love, and we found Br. Petrum [Peter Böhler] somewhat sickly.

June 21, 22, 23, 24

In New York I visited all of my old acquaintances, and the Savior was with me, and I had an innermost sense of comfort going about the work. I was gladdened by most things, but also saddened by some.

♂ [Tuesday], June 25

I departed from New York with my Anna. On the way we visited Mr. Debaut. He and she [his wife] acted very amicably toward us. Moreover, something came over me today so that I took my road to Pachgatgoch by way of Rhinebeck. This evening I came to take up quarters with rather fine people.

☿ [Wednesday], June 26

I came as far as the Highlands, where I found a Jew at the inn who immediately availed himself of my company, and [who] acted quite amicably and in a temperate manner. He assured me that he had every respect for the Brethren.

♃ [Thursday], June 27

My Anna did not feel altogether well today, moreover, such heavy rains set in that I was unable to reach Rhinebeck, requiring me to stay overnight in a miserable house 10 miles from there [Rhinebeck]. It was certainly not unlike a murderers' den, but the Savior comforted us by His nearness to our hearts.

♀ [Friday], June 28

Today my host and his wild company were very humble; they were sensible of their ways. I remained stern toward them, and [I] visited Streit today, who was very glad to see me again. Afterward, [I visited] Zacharias Haber, and Jacob Maul, Christ. Führer, and Heinrich Martin. They were very happy to see me, Führer in particular. I remained the 29th and the 30th of June among these people[d], also because my Anna was somewhat indisposed.

☽ [Monday], July 1

I departed with my Anna from Rhinebeck; Christian Führer traveled with us. I revisited my dear old Shekomeko. Visited my old Johannes Rau Sr. He was very happy to see me, and I stayed overnight with young Johannes Rau, who is living in our house.[5] They rendered us a great deal of kindness.

♂ [Tuesday], July 2

I departed with my Anna and Christian Führer from Johannes Rau Jr. On the way to Pachgatgoch, visited Philip, Wilhelm, and Nicolaus Rau; we took our midday meal with the one mentioned last. They were quite pleased to see me. On leaving Rau's we encountered rain and a bad road. My Anna's horse stumbled, causing her to fall off. At that moment the dear helping spirits[d] performed their office so faithfully that she did not suffer even the least bit of harm. In the afternoon we arrived at Pachgatgoch. Brother and Sister Büninger received us with much love. Those Indian brethren and sisters who were at home right away came running to welcome us. They were happy. We spent the remainder of the day in quite a loving manner. In the evening Br. Büninger conducted the quarter-of-an-hour.

☿ [Wednesday], July 3

Br. Büninger delivered the morning blessing. Christian Führer stayed here until noon. I had a in-depth conference of the heart with him. He departed from here following the midday meal. I visited the winter huts with Br. Abraham Büninger, and had a conference with him [on] 1.) how the congregation was doing and how it was generally going in Pachgatgoch, 2.) how he was doing and how he was disposed toward the congregation, and 3.) how his wife was doing. The Savior was in our midst. He shed many tears in front of me and my heart was greatly stirred to love him very much. I also visited a sick sister today, Gideon's daughter Johanna; she is longing to go home. Br. Büninger conducted the quarter-of-an-hour in the evening. Afterward, I gave him Joseph's [Spangenberg] letter.

♃ [Thursday], July 4

Br. Abraham Büninger delivered the morning blessing. Afterward, I had Joseph's letter read to the conference by Br. Abraham. It having been read, I asked them if they had understood it well and taken it to heart. The response that I received to this question told me a great deal about the present situation at Pachgatgoch. I said no more and had the conference break up, and I hid myself alone in the woods to confer with the Savior, and so I spent the entire day engaged in meditation. Also, 2 drunken Indians arrived here; they sang their drinking songs in plain Indian and then took off again. Br. Abraham conducted the quarter-of-an-hour in the evening.

♀ [Friday], July 5

In the morning Br. Abraham delivered the morning blessing. The sick Sister Johanna, Gideon's daughter, sent for our sisters, as she desired to speak with them about her heart. I had many a heartfelt discussion and conference with Brother and Sister Büninger. My heart felt well to me on that occasion.

♄ [Saturday], July 6

Br. Büninger delivered the morning blessing today. Afterward, he went to the mill for some flour. He returned home in the evening, and our sisters had gone visiting today. I, however, remained in a state of blissful tranquility, and was in conference with the Savior about the circumstances in Pachgatgoch. Also, Br. Abraham conducted the quarter-of-an-hour in the evening.

☉ [Sunday], July 7

Brother Abraham delivered the sermon today. I conducted a quarter-of-an-hour for the communicants and testified to what the Savior saw as being important among them. In my heart I felt compelled to openly speak the truth. And one was able to notice about the brethren and sisters who were present that, in the close presence of the Savior, they felt something that penetrated [them] to the very marrow. In the evening Br. Joseph's letter was read to all of the baptized ones. In the end, Gideon had to prophesy.[6] Something extraordinary overcame him; the Savior wanted to have it this way. *Drum bleibts warheit, Er kann alles waß Er will, im himmel und auf Erden, und durch Menschen wie Er sie Eben Nimmt.*[7] Later, an English man with his wife came to visit us. They would have liked to have learned from me much that was new.

☽ [Monday], July 8

At 1 o'clock I had the communicants assemble again, and spoke to them warmly and in depth, and declared to them the Jesus of those who are genuine. And this we had to stress with the Indians, as truly, and firmly, and surely, as we were the man servants of the Lord Jesus. And he who in keeping with heathenish desire intended to live in every nastiness, allowed himself to be tormented by the devil, and chose the miserable life over the state of bliss inside Jesus' wounds, trampled upon our beloved Savior and us as well. And such poor, ignorant children made our work among the Indians difficult with their insubordination. With sighing, and pained hearts, we would have to look at them and think: Ah! How greatly will this hurt our beloved Savior—the Indians who have cost Him His precious blood, for whose life and welfare He has hungered and thirsted for so long—He is given bile to eat and vinegar to drink, p[p]. Today's watchword was, in the end, my text. I also informed them [the Indians] of the departure of Brother and Sister Büninger; [and of] my and my Anna's staying; the feelings of my brethren and sisters in Bethlehem for the Indians; [and] the mind of the beloved Jünger[s] and his fellow laborers in Europe. I furthermore told them about Gnadenhütten, and about those who had moved to Wyoming, and that we had not sent them there, but that they had chosen this for themselves. And after this occasion Abraham Büninger left to still pay off some debts. He returned home in the evening. I conducted the quarter-of-an-hour and afterward held an in-depth conference with Samuel about his being a servant among the assembly here, and at this opportunity, I came to speak with him about various matters. He became persuaded by several [of these], rendering him all soft in his heart.

♂ [Tuesday], July 9
In the morning, Brother Abraham delivered the morning blessing. Afterward, I went visiting with him and still had to confer with him about this and that. In the afternoon he departed from here with his wife, quite sinnerlike, soft, and melted. I accompanied them for a distance, and Br. Samuel went with them as far as Rhinebeck. This evening we were paid a visit by several Indian sisters. [I] conducted a quarter-of-an-hour for them in the evening.

☿ [Wednesday], July 10
Two English women visited us; they had many questions. I went into the woods to get wood. They stayed until almost noon. Past noon still another one came to visit; she stayed until the evening. [I] conducted the quarter-of-an-hour this

morning and evening, and therein have demonstrated to them the loving heart Jesus.

♃ [Thursday], July 11

[I] delivered the morning blessing. At the 10th hour a minister by the name of Mr. Schmit,[9] having learned of my presence here, visited us; he acted very amicably and in a temperate manner. He wished me many 1000s of blessings among the Indians [and] that I may experience among them much joy in exchange for my faithfulness and industry. Afterward, he went to visit Mr. [Cyrus] Marsh. Br. Gideon came to visit me in the evening; he told me that the brethren intended to go in their sweat house[10] this evening. Thus, I should please ~~postpone~~ suspend the quarter-of-an-hour for this evening. At midnight Br. Samuel returned home from Rhinebeck. He brought a letter[d] for me from Br. Büninger.

♀ [Friday], July 12

This morning [I] conducted the early service. Today I was greatly troubled by white people's visits. Several among them were quite rude, and impudent, and forward, asking all sorts of things. I visited Martin today and had a heartfelt conversation with him. He also attended the quarter-of-an-hour this evening. He had made two crutches for himself today, for he had hungered so for the Savior's word, having been unable to come in a long time. After the quarter-of-an-hour Petrus and his Thamar came to us. They had a longing to speak with us about their hearts. They were upright and sincere, and my heart was quite open toward them. They were with us for about 2 hours and parted from us quite heartily.

♄ [Saturday], July 13

[I] conducted a quarter-of-an-hour this morning. I had only few [people in attendance]. I and my Anna went visiting today, and in the evening [I] conducted the quarter-of-an-hour.

☉ [Sunday], July 14

[I] held the general meeting today with a warm heart; I had a rather large number of hearers and was not troubled with any visits from white people today. Also today, I conducted a quarter-of-an-hour for the children, and in the evening for all of the baptized brethren and sisters. And I had an in-depth conversation of the heart with the conference brethren today. My wife also spoke

with several sisters today, who expressed themselves with sincerity and up-
rightness toward her.

☽ [Monday], July 15

In the morning, [I] conducted a quarter-of-an-hour. I spoke quite openly with
them [about] how much effort the Savior had expended with the Indians in
Pachgatgoch for some years. I went into the woods today to procure some firewood. In the evening an English man came to me; he held a claim of a debt
against Abraham Büninger. I satisfied him and ~~afterward~~ later delivered the
evening blessing.

♂ [Tuesday], July 16

[I] delivered the morning blessing and committed the poor torn hearts to the
care of the faithful and loving Lamb[d]. In the afternoon my dear old Michael[11]
arrived here as courier from Gnadenhütten. He was full of joy and love. He
brought me letters from Joseph [Spangenberg], Martin [Mack], and [Johann
Jacob] Schmick. He soon began to talk about Gnadenhütten and about his joyful and safe journey, and how close to his heart he had felt the Savior along the
way. There were several Indians present who blushed with shame during his account. Among other things, he said that a *böstern Mann*[12] had tried to entice him
into drinking *romm* [rum], but the Savior in his heart had been stronger than
the corruptor, and had preserved him. In the evening [I] conducted a blessed
quarter-of-an-hour and warmly passed on the greetings that I had.

☿ [Wednesday], July 17

In the morning I delivered the morning blessing and later spoke with Samuel
and Joshua, but especially spoke at great length with Gideon; my heart was
quite open toward him. Moreover, he was particularly disposed to hearing me
today. I also spoke extensively with Br. Michael, Martin, and Petrus today. Martin in particular became fairly soft over my discussion with him. In the evening
[I] conducted a rather blessed and most special quarter-of-an-hour. My main
theme was that I wished for them that the blood of Jesus may seize their hearts
as hot as fire. Many a person sighed very deeply on this occasion.

♃ [Thursday], July 18

In the morning, [I] delivered the morning blessing. My Anna and I went visiting today. Michael came to me today and told me how he was feeling here in

Pachgatgoch, who of the brethren he was feeling, and who appeared to him to be cold and dead. In the evening [I] conducted the quarter-of-an-hour. Afterward, I had another conversation with Br. Michael.

♀ [Friday], July 19
In the morning I delivered the morning blessing. Today one of our finest neighbors came to me, having much to ask. I answered his many questions with one reply, causing him to immediately look down and blush with shame, and with that he went his way. Gideon informed me today that he intended to travel to Gnadenhütten with Br. Michael. Today I also spoke with Samuel openly and in depth, who throughout it was feeling, and in the evening my dear Michael visited me again. My Anna went visiting today as well. Gottlieb and his wife and children went out today to earn something by means of the harvest, which began yesterday in this area, recommending themselves to our thoughts. [I] conducted the quarter-of-an-hour in the evening.

♄ [Saturday], July 20
In the morning, I delivered the morning blessing. Br. Michael visited us today and told us of his concern, [namely,] that he is finding so little love among the brethren and sisters in Pachgatgoch. My Anna and I also went visiting in the winter huts today, but we did not find much there that was pleasant, and returned home with sorrowful hearts. In the evening, [I] conducted the quarter-of-an-hour.

☉ [Sunday], July 21
I had a meeting that was attended by many. I preached with quite a warm heart on the words [from] *Acts* 26, verse 18. Past noon I went visiting a bit, and toward evening [I] conducted a quarter-of-an-hour for all the baptized ones. On this occasion [I] spoke with emphasis on the words _wer in Christo Jesu ist, der ist eine Neue Kreatur,_[13] _p[p]_. Following the quarter-of-an-hour, Br. Michael stayed on with us for a long time visiting. He wished that all the Indians of Pachgatgoch may recognize how well and blessed they could live near the wounds of Jesus.

☽ [Monday], July 22
In the morning, [I] delivered the morning blessing. Afterward, Joshua came

to me and told me that he would go out today to help the white people with the harvest. I seized the opportunity to speak with him so as to affect his heart. We had many visitors today who did not have anything to tell us, however, except that they were going out. Thus Pachgatgoch came to be nearly vacant. After they all had departed, I wrote to Br. Joseph, Martin, and Schmick, as Brother Michael intends to leave from here tomorrow. I did not conduct a quarter-of-an-hour today, nor on Tuesday, the 23rd of July. Br. Gideon visited me, as well as Br. Michael, telling me that they both intended to leave today. I spoke with them with affection. But beforehand they went from hut to hut to say farewell. Afterward, Michael came to me once again and I supplied him with what he needed for his journey, and with that let him go in peace. He was full of joy and declared that being here had made his Gnadenhütten so much the more dear and important to him. Also, Martha, Erdmuth, Justina, [and] Thamar visited my Anna today. In addition, Mr. Mills came this evening to visit us.

☿ [Wednesday], July 24
My Anna visited several sisters who were yet at home. I too went visiting today and some came to visit us.

♃ [Thursday], July 25
I visited Martin. He and she both were quite affectionate and full of light. Several Indian women came to visit us today, among others one by the name of Hannah, whom an English preacher had baptized. She thought of herself as very holy and righteous. She told us how devout she was. She was not at all haughty, and had not laughed in 9 years. She was often full of sorrow over the Indians here. She has lived with them for only one year, as of yet she has [neither] seen nor heard anything good among them; we are quite deceived by these people [she said]. As long as they were at the meeting and at Communion they were good, yet once they got to be among the white people they were much more ungodly than they had been before. Our work was completely wasted on these wicked people. She also complained that she was seen by the Pachgatgoch Indians as mad and a witch. My wife issued her a sharp admonition, and with that she went back home. My Anna and I paid a visit to Samuel's hut [where his] little Timotheus is very ill and from all appearances will go home. Furthermore,

3 drunk Indians arrived here toward evening; among them was one Schirÿ. They danced and created a horrible racket, causing everyone to flee from their houses. I felt completely secure, and was left alone this evening as well. They sang their drinking songs and at times cursed much like barbarians.

♀ [Friday], July 26

At daybreak Schirrÿ came to our door, calling me, [that] I should open the door—he needed to speak with me about his heart, he wanted to be baptized. I told him he should sleep himself sober first, then he should come back. Besides, I intended to sleep longer myself. [Yet] it was of no use; he threatened me [that] if I did not open the door for him, he would break it in two and strike me dead. I got up, got dressed, opened the door, and spoke with him sternly. He was very humble and paid [me] many compliments, telling me what the white people and also the Indians thought of me; moreover, telling me openly all of his most secret thoughts of the heart. Then he stumbled back into his house and soon after went out for more romm [rum]. He has made up his mind to drink for 14 days at a stretch. Today my Anna paid a visit to Johanna and to Samuel's hut. It was there that she learned that Magdalene, Priscilla, and Benigna, as well as old Simon, had gotten very drunk at Sackett's, and had carried on an absolutely abominable existence [there], having danced through an entire night. Moreover, Erdmuth came to our house and told us the same story, with many frightful gesticulations, and did so very faithfully. Oh, yes! Poor Pachgatgoch is a sad, deplorable place. I likewise received word on Sarah today, that she is drunk. I called on Martin and [took] my leave of him; he was affectionate. In addition, my Anna visited Samuel's people. During the night Samuel came and informed me that his son was going to the Savior right at that moment. I got up and went there. Yet, in the course of the singing the little heart revived.

♄ [Saturday], July 27

In the morning, Br. Samuel visited me, telling me about his child, how sweet it was. At this opportunity I spoke with him with affection. My Anna visited Johanna, and thereafter I set out from Pachgatgoch, recommending to the Savior my Anna and the souls [here] for [His] protection and preservation.

Abraham Büninger and Christian Heinrich Rauch
25 July to 31 December 1754

Abraham Büninger's *Diarium*, and Christian Heinrich's, of Pachgatgoch.[1]

Thursday, July 25, [17]54

I arrived in Bethlehem from Pachgatgoch together with my wife. Brother Joseph [Spangenberg] and all of the brethren and sisters welcomed us with heartfelt love, charging me at once with returning to Pachgatgoch and resuming care of the Indian brethren and sisters. Brother Christian Heinrich [Rauch] and his dear Anna, who were there [in Pachgatgoch] caring for the Plan[2] in the meantime, are to come to the synod, which is to be held in Gnadenhütten on August 6. And I was to stay there [in Pachgatgoch] until they or someone else would relieve me. To that end I left Bethlehem that very day and stayed overnight with the dear brethren in Christiansbrunn.

The 26th

I was delayed for a long time at the Delaware as no one would take me across, so that in the end I was forced to swim [across] the river. After that I also missed the right trail into the woods; thus, I did not get as far that day as I had thought I would. This caused me to arrive in Pachgatgoch almost one day later than I would have otherwise expected.[3]

The 27th

I got back onto the right trail and traveled my road happily and with good courage.

[No entry for the 28th]

The 29th

I reached the North River but had to wait for several hours until I was able to get across. I stayed overnight at the river, on this side.

The 30th

I came as far as 4 miles from Pachgatgoch.

Wednesday, July 31

I came to Pachgatgoch at an early hour. The watchword read: *Sicher alleine,*[4] 5th Book of Moses 33.28. *Nun kan uns kein Feind schaden mehr.*[5] Thank God, I also experienced this on my journey.

The dear Brother Christian Heinrich [Rauch] had already left for Bethlehem the previous ~~Friday~~ Sabbath. He had left his dear Anna behind ~~to look after~~ to keep an eye on the place and the *Plan,* also because most of the Indian ~~brethren and sisters~~ brethren were helping white people with the harvest, and the sisters [were] at home. Sr. Anna told me that on July 29 little Timotheus, Samuel and Lucia's son[d], had gone to the Savior, [and] that she, at the time, had sung to him several Indian verses[d]. He was buried on the 30th; Sr. Anna sang a number of Indian and German verses[d] at that time. ~~See~~ The child's grandfather had to carry the child to the grave himself, as no baptized Indian brethren were at home.

That day Martha[6] visited Sr. Anna. She poured out to her her sorrow and hurt about Pachgatgoch, because the brethren and sisters were presently acting so badly. Martha said it has been going on like this for 5 years, [i.e.,] that they were all back to their old affairs. Gideon has been repeatedly wanting to remove his daughter Christina from the Single Sisters' House.[7] But she [Martha] did not desire to have her back here, and she wished that all of the brethren and sisters would tell her this, that her mother did not wish to have her back in Pachgatgoch.

After little Timotheus had gone to the Savior, it occurred to Br. Samuel and Lucia that now they had the time and opportunity to go to Gnadenhütten for a visit and to visit the brethren there; [they] would also get there in time for the *synodo.* Br. Samuel told me his thoughts on this, and Lucia spoke with Sr.

Anna. This pleased us and we helped them with the journey. At the same time we wrote to our dear brethren and sisters in Gnadenhütten.

Thursday, August 1
They [Samuel and Lucia] set out on their journey.

♀ [Friday], the 2nd
Most of the brethren and sisters returned home. Br. Joshua visited us; we spoke with him a great deal about their present circumstances. He was very impudent, however.

♄ [Saturday], the 3rd
Christian Führer from Rhinebeck visited us. Also, the remaining brethren and sisters came home.

☉ [Sunday], the 4th
I held only a general meeting for the brethren and sisters and spoke on the text. Next I visited the brethren in their huts.

☽ [Monday], the 5th
Christian Führer went back to Rhinebeck. Old Erdmuth went to Newtown; Thamar also went out for several days. In the evening there was a quarter-of-an-hour.

♂ [Tuesday], the 6th
The morning blessing was at an early hour. Caritas and Gottliebe returned home. They had been to the seaside; from what we are hearing, they have conducted themselves poorly. In the evening there was no quarter-of-an-hour.

☿ [Wednesday], the 7th
During the early quarter-of-an-hour I spoke about the blessedness that one may experience near Jesus' wounds, if one stays close to Him. Sr. Anna visited the sisters who were at home. Agnes complained to her about her corrupted heart, saying that it was nearly dead.

♃ [Thursday], the 8th
The morning blessing was at an early hour. I visited Br. Jeremias, asking him how he was. He said, I am in a bad state. I am growing worse by the day. I asked

him if he did not think it was time to turn back to the Savior and to give Him his whole heart. He replied [that] it was high time for him. I spoke a great deal with him about this subject. I also visited Br. Martin. He said that his heart was well and happy. Also, Anna communed with Magdalena; she was straight and sincere.

♀ [Friday], the 9th

The morning blessing was at an early hour. Thamar, who had been away for several days, came home. I visited the brethren who were at home. Old Erdmuth, who had visited her cousin[8] in Potatuck, came home; so did Martha.[9]

♄ [Saturday], the ~~9~~ 10th

Joshua returned home with his family. He had been in the woods building a *cannue* for himself. I visited him, spoke with him about his bad conduct up to now. However, he was not at all a sinner and laid the blame on others.[10] But I told him, and demonstrated to him, the whole truth and the danger to which he was exposing himself. In the evening there was a quarter-of-an-hour. That day we thought of our brethren and sisters in Gnadenhütten a great deal, wishing to be there. ~~Erd Martha came from the seaside[.]~~

☉ [Sunday], the 11th

During the general meeting [I] spoke on 1 Jn. 2, verse 15: *Habt nicht Lieb die Welt,*[11] and so forth. Afterward, I called on Br. Martin and Jeremias. Sr. Anna visited Elisabeth and communed with her thoroughly. She was entirely straight and admitted [that] her heart was dead and had again fallen in love with sin. While it often occurred to her to return to the Savior, she saw that her heart was not willing to do so. She is truly hardened.

☽ [Monday], the 12th

At the early quarter-of-an-hour I spoke on the daily covering[12] that the dear Savior grants us and has us experience.

Martha went to the seaside to bring back from there a sick Indian woman. The Indian woman lives here. I went to Gaylords, visiting Magdalena at the same time; she is very ill.[13] Petrus left yesterday, so that no one knows where he went. He has resumed drinking and stealing.

♂ [Tuesday], the 13th

We put ourselves in mind of the congregation's memorial day.[14] Sr. Anna was paid a visit by Justina, who spoke with her about her heart. Sr. Anna was very sorry that Justina has adopted so many things and expressions from the Presbyterians. The majority here are corrupted by that poison.

☿ [Wednesday], the 14th

[The] quarter-of-an-hour was at an early hour. Johanna, who had been ill for a long time, for the first time visited Sr. Anna in our house.

♃ [Thursday], the 15th

[The] quarter-of-an-hour was at an early hour. Menzero, an Indian from Potatuck, came here for a visit. I went to the mill, returning home in the evening.

♀ [Friday], the 16th

The morning blessing was at an early hour. Our Indian sisters told us that Magdalena, the wife of old Seyakes's son, was so ill that she will soon go home. Sr. Anna at once resolved to visit her, 6 miles from here, for she is a soul who is one of us, and was baptized by the Brethren. And in former times, while she lived with the Single Sisters' Choir in Bethlehem, she had joined the congregation for Holy Communion. Justina and Priscilla went with her to see her once more. Sr. Anna said that she had found her very weak and faint, but had been happy to ~~see~~ find her a sinner, and [that] she tearfully recognized her misery and bad circumstances that she had brought upon herself. Sr. Anna directed her as a poor sinner to the Savior and his bloody wounds, ~~and~~ returning that evening, as did the 2 Indian sisters. *So ists war, Es läufft am abgemeßnen Ende, ihm doch alles in die hände.*[15]

♄ [Saturday], the 17th

Nothing special happened here. We were hoping to see Br. Christian [Rauch], but he did not yet come that day. Br. Joshua, along with his family, came from out of the woods where he had worked on his *cannus* this week.

☉ [Sunday], the 18th

During the general meeting I spoke on the watchword. The Savior was near me and strengthened me. Afterward, Sr. Anna visited the Indian sisters, and I [Büninger] the brethren.[16]

I [Rauch] arrived at Rhinebeck yesterday at noon. And because one is not permitted to travel here on [Sunday], and having experienced strong rains for the past 2 days, I stayed in Rhinebeck through Sunday and dried my things; and besides, [I] had the one or another business to attend to here.

☽ [Monday], August 19

I departed from Rhinebeck. Christian Führer accompanied me for several miles. In the evening I arrived at Pachgatgoch in good time. My Anna came to meet me partway; she was happy with all her heart to see me again. Abraham [Büninger] too was glad to see me again, and the Indians who were at home also came running right away to welcome me. Abr. B. has done things rather well, and my Anna is well satisfied with him.

♂ [Tuesday], August 20

Today I had my Anna and Br. Abrah[am] tell me how things had gone among the Indians during my absence. Hence, I got to hear many a sad piece of news concerning the deplorable circumstances here, so that I had a mind to suspend all of the occasions and to hold nothing but a public sermon on Sundays, and to conduct frequent house visits. Br. Gideon, and Samuel, along with his wife, arrived here today from Bethlehem, bringing me a letter[d] from my dear [Brother] Joseph. I soon went to visit them, and Abrah[am] ~~and my~~ did likewise. My Anna also visited Samuel's wife.

☿ [Wednesday], August 21

Today we again heard all sorts of sad stories. Gideon brought the entire place into a state of unrest over [the issue] that Andreas's wife in Gnadenhütten was treating his daughter's child so barbarically.[17] Once she reportedly nearly beat him to death. Lucia, Samuel's wife, furthermore reported [that] in Gnadenhütten people did not even deign to look at her; all of the sisters had been spoken with [in preparation] for Communion except her. However, as I knew just the opposite about this matter, I had her harshly admonished through her husband not to lie so shamelessly, for she had gotten involved in something in Gnaden-hütten, through Lidia, and this I knew.

♃ [Thursday], August 22

Br. Abraham Büninger decided to leave from here for Bethlehem today. Before-hand he paid a visit to the huts and I wrote a letter to dear Br. Joseph. Then he left here in rather good spirits. I accompanied him for a distance and had the one or another heartfelt conversation with him. Later we were visited by sev-eral Indian brethren and sisters with whom I had the opportunity to speak in depth and with affection.

♀ [Friday], August 23

I went visiting today, and I was visited in turn. Otherwise nothing happened.

♄ [Saturday], August 24

We were paid a visit by various Indian brethren and sisters, and the Savior made it so that I was welcome to speak to them convincingly about many a matter. I had visitors until very late into the night.

☉ [Sunday], August 25

This morning the captain of Cent Kent came to this place, ordering the Indi-ans to help find a mad person today, who had escaped from them and is sup-posed to be somewhere hereabouts in the woods. Their order was very strict and sharp. Several [Indians] came and reported to me—they would have to go. My Anna said to Samuel, You poor brethren in Pachgatgoch. You boast so much of your freedom; one can tell [just] how free you are. Do not ever rail against the Gnadenhütten brethren again, else you sin [against them], for they are 1,000 times more free [than you]. They do not boast of it, but are [free] nonetheless. You [on the other hand] boast of freedom, and do not have it. He said, It is true, sister. I, however, told them, Be submissive to that authority which has power over you, and go.[18] Then they went. Today I preached from the words on how the dear Savior cleansed 10 lepers and how 9 showed themselves to be so un-grateful toward Him.[19] Br. Martin interpreted for me today. (At present I can no longer use Joshua for interpreting; he is an impudent, corrupting soul.) The Savior was right close to me, and my hearers, of whom there were only a few today, were quite broken and like sinners at this time. But I had opened my heart to them quite a bit to be sure, which caused Martin, my interpreter, to melt to tears, so much so that he was no longer able to speak, and then my meeting was over. During the remainder of the day all was very quiet. In the evening the brethren returned home from their compulsory service.[20] Then the others told them what had come to pass today. Thus, I was right away visited by several [brethren] who came wanting to get something from me as well. Among other things, I thoroughly and at great length spoke with Samuel, who was quite soft and melted.

☽ [Monday], August 26

Gideon visited me this morning; I kept him with me ~~me~~ to have breakfast at my place. He told me that today he, together with the brethren, intended to bring sick Magdalena to the winter huts; she was reportedly very ill. She believed [that] she would go to the Savior and was said to be longing so to go home here. I told him that I would be very pleased if he did this. I went to Mr. Mills on account of outside business. We also had many white people for visitors today. One of them was so bold as to want to direct me to capture the mad person with the help of the Indians and then to deliver [the person] to them. I said to him, ~~Dear~~ friend, I am presently the *minister* at this place and not the *captain*, and I thought you would know who the *captain* is. How am I to understand this, that you want to demand of me something of this nature which is not at all my affair? He went on his way and said not another word. In the evening Samuel paid me a visit and stayed with me for a long time.

♂ [Tuesday], August 27

Br. Jeremias visited me this morning and looked very much confused. I spoke with him a bit and did so quite affectionately. He was feeling so because of his faithlessness toward the Savior. Today I traveled to Nicolaus Rau to buy provisions for myself there. My Anna, along with several Indian sisters, visited sick Magdalena. She felt right comfortable with her. She [Anna Rauch] is said to be very soft, affectionate, and childlike, and quite edifying for everyone she visits. She preaches to many with her hot tears of a sinner. I came back home in the evening. Old Erdmuth visited us this evening and stayed with us for a long time. However, this woman is so rich and satiated, and at the same time so dead in her heart, that there is not much to be affected on her at this time.

☿ [Wednesday], August 28

We again received frequent visits from the Indian brethren and sisters, and I visited several in turn. White people again visited us as well.

♃ [Thursday], August 29

Thamar returned home today, but her husband Petrus did not. She at once visited my Anna and spoke with her in a very sisterly way about her heart. Several more sisters paid a visit to my Anna today, such as Johanna, Elisabeth, Justina, Lucia, Magdalena, Agnes, etc. My Anna also visited Benigna, that is, Priscilla's daughter, and spoke with her thoroughly.

♀ [Friday], August 30

Br. Martin visited me today and spoke with me about his heart in quite a brotherly way. In addition, we received a visit of rank today. The minister of Kent, Mr. Marsh, and his wife, were here today, and a doctor,[21] and Mrs. Mills, and another man. But they acted quite amicably, courteously, and in a very temperate manner, asking no questions and merely assuring us of their love and friendship. And we too acted right pleasant toward them. They stayed here with us almost until evening, paying visits to all of the Indian huts hereabouts, and when taking leave, warmly inviting my wife and me for a visit. Whether it would come to pass—I did not promise them. Br. Jeremias visited me in the evening, and my Anna called on Justina. I spoke with Jeremias right thoroughly and from the heart, reminding him of the way I knew him, 10 and 11 years ago.[22] He wept hot tears, and my heart harbors great hopes for him that he will return to the arms of his good Shepherd. He hears, feels, and understands me quite well. He knows himself, and knows of all of his unfaithfulness; also, what he has lost as a result and what harm he has suffered.

♄ [Saturday], August 31

Martin visited ~~visited~~ me this morning, thereafter Samuel, and after that Gideon, Erdmuth, and Elisabeth. The one mentioned last said to my wife [that] she had no words and could not find any that expressed her poor and miserable heart; she had lost much, [she said]. I and my Anna spoke with her very affectionately and in a straightforward way.

☉ [Sunday], September 1

Br. Martin visited me at an early hour. Today I preached with a great deal of palpable grace and affect on the Indian hearts. I dare say, something extraordinary overcame me today; I was as if inspired. Following the sermon all was very quiet. I and my Anna visited sick Magdalena in the winter huts; she is improving. She was quite friendly toward us. In the evening we were paid a visit by one or another of the brethren and sisters. During the night there was an alarming noise at our place, and on wanting to learn what it was about, [I found out that] it was a ~~false~~ mighty alarm about the war, and that the French Indians were making inroads, having struck dead and scalped[23] 4 people near Westenhook.[24]

☽ [Monday], September 2

There was much for me to do to console my people; they were in a complete state of fear and terror. I was visited by them quite frequently today. In the evening 2 English [people] from New Milford came to us. They had a good mind to enter into a disputation with me. They made use of all sorts of cunning tricks to get to me. I was short with them, however. They were 2 rather rude, brazen people. They thought for sure I was Pyrlaeus.[25]

♂ [Tuesday], September 3

I went visiting in the huts today, and my Anna did the same. I especially spoke a great deal with old Simon and Martin. Petrus also returned home today. Many wanted to go to the seaside today, but old Gideon issued them an order [so] that they had to stay. For some time he has been diligently preaching to them repentance. He went from hut to hut exhorting them.

☿ [Wednesday], September 4

Samuel visited us and so did Thamar. Samuel had a number of concerns about which he spoke with me. Old Erdmuth also visited us today. Also, the doctor and the minister from Kent came to visit me today. They acted exceedingly friendly toward me. My Anna visited the sisters at work today. They started making *argritgens* today. Also, several brethren came home in the evening. In addition, Zacharias Haber came from Rhinebeck to pay us a visit, bringing me a letter[d] from Führer, by which he informed me of Br. Leighton and his wife's arrival in Rhinebeck.[26]

♃ [Thursday], September 5

Haber stayed with us today as well. Throughout the entire day we received many visits from Indian brethren and sisters. I also wrote a letter[d] to Hendrick van Vleck today, and had many a heartfelt conversation with Haber.

♀ [Friday], September 6

Old Zacharias Haber departed from here today. Br. Gideon called on me today. I also went visiting in several huts today. My Anna was paid a visit by several sisters.

♄ [Saturday], September 7

Today we were visited by a number of Indian brethren and sisters. My Anna especially spoke a great deal with Elisabeth today, and I with Br. Martin and Jeremias.

☉ [Sunday], September 8

I preached today, and the Savior was especially close to me, and my hearers were very attentive at this time. Moreover, it was so very quiet in Pachgatgoch today, as if there was not one human being here. Br. Martin came to visit me, with whom I had a right thorough and affectionate conversation. My heart was very open toward him. My Anna went visiting in the huts.

☽ [Monday], September 9

Today 3 Indians, who for some time had been bear hunting near Shekomeko, came home. They had shot 4 bears and a number of deer.[27] Also, several [Indians] went out today. Today the sisters were again busy making *argritchens*. We went visiting quite often today.

♂ [Tuesday], September 10

Old Gideon called on me today. He intended to hold a conference with the brethren and sisters this evening, on the issue of strict and good order, also with respect to the upbringing of children. Also, several sisters came to visit my Anna today.

☿ [Wednesday], September 11

Gideon visited me this morning and spoke with me a great deal, and I with him. I told him of my concerns about a number of matters. Everything was quite clear to him. Also, several [Indians] came to us today, who reported that they intended to depart for the seaside today to sell their baskets and brooms there, *etc.* Gideon said he feared [that] they would probably do some hard drinking again. He admonished them very earnestly.

♃ [Thursday], September 12

Old Marie visited us today. And Br. Martin's wife Justine was happily delivered today, giving birth to a young daughter. My Anna visited her a number of times today. I also went visiting in several huts today.

♀ [Friday], September 13

A number of the Indian brethren and sisters visited us today. Thamar and her husband both went into the woods today. Mr. Mills called on us in the evening. My Anna visited Justina. Also, old Erdmuth paid us a lengthy visit today.

♄ [Saturday], September 14

I and my Anna went visiting today. Moreover, we longingly expected someone from Bethlehem. Martin and his Justina declared herself toward my Anna today, [that] it would be a great mercy to her [Justina] if I baptized her poor child.[28] He, Martin, visited me today, but he did not discuss anything with me regarding the baptism of his child.

☉ [Sunday], September 15

At a very early hour Br. Martin visited me and spoke to me, much like a sinner, about the baptism of his child. At this opportunity I spoke with him very openly, pointing out to him the sad examples that made it evident that the baptized children in Pachgatgoch were godlessly ruined by their parents and kin,[29] yes, as if murdered with respect to their tender hearts, and dragged into every vice and abomination. For that reason I had scruples baptizing any children here at this place, and told him, at the same time, [that] I had only baptized one Indian child, Joshua's, and this had occurred in Bethlehem. At the place of a congregation where God's divine laws were observed, I would not have such great scruple[s]. However, he remained persistent in his request and his eyes filled with tears, and [he] emphatically declared that they both had promised their child to the Savior for His eternal possession, even before it was born. Thus, I encouraged him to wait for 8 more days, as I was expecting a brother from Bethlehem who may be coming here to stay. He should baptize his child for him, and I, from this day forward, intended to care for it as if it were my child. For it was indeed more appropriate for a brother who was staying here [to baptize the child], and [who] could also keep an eye on how the child was dealt with, than for me who was only here for a sojourn and visitation. Afterward, I preached, but I had few hearers. Yet the Lamb[d] was right near me. The words on the _offnen brunnen, wieder alle Sünden und Unrei[ni]gkeit p[p]._ were my text.[30] There was a pleasant feeling present during the meeting. After the sermon Joshua and his wife Elisabeth paid me a visit. No sooner had I begun speaking with her husband, an angel (so I believed) commanded her to leave. It was the right moment for me to point out to him his misery. At first he showed himself to be very hard, but the Savior granted me victory over him in that he said, with sadness, Brother, you have hit it right. I am just the way you say. I am an enemy of the Savior. I no longer love any brethren, you neither. I am in love with sin, and I love it so much that I do not seek help from the Savior. What I did to Br. Abr[aham] B[üninger] I regretted at once. It was too harsh, I must admit. But I was quite angry that day. My father-in-law, Petrus, had told me something about Abr. B. which had made me so angry [that] I could have hit him.[31] Thereupon I [Rauch] pointed out to him the reason why Satan had so much power over him at present. I declared myself about this at length toward him. He took hold of me, also wanting to feel me. Then I fell about his neck, kissing him with sadness. In the name of Jesus, I promised him mercy as soon as he would be in need of it and could no longer stand being tormented in Satan's murderous clutches. And I firmly insisted that he belonged to the Savior, and not to the devil. Afterward, I thought on and spoke about various matters ~~with~~ concerning the Savior, on account of this poor child and whoever is here of its kind. I regretted only one thing, that he [Joshua] is going to the seaside, and that cannot be changed.

☽ [Monday], September 16

I cut firewood in the woods for myself and carried it home, for it is already quite bitterly cold here, and I spent the day with this. My Anna—she went visiting, that is true. A[nna] has been used by the Savior as his tracking dog[d] throughout this time in Pachgatgoch.

♂ [Tuesday], September 17

Joshua visited me again and took leave of me so as to depart for the seaside right away. I told him what the Savior was dictating into my heart for him. He left agreeably; I kissed him with affection. But when he will come back—God knows. Afterward, many more [Indians] who are also traveling to the seaside in *compangnie* with Joshua came to take leave, and thus, poor Pachgatgoch grew entirely empty. Toward noon Br. Abr[aham] B[üninger] arrived here from Bethlehem, to our great joy. He was welcome to us most warmly, and then we were visited by the few Indians and children who were still at home, and we spent the remainder of the day together quite blissfully.

☿ [Wednesday], September 18

Br. Gideon and Simon and Samuel visited us. The first asked Abr. B. a number of things [about] what the brethren in Gnadenhütten and Bethlehem were doing, whether they were still so successful in their hunt, *etc.* Here, he [Gideon] continued, our Indians have no hunt other than the hunt for *seider* [cider] and *romm* [rum]. He was afraid that all of them would return home from the seaside in a wounded state. My Anna visited several sisters today. Petrus and Thamar also returned home.

♃ [Thursday], September 19

Today Br. Abraham Büninger traveled to Potatuck for a visit. I had weighed it [the visit] in my mind between me and him; however, given the circumstances, it so happened that he went. My Anna went visiting today, and the Savior had accompanied her visit. She spoke quite openly with several [of the sisters]. I also spoke with Petrus very thoroughly and sharply today.

♀ [Friday], September 20

I and my Anna went visiting today. This evening Br. Abraham Büninger returned home from Potatuck. He had found the old man Maqua all alone at home, and had spoken with him at length. However, in the end, he, Maqua, had declared himself toward Abraham in brief and to the point. He did not like hearing about the Savior, for this reason: because he wanted to remain a true Indian and die as such. *Kiery eleison* [*kyrie eleison*][32] (a wretched candidate for baptism).

♄ [Saturday], September 21

Br. Martin visited us again today. He was affectionate. Br. Abrah[am] summoned several brethren and sisters for a conference that he is to hold with them this afternoon. I and my Anna went visiting in the winter huts, and Br. Abraham held the conference; the Savior laid His blessing on it.

☉ [Sunday], the 22nd[33]

[No entries for the 22nd and 23rd]

Diarium of the Indian brethren and sisters in Pachgatgoch, starting September 24, 1754.[34]

♂ [Tuesday], September 24

The dear hearts Christian Heinrich [Rauch] and his Anna departed from here to return to Bethlehem. They took a heartfelt and friendly leave of all the Indian brethren and sisters, recommending them to the Lamb[d] and His bloody wounds. Br. Christian also gave me the necessary instructions as to how Pachgatgoch can most effectively be dealt with for now, for the [benefit of the] dear Savior. Thereupon we took an affectionate leave of one another. Because I was in need of provisions I rode on horseback to N[icolaus] Rau. Yet it got to be too late for me to get home that day.

☿ [Wednesday], the 25th

The brethren and sisters who had been to the seaside came home.

♃ [Thursday], the 26th

Br. Gideon and Samuel visited me. I had an affectionate conversation with them, expressing to them my heartfelt desire to see the brethren and sisters on a blessed course, that everyone may enter into a close fellowship with the dear Savior. Br. Gideon went to New Milford, and Samuel to Sharon.

Friday, the 27th

Br. Jeremias visited me; the dear Savior guided me into a beneficial conversation with him. He admitted the danger to which he has been exposed up until now. He said, Now I do not know how to help myself. I spoke with him affectionately and directed him to the dear Savior. I also visited Magdalena. She reported to me of her journey to the seaside.

♄ [Saturday], the 28th

Br. Joshua visited me, telling me that he intended to visit Gnadenhütten as soon as he was able to get ready. He said his heart was always telling him that he was too much removed from the acquaintanceship with the brethren in Gnadenhütten and Bethlehem. I also went visiting in the winter huts. I was able to speak quite beautifully with sick Magdalena about the Savior and his wounds, and to make her aware of her present circumstances. Wenemo's wife said, It often occurs to me that I belong to the Savior. She had also wanted to attend the sermon on Sunday, but her husband did not want to let her go.

☉ [Sunday], the 29th

During the meeting I spoke on Heb. 10.22, 23, 24. My dear Savior was powerfully near me and strengthened me, enabling me to speak with a warm heart. Past noon I went visiting in several huts. My heart frequently thought of dear Bethlehem and the joy that the children will experience on the occasion of their angels' festival.[35]

☽ [Monday], the 30th

I again started holding school with the children in the order in which it was held before, that is, first with the boys and then with the girls.

♂ [Tuesday] 1 October

The brethren went bear hunting.

☿ [Wednesday], the 2nd

I went visiting in all of the huts. I happened to come at a favorable time. It was just as if the dear Savior had cleared the path before me, in the huts as well as in the hearts of the brethren and sisters. They all were openhearted and trusting, telling me how matters stood with them. Moreover, the dear Savior was exceptionally close to me, and granted me new grace from his bloody wounds with each one of them, enabling me to advise each one according to his situation. The account would be too long if I were to report everything in detail. In short, the dear Savior let me find open hearts.

Also, the brethren came from bear hunting.

♃ [Thursday], the 3rd

Seeing that the children enjoy learning, I felt especially well holding school. I also think that it is the best opportunity to tell the children about the dear Savior.

I also spoke with Petrus. He greatly lamented that some time ago he had started straying so very far from the dear Savior. I spoke with him thoroughly and with affection, telling him that it had saddened me deeply when I saw him running about at the reins of the wicked enemy. He promised me that he would amend his ways; I should forgive him for this. I directed him to the dear Savior, that he should stay near Him; He would be able to free him to be sure.

The brethren again went hunting.

♀ [Friday], the 4th and ♄ [Saturday], the 5th

I had all that I could do to get some Indian corn ground. I had to go for 10 miles, because all of the mills around here are standing dry. The brethren came from hunting, having gotten 2 deer.

☉ [Sunday], the 6th

I spoke on the words: *Wer mir nachfolgen will, der muß sich selbst verläugnen,* Lk. 9.23.[36] The Lamb[d] ~~was~~ was powerfully near me and to those present. When speaking, my aim was to show why the beloved Savior enjoyed preference over all other matters and creatures, namely, because He died for us and shed His blood for us. And our little church[d] was full of people; many unbaptized ones attended the meeting. Visiting, I sensed a right sinnerlike feeling with several of the brethren and sisters. I also had the opportunity to speak with Christian. I did so thoroughly and with affection, just as I had been instructed to by Br. Chr. Heinrich [Rauch], for he [Rauch] did not get to speak with him himself.

☽ [Monday], the 7th

The brethren went hunting.

♂ [Tuesday], the 8th

Sick Magdalena came from the winter huts and once again visited the sisters here.

The brethren returned from hunting, but had not gotten anything.

☿ [Wednesday], the 9th

They again went hunting; got a bear.

♃ [Thursday], the 10th

Moses Woncopāsch's wife was delivered of a young son in the winter huts. These are unbaptized people.

I finished gathering my Indian corn. It is a bad year for Indian corn throughout New England.

Brother Leighton came from Salisbury to visit me. He told me that the people there were very fearful of the Indians because 4 people recently had been murdered in Stockbridge,[37] and it was not yet known whether [the] *Fransche* [French] or English Indians had done it. They sent us *exprse* [express] words from Sharon that no Indian from here should show his face in their township, and where it happened, given these times, they would shoot him.

♀ [Friday], the 11th

Br. Leighton traveled back to Salisbury.

♄ [Saturday], the 12th

I went to the winter huts. In several places the dear Savior granted me the opportunity to bear witness to Him. Gihur said he could not forget the brethren; he was constantly reminded of what he was hearing about the Savior.

Toward evening the wife of young Tam Torkis was delivered of a son[d]. It was very difficult for this poor woman. She was in labor for 3 days; all of the sisters here thought that she would have to die. But they got an English midwife; hence, the child was soon born.

☉ [Sunday], the 13th

During the sermon I spoke on Eph. 4.15. Brother Joshua and Samuel visited me; we had a beneficial disc[o]urse during which I read to them extensively from the Bible. Visiting, I had in several places a favorable opportunity to speak of the Savior.

☽ [Monday], the 14th

The brethren went hunting on the mountain—got nothing.

♂ [Tuesday], the 15th

The Indian brethren started bringing their Indian corn home. They all have very little, as it is a bad year and our fields are old and barren. The first land that they cultivated has been planted on for 17 consecutive years.[38]

☿ [Wednesday], the 16th

Late at night 5 men came from Sharon and 3 from our neighborhood, among whom was Esq. Ensam [Ransom] of Kent. The reason for their coming was that the people in Sharon are in a state of fear because of the Indians, for several white people recently had been murdered in Stockbridge. The English suspect that the Indians in Stockbridge themselves did it.[39] That is why they are in such great fear. These men said that about 10 days ago, at night, 2 Indians had been seen at the place where Wechquadnach had stood.[40] Mr. Barns and another English man are said to have taken shots at them, wounding one.[41] He [the Indian,] supposedly came here, died here, and last week we buried him, and were silent about it. Now they wanted to see if this was true or not. I told them that there was no truth to that entire story. Moreover, I assured them that our Indians here had no connection to Stockbridge, that no Indian from there had been here in 12 months. These men looked over all of the Indians that very evening. The brethren, for their part, were so very much relieved that they [the men] saw that there was no truth to this.

♃ [Thursday], the 17th

Most of the aforesaid men returned today to gain even better *satisfaction*. Br. Joshua, Samuel, and Martin led them to the burial ground and showed them all of the graves so that they, on no account, shall have any more *scruple* [i.e., doubts]. They were completely satisfied and recognized this as a lie that was told about us. Next they demanded a list of all the Indians here, and because they carried orders from the *magistat* [magistrate] in Sharon,[42] I made one for them.[43] They then took a cordial leave, asking that we do not take it ill. We assured them that, as for our part, they had nothing bad to fear, but instead [could expect] goodness and kindness.

♀ [Friday], the 18th

The following brethren and sisters went to Potatuck to catch eels:[44] Petrus, Thamar, Jeremias, Philippus, and Lucas. All of this fall they had also gotten many [eels] here [at Pachgatgoch]. I went to the winter huts but did not find anyone at home except Sarah. She very much mourned over her corrupted heart, that she kept straying from the Savior.

♄ [Saturday], the 19th

The brethren helpéd Samuel place his house in a different spot, because the old one is standing too close to the public road for him.[45] I frequently visited them at work.

☉ [Sunday], October 20

At the general meeting I spoke on Mic. 7.7. The dear Savior was especially near to us; I felt indescribably well in my heart.

Toward evening I had all the brethren and sisters assemble, pointing out to them the circumstances that have come to pass, making it clear to them how important it was during these times that they always report to the brother living here whenever they want to go out, as inquiries about them [the Indians] invariably are first made with the brethren; and if he [the Moravian brother] is unable to give *satisfaction* to the people, he is under suspicion along with the Indians. The matter was understood by all of them so that they have decided henceforth to report properly when they want to go somewhere.[46]

517

Visiting, I had a favorable opportunity to speak with Martin and Justina; likewise with Gottlieb, in our house.

From the 21st until [the] 26th nothing special happened. The brethren and sisters who had gone to Potatuck came back, yet had gotten few eels. I visited the huts several times, and when there was the opportunity, talked about the Lamb^d and his wounds. I wanted to visit in the winter huts but learned that all of them [the Indians] had gone to New Milford. In addition, school proceeded in due order.

☉ [Sunday], the 27th

At the meeting I spoke on 2 Tim. 1.9. Our Lamb^d of God was with us. Past noon I visited the brethren and sisters. I have not felt this well during a visit in a long time.

☽ [Monday], the 28th

Joshua visited me, telling me that soon he will be ready for his visit to Gnadenhütten and Bethlehem.

♂ [Tuesday], the 29th

Joshua helped me bring in my hay.

☿ [Wednesday], the 30th

I wrote to my dear brethren in Bethlehem, informing them of the circumstances at this place.

♃ [Thursday], the 31st

Joshua, together with his Elisabeth, his little Rosina, and [his] eldest son, departed from here for Bethlehem.

♀ [Friday], November 1

Jerry visited me; I spoke with him at length about the dear Savior. He indeed listens in a temperate manner to what he is being told. Br. Gideon called on me as well. He had a good number of things to tell me.

The brethren left to go hunting. At present, they only go so far [as to ensure] that they can be back home in the evening.

♄ [Saturday], the 2nd

I very much thought about the beloved Bethlehem, wishing for the blessing and joy of my dear brethren and sisters, hoping that I would be visited soon and be given the pleasure of blessed news.

☉ [Sunday], the 3rd

I felt exceptionally well and blessed during the meeting. My text was Eph. 4.15, 16. The dear Savior enlightened me quite beautifully and graciously about the subject matter. The rest of the time I spent visiting. Br. Martin told me about the old Woncabasch, that she reportedly said she hardly knew any more where she stood with respect to the old Indian ways; if what the Brethren were preaching was true, then she was entirely *miß* [amiss].

☽ [Monday], the 4th

Christian went with his family to Woodbury; he intends to stay there for several weeks. Br. Jeremias visited me; I had a heartfelt conversation with him.

Tuesday, the 5th

Lucas, Jerry, Wittly, and several other young people went hunting across the North River.

Br. Gideon visited me, telling me his worries about Pachgatgoch. It is true, the enemy is busy in all sorts of ways, obstructing the dear Savior's work of grace. Martin and Justina visited me. They are a couple of rather dear hearts who are cleaving to the Savior with body and soul. Samuel went to Sharon.

☿ [Wednesday], the 6th

The brethren and everyone who is able to hunt went hunting. Should difficulties arise, they intend to build *cannous*.[47]

The 7th and 8th

I chinked the cracks in my house[d] with clay.

♄ [Saturday], the 9th

The brethren returned from hunting but had not gotten anything. Also, Samuel came from Sharon.

☉ [Sunday], the 10th

During the meeting [I] spoke on Phil. 1.6. The dear Savior was powerfully near us. Mr. Paine, a neighbor, visited me; that was a hindrance to my visiting [the brethren and sisters].

☽ [Monday], the 11th

Jeremias and Gottlieb went into the woods to build a *cannoue*. I again did some chinking on my house[d].

♂ [Tuesday], the 12th

Martin, Priscilla, and her daughter Salome went to New Milford. I went to Mr. Mills on account of business.

☿ [Wednesday], the 13th

It was the day of *Genneral Thanks Giving* in [the] Connecticut *goverment*. As is always customary, most [of the Indians] went out into the neighborhood since they are always presented with food and drink by the English on that day.

That morning Benigna, the wife of Philippus, was delivered of a young daughter. I used this day for the benefit of my heart; paid homage to my faithful Chief Elder anew, to remain true to Him as long as I shall live.[48]

♃ [Thursday], the 14th

Several [Indians] returned home. The rest came on the 15th and 16th. The *Thanksgiving* had caused that no school could be held this week.

[No entries for the 15th and 16th]

☉ [Sunday], the 17th

During the meeting I intended to speak on 1 Tim. 1.15., but was right away prevented from doing so by the screaming of the children, so that I soon had to close [the meeting]. Visiting, I noticed that the brethren and sisters are greatly longing for someone to come from Bethlehem soon.

☽ [Monday], the 18th

It was a very stormy day, making it impossible for me to hold school. The rainstorm washed all my chinking down the exterior of my house[d].

Thamar visited me toward evening, telling me how she had fared until now, that she had strayed with her heart from the Savior. I directed her back to the Savior and his bloody wounds.

♂ [Tuesday], the 19th

The brethren went hunting. I held school.

☿ [Wednesday], the 20th

I went visiting in several huts. I thought especially often of dear Bethlehem and my dear wife.

♃ [Thursday], the 21st

Several brethren and sisters went out into the neighborhood and came home on the Sabbath, the 23rd, as did the brethren who had been hunting nearby. I observed a rather blessed Sabbath.

☉ [Sunday], the 24th

During the meeting I spoke on Col. 1.13, 14. The dear Savior was especially near me. Visiting, I was able to speak with several brethren very much from the heart.

☽ [Monday], the 25th

I again held school. Br. Samuel visited me in the evening; the dear Savior with His bloody wounds was no doubt powerfully near both of us.

♂ [Tuesday], the 26th

Br. Gideon went to New Milford, Samuel and his brother Jeremias into the woods to build a *cannuoe*.

☿ [Wednesday], the 27th

Br. Martin went to the mill for me as I did not have the time myself. Gideon came home.

♃ [Thursday], the 28th

Thamaseed, the son of Sim[on], and another Indian stranger came from the seaside.

[No entry for the 29th]

♄ [Saturday], the 30th

Because I have not been feeling well for several days, and have been unable to do anything, I brought in some wood today. However, Jeremias and Samuel took pity on me, and each one brought me a sled full.

☉ [Sunday], December 1

At the meeting I spoke about the Sunday's Epistle. In the afternoon I visited the brethren and sisters in their huts. Jeremias and Martin called on me in the evening. They had me read to them from the Bible. The dear Savior was with us.

☽ [Monday], the 2nd

Esqr. Ensam [Ransom] of Kent sent me, through Br. Samuel, his *law* book for several days. The ordinance that the *Assamble* [Assembly] passed concerning the Indians is indeed a commendable ordinance. If only it would be adhered to, then the Indian brethren and sisters would be well able to provide for themselves before the Savior. Upon the request of the brethren I read to them this *acte* [act], as well as the one concerning Sunday observance.[49]

[No entry for the 3rd]

☿ [Wednesday], the 4th

Several brethren visited me. We enjoyed a blessed *discurs* together, which they will not forget for some time, I hope.

♃ [Thursday], the 5th

Samuel, Philippus, Makwa, Simon's sons, and also an Indian stranger went hunting 20 miles from here. The *Gen. Assamble* [General Assembly] created *bounds* where the Indians are at present permitted to hunt.

[No entry for the 6th]

♄ [Saturday], the 7th

A white man with his wife called on me, requesting that I please give them something to eat. And fortunately I had [food], making it possible for me to give them some. Last Wednesday a *justus* [justice] lodged with me, having been overtaken by the night; to him I was unable to give anything.

☉ [Sunday], the 8th
During the meeting I spoke on the common Epistle, Rom. 15. The dear Savior was near us. And anyone who could possibly come attended the meeting. During the remainder of the day I went visiting in the huts.

☽ [Monday], the 9th
I held school and set myself up for cutting firewood.

♂ [Tuesday], the 10th
Brother Martin visited me. He spoke with me a great deal about his heart. He said, Brother, I do not know what will become of me. I often sense my heart to be so ill-mannered and *stuborn*, that it is not as *gntle* [gentle] as that of a head of cattle. Then he said, If a man who owns a horse that is very wild can get the horse to take salt from his hand just once, it will always come back to him for more. Now, I feel my heart is not like that toward the dear Savior. He keeps holding out to me the hand with His grace. I once before have taken grace from that hand, yet my heart wants to keep running from Him, and I frequently run from Him when He puts the hand bearing His grace in front of me. This is how dumb we Indians are, he said, that we do not have as much sense as the beast, [for] it right away comes running when it sees salt on the hand. But we are so proud that we resist taking the grace from the hand of the dear Savior. That is when I invariably recall the words of the Savior that I have once heard: It is easier for a *cammel* to go through the eye of a needle than for a rich, that is, proud person to come to the Savior and take grace from Him. He declared himself in this manner for a good while. I spoke with him a great deal on that occasion.

☿ [Wednesday], the 11th
Priscilla and Caritas went to Sharon to sell baskets.

♃ [Thursday], the 12th
Nathan Gaylord of New Milford visited me. He is our good friend and a kind man who loves the Savior.

[No entry for the 13th]

♄ [Saturday], the 14th

To my greatest joy Br. Post and Ludwig Hübner arrived from Bethlehem, bringing me the spirit and the peace of my dear brethren. My heart rejoiced indescribably over the loving remembrance in which my dear brethren keep me and all the brethren and sisters in Pachgatgoch, for they sent us dear Br. Ludwig Hübner that he may stay with me ~~this wint[er]~~. Our Indian brethren and sisters were most heartily delighted to see their old Achamawant.⁵⁰

[*Page break*]

Pachgatgoch *Diarium*.⁵¹

☉ [Sunday] 15

During the general meeting I spoke about the common Epistle, Rom. 13. The dear Savior was powerfully near us with His bloody wounds. Next I, together with Br. Achamawant, visited several Indian brethren and sisters. We had a favorable opportunity to remind the brethren and sisters of their initial time of grace. I hope it was a blessing for the dear hearts; several acknowledged this with tears.

☽ [Monday], the 16th

We celebrated a blessed love feast with all of the baptized brethren and sisters. At this time Br. Achamwant passed on the heartfelt greetings that he was bearing from the beloved Jünger [Zinzendorf], and Johannes [von Watteville], and from other dear brethren and sisters in Europe, as well as the warm greetings from the dear hearts in Bethlehem. All of the brethren and sisters showed themselves grateful for the loving remembrance in which their dear brethren and the entire congregation kept them. Moreover, Brother Achamawant expressed his joy and pleasure at seeing his old familiar friends⁵² and all of the brethren and sisters together. We conversed a great deal about our Lamb^d of God, about His sufferings, and the claim that He has to each heart, as well as about the close fellowship that we may enjoy with Him as sinners.

Late in the evening Samuel [and] Philippus, along with several unbaptized ones, came from hunting.

♂ [Tuesday], December 17

After school I, together with Brother Achamawant, visited the brethren and sisters in the winter huts. The dear Savior Himself made for the opportunity that we could speak with each one separately about his heart, and the brethren and sisters were open-hearted. Leah wept silently and bemoaned [that] because she was such a great sinner, she believed that she could no longer go among her brethren and sisters. We affectionately directed her to the Lamb[d] and His bloody wounds. At the same time Br. Achamawant took leave of the brethren and sisters. They sent with him many heartfelt greetings for the brethren and sisters in Bethlehem and Gnadenhütten.

☿ [Wednesday], the 18th

We were paid a great many visits by our Indian brethren. Toward evening I went with Achamwant to visit Mr. Mills and she [his wife], as they have very much requested this of us, and are old acquaintances of Achamwant. They acted exceedingly joyful and courteous. We had also an opportunity to say a good word[d] about our Lamb[d] of God.

♃ [Thursday], the 19th

We were busy writing letters[d] to our beloved brethren and sisters in Bethlehem, and Achamawant prepared himself for his return journey.

♀ [Friday], the 20th

He [Post] bade us and all of the Indian brethren and sisters a heartfelt farewell. We sent with him many greetings and kisses for our dear brethren and sisters. [Br.] Abr[aham] accompanied him to Nicolaus Rau, and they stayed with him that night.[53]

♄ [Saturday], the 21st

We took a heartfelt leave of each other and set out to continue attending to our calling. Abr[aham] returned to Pachgatgoch in good time. I observed the first Sabbath here with my dear Ludwig [Hübner].

☉ [Sunday], the 22nd

During the general meeting I spoke on Phil. 4.6, 7. Our Lamb of God was powerfully near us. Following the sermon all of the baptized brethren and sisters

525

reassembled in the hall where our dear Brother Nathanael's [Seidel] letter was read to them. All of the brethren and sisters were delighted and encouraged by their brethren and sisters in Bethlehem keeping them in loving remembrance. Moreover, I informed them of the forthcoming Christmas celebration, and in what way we intended to celebrate it for [the benefit of] our hearts, so that it may be a blessing for us all. Br. Jeremias visited us in the evening. He is in a blessed state at present; may the dear Savior preserve him in it.

☽ [Monday], the 23rd

School was resumed. Christian returned with his family from out of the woods. In the evening the dear Savior delighted us with the visit of Br. Martin.

♂ [Tuesday], the 24th

In the evening the dear Savior provided us with a most heartfelt joy through the visit of several brethren and sisters whom we told a great deal about our Jesus[d], that He came into the flesh for our sake. It was a blessed conversation, giving us comfort and joy. I and dear Brother Ludwig observed a most blessed night watch together.[54]

☿ [Wednesday], the 25th

To our delight, all of the unbaptized ones and baptized ones assembled in our hall[d] on Christmas. The dear Savior was powerfully near us and had us feel His loving heart. First we sang a number of Christmas verses[d] in English. Afterward, I read to them the story of our Savior's coming into the flesh, from Luke, chapter 2. Next, I spoke with a warm and feeling heart of His great love for us poor sinners. This meeting having ended, all of the children, 30 in number, assembled. I also told them something about their Jesus[d], and that He was a child[d] born for them. They were very *attent* [attentive]. I promised them to again conduct a quarter-of-an-hour every Sunday hereafter. Afterward, we had many visits from the brethren and sisters, at which time we pointed out to them the importance of this day. In the evening, to our great delight and to that of all of the brethren and sisters, our dear heart Martin [Mack] arrived, and with him our Br. Jonathan from Gnadenhütten. He brought us many heartfelt greetings and kisses from our dear brethren and sisters.

♃ [Thursday], the 26th

All of the brethren and sisters came and welcomed their dear Martin, and were happy to see him here once again. Afterward, he visited them in their huts. Also, Br. Lucas came from hunting, likewise Br. Joshua and Elisabeth from his [their] visit to Bethlehem and Gnadenhütten. I hope the visit will be a true blessing for them.

♀ [Friday], the 27th

We began speaking with the brethren and sisters [in preparation for Communion]. Br. Martin [Mack] at once informed them of the reason for his coming and why his dear brethren sent him here, namely, to see and hear what our dear Indian brethren and sisters are doing and in what state they are. To our delight we found that the brethren and sisters were openhearted and straightforward, telling us about their hearts and minds under the present circumstances. At the same time we saw various traces of grace of the faithfulness and love of our Lamb[d] for our dear brethren and sisters, also that He seeks to bring all onto the right track.

♄ [Saturday], the 28th

We were busy all day long speaking with the brethren and sisters [in preparation for Communion]. We were again able to see clearly the dear Savior's work of grace. Anna, Petrus's daughter, Sarah's son's wife, was delivered of a young son[d].

☉ [Sunday], the 29th

Dear Br. Martin preached with much blessing and grace on the words of the dear Savior: *Ich bin der Weg die Wahrheit und das Leben.*[55] Our little hall[d] was as full as it could be with people, all of whom were very *attent*. After the sermon Br. Martin also conducted a quarter-of-an-hour for the children, during which we felt the nearness of the Lamb[d] as well. We then went on to visit several brethren and sisters in their huts.

☽ [Monday], the 30th

We again spoke with several brethren and sisters [in preparation for Communion], yet were unable to finish with all of them as some had gone out into the neighborhood. Past noon we hauled home wood for ourselves because it was icy. Jeremias and Samuel visited us in the evening.

♂ [Tuesday], the 31st

In the forenoon we spoke with several more brethren and sisters who openly told us about their hearts and minds, how they felt, and how they had fared until now. They all recognized themselves to be poor sinners who frequently have done wrong. We touched them with our love and directed them to the bloody wounds of Jesus, the fountains of grace for poor sinners.

Because we would like to celebrate a love feast and a small night watch at the closing of this year, we sent Br. Christian, who had volunteered to do this, down to the winter huts to inform the brethren and sisters to that end. Past noon we prepared for the love feast.

In the evening, at nightfall, all of the baptized brethren and sisters gathered. Our dear Brother Martin gave a brief but blessed address, at the same time informing them the brethren and sisters that we intended to celebrate a love feast and a small night watch.

The brethren and sisters assembled around 10 o'clock. We opened by singing a number of German and Indian verses. At the love feast, many useful matters were discoursed upon. For example, we reminded the brethren and sisters of their baptisms and the grace that the dear Savior bestowed upon them back then; moreover, that we are brethren because we partook of His blood, [and] that we are no longer to look upon one another as foreigners or strangers, but as brother[s].

On this occasion, we also put ourselves in mind of all our brethren and sisters, here and in Europe, and wherever else we are dispersed in this world. Next we asked them if they indeed knew how many brethren had visited them over time. They were able to name all of them from the beginning. Then the circumstances that had come to pass in the course of the past year were recalled and committed to the care of the brethren and sisters. We found many reasons to lay ourselves at the feet of the Lamb[d].

Afterward, Brother Martin gave a blessed address during which he described, [in a manner] quite lively and with feeling, the Lamb[d] with his bloody wounds,[56] praising to everyone his loving heart. Then we all fell on our knees, and Br.

Martin beseeched our God and Lamb for absolution and the forgiveness of all [our] previous faults and trespasses, that He may wash away everything with His blood and take us into the new year as pardoned poor sinners, enabling us to serve Him with all our hearts and all our souls. Then we again sang a number of Indian and German verses[d] and ~~again~~ happily laid ourselves down to sleep inside the bloody wounds of the Lamb[d].

Abraham Büninger and Carl Gottfried Rundt

1 January to 7 December 1755

Pachgatgoch *Diarium*[1]

Wednesday, January 1, 1755

After the brethren and sisters came up from the winter huts, a general meeting took place. Brother Martin [Mack] spoke on Jn. 12.46, on blissfully walking in the light and near our Lamb[d] of God and His bloody wounds. Afterward, Abraham [Büninger] and Martin visited a sick child in Gideon's hut who has been ill throughout the entire autumn with paralysis of the nerves,[2] [so] that she is now completely lame on one side. Amid all of her pains she told us how she felt in her heart. She said, I entreat the *Pachtamawos* at all times that He may wash my heart with His blood. I am a poor child, I feel my heart, yet I often grow impatient. I am unable to help myself; the *Pachtamawoos* must help me.[3] Please entreat the Savior that He may soon help me and wash me with His blood. Br. Martin told her about the Savior's wounds, that He died for her[4] and shed His blood for her, [and] that the Savior wanted to take her to be His child. For this she thanked Br. Martin and asked that we think of her always. That day we had observed a particularly blessed way about our brethren and sisters, full of light; many visited us and demonstrated that they were quite blessed.

In the evening we had a separate meeting with all of the baptized, for we wanted to hear their thoughts about their circumstances up until now, especially because the quarter-of-an-hour services in the morning and in the evening had been discontinued. They all declared that they regretted that it had turned out this way, [and they] wished that the Savior would show mercy on them and let them hear His words as before. Br. Martin informed them of the congregation's heart and mind [regarding this matter]. Also promised them that the quarter[-of-an-hour services] in the morning shall be reinstituted, which caused a great deal of joy among all of the brethren and sisters.

♃ [Thursday], the 2nd

Brother Martin conducted the early quarter-of-an-hour for us on the verse[d] *Bless this Day Lord and Savior[,] etc.* Afterward, Martin and Abraham went to the winter huts and there visited the brethren and sisters.[5] The dear Savior was with us. We had a favorable opportunity to bear witness to His blood and wounds. Br. Martin conducted the quarter-of-an-hour in the evening.

♀ [Friday], the 3rd

Abraham delivered the morning blessing. Br. Martin visited the brethren and sisters. Abraham went to our neighbor Mills to buy some Welsh corn.

♄ [Saturday], the 4th

We observed a rather blessed Sabbath together, which we white brethren concluded with a small love feast. We also wrote letters[d] to our dear brethren in Bethlehem.

☉ [Sunday], the 5th

Brother Martin preached on the words *Wache auf der du schläffest,*[6] [words crossed out] with much grace and blessing. After the sermon there was [the] children's quarter-of-an-hour, in the course of which Brother Martin baptized the son[d] of Jeremias and Agnes, giving him the name Anton. It was an exceedingly blissful and blessed *actus*, which was a great blessing for all those present, especially for the children.

In the evening Brother Martin still conducted a quarter-of-an-hour for the baptized, during which he pointed out and reminded them about several matters; for example, about [their] leaving and selling of the wares that they make, also about school, and that they are to make sure to report [to us] properly when they leave.

☽ [Monday], the 6th

At the early quarter-of-an-hour our dear heart Martin put the brethren and sisters in mind of the Lamb[d] and His bloody wounds, and that they are to cleave to Him with their hearts. He, at the same time, took leave of them. They gave

531

him many heartfelt greetings for the beloved brethren and sisters in Bethlehem and Gnadenhütten. I and Brother Ludwig [Hübner] accompanied him for a mile and bade him a warm and tender farewell.

♂ [Tuesday], the 7th

In a heartfelt prayer we recommended ourselves to the Lamb[d] and His bloody wounds. Then our dear brethren and sisters and we blessedly carried on in our course throughout the entire day. In the evening the brethren went sweating in the sweat house.

☿ [Wednesday], the 8th

At the early quarter-of-an-hour I read the first chapter [of the letter] to the Ephesians. Nothing noteworthy occurred that day. In the evening [I] spoke on the words *Er ist nicht alleine vors Volck gestorben, sondern das Er alle Kinder Gottes zusamen brächte.*[7]

[*No entry for the 9th*]

♀ [Friday], the 10th

Anna, a girl who had lived with Gideon, went to the Savior.

♄ [Saturday], the 11th

We wanted to bury her, but were unable to, for it was very stormy all day long. We observed a blessed Sabbath together, remembering our dear brethren and sisters in Bethlehem.

☉ [Sunday], the 12th

During the general meeting [I] spoke on Eph. ~~2.20, 21, 22~~ 3.16, 17. Afterward, there was [the] children's quarter-of-an-hour, and at the same time, the burial of our little Anna. She was a girl of about 10 years of age [and] had been baptized by Mr. Graeham[8] in Southbury when she was still very young. Her father lives in Potatuck, where she was born. Her mother died when she was still a small child. Her father then gave her to Hannah, the wife of Timotheus in ~~Gnadenhütten~~ Wechquadnach. But when Timotheus moved to Gnadenhütten, she [Hannah] gave Anna to Erdmuth and Martha, Gideon's wife, who then took her in and kept her until her blessed end.

☽ [Monday], the 13th

At the morning blessing we recommended ourselves to the Lamb[d] and His precious wounds by means of a heartfelt prayer. At the quarter-of-an-hour in the evening I read aloud the 4th chapter [of the letter] to the Ephesians. The whole assembly was very *attent* [attentive].

♂ [Tuesday], the 14th

At the early quarter-of-an-hour [I] spoke on Eph. 4.13. Our Lamb of God makes Himself known to us, quite mercifully and near. We sledded some firewood from off the mountain for ourselves. There was no quarter-of-an-hour in the evening because the brethren went into the sweat house.

☿ [Wednesday], the 15th

At the early quarter-of-an-hour [I] spoke on the text. Our Lamb[d] of God was powerfully near us and let us feel His loving heart. Br. Joshua visited us. He spoke much with me about his heart. The dear Savior has affected a great deal in him up until now. He [Joshua] also told me about several things that had occurred here, [and] that he is hopeful that matters will improve in Pachgatgoch. Br. Samuel went to Sharon. During the evening quarter-of-an-hour I read aloud the last 2 chapters of the epistle to the Ephesians.

♃ [Thursday], the 16th

At the early quarter-of-an-hour [I] spoke on the beautiful text. Br. Gideon went to New Milford [and] Gottlieb to Sharon. In the evening, following the quarter-of-an-hour, Br. Joshua and Martin visited us. The dear brothers are lacking suitable words in their language to express themselves when interpreting. For example, they do not have any fitting words for *grace, blessing, and redemption.* We advised them to incorporate these particular words into their language, as one language often borrows one word from another language. We spent quite a blessed evening together.

♀ [Friday], the 17th

At the early quarter-of-an-hour [I] again spoke on the text. Abraham went out into the neighborhood to see whether he could buy some Welsh corn but did not get any. Br. Ludwig held school with the children, and in the evening, the quarter-of-an-hour. It was the first ~~address~~ meeting that he held in the English language.

♄ [Saturday], the 18th

After the morning blessing we went visiting in the winter huts. The Savior granted me an especially favorable opportunity to speak at length with Gottlob. And he expressed himself in great detail about how he feels in his heart. He said, I often recall what the brethren told me when I wanted to move away from Pachgatgoch, and afterward came to live here [at the winter huts]. They fully predicted how I would feel. And everything happened just exactly the way they had told me. My heart has become deathly ill and cold toward the Savior. I have succumbed to sin [so] that I now no longer know how to help myself at all. We spoke with him quite brotherly-like and with affection, presenting to him in prayer the merciful heart of the dear Savior. Our other visits were of great joy to us; we were able to most heartily give thanks to the Lamb for the mercy He is bestowing on this small poor flock. Having finished visiting, we prepared a small love feast for ourselves, rejoicing together, and remembering our dear brethren at the *synodo*.

☉ [Sunday], the 19th

At the general meeting [I] spoke on [blank]. Afterward, the children's quarter-of-an-hour took place; then, we still went visiting in several huts. Our hearts were made to feel ashamed and humbled over the work of grace that the Savior is at present engaged in with the dear brethren and sisters. In the evening we had a blessed singing service[d] together. Then we went to sleep inside the nearby wounds of the Lamb.

☽ [Monday], the 20th

Br. Ludwig went to Salisbury to visit Br. Leighton. I held school. Throughout the day [I] was visited several times by ~~brethren and sisters~~ brethren. At our morning and evening quarter-of-an-hour services the dear Savior was powerfully near us.

[No entry for the 21st]

☿ [Wednesday], the 22nd

Br. Ludwig returned home. Christian went to New Milford.

♃ [Thursday], the 23rd

At the early quarter-of-an-hour [I] spoke on the words *Durch seine Wunden sind wir geheilet.*[9] Nothing noteworthy occurred that day. The brethren and sisters blessedly proceeded on their course. We had a blessed quarter-of-an-hour[d] in the evening.

♀ [Friday], the 24th

At the morning blessing we recommended ourselves to the Lamb and His bloody wounds by means of a heartfelt prayer. Sr. Rebecca, David's wife, was delivered of a young daughter that morning. Br. Samuel's house caught on fire because of his children's carelessness, but [the fire] was right away extinguished by the brethren [so] that he suffered no additional damage. At the quarter-of-an-hour in the evening [I] spoke on the text.

♄ [Saturday], the 25th

After the early quarter-of-an-hour we went to the winter huts to visit. Sarah complained about her children, that they were lazy and ill-mannered, and did not want to do any work. In the past she had frequently admonished them in that regard, and seeing that it was of no use, she had told them [that] they should then go ahead and see where they would get something to eat for themselves. She very much wanted to hear our thoughts on this matter. We told her the following during the Bible hour: That he who does not want to work also should not eat, and her children were big enough to earn their keep; she should not agonize over this. Leah said [that] she had felt blessed this week. ~~We also spoke~~ I also spoke with Rebecca.

☉ [Sunday], the 26th

For the general meeting our little church[d] was completely filled with brown sheep[d], old and young, for which we heartily praised the dear Savior. I spoke on Jn. 6.27, 28, 29. Our bloody Lamb[d] was powerfully near me. Moreover, He made the hearts of all those present favorably disposed to what was spoken and testified about Him. Next, there was [the] children's quarter-of-an-hour.

And they all came so that almost no one was missing; our beloved Lamb^d was in our midst, granting us a blessing.

Past noon we visited the brethren and sisters in their huts.

☽ [Monday], the 27th

At the morning blessing our Lamb^d of God was powerfully near us. Petrus and Thamar reported to us that they needed to go out this week to work, for they had nothing more to live on; their corn was used up. He [Petrus] said, Brother, it is difficult for me these days. Not only do I have to provide for myself, but also for my grandchildren, those of Caritas—who has 4 children and cares for them poorly. At the quarter-of-an-hour in the evening [I] spoke on the text. Right after the quarter-of-an-hour a young Indian visited us, who is bound to a neighbor until he is of age. Not long ago I had presented him with the *Pilgerbrief*. He said that in reading it, it came to him that he should visit Bethlehem. He intends to do so as soon as he is free, which will be this coming April. He is of the *Mohik*. [Mohegan] *nation*; does not live far from Boston.

♂ [Tuesday], the 28th

At the evening quarter-of-an-hour I read aloud chapter 10 [and] 11 in John.

[No entries for the 29th and 30th]

♀ [Friday], the 31st

Joshua and Elisabeth went to Quaker Hill to sell their utensils.

♄ [Saturday], February 1

This month was begun with a heartfelt prayer and supplication to our Lamb^d of God. Then we went to the winter huts. The main purpose of our visit was to speak with David. He said that he was reluctant to come to us any more because he had done wrong and had stayed away from us for so long. I told him that he had done this on his own; we had not told him to stay away. The door to us had always remained open for him and shall not be closed to him, to be sure. He said, I want to come back tomorrow. I told him [that] he had to promise me this solemnly, which he did. Rebecca and Maria acted very amicably. Anna and

Sarah said that they had been in good spirits this week. In the evening Samuel visited us and related to us the beginning of his awakening. The dear Indian brethren feel the same way we do; their hearts feel humbled before the Savior each time they call to mind the initial time of grace.

☉ [Sunday], the 2nd

At the general meeting [I] spoke on the words [from] Acts 16, *Glaub an den Herrn Jesum so wirstu sel.*[10] Our Lamb[d] of God invigorated me quite strongly. The Indians, baptized and unbaptized, were very *attent* [attentive]. During the children's quarter-of-an-hour I described the dear Savior's childhood, how He as a child had conducted Himself in the world. Then [I] said that through His bloody death He had purchased the grace for us to become like He was. Past noon we had quite a joyful visit at the brethren and sisters'.

☽ [Monday], the 3rd

During the morning blessing we recommended ourselves to our faithful Lamb[d] of God, appealing to Him that this week He may shelter us inside His holy wounds and bless us. Br. Gideon went to New Milford to sell [some] of the utensils he had made. Abraham went to the mill in Kent to mill some Indian corn. In the evening the brethren went into the *peesponk*.[11] Later, Br. Martin visited us and told us what discourses had taken place between the brethren while sweating. He said, Brother, we have decided among ourselves that we want to frequently remind one another about the Savior and His wounds, so that we will not return to our former ways from which the Savior has redeemed us. Afterward, he still told us a great deal about his heart and that the Savior helped him out of the poor circumstances in which he found himself this last summer, [so] that now he was able to be very grateful to the Savior.

♂ [Tuesday], the 4th

At the early quarter-of-an-hour the text was discussed some. Joshua and Samuel went to Sharon upon the request of several men who have been appointed to a *comitee* by the *General Assembly* to put in order the land affairs of the Wechquadnach Indians.[12] In the evening [I] spoke on the words: *Er ist die versöhnung für unsere Sünden.*[13]

☿ [Wednesday], the 5th

Gottlieb's family went into the woods to work because they have absolutely nothing more to eat; we were sorry for the children, for they have to do without school. They were well into the course of learning.

In the evening [I] spoke on the words *Also hat Gott die Welt geliebet, daß etc.*[14] Our Lamb[d] of God was powerfully near us with His bloody wounds.

♃ [Thursday], the 6th

At an early hour there was [the] quarter-of-an-hour. Br. Joshua came back from Sharon. Nothing was done about their [land] affair because the *committe* was unable to come to any conclusion other than to take this matter before the *court* in Litchfield. To this end Br. Samuel was sent by the *committee* to Stockbridge to inform Timotheus that he is to appear before the *court*. The *committee* was of the opinion that several of the Indians here should go to the *court* in Litchfield and see to it that the matter was dealt with fairly, because several brethren here are acquainted with the circumstances concerning the Wechquadnach land.[15] At the quarter-of-an-hour in the evening [I] spoke on the text.

♀ [Friday], the 7th

At an early hour [I] spoke on the words *Du solst lieben Gott Deinen Herrn von Gantzen herzen — und den Nächsten als dich selbst.*[16] The dear Savior was exceedingly close to us. Because some snow had fallen, we were busy sledding home firewood. It [the snow] was gone again by noon. At the quarter-of-an-hour in the evening [I] spoke on the text.

♃ [Thursday], the 8th

After the morning blessing we went visiting in the winter huts; there were not many at home, however. Nothing noteworthy occurred. Brother Jeremias visited us; we discoursed on many matters. He especially enjoys hearing someone speak or read to him from the Bible. He also declared himself to be very satisfied, thanking the Savior for the school, because his children have the opportunity to learn something and are so willing to do so. Also, the brethren built a *cannue* for themselves, as the high waters this week had carried away their old one.

☉ [Sunday], the 9th

During the general meeting [I] spoke on 2 Th. 1.11, 12. Our church[d] was again filled with people. For some time now the unbaptized have diligently attended the meetings, and it can be observed that the dear Savior is working on several hearts. At the children's quarter-of-an-hour [I] spoke on the verse[d] *Christi Blut u. Gerechtigkeit, etc.*[17] Past noon we went visiting in the huts. Thus [we] saw the work by the dear Mother[18] on the hearts of the dear brethren and sisters.

The 10th

Abraham went to Nicolaus Rau to get some wheat and corn flour. Br. Ludwig Hübner conducted the quarter-of-an-hour services in the morning and in the evening, and held the schools. The brethren finished their new *cannue* and hauled it into the water.

♂ [Tuesday], the 11th

At the early quarter-of-an-hour [I] spoke on the text. Gottlieb went to his family in the woods, as did Philippus with his wife. Petrus and Thamar also went into the woods to work. We visited them all and exhorted them to cleave to the Savior and His wounds.

☿ [Wednesday], the 12th

Brother Samuel came from the court in Litchfield. However, it [the court] has not yet arrived at a decision; instead, [the question of the land] shall be settled on next week in Sharon. Timotheus came along with Samuel. At the quarter-of-an-hour in the evening [I] read aloud the 5th chapter in Matthew.

♃ [Thursday], [the] 13th

At the early quarter-of-an-hour [I] spoke on Mt. 5.7, 8, 9. In the evening, after the quarter-of-an-hour, Joshua visited us with Martin. We had a favorable conversation about a great number of matters that so happen to occur inside the kingdom of the dear Savior.

♀ [Friday], [the] 14th

At the early quarter-of-an-hour [I] spoke about the verse "O! Haupt voll,[19] p[p]." Br. Samuel reported to us in detail on his journey to Stockbridge. We are very pleased and see it as the divine will of the dear Savior that Samuel arrived there. This way we learned in good time about the plans that they have: They [at Stockbridge] would very much like to have our young folk from here go to Stockbridge as soldiers to guard their new ford [fort]. Several chi[e]fs as officers of the Indians intend to come to us before long, wanting to see whether they can recruit some [Indians here]. At the quarter-of-an-hour in the evening [I] spoke on the text.

♃ [Thursday], [the] 15[th]

At an early hour there was the morning blessing, then we went visiting. Br. Ludwig went to the winter huts, and Abraham into the woods to [visit] Gottlieb's family. The brethren and sisters are yet satisfied and in good spirits [as they proceed] on their course.

☉ [Sunday], the 16th

At the meeting [I] spoke on 2 Cor. 6.1, 2. I was once again greatly disturbed by the restless children; I was deeply sorry for it, but could not help it. Brother Ludwig conducted the children's quarter-of-an-hour on the verse[d] *Here by the Cross then will I stay, coll[ect] N[um]. 70.5.* At the visit, Br. Joshua told us that the brethren intended to hold a conference about the intelligence that Samuel had brought from Stockbridge. The dear brethren are truly at a loss about this place[d] here.

☽ [Monday], the 17th

The quarter-of-an-hour took place early, afterward [was] school. Next, we hauled home some wood for ourselves, for it had snowed some. In the evening during the quarter-of-an-hour [I] spoke on the words *Ich glaube Herr hilf mir wieder meinen Unglauben.*[20]

♂ [Tuesday], the 18th

After the morning quarter-of-an-hour the following brethren went to Sharon: Gideon, Joshua, Samuel, Martin, and Jeremias. They have been called by the *commitee*, because the matter concerning the Indian land in Wechquadnach is to be brought to a close now.

☿ [Wednesday], the 19th

Was [the] morning blessing. Elisabeth, Priscilla, and Caritas went to Sharon to sell brooms and baskets. In the evening I read aloud chapter 3 in John.

The 20th and 21st

There was hardly anyone at home. Because some fair amount of snow had fallen, we worked hard hauling home some firewood for ourselves. The schools proceeded in due order, as usual.

♃ [Thursday], the 22nd

We went visiting in the winter huts, but found only 4 people at home.

Toward evening the brethren and the rest of the company came [back] from Sharon. The *committee* has decided on the matter concerning the land at Wechquadnach. Timotheus received about 76 sh. [shillings] *Yörksch* [New York] currency for the claim that he had laid to the land, and was obliged to give [in return] a lawful *deed* for more than 200 acres of land.

Now it is also clear who had played the trick in Wechquadnach that was imputed to our brethren here. It is one of their [the colonists'] own bad boys in Sharon who did it in order to frighten the people.[21]

☉ [Sunday], the 23rd

At the meeting [I] spoke on Lk. 9.24, 25. The dear Savior assisted me quite mercifully and invigorated me, and the entire assembly was *attent* [attentive] and orderly. Past noon we had a rather joyful visit; Lucas visited us in our house. Br. Ludwig spoke with him affectionately.

☽ [Monday], the 24th

Because it had snowed heavily during the night, there was no quarter-of-an-hour in the morning, and because it continued snowing, there was also no school that day. We visited the brethren and sisters in their huts. Most of them poured out their hearts to us on account of their poverty. Gottliebe was boiling her last corn. Joshua said he had not one *päck* [peck] left. Petrus, Martin, Jeremias, and Samuel have had to buy [corn] for a long time. Yet, the Savior is nonetheless blessing them in their tremendous poverty, [so] that not one is discontented or morose. When one consoles them in their poverty they say, *Yes Brother the Savior will Help us through*. We had a blessed quarter-of-an-hour[d] in the evening; I spoke on Heb. 5.9.

541

♂ [Tuesday], the 25th

At the early quarter-of-an-hour [I] spoke on the beautiful Indian text. Thereafter I spoke with Caritas, for she is conducting herself so badly, and, moreover, does not show any concern for her children. I quite heartily exhorted her to turn back from her wicked ways. But her reply to me was, I still like it quite well this way, I cannot turn back yet. If I did not like it this well, I would have turned back a long time ago. At the quarter-of-an-hour in the evening the reading of the passion story was begun.

☿ [Wednesday], the 26th

At an early hour there was the morning blessing. Next, several brethren and sisters went out to see where they could get provisions. Poverty is fast gaining ground among them. In the evening we felt a lovely air of grace emanating from Jesus' bloody wounds. The brethren and sisters indeed all attended the meeting.

♃ [Thursday], the 27th

At an early hour there was the quarter-of-an-hour. Nothing noteworthy occurred that day. At the quarter-of-an-hour in the evening [I] spoke on Mt. 18.14.

♀ [Friday], the 28th

At the early quarter-of-an-hour I spoke on the words *Gleich wie Moses eine Schlange erhöhet hat, in der Wüsten; also muste der hld. erhöhet werden, auf das ein jeder der an Ihn Glaubt[,] p[p].*[22] At the quarter-of-an-hour in the evening I read aloud chapter 26 in Matthew.

Sabbath, March 1

At the morning blessing we felt the nearness of our dearest Lamb[d]. We recommended ourselves to His merciful protection by means of a heartfelt prayer. Next, we went to the winter huts. The brethren and sisters are quite lively and blessed [as they proceed] on their course, [and] are very glad when one visits them. On returning home, Martin, Petrus, and Thamar visited us. Their reason was to tell us that they feel rather well and blessed near Jesus' wounds. Br. Martin said, When I look at Pachgatgoch, I think that we are like a seed that a man sticks into the ground. First it lies in the ground for a while, then it sprouts, soon it gets hoed around and hilled, then it [grows] ears and becomes mature.

The Brethren and the Savior have planted a seed such as this in Pachgatgoch, and this kernel has sprouted. Presently, it is being tended and cared for. I wish that all of us will turn out well and bear fruit for the Savior.

☉ [Sunday], March 2

At the meeting [I] spoke on Gal. 1.4, 5; the Savior manifested Himself to us quite mercifully, likewise during the children's quarter-of-an-hour.

Past noon we visited all of the brethren and sisters in their huts. In the evening Br. Samuel visited us. He told us about all sorts of disquieting circumstances, making us realize [that] the wicked enemy[23] is very busy disturbing the brethren and sisters on their blessed course on which they have proceeded for some time, robbing them of their peace. By way of closing the day, we prayed the church litany together.

☽ [Monday], the 3rd

At an early hour there was the morning blessing. Br. Martin went to New Milford on business, and Lucas to Stockbridge. The remaining brethren went to the winter huts, as Sarah had asked them for one day of work.

Br. Ludwig went to Nicolaus Rau, for we were hoping that the items that our dear brethren and sisters had sent us from New York had arrived from Rhinebeck. They had not come, however. At the quarter-of-an-hour in the evening [I] spoke on the words *Christus wird Euch vor die Augen Gemahlt*.[24] Caritas left here with 3 of her children; she gave her little Gabriel to her father, Petrus. She shed many tears as she took leave of her parents. David along with his family also went into the woods.

♂ [Tuesday], the 4th

Because it was such stormy weather, we were neither able to conduct [the] quarter-of-an-hours nor [the] schools.

☿ [Wednesday], the 5th

The storm continued until about evening. We visited our brethren and sisters. This has been difficult for them. We had a blessed quarter-of-an-hour[d] in the evening.

♃ [Thursday], the 6th and ♀ [Friday], the 7th

Nothing noteworthy occurred. The quarter-of-an-hour services and the schools proceeded in due order. Also, Martin came from New Milford, with great effort, for the snow is so very high.

♃ [Thursday], the 8th

To our delight, and that of all of the brethren and sisters, our dear Brother Martin [Mack] came from Bethlehem, and with him dear Brother and Sister Jungmann, as well as Gottfried Rundt. They were welcomed by us with affection and much love.

☉ [Sunday], the 9th

The rest of the brethren and sisters, who had not been able to come here yesterday evening, came and welcomed the dear ~~hearts~~ brethren and the sister[25] who were coming to us. The dear Brother [?][26] conducted the general meeting; he spoke on Is. 53.5. He described the Lamb[d] in terms of His great love for poor sinners quite beautifully and lovely. Next, there was the children's quarter-of-an-hour. They were told about the Savior's suffering and dying, and what blessedness He has therewith purchased for us. Past noon there was a quarter-of-an-hour for all of the baptized brethren and sisters. Dear Brother Martin passed on to them the congregation's heartfelt greetings. He also gave *relation* of the baptism of dear Sr. Elisabeth, the wife of PakSchanos. This was a great blessing for the dear brethren and sisters and [it] raised their spirits.[27]

☽ [Monday], the 10th

Br. Büninger went into the neighborhood on account of some business.

The Indian brethren and sisters visited us, and in turn were visited by us.

Br. Martin conducted the evening meeting.

Also, this morning Br. Ludwig Hübner ~~went~~ had gone from here to Br. Leighton in Salisbury with several letters that had been brought for him from Bethlehem. ~~Also,~~ Br. Rundt ~~wrote~~ likewise wrote to him, reporting to him the most noteworthy news from the congregation.

♂ [Tuesday], the 11th

In the afternoon Br. Martin went to visit the Indian brethren and sisters in their huts.

Toward evening Br. Hübner returned from Salisbury, bringing us heartfelt salutations from Brother and Sister Leighton, having found them well and in good spirits. Their joy had been immeasurable when they learned that they are to see and enjoy Bethlehem again.

Soon after we had a delightful and joyous love feast with all the baptized of this place, adults and children. At this time, Br. Martin informed the brethren and sisters of Brothers Abraham Büninger and Ludwig Hübner's departure from here for Bethlehem tomorrow, and in the end delivered a blessed address to them. On this occasion several Indian brethren expressed themselves very affectionately, openly, and emphatically with respect to their hearts and their present condition, desire, and longing.

Following everything, we white brethren and sisters celebrated a very blessed Holy Communion, previous to which we knelt before the heart of our faithful and merciful Savior and let ourselves be absolved by His pierced hands, and afterward, with delight and h[oly?] trembling, we ate from the body that was committed into death for our sins, and drank from the blood of the Lamb wherein life and God's powers are found.

Thereupon we retired in the soft bed^d of the holy side of our Bridegroom of the Souls.

Pachgatgoch *Diarium*, from *Mart[ius]* 17 to May 20, 1755

☽ [Monday], the 17th

At an early hour, having held a blessed early service, and having taken an affectionate leave of us and of all of the Indian brethren and sisters, he [Martin Mack] left from here for Bethlehem. We accompanied him with our love and remembrance, and gave him several letters for Bethlehem to take with him.

Sister Jungmann visited the Indian sisters and we, having held school, hauled some wood to this place. The Indian brethren worked in the woods nearby.

At the evening meeting the brethren and sisters were reminded of the many good and wholesome words about our Savior's love for sinners, as well as [His] mercy, blood, wounds, and death, which they have heard *privatim* [Latin: privately] and publicly through Br. Martin since his presence here, and it was wished for them that the same [words] would sink deeply into their hearts, and as if in a fine [and] good soil, bear the desired fruit.

In the course of this occasion, Br. Christian's wife Gottliebe was delivered of a young daughter[d].

♂ [Tuesday], the 18th

Shortly after the morning blessing Sr. Jungmann visited Brother Christian's wife and found her, along with her child, well. The father [Christian] had declared himself toward her in this way: that he wanted to give this child, who was given to him by the Savior, back to Him to be His possession, and to that end wished that it may soon receive the grace of holy baptism. He had expressed himself in the same way already yesterday toward Br. Martin, [the] Indian. Br. Gottlieb and his Magdalena went into the woods, 4 miles from here, to work there for a while.

Br. Jungmann went to the mill in Kent during school hours, and in the afternoon Br. Rundt went to meet him with a horse, to bring home the flour.

Yesterday and today our Indian brethren were busily at work; they jointly built a new *fence* around a piece of fresh ground near their houses, which they intend to have broken in order to be used by them.

At the evening meeting, guided by 1 Jn. 4.7–11, the brethren and sisters were put in mind of the love of our Lord, with which He loved us to His death, and for this reason [they] also were reminded of the warm, brotherly love toward and among one another.

Br. Joshua and Samuel visited us in the evening for a short hour.

☿ [Wednesday], the 19th

At the early service we reflected on Is. 53, 4–7. Soon after, Br. Jungmann and Rundt went visiting in Br. Christian's house.

Br. Jungmann obtained some things in the neighborhood necessary for our household.[28]

♃ [Thursday], the 20th

At the early service Heb. 2, 14–17, was spoken about, that is, about our Redeemer's great love for us, about His great humiliation, through which He assumed not the nature of angels but that of the poor, fallen people, [and] about His faithful and pitiful heart for all sinners who feel sick, weak, and needy, p[p].

All of the Indian brethren and sisters were visited by Brother and Sister Jungmann, who found them all well and industrious. Br. Joshua went out today to get wood for brooms, returning home in the evening.

Lucia, Samuel's wife, visited Sr. Jungmann in the evening and conversed with her warmly.

The facility with which God's commandments are kept, once a person has started to believe in Jesus and has gained a fresh heart, was discussed at the meeting in the evening in accordance with 1 Jn. 5.3 & 3.23.

♀ [Friday], the 21st

During the morning blessing we recommended, by means of a heartfelt prayer, all of our small Indian flock here to the faithful wounds of our beloved Lord and to His faithful hands, to bless and preserve.

Br. Jeremias went with several crafted wooden utensils to New Milford; Philippus went with him.²⁹

At the evening meeting, as had occurred last Friday, the reading of our Savior's passion story [was] continued.

Br. Samuel visited us afterward, and because our discussion with him offered the opportunity, several circumstances that had taken place during the Savior's passion, death, and resurrection were read to him from the Bible, to which he listened with thorough *attention* and deep feeling.

♃ [Thursday], the 22nd

In the forenoon Br. Rundt visited all of the huts, finding the brethren and sisters in good spirits, and where the opportunity presented itself, he reviewed with the boys their school lesson[s].

We seasoned our midday meal with a song suited to our circumstances. Past noon Brother and Sister Jungmann went to the winter huts and visited the brethren and sisters there, but did not find all of them at home.

Several sisters had gone out today, but returned home before the evening occasion, it[em] Br. Jeremias and Philippus.

At the evening meeting the words from Jn. 2.24, 25 were considered, *Jesus knew all Men & knew what was in Man.*

☉ [Sunday], the 23rd

There was the sermon at the regular time, on Acts 4, verse 12, *There is none* [sic] *other Name under Heaven given among Men, whereby we must be saved, than the Name of Jesus.* A man from our neighborhood was present at this.

At 2 o'clock there was the children's meeting, in the course of which several words of our Savior concerning the children were read to them from Mt. 18, and then were discussed some; Br. Joshua interpreted.

Immediately thereafter Brother and Sister Jungmann went visiting in all of the huts and conversed especially with the brethren and sisters who had come up here from the winter huts for the sermon.

After 3 o'clock, in the course of a small love feast, we had a heartfelt conversation with Brothers Gideon, Joshua, Samuel, and Jeremias, and held a *Bande* with them.[30] Rather delightful subjects came up: for example, about their first awakening; [their] acquaintance with the Brethren; about their baptism; and since then, the various manifestations of the Savior's grace in their hearts in different situations; about the brotherly and tender love among them; and so forth. Finally, [we] also spoke about this or that word and *expression* in the Bible that our brethren here are unable to express with <u>one</u> word when translating into their language, thus having to circumscribe them, and explained to them as best as possible the true meaning of these. On this occasion, we proposed to them to hold in our house, whenever possible, a meeting such as this each Sunday toward evening, and they all thought this to be very good and beneficial. And with that the brethren went home, newly bonded to one another by love. Soon after Br. Martin also came to us, of his own accord, with whom we had likewise a very affectionate *discours*. This day was quite a blessing for us as well as for the Indian brethren, and our good Lord was in our midst, in keeping with His promise.

During our singing service[d], which we three always hold in the evenings before going to bed, we celebrated in song, through beautiful verses, the subject of today's general text in the presence of our Bridegroom of the Souls, at which time we smelled the sweet fragrance of His name, which fell like dew upon us poor sinners also at that hour.

☽ [Monday], the 24th

At the morning blessing the brethren and sisters were reminded that this week had been our Savior's passion week. At this time they were dearly entreated, especially this week, to cleave with their hearts to the Savior and His wounds, to occupy themselves with Him, and to appeal to Him for a special blessing.

Br. Philippus went with his Benigna and [with] Priscilla to Dover, to work there this week.

Br. Gideon likewise went out, with Br. Petrus; the former to New Milford and thereabouts. Petrus returned home in the evening.

♂ [Tuesday], the 25th

At the morning blessing [we] spoke about keeping Jesus and the bloody form of His martyrdom constantly on one's mind, and how this was the sole means by which to preserve our hearts in a perpetual state of blessed feeling.

At breakfast we remembered today's congregation festival,[31] singing our *Ave* and *Gloria* to the son of God and Mary, who saw our suffering and did not shun a poor woman in order to become man in her womb.

Br. Joshua and Martin went out several miles from here with some handiwork, to procure with it some provisions.

In the afternoon Johanna along with her daughter visited Sr. Jungmann, and in the evening, Br. Samuel spent a short hour with us.

During the evening occasion we reflected upon the words from 1 Tim. 1.15, *This is a faithful Saying-that C. J. [Christ Jesus] came into the World to save Sinners[,] p[p]*.

☿ [Wednesday], the 26th

At the morning blessing, guided by the words of Paul, 1 Cor. 2.2, the knowledge of Jesus crucified as the sole and highest wisdom of God's children was spoken about.

Br. Joshua and Martin came home in the afternoon, as did Br. Gideon. Br. Jungmann reported to the one mentioned last, requesting of him an acre[32] of new land to be used by us.

During the evening occasion we availed ourselves of the words of David, ♄ [Psalms] 16.8, *I have set the* LORD *always before me—Therefore my heart is glad,* for the benefit of our hearts.

♃ [Thursday], the 27th

In the forenoon one of our neighbors called on us for a while. Among other subjects of his *discourse*, he gave us to understand [that] we should remind our Indians here that none of them is to go to Stockbridge; the *government* did not want it. The current talk is that one Indian from Pachgatgoch had gone up there regardless. (This is Lucas, who went there against Br. Gideon's reminder, even before we arrived here.) There was concern that a complaint about this would reach the *government*. Afterward, we spoke with our Indian brethren about this subject.

Br. Martin told us today [that] last night he lodged with a separatist who had attended our meeting several times. He [the separatist] had acted and declared himself very amicably toward him. He very much loved those Indians who love the Savior. When Br. Martin, at this opportunity, declared himself toward him [the separatist] on what the Savior had affected in his own heart, how important the Savior's life and death were to him now, [and] how much he loved Him, p[p]., the *separatist* reportedly turned to his 2 children, who were present, and said to them, You Children! Are you listening carefully to what the Indian is saying? I wish you would become like this Indian. Their *discours* is said to have lasted until after midnight.

In several other houses Br. Martin was frequently asked, for example, How do matters presently stand concerning the war with the French? He reportedly answered: I do not know anything about it. Question: Are you not afraid of the war? Answer: No! The Savior will surely preserve me. Question: But in this area all of the people are afraid of the war. Answer: The people have a bad conscience and do not know their Savior; that is why they are afraid. Question: But are you not afraid of death? Answer: No! My Savior died for me on the cross. I believe in Him and will not die but live forever; so He spoke. Thus the people marveled at him and said, This is an exceptional Indian.

♀ [Friday], the 28th

During the early meeting on the day of the death of our Lamb of God, the particulars of what happened to the Savior on the cross, and especially His last 7 words (on which occasion only a little was noted here and there) were read aloud to the brethren and sisters with deep feeling, and were listened to by them in the same way. Br. Joshua interpreted. This occasion was accompanied by a special blessing for all of our hearts. Soon after, at the visit, Br. Gideon declared himself thus: His heart had been all in tears at the time. Martha, his wife, reportedly said, in like fashion: This time she had felt so well in her heart, [just] like when she had heard these words about the Savior's suffering and death from us for the first time in Shekomeko. Several brethren and sisters regretted that they were not present at the early service and did not also benefit from the blessing. We visited those afterward and repeated with them this important matter, and indeed, not without the blessing for their hearts.

As for the rest, this day was spent in quietude. And in the evening meeting we saluted and kissed our Lord's bloody wounds, again reflected on His death and the reason for it, and submitted to Him our poor heart as an offering of gratitude.

Late in the evening Br. Rundt visited Br. Martin, and because Br. Jeremias was present as well, this yet provided the opportunity for quite an affectionate and edifying *discours*.

♄ [Saturday], the 29th

At the early meeting the circumstances surrounding our Savior's burial were read aloud, and were listened to with *attention*. Soon after Br. Rundt went visiting in all of the huts.

In the afternoon Br. Jungmann and Rundt visited the brethren and sisters in the winter huts, and very late in the evening Br. Rundt still visited Br. Samuel and had a heartfelt conversation with him.

Thus far, school and the visits to the brethren and sisters were continued daily. The children are learning with joy, and the visits surely have not been without blessing.

☉ [Sunday], the 30th

After 11 o'clock on Easter Day the regular sermon was delivered on the words *I am he that liveth & was dead — & have the Keys of Hell & of Death*, Rev. 1.18.

Having disbanded at half past twelve o'clock, there still came 8 persons from our neighborhood to hear the sermon,³³ who did not know exactly what time it was, and [given that they were too late,] were obliged to turn back after they had stayed with us for a while. Br. Joshua interpreted for the children's meeting, and immediately afterward, there was a general meeting during which the story of our Savior's resurrection, according to the harmonious account of the Evangelists, was read aloud and listened to with blessing.

Next, Brother and Sister Jungmann, along with several Indian brethren and sisters, went to the winter huts to visit Leah's child, who is very ill. Br. Jungmann had the opportunity to speak quite affectionately with the 2 unbaptized [Indians], Sarah's husband Kihor and [their son] Wenemo, about their innermost state.³⁴

We felt the close presence of our good Lord during all of our occasions, [and] altogether had a rather blessed day, frequently thinking of our beloved brethren and sisters in Bethlehem and at other places; and at our singing service in the evening [we] sang, with a very joyful and grateful heart, to Him who lives and was dead, the [hymn] *Allein Gott in der Höh sey Ehr! p[p].*³⁵

☽ [Monday], the 31st

During the morning blessing ~~was~~ one section from the church litany was recited in prayer, as far as to the words *with thy holy Resurrection comfort us D. Lord & god.*

Thereupon Br. Jungmann rode on horseback to the mill and came home early in the afternoon. Today Br. Petrus, Thamar, and Benigna went out [to a place] several miles from here to work. Br. Gideon went to visit Br. Gottlieb and his family, who for the past several weeks have been living and working in the woods about 4 miles from here.

April.

♂ [Tuesday], the 1st

During the early occasion we reflected on the words *Ye Know that He was manifested to take away our Sins[,] p[p],* 1 Jn. 3.5, 6, 8, 9.

Br. Samuel rode on horseback to [the] Oblong with handmade wooden utensils. Br. Gideon came home from his visit; brought us greetings from Br. Gottlieb and his Magdalena, reporting that their child's illness had been the reason that they did not come here for the meeting last Sunday. Sr. Johanna also went there today to visit them.

The evening meeting was suspended today, for the brethren had gone sweating.

☿ [Wednesday], the 2nd

During the morning blessing we recommended ourselves and our absent Indian brethren and sisters to our Savior's faithful and wounded heart by means of a heartfelt and devout prayer.

In the afternoon Br. Joshua went out several miles from here.

♃ [Thursday], the 3rd

Our meetings were not attended by many because so many brethren and sisters had gone out.

Br. Samuel came home in the forenoon, it[em] Br. Joshua. In the evening Eph. 2.1–5 was spoken about, *You hath he quickened, who were dead in trespasses and Sins &c.*, and on [Friday], the 4th, early, that day's text, *The Lord God is a Sun.*

After the midday meal Br. Rundt went to the winter huts but found few persons at home. Leah was glad that matters have improved with her sick child, and said on this occasion [that] she would have been pleased to give the child up to the Savior, had only the child been baptized before.

Today the Indian brethren were busy working on their new *fence.*

♄ [Saturday], the 5th

Br. Jungmann went out, about 3 miles from here, to purchase some wood necessary for his trade.[36] He took Br. Martin along and afterward paid a visit to the winter huts.

Several Indian brethren and sisters who had been out for several days returned home today, such as Petrus, Thamar, Jonathan, p[p]., it[em] Tsherry, who had been gone for a while.

At the evening meeting we had for our blessed reflection the words of John, chapter IV, [verse] 19, *We love Him, because he first loved us,* and concluded this week with [our] hearts feeling grateful to our lovely and faithful Lord, who let us experience His mercy, His nearness, as well as His assistance in spirit at the daily visits to the brethren and sisters, [and] in school, and everywhere else.

☉ [Sunday], the 6th

The sermon was at the usual time. Today's Sunday gospel on the Savior's appearance among His disciples after His resurrection, according to Jn. 20.19–30, was read aloud, and then Thomas's exclamation *My Lord and my God!* was mainly spoken about.

The children's meeting was at 2 o'clock; Br. Samuel interpreted. Afterward, all of the Indian brethren and sisters were visited.

Brothers Jeremias, Samuel, and Martin visited us toward evening, at which time we had a very joyous conversation with them, ending with a humble and grateful remembrance of what God had us experience, and [about] His great miraculous deed, and [about] what He has ransomed for us at such a high price.

☽ [Monday], the 7th

Br. Joshua came to us shortly after the morning blessing, and it so happened that we came to engage in a quite affectionate and edifying conversation with him. This was brought on by the sermon that had been heard yesterday. In the course of this, one also came to speak of the Savior's appearing among His apostles following His resurrection, of His warm and loving way toward them, about His ascension, and [about] what powers of God were still present at Pentecost during the sermon of the disciples about the death of the Lord. All of this was read to him [Joshua] from the Acts of the Apostles for additional testimony. He very much rejoiced to hear all of this in its entirety, and immediately upon arriving at home, he joyfully told his wife about this.

The Indian brethren were busy working on their new *fence*, and were presented with a half *bushel* of corn by us, for they have so little in store at home.

♂ [Tuesday], the 8th

In the forenoon we got to hear the bad news that yesterday the unbaptized husband of Benigna, Simon's daughter, by the name of Wittli, drowned 2 miles from here in the *river* that runs here past Pachgatgoch. He and another unbaptized Indian, named Paschqua (by the English [he is called] John), Anna's husband, had intended to go home to the winter huts in their 2 *canoes*. However, they had drunk too much rum; thus Wittli drowned and the other one came close to it.

In the afternoon Br. Jungmann went a few miles from here on account of some business; his wife went with him.

Soon after, it happened that the daughters of Br. Christian and Joshua, 2 unbaptized girls [and] both in one *canoe*, fell into the *river*, as the first intended to collect her father and take him across the *river*, it being very high presently. They had suddenly run onto a tree branch; the *canoe* capsized and drifted off. The Savior, however, showed them mercy and preserved them until someone was able to come to their aid, in part with another *canoe* and in part by other means, so that in the end, they escaped with their lives.

Br. Gottlieb came home, having left his wife and children in the woods, safe and in good health. He will return there tomorrow.

At the evening meeting Lk. 12.36, 37, 40 was spoken about, about the necessary watchfulness of God's children and their willingness to joyfully meet their Lord when He calls them home to Him.

☿ [Wednesday], the 9th

In the morning, the text of the day, from Jn. 8.12, *I am the Light of the World*, was reflected upon.

The Indian brethren went out to look for Wittli's body but did not find it; they did find the 2 *canoes*. Today his wife Benigna moved up here from the winter huts. She will live with her father, Br. Simon. When the brethren came home, they brought home a live deer of considerable size that they had seen swimming in the *river* and caught there.

During the meeting in the evening we had for our blessed *meditation* the Savior's words according to Jn. 15.4–7, *Abide in me & I in you &c.*

♃ [Thursday], the 10th

In the forenoon several brethren and sisters went out, some to Sharon, some to Dover, to sell their handiwork. The lack of corn is already widespread among them. Br. Martin's wife Justina went to New Milford along with Christian's daughter.

At the meeting in the evening, occasioned by today's text, the Savior as the light of the heathens, rendering them children of the light, was reflected upon.

♀ [Friday], the 11th

Magdalena, who until now has lived with her unbaptized husband in Danbury, visited Sr. Jungmann. Br. Jungmann and Rundt had gone to the winter huts. Magdalena will live here with her husband once the time for planting approaches. Now they are returning to Danbury.

Br. Joshua worked in our neighborhood today and returned home late in the evening.

During the evening meeting, the faithful and merciful heart of our Savior toward His children and members in the face of everything that occurs to them was discussed.

♄ [Saturday], the 12th

The brethren and sisters who had been in Sharon, Dover, and New Milford returned home, as did Br. Gottlieb with his family, from out of the woods. In addition, several of Wittli's relatives, who had learned of his death, came here for a visit.

In the afternoon Brother and Sister Jungmann went visiting in the winter huts, and there [they] had spoken quite affectionately with the baptized and unbaptized.

In the evening we reflected on *Where the Spirit of the Lord is, there is Liberty*, from 2 Cor. 3.17.

☉ [Sunday], the 13th

The sermon was on John XX.31, *The Gospel was written to this End, that ye might believe, that Jesus is the Christ* &c. The meeting was attended by many, and the Savior did not remain unmanifested among us. The Indian strangers were quite *attent* [attentive].

The children's meeting also was blessed.

In the afternoon we were visited by a number of brethren and sisters, in particular by Br. Joshua, Samuel, and Martin.

☽ [Monday], the 14th

After the morning blessing the Indian brethren measured out 2 acres of new land for Br. Jungmann for our use. We prepared one of these acres for this year.

Several sisters went out with handiwork but returned home in the evening. Our good Lord was quite close to us during the evening meeting, and everyone, young and old, attended the occasion.

♂ [Tuesday], the 15th

We had our land broken open after the Indian brethren had helped us, of their own accord, to clear it by the time for breakfast, in return for which we entertained them with breakfast.

In the evening the 15th chapter of John was read to the brethren and sisters. Afterward, Br. Samuel visited us for a short hour.

☿ [Wednesday], the 16th

Several brethren went out, who, however, returned in the evening before the meeting, in the course of which the familiar words of David, Ψ [Psalms] 73.25, 26, were spoken about, *Whom have I in Heaven but Thee? & there is none upon Earth that I desire besides Thee.*

[No entry for the 17th]
♀ [Friday], the 18th

Wittli's body was found not far from the winter huts where the current had thrown it ashore, and [it] was also buried in that area.

♄ [Saturday], the 19th

The brethren and sisters here, as well as in the winter huts, were visited [by us], and many a word concerning our Savior's love, faith, and mercy for His people was recommended to them. Br. Jungmann celebrated his 36th birthday today, and Br. Rundt congratulated him on it by means of several verses.

In the afternoon Azariah Smith of Salisbury visited us and brought back to us several items from here that had been on loan to Br. Leighton. He was in rather good spirits, and used his time here with us to his benefit; demonstrated to us that he, as well as several other friends there [in Salisbury], very much regretted Br. Leighton's recall from Salisbury. They were resolved to soon write to the congregation in Bethlehem regarding this matter.

At the evening meeting today's text, Jn. 6.33, was considered: The Bread of god is he which cometh down from Heaven, p[p]. The dear Savior could be felt to be very near, and the meeting was attended by many, because all of the brethren and sisters were at home.

☉ [Sunday], the 20th

The sermon was delivered on the following 2 passages: Is. 53.6 and Jn. 3.16, 17: *All we like Sheep have gone astray: we have turned every One to his own Way; But God so loved the World that he gave his only begotten Son &c.* Before the sermon, part of the church litany was recited in prayer.

Soon thereafter, Azariah Smith left us again for Salisbury.

Br. Jungmann conducted the children's meeting. Afterward, we were paid a visit by several brethren and sisters.

☽ [Monday], the 21st

After the morning blessing many brethren and sisters went out, some to New Milford, as well as to other places, to earn there something with their work, and to procure provisions for the time of planting that is approaching. We recommended them to the Savior and wished them His blessed nearness and merciful preservation wherever they are.

Brother and Sister Jungmann went several miles from here to Nicolaus Rau, where he had some business, and returned home before the evening occasion.

After school Br. Rundt visited the brethren and sisters who had stayed at home.

At the meeting in the evening, 2 Cor. 5.17 was discussed: *If any Man be in Christ, he is a new Creature, old things are past [sic] away &c.*

♂ [Tuesday], the 22nd

After school, and having visited the brethren and sisters, which occurs daily, we started on our garden work.

In the evening, the story of the woman who had suffered from a hemorrhage [Mt. 9.20] was read aloud and applied for the benefit of our hearts.

☿ [Wednesday], the 23rd

Br. Gideon, as well as Joshua and his Elisabeth, came home in rather good spirits.

During the evening meeting, witness was borne to [the notion] that the life, power, and blessedness of God's children only exists because they do not turn their eyes and hearts away from the Martyred Husband, from His face that was spit on, and [from His] open, bloody wounds.

Several sisters, who had left on Monday with some handiwork to sell, came home well and in good spirits, whereas Br. Martin left with his Justina and Br. Samuel. David's family arrived at the winter huts, yet he himself [David] did not, for the time being. His son, about 16 years old, died 3 days ago not far from Old Fairfield, and had been baptized there by an English minister.

In the afternoon, Wenemo, Sarah's unbaptized and married son, visited us and declared toward us his desire to be baptized by the Brethren. He, along with his wife, has had a mind to that end for a long time. He would like to be freed from sin and the enslavement to sin. He felt that he was not able to help himself. He was spoken with most affectionately, and the Savior's merciful and faithful shepherd's heart for all the poor and lost sinners and strayed sheep was recommended to him. In the evening we had quite a blessed meeting near our good Lord. Rom. 14.7, 8[,] was discussed: *None of us liveth to himself, & no Man dieth to himself.*

♄ [Saturday], the 26th

All of the remaining brethren and sisters who had gone out this week also came home. When visited, several [of them] told us, to our delight, [that] on the way they had beforehand discussed with the Savior the things[d] they intended to sell on the one hand, and to buy on the other. And He had made everything happen just the way they had desired, [so] that they would have to give thanks to Him for this. The Indian corn is already scarce and difficult to come by in this area.

On the days of this week we have been paid the one or another visit by people from our neighborhood, and today by the English minister of New Fairfield.[37] They all had presented themselves in an amicable and temperate manner.

The schools are attended by the children with joy. The children benefit in their own way, and their parents rejoice when they, at times, hear them read a verse[d].

At the evening meeting we had the declaration of Paul from 1 Cor. 2.2 and Gal. 6.14 for our blessed reflection.

Before going to bed, the three of us celebrated in song, with hearts that are poverty-stricken but in love with the Man of Affliction, this heavenly sweet subject, and then laid ourselves down to rest inside His wounds.

☉ [Sunday], the 27th

At the usual time was the sermon on 1 Pet. 1.18–19: [Y]e know that ye were not redeemed with Silver & Gold-but with the precious Blood of Christ &c. The children's meeting [was] in the afternoon, and then the brethren and sisters were visited.

☽ [Monday], the 28th

The Indian brethren worked partially on their new and partially on their old fences, and were in rather good spirits while doing so.

At the evening meeting the brethren and sisters were read to from Jn. X, on the subject of when the Savior presents Himself as the only good shepherd, and His people as His sheep, and this was discussed some.

[No entries for the 29th and 30th]

Majus.

♃ [Thursday], the 1st

At the morning blessing [the belief] that one could be kept and preserved nowhere safer and happier than inside the wounds of our Lamb of God was discussed.

Br. Samuel and Joshua went several miles from here to work. In addition, several sisters went out to sell their handiwork.

In the afternoon, Brother and Sister Jungmann went to the winter huts to visit but found few at home.

A New Englander, a captain and recruiter, came to this place and inquired whether any of the Indians wanted to serve in the war for money. But no one had a mind for that trade.

[No entry for the 2nd]

♄ [Saturday], the 3rd

Br. Samuel and Joshua, as well as several other brethren and sisters, returned home today. When [we were] visiting the winter huts, only a few of the unbaptized were found at home.

At the evening meeting the words [E]very Spirit that confesseth that Jesus Ch. is come in the Flesh, is of god[,] p[p]., 1 Jn. 4.2, were discussed.

Just as this occasion was getting started, our dear Br. Christian Seidel, in the company of Br. Wilhelm Böhler, arrived here entirely unexpectedly and to our particular joy. As soon as the occasion was over, we as well as all of the Indian brethren and sisters and children greeted them most warmly. Afterward, we were much cheered by many a good tiding from the congregation, in part through our dear Br. Christian Seidel's relation by word of mouth, [and] in part through the various letters from our dear brethren and sisters in Bethlehem; and [we] spent a very joyous evening together.

☉ [Sunday], the 4th

Before it was time for the sermon, which he delivered on Lk. 12.49, I am come to send fire on the Earth, & what will I, if it be already Kindled, Br. Christian received several visits from the Indian brethren and sisters.

He likewise conducted a passionate quarter-of-an-hour for the children in the afternoon. At this time, Benigna, Simon's daughter, was delivered of a daughter[d].

Following this there was also a general occasion, in the course of which Br. Christian passed on to the small brown flock here the heartfelt greetings from our dear brethren and sisters in Bethlehem, Nazareth, and Gnadenhütten. Next, the letters from our dear Br. Joseph [Spangenberg], Petrus [Böhler], Martin [Mack], Grube, and those of several Indian brethren and sisters in Gnadenhütten were read aloud, at which everyone greatly rejoiced.

In the evening, moreover, Br. Christian had a passionate and heartfelt conversation with Brothers Gideon, Joshua, and Samuel in our house.

☽ [Monday], the 5th

In the afternoon Br. Christian and Rundt went visiting in all of the huts here, and Brother and Sister Jungmann, at the same time, went to the winter huts to pay a visit.

Br. Christian conducted the evening occasion, and before going to sleep [also held] a passionate quarter-of-an-hour for us white brethren and sisters on to-day's text, *Er ist Richter der Gedanken u. Sinne des Herzens*,[38] along with the added evening blessing.

♂ [Tuesday], the 6th

A number of the Indian brethren and sisters visited us. Br. Christian conducted the evening occasion on Apocalypse [Revelation] 3.20: *Behold, I stand at the Door, & knock &c.*

☿ [Wednesday], the 7th

Br. Joshua and Elisabeth went to [New] Milford to sell their handiwork.

♃ [Thursday], the 8th

Br. Seidel delivered the morning blessing. Br. Jungmann went 10 miles from here on account of business, returning home in the evening.

Sr. Martha, who last week had gone out along with Johanna and Salome, re-turned[39] home today, in rather good spirits.

Br. Christian, along with Br. Rundt and Böhler, visited the brethren and sis-ters in a number of huts.

In the evening, the story of the Savior's ascension was read aloud to the brethren and sisters.

♀ [Friday], the 9th

Br. Christian delivered the morning blessing, and shortly thereafter, in the pres-ence of Brother and Sister Jungmann, began to speak with all of the baptized brethren and sisters [in preparation for Communion]. In the evening he spoke on today's text, Apocalypse 5.6: *I beheld, & lo, in the midst of the Throne—stood a Lamb, as it had been slain.*

♄ [Saturday], the 10th

Br. Jungmann delivered the morning blessing. In the afternoon Br. Christian, who had not been able to go out much throughout this week because of his swol-len feet, went with Brother and Sister Jungmann to the winter huts, speaking there with the baptized and unbaptized.

During the evening occasion he [Seidel] spoke most warmly on the text *Die Liebe Gottes ist ausgegoßen in unser Herz durch den h. Geist.*[40]

☉ [Sunday], the 11th

Right after breakfast Br. Christian held a conference with Brother and Sister Jungmann, in the course of which today's candidates for baptism, today's Communion, and other occasions were conferred about; see enclosure.[41]

At noon he preached on Jn. 15.4: *Abide in me, & I in you.* A few people from our neighborhood were present for this.

At about 2 o'clock, the children's meeting was conducted by Br. Christian, for which all the children and adults were present, and the following 3 children were baptized by him into the death of Jesus: Gottlob and Leah's, a boy[d] nearly 1 year old, with the name Jonas; the child of Simon's daughter Benigna, a girl, 8 days old, with the name Anna Rosina; and David and Rebecca's daughter[d], 4 months old, with the name Elisabeth.[42] Br. Rundt stood sponsor to the boy, and Brother and Sister Jungmann to the other two children.

Soon after there was a love feast for all the baptized, 35 adults and 16 children in number, at which Kihor and Tsherry, who are currently awaiting the grace of holy baptism, were present as well. On this occasion, Br. Christian discoursed upon various matters, and in particular told the brethren and sisters just how much Pachgatgoch and the small brown flock here are being remembered in prayer before the Savior in Bethlehem, day and night. He then also read aloud several letters from the Indian sisters in Gnadenhütten to the sisters here, which were listened to very attent[ively].

Immediately thereafter a general meeting took place, at which time Sarah's husband, named Kihor, some 70 years old, as well as Tsherry, also a husband of quite an advanced age, both of whom had come to know the Brethren before in Shekomeko, were baptized by Br. Christian into His death amid the palpable presence of the Savior—the first one with the name Abraham, the 2nd, Solomon. The persons to be baptized were *in albis* [Latin: in white], and were led by Br. Jungmann and Rundt to, as well as from, the meeting.

In the evening, we, in the end, partook of the blessed enjoyment of the martyred corpse and the blood of our Lord in holy sacrament, with 20 brown brethren and sisters, namely, 7 brethren and 13 sisters; together with us 5 white brethren and sisters, 25 persons in all. And then, having been flooded with grace and the blood from the wounds, we blessedly laid ourselves down to rest in the arms of our Husband of the Souls and Martyred Husband.

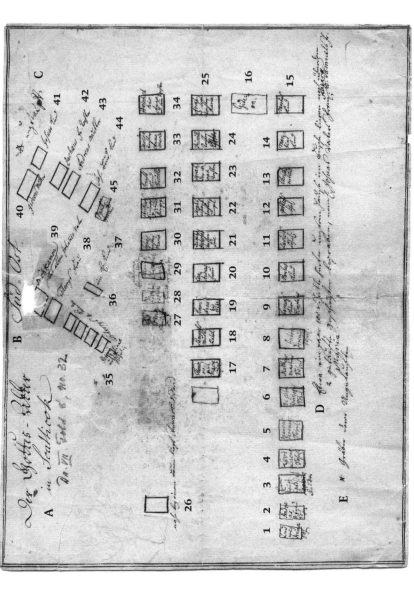

Fig. 4. God's Acre, the cemetery at Pachgatgoch.

From the collections of the Moravian Archives, Bethlehem, Pennsylvania.

LEGEND
Fig. 4. God's Acre,
the cemetery at Pachgatgoch.

(A) God's Acre in Scatticok

(B) Southeast

(C) * Unbaptized

(D) About a couple of 100 paces behind
our house in the woods lie buried,
in addition, 2 baptized *Geschwister*
[brethren and sisters], namely,
Joshua's father's wife Lazara, and
Samuel's wife Maria.

(E) * Graves of the unbaptized

(1) Ludwig[,] Anna's son

(2) Andreas[,] P.'s wife's son

(3) A candidate for baptism[,]
Sophia's brother

(4) Levi[,] Lucas's little son

(5) Marcus[,] Jeremias's little son

(6) Jephta, Christoph's little son

(7) Matthias[,] Martin's little son

(8) Anton[,] Jeremias's little son

(9) Samuel's child Timoteus

(10) Paulus's child

(11) David's little son

(12) Gottlieb's little son

(13) Christian's child

(14) Martin's child

(15) Martin's child

(16) Gideon

(17) Theodora[,] old Marie's sister

(18) Samuel's mother Rahel

(19) Simon's Anna [Hannah?][,] *his wife*

(20) Lea[,] Andreas's wife

(21) Old Hetschet's daughter Söre

(22) Sarah's sister's daughter[,]
unbaptized

(23) Sarah[,] Sarah's daughter

(24) Priscilla's daughter Esther

(25) abrah, and Sarah's daughter Maria

(26) Near a tree lies Andreas's child, David

(27) Rosina[,] Paulus's wife's child

(28) M. Elisabeth[,] Sophia's sister

(29) Salome[,] Salome's little daughter[.]
Maria Elisabeth[,] Sophia's sister
[line drawn through this notation]

(30) Josua's daughter Maria

(31) Christian's child, went home [died]
after birth

(32) Jonath.'s child Priscilla

(33) David's daughter Anna Maria

(34) Hetschet his Anna[,] or his daughter

(35) Petrus and Juliana's little son

(36) Tsherry's 4 children

(37) Tsherry's wife

(38) [Tear in document] N[ ]chkamon[,]
old Johannis's father

(39) Gideon's mother

(40) Josua's child

(41) Zachaeus's wife's daughter

(42) Andreas's mother

(43) Jos.'s brother's child

(44) Paulus's wife

(45) A small child

Note: The drawing of the tree is in pencil.

☽ [Monday], the 12th

At the morning blessing 2 Tim. 1.12 was discussed: *I know, whom I have believed.* Shortly thereafter, in the course of a separate occasion, the daughter[d] of Brother Samuel and Sister Lucia, born tonight, was baptized into the death of Jesus by the name of Anna Maria.

We began planting Welsh corn on our new land.

In the afternoon, Br. Christian had Brothers Gideon and Joshua give him the names of the brown brethren and sisters who are lying in our God's Acre at this place, and made a drawing of God's Acre.[43] Br. Rundt visited Solomon and conversed with him warmly.

Br. Christian conducted the occasion in the evening, and before going to bed, [delivered] the evening blessing to us white brethren and sisters.

♂ [Tuesday], the 13th

Br. Christian delivered the morning blessing and shortly thereafter departed from here for Salisbury and Rhinebeck, along with Brother and Sister Jungmann.

Brother Joshua went several miles from here, as did a number of other brethren and sisters.

At the evening meeting it was discussed that, for those children of God who drew their spiritual life from Jesus' blood, everything else that does not sprout forth and come from the wounds of the Lamb of God is dry and without taste. Moreover, that they season, sanctify, and anoint all of their lives' circumstances, affairs, places, and the like with the subject of His blood, wounds, and death.

☿ [Wednesday], the 14th

Yesterday and today Br. Böhler and Rundt continued planting Welsh corn.

Br. Joshua and the other brethren and sisters who had left yesterday returned home today.

Toward evening Br. Rundt visited the brethren and sisters in the huts, finding them in good spirits and full of light. Solomon went out today.

[No entry for the 15th]

♀ [Friday], the 16th

In the evening a Bible lesson from Jn. 14 was read to the brethren and sisters as an advance reminder of the upcoming feast of Pentecost, with a few matters being remarked upon in the course of this.

♄ [Saturday], the 17th

Right away in the morning Br. Rundt visited the brethren and sisters in the winter huts, and afterward also the brethren and sisters at this place.

The girls' school was suspended this week.

Toward evening Br. Christian Seidel returned home, along with Brother and Sister Jungmann. The Indian brethren and sisters welcomed them.

During the evening occasion Br. Christian passed on to the Indian brethren and sisters of this place the heartfelt greetings from our friends in Salisbury and Rhinebeck.

☉ [Sunday], the 18th

The sermon was delivered by Br. Rundt at the usual time.

Br. Christian, [the] Indian, came home, together with his family and Solomon.

Br. Christian conducted the children's meeting, and in the evening also a general occasion, which shall be continued henceforth every Sunday evening.

Finally, before going to sleep, he delivered to us white brethren and sisters a brief and passionate address based on today's festival texts, as well as the evening blessing.

☽ [Monday], the 19th

At the morning blessing Br. Christian baptized the daughter[d] of Br. Christian and Gottliebe, born on March 17 of this year, into the death of our Lord, with the name Dorothea.

Following this, several Indian brethren and sisters came to Br. Christian to dictate their letters to him that they want to write to the brethren and sisters in Bethlehem and Gnadenhütten; several brethren came to Brother Rundt and did the same.

Today Br. Gottlieb went out with handmade utensils; *item* Br. Samuel in the afternoon, who, however, returned home this very night.

One of our friends from the Oblong, named James Allworth,[44] visited us, bringing a letter from there for the congregation, which he delivered to Br. Christian, returning thither soon after.

Br. Christian conducted the evening occasion.

♂ [Tuesday], the 20th

Immediately after the morning blessing, Br. Christian and Brother and Sister Jungmann had to speak with and agree upon the one or another matter with several of the brethren and sisters.

We wrote to our dear brethren and sisters in Bethlehem. Our Indian brethren began planting their Welsh corn over the course of these days and were very industrious at that. We had an acre of old land plowed today.

Our dear Br. Christian prepared for departure along with his companion.

During a general occasion in the evening, took ~~David's son, called Wawampékum, and his wife, Johanna's daughter, called Salome, were baptized by Br. Christian into the death of the Savior; the first with the name Johannes, and she with the name Zipporah.~~[45]

Immediately afterward, there was, moreover, a separate occasion for all of the baptized brethren and sisters, in the course of which David's son, otherwise called Wawampékum, and his wife, Johanna's daughter, otherwise called Salome, were baptized by Br. Christian into the death of the Savior. He received the name Johannes and she the name Zipporah.

As soon as the newly baptized were led from the meeting by Br. Jungmann and his wife, Br. Christian proposed to the brethren and sisters his intention, to wit, to divide the brethren and sisters into small fellowships, or *Banden*,[46] including their purpose, and the hopefully resulting advantage, benefit, and blessing of these *Banden*, collectively as well as for each one individually. Thereupon he read aloud the names of the brethren and sisters and their grouping.[47]

Finally, we white brethren and sisters yet enjoyed the blessed meal of the Lord. And in the course of this feast of the body and [of the] blessed drink from the wounds, we submitted anew [our] hearts and hands to our precious Lord, and pledged ourselves to remain His faithful souls until the end.

☿ [Wednesday], the 21st

During the morning blessing Br. Christian still baptized the son[d] of Anna and Paschqua into the death of Jesus by the name of Ludwig. And then he [Br. Christian] fell upon his knees and prayed in the German language, recommending the entire small brown flock of this place in the most supplicating manner to the heart and precious wounds of our Lamb of God.

Pachgatgoch *Diarium*, from
May 21 to August 3, inclusive, 1755.

☿ [Wednesday], the 21st

Shortly after the morning blessing, having taken a tender leave of us and all the Indian brethren and sisters and children, our dear Br. Christian Seidel, along with his companion Br. Wilhelm Böhler, went back to Bethlehem by way of New York. Br. Jungmann, Rundt, and the Indian Brother Joshua accompanied them for several miles, and then the first two turned back. We gave thanks to the Savior for this visit and for all the grace that He granted us since the presence of Br. Christian among us.

Immediately afterward, we began planting corn on our old land.

During the evening occasion the Indian brethren and sisters were once again saluted from Br. Christian, and then they were warmly reminded to preserve well in their hearts everything that they have heard, felt, and enjoyed in the course of these days.

♃ [Thursday], the 22nd and ♀ [Friday], the 23rd

Both days were spent quietly by us and the Indian brethren and sisters with field and garden work. On the first evening following the occasion, Br. Samuel visited us for a short hour and Br. Joshua did the same on the second.

♄ [Saturday], the 24th

Br. Rundt rode on horseback to the mill several miles from here, and Brother and Sister Jungmann went visiting in the winter huts.

At the meeting in the evening, Phil. 1.6, *I am confident of this very thing, that he which hath begun a good Work in you, will perform it* &c., was discussed and applied to our baptized brethren and sisters, as well as the good work which the Savior has begun also in them, and has continued up to this point.

☉ [Sunday], the 25th

The sermon took place at the usual time, on 2 Tim. 1.12, *I Know, whom I have believed* &c., and the meeting was attended by many.

569

Immediately after the midday meal the *Banden*, such as had been established here by Br. Christian before his departure, were begun with all of the baptized brethren and sisters, in the name of the Savior. We felt well on this occasion; the brethren and sisters were upright and openhearted with one another, and in part quite glad about this opportunity. And we had but one wish: that the Savior may continue to further guide them in this simple and affectionate direction, and [that] He may make ever more clear and weighty to them the reality and the blessedness of this occasion.

Next Br. Jungmann conducted the children's meeting.

Afterward, we were paid a visit by several brethren and sisters. In particular, those who live in the winter huts reported that they all wanted to go fishing in New Milford this coming week. We recommended to them the close communion with the Savior, who can and will preserve and bless their souls everywhere.

In the evening there was also a general singing service.

☽ [Monday], the 26th

During the early occasion it was discussed that the Savior had made the particular promise to His people, and to each and every soul that belongs to Him, that He Himself wanted to protect and preserve them from evil, from sin, and [from the] world, and that no one can, nor shall, tear His souls from out of His hands, as long as they stay well at home inside His wounds.

In the afternoon the *merchant* from Kent, a European Jew, who speaks German well, having settled there not long ago, called on us with 3 unmarried English women from our neighborhood.⁴⁸ Brother and Sister Jungmann led them round at this place and into the Indian huts. They had a mind to attend our evening meeting, but it was a bit too late for them.

In the evening Phil. 3.1, *To preach the same things to you, to me indeed, is not grievous, but for you it is safe*, was spoken about; the Savior let Himself be especially felt with His nearness.

♂ [Tuesday], the 27th

Br. Christian with his family, also Br. Samuel with his, [as well as] Br. Joshua and his wife, and many more brethren and sisters went out today, the majority to New Milford to fish.

☿ [Wednesday], the 28th

At an early hour today's name of the Savior was talked about a bit: *He is the Prince of the Kings of the Earth*.

Because today everyone of this place went to New Milford, except for 2 brethren and about 3 sisters, Br. Rundt set out as well, following his parishioners and school children to that place. Just as he arrived there the brethren were making a catch of some 80 *shet* [shad] fish.

♃ [Thursday], the 29th

They did the same, but got only half as many, because it was cold and the water had risen owing to the heavy rains. As for the rest, the brethren and sisters were quiet, orderly, and made brooms and other pieces of work besides.

After sunset Br. Rundt conducted the occasion for them; Br. Joshua interpreted. The brethren and sisters sat on the elevation next to the *river*, on the green grass by the road, in rows, as is usual otherwise. About 4 people from the nearest houses, who have been coming toward evening to visit the Indian brethren and sisters and observe their economy, sat down with them and listened *attent[ively]*. The orderly and quiet manner of the old and young during the meeting had quite impressed them. [*Lines crossed out*]

♀ [Friday], the 30th

Because the fish catch did not yield much, several of our Indian brethren went to the white people to work. Others changed their place, and Br. Rundt and Gideon went back home. During these 2 days Br. Jungmann had delivered the evening and morning blessing for the few brethren and sisters and children there [at Pachgatgoch]. Also, throughout yesterday afternoon Brother and Sister Jungmann had one of our nearest neighbors for a visit, along with his wife.

Tonight another one of our nearest neighbors, whose wife had given birth, requested through a messenger that Sr. Jungmann come to him, and at the same time sent along a horse for her.

She had her reasons to decline this errand; went there, however, early on [Saturday], the 31st, together with her husband. Afterward, Br. Jungmann continued on as far as 10 miles from here on account of other business, returning home in the afternoon.

Last night we had such a hard hoarfrost that it caused most of the field and garden plants that were already above ground to freeze. Even the foliage on many trees looked as if it had been burned off by fire.[49]

Br. Joshua, Samuel, and Martin, with their families, as well as Salomon, Sr. Thamar, Johanna, and Caritas, came home before the evening occasion today.

Julius

☉ [Sunday], the 1st

The sermon was on Jn. 14.19: *Because I live ye shall live also.* Afterward, the *Banden* were held with the few brethren and sisters who were at home, and immediately thereafter the children's meeting [was held].

During the evening occasion a Bible lesson was read aloud to the brethren and sisters, namely, the 5th chapter from Ephesians as far as to the 4th v[erse] of the 6th chapter. Thereupon we again fell upon our knees, and by means of a supplicating prayer, Br. Rundt recommended the entire small brown flock of this place, those absent and present, baptized and unbaptized, to the care of the beloved, faithful, and wounded heart of our Lord and Savior, whose nearness could be felt among us.

☽ [Monday], the 2nd

We used [this day] to haul wood to this place for our use.

♂ [Tuesday], the 3rd

Br. Joshua, with his eldest son, and Br. Gottlieb went out into the woods today. Br. Jungmann went to the winter huts, for we had heard that several brethren had returned home from Milford; yet they were going back there right away. In the evening Col. 3.11 was spoken about: *Christ is all, & in all.*

☿ [Wednesday], the 4th

Br. Samuel and Martin went out today but returned before the evening occasion, for which we had the 16th verse from Ψ [Psalms] 66 for our blessed reflection: *Come & hear, all ye that love God, & I will declare what he hath done for my Soul.*

♃ [Thursday], the 5th

At the morning blessing we reflected on the words of our Savior: *Without me, ye can do nothing.*

Br. Joshua returned home with his son today. In the evening a Bible lesson from the Savior's sermon on the mountain was read aloud to the brethren and sisters.

♀ [Friday], the 6th

Br. Gottlieb, as well as Johannes and his Zipporah, came home today.

Br. Rundt went to the mill several miles from here and had corn milled.

During the evening occasion 1 Jn. 5.18 was discussed: *He that is begotten of god, Keepeth himself, & that [sic] Wicked One toucheth him not.*

♄ [Saturday], the 7th

At the morning blessing the 95th psalm, from which today's name of the Savior was taken, was read aloud up to the 7th verse. Hereafter, our King's virtue and power of love, which led Him from God's throne down to the cross, was celebrated in song, with deep feeling.

We used this day today in particular to do work in the garden; also had an acre of old land plowed for our use, to be sown with buckwheat.[50]

This week school was continued with the children as usual, even though hardly half of them are at home.

☉ [Sunday], the 8th

During the regular sermon the summary content of the 2nd chapter [of the letter] to the Ephesians was considered and applied for our edification.

The *Banden* were held with those brethren and sisters who are at home, with blessing.

Next Br. Jungmann conducted the children's meeting, and in the evening we also had a blessed meeting.

☽ [Monday], the 9th

Br. Jonathan came home from Milford with his wife. During the evening occasion 1 Cor. 1.18 was discussed, about how powerful the word of the cross is to those who are becoming blessed, but folly to those who are perishing.[51]

♂ [Tuesday], the 10th

Today we hoed the Welsh corn on our new land. The Indian brethren and sisters who were at home and had time helped us with it, and we fed them in return.

☿ [Wednesday], the 11th

Yesterday during the evening occasion, as well as early today at the morning blessing, it was discussed, according to Rom. 5, that just as sin and death came into this world through the first man's transgression and spread to all men, so too reign righteousness and eternal life through the gracious death of the one man, which will be experienced and enjoyed by all those who believe in Him and are in Him. Sr. Jungmann was called to a woman in our neighborhood who was in the process of delivering.

♃ [Thursday], the 12th

Having held school, Br. Rundt went to the mill 10 miles from here, and while there, [he] took care of several other matters concerning our house economy. He returned home in the evening.

♀ [Friday], the 13th

At the morning blessing it was demonstrated [to the brethren and sisters] that actions of God's children are done in God, for they are never alone, but the Savior lives and moves in them, and they in Him, and that none of them, having his wits about him, could allow sin the slightest liberty over him, not even in thought.

Br. Gideon went to Sharon, and Samuel to New Milford.

♄ [Saturday], the 14th

Most all of our Indian brethren and sisters, who until now had been at the falls near New Milford for fishing, returned home, as did Br. Gideon and Samuel. Today we learned that Christian, Gottliebe's husband, let himself be recruited into English service and took enlisting money; this happened in New Milford.

In the afternoon Brother and Sister Jungmann went to visit some of our nearest neighbors.

☉ [Sunday], the 15th

The regular sermon was on Heb. 2.14, 15: *As the Children are Partakers of Flesh & Blood; he also himself likewise took part of the same, &c.*

Because several of our Indian brethren and sisters from the winter huts had not come up for the sermon, Br. Jungmann went there to visit them right after the meal.

Then the *Banden* were held amid the feeling of our Lord's nearness, and immediately thereafter the children's meeting.

We were visited by several brethren.

During the evening occasion the church litany was recited in prayer, and with that, this day was blessedly brought to a close.

☽ [Monday], the 16th

Today our Indian brethren together built a new house for old Simon.

Sisters Elisabeth and Thamar went to the seaside.

♂ [Tuesday], the 17th

Several sisters again went to New Milford, such as Salome, Benigna, p[p]. The remaining brethren and sisters jointly started to hoe their corn, and we, likewise, busied ourselves in the field during these days.

The minister of Kent [Cyrus Marsh] called on us for a little while, and was very courteous and amicable.

Today, Brother and Sister Jungmann especially remembered the birthday of their youngest son^d, Johann Jacob, and we sang him a few verses in the course of a small love feast.

In the evening we in particular felt the nearness of our Lamb^d of God when discussing the verse: *In the same Form to me appear, wherein-Thou-to Death thyself didst bleed.*

[*No entry for the 18th*]

♃ [Thursday], the 19th

Venemo's wife came home to this place, along with several of her relatives, *item* David with his family, and Sr. Magdalena, Gottlieb's wife, with her children, who all had been away until now.

575

Brother and Sister Jungmann spoke with Venemo's wife, pitying her loss that she had brought on herself by leaving here and [by] separating from her husband. Before Br. Christian Seidel's arrival she, along with her husband, had the desire to be baptized, but now he has again joyfully given himself wholly to sin; [he] has, moreover, taken another wife.

♀ [Friday], the 20th

Today Brother and Sister Jungmann paid a visit to several of our neighbors; the girls' school was therefore suspended.

During the evening occasion the verse *Grant, o Christ! thou Son of god — that we always weigh the Cause of thy Death & Suff'ring &c.* made for the opportunity to speak, with a blessing for our hearts, about the death of our Lord and its cause.

♄ [Saturday], the 21st

Brother and Sister Jungmann went visiting in the winter huts. Magdalena, Gottlieb's wife, and Sarah were issued warm and earnest reminders about a number of things that they have been heard saying, and both were put in touch with their hearts. Venemo came here with his 2nd wife to live in the winter huts.

In the evening the close and near *connexion* [connection] was discussed, [one] that each heart needed to have and maintain especially with the Savior if it wanted to feel [nothing] but blessed, have the peace of God within itself, and remain preserved from sin.

☉ [Sunday], the 22nd

The sermon was on 1 Tim. 2.4,5,6, *God our Savr. will have all Men to be saved &c.*, about the redemption that was brought about through Jesus and of what it consists; beforehand the church litany was prayed. One of our neighbors, who had never before attended our meeting, was present for it.

Many requests for medicine are being made to us by English people — and whether a doctor was going to come here again soon — like now, just before the sermon, when someone in quite a hurry came to ask for medicine.

The *Banden* and children's meeting afterward went on as usual. Because Sarah has been stirring up bad quarrels for several weeks, and especially yesterday, between her children and [her] sister's children, baptized as well as unbaptized, also having drawn her husband Abraham into it, there first came [to us] in the afternoon Brothers Joshua and Samuel, by their own painful impulse. And afterward, prompted by them, [there] came with them Brothers Gideon, Martin, and Jeremias, along with Sr. Elisabeth, for the same reason, inquiring about our thoughts [regarding this matter] and what was to be done. We conferred on this, and it was agreed that Brother and Sister Jungmann, along with Br. Gideon and Joshua, should go to her [Sarah] tomorrow and ask her, in the name of the Savior and [of] the brethren and sisters of this place, if she intended to submit herself wholly to sin and sacrifice herself to the enemy, or if she wanted to be the Savior's to whom she lawfully belonged. Her acting the hypocrite, looking for excuses, and apologizing were loathsome to all of the brethren and sisters here. Moreover, David as well as Leah are to be spoken with warmly and severely about the state of their hearts.

In the evening there was still the singing service, which was concluded with a short prayer to our only Lord and Head.

☽ [Monday], the 23rd

After the morning blessing the aforementioned brethren and sisters went to the winter huts and carried out their commission. Sarah wept about herself, and the other ones also admitted the poor condition of their hearts, wishing to be freed from it.

Today the Indian brethren and sisters finished hoeing their Welsh corn, [a task] in which they have been jointly engaged every day until now.

At the evening meeting it was discussed that every faithful child of God neither could, nor should, let these 2 considerations leave his heart: 1) I am a poor sinner, a fallen person, I have sin and misery in and about me, [and] I can no longer rely upon myself in the least; but 2), I am atoned, I am a redeemed and saved sinner, much was forgiven me, [and] now I am able to love a great deal. He to whom I lawfully belong, [and] who ransomed me, shall have me wholly as His own, just the way I am. He can, wants to, and will preserve me in a state of blessedness.

♂ [Tuesday], the 24th

Christian, Gottliebe's husband, went to Woodbury today, to his [militia] captain. He had received from him several days leave to come here in order to hoe his Welsh corn, and so he did. We spoke with him with affection. However, he is dry in his heart and fearful of us, so much so that indeed he cannot be gotten into our house. His wife and children are staying here for the time being.

In the evening the example, based on Lk. 10, 38–42, of Mary, who had chosen the good portion, was reflected upon with blessing.

☿ [Wednesday], the 25th

Br. Martin and his wife went out to Sharon for a couple of days, as did Philippus and his wife, and Benigna, Simon's daughter, to sell their handiwork there.

Today's text was discussed during the evening occasion.

♃ [Thursday], the 26th

Old Erdmuth and Salome went to the area of Shekomeko today.[52]

Br. Rundt visited the few brethren and sisters who were at home in the winter huts, reminding them of what the Savior has done for and affected in them. Old Abraham had gone to Woodbury with his Sarah, where they will stay for a couple of weeks, for they have nothing more to eat here. On the whole our Indian brethren and sisters are having a difficult time now because victuals are very expensive and scarce here and they have nothing more stored.

Br. Martin and his Justina returned home, it[em] old Erdmuth.

[No entry for the 27th]

♄ [Saturday], the 28th

Right after the morning blessing Br. Jungmann went 10 miles from here with some handiwork [he had] made from pine, taking it to several of our acquaintances there who had ordered it from him. At the same time he had visited several of our Indian sisters, as well as some of the unbaptized from here, who had pitched their huts in the woods along the way and were working. He returned home in the evening.

Venemo's first wife, along with her mother (a widow baptized by the Presbyterians) and several more of her unbaptized relatives, moved up here from the winter huts, for they had been treated there very badly by Sarah and her family.

In the evening the verse *O dearest Savr. might my Heart be quite giv'n up to Thee! O might it, to be always Thine, my highest Pleasure be!* was discussed.

☉ [Sunday], the 29th

The sermon was delivered on Is. 35.4: *Behold, your God will come, he will come and save you.* Eight persons from our neighborhood, who had never before attended the meeting of the brethren, joined in.

The *Banden* and [the] children's meeting were in the afternoon, as usual, and the brethren and sisters were visited in their houses.

During the evening occasion the church litany was prayed.

☽ [Monday], the 30th

Following the morning blessing Petrus went with his Thamar to the area of Stissing to work there. We had already yesterday shared some food with them, for they had nothing at all, and so it happens sometimes that we have to help out the brethren and sisters with food for half or whole days.[53] Br. Samuel with his family, likewise Br. Gideon, went out as well, about 10 miles from here; those mentioned first intend to work there in the woods this week. The German Jew from Kent, a *merchand* [merchant], along with several women from our neighborhood, visited Brother and Sister Jungmann.

Julius.

☿ [Wednesday], the 2nd

Br. Gideon came home and gave us greetings from our brethren and sisters who are working together in the woods in the area on the way to Sharon.

Brother Jungmann tilled a piece of land of 5/4 acres, and sowed it with buckwheat.

The few brethren and sisters who were at home here were industrious and tended their corn.

Today an Indian (it was the brother of David's wife) came from Stockbridge with a *String of Wampum* as a messenger from the Indians there. He reported to Br. Gideon, calling for all of the adult men of this place to go there within 6 days and hear their *propositiones* concerning the present war situation. They would have a conference about this with all of the Indians living in these parts. Moreover, a messenger is to go immediately from here to Potatuck, and to the Indians in the Highlands, and relate there the same [message]. Even before we

579

knew anything about the arrival of the foreign Indian, Br. Gideon had sent Br. Martin to Potatuck.

Br. Rundt rode on horseback to the mill 5 miles from here, and at the same time went visiting in the winter huts, where the foreign Indian was lodging with his sister [Rebecca] today.

He [the foreign Indian] was also present at the evening occasion, in the course of which 1 Jn. 5.18 was discussed: *Whosoever is born of God sinneth not.*

♃ [Thursday], the 3rd

The foreign Indian went back to Stockbridge in the morning. Lucas went to the Indians in the Highlands.

Our Indian brethren and sisters who have been away until now all came home today, prompted by a messenger sent to them by Br. Gideon.

In the evening, according to the text Col. 3.17, *Whatsoever ye do in Word or deed do all in the Name of the Lord Jesus,* it was said that the unspiritual people who neither knew nor loved the Savior, and were slaves to sin, were able to do anything they longed for or that came to their minds. This, however, was very different with the child of God, who was freed from sin through Jesus' blood. That [child] had a very different nature. Its heart, mind, thoughts, intentions, and actions, in small as well as in large matters, were at all times focused on the Savior and His heart, mind, will, word, and example. At every undertaking it [the child of God] would first inquire if this was the Savior's will; was he able to execute this or that affair in His name; would the Savior advise him to that end if He were to stand there in person, p[p].?

♀ [Friday], the 4th

Even before our Indian brethren agreed among themselves which one of them was to go to Stockbridge, both of us brethren spoke with Br. Joshua, reminding him that in their conference to be held, he is to earnestly point out to our Indian brethren to be sure to be very careful, and not undertake or agree to anything that went, even in the least, counter to the King of England, as our overlord, or [against] the *governement* here. We were even worried about their merely going up to Stockbridge, for we had learned that last winter our Indians had been forbidden by the *governement* here to go to Stockbridge. Br. Joshua replied [that] they too had already thought about this and would continue to do so. He thought that they would report to the nearest *justice of* [the] *peace*, to point out their intentions to him, and [to] hear his thoughts on this, which satisfied us.

During these days, both of us brethren again hoed our Welsh corn and other garden fruits.

In the evening the story from Lk. 7, about the woman who, in the Pharisee's house, anointed the Savior with ointment and wept over His feet, was read to the brethren and sisters, and the heart, love, urge, as well as the sinnerlike feelings that were present in this woman were wished unto them.

♄ [Saturday], the 5th

Brother and Sister Jungmann went visiting in the winter huts but found only 2 sisters at home. They had most affectionately spoken with Leah, who came right out and said [that] her heart had been in a bad state before, even before she was caught up in the most recent quarrel between her mother and her brother's wife.

At the evening occasion the brethren and sisters were put in mind of the various manifestations of grace, [the] blessing, [the] faithfulness, and [the] acts of kindness by the Savior that we have experienced here together throughout an entire week, spiritual and physical, inward and outward, not to mention that which each one experiences separately for himself. Moreover, their hearts were encouraged to henceforth show humbleness, gratitude, thankfulness, love, and complete surrender to Him.

☉ [Sunday], the 6th

At the sermon, it was demonstrated—guided by the summary content of the 6th chapter [of the letter] to the Romans—that all men were from the start sinners by nature, and had participated in the fall of the first man. [Moreover,] that all of those who did not want to accept the redemption in Jesus' blood, secretly or openly, necessarily remain slaves to sin, have Satan as their lord and master, and ultimately would have to expect their reward from him [Satan]. However, that the children of God, who through grace were freed from sin in the blood of Jesus, have sin to be sure, yet they do not let sin rule inside their mortal bodies;

instead, they live by the will of Him who died and rose for them, and in the end inherit the gift of God—eternal life.

Right after the meal were the *Banden*. Br. Gideon felt uncomfortable that he had accepted the message from Stockbridge and had entered into a promise with the Indians at that place to send there several persons from here. He had simply been in too much of a hurry, and had not told us anything about it, and now that he was conferring with his brethren, no one wanted to go up. Brother Jungmann later conducted the children's meeting, and in the evening there was also a singing service.

☽ [Monday], the 7th

Immediately after the morning blessing Br. Gideon and Salomon reported that they would go to Stockbridge now. We recommended them to our Savior's guidance and preservation, and reminded them once again not to pass by the *justice* in Kent but to properly report to him. Br. Gideon requested from Brother Rundt a letter for the *justice*, but he [Rundt] was not able to grant him his request, for he did not want to meddle in this affair at all, not even from afar.

After school Br. Rundt rode on horseback 10 miles from here to get some provisions for us. Today our Indian brethren and sisters helped us hoe our Welsh corn on our new land, and we fed them in return.

Old Erdmuth went to Potatuck to visit her brother, and several other sisters went some miles from here, wanting to work there.

[*No entry for the 8th*]

☿ [Wednesday], the 9th

The Indian brethren and sisters again set about [tending] their corn, hoeing it. This year it very much looks like there will be a plentiful harvest.

In the afternoon we had visitors from our neighborhood, a woman with several of her children. Today a general day of fasting was observed in this *government* on account of the present war situation.[54] They say that the *gouverneur* of here [this province] took to the field in person.

♃ [Thursday], the 10th

Br. Jungmann delivered the morning blessing, and immediately afterward, David left from here for Danbury, along with his Rebecca and his children, where they intend to stay for a while to earn something to satisfy their needs.

[No entry for the 11th]

♄ [Saturday], the 12th

Sr. Elisabeth, Joshua's wife, was delivered of a daughter[d] last night.

In the afternoon Brother and Sister Jungmann went visiting in the winter huts but found only 3 brethren and sisters at home. Meanwhile, Br. Rundt was visited by several brethren and had the opportunity to especially speak with Petrus openly, thoroughly, and with much compassion about the present poor state of his heart. Old Sr. Erdmuth came home.

☉ [Sunday], the 13th

The sermon was on Jn. 1.41, *We have found the Christ*, about the threefold office of our Anointed One. An English woman [from] about 3 miles from here was present as well, along with some of her children, it[em] a foreign Indian family.

The *Banden* for the brethren were held after the meal by Br. Rundt; the ones for the sisters were suspended because of the foreign family that stayed with us until about evening.

Then the children's meeting was held by him [Rundt], and this day was concluded with a singing service.

☽ [Monday], the 14th

During the morning blessing it was rather concernedly recommended to the brethren and sisters to stay also during this week quite close to the Savior with their hearts, cleave to His wounds, avail themselves of His spirit's teachings and reminders, and generally, to mix the Savior into all of their affairs and outside work. Immediately thereafter most of the brethren and sisters left; the brethren in order to work here and there, and the sisters to pick blueberries.[55] They have now finished hoeing their Welsh corn.

These days we frequently thought of Br. Gideon and Solomon who had gone to Stockbridge and have already been gone for several more days than they had expected.

[No entry for the 15th]

☿ [Wednesday], the 16th

At the morning blessing it was discussed that it was the purpose of our creation and redemption, and [that it] was [for the benefit of] our own blessedness, that we cleave to the Lord and live by His will.

The Indian children, big and small, were fed by us today, for they had helped us carry to this place the clay to build a new fireplace in our meeting house.

From Br. Gideon, who came home yesterday (Salomon had to lay by on the way and came only today), we learned that the Indians in Stockbridge had neither approached nor agreed upon anything special with him; they had merely asked that our Indian men go up to them and let themselves be used as soldiers in the present situation, to which he was not able to consent. They are living in a state of insecurity in that area, and white people as well as Indians are keeping watch night and day. They say [that] the French Indians have already committed violent acts in those parts as well, and have even killed people.

Yesterday and today Brother and Sister Jungmann had visitors from our neighborhood.

The participation in another man's sins was spoken about during the evening meeting.

Immediately afterward, we spoke with Br. Gideon and Joshua, urgently requesting that they assist us and not tolerate old Indian practices and abominations to again appear out in the open here in Schaghticoke. We had learned that Priscilla, against all admonitions and [her] better sense, had again brought rom [rum] here in order to entertain with it the foreign Indians who she was expecting at this place. They [Gideon and Joshua] promised to do so. Indeed, Br. Gideon issued her a reminder later on; however, she showed herself obstinate and voiced threats.[56]

♃ [Thursday], the 17th

Christian came here again with his family, with the permission of his captain, to hoe his Welsh corn for the 2nd time.

♀ [Friday], the 18th

On the days of this week Br. Jungmann worked on our new fireplace,[57] and today several Indian brethren helped him with it, who we fed in return.

In the evening the words *Keep Jesus Chr. in Remembrance* were discussed, and this reminder of the apostle was, in the most moving manner, committed to the care of the brethren and sisters.

♄ [Saturday], the 19th

Br. Martin, who for most of the week had worked in the neighborhood helping with the wheat harvest, came home today, whereas Br. Jeremias went to New Fairfield. The other brethren, who had worked for the English people in the nearby area, had come home previously in the course of this week. Abraham and his Sarah also returned home from Woodbury.

☉ [Sunday], the 20th

The regular sermon was delivered on Jn. 3.18, 19, *He that believeth on* [sic] *him, is not condemned &c.*, at which time the true form and nature of a believer and a nonbeliever were demonstrated. First, witness was borne against the false presumption that one could be a believer today, tomorrow a slave to sin, the next day once again a believer, and could continue in that way. Because we ran out of time, the 2nd part was postponed until the evening occasion.

Afterward, at the regular time, the *Banden* for the brethren and [for the] sisters, as well as the children's meeting, were as usual. During the last mentioned [occasion], *Thy Blood-Sweat dear Savr. rain on her like Water &c.* was sung for Br. Joshua's little daughter[d], who his wife brought to the children's meeting today for the first time.

In addition, the brethren and sisters were visited separately in their houses by Br. Jungmann. Brother and Sister Jungmann remembered the birthday of their son[d] Johannes today.

☽ [Monday], the 21st

The morning blessing was delivered quite early, for immediately afterward, most of the brethren went to work in the neighborhood here and there, gathering in the crop.

Christian with his family went back to Woodbury, to his [militia] *compagnie*.

A couple of English men came here to inquire whether some Indians would like to have themselves recruited as soldiers. [They] also had asked Br. Jungmann about it, whom they met, but none of our adult menfolk was at home.

♂ [Tuesday], the 22nd

In the morning our brethren again went to work where they had been yesterday. They always return home before the occasion in the evening.

During the evening occasion Jn. 6.68, 69, *Lord, to whom shall we go: thou hast the Words of eternal Life* &c., was discussed; [that is,] that those hearts who believe and are in love with the Savior could not be removed from Him or His wounds till the end of time.

[*No entry for the 23rd*]

♃ [Thursday], the 24th

In the course of these days both of us brethren made a scanty supply of hay for the winter.

Br. Jeremias returned from New Fairfield.

Br. Rundt went to visit Abraham in the winter huts, who was found there all alone, and reminded him warmly of his baptism and of what the Savior had done for him on the cross. He feels uneasy at heart, for he committed a transgression after his baptism.[58] In the evening a lesson from the Bible, Phil. 2, was read aloud.

♀ [Friday], the 25th

Magdalena, the daughter of Lydia's sister, came here together with her husband Stephen but immediately left again. She did not want to engage with us at all, nor answer us.

Driven by his own conscience, Solomon has stayed away from all our meetings ever since his return from Stockbridge. He says he could not do as the other baptized Indians did, those who also get drunk and attend the meeting and go to Communion regardless.[59]

Br. Jeremias brought from New Milford, from a *justice of [the] peace* there, for our Indians here, a copy of the response and *resolution* of the *General Assembly of Connecticut* concerning their [the Indians'] demonstration and request made to them in the month of May, 3 years ago, for additional land for their own use. In it 1 1/2 lot are granted them with these words, to wit: *[F]or their Improvement & for the Cutting of Wood & Timber for their own Use only — during the Pleasure of this Assembly.* The copy was signed by the *secretair* [secretary] of the *Gen. Assembly* by the name of George Wyllys. (The copy *in extenso vid.* [Latin: see at full length] in the enclosure.)[60]

♄ [Saturday], the 26th

Brother and Sister Jungmann went for a visit in our neighborhood.

Brothers Martin, Jeremias, and Samuel have several times before expressed to us that they had a mind to pay a visit to Bethlehem as soon as their circumstances at home allowed it. We do not want to either encourage or discourage them in this regard.

Occasioned by the verse *Stream thro' the Bottom of my Soul Blood of the Son of God* &c., the all-seductive, invigorating, sanctifying, and strengthening power of Jesus' precious blood was discussed at the evening meeting.

(Belonging to the 25th of July.)

*At a General assembly holden at Hardford in the Colony of Connecticut on the 2 Thursday of May Anno dom. 1752.**

Upon the Memorial of Gideon an Indian and Several other Indians living on the Country Lands on the West Side of Ousatunnik River at a Place called Scatacook Praying this assembly to Grant to them some Lands at or near said Scatacook for their Improvement and for Timber &c. Resolved by this Assembly that the said Indians the Memorialists shall have the Liberty and they have hereby Liberty Granted to them for their Improvement and for the Cutting of Wood and Timber for their own Use only, the whole of the Twenty fifth Lot as the Lots are now laid out and also the Equal half of the twenty fourth Lot on the Southward part thereof adjoining to said twenty-fifth Lot and this to be improved by said Indians as afore— said during the pleasure of this Assembly

A True copy of Record

Test George Wyllys Secretary

* This [line] and the last 2 lines were written in the secretary's own hand.

☉ [Sunday], the 27th

The sermon was delivered on Heb. 8.10, 11: *This is the Covenant that I will make with them, saith the Lord: I will put my Law into their Mind[s] — they shall be to me a People — all shall Know me, from the least to the greatest.* It was demonstrated that he who [word crossed out] was one of the people of God and could be called a Christian, a brother or sister, surely behaved himself in the same way He had walked on earth. He about whom this was found not to be so, still had an understanding with and a connection to Satan, the world, and sin. It was the inspiration and persuasion of the wicked enemy when baptized Indians thought [that] the white brethren and sisters were well able to attain the grace to be free from the domination of sin, but they, as born Indians, were not. A foreign Indian who understands English well also attended the sermon.

After the *Banden* had been held with the brethren and sisters, there was right away the children's meeting.

Afterward, all the baptized parents also gathered. Br. Rundt put them in mind of several matters in regard to their children, in a concerned and thorough manner.

Then Br. Jungmann went to the winter huts and visited old Abraham, who did not come to the sermon today. He found him somewhat sick.

In the evening there was still a singing service.

☽ [Monday], the 28th

Solomon again attended the occasions.

Most of our Indian brethren went out into the neighborhood to help the English people with their harvest, and through this earn a little for themselves until their Welsh corn is ripe. Moreover, they will not come home for several nights because it is too far.

At 8 o'clock in the morning our dear old Haber came from Rhinebeck, bringing us, to our particular joy, pleasant letters from Bethlehem from Br. Joseph [Spangenberg], Matthew [Hehl], p[p]., it[em] several *Gemeinnachrichten* from Pennsylvania, Greenland, Jamaica, etc. These had been given to him last Friday by Br. David Nitschmann who had come there by way of New York. He [Haber] went back in the afternoon, and through him Br. Rundt wrote to our friends there. Thereafter the latter [Rundt] went to the mill with my [his] corn, returning home before the evening occasion.[61] In the meantime, Brother and Sister Jungmann had been paid a visit by some women from our neighborhood.

It was a pity that because so few brethren were here, one was unable to pass on, still warm, the good tidings received by us to the brethren and sisters during the evening occasion. Meanwhile, most hearty greetings were passed on from the congregation, and the rest will be communicated to them little by little at a favorable opportunity. This will be surely quite a feast for them.

♂ [Tuesday], the 29th

Sr. Justina, Martin's wife, had declared herself to Sr. Jungmann in the following manner during these days: While picking blueberries in the woods, she reportedly conversed with her heart, and it became very apparent to her that her heart was indeed quite hungry and thirsty for Jesus' flesh and blood. (She meant the enjoyment in holy sacrament.) Thus she reportedly said further to the beloved Savior: Will it be much longer before we eat your flesh and drink your blood? Sometimes I indeed feel as if I could not stand it any longer. Several other sisters also had indicated their heartfelt longing for the holy sacrament.[62] Also, the majority of the sisters went out for several days today, some to the places where their husbands are working, some into the woods to procure a supply of rushes with which they weave mats, p[p].

[No entry for the 30th]

♃ [Thursday], the 31st

Br. Jungmann went 10 miles from here to get some provisions for us, returning home in due time.

Christian's wife, Gottliebe, came back here with her children; her husband is now on the march.[63]

Augustus

♀ [Friday], the 1st

Brother and Sister Jungmann went visiting in the winter huts; there were only 3 people at home.

♄ [Saturday], the 2nd

Our Indians returned home little by little. During the evening occasion the heart-felt greetings from Br. Joseph, Matthaeus [Hehl], etc., indeed, from the entire congregation in Bethlehem, were passed on to them; they were informed of the forthcoming *synodus* in Warwick,[64] and at the same time, it was announced that Br. Rundt will be departing for that place next Monday, on the 4th of this [month]. Then the reading of the *Memoirs from Bethlehem* was at once begun. The brethren and sisters were extremely pleased to hear about everything, especially this: that Br. Matthew [Hehl] had made arrangements in New York that, hence-forth, we may expect good tidings of this kind from there. In the end we sang *Lord Jesu, — did the whole Earth but feel thy Flame! O Kindle it in every Place thro' the good Tidings of Free Grace.*

☉ [Sunday], the 3rd

The reading of the Gem[ein] *Nachrichten* that we had received was continued, so that we completed everything in 4 sessions in the fore- and afternoon, to the special joy of all of the brethren and sisters. Having heard the *relation* from Jamaica, we sang *Think on our Brethren, Lord, who spread the Gospel Word, in Spirit free & bold, in Perils, Heat & Cold.*

At noon 4 people came here from New Fairfield. They had heard something about a new preacher here — they wanted to hear him. However, because the regular sermon was suspended today, they soon turned back to return home.

The children's meeting was held by Br. Jungmann at the usual time.

Several Indian brethren had short and heartfelt letters[d] written to Bethlehem. Upon his earnest request, Joshua was given permission to go to Bethlehem and to attend the *synodum*. He intends to leave here in a couple of days.

Toward evening there also was an occasion for all the baptized brethren and sisters, in the course of which Br. Rundt recommended them as a whole to the precious wounds of the Lamb, advising them to keep our eternal object of the heart inside their hearts and before their eyes for their blessing, life, advance-ment, and preservation. Thereupon the church litany was prayed. At the words *O Christ, Almighty god Have Mercy on us!* we fell on our knees and sang *The Son of Christ, p[p]*. With that Br. Rundt thus concluded our blessed day today and im-mediately thereafter took a particularly heartfelt and tender leave of all of the brethren and sisters.

Brother Jungmann's account about what occurred here in Schaghticoke in the month of August.[65]

August 4

In the morning Br. Rundt departed from here for Bethlehem by way of New York, to go from there to the *synodum* at Warwick. Soon after I delivered the morning blessing, in the course of which I reminded the brethren and sisters to frequently remember before the Savior the two of us, and Br. Rundt, as well as the *synodum* to be held by the Brethren this month. Today we were often visited by our Indian brethren and sisters and had heartfelt conversations with them. At the meeting in the evening I wished for them that they too may truly feel the Savior in their hearts as <u>their vital strength</u>.

The 5th

Br. Joshua left from here today for a visit to Bethlehem, and I went to Kent, on account of some business there. Old Sr. Erdmuth went with her daughter Martha to Potatuck, the former to visit her very old brother there.

The 6th

We were paid a visit by a doctor and a merchant, both English; they acted in very temperate manner, and in the end, took a friendly leave of us.

The 7th

After the morning blessing I visited the sick boy Gabriel, Caritas's son, who is baptized. He had a high fever, and in a dream during the night before, he had seen the Savior, which he later joyfully related to his grandmother [Thamar].

[No entry for the 8th]

♄ [Saturday], the 9th

After the morning blessing I went to the mill, 10 miles from here, returning home in the evening; and in the evening, by means of a heartfelt prayer, committed all of our brethren and sisters to the care of the faithful heart of the Savior.

☉ [Sunday], the 10th

In place of the sermon, I read the 1st chapter from John as far as the 30th verse. Later on a couple of people from the neighborhood came for the sermon, but soon went back home, for none was being held. In the afternoon I spoke with the children about the Savior's love for them.

☽ [Monday], the 11th

Today we were paid many visits by people who were passing through, who all acted courteously and in a temperate manner. Cap[tain] Marsh[66] inquired about many things in Bethlehem, and was *well satisfied* with our brief reply. At the evening meeting I spoke somewhat about the Savior's name for today, *Mein Gott! u. ward ein armer Mensch wie ich,*[67] [and] that no one may say this save he who has found forgiveness of his sins in Jesus' blood. And for becoming a poor human being, He is now to have our whole heart.

♂ [Tuesday], the 12th

After the morning blessing we went visiting the brethren and sisters in the huts. When later on I went into the woods to search for brushwood,[68] I found our mare there, dead. She had gotten her hind foot entangled in a wild vine, [so] that she had to die of hunger on the spot. Her foal perished along with her. This is quite a loss for our house, because here we have to get everything we need for running the household from afar; [we] have [it] far to the mill, and soon had intended to haul with her some wood for the winter to this place.

☿ [Wednesday], the 13th

At the morning blessing I once again put the brethren and sisters in mind of the *synodum*, which begins today, saying [that] they should please appeal to the Savior for a good blessing for our brethren and sisters at the *synod*[um]. The Savior liked to see us think of one another, especially on such occasions; they would get to enjoy it [the synod] as well. I went with my Anna to several of our neighbors, who love us and have repeatedly asked us to visit them.

[No entry for the 14th]

♀ [Friday], the 15th

At the morning blessing I read to the brethren and sisters the beautiful names of the Savior that we have enjoyed since the 11th, such as *Mein Gott[,] p[p], Lieber Vater[,] p[p], Du Meister meiner Jugend[,] p[p], Ach Bruder[,] p[p], Mein Lieber[,] p[p]*, and in the evening, from the 1st Epistle of Peter 1.18, 19, *Wißet daß ihr nicht mit vergänglichem Silber oder Gold erlöset seyd[,] p[p].*[69]

♄ [Saturday], the 16th

Today we learned that Salome, Jonathan's wife, was delivered of a child 20 miles from here, in the area of Danbury; also, that both mother and child had been close to going home [dying], but matters had now improved somewhat with the mother.

☉ [Sunday], the 17th

I read a little to the brethren and sisters from Matthew, chapter 18, and reminded them of how the Savior had searched for us as well, and had deceived us so as to be able to render us blessed. In the afternoon I told the children that the kingdom of heaven was theirs, and that the dear Savior had ransomed it for them with His blood; they shall be sure to come to love Him dearly. Because many brethren and sisters were not at home, the fellowships were suspended, and we visited the remaining ones [Indians] in their huts.

☽ [Monday], the 18th

Soon after the morning blessing Jonathan arrived with his wife, it[em] Priscilla, Gideon and his wife, and several others who had gone to Danbury, bringing with them Jonathan's child, who had gone home [died] there, to be buried here, which is what happened later.

♂ [Tuesday], the 19th

At the evening quarter-of-an-hour we reflected on the Savior's words on the cross: *Mich dürstet!*[70] I said these were such sweet words, that he whose heart was not immediately seized by this had to be as hard as stone in his heart. Br. Martin visited me afterward, with whom I carried on a blessed conversation about our Savior's death and sufferings. He said he had felt his heart to be quite soft during the quarter-of-an-hour.

593

☿ [Wednesday], the 20th

Today I visited Br. Jeremias and had the opportunity to speak with him about various matters. He declared himself most agreeably toward me. At the evening quarter-of-an-hour I demonstrated how a poor sinner always concerned himself with <u>himself</u> and cannot so occupy himself with his brother or sister that he would forget his own heart over this.

♃ [Thursday], the 21st

I and my Anna went to visit all of the brethren and sisters today, for nearly all of them were presently at home.

♀ [Friday], the 22nd

At the morning blessing we presented ourselves to our good Lord just the way we are, asking Him for His nearness on this day. We immediately felt that He was in our midst. Today one of our neighbors, who loves us, came to visit us from 5 miles away. In the evening I conducted a brief singing service[d]. A man from Kent was present for it, staying on with us afterward for another hour. He desired to read something from the speeches of our dear *Jünger*, and said he had read several before. I gave him the *Berlinische Reden*[71] to take with him.

♄ [Saturday], the 23rd

Today a *minister* from the high English church in New Milford called on us and inquired about various matters.[72] For example, if the *Moravians* were living here; if I was one; if I taught the Indians; where the *minister* was; if I did work from pine; where the worshipful[73] Gr. v. Z.[74] was presently; and so forth. He said he had been to London the past winter and had visited Lindsey House; it was a very beautiful house.[75] He acted in a temperate manner, in the end wishing me good luck and blessings, saying he believed we would not be among the people here without blessing.

☉ [Sunday], the 24th

At the meeting I spoke of the love that the father of our Lord had felt for us, that He gave His only son so that everyone who believed in Him was not lost, but had eternal life.

During the fellowships many brethren and sisters demonstrated a hunger for Holy Communion, for which we gave them fair hopes. Then the children's meeting took place, and in the evening we had yet a meeting, which was attended by many.

[*No entry for the 25th*]

♂ [Tuesday], the 26th

At the morning blessing I read to the brethren and sisters from Jn. 6, from v[erse] 47 to 54, and said, if one did not nourish himself daily with the Savior, eating His flesh and drinking His blood, one's heart would become sick, and in the end, would even have to die.

☿ [Wednesday], the 27th

At the early quarter-of-an-hour I discussed that the Savior loves His poor sinners so that He is unable to forget even a single one; they have cost Him too much, and His death and sufferings are yet fresh in His mind.

[*No entry for the 28th*]

♀ [Friday], the 29th

Today I went to the mill in Sharon,[76] and returned home in the evening and conducted the quarter-of-an-hour. Some time during the night our Br. Joshua arrived here with rather beautiful letters and tidings from Bethlehem, with which he delighted us a great deal. We gave thanks to our Savior for everything that He does, especially for His congregation, but also for the entire country.

♄ [Saturday], the 30th

Br. Gideon, who had been called to a sick person yesterday, returned home today, as did Solomon from his work, where he had gone last Monday.

☉ [Sunday], the 31st

At the meeting I spoke on the 1st verse from 1 Jn. 3: *Sehet, welch eine Liebe hat uns der Vater erzeigt, daß wir Gottes Kinder seyn sollen.*[77] Afterward, there were the children's meeting and the fellowships, as usual. During the latter we felt especially well, and the Savior was in our midst; our hearts felt it.

September

☽ [Monday], the 1st

At the morning blessing we most heartily appealed to the beloved Savior, that He take us anew into His wounds and preserve us there, also during this week. At 5 o'clock in the morning something of an earthquake could be felt at this place as well as in the surrounding area. Our house and our bedstead, p[p].[,] inside of it moved noticeably. At the same time something resembling a thunderstorm could be heard through the air.[78]

Br. Gideon and old Sr. Erdmuth went 4 miles from here to visit one of her sick relatives, returning home on [Tuesday], the 2nd. During the evening occasion a man from Kent, who knows the Brethren, was present.

☿ [Wednesday], the 3rd

At the morning blessing I talked about this as something that came to the mind of a child of God first thing in the morning: *O mein H[ei]land! laß mich doch deine Nähe diesen ganzen Tag fühlen. Sey mir doch in deinem Xzes-Bilde stets vor den Augen u. Herzen.*[79] And he who has this always feels afterward blessed and preserved for the entire day. I went to the winter huts to visit but found only Sr. Anna, Paschqua's wife, at home.

♃ [Thursday], the 4th

Our good Lord was very much near us during the morning blessing. Today many brethren went out on account of their business to New Milford, Kent, and into the woods.

In the evening, we availed ourselves of the description of the opening in Jesus' side for the benefit of our hearts, according to Jn. 19.34,35. *Der Seiten-Schrein, ist doch unser liebstes Pläzelein.*[80]

♀ [Friday], the 5th

Br. Gideon returned home. In the evening I spoke about the election by grace that we have found in His blood for so many other 1,000 people, and reminded our Indian brethren and sisters to realize the importance of belonging to the Savior's church, being permitted to know the Savior and to love Him.

Pachgatgoch *diarium*, from
September 7 to October 6, 1755.[81]

Sunday, the 7th [September]

Very early in the morning Br. Rundt arrived here at our place from Bethlehem with letters from Br. Joseph, and other brethren and sisters there, which were quite pleasing to us. Right away he was warmly welcomed by our Indian brethren and sisters, and children.

He delivered the sermon at the usual time, and afterward read aloud Br. Christian's letter that he had written to the Indian brethren and sisters here. Next he conducted the other occasions, and visited all the brethren and sisters in their huts.

☽ [Monday], the 8th

The school children quite rejoiced that their school was resumed today.

[No entry for the 9th]

☿ [Wednesday], the 10th

Our Br. Martin departed from here for a visit to the congregation in Bethlehem, of which he has heard and enjoyed so much, yet which [he] has never seen before. At the morning blessing we sang for him *In Thy Five holy Wounds so wide let Him as in his Rock-holes hide &c.*, and gave him several letters for our dear brethren and sisters in Bethlehem.

Because the weather was rather warm these days, our Indian brethren and sisters prepared for themselves a supply of sweet corn for winter. We did the same.

Throughout this week we heard one kind of intelligence after the other that a large number of the menfolk from our neighborhood have been ordered by the authorities to come to Albany right away, thence to be used in current military operations. We were sincerely grateful to our dear heavenly Father for the outward peace and quiet we have been able to enjoy here thus far, for the sake of His son and His cause.

♄ [Saturday], the 13th

Brother and Sister Jungmann went visiting in the winter huts but found few brethren and sisters at home.

☉ [Sunday], the 14th

During the regular sermon, according to 1 Tim. 3.16, *Great is the Mystery of Godliness: God was manifested in the flesh*, the main reason for God to appear in the flesh, that is, to reconcile the world to Himself, was reflected upon.

At the *Banden* in the afternoon, several brethren and sisters expressed their deep longing for Holy Communion.

[*No entry for the 15th*]

♂ [Tuesday], the 16th

At an early hour today's name of the Savior, *He is thy Lord*, and in the evening the word of the Savior, *All the Churches shall Know Me*, were discussed some.

[*No entry for the 17th*]

♃ [Thursday], the 18th

Three English recruiters came here. They inquired in all of the Indian huts whether anyone wanted to let himself be enlisted to go up to Crown Point; however, they found no one willing to do so.

Today there was again a general day of prayer and fasting in this *governement*, on account of the present war situation.

♀ [Friday], the 19th

Today the two Indians, Moses and Johannes, departed from here for Crown Point, for the war. They had allowed themselves to be recruited as soldiers somewhere in Newtown, and last night lodged at this place.

♄ [Saturday], the 20th

At the morning blessing, with blessing for our hearts, we reflected upon the Savior as the only shepherd for the multitudes ransomed with [His] blood.

Several brethren and sisters who had left for a couple of days with crafted wooden utensils to sell returned home in good spirits today.

☉ [Sunday], the 21st

The sermon was on Jn. 1.12, *As many as received him, to them gave he Power to become the Sons of God*. We especially felt our Savior's nearness at this time.

Br. Jungmann held the children's meeting. Later on the *Banden* were held with the brethren and sisters, and then we closed this day with a singing service.

[No entry for the 22nd]

♂ [Tuesday], the 23rd

Br. Gideon, who had gone to New Milford yesterday, returned home today. Brother and Sister Jungmann went into our neighborhood for a visit.

Lucas, who had been to the seaside, came home, at the same time bringing himself a wife from there.

In the evening it was discussed how blissful and happy one is in every situation, and throughout all changes in this life, if one stays quite close to the Savior's heart and remains in continual, uninterrupted communion with Him.

[No entry for the 24th]

♃ [Thursday], the 25th

This week our Indian brethren and sisters, and we as well, busied ourselves with harvesting several crops from the field. We in particular brought in our buckwheat, which turned out well.

In the evening we reflected upon the name of the Savior for today, *Er ist der große Prophete.*[82]

An unbaptized Indian and relative of old Sr. Erdmuth arrived here, who, based on his account, was recently wounded at Crown Point. He wants to stay here for a while until he has recovered.

[No entries for the 26th and 27th]

☉ [Sunday], the 28th

The sermon according to Is. 55.1–9 was delivered at the usual time. Several strangers from our neighborhood came and joined us, but only at its [the sermon's] closing.

At 2 o'clock in the afternoon, when the children's meeting was about to start, our dear Br. David Zeisberger arrived here completely unexpectedly and to our heartfelt joy, as well as that of the Indian brethren and sisters, bringing us pleasant letters and news from the congregation. He was immediately welcomed warmly by the Indian brethren and sisters and children, and soon after he went and visited them in all of the huts.

Br. David conducted the evening occasion, and at the same time, passed on to our small brown flock here the heartfelt greetings from the congregation in general, and from a number of brethren and sisters in particular.

Later on our dear Br. Joseph's letter to the communicant members concerning the forthcoming Holy Communion, p[p]., was read to them by Br. Rundt, and was listened to by them with a great deal of attention.

☽ [Monday], the 29th

Br. Jungmann delivered the morning blessing.

Thus far our Indian brethren and sisters have caught a large number of eels in this river, and we have been able to enjoy this along with them.

In the evening Br. David spoke about the undying blessedness that the heart of a poor sinner could bear, possess, and enjoy in Jesus' wounds, if it [the heart] cleaved to Him.

♂ [Tuesday], the 30th

At the morning blessing Br. Rundt spoke on Jude, verse 24, [G]od our Savr. is able to keep you from falling &c., discussing that our Savior was neither lacking the will or inclination, nor the ability, to preserve His people until one day He is able to present them, without blemish, before the presence of His glory with rejoicing.

Br. Jungmann departed for Rhinebeck in order to bring several items from there that had been sent to that place for us from New York. He returned late [on] [Thursday], the 2nd of October, and to our heartfelt joy, brought with him our dear Br. [Jacob] Rogers, whom he had met on the road. Through the latter we at the same time received a couple of letters from our dear Br. Petrus in New York, addressed to us and the Indian brethren and sisters.

♀ [Friday], the 3rd [of October]

Br. Rundt delivered the morning blessing and declared himself with respect to the verse: My Heart is glad & I know why; it is, because a Lamb did die for me, &c.

Today our Indian brethren and sisters, one after the other, visited Br. Rogers, being quite joyful about his visit.

Br. Rogers conducted the occasion in the evening, *simple*, with passion, and full of feeling.

And a short while after this, a quarter-of-an-hour was conducted by Br. David [Zeisberger] for all of the communicant members.

♄ [Saturday], the 4th

Br. Jungmann delivered the morning blessing.

At noon Br. Rogers again went back to Salisbury to preach there tomorrow, in keeping with his promise.

In the afternoon the Indian brethren and sisters were spoken with by Br. David [in preparation] for Holy Communion, in the presence of Brother and Sister Jungmann.

☉ [Sunday], the 5th

Br. Rundt preached on Eph. 1.7, *In J. C. we have Redemption thro' his Blood, the forgiveness of Sins, according to the riches of his grace*, about the redemption that came about through Jesus Christ, and how one was able to share in it. About 11 strangers were present for this.

At the children's meeting in the afternoon the daughter[d] of Brother and Sister Joshua, born on July 12, was baptized into the death of the Savior by Br. David, with the name Elisabeth. At 4 o'clock there was a love feast for all the baptized. This time 23 adults and 19 children were present for this. On this occasion several letters from the congregation were read aloud, such as the letter from Br. Petrus [Böhler] to the Indian brethren and sisters here, which we had received through Br. Rogers, likewise, Br. Christian Seidel's and Christian Heinrich's [Rauch] letters to them. In addition, Br. David told them several things about our Negro brethren and sisters on St. Thomas, p[p].

In the evening we gathered for holy absolution with our communicants [who were admitted] at this time, only 11 in number,[83] because the majority was not at home this time, and right afterward, we partook of the blessed enjoyment of the body and blood of our Lord in holy sacrament.

☽ [Monday], the 6th

Br. Jungmann delivered the morning blessing.

We as well as our Indian brethren and sisters wrote letters to the congregation in Bethlehem today.

In the course of the evening occasion, the mother of our Solomon, an old widow, was baptized by Br. David into the death of the Lord, with the name Gertraud.

♂ [Tuesday], the 7th

At the morning blessing Br. Dav. Zeisberger yet committed this entire small flock to the Savior and His wounds, and after a heartfelt farewell he departed to return to Bethlehem ~~from here~~ by way of New York.

Pachgatgoch *Diarium*, from October 7 to December 7 incl. [inclusive], 1755[84]

♂ [Tuesday], the 7th

Immediately after having delivered the morning blessing, our dear Br. David Zeisberger took a heartfelt leave of us and the Indian brethren and sisters, and set out on his return journey to Bethlehem. Br. Rundt accompanied him for several miles.

Joshua and his wife, as well as several other Indian brethren and sisters, went out[85] into the area of Potatuck and to the seaside. For this reason our daily occasions were not attended by many.

Br. Rundt made a modest beginning with the boys in school to read written script.[86] The girls' school was suspended this week on account of Sister Jungmann's indisposition. She was caused much discomfort by a cough.

[No entry for the 8th]

♃ [Thursday], the 9th

Br. Petrus and his Thamar, as well as Caritas, who had been out into their 4th week, returned home today.

♀ [Friday], the 10th

Br. Martin [the Indian] arrived back here from his visit to Bethlehem, in good spirits and full of light. Along with the many heartfelt greetings from the congregation, he also brought us several letters from Br. Matthew [Hehl], Pezold, Grube, etc., as well as several *Gemeinnachrichten*. It was something very special for us here to receive letters and news from Bethlehem twice within a period of 13 days through persons coming from there. The new English hymnal, which we received at the same time, was a pleasant *present* for us.

♄ [Saturday], the 11th

Br. Jungmann went 10 miles from here to procure several items for our household.

Br. Joshua and his Elisabeth returned home, along with several other Indian brethren and sisters from here and from the winter huts, who had been absent for some weeks, so that our assembly at the evening occasion was again more numerous, in the course of which the 5th supplication from the Lord's prayer was discussed and a brief reminder was issued as regards the Indians' singing along during the meeting.

☉ [Sunday], the 12th

The sermon was on 1 Pet. 2.25, *Ye were as Sheep going astray, but are now returned unto the Shepherd and Bishop of your Souls*, about the unblessed state of those souls who are living in this world without Jesus, and about the blessed state of those who have come to Him and His wounds. Several English strangers were present as well.

At the children's meeting in the afternoon, for which, however, our entire brown flock here was present, the letters to our Indian brethren and sisters that had been received from Bethlehem through our Indian Br. Martin, were read to them, and were listened to with pleasure and *attention*.

Later on Br. Martin visited us, and we gave him the opportunity to pour out [i.e., express without restraint] everything that he has seen and heard at the congregation, and that which he has felt in his heart, which hitherto he has not been able to do. He admitted not being able to sufficiently express himself about everything.

Br. Jungmann visited several brethren and sisters.

☽ [Monday], the 13th

At the morning blessing it was pointed out that in all of our affairs, business, and labors, Jesus needed to be the beginning, the middle, and the ending if something that is beneficial and blessed is to be the result. Thus, we wanted to begin this week's business in His name, then the middle, and end it in His presence.

At the evening meeting the words of the Savior, Jn. 4.34, *My Meat is to do the Will of him that sent me*, provided us the opportunity for a blessed reflection upon His love of man and [His] hunger for our blessedness, giving rise to our self-searching, feeling shame in His presence, and submitting ourselves to Him anew, so as to mold ourselves in such a way that to do His will may become our nourishment and heart's joy.

♂ [Tuesday], the 14th

We harvested our Welsh corn, and the Indian brethren and sisters began to do the same. Our Welsh corn turned out tolerably well; that of the Indians for the most part better.

In the evening today's word of the Savior was discussed some: *They are not of the World, even as I am not of the World.* [Jn. 17.16.]

[*No entries for the 15th and 16th*]

♀ [Friday], the 17th

At the evening occasion we began using our new English hymnal, and in the beginning, Br. Rundt read aloud the excellent hymn: *Dear People of the Lamb our Head, be of his Wounds for ever glad* &c.

[*No entry for the 18th*]

☉ [Sunday], the 19th

The sermon was delivered on Rom. 14.9: *To this End Christ both died & rose, that he might be Lord both of the Dead* &c. There were again English strangers present, also a man from New Fairfield. Soon after we also had a visitor from our neighborhood.

☽ [Monday], the 20th

Today Sr. Jungmann again started the school for the girls, which she was obliged to suspend for a couple of weeks owing to her being indisposed. She also received a visit from Sr. Thamar, who has been ill until now.

David's entire family, which had come here from the seaside to harvest their Welsh corn, again departed thither, it[em] [the] Gottlobs and [the] Abrahams went out.

During the evening occasion part of yesterday's text was taken up again, and special mention was made that Christ had also died so that he may be Lord over the <u>dead</u>.

♂ [Tuesday], the 21st

At the morning blessing, in remembrance of today's watchword, <u>Jacob betete</u>,[87] we recommended ourselves and our entire small flock here by means of a humble and childlike prayer to our faithful Lord and Savior, [for Him] to bless, guide, and preserve [us]. And in the evening, the familiar words of David were discussed: *Whom have I in heaven but Thee? & there is none upon Earth that I desire besides Thee* [Ps. 73.25]. Throughout this our dear Savior could be felt quite near us.

[*No entries for the 22nd and 23rd*]

♀ [Friday], the 24th

Br. Jungmann went several miles from here on account of business for our house, and at the same time visited in the winter huts the few people he found there.

In the evening we had for our reflection from 1 Pet. 1.5: *We are kept by the Power of God thro' Faith unto Salvation*.

♄ [Saturday], the 25th

At the morning blessing today's name of the Savior was discussed: *He is the Life &c.* Brother and Sister Jungmann went visiting in our neighborhood.

Most of our Indian brethren and sisters had stayed home throughout this week, having busied themselves with harvesting the blessing that our dear Father in heaven has presented them. We did the same. The schools proceeded every day in their usual course.

In the evening we closed this week reflecting on the word of the Savior: *Watch ye & pray always* [Lk. 21.36].

☉ [Sunday], the 26th

During the sermon the beautiful song *See World, upon the bloody Tree thy Life there sinks in Death*[,] p[p]. was discussed. A couple of English strangers from the farthest end of Kent were present; [they] also stayed with us for the meal.

Because our *Banden* had been suspended for a couple of Sundays, in the afternoon we spoke with those leading the *Banden*, renewing in them the purpose and benefit of our small fellowships, on which they agreed with us wholeheartedly. We asked that each one of them do the same with his brethren and inquire with them if it would please them and be a blessing for the heart if the *Banden* were continued the way we had done thus far. They did so, and in the evening brought us the reply: that each one whose heart had life had declared himself in favor of ~~keeping~~ the *Banden*. Sr. Jungmann assembled those Indian sisters who are to lead the *Banden*, and did the same with them.

Br. Samuel, who for some time now has not had a light and lighted heart, to which he also admits, was most warmly advised to throw himself at the Savior's bloody mercy, just the way he is.

In the evening the first 2 verses of the song *Ye Hands of Love once pierc'd with Nails* &c. gave us the opportunity for a refreshing reflection, and then we blessedly laid ourselves down to rest in these hands of love.

[*No entry for the 27th*]

♂ [Tuesday], the 28th

Br. Gideon went to New Milford. Several Indian sisters visited Sr. Jungmann.

[*No entry for the 29th*]

♃ [Thursday], the 30th

Br. Gideon returned home. In the evening Br. Martin visited us, with whom we carried on a brotherly and heartfelt *discours*.

At the evening occasion the words *Lord, thou Knowest all Things* were discussed, and it was demonstrated how consoling this truth was for a true child of God, but also how frightening it must be for all those who do not follow the truth and live in such a way as to cast disgrace upon the Gospel through which they were called upon.

[*No entry for the 31st*]

♄ [Saturday], November 1

At the morning blessing we reflected on today's name of the Savior, *He is the God of all Gods*, and in the evening today's word of the Savior was discussed: *To whom Little is forgiven, the same loveth little* [Lk. 7.47].

In the course of this last occasion our dear Heinrich Martin arrived here from Rhinebeck. He brought some things up for us that had been sent to him from New York for our use. At the same time, we received pleasant letters from Br. Joseph and some news from the congregation.

☉ [Sunday], the 2nd

The sermon was delivered on Eph. 4.24, *Put on the new Man, which is after God created in Righteousness & true Holiness*, which was used to demonstrate, in part, how wisdom, righteousness, and holiness fared with the unspiritual people, and then, what makes up the true and eternal wisdom, righteousness, and holiness of the children of God.

The *Banden* for the brethren were held by Br. Rundt in the afternoon (those for the sisters were still suspended). The poor condition of their hearts was pointed out to Petrus and Philippus, and they were movingly entreated to allow themselves to be seized by the Savior together, and to be brought to His wounds.

Br. Jungmann held the children's meeting. In the evening there was still the singing service.

☽ [Monday], the 3rd

Henrich Martin went back home at an early hour. Br. Rundt wrote a letter[d] to Br. Hendrick van Vleck in New York [to be delivered] through him.

At the evening occasion Br. Joseph's letter was read to the Indian brethren and sisters, which could not happen yesterday because a stranger was present. In addition, the news of the blessed going home [death] of several children from the European institutes,[88] etc., was related to them, and contentedly listened to by them.

♂ [Tuesday], the 4th

Br. Joshua and his eldest son, it[em] the son of Simon, went out to build canoes today. In the evening Br. Sauter's account about his journey to Wachovia[89] was read to the Indian brethren and sisters.

☿ [Wednesday], the 5th

Today the Brothers Martin and Gottlieb, it[em] Lucas and Jonathan, followed Br. Joshua to [also engage in] the above-mentioned work.

Br. Samuel, who had been out for a couple of days, came home. Br. Rundt visited him soon after, and had the opportunity to engage in a heartfelt and in-depth *Bande* with him. He [Samuel] felt like a sinner, was humbled, and admitted that nothing else but his own righteousness had, up to now, prevented him from enjoying the grace and kindness of the Savior and the sweetness and power of His wounds.

♃ [Thursday], the 6th

Br. Jungmann delivered the morning blessing. Old Sr. Erdmuth went to Newtown. Benigna, the daughter of Simon, also left, for a different area. Br. Martin returned home this very same evening.

[No entry for the 7th]

♄ [Saturday], the 8th

Br. Joshua and Gottlieb, along with those who had been part of their *compagnie*, returned home. Today Br. Jungmann went to the area of Sharon on business for our house, and came back late.

☉ [Sunday], the 9th

The sermon was at the usual time; the *Banden* were suspended. Brother and Sister Jungmann went into several huts to visit the Indian brethren and sisters. Br. Rundt discussed matters with Br. Joshua and Martin regarding their boys, and showed them how to animate and encourage them, in a loving manner, to learn their written verses[d] that they bring home from school, and to sing along during the meeting. The latter is difficult for them, just as it is for the old.

At the evening occasion the church litany was prayed.

☽ [Monday], the 10th

At the morning blessing the apostolic salutation and closure of all the letters of Paul, *The Grace of our Lord J. C. be with you all*, was what was most warmly wished upon our Indian brethren and sisters when starting with their weekly tasks and business.

♂ [Tuesday], the 11th

Br. Gideon and Samuel went to New Milford. In the evening, guided by yesterday's and today's word of the Savior, it was discussed that we were 1.) created by Him, and 2.) were ransomed with His own blood in order to live here with Him in the close *connexion* [connection] of a bride, and one day to rest eternally in the arms of our Husband of the Souls.

☿ [Wednesday], the 12th

Br. Martin and Gottlieb, as well as several sisters, went out with handiwork; and in the evening Br. Gideon returned home still before the occasion, in the course of which today's word of the Savior, *Continue ye in my Love,* [Jn. 15.9,] was reflected upon.

♃ [Thursday], the 13th[90]

At the morning blessing it was pointed out to the few of our baptized people who were at home—the majority having left yesterday, and indeed without our knowledge,[91] given that there is today in the *Connecticut colony the day of general thanksgiving*—what the true offering of thanksgiving to our God consists of; also for a blessed harvest and all the other temporal gifts.

We, at the same time, spent this day blessedly in quiet, praying to our precious Chief Elder, having ourselves absolved and blessed by Him anew, and appealing to Him for the favor to remain His faithful souls until the very end.

♄ [Saturday], the 15th

Brother and Sister Jungmann visited someone in our neighborhood, 3 miles from here. Little by little our small flock came home; hence all of them—except for those who live in the winter huts, of whom we have seen no one in several weeks, and who are said to be in Potatuck—were present for the sermon [on] [Sunday], the 16th, in the course of which 1 Cor. 11.26 was discussed: *Ye should shew forth the Lords Death till he come.*

Right after the meal there was another occasion. In it Rom. 8.32 was discussed: *He that Spared not his own Son—; how shall he not with him also freely give us all Things.* Only the baptized were assembled, to whom, in the end, it was demonstrated, warmly, yet in earnest, that they had cast disgrace upon the Savior, the congregation, and this place with their running out to the worldly people and begging them in importunate ways for some food and drink, such as we, not without feeling, had to experience with them last week, especially given that God gave them such a plentiful harvest and they all are healthy and able to work.[92] Furthermore, they had acted against instructions [by] not reporting to us, and had sought out themselves the opportunity for their hearts to suffer harm most easily. Some were at once deeply affected, and they recognized their wrongdoing.

Right afterward, Br. Jungmann conducted the children's meeting. Several brethren and sisters also were visited, and during the evening occasion, the church litany was prayed.

☽ [Monday], the 17th

Toward evening we experienced an unexpected joy. Our dear Azariah Smith visited us from Salisbury, bringing us a small *paquet* [packet] from Bethlehem that had been given to him by Elijah Colver[,] who has been there recently for a visit to the congregation. In it we found a letter from our dear Br. Matthew [Hehl], the statement of the arrival and departure of the mails[93] from Bethlehem, from September 27 to October 17, and the new, excellent liturgy book[d], for all of which we felt a deep gratitude.

At the evening occasion we had for our blessed reflection the words of the apostle: *Keep J. C. in Remembrance.*

Tonight, around the 3rd hour, we experienced here a very strong earthquake, lasting for more than 3 minutes.[94] Our house and the furniture inside it was cracking all over, and although we were not moving on our bedsteads, we nevertheless felt the movement so strongly as if we were thrown with great *force* from one side to the other. The weather was very clear and moonlit. The beginning of the earthquake reportedly sounded (according to how Br. Jungmann observed it, who was awake at the time) as if a party of about 10 horsemen was advancing at great speed.[95]

♂ [Tuesday], the 18th

Because everyone, young and old, appeared today for the early occasion, as is otherwise the case for the sermons on Sundays, an address was delivered on Rom. 14.7, 8, *None of us liveth to himself, & no Man dieth to himself. For whether we* live, [one or two words crossed out and illegible] we live unto the Lord &ca., and the happiness of those people who know their Lord, are in love with Him, who live by His will, and are daily looking out for His second coming with 1,000 joys, was pointed out [to the Indians]. Moreover, how sure these [people] are in their souls that neither death, nor life, neither that which is present, nor that which is in the future, and so on, can separate them from His love. However, how, on the other hand, the hearts of those people tremble who disobey the Gospel of J. C., and their loins tremble, when only they think about it that one day they have to appear before the Lord.

Toward noon Azariah Smith again returned to Salisbury, in quite good spirits. It pleased us that we were able to entertain and delight him by reading to him several tidings from the congregation which we had here in English.

Sr. Erdmuth returned home from the area of Potatuck.

[No entry for the 19th]

♃ [Thursday], the 20th

Br. Joshua went hunting above Kent with his eldest son, as well as Jeremias, Jonathan, and old Simon's son. They intend to stay there until Christmas.

At the evening occasion we reflected upon the Savior's word for this day: *This thou hast, that thou hatest the Things, which I also hate* [Rev. 2.6]. Br. Gottlieb had also left today to go hunting with his eldest son.

♀ [Friday], the 21st

Br. Jungmann went 3 miles from here to select some wood for his *profession*. He returned home in the evening.

The minister of Kent called on us and saluted us, and late this evening we also were paid a visit by 4 English people from our neighborhood.

♄ [Saturday], the 22nd

At the morning blessing we recommended all our present and absent Indian brethren and sisters to the faithful Savior by means of a childlike and devout prayer, to be blessed and mercifully preserved by Him, while at the same time committing to His merciful heart especially those, who, their baptism notwithstanding, have been walking about for quite some years without life and [without the] feeling of His bloody mercy and power.[96] At the same time [we] remembered, with tender love, our precious brethren and sisters and witnesses to the Lamb in America and Europe before our Savior. In the evening, at about 9 o'clock, there was again something of an earthquake felt.[97]

☉ [Sunday], the 23rd

The sermon was on Eph. 5.1: *Be ye followers of god, as dear Children.* Br. Martin interpreted.

After the children's meeting, Brother and Sister Jungmann visited the Indian brethren and sisters in the[ir] huts.

In the evening the words *Such a One is my Beloved* were spoken about, without an interpreter.

[No entries for the 24th and 25th]

☿ [Wednesday], the 26th

Br. Jungmann went to Sharon on business for our house; Br. Gideon to New Milford. Caritas came back home with her eldest son, and Solomon went to Stockbridge to sell some mats. We advised him against it to be sure, but he was of the opinion [that] he needed to go there.[98]

Circulating in this area, for some time now, are very different, false, and contradictory reports about our brethren in Bethlehem. Thus, several weeks ago, for example, a rumor spread, [that] the *Moravians* in Bethlehem had supplied the French with battle ammunition.[99] And today, Br. Jungmann was told everywhere in Sharon that the people in Bethlehem had all been slain by the French. Some, however, reportedly subtracted a large part of this number, saying, only 100 persons of them had been killed, but that was absolutely certain.[100]

[No entry for the 27th]

♀ [Friday], the 28th

Br. Gideon returned home. On a couple of days during this week Br. Jungmann prepared for himself some wood for his *profession* 3 miles from here. Sr. Jungmann had a number of visitors from the neighborhood.

♄ [Saturday], the 29th

Sr. Jungmann closed her girls' school for now and gave the biggest ones their school book^d to take home to practice there on their own. Br. Jeremias returned from hunting, having shot a deer.

☉ [Sunday], the 30th

For the sermon a couple of strangers, from 6 miles distant, were present, who also stayed with us for the midday meal. After the meal Br. Rundt visited all the brethren and then held the children's meeting.

Sr. Jungmann visited the Indian sisters and took leave of them for a while.

☽ [Monday], December 1

Sr. Jungmann also was present for the morning blessing, which she had not attended in a couple of months.

Soon after, Br. Jungmann departed from here for Rhinebeck with his wife. There she will await her delivery in the house of our dear Henr. Martin.

In the evening Br. Samuel visited me for short hour. Johannes returned home from the war.

♂ [Tuesday], the 2nd

Toward evening, all the brethren who had gone hunting on the 20th of the previous month, already returned home. All of them together had shot about 6 deer.

After the evening occasion, when I had Br. Joshua join me to inquire of him how things had gone at their place of hunting, our conversation was right at the beginning pleasantly interrupted by the visit of our dear Brothers Christian Seidel and Utley.[101] Along with their delightful presence, we also received a number of letters from Bethlehem, from our precious Br. Joseph and several other brethren and sisters there, it[em] from New York, and several *Gemeinnachrichten*, all of which were very pleasing to us.

☿ [Wednesday], the 3rd

At the morning blessing Br. Christian Seidel greeted our small flock here quite affectionately, not only from the congregation as a whole, but also from several brethren and sisters by name, and appealed for them, and for himself, for the Savior's special presence of grace and the plentiful flooding from His wounds for the duration of his stay.

Afterward, all of the Indian brethren and sisters and children came to welcome our pleasant guests.

In the afternoon, Br. Utley and Rundt went to Kent, and in the meantime, Br. Christian visited the Indian brethren and sisters in their huts.

For the evening occasion Br. Christian read dear Br. Joseph's letter to the conference brethren and sisters, and in addition, informed them that a love feast would be held next Sunday for all baptized, and 8 days thereafter, Holy Communion. Both of which were also announced soon afterward in the course of the occasion that he conducted on today's word of the Savior: *Hold that fast which thou hast* [Rev. 2.25].

♃ [Thursday], the 4th

Br. Utley delivered the morning blessing, and with a great deal of feeling bore witness to the truth that if one had Jesus and enjoyed His blood and wounds, one had and possessed everything to give us eternal joy. He closed with a childlike and inspiring prayer.

Br. Rundt remembered, with a heartfelt expression of gratitude before the Savior, his arrival in America 4 years ago today. He conducted the occasion in the evening. Br. Jungmann came home late from Rhinebeck today, bringing us warm greetings from our friends there.

♀ [Friday], the 5th

Br. Jungmann delivered the morning blessing. Later on several Indian brethren visited Br. Seidel. In the evening he spoke on the text from the Old Testament.

♄ [Saturday], the 6th

Br. Christian and Utley visited the boys' school. The former promised to soon send new books as a *present* for the bigger boys in the reading class, to which they are looking forward very much. Solomon came home from Stockbridge today.

At the evening occasion Br. Christian spoke on the text from the New Testament for today: *I have a few Things against thee* [Rev. 2.14].[102]

Sunday, the 7th

Br. Rundt delivered the sermon on Isaiah 35.4, 5: *Say to them that are of a fearfull Heart, fear not: behold, your God will come & save you.*

In the afternoon Br. Christian held the *Banden*, and Br. Utley, the children's meeting.

Toward evening Br. Christian celebrated a love feast with all the baptized. First, he related to them many a delightful matter from the congregation. Afterward, he read aloud to our Indian brethren and sisters here the letters from several brethren and sisters from the congregation, and finally, Br. Joseph's [letter], which contained, among other things, Br. Rundt's recall from here to be at the *synodo* in York [Pennsylvania], on the Catores [Codorus River], on the 18th of this [month]; and in the end, he spoke with a great deal of feeling about the verse: *Love[']s Smart will I feel for ever for the Side-Hole I'll be sick.*

Following everything, we, as well as our Indian brethren and sisters, wrote letters to the *synodum*, and [to] several other brethren and sisters.

We enjoyed overall quite a joyous and blessed day.

Aufs Aeltsten-Fest der Gemeine den
13*ten* Novbr. 1755. in Scatticok[103]

Text aus dem a. T.: *Von der Zeit an, segnete der herr das*
Haus, u. war eitel Segen des herrn in
allem, zu hause u. zu Felde, Gen.39, 5.
Dein Gnad u. all's Vermögen in uns
reichlich vermehr.
Name des heildes: *Der Alte der Tage*, Dan.7, 9.
Nach den Jahren und nach dem merito.
Text aus dem N. T.: *Ich habe die Schlüßel:* Apoc.1, 18.
Authoritaet zu Schluß und Sperr.

I.

Du, den man an den Wunden kennt,
durchs Geistes Offenbahren;
und den man, mit der Bibel, nennt
den Aeltsten nach den Jahren,

615

dem schon vor allen Zeiten so
wie heut der Nahm' gebühret,
und der auch nach dem merito
den Aeltsten-Titel, führet.

2.

Du, der sein Da-und Nahe-seyn
beweist, mit Gottes-Kräfften
in seinem haus, in der Gemein,
und den Gemein-Geschäfften;
Der du mit Einem Blick durchsiehst
die Zeit und Ewigkeiten,
und dennoch dich so sehr bemühst
mit deinen Creuzes-Leuten

3.

Wir sinken vor Dir heute hin
Du Aeltster aller Chöre!
Wir beten an mit Herz und Sinn
und geben Dir die Ehre,
du Herzog deiner Zeugen-Wolck:
Wir thuns in Geists-Gemeinschafft
mit deinem Bethlehemschen Volck
und ihrer Herzens-Freundschafft.

4.

Was thust Du? Was hast Du geschafft
bey deiner Blut-Gemeine,
die selig, fröhlich, sünderhaft,
arm, mangelhaft; Doch Deine.
Sie lebet in dem Wunden-Meer:
Noch mehr! Sie sieht jezunder
auch noch dazu ein ganzes Heer
von lauter Gnaden-Wunder.

5.

Stammst Du /: O Weisheit, Gnad und Ehr!:/
gleich her aus unserm Mittel,
    uns bleibt doch heilig, hoch und hehr
    dein Stab, Stuhl, Amt und Titel
        Dein Da-seyn in der Creuz-Gestalt,
    dein unter uns Regieren,
        mit Licht, Recht, Gnad und Liebs-Gewalt,
    ists was wir veneriren.

6.

Ach absolvire, pardonir,
wasch, heilige und stärke
    mit deinem Blut uns alle hier,
    daß jedes Herz es merke.
        Erneure mit dem Dornen-Stich,
    auch ganz besonders heute,
        an uns den Blut-und Sünder-Strich:
    Wir sind ja deine Leute.

7.

Gib Gnad, daß künftig immerdar
wir uns Dir überlaßen,
    daß Herz, haupt, Händ' und Füße gar
    in deine Absicht paßen,
        damit, nach deinem ganzen Sinn,
    wir Dir noch brauchbar werden,
        /:für deine Arbeit zum Gewinn:/
    zum Dienst bey deinen Heerden.

8.

Es ist wohl nicht der Rede werth,
was wir zu Lieb Dir machen;
    Doch du bist der, der's Herz begehrt,
    sieh'st nicht auf große Sachen.

Du brauchst uns nicht: Gnad ist es nur.
Du willst uns dadurch ehren,
und manches nöth'ge auf der Spuhr
an uns und andern lehren.

9.

Es halte unser Aug und Herz
dein Todes-Blick stets munter,
und misch auch unter unsern Schmerz
den Wunden-Honig drunter.
Dein Da-Bey-Um-und In uns seyn
laß uns beständig haben,
so außer als in der Gemein,
samt allen nöth'gen Gaben.

10.

Der du allein die Schlüßel führst
zum Auf-und zum Zuschließen,
und Gottes Schätze dispensirst
und mittheilst zum Genießen,
wo man auf deine Hände schaut,
bleib hier in unsrer Mitte,
wo doch manch Steingen wird behaut
zu deiner ew'gen Hütte.

11.

Bespreng mit Blut hier diese Stätt
und die Gelegenheiten,
die Herzen, Banden, das Gebet,
ja unsre Kleinigkeiten.
Sey deinem kleinen Dörfflein hier
sehr gnädig und gewogen:
Du bist ja doch in dis Revier
einmal schon eingezogen.

618

12.

Authoritaet zu Schluß und Speer
hast Du an allen Orten;
   Du heißt und bist und bleibst der Herr:
Schleuß zu des Satans Pforten.
Versperr dem Feinde seinen Paß
zun Indianer-Seelen,
   die schon einmal geschmecket was
aus deinen Wunden-Höhlen.

13.

Gedenk an die Gemein, dein haus:
Laß drinn seyn eitel Segen.
   Breit deine gnade drinnen aus:
Vermehre all's Vermögen.
   Laß es dein Lob seyn in der Zeit,
ein Shelter armer Sünder,
   des Satans Schreck, der Engel Freud
und aller Gottes Kinder.

14.

Du Bischoff einer jeden Seel
des Volcks, die deine Glieder;
   Du Aug und Wächter Israel,
der Unitaet der Brüder,
   sey deinen Seelen allerseits
stets gut für allen Schaden:
   Und weid' sie mit dem Wort vom Creuz.
Thu es aus lauter Gnaden.

15.

Du, deiner Jünger Fürst und herr,
ihr Principal und Führer,
   ihr specialer Aeltester,
Hirt, Meister und Regierer,

der du, dem Amt nach, Vater bist
auch Priester und Erz-Engel,
    der wesentlich zugegen ist
in jedem Kirchen-Sprengel.

16.
Siz in dem Rath der Jüngerschafft
als Chef und Praesidente:
    Besorg' das Volck der kleinen Krafft,
als wahrer Creuz-Regente.
    Sez ihnen deine Liebes-Absicht,
mit manchem Ort und Lande,
    noch immer mehr in hellers Licht
und bring sie selbst zu stande.

C.G.R.

Notes

Abbreviations

DHNY *The Documentary History of the State of New York, Arranged under Direction of the Hon. Christopher Morgan, Secretary of State,* ed. E. B. O'Callaghan

MAB Moravian Archives, Bethlehem, Pennsylvania

NYCD *Documents Relative to the Colonial History of New York; Procured in Holland, England, and France by John R. Brodhead,* ed. E. B. O'Callaghan

PRCC *The Public Records of the Colony of Connecticut, from April 1636 to October 1776 . . . transcribed and published, (in accordance with a resolution of the General assembly),* eds. James Hammond Trumball [vols. 1–3] and Charles J. Hoadly [vols. 4–15]

RMM Records of the Moravian Mission among the Indians of North America (Cited by reel/box/folder/item number, and date, where available)

UAH Unity Archives, Herrnhut, Germany

Introduction

1. Thomas Jefferson to William H. Harrison, 27 Feb. 1803, Thomas Jefferson Papers, Series 1, General Correspondence, 1651–1827, Library of Congress. The epigraph to this chapter [emphasis added] is from the same source.

2. Wojciechowski, *Paugussett Tribes,* 231–49.

3. PRCC, 8:38. The lands at Pachgatgoch do not appear to have been expressly granted to the Indians until 1752 (PRCC, 10:108).

4. Trumbull, *Indian Names,* 43.

5. Leach, *Flintlock and Tomahawk;* Jennings, *Invasion of America;* Lapore, *Name of the War.*

6. Jennings, *Invasion of America,* 325; Mandell, *Behind the Frontier,* 2.

7. Campisi, *Mashpee Indians;* Mandell, *Behind the Frontier;* O'Brien, *Dispossession by Degrees.*

8. Axtell, *Invasion Within,* 135.

9. RMM 30/225/3/1, 21 Dec. 1748.

10. Salwen, "Indians of Southern New England"; Conkey, Boissevain, and Goddard, "Indians of Southern New England"; Snow, *Archaeology of New England.*

11. Salwen, "Indians of Southern New England"; Snow, *Archaeology of New England;* Bragdon, *Native People;* Starna, "Pequots."

12. Salwen, "Indians of Southern New England," 168; Conkey, Boissevain, and Goddard, "Indians of Southern New England," 177–78, 181–84; Wojciechowski, *Paugussett Tribes;* Grumet, *Historic Contact,* 153–58.

13. PRCC, 2:419.

14. Jennings, *Invasion of America,* 300–302; PRCC, 2:369.

15. RMM 1/111/4/4, 14 June 1743.

16. Readers interested in the origins and history of the Moravian Church, and generally its mission to the Indians of North America, should consult J. Müller, *Geschichte;* K. Müller, *200 Jahre;* Hamilton and Hamilton, *History of the Moravian Church;* Beck, *Brüder in vielen Völkern;* Meyer, "Zinzendorf und Herrnhut"; [Neisser], *History of Moravian Work;* Loskiel, *History of the Mission;* Heckewelder, *Narrative of the Mission.*

17. Fries, *Moravians in Georgia;* Schwarze, *History of the Moravian Missions,* 5–14; [Neisser], *History of Moravian Work,* 19–20; Fogleman, "Decline and Fall"; Jones and Peucher [Peucker], "'We Have Come to Georgia.'" The Moravians returned to the South—the Winston-Salem area of North Carolina—in the early 1750s but were unsuccessful in establishing a dedicated Indian mission until 1801, this among the Cherokees (McLoughlin, *Cherokees and Missionaries*).

18. [Neisser], *History of Moravian Work,* 9–11. Rauch was supposed to have traveled with another brother, but this person fell ill and was unable to make the journey (UAH R.8.33.a.3.a, 10, 30 Dec. 1739; RMM 29/221/21/1, 1739–51, 1/111/1/1, 1739–46).

19. These Indians were part of a delegation that had come to New York to meet with the colonial governor, George Clarke, an original patentee of the Little Nine Partners patent within which Shekomeko and the lands there contested by the Indians, in particular Shabash, later baptized Abraham, were located (UAH R.15.H.I.a.1.1, n.d.). See discussion at note 35.

20. Martinus Hoffman (b. Kingston NY, 1707, d. 1772). A major landholder, miller, wheat merchant, militia officer, and justice of the peace in Dutchess County who figured importantly in land disputes involving Shekomeko (Reynolds, *Genealogical and Family History,* 1:89–90; Bonami, *Factious People,* 169; DHNY, 4:134).

21. RMM 1/111/1/1, 1739–46.

22. See Kittle, *Palatine Emigration,* 268; Otterness, *Becoming German.*

23. UAH, Christian Heinrich Rauch to Petrus Böhler, R.15.H.I.a.2.1., 12 Jan. 1741.

24. UAH, Christian Heinrich Rauch to Petrus Böhler, R.15.H.I.a.2.1., 12 Jan. 1741; RMM 1/111/1/1, 1739–46; W. Reichel, *Memorials,* 54.

25. The Esopus or Sopus Indians occupied the west side of the mid-Hudson Valley, while the Highland Indians, in particular the Wappingers, the areas of Dutchess and Putnam counties on the east side (Goddard, "Delaware," 213–14). The Moravians identified the Indians from Pachgatgoch and vicinity, that is, the middle stretch of the Housatonic Valley, as either Wampanoags or, more frequently, Wompanoos. We use "Wompanoos," the singular form of which is "Wompanoo," to avoid any possible confusion with the Wampanoags (Pokanokets) of southeastern Massachusetts. "Wampanoo" (*wá·pano·w: easterner) is a Munsee term for the native people living to their east. See Goddard, "Ethnohistorical Implications"; Salwen, "Indians of Southern New England," 175.

26. RMM 2/112/17/1, 1745. See also W. Reichel, Memorial of the Dedication, 63.

27. Nelson, "Boehler's Reminiscences"; Smaby, Transformation, 9.

28. These Indians were Seim and Kiob, both Wompanoos, and Shabash, a Mahican (UAH R.15.H.I.a.1.2.a, 1742–49).

29. RMM 26/211/5/1, Dec. 1741, Jan. 1742. In a letter dated 18 Dec. 1741, Rauch informed Zinzendorf of his wish to visit him and the brethren and sisters in Bethlehem, bringing along these three Indian men. Before the letter could be delivered, however, Büttner had been ordered to Shekomeko (RMM 29/221/4/5, Dec. 1741).

30. Early on, the Moravians referred to Stockbridge by its geographic location, Westenhook, the far southwest corner of Massachusetts and the adjacent part of New York (RMM 26/211/5/1, 25 Jan. 1742; see Wm. Alexander, "A Map of the lands in Controversie Between The Province of New York and Massachusetts," 1754, CO 700/New York 21, Public Record Office, Kew, United Kingdom).

31. RMM 29/221/4/5, Dec. 1741, 1/111/1/1, 1739–46. On Zinzendorf's journey to Shekomeko, see W. Reichel, Memorials, 45–61.

32. RMM 1/111/1/1, 1739–46. In the entry under Rauch's name, Träger and Träger-Große, Dienerblätter, furnish the New Style date for his ordination as 22 February. See also W. Reichel, Memorials, 145n.

33. RMM 26/211/5/1, Jan. 1742, 1/111/1/1, 1739–46. Seim also carried the name Otabawánemen (W. Reichel, Memorials, 145).

34. See NYCD, 7:246. On Abraham's land, see RMM 3/113/5/4, n.d., 3/113/5/6, 16 Oct. 1743.

35. Jeannette or Johannetta Mack, née Rau. See Linn and Egle, Marriage Register, 119. See also [Neisser], History of Moravian Work, 7. At least a dozen Moravian brethren, several with their wives, passed through Shekomeko during the first four years of the mission.

36. RMM 29/221/4/5, 18 Dec. 1741, 1/111/2/1, 21 Feb. 1743. At this early period of

their mission to the Indians, the Moravians were much more liberal in terms of what was required of an individual to be baptized.

37. That an unknown number of Indian people were settled at a place called Shekomeko [Shekomakes] is first documented in 1724 (RMM 3/113/5/2, Sept. 1743; see also 3/113/5/6, 16 Oct. 1743, 3/113/5/11, n.d.). By the early 1740s the community's mixed Indian composition, the uncertainty about who its leaders were, and the sense that its membership was not only fluid but unconsolidated suggest that it had become a gathering place for Indians who had surrendered or been forced from their lands as a result of expanding colonial settlement and population loss from disease. An indication of how quickly non-Indians moved into the region is reflected in census data from Dutchess County. A total of 445 "inhabitants and slaves" was counted there in 1714; 1,727 in 1731; 3,418 six years later; and by 1746, 8,806 (DHNY, 1:240, 471, 472). For references to leaders at Shekomeko, see RMM 29/221/21/1, 1739–51.

38. This is Tschoop, a.k.a. Wasamapah (W. Reichel, *Memorials*, 55). Abraham was appointed elder (*Ältester*), Jacob exhorter (*Ermahner*), Isaac sexton or servant (*Diener*), and Johannes teacher (*Lehrer*).

39. RMM 26/211/5/5, Oct. 1742.

40. W. Reichel, *Memorials*, 32–33, 57, 64–66. Zinzendorf never visited any of the Iroquois communities, although several other Moravians did. See Beauchamp, *Moravian Journals*.

41. RMM 26/211/5/1, Oct. 1742.

42. RMM 29/221/4/1, 4, 1743. The minister Rauch encountered was in all likelihood the Reverend John Jacob Ehl (Ehle, Ehlig, Oehl, Oël) (1685–1777), a Palatine German whose homestead was just east of modern Nelliston. See Lydekker, *Faithful Mohawks*, 63–64; Corwin, *Ecclesiastical Records*, 3:2232–33.

43. RMM 1/111/1/1, 9, 10, 15 Aug., 2, 8 Sept. 1743, 29/221/4/1, 4, 1743.

44. RMM 1/111/1/1, Jan. 1743. On 19 August 1742, a number of Indians traveled a short distance from Pachgatgoch to a place where they were preached to by the yet unordained "New Light" David Brainerd. "New Lights" were practitioners of the religious revival known as the First Great Awakening. See UAH, Cammerhoff to Zinzendorf, R.14.A.28.1, 22 May 1747; Edwards, *David Brainerd*, 175–76; W. Reichel, *Memorials*, 27–28n. Reichel, however, is mistaken in his belief that this event took place while Brainerd was at Kaunaumeek. His mission did not begin there until April 1743, after the Moravians had begun baptizing Pachgatgoch Indians. The Moravian bishop Johann Christian Friedrich Cammerhoff believed that it was Brainerd who had awakened these Indians; however, there had been earlier contacts with local Presbyterian clergy. See *The Law Papers*, 1:42–43; PRCC, 8:480–81; Wojciechowski, *Paugussett Tribes*, 252.

45. The discussion that follows of the Macks' visit to Pachgatgoch and Potatuck is from RMM 1/111/3/1, 27 Jan.–18 Feb. 1743, 1/111/3/3, 26 Jan.–18 Feb. 1743.

46. See [Indian Papers], 1st ser., 1:118–118b; PRCC, 6:551, sec. 5 [11 Aug. 1725], viz., "If any Indian or Indians shall assault or threaten to kill, or anyways unlawfully terrify and disquiet any of his Majesties subjects . . . the said authority are ordered to commit such Indian or Indians to the common goal [jail]."

47. Jeannette Mack, who grew up next door to the Indians at Shekomeko, spoke Mahican, as did her brother Wilhelm. See RMM 30/225/3, 17 Dec. 1748. The available evidence indicates that the inhabitants of Pachgatgoch and Potatuck spoke Wampano, an eastern dialect of Munsee. Nevertheless, given the exposure these Indians had had to surrounding native speech communities, a degree of mutual intelligibility must have developed between many of the region's Mahican, Quiripi-Naugatuck-Unquachog, and Wampano speakers. See Goddard, "Eastern Algonquian Languages," 72–73; Goddard, Review of *Mahican Language Hymns*; Salwen, "Indians of Southern New England," 160. The claim that Jeannette spoke Mohawk, which is traceable to W. Reichel, *Memorials*, 100–101n, and has been repeated by others, cannot be substantiated. See Carter, *Early Events*, 90; Merrell, "Shamokin," 19; Merritt, *At the Crossroads*, 75.

48. Büttner asked the headman whether he and the others wanted to have their baptisms conducted in English or in their own language, and whether they wished to choose their Christian names for themselves. Maweseman replied that he did not care one way or the other, and in any case, the Moravians knew how to proceed with such matters better then he. In addition to Gideon and his son, whose Indian name was recorded as Schoop, Büttner baptized Gideon's daughter Maria, the widow Rachel, Amos (Hiop, also Kiop/Kiob), and Samuel (Buicke) (RMM 1/111/3/3, 1/111/2/1, 13 Feb. 1743).

49. The discussion that follows on Mack's second journey to Pachgatgoch and Potatuck is from RMM 1/111/3/2, 4, 22 Feb.–11 Mar. 1743.

50. The diaries strongly suggest that the mother of Chuse and Martin, and Joshua's mother, were not the same woman.

51. RMM 26/211/5/1, 8, 15–16 Apr. 1743.

52. Characterized as the "Chiefe Sachem of the indians in these parts," Metoxson figured prominently in several land transactions in Connecticut in the 1720s and 1730s, where he was identified as Corlar (var.) and also Collonel ([Indian Papers], 1st ser., 1:244–244c). The Iroquois had favored Governor Edmund Andros with the honorific "Corlear" in about 1675, and with the exception of Benjamin Fletcher, who was styled "Swift Arrow," it has been used ever since in addressing New York's chief

executive. The name is traceable to Arent van Curler, who in 1643 negotiated the first treaty between the Mohawks and the Dutch (Jennings et al., *Iroquois Diplomacy*, 235, 237; Gehring, *Court Minutes*, 457). How it was that Metoxson appropriated or perhaps was given this name is unknown. Whatever the case, the name may have functioned to buttress his actual or assumed status of head sachem. Büttner describes Corlaar or Metoxson as being about seventy years old in 1743 (RMM 1/111/2/1, 21 Feb. 1743). The date of his death is undocumented.

53. RMM 1/111/2/1, 15, 21 Jan. 1743.

54. Whether the number of miles is fifty or sixty is unclear in the German-language document. See RMM 1/111/2/5, 16 Aug. 1743. It is definitely not thirty, the figure found in the English translation (RMM 1/111/2/8, 16 Aug. 1743). See also Hamilton and Madeheim et al., *Bethlehem Diary*, 2:244. Other than what the Moravian records provide, there is nothing known about this Indian community.

55. RMM 26/211/5/1, 6 Oct. 1743, 1/111/2/8, 6 Nov. 1743, 29/221/21/1, 1739–51.

56. This legislation, written in support of the "Old Light" religious establishment in western Connecticut, was introduced by Jonathan Trumbull, a member of the assembly who would serve as governor from 1769 to 1784. See PRCC, 8:521–22.

57. Abel Wright (d. 1770) was one of Kent's leading citizens, an original proprietor who served at one time or another as captain of the militia, selectman, town agent, and moderator. He also was a charter member of Kent's Congregational church. In early July, following the arrests of the Moravians, and after having invited "'notoriously corrupt'" New Light preachers into his home, he was suspended from gospel privileges, with the Reverend Cyrus Marsh prominent on the list of prosecutors. Rejecting a call to confess, he turned to the teachings of the Moravians, causing himself further trouble with the locals. The next year, he moved to Fairfield, Connecticut. In 1760 he returned to Kent, running the town's general store until his death (Grant, *Town of Kent*, 165–66).

58. RMM 1/111/4/2, 1–18 June 1743, 1/111/4/4, June 1743; UAH, Spangenberg to Zinzendorf, R.15.H.I.a.7.3.f, 14 May 1752.

59. UAH, Spangenberg to Zinzendorf, R.15. H.I.a.7.3.f, 14 May 1752.

60. RMM 1/111/4/4, June 1743.

61. RMM 1/111/2/1, Feb. 1743.

62. RMM 29/221/21/1, 1739–51.

63. DHNY, 3:613. It is not known whether colonial officials in Connecticut and New York were in contact and sharing information in regard to Moravian activities and how best to deal with them, although we believe it likely.

64. DHNY, 3:613.

65. A description of this visit and its aftermath is drawn from Büttner's personal diary (RMM 26/211/5/1, 16–19 June 1744, 1/111/1/1, 16–19 June 1744), which is summarized in Hamilton and Madeheim et al., *Bethlehem Diary*, 2:112–15.

66. RMM 26/211/5/1, 16–19 June 1744, 1/111/1/1, 16–19 June 1744. As one of its many responses to King George's War, the Connecticut assembly passed an ordinance in October 1744 in respect to Indians residing within the colony "appointing the limits where such Indians may range and the badge by which they shall be known." This was to "prevent their being mistaken for the enemy Indians and fired upon as such." The efficacy of this directive, and the extent to which it was complied with by Indians or colonists, is unknown (PRCC, 9:76).

67. RMM 2/112/6/6, 19 June 1744. The Reverend Peter Pratt also acted as an agent for the town of Sharon in an early and controversial land deal with the Indians. He was removed as minister in 1747 following charges of intemperance (Sedgwick, *General History*, 37, 42–43).

68. There is minor disagreement in the record concerning the date on which the Filkins and their associates visited Shekomeko, and also on the number of men in the posse. According to colonial authorities, it was 17 June and 18 June. Büttner wrote that it was 19 June. The governor's letter maintained that ten men were in the posse, while Büttner reported numbers of eleven and thirteen. See DHNY, 3:613–14; RMM 26/211/5/1, 19 June 1744. Büttner, and soon other Moravians, refused to take "the Oaths by Law appointed to be taken, in Stead of the Oaths of Allegiance and Supremacy, Subscribe the Test, and make, repeat and Swear to, and Subscribe the abjuration Oath" required under "*Das Act die Naturalisation*" [The Act of Naturalization], as Johannes von Watteville identified it in 1748. See RMM 30/225/3, 26 Dec. 1748. First promulgated in 1683, the 1715 revision of this statute is titled "An Act declaring that all Persons of Forreign Birth heretofore Inhabiting within this Colony and dying Seized of any Lands Tenements or Hereditaments shall forever hereafter Deemed Taken and Esteemed to have been Naturalized, and for Naturalizing all Protestants of Forreign Birth now Inhabiting within this Colony" (*Colonial Laws of New York*, 1:123–24, 858–63). To "Subscribe the Test" was to take the oath stipulated in the Test Act of 1691, which repudiated transubstantiation, the invocation or adoration of the Virgin Mary, and the sacrifice of the Mass (See Corwin, *Ecclesiastical Records*, 2:1012–13). In New York, the Test Act led to the passage in 1700 of a particularly odious piece of legislation, "An act against Jesuits & popish priests" (*Colonial Laws of New York*, 1:428–30). The Abjuration Oath was prescribed by laws put into force by William III, George I, and George III opposing the right of the Stuarts or other pretenders to the crown.

69. RMM 26/211/5/1, 2 July 1744. See Hamilton and Madeheim et al., *Bethlehem*

Diary, 2:114, 178. The other patentees living at this time were George Clarke, New York's colonial governor from 1736 to 1743, and Rip van Dam, a former member of the colonial council and a former acting governor. F. Franconier was still alive in 1742. Henry and Francis Filkin's father, Henry Sr. (1651–1713), had been a patentee of the Great Nine Partners patent of 1697, the lands of which lay adjacent to and south of the Little Nine Partners patent.

70. RMM 26/211/5/1, 1–2 Aug. 1744; DHNY, 3:614–17. Sensemann may have had the easier time of it; he knew very little English and thus could not readily understand or be understood by his inquisitors (RMM 2/112/6/2, 13 Aug. 1744, 1/111/1/1, 18 Aug. 1744).

71. Hamilton and Madeheim et al., Bethlehem Diary, 2:133–34.

72. Colonial Laws of New York, 3:424, 428. The oaths required under this 1744 statute were one of allegiance to "his Majesty King George the Second," a second repudiating any assumption of authority by the Sea of Rome or any "foreign Prince, person, Prelate, State or Potentate," and a third rejecting claims of pretenders to the Crown (Colonial Laws of New York, 3:425).

73. Hamilton and Madeheim et al., Bethlehem Diary, 2:175.

74. DHNY, 3:617. The act would expire one year later, on 21 September 1745. A first violation carried with it a fine of forty pounds and six months' imprisonment without bail or surety. Expulsion from the colony would follow a second offense, and if such an order was ignored, it was decreed that the offender "shall Suffer Such Punishment as shall be Inflicted by the Justices of the Supreme Court, not Extending to Life or Limb" (Colonial Laws of New York, 3:424, 428).

75. RMM 26/211/5/7, 19 Dec. 1744.

76. Hamilton and Madeheim et al., Bethlehem Diary, 2:198.

77. This money may have been a part of that appropriated by the Connecticut assembly in May 1742.

78. RMM 26/211/5/1, 7 July 1743.

79. RMM 26/211/5/1, July–Dec. 1743. For Lazara's baptism, see RMM 26/211/5/1, 13 Aug. 1743. See MAB, Maps and Architectural Drawings, drawer 7, folder 8, no. 32 [fig. 4]. Shortly after Lazara's death, Gideon married Martha, a Potatuck Indian who had been baptized by Mack on 3 January 1744 (RMM 26/211/5/1).

80. RMM 26/211/5/1, 28 Dec. 1743, 2 Jan. 1744; W. Reichel, Memorials, 144, 148.

81. See Hamilton and Madeheim et al., Bethlehem Diary, 2:36, 48; Stocker, History of the Moravian Church in New York City, 62.

82. "de gayeté [gaieté] de Coeur" (French): out of sheer wantonness.

83. NYCD, 6:270.

84. NYCD, 6:279.

85. NYCD, 6:311. See also DHNY, 3:619–21.

86. Hamilton and Madeheim et al., *Bethlehem Diary*, 2:203, 213.

87. Hamilton and Madeheim et al., *Bethlehem Diary*, 2:233; W. Reichel, *Memorials*, 138n. During their visit to Shekomeko in 1748, the Moravian bishops Johannes von Watteville and Johann Christian Cammerhoff counted twenty-five graves in the cemetery: Büttner's, those of twenty-three Indians, and that of Robert Bos or Boss (d. 26 June 1745), a white man "who loved the brethren" and had asked to be buried in Shekomeko's God's acre (RMM 30/225/3, 15 Dec., 1/III/1/1). A Robert Bos, also Boos, appears on tax lists from Dutchess County in 1736 and 1737, and again in Rhinebeck precinct from 1738 to February 1745 (Frank Doherty, personal communication, 2004; see also Jones, *Palatine Families*).

88. RMM 2/112/16/7, 10/1, 21 Mar. 1745. Although we cannot be sure, this may have been Henry Livingston (1714–1799), Henry Beekman's cousin and confidant. See Bonami, *Factious People*, 167–68.

89. About this incident, see RMM 2/112/16/7, 21 Mar. 1745, 2/112/10/1, 1–5 Mar. 1745; Hamilton and Madeheim et al., *Bethlehem Diary*, 2:237.

90. RMM 2/112/8/1, 2, 1 Feb.–Aug. 1745, 1/III/1/1, Nov. 1745–July 1746.

91. RMM 29/221/21/1, 1739–51.

92. Hamilton and Madeheim et al., *Bethlehem Diary*, 2:306. Two years earlier, Büttner had characterized Hoffman as "having acted upright" in the controversy over Abraham's land (RMM 3/113/5/6, 16 Oct. 1743).

93. Zeisberger and his companion Brother Post had been released from confinement in New York City several weeks earlier; they had been held there since their arrests in Mohawk country in early February 1745. Both men returned to Bethlehem on 16 April (Hamilton and Madeheim et al., *Bethlehem Diary*, 2:228–30, 273, 275; RMM 29/221/21/1, 1739–51).

94. RMM 29/221/21/1, 1739–51; Beauchamp, *Moravian Journals*, 12–13; Wallace, *Conrad Weiser*, 219–22.

95. RMM 29/221/21/1, 1739–51.

96. RMM 1/III/1/1, 1739–46. Reports reaching Shekomeko and Pachgatgoch about the alleged abusive manner in which the Moravians were treating the Indians in Gnadenhütten and Bethlehem were a cause of some concern (MAB, *Epistola Tertia Johannis Friederici Cammerhoffii*, Cammerhoff: Letters to Zinzendorf & al.: 1747–51). Gnadenhütten was destroyed in an Indian attack on 24 November 1755.

97. RMM 3/113/1/5.

98. RMM 3/114/1/1.

99. MAB, Bethlehem Diary, 1747, 7, *Beylagen*, 1 July.

100. W. Reichel, *Memorials*, 34; RMM 4/116/1/1, 19 Aug., 2 Sept. 1747.

101. MAB, Bethlehem Diary, 1747, 7, *Beylagen*, 3 July, 1 Sept.; RMM 4/116/1/1, 2 Sept. 1747.

102. UAH, Bethlehem Diary, R.14.A.a.3, Aug.–Sept. 1747; RMM 4/116/1/1, 2 Sept. 1747, 29/221/21/1, 1739–51; MAB, Bethlehem Diary, 1747, 7, *Beylagen*, 24, 31 Oct. 1747.

103. [*Acta Fratrum Unitatas*], 634–38.

104. RMM 30/225/3/1, 15–16 Dec. 1748; UAH, Bethlehem Diary, R.14.A.a.4, 18 Mar. 1748.

105. RMM 3/114/8/1, 1, 20 July 1753.

106. RMM 3/114/8/1, 16, 20 Dec. 1753, 26/211/7/1, 3/114/1/2; UAH, Bethlehem Diary, R.14.A.a.5, 16 May, 15 Sept., 21 Oct.–1 Nov. 1749, R.14.A.a.6, 26 Feb. 1750.

107. The discussion on the location and layout of Pachgatgoch that follows is from Dally-Starna and Starna, "Picturing Pachgatgoch." Not considered here are the movements of missionaries and Indians to and from communities in western Connecticut and eastern New York, and also those in Pennsylvania, namely, Bethlehem, Friedenshütten, and Gnadenhütten.

108. MAB, Bethlehem Diary, 1768–71, 28:548.

109. MAB, Bethlehem Diary, 1765–67, 27:531. See also MAB, *Protocoll der Oeconomats Conferenz*, 1767–74:168–69. There had been deliberations among church leaders in Bethlehem about closing the mission in 1768, and a suggestion to consider doing so two years before that (*Protocoll der Oeconomats Conferenz*, 115–17; MAB, Joachim Sensemann to Nathanael Seidel, P.H.C. 1755–75, Letters from Sichem and Kingsbury NY, 31 Dec. 1765; UAH, Joachim Sensemann to Nathanael Seidel, R.15.H.I.a.2.95, 2 April 1766, R.24.B.16.35, April–July 1765).

110. MAB, Bethlehem Diary, 1772–74, 29:177.

111. Hamilton, *John Ettwein*, 252.

112. RMM 1/111/2/1, 21 Feb. 1743.

113. The description of Pachgatgoch that follows is from the von Watteville–Cammerhoff journal (RMM 30/225/3/1, 20–21 Dec. 1748).

114. We translate the German "Hütte" as "hut" rather than attempting to add unwarranted specificity to the type of dwelling referred to; for example, by translating "Hütte" as "cabin" or "wigwam," terms the Moravians supplied when they thought it necessary. The word "fireplaces" (*Feuerplätze*) used here is meant to suggest an open hearth, not a stone structure at the base of a chimney.

115. "kill" (Dutch): creek. Distances reported by the Moravians were probably based on the time it took them to travel from one point to another. Even so, and

almost without exception, their estimates closely match those of measured statute miles.

116. Gideon had remarried after Lazara's death in September 1743 but before the first days of January 1744 (RMM 26/211/5/1, 3 Jan. 1744).

117. Seven years earlier, in July 1741, Indians at "'Scaticook'" sold a large parcel of land "'on Stratford [Housatonic] river at a place called Sassucksuck, northward from the place where the Ten Mile river falls into the Great River [also the Housatonic]'" (Orcutt, *History of the Towns*, 17). Written "Sasaksuk" by Cammerhoff, this was a large falls on the Housatonic just upriver from Bulls Bridge.

118. Insofar as we have been able to determine, there is no similar structure described in the literature from southern New England or adjacent New York for any time period.

119. In 1904 a hydropower plant was completed at Bulls Bridge, impounding upstream waters and elevating the river surface. In addition, an overflow channel for the power canal was created on the west side of a landform that is today called Bulls Bridge Island.

120. RMM 3/114/5/1, 28 Jan. 1752, 11 Dec. 1751.

121. RMM 3/114/4/1, 19–20 Sept. 1751.

122. RMM 3/114/4/1, 23 Sept. 1751.

123. RMM 3/114/5/1, 30 Dec. 1751.

124. RMM 4/115/9/1, 11 Dec. 1759. Gideon died on the mountain on 28 January 1760.

125. RMM 4/115/11/1, 1 Apr. 1761.

126. RMM 4/115/12/1, 26 July, 9 Sept., 3 Dec. 1762.

127. In early 1756 Bishop Spangenberg reflected on the use of the name "Pachgatgoch," writing: "we do not want to abandon this name, for it is better known to the congregation than this: Scatticock" (RMM 4/115/15/18, n.d. [ca. May 1756]). See appendix 4, "Lists and Correspondence."

128. RMM 4/115/10/1, 25 Oct. 1760.

129. RMM 4/115/10/1, 3 Jan. 1761.

130. RMM 4/115/2/1, 19 Oct. 1754.

131. [Indian Papers], 1st ser., 2:77.

132. Barber, *Historical Collections*, 470.

133. RMM 4/115/2/1, 15 Oct. 1754.

134. RMM 4/115/11/1, 20, 23 Jan. 1761.

135. RMM 4/115/11/1, 14 May 1761, 4/115/12/1, 20 Feb. 1762.

136. RMM 4/115/6/1, 15 May 1756.

137. UAH R.15.H.I.a.5.8, 13 Mar. 1749.

138. RMM 2/112/17/1, 1745; W. Reichel, *Memorial of the Dedication*, 63.

139. RMM 30/225/3/1, 20 Dec. 1748; McBride, "Archaeology."

140. RMM 3/114/2/1, 8, 29 June, 28 Oct. 1750.

141. MAB, Journals, Box JE: Letters S, Box JE III 2c, Oct. 1760–May 1761.

142. RMM 3/114/6/1, 19 Apr. 1752.

143. Quoted in Hopkins, *Housatonic Indians*, 137.

144. RMM 4/115/3/1, 12 May 1755.

145. For grave number 29, the notation "Maria Elisabeth[,] Sophia's sister," was crossed out and replaced with "Salome[,] Salome's little daughter." Maria Elisabeth's grave is number 28.

146. RMM 30/225/3/1, 15 Dec. 1748; Gollin, *Moravians in Two Worlds*, 67–89, 109.

147. The placement of Gideon's grave should not be interpreted as reflecting his headman status in the community; it indicates only that he was an adult male and as such was not to be buried with children of either sex or with women.

148. RMM 3/114/2/1, 9 July 1750, 3/114/5/1, 8 Jan. 1752, 3/114/7/1, 22 Nov. 1752, 4/115/9/1, 10 Aug. 1760.

149. RMM 1/111/1/1, 13 Feb., 13 Aug., 24 Sept. 1743, 27 Sept. 1744.

150. RMM 34/3191/1/1; MAB, Edward Thorp to John Ettwein, P.H.C. 1765–75, Letters from Sichem and Kingsbury NY, 13 May 1770.

151. We do not include Lazara and Maria in our calculations, as their graves are not within the boundaries of the cemetery. Neither do we include the one unlabeled grave.

152. RMM 2/112/17/1; W. Reichel, *Memorial of the Dedication*, 63; Sabathy-Judd, *Moravians in Upper Canada*, xxx, figure facing 310.

153. W. Reichel, *Memorial of the Dedication*, 71, 73–76; Johnson, *Register of Some of the Families*.

154. W. Reichel, *Memorial of the Dedication*, 71, 76–77.

155. RMM 4/115/10/1, 25 Oct. 1760.

156. W. Reichel, *Memorial of the Dedication*, writes: "As at Pachgatgoch (as we ascertained later), so here [Shekomeko] the Indians buried their dead on low ground; whether these were exceptional instances, or whether it was a custom, is a question of interest yet to be decided" (70). We would only caution that, in respect to the location of the cemetery at Pachgatgoch, the Moravians were relying on Beardsley's word.

157. RMM 4/115/11/1, 18 May 1761.

158. MAB, Joachim Sensemann to Nathanael Seidel, P.H.C. 1755–75, Letters from Sichem and Kingsbury NY, 31 Dec. 1765.

159. Todd, *Olde Connecticut*, 215.

160. The count of Indians that Gideon gave to Cammerhoff in 1748 should be considered conservative, as it may have represented only those who were at the winter huts that day. Eighty Indians, "not including the children," were in attendance for a sermon delivered at Pachgatgoch in 1752 (RMM 3/114/6/1, 21 May). Ezra Stiles restates the figure of 127 Indians living at "the upper end of Kent on the west side of the Oustonnoc river" found in the 1762 census ([Stiles], *Collections of the Massachusetts Historical Society*, 10:112). Brother Edward Thorp, the last missionary at Pachgatgoch, reported a population of ninety-four in mid-1770 (MAB, Edward Thorp to John Ettwein, P.H.C. 1755–75, Letters from Sichem and Kingsbury NY, 13 May 1770 resp[ectively], 24 July). The 1774 colonial census lists sixty-two Indians in the town of Kent (PRCC, 14:490).

161. RMM 3/114/8/1, 16 Jan. 1754, 3/114/9/1, 22–23 Apr. 1754, 4/115/6/1, 2 Aug. 1756, 4/115/12/1, 27 Apr. 1762.

162. [Indian Papers], 2nd ser., 2:66–68d.

163. The discussion that follows is drawn from Dally-Starna and Starna, "'Amongst the Brown Flock'"; Dally-Starna and Starna, "American Indians and Moravians."

164. In 1725, after learning that the Indians at New Milford [Weantinock] and Potatuck "had lately several dances, and sundry of them have painted themselves as is usual for Indians to do that design war," Connecticut took steps to discourage such behavior: "It is therefore resolved, that if any Indian or Indians within the Colony shall be seen painted. . . . They shall be taken for enemies and proceeded against as such" (PRCC, 6:551). We suspect that this edict, along with other less obvious, but perhaps equally effective signals from the colony's inhabitants in the form of prejudicial words and actions, may have inhibited other similarly visible expressions of Indian culture.

165. MAB, Journals, Box JA I 11, 24 Sept.–4 Nov. 1745.

166. MAB, Bethlehem Diary, 24 July 1758, 19:56 [60]. That the image on Michael's jaw was of a wild boar is doubtful. It was most likely a rude rendering of a bear or perhaps a wolf's head.

167. It is an anthropological axiom that in areas where horticulture—farming—is dominant, so too is matrilineality. This correlation stems from the fact that women controlled and managed virtually all elements of this form of subsistence.

168. See Salwen, "Indians of Southern New England"; Snow, *Archaeology of New England*; Bragdon, *Native People*; Starna, "Pequots."

169. Spangenberg, *Account*, 91; Gollin, *Moravians in Two Worlds*, 67–89; Smaby, *Transformation*, 10–13.

170. Smaby, *Transformation*, 11–13.

171. There was a trend in Indian communities at this time toward bilateral descent.

172. Uttendörfer, "Missionsinstruktionen," 22–23; UAH R.3.A.8.2.a, Dec. 1740; RMM 4/115/15/18, n.d. [ca. May 1756]. See appendix 4, "Lists and Correspondence."

173. When visiting with Indian women, a Moravian was always in the company of other Indians, his wife, or the wife of a brother.

174. Axtell, *Invasion Within*, 81.

175. RMM 4/115/15/18, n.d. [ca. May 1756]. See appendix 4, "Lists and Correspondence."

176. UAH, Bethlehem Diary, R.14.A.a.3, 13 Dec. 1747; RMM 3/114/6/1, 16 Apr. 1752, parenthetical statement in Bishop Spangenberg's hand.

177. RMM 4/115/3/1, 16 Jan. 1755.

178. Uttendörfer, "Missionsinstruktionen," 51n120. For examples, see Masthay, *Mahican Language Hymns*.

179. RMM 3/114/7/1, 5 Dec. 1752.

180. See, generally, Cronon, *Changes*; Jordan and Kaups, *American Backwoods*. See also Starna and Relethford, "Deer Densities."

181. Axtell, *Invasion Within*; Campisi, "Fur Trade and Factionalism."

182. Axtell, *Invasion Within*, 78.

183. RMM 3/114/7/1, 3 Nov. 1752.

184. UAH, Martin Mack to Petrus Böhler, R.15.H.I.a.2.54, 14 Aug. 1760; Martin Mack to Joseph Spangenberg, R.15.H.I.a.2.55, 4 Sept. 1760.

185. RMM 3/114/2/1, 21 Aug. 1750.

186. Axtell, *Invasion Within*.

187. See Mancall, *Deadly Medicine*.

188. Axtell, *Invasion Within*; Frazier, *Mohicans of Stockbridge*; Mandell, *Behind the Frontier*.

189. RMM 3/114/5/1, 20 Feb. 1752.

190. Axtell, *Invasion Within*, 286.

191. Spangenberg, *Account*, 42.

192. Axtell, *Invasion Within*, 91.

193. Axtell, "Indian Conversions," 114. Quoted passage cited in Axtell, *Invasion Within*, 122–23.

194. Quoted passage cited in Axtell, *Invasion Within*, 133. Axtell's work is the most complete and best discussion on Protestant mission efforts in New England.

195. Uttendörfer, *Missionsinstruktionen*, 53, citing August Gottlieb Spangenberg's 1754 essay "Von der Arbeit der Brüder unter den Hieden in genere."

196. RMM 30/225/3, 14 Dec. 1748.

197. RMM 4/115/15/16, 6 Oct. 1755. See appendix 4, "Lists and Correspondence."

198. See Salisbury, "Embracing Ambiguity," 257.

199. Axtell, "Indian Conversions"; Axtell, "Some Thoughts"; Salisbury, "Embracing Ambiguity"; Salisbury, "Red Puritans."

200. Salisbury, "Embracing Ambiguity," 257–58.

201. See Fenton and Moore, Customs, 207–13; Heckewelder, History, Manners, and Customs, 225–26.

202. Fogelson, "History of the Study of Native North Americans," 147. On the topics of secularism and nonbelief in "traditional" societies, see Douglas, "Primitive Religion"; Radin, Primitive Man.

203. Berkhofer, Salvation and the Savage, 117.

204. There was no native American ordained a minister of the Moravian Church until 1946. The Roman Catholic Church, which had begun its missions a century earlier, waited until 1913. English Protestants, on the other hand, had, by the time of the Revolution, ordained 133 Indians in southern New England (Schwalbe, Dayspring on the Kuskokwim, 234; Axtell, Invasion Within, 225).

205. Berkhofer, Salvation and the Savage, 123–24, 159; Axtell, Invasion Within, 210. See also Campisi, Mashpee Indians; Mandell, Behind the Frontier; O'Brien, Dispossession.

206. Barth, Ethnic Groups; Axtell, Invasion Within, 285. See also Campisi, Mashpee Indians; Mandell, Behind the Frontier; O'Brien, Dispossession.

207. Unlike in other mission situations, there is no unambiguous indication that at Pachgatgoch baptized Indians or those seeking the sacrament were targets of ridicule or violence at the hands of their unconvinced traditionalist kith and kin. See discussions in Axtell, Invasion Within; Berkhofer, Salvation and the Savage.

208. The Law Papers, 1:42–43; [Indian Papers], 1st ser., 1:242–43; PRCC, 8:480–81; Wojciechowski, Paugussett Tribes, 252. It was probably these same clergymen who had gone to the Indians at Pachgatgoch the following summer in an attempt to divert their attention from the Moravians, enticing them to attend their sermons with promises of money and assistance with "outside matters" (RMM 1/III/1/1, 7 July 1743).

209. MAB, Epistola Tertia Johannis Friederici Cammerhoffii, Cammerhoff: Letters to Zinzendorf & al.: 1747–51; RMM 4/116/2/1, 1 Aug. to 3 Sept. 1747; UAH R.14.A.a.3, 21 Aug. to 17 Dec. 1747.

210. RMM 30/225/3/1, 20 Dec. 1748.

211. RMM 4/115/9/1, 30 Jan. 1760.

212. RMM 1/III/3/3, 1 Feb. 1743. See also the diary entry for 12 June 1751.

213. A perfect example of this is Gideon's effort to persuade David Warrup (Warrups, Warop, and var.) to be baptized while his wife Martha was speaking to Caritas about the state of her heart (RMM 3/114/3/1, 21 Mar. 1751; see also the entry for 6 May 1751).

214. See Trigger, *Natives and Newcomers*, 254–55; Axtell, *Invasion Within*, 282–86; Richter, *Ordeal of the Longhouse*, 115–16. See also Starna, "Biological Encounter."

215. For Iroquoian examples, see Richter, *Ordeal of the Longhouse*, 117, 126. See also Trigger, *Children of Aataentsic*, 1:51.

216. Axtell, *Invasion Within*, 279.

217. MAB, Joachim Sensemann to Nathanael Seidel, P.H.C. 1755–75, Letters from Sichem and Kingsbury NY, 31 Dec. 1765.

218. UAH, *Diarium von Pachgatgoch vom Monat April 1765* [to July], R.24.B.16.35.

219. See Gollin, *Moravians in Two Worlds*, 50–63.

220. MAB, Edward Thorp to Nathanael Seidel, P.H.C. 1755–75, Letters from Sichem and Kingsbury NY, 21 May 1764.

221. MAB, Edward Thorp to John Ettwein, P.H.C. 1755–75, Letters from Sichem and Kingsbury NY, 13 May 1770, resp[ectively], 24 July.

222. MAB, *Protocoll der Oeconomats Conferenz*, 1767–74:115–17, 155–56, 168–69.

223. MAB, Extract, September and October 1770, Records of Town and Country Congregations, 1768–70, Francis Böhler to Nathanael Seidel, P.H.C. 1755–75, Letters from Sichem and Kingsbury NY, 13 Oct. 1770.

224. Mandell, *Behind the Frontier*, 130–31.

225. Gideon's effort to encourage men to join the militia was in contravention of the wishes of the Indians, who "had met on that account and thought about what there was to be done in this case, and had discussed matters and come to an agreement among themselves: they did not want to involve themselves in this war, but wanted to stay out of it, which was to the satisfaction of all the young people" (RMM 4/115/10/1, 16 Nov. 1760).

226. See Frazier, *Mohicans of Stockbridge*; Jennings, *Empire of Fortune*, 199–200.

227. RMM 4/115/9/1, 21, 23 May 1759. See fig. 4, grave number 44. Paulus had lost a wife and child at the hands of colonial assailants in Orange County three years earlier (RMM 4/115/6/1, 20 Apr. 1756).

228. See Hagedorn, "Brokers of Understanding"; Richter, "Cultural Brokers"; Merrell, *American Woods*.

229. See Wojciechowski, *Paugussett Tribes*, 242–59.

230. See MAB, Nathanael Seidel to the congregation at Sichem, P.H.C. 1765–75, Letters from Sichem and Kingsbury NY, 5 Aug. 1772, and letters from the

congregation at Sichem, P.H.C. 1765–75, Letters from Sichem and Kingsbury NY, 26 Sept. 1772, 11 Aug. 1773, 12 May 1775.

231. MAB, *Diarium von Sichem*, Lititz Records, Sichem NY, Nov. 1771.

232. One early source asserts that Pachgatgoch—the "Scatacook tribe"—"furnished 100 warriors" during the Revolution, but this number is not supported by census data from the period (Barber, *Historical Collections*, 471; PRCC, 14:490).

233. [Indian Papers], 2nd ser., 2:66–68d.

234. Todd, *Olde Connecticut*, 214, 208.

Bischoff: 18 May to 5 June 1747

1. RMM 3/114/1/1. This travel diary, covering the period from 18 May to 5 June 1747, is by Johann David Bischoff, who had gone to Pachgatgoch to escort a number of Indians to Bethlehem and thence to Gnadenhütten. While in the area, he spoke to several of the Indians living at Shekomeko and Wechquadnach, who also expressed a wish to move.

2. Samuel Green Sr., who lived at Hope, New Jersey, or Samuel Green Jr., whose home was a few miles north on the Paulins Kill (Hamilton and Hamilton, *History of the Moravian Church*, 222, 232).

3. This may be the Indian woman described by Johann Christopher Pyrlaeus as the wife of a free Negro and baptized by Johannes von Watteville during his visit to the colonies in 1748. Given the name Anna Elisabeth, she was the daughter of Hannibal, a headman on Long Island (RMM 29/221/21/1, 1739–51).

4. The Hudson River. In their diaries the Moravians refer to the Hudson River as the North River, the name given it by the Dutch early in the seventeenth century (*Noortrivier*). We retain this usage throughout.

5. "*Plan*": "An agreed role or set of instructions (in accordance with the Saviour's intentions) and the place or area where it is to be carried out" (Faull, *Moravian Women's Memoirs*, 154). This term can be translated as "call," "post," "mission," or "charge" (Hamilton and Madeheim et al., *Bethlehem Diary*, 2:392).

6. Although Bischoff writes "Rauch," the context suggests that this is Johannes Rau. Subsequent occurrences of this spelling have been silently corrected.

7. The bark-covered house that the Moravians had built for themselves at Shekomeko, which they described as being very cold and smoky (RMM 1/111/1/1, 9 Oct. 1742).

8. In 1742 the reported Indian population of Sharon/Salisbury, where Wechquadnach was located, was forty-five: fifteen adult females, thirteen adult males, and seventeen children ([Indian Papers], 1st ser., 1:244c).

9. See the glossary.

10. "O Lord, save us, O Lord, deliver us." A satisfactory translation of this verse is found in Eberhardt's diary: "Bless both my Thought & Action, afford me thy Direction to thee alone be tending, Beginning, Mid[d]le, Ending." See entry for 8 May 1756.

11. "*Es Kammen auch gar von Wechquatnach Bartelmeus bruder Jonge Johannes Moses sein sohn zu uns.*"

12. The inference is that at Gnadenhütten, the Indians would have to provide entirely for themselves rather than make up for any shortfalls by working as wage laborers for surrounding colonists.

13. In Moravian spiritual discourse, the "enemy" is Satan. See the glossary.

14. Several families in the Rhinebeck area, including those of Jacob Maul, Zacharias Haber, and Christian Führer, had requested that the Brethren care for them and their children, and that they be permitted to build a school for themselves (MAB, *Epistola Tertia Johannis Friederici Cammerhoffii*, Cammerhoff: Letters to Zinzendorf & al.: 1747–51, 8–23 Mar. 1747).

15. This may be Martinus Hoffman. See the introduction.

16. A catalog of names, Indian and Christian, of those persons who are reported to have arrived in Bethlehem about a month later, is in RMM 3/114/10/1, 20 June–1 July 1747.

17. "She," in the context here and elsewhere, is a reference to "wife" or "companion."

18. Bischoff writes "*groß kinder*" (grandchildren). However, the catalog cited earlier specifies that it was this couple's children who accompanied them to Bethlehem in June of that year.

Bruce: 6 March to 5 May 1749

1. RMM 3/114/1/2. "*St. vet.*" is written below this line. This diary is by David Bruce, residing at Wechquadnach. The last entry is 5 May 1749. On 23 January–3 February 1749, Bruce had set out for Wechquadnach accompanied by Christian Frederick Post, Johannes, an Indian from there, and young Wilhelm Rau, who had traveled to Bethlehem the previous December in the company of von Watteville and Cammerhoff (UAH, Bethlehem Diary, R.14.A.a.5, Feb. 1749).

2. During their visit to the area in March 1749, Cammerhoff and Pezold baptized thirteen Indians at Wechquadnach and Pachgatgoch (RMM 26/211/7/1).

3. See Masthay, *Mahican Language Hymns*.

4. Bruce may have intended to cross out one of these names.

5. The Indians apparently were making maple sugar in the vicinity of Wechquadnach. For a description of this activity as reported near Stockbridge, see Hopkins, *Housatonic Indians*, 38n1. There are no mentions of sugar making at Pachgatgoch.

6. For the most authoritative discussion on the feminization of Christ in the Moravian Church, see Fogleman, *Jesus Is Female*. A treatment of the language peculiar to the Sifting Period is found in J. Reichel, *Dichtungstheorie*. See "Translation and Editorial Comments."

7. Bruce writes "*zugar schwamm*," and elsewhere "*zugar schwammp*," probably for the English "sugar swamp." In German "*Schwamm*" translates as "sponge" (and "fungus"), but it is also a reference to wet or soggy land, as it is in English. In colonial American English, "swamp" denoted "a tract of rich soil having a growth of trees and other vegetation, but too moist for cultivation" (OED). The Indians at Wechquadnach are preparing to go to a sugar bush.

8. "Side hole^d, thou art mine."

9. Erdmuth was also the name of Zinzendorf's first wife (Fries, *Moravian Heroes*, 44). "Body and soul enter into thee."

10. "Hut," as a neutral translation for "*Hütte*," is applied throughout. Elsewhere in the records diarists were more specific, employing terms such as "house" or "wigwam."

11. New Lights were practitioners of the religious revival known as the First Great Awakening.

12. There is no evidence, nor would it have been likely, that the Indians purchased the land in Sharon that Skinner offered to sell. For an early discussion of this matter, see DeForest, *History of the Indians of Connecticut*, 400–403. See also [Indian Papers], 1st ser., 1:244–46, 1st ser., 2:19–21, 2nd ser, 2:103–4.

13. "Low German" (*Niederdeutsch*), that is, Dutch.

14. This Martha is not to be confused with Gideon's wife.

15. At this council Martha was afforded the opportunity to seek redress for her son's death through revenge, a native practice that had endured despite decades of contact and social change. Although such an act would not have been condoned by the Moravians, there is no indication that Bruce intervened in this extremely serious matter. Nonetheless, in reaching her decision, Martha seems to have placed considerable reliance on the church's teachings.

16. With a small number of exceptions, there is little evidence that the Moravians stationed in the Housatonic Valley or the surrounding region had much success learning the local Indian languages. They, along with many of the Indians, spoke English. The language of the Pachgatgoch Indians was Wampano, an eastern dialect of Munsee. See Goddard, *Review of Mahican Language Hymns*; Dally-Starna and Starna, "Comment," 62, 64; DHNY, 3:614–16; and the introduction.

17. Martin or Andreas.

18. Justina or Elisabeth.

19. This sentence reads, "*Paulus hat ein Ledige brud: sie und der heiland fuhrte auf den rechte spur*," which is incomplete and thus unclear. Perhaps Bruce intended to establish a connection between this and the previous sentence: that is, Gottlob's wife, along with Paulus's brother, is being led onto the right path by the Savior.

20. "Flown home": that is, died.

21. The last two weeks of Lent.

22. Possibly one of Friederich Streit's sons, Johann George (b. 1721) or Friederich (b. 1722).

23. "Occasion" is frequently used by the Moravians when referring to a religious gathering or event; however, it is not a liturgical or theological term. See the glossary.

24. There is no evidence that the Moravians wore or affected Indian styles of dress. Of course, this statement is meaningful only if Indians in mid-eighteenth-century southern New England actually outfitted themselves in a noticeably different way from colonists in the first place. In February 1742 Büttner writes that while on the trail with a group of Indians from Shekomeko, he was taken for one of them by colonists, probably because he was wrapped in a blanket to protect himself from the cold like the others (RMM 1/III/2/1, 14 Feb. 1742). Elsewhere in their diaries, the Moravians remark that they purchase or receive their clothing from benefactors in New York City, wash their "shirts" and "whites," and repair their "shoes," none of these items resembling anything that can be identified as exclusively Indian apparel. At no point in the Pachgatgoch records do they describe "traditional" Indian attire or hair styles; indeed, they offer nothing at all in the way of physical descriptions of native people. In one diary entry from Pachgatgoch, the Indians are said to have walked barefoot until it became cold; in December 1755, an Indian woman asks "permission" to go out and make brooms so that she can get a pair of "shoes" for herself. Moccasins were most likely worn by the Indians, although white-tailed deer and, thus, deer hides normally used to make such footwear were in short supply. See Cronon, *Changes*, 101; and the introduction. For a sketch of a Stockbridge Indian wearing what appear to be moccasins, see figure 2. Indians who hired themselves out to nearby farmers were sometimes paid in clothing, and they often exchanged the wooden wares they made for clothes and blankets. In the diary entry for 20 April 1752, children at Pachgatgoch are reported to be wearing "a piece of shirt" that Brother Rundt describes as flapping above their heads as they ran to school.

25. This is most likely Joshua, formerly Nanhún, from Shekomeko. Baptized by Gottlob Büttner in 1742, he moved to Gnadenhütten on 25 April 1746 (RMM 1/III/1/1).

Joshua had departed Bethlehem for Wechquadnach on 21 March/1 April 1749 with letters for Bruce and the intention to bring back several of the brethren and sisters from there, his relatives in particular (UAH, Bethlehem Diary, R.14.A.a.5, Apr. 1749).

26. Martha, Gideon's wife, was originally from the Indian community of Potatuck (RMM 1/III/1/1, 3 Jan. 1744).

27. The land mentioned is that in dispute near Sharon. Two years earlier, in May 1747, Moses, or Qotomuck, had been a signatory to a petition by the Indians there, requesting a grant of land, "as we being In fear of being turned off by Some person or other." The Indians also asked to be schooled ([Indian Papers], 2nd ser., 2:103–4; see also PRCC, 9:308).

28. Bruce writes, "*mit den andern verdorbene gesetzliche leute.*" "*Gesetzliche Leute*" are persons who follow Mosaic law and exhibit a superficiality of character, particularly with respect to religious practice.

29. Jonathan Moore (b. Windsor CT, 1680, d. Salisbury, 1770). Moore's name appears on a 1749 petition to the Moravians requesting a minister, and later, on a list of members of the congregation at Sichem, in the Oblong (W. Reichel, *Memorial of the Dedication*, 68; MAB, Memorabilien, Lititz Records, Diarium, Sichem NY, Nov.–Dec. 1769).

30. See the introduction.

31. This is a continuation of the land dispute mentioned earlier.

32. The "shore," or, more commonly, the "seaside," are general references to Long Island Sound, but in particular to the area near the mouth of the Housatonic River and Milford, Connecticut, that the Moravians sometimes designated Old Milford. Living in and around the colonial settlements on the Sound was an unknown number of native people. Indians traveled there on foot or by water to sell brooms, baskets, canoes, and other items that were manufactured at their upper Housatonic locations. Frequently staying for weeks at a time, they visited and may have lodged with relatives, who, in turn, would journey north to Pachgatgoch and elsewhere upriver. Strong kinship and economic ties linked these communities, and on occasion, families or individual family members would relocate from the seaside to Pachgatgoch, or the reverse. In several cases, children whose parents lived and worked at the seaside were taken to Pachgatgoch and cared for there by relatives.

33. Bruce's expressions of pessimism and despondency are understandable given the fact that the land around Wechquadnach was being sold, placing the Indian community there under certain and immediate threat.

34. See the glossary.

35. Farm work.

36. In 1743 Isaac Yanarem or Vernernum (probably Van Arenan or Van Aarnem, see Sedgwick, *General History*, 39) from "Alobeck," an unidentified location in Dutchess County, New York, purchased some 2,000 acres of land in Connecticut from "Stephen John Indian, of Squampamack [Ghent, New York] in the county of Albany." Two years later the land was conveyed to Joshua Lazell and Joseph Fuller of Kent, who then petitioned the Connecticut assembly that they be compensated for their "trouble" in obtaining for the colony the Indian title to what was actually 4,820 acres of land on the west side of the Housatonic River, bounded on the south by the "country" lands at Kent and on the north by the town of Sharon (PRCC, 9:139–40, 10:25, 138–39). In 1749 "Vanarenem" received a notice from John Williams, the Sharon "register" or town clerk, informing him that the land on which the Indians were living belonged to Joseph Skinner and adding: "I would be glad You would let the Indians know how the Case is; I Should be glad of it had been otherwise but I cannot do more for them than I have done" ([Indian Papers], 1st ser., 2:23).

37. The indication is that Skinner paid the Indians for improvements they had made to the land.

38. Possibly Joseph Park, originally from Middletown, Connecticut (Sedgwick, *General History*, 144).

39. A colonial official in New Milford, perhaps the justice of the peace, Samuel Canfield.

40. Bruce confuses the days of the week and the corresponding dates: 20 and 22 April appear twice, 21 April not at all.

41. Or "them."

42. The German noun used by Bruce throughout his diary is "*Karig*," or "*Karrig*," suggesting a two-wheeled vehicle.

43. Or "relative."

44. Or "their."

45. Bruce writes "*von gorigen hehr*," perhaps intending to write "*von vorigen her*" (from previous times).

46. "This is my heart, locked up in God's wounds, also in the side."

47. On the Paulin's Kill, New Jersey.

48. The Moravians crossed the Delaware at about Columbia, New Jersey, and Portland, Pennsylvania.

49. On this day, word was received in Bethlehem that Bruce had arrived in Nazareth with twenty-nine Indians from Wechquadnach, who later were taken to Gnadenhütten. Some would live in Gnadenhütten proper, others in a nearby house that the Pachgatgoch Indians had built during their brief stay in 1747, at a place they

called "Gnaden-Hügel" (Hill of Grace). A list of these Indians, and also one of a second party that arrived some three months later, survives (UAH, Bethlehem Diary, R.14.A.a.5, 5/16, 10/21 May, 5/16 Aug. 1749).

Büninger: 29 March to 6 December 1750

1. RMM 3/114/2/1. Abraham Büninger kept this diary from 29 March to 6 December 1750; there are no entries for September. Although he was first sent to Pachgatgoch in September 1749, no diary for the period before March 1750 has been located. Büninger's primary duty was to serve the Indians at Pachgatgoch, but also to care for those remaining at Wechquadnach. The brethren were instructed that the house there could be used for meetings and services until Pachgatgoch was properly set up. Once in Pachgatgoch, Büninger resided first in Gideon's house, initiating what would be more than thirteen years of nearly continuous reporting on this mission (UAH, Bethlehem Diary, R.14.A.a.5, 4–15 Sept., 24 Sept.–5 Oct. 1749). Written above the line: "st. vet."

2. Although Büninger writes "Rauch," this person is Johannes Rau, who by 1755 had acquired the title to the land on which Shekomeko had been located (UAH, Br. Christian Seidel's Diarium v. seiner Reise u. Arbeit nach u. in Pachgatgoch, R.15.H.I.b.5.16, 13 May 1755).

3. "Wood," that is, logs. From Pachgatgoch's location just west of the Housatonic River, the land rises steeply in elevation, some nine hundred feet over a horizontal distance of a little more than one-half mile.

4. Details on how this structure was assembled are unknown. Moravian log-building techniques developed in Europe, which were later used in America, are discussed in Jordan, "Log Construction." See Dally-Starna and Starna, "Picturing Pachgatgoch"; and the introduction.

5. These are dugout canoes, the traditional watercraft of Indians in southern New England, routinely shaped from white pine (Pinus strobus) or American chestnut (Castanea dentata). Other woods used by native boatmakers in the region over time included yellow poplar, or tulip tree (Liriodendron tulipfera), and eastern cottonwood (Populus deltoides). Metal tools significantly reduced the time and effort required to hollow out and finish such boats, which were narrow and low-board and, when used on freshwater rivers, probably less than twenty feet in length. Indians in the Housatonic Valley manufactured canoes for their own use and also to sell or barter, most often on their trips to Long Island Sound and the Milford area.

6. Indians often hired themselves out to surrounding colonial farmers. See the introduction.

7. This and the schoolhouse are the same building.

8. On a number of occasions the Moravians traveled to Stockbridge to meet with Indians who resided there. However, visits of Stockbridge Indians to Pachgatgoch, or elsewhere in the Housatonic Valley, were somewhat more frequent, fostered, it . seems, primarily by political concerns, but also by kinship ties.

9. People who had left the traditional Protestant Church in response to the First Great Awakening.

10. This is probably the Reverend Samuel Hopkins (1693–1755), an influential figure in the establishment of Stockbridge (Colee, "Housatonic-Stockbridge," 37–38; Frazier, *Mohicans of Stockbridge*). See also the entry for 17 February 1751. Hopkins's wife was Esther Edwards (1695–1766), the daughter of the Reverend Timothy Edwards (1669–1758).

11. Possibly a reference to the Indian William from "Westenhoek or Wanachquatico," baptized in Bethlehem before September 1749 (UAH, Bethlehem Diary, R.14.A.a.5, 4/15 Sept. 1749).

12. Sankiwenecha (also Zankewenachek) appears most often in the records as Umpachenee (var.) (b. ca. 1696, d. 22 Aug. 1751), who, before the establishment of Stockbridge, was one of two documented headmen of the Housatonic Indians. His village of Skatehook was located near Sheffield, Massachusetts. The other headman was Kunkapot (var.) (b. ca. 1690, d. 1763–1766), from the village of Wnahktukook or Whahktukook. They later shared headman status at Stockbridge. Umpachenee's Christian name was Aaron, and he is known in English-language documents as "Lieutenant" rather than "Captain," a designation that is attributed only to Kunkapot (whose Christian name was John). Both men apparently received commissions in the Massachusetts militia, which may account for their officer titles (Hopkins, *Housatonic Indians*, 14–15, 17; Colee, "Housatonic-Stockbridge," 3, 123–35; UAH, Bethlehem Diary, R.15.A.a.5, 2/13 Aug. 1749).

13. 1 Tim. 3.16: "Great indeed, we confess, is the mystery of our religion: He was manifested in the flesh."

14. Shaking or touching and pressing hands was a greeting and parting behavior practiced by Indians throughout eastern North America. See Axtell, "Imagining the Other," 43–45.

15. Or "relatives."

16. Büninger is referring to Oswegy, Owegy, or, often, Owego, at present Owego, New York. This was one of several mid-eighteenth-century mixed Indian communities that lay along the Upper Susquehanna River in southern New York and northern Pennsylvania, namely, Tiogy (Tioga), Otsiningo, Onoquaga, and Unadilla, where

numbers of Conoys, Shawnees, Nanticokes, Tuscaroras, Oneidas, Onondagas, Cayugas, Delawares, Mahicans, and southern New England Algonquians had taken refuge (See Elliott, "Otsiningo"; Gillette and Funk, "Upper Susquehanna"; Mancall, *Valley of Opportunity*; Grumet, *Historic Contact*, 424–30).

17. This may have been Timothy Woodbridge.

18. Probably Martin Kellogg (b. Deerfield MA, 1686, d. Newington CT, 1758), a militia captain, farmer, interpreter, and former Mohawk captive regarded by most to be an incompetent (Frazier, *Mohicans of Stockbridge*, 101; Axtell, "Scholastic Frontier," 69–70.)

19. This is "An Act for encouraging the People known by the Name of *Unitas Fratrum* or *United Brethren*, to settle in his Majesty's Colonies in *America*," promulgated by the British Parliament on 24 June 1749 ([*Acta Fratrum Unitatas*], 635–38). See the introduction.

20. The act named previously reads, in part, that "the said Congregation [*Unitas Fratrum* or United Brethren] are an ancient Protestant Episcopal Church" ([*Acta Fratrum Unitatas*], 635–36).

21. "*Leimen*": clay, also loam.

22. "*Feür Mauer*," in modern German "*Feuermauer*," can refer to a chimney, a chimney shaft, or to the protective wall behind a fireplace.

23. The clay or clayey soil that the Indians carried in was mixed with water and possibly other materials, such as grass, and used to chink the open spaces between the logs and roof elements, and also to cover surfaces that would be exposed to the heat of a fire.

24. The Moravians' crop land—one- or two-acre plots—was allotted to them by the Indians. The brethren arranged to have the land plowed by colonial farmers living nearby or, in a few instances, by an Indian.

25. There are a number of instances in which the Indians at Pachgatgoch helped the Moravians plant and work their fields. There is little indication, however, that the brethren reciprocated to any degree; nor did they depend on the Indians to provide them with what they could grow for themselves. See the introduction.

26. A term used in the past to describe a nonspecific chill or fever.

27. Büninger was sufficiently acquainted with the nature of Indian child-rearing practices—which were characterized by positive inducements rather than punishments—to know that any application of the disciplinary measures with which he was familiar would be counterproductive.

28. The falls at New Milford—known locally as "The Great Falls"—stood two and one-half miles downriver from New Milford, at the hamlet of Still River. The Shepaug

dam, built on the Housatonic in the town of Southbury in the mid-1950s, raised water levels to form Lake Lillinoah, submerging the falls. Indians from Pachgatgoch fished at this location throughout May and into early June of each year for the migratory common shad (*Alosa sapidissima*) and lampreys (*Petromyzonidae*).

29. Indians and colonists alike grew a variety of bush and pole beans.

30. The Moravians expressed concern any time that the Indians left Pachgatgoch and traveled beyond their influence, fearing the worst when it came to the temptations they might encounter, especially where alcohol was concerned.

31. The suggestion here is that the Indians had to portage for a distance of three miles, from an unknown point above to somewhere below the Great Falls at New Milford. Downriver from the falls, the Housatonic flowed through a steep-sided gorge, making access to its waters difficult.

32. Büninger hesitates to hold a service because he did not have anyone to interpret for him. The Indians remind him, however, of their ability to understand English.

33. In Moravian religious discourse, "Mother" refers to the Holy Spirit. See the glossary.

34. This location would be near Gaylordsville.

35. Lengths of logs were probably squared with an adze and then split into planks.

36. "Quarter-of-an-hour" (*Viertelstunde*), a religious service or devotion named for its duration. See the glossary.

37. There are frequent references in the records to Indians hunting, but nothing points to the Moravians at Pachgatgoch doing so. There is a single exception from Shekomeko, where Rauch and Büttner went out to find ducks (RMM 1/III/1/1, 5 Oct. 1742). The Indians sometimes supplied the brethren with deer and bear meat, as well as with fish, which were used to supplement the foodstuffs they purchased from nearby merchants and farmers. There is one mention of a Moravian fishing on his own (RMM 3/113/1/5, 1 Aug. 1746).

38. June 24 (New Style) is Witness Festival in the Moravian Church, the saint's day for John the Baptist.

39. Children, perhaps relatives, for whom Erdmuth apparently cares.

40. Gnadensee, the name the Moravians gave present Indian Lake/Pond, on which Wechquadnach was located. It is bisected by the New York–Connecticut line (Dutchess County, New York; the town of North East; and Litchfield County, Connecticut, town of Sharon). See the gazetteer.

41. "As many as touched Him were made well." After Mt. 14.36: "If you had faith."

42. Büninger may have intended to use bark as building or roofing material.

43. Rom. 9.5: "God who is over all be blessed for ever."

44. Although Büninger's use of the plural "*Hütten*" may be a reflection of his Swiss dialect, there are indications in the diaries that Gideon occupied attached huts, elsewhere in Connecticut described as "double" huts (houses or wigwams). See the introduction; and Dally-Starna and Starna, "Picturing Pachgatgoch," 9; [Indian Papers], 1st ser., 1:101.

45. In his use of the term "*Fremde*" (strangers), Büninger is most likely referring to Indians who are from outside the community.

46. The New Style Gregorian calendar was not officially adopted in the British-Atlantic empire until 1752. Büninger's shift to this calendar, which had taken place in the German Protestant states fifty years earlier, was so the daily watchwords and festival days celebrated in the colonies would correspond to those of the mother church. German Protestants, however, retained the Old Style dating of the movable festival of Easter until 1776.

47. Rom. 6.10: "The death He died He died to sin, once for all." "That through His death we may have life."

48. An unfinished word beginning with the letters *hu* is placed before "sickly," perhaps for "*Husten*" (cough).

49. A floor for the loft.

50. On 16 February 1750, "Maywhehew sachum Indion of Caticock . . . with the Con sent of ye Companey of Indions in sd Scaticook" sold some 600 acres of land, for 110 pounds, to one Samuel Alger, representing the Nine Partners patentees of Dutchess County, New York. On the same day, Alger conveyed the identical parcel, for the same price, to John Mills of Kent ([Indian Papers], 2nd ser., 2:44–45b). Elsewhere in the Moravian records, Mills is described as a "neighbor" and sometime visitor to the Indians at Pachgatgoch (Schaghticoke), who he occasionally hired to work for him. Büninger's estimate of the sum that the Indians received per acre of land—about two pounds—does not correspond to the price paid in the February 1750 transaction. In October of that year, the Connecticut General Assembly appointed a committee to look into a purchase from the Indians of "many hundred acres" of land, made "without any liberty" by "several persons living in New York Province," who then "made conveyances of some part thereof to others" (PRCC, 9:566).

51. "~~Thou bloody hands, bless us, etc.~~" Jn. 3.16: "For God so loved the world."

52. "Thou bloody hands, bless us."

53. Jn. 6.57: "He who eats me will live because of me."

54. There are several instances in the records where a shortage of provisions is

mentioned, particularly during the late winter and spring, which was the hungry time for Indian people.

55. The manufacture and sale of baskets and brooms was a mainstay of the cash-and-barter economy of the Pachgatgoch Indians. From all indications, both were woodsplint-fashioned items. Black ash (*Fraxinus nigra*) was the preferred material for making woodsplint baskets in this part of New England, although white oak (*Quercus alba*) and maples were also used (Turnbaugh and Turnbaugh, "Weaving the Woods," 84; McMullen, "Interpreting Woodsplint Basketry"; Richmond, "Schaghticoke Basket-Making"; and generally, McMullen and Handsman, *Woodsplint Baskets*). Brooms were typically made from silver/gray birch (*Betula alleghaniensis*) or black birch (*B. lenta*), and sometimes white oak (Speck, "Notes," 189).

56. "Going home," often "go home," that is, to die. See the glossary.

57. Rachel's burial in a coffin is a departure from native practice and reflects Christian influence. In the past, the body of a deceased person was drawn into a flexed position—knees to the chest and arms placed around the knees—and wrapped in a mat, or possibly hides or furs, and then buried in a circular, relatively shallow grave. Archaeological data from southeastern Connecticut demonstrate the persistence of traditional burial practices as late as 1720, which changed during the First Great Awakening of the 1740s and the appearance of Christian missionaries (Kevin McBride, personal communication, 2002). There are, however, few mortuary data reported or published from western Connecticut or the Housatonic Valley.

58. The reason is not given; however, the Moravians often postponed religious services when colonists were present.

59. Brother David Bruce died in Wechquadnach on 9 July 1749 (MAB, Bethlehem Diary, 1749–Apr. 1750, 8:479).

60. Heb. 9.12: "[H]e entered once for all into the Holy Place, taking [. . .] his own blood, thus securing an eternal redemption."

61. Wechquadnach was without a resident Moravian at this time.

62. Lk. 12.36: "Be like servants who are waiting for their master."

63. The Indians apparently had been hired to cut wheat or oats.

64. The meaning behind the phrase "*ganz Indianisch*" (entirely in the Indian fashion) is unknown.

65. Rushes or cat-tails were woven/stitched together to create mats, not only to use as bedding, but also as wigwam coverings. They were sometimes decorated.

66. The German verb used here is "*fahren*," which excludes horseback riding as a mode of transportation. Travel might have been by canoe.

67. Büninger, the Indians at Pachgatgoch, and people living nearby, Indians and

colonists alike, were probably suffering from influenza. Classic symptoms, so well described by Büninger, include a hard paroxysmal cough, severe headache, fever, lassitude, malaise, prostration, anorexia, and nosebleed, in addition to the common complication of a middle-ear infection.

68. There is little in the records to suggest that the Moravians stood in opposition to or disparaged Indian medicinal practices. In addition to the assistance rendered Büninger, Sensemann receives a remedy that, in his diary, he identifies simply as "besson" [béson: medicine]. See Masthay, *Schmick's Mahican Dictionary*, 164. Still, on another occasion, Sensemann is critical of a young Indian woman for searching out an "Indian doctor." *Béson* was also used to mean something imbued with power, such as an amulet or charm, or a poison; the word is found widely in the Moravian records. See, for example, Zeisberger, "History of the North American Indians"; Gipson, *Moravian Indian Mission*. Gideon is a central figure at Pachgatgoch, where the treatment of ailments and afflictions is concerned. For example, in the entry for 14 August 1751, Büninger reports that an Indian woman bitten by a rattlesnake "was still very ill, because no one was able to extract the venom as well as Brother Gideon." See also Spangenberg, *Account*, 104. A colonist living nearby visited Pachgatgoch to ask Gideon for advice about his joint pain, which no local physician had been able to alleviate. He recommended that the man use a sweat house, which Gideon undertook to build for him. In addition, the Moravians applied their medical skills, primarily bleeding, in an attempt to aid Indian people. Nonetheless, when neither native practitioners nor the Moravians could effect a cure, the Indians did not hesitate to seek outside help, going to colonial doctors in New Milford or Woodbury. As an important aside, none of the Moravians reported any firm evidence for shamans (*powwows*) or their ceremonies in the Indian communities where they lived or visited. See Simmons, "Shamanism," for a perspective on *powwows* in southern New England. However, while among the Housatonic Indians in far southwestern Massachusetts during the winter of 1735, Timothy Woodbridge did attend and describe what was clearly a shamanistic ritual (Hopkins, *Housatonic Indians*, 35–37).

69. A New Style/Old Style date.

70. The swelling may be from Büninger's middle-ear infection.

71. Given the choice, the Moravians preferred preparing foods they were familiar with, using ingredients purchased from nearby merchants and what they could grow in their gardens, such as corn, beans, turnips, currants, cucumbers, potatoes, and cabbages, from which, on at least one occasion, they made sauerkraut (UAH, Martin Mack to Petrus Böhler, R.15.H.I.a.2.61, 28 Oct. 1761; RMM I/III/I/I, 14 May 1745).

72. "Tabernacle" is a reference to the living body, the temporary shelter of the soul. See the glossary.

73. *"Gichter"* (convulsions). Like so many others at Pachgatgoch, this child may have contracted influenza, suffering convulsions caused by high fever. Death from this disease is common in infants under one year.

74. Nicolaus Rau.

75. Rapid recovery from influenza, which Samuel probably had also contracted, is the usual case, at least in modern populations; however, some individuals nonetheless experience lassitude for weeks or months after the acute stage of the disease has passed, which might have suggested to Büninger a return of the illness.

76. The upper floor is in the loft.

77. August 13, the festival day commemorating the spiritual renewal of the *Unitas Fratrum* in 1727.

78. The Moravian Church maintained a mission among the Inuits in Greenland from 1733 until 1900, when it was turned over to the Danish Lutheran Church. Gideon's question concerning the brethren there stems from the constant flow of information that circulated among Moravian congregations, making its way to native people, about their missions elsewhere in the world. To illustrate, when the news of the destruction of Gnadenhütten in 1755 reached the Greenland missions, "the Eskimos brought skins and blubber [to the missionaries] for their faraway fellow believers" (Hamilton and Hamilton, *History of the Moravian Church*, 52, 260, 499–500; see also RMM 30/225/3/1, 21 Dec. 1748).

79. Jn. 3.7: "You must be born anew."

80. "I am the door [. . .] and to him who knocks it will be opened." Jn. 10.7, Mt. 7.8.

81. Mt. 11.5: "The poor have good news preached to them."

82. "If only with my Husband alone."

83. "Christ's blood and righteousness."

84. The sweat house was a prominent feature of native life at Pachgatgoch and was frequented by segregated groups of men and women.

85. This was probably a catted chimney, made of horizontally laid, small-diameter lengths of wood. The spaces between would have been chinked inside and out.

86. Büninger was chinking the interior of this log house.

87. The books mentioned here attacking the Moravians and Zinzendorf were written by Jacob Lischy (b. 1719, d. Codorus PA, 1781), a Swiss-born Moravian minister who left the church in 1747, joining the German Reformed Church of York, Pennsylvania (W. Reichel, *Memorials*, 25–26n; and W. Reichel, "Register of Members," 334). The first was printed in German in 1749 and the second, written with Gerardus Kulenkamp, in Dutch in 1750. See *Eine warenede Wächter-Stimm an alle Gott und Jesum liebende Seelen. Hergenommen aus dem überaus wichtigen Evangelio von den Falschen Propheten*

zuerst in einer predig am 8 Sonntag nach Trinitatis der Reformirten Gemeinde an der kleinen Catores mündlich zugeruffen und hernach solches mit kurzen doch gründlichen Anmerckungen von den sogenandten Währischen [sic] Brüdern oder Zinzendörffern beträffeiget: und auf vielfältiges Begehren, zu desto allgemeinerer Warnung und Erbauung [Germantown PA]; and Anatomie der Herrnhuthsche secte: of gewigtige gedenk stukken meest van gewezene vrienden, en voorname leden dier gesinte uitgegeven, ontdekkende hare grouwelyke geheimen der Godloosheit zo wel in de Lere, als voornamelyk in de praktyk: uit het hoogduitsch vertaalt: met nodige en uitvoerige aanmerkingen voorzien, en met een voorbericht, waar in, onder anderen, een Boekje, onlangs van . . . J.F. Beyen [Amsterdam, The Netherlands].

88. "[T]he result of righteousness, quietness and trust for ever." "Let us rest utterly secure."

89. There is no hint about the purpose of these journeys.

90. Also "acritches," "akritches," "acritjes," "argritgens," and others. The word appears in entries written in the months of September and October. Masthay, Schmick's Mahican Dictionary, 76, lists "Akridges, Akridches" with the suggested meanings of "grits, hominy, pone," but also "potatoes." We are unsure whether it is a "slightly Germanized, English word," as Masthay contends. In von Watteville and Cammerhoff is found "Acritgens," a food that is not described but is eaten along with bear's fat (RMM 30/225/3, 7 Dec. 1748). However, in examining the contexts in which this word and its variations appear in the Moravian records, and by drawing analogies to known native foods in the region, we propose that this is roasted, hulled, and then cracked corn. The meal that was produced stored well and was easily carried by people on the trail. It could be stirred into water and drunk, boiled to make a porridge (often with other food ingredients added), or mixed with sugar or dried fruits and eaten as is.

91. Cammerhoff and David Zeisberger had traveled from Bethlehem to Onondaga in May–June 1750, returning in August (Beauchamp, Moravian Journals, 24–105; see also Doblin and Starna, Journals of Claus and Weiser).

92. Heb. 9.12: "He entered once for all into the Holy Place, taking [. . .] his own blood, thus securing an eternal redemption."

93. Büninger married Martha Mariner in 1746.

94. White wampum (wampumpeag) beads were made from whelks (Busycon canaliculatum and B. carica); purple or "black" wampum, which appeared somewhat later in time, from the quahog or hard-shell clam (Mercenaria mercenaria). Strings of wampum were used to announce urgent and important business, to accompany the "words" of a message brought to a meeting or treaty conference, and to affirm that message (See Ceci, "Value of Wampum"; Fenton, Great Law; Jennings et al., Iroquois Diplomacy).

95. The homeland of the Iroquoian-speaking Mohawks was in the middle Mohawk Valley of New York State, west of Albany.

96. No record of this conference has been located.

97. "Wiping away the tears," an expression that has its origins in native funerary rites, became an integral part of Eastern Woodlands diplomatic protocol soon after contact. Before a council could begin, the assembled participants would metaphorically "wipe away the tears," that is, publicly condole the deaths that had occurred among them since their last meeting (See Jennings et al., *Iroquois Diplomacy*). Algonquians in New England practiced forms of treaty protocol similar to those of the Iroquois.

98. The record suggests that the Indians residing in the Housatonic Valley of Connecticut did not see themselves as politically aligned with those at Stockbridge, some of whom were their kin. However, this was apparently not the view of the headmen at Stockbridge, who on a few occasions issued directives to the Indians at Pachgatgoch, which were received with indifference.

99. "Everyone then who hears these words of mine and does them will be like a wise man."

100. These three persons are siblings.

101. 1 Jn. 1.7: "And the blood of Jesus His Son cleanses us from all sin."

102. Lk. 22.44: "And being in an agony [. . .] his sweat became like great drops of blood falling down upon the ground."

103. Eph. 5.23: "Christ is the head of [. . .] his body, and is Himself its Savior."

104. That is, there were no interpreters available.

105. Acts 4.12: "And there is salvation in no one else, for there is no other name under heaven given among men by which we must be saved[,]" "than the name Jesus Christ."

106. The mill in Sharon was owned and operated by Gerhard Winegar.

107. This may be Jonathan Sackett (b. Westfield MA, 1695/96, d. Kent CT, 1773), or perhaps his son Jonathan (b. Tolland CT, 1727, d. Kent CT, 1777). See Grant, *Town of Kent*, 68.

108. Büninger may have suffered from a food-related illness. Gideon's medicine was probably a tea, made from any number of wild plants, that acted as a demulcent. For an important discussion of native remedies, see Herrick, *Iroquois Medical Botany*.

109. 1 Jn. 4.19: "We love, because he first loved us."

110. 1 Jn. 4.19: "He first loved us."

111. The cemetery, after the hill on which the cemetery at Herrnhut was located.

112. A reference to Jesus Christ. See the glossary.

113. "He who believes in me will not be put to shame." After Rom. 9.33.

114. Büninger apparently was not confident that his preaching in English would be fully understood by the Indians without the use of a native translator.

Sensemann: 12 February to 16 June 1751

1. RMM 3/114/3/1. This diary, covering the period from 12 February to 16 June 1751, was written by Joachim Sensemann. There was no missionary at Pachgatgoch between the time of Büninger's departure on 30 November 1750 and Sensemann's arrival. Sensemann provides marginalia and interlinear text to be inserted in his diary entries, which are noted.

2. "So Israel dwelt in safety." "This child shall be unharmed."

3. "I will set them together like sheep in a fold." "No evil shall come upon you, this the Lord's protection will ensure." After the seventh verse of "Ich heb mein Augen sehnlich auf," by Cornelius Becker. See Julian, Dictionary of Hymnology, 1:121, 711.

4. This is the "helpers'" or "workers' conference," whose members were leaders and influential persons in Pachgatgoch. Matters of importance would be discussed by this group before being communicated to the community at large. It first met on 11 October 1750. See the glossary.

5. Two of Gideon's daughters had gone to Bethlehem: Maria, who married there in 1744, and Christina, who had left with von Watteville in 1748. See the introduction; RMM 30/225/3, 21 Dec. 1748.

6. We have not identified this alleged land owner.

7. Information on an Indian community at "Westenhook" is scant and somewhat confused. In earlier literature the term "Westenhook" is equated with Stockbridge. It has also been applied to a group of Indians who sold land on Kinderhook Creek in New York colony in 1679; as a locale on the boundary of New York and Connecticut in 1726; and as a name for the Housatonic River (Colee, "Housatonic-Stockbridge," 115). A 1705 land patent also carries the name (Kim, Landlord and Tenant, 283–84). Sauthier's 1779 map places Westenhook in the area between Copake Falls, New York, and South Egremont, Massachusetts, just east of the New York–Massachusetts line (DHNY, 1, map facing 526). A Moravian reports that the Indian Joshua traveled "some 40 miles" on the day he had returned to Pachgatgoch, presumably from Westenhook, where he had been visiting. See entry for 24 April 1752. This would put his starting point in the far southwestern corner of Massachusetts, possibly in the vicinity of Sauthier's "Westenhook." Gideon's son Joshua delivered a message from Sir William Johnson to the Indians here in 1758 (UAH R.15.H.I.b.5.15.a, 28 Apr.). In 1675 certain Mahican headmen drew a distinction between their people — "we

Mahikanders"—and "'western corner' Indians," which suggests that the Indians living at Westenhook were probably Housatonics (Leder, *Indian Records*, 37). "Westenhook" is the English spelling of the Dutch "*Westenhoeck*" (western corner).

8. "And no inhabitant will say, 'I am sick'; the people who dwell there will be forgiven their iniquity." "Grace seemed to awaken us, grace kissed, grace slumbered, could be felt, could be savored, grace also made things go awry."

9. "God knows that you may charge your children and your household after you to keep my way." After Gen. 18.19. "And another 1000 hearts."

10. "*Welsch Hu[h]n*." This may be a wild turkey (*Meleagris gallopavo*).

11. Mack's first wife, Jeannette/Johannetta Rau, had died in 1749.

12. The minister mentioned is perhaps the Reverend Samuel Hopkins, a student of Jonathan Edwards, who served the communities of Great Barrington and Sheffield from 1743 until 1769. He was the nephew of Samuel Hopkins (Colee, "Housatonic-Stockbridge," 37–38; Marsden, *Jonathan Edwards*).

13. Or "relatives."

14. "[F]an *kuchen*," in modern German "*Pfannkuchen*." This may be a kind of pan bread made from corn meal or wheat flour.

15. "Thus says the Lord God, who gathers the outcasts of Israel, I will gather yet others to him besides those already gathered." "Hail, enter the house."

16. "*Quasten*": tassels. We are unable to identify this plant.

17. "Remember not the former things, nor consider the things of old. Behold, I am doing a new thing." "For at no other time of the church did the side sparkle so bloody."

18. "Then the nations will know that I the Lord sanctify Israel." "And that the kingdom of Jesus has not been a fantasy and an empty dream."

19. For insertion here: "for she expected to be delivered of a child soon."

20. "Papa" is Zinzendorf.

21. For insertion here: "a blessing."

22. "[T]his is the covenant [. . .]: I will put my law within them, and I will write it upon their hearts." "Your sweet gospel is pure milk and honey" (from the second verse of the hymn "*Wie schön leuchtet der Morgenstern*," by Philip Nicolai, in Julian, *Dictionary of Hymnology*, 1:806).

23. See the introduction.

24. "[N]ow it shall be said of [. . .] Israel, 'What has God wrought!'"

25. Or "her."

26. Pach-qui-ack, Pachquayack, Paskoecq, and Pachquyak. A flat on the north side of Catskill Creek, Greene County, New York, mentioned in land purchases made

from Indians in 1675 and 1678 (Van Laer, *Early Records*, 1:107, 2:19–20; Beauchamp, "Place Names," 85).

27. Perhaps the daughter of the Nimham who, along with "Conkepot" [Kunkapot] and several other Housatonic Indians, was a signatory to a land purchase agreement in 1724 (Grumet, "Nimhams," 85–86). In 1742 the Moravian Gottlob Büttner writes of meeting "King Nimham," a man more than seventy years old, who is living at an unknown distance from Shekomeko (RMM 26/211/5/1, 12 Jan. 1742). This may be the Nimham who died in 1745–46 (Grumet, "Nimhams," 86).

28. Word ending crossed out and replaced with "qutaticok." This is evidence that Wanachquaticok (var.) and Stockbridge are the same place. "Wnahktukook," also "Whahktukook," was the name of the village of the Housatonic headman Kunkapot, near where Stockbridge was founded in 1739 (Hopkins, *Housatonic Indians*, 15; Colee, "Housatonic-Stockbridge," 3).

29. A cemetery.

30. Rau's first daughter, Jeannette/Johannette, Martin Mack's wife, had died in 1749.

31. See entry for 1 October 1750.

32. "[H]e will destroy on this mountain the covering that is cast over all peoples." "He glows in the middle of the night."

33. This family is mentioned by von Watteville and Cammerhoff in their travel journal of 1748: Wampchom and his wife Schachquanoà, who is the mother of Joseph of Gnadenhütten, and her daughter, Joseph's half-sister, at the time about eleven years old (RMM 30/225/3, 17 Dec. 1748). Sensemann counts only the adult Indians.

34. "Listen to me, my people." "Here I lie face down, recommending myself to your mercy."

35. "And they sang to them: Sing to the Lord." "Bring together all tongues into one faith, Amen."

36. "*Weiberhütter*," a dangler after women (OED); that is, a philanderer.

37. "Though I scattered them among the nations, yet in far countries they shall remember me." "That one may experience there too one's *animum efflare*" [Latin: "the spirit flows out," i.e., death].

38. Is. 51.5: "[T]he coastlands wait for me." "One has Him where one weeps for Him."

39. "Thy will be done." "Through the flocks of the Lamb."

40. Mameho (Mamaho, Mamoho) is recognizable as a Pequot name, one that was carried by a sachem at Mystic, Connecticut, in the 1630s (McBride, "Archaeology," 101).

41. "*Vetter*": cousin. Historically, in German, this noun can apply to male relatives on the father's and the mother's side of the family. In this case, the entry on the 24th provides a more specific context: "the son of Schiri's brother."

42. "[W]e are bondmen; yet our God has not forsaken us in our bondage." "Who according to the laws of nature would have become embittered at home."

43. The Indians at Pachgatgoch erected fences to protect their fields from the pigs that they and the Moravians raised.

44. "Let thy work be manifest to thy servants." "Thus we too want to be diligent and delight you every hour."

45. In the margin: "His brother's son from Farmington was going with him as well."

46. "The Lord builds up Jerusalem; he gathers the outcasts of Israel." "Thy work no man can hinder." From the fourth verse of the hymn "*Befiehl du deine Wege*," by Paul Gerhardt (Julian, *Dictionary of Hymnology*, 1:125–26).

47. Ps. 36.10: "O continue thy steadfast love to those who know thee." "Make us into your congregation."

48. "Consider too that this nation is thy people." "You have purchased us."

49. "[N]ot for the nation only." "But gathers through the ransom the created and redeemed first fruits from among the whole world."

50. This place-name is as Sensemann wrote it. Read as a German-language phonetic rendering of an English word, it most closely resembles "Saybrook," a colonial settlement at the mouth of the Connecticut River. There is the outside possibility that he heard "Seabrook," perhaps Seabrook, Massachusetts, on Cape Cod. Whether Sensemann used the term "friends" to identify the two men as intimate acquaintances, as Quakers, or as both, is unclear.

51. "Tomorrow is the Sabbath of solemn rest of the Lord's exodus. Now let us joyfully sing the *consummatum est*" [Latin: "it is finished"].

52. This is Roeliff Jansen Kill, which empties into the Hudson River at Clermont, Columbia County, New York. The variation of the name apparently offered here by Bartholomew, an Indian living at Stockbridge, who uses an l for both r and l, suggests that he may have been from a central Massachusetts native community or was a speaker of Munsee (Ives Goddard, personal communication, 2002).

53. "[S]he" is companion or wife.

54. The Moravians used a trombone (German: *Posaune*), an instrument that more resembled a trumpet, to summon the faithful to services.

55. "Shepherd thy people with thy staff." "Rediscovered at the graveside."

56. "To thee have we committed our cause." After Jer. 11.20. "We serve you according to your will."

57. In the margin, for insertion here: "her very unexpected going home." This is Juliana Haberland Nitschmann (b. Schönau, Moravia, 1712), "Mother of Pennsylvania," who had died in Bethlehem on 22 February 1751 (MAB, Church Register, 1:215–16).

58. "[T]he Lord will plead their cause." "He gladly keeps His word."

59. Sensemann begins to sometimes write in the third person.

60. Ps. 34.19: "[He] delivers him out of them all." A reference to the seventh stanza of the hymn "Mache dich, mein Geist, bereit," by Johann B. Freystein (Julian, Dictionary of Hymnology, 1:397).

61. "The enemy said, 'my desire shall have its fill of them.'" "Grant me steadfast love for all those who hate us."

62. "And the Lord hears it." After Num. 12.2.

63. "He is wonderful in counsel, and excellent in wisdom." "Before one is aware, more has come to pass than one ever expected of Him."

64. "Welsh corn" is one of many names given by Europeans to Zea mays Linn., maize or corn, the New World domesticated plant. Others include Turkish wheat, Virginia wheat, Indian wheat, Egyptian corn, and Spanish corn. Moravian diarists wrote either "Welsch Korn" or simply "Korn," that is, "corn." There are occasions, however, when "Korn" was used in reference to other grains, for example, wheat or oats.

65. In the margin: "Samuel came home in good spirits and full of light."

66. Is. 42.14: "For a long time I have held my peace, I have kept still." "And [it] will be done, regardless."

67. For insertion here: "or quarter-of-an-hour."

68. "For Zion's sake I will not keep silent [. . .] until her salvation [goes forth] as a burning torch." "How beautifully glows the wounds' star!"

69. "The sons of those who oppressed you shall come bending low to you; and all who despised you." "They will be greatly frightened by your salvation."

70. "'O afflicted one, storm-tossed, and not comforted.'" "Alas, now God is comforting you!"

71. The Indian Wilhelm.

72. Ps. 47.9: "The princes of the peoples gather as the people." "The old Unitas Fratrum."

73. "Seal the servants of God." After Rev. 7.3: "Pale Lips, kiss them on their heart."

74. "'Prepare the way, remove every obstruction from my people's way.'" "An unobstructed path."

75. Gideon was a signatory to several land sale agreements made before 1751. One of these, where his name appears as "Mauhehu," was in 1716, and another, as

"Mawehew," in 1720, thus corresponding to the "30 years ago" date mentioned in this entry. Both of these transactions dealt with Indian lands that lay *east* of the Housatonic River. However, Gideon said he was going to Dover, in the colony of New York, *west* of the river, to point out the boundary of what must have been a different sale of land, one in which he may have been involved. This could be the 24 April 1729 purchase of Indian lands in the Sherman–New Fairfield area, which abutted those in the town of Dover. In the deed to the sale, "Mawwehue" and "Cockkenon" are entered as the owners and sellers (Wojciechowski, *Paugussett Tribes*, 242–44, 247–49).

76. Possibly seed beans for planting.

77. "'Surely they are my people, sons who will not deal falsely.'"

78. In the margin: "and Petrus."

79. For insertion here: "Petrus."

80. "Thanks be to God for his inexpressible gift!" "That one has now found the trade wind of the breeze coming from the body."

81. Ps. 77.13: "Thy way, O God, is holy." "We have walked it now for many a year, and the heart now understands you quite well."

82. "We departed, being commended to the grace." After Acts 15.40: "Over land and sea."

83. The letter P may be a slip of the pen, or perhaps it was meant to be the first letter of the name of Captain Aaron's son. It is not known how many sons Aaron had. In 1734 John Sergeant identified the eldest, about eight years old at the time, as "Etowaukaum." Etowaukaum also was the name of the boy's maternal grandfather, a man renowned as one of the "Four Indian Kings" who were taken to London in 1710 and painted by Jan Verelst. Jonas, a name recorded in 1749, appears to have been another of Aaron's sons (Hopkins, *Housatonic Indians*, 29–30; Fenton, *Great Law*, 369–76; UAH, Bethlehem Diary, R.14.A.a.5, 2/13 Aug. 1749).

84. "*Pforte*": gate, possibly a phonetic rendering of the English "fort." Stockbridge was laid out like a New England town, with a number of fenced properties and framed homes, one of which may have been fortified, interspersed with wigwams and other buildings. At the very least, a physical distinction could be made between being either inside or outside the town.

85. Or "relatives."

86. Or "relatives."

87. Or "relatives."

88. John Sergeant, the minister at Stockbridge, had died on 27 July 1749.

89. "Even to your old age [. . .] I will carry you." "With the church in Holy Spirit."

90. Inserted here: "or food that was too poor."

91. Sergeant had completed construction of a boarding school at Stockbridge in the summer of 1749, shortly before his death. With his encouragement, twelve Indian boys who had been enrolled at Martin Kellogg's school in Newington, Connecticut, were transferred there. However, because of Kellogg's failure to clothe, feed, and treat the boys properly, they soon left (Axtell, "Scholastic Frontier," 63–65; Frazier, *Mohicans of Stockbridge*, 101).

92. Also before his death, Sergeant had contacted William Johnson, the Indian agent for the colony of New York, asking his help in persuading the Mohawks to send their children to Stockbridge. By the end of 1751, some ninety-five Mohawk, Oneida, and Tuscarora boys were enrolled in the boarding school. But disputes between those involved in running the school, who used and misused the Indians in their political battles, caused many of the Indians to leave Stockbridge. In spring 1753, the Mohawk headman Hendrick ordered all of the Iroquois there to return to their communities (Frazier, *Mohicans of Stockbridge*, 98–103; see also Marsden, *Jonathan Edwards*).

93. "The Lord [. . .] has met with us." "Here are we, and a thousand more peasants."

94. "Look to the rock from which you were hewn, and to the quarry from which you were digged." "There God's suffering was born."

95. "[T]he Father himself loves you." "Thou art our dear Father, for Christ is our Brother" (from "*Bescher uns, Herr, das tägliche Brot*").

96. Cammerhoff died in Bethlehem on 28 April 1751.

97. "'I have loved you.'" "Pair of cheeks, wet from a million tears shed by the love-struck church."

98. The content of this crossed-out section, at the top of a manuscript page, is reported on 2 June.

99. This matter appears to bear on the impending marriage of Esther and Augustus.

100. Ex. 22.31: "'You shall be men consecrated to me.'" "Here you have your *privilegium!*" [Latin: privilege, special law].

101. Augustus, a.k.a. Memenowal and George Rex, the Delaware headman of the Indian town of Meniolagomekah, was baptized in April 1749. His first wife, Anna Benigna, died in May 1750. See RMM 29/221/21/1, 1739–51; Merritt, *Crossroads*, 90, 92, 331.

102. Inserted here: "other marriages."

103. In the margin: "MSegan came to me in the morning, asking for Jonathan; he would very much like to see him. He went to Wechquadnach."

104. "Do not be anxious." "Bestow your peace upon us, O Jesus!" (from the Lutheran hymn "*Herr, gib uns deinen Frieden*," in Julian, *Dictionary of Hymnology*, 1:418).

105. "The peasantry ceased [. . .] until you arose [. . .] as a mother in Israel."

106. "My cities shall again overflow with prosperity." "For the dear ones of yours to decide."

107. The Moravians' house.

108. See "Translation and Editorial Comments" for a discussion of the meaning and use of this word.

109. "They shall not build and another inhabit [. . .] for like the days of a tree shall the days of my people be." "Eternal wounds of Jesus! My house in which to dwell. You will still be fresh in a million eternities."

Büninger: 27 June to 11 December 1751

1. RMM 3/114/4/1. This diary is by Abraham Büninger. It covers the period from 27 June to 11 December 1751, leaving a break of ten days between its first entry and the previous diary. The letters A to E are written sequentially at the bottom of several pages of the manuscript. Vertical lines and brackets penciled in the margins are found throughout; they are not reproduced here.

2. This is probably Asher or Simeon Ross, brothers and farmers living in Kent (Grant, *Town of Kent*, 72–74).

3. Mt. 7.7: "Ask, and it will be given you."

4. Mohegan, an Indian people located on the Thames River in southeastern Connecticut.

5. "He is who God made our righteousness" (after 1 Cor. 1.30). "With this we want to stand before God."

6. Perhaps Conrad Schwartz, originally from the congregation in Nazareth, Pennsylvania. See W. Reichel, "Register of Members," 385.

7. This is the first and only mention of a woman acting as an interpreter.

8. "He is the great shepherd of the sheep." After Heb. 13.20.

9. "Will I not soon be yours; devoted, blissful, indefatigable, enclosed by the etc."

10. This sentence, "*Arbeitete was vor mein häussel,*" could also be read to say that Büninger did some work in front of his house.

11. 1 Cor. 6.20: "So glorify God in your body." "And in your spirit."

12. "Deep, so deep, into the side[d]."

13. Büninger writes "*Heydelbeern Brodt,*" in modern German "*Heidelbeerbrot*" (blueberry bread).

14. Joshua and Samuel were needed as interpreters.

15. The sentence "*Abends besuchte br. Gideon*" may also be interpreted to mean that Büninger, who in his diary often leaves out pronouns, visited Gideon.

16. See the introduction.

17. Büninger writes "cousin" phonetically in English ("cussin"), suggesting that he had heard this word from someone else. In other contexts the Moravians use "Vetter," a German word for "cousin." See, for example, the entry for 27 March 1751. The "cousin" relationship said to exist between Aaron [Umpachenee] and Gideon might be a fictive rather than a biological one—a rhetorical device employed by natives in social and political discourse. The precise meaning of the term as understood by the Indians of southern New England and southeastern New York at this time is unknown. See Jennings et al., *Iroquois Diplomacy*, 119–20; Bragdon, *Native People*, 161–68.

18. "God sent his own Son in the likeness of sinful flesh, and condemned sin in the flesh." After Rom. 8.3.

19. "I believe [in] a holy Christian Church."

20. The new minister would be Jonathan Edwards (1703–1758). See Frazier, *Mohicans of Stockbridge*, 89; Marsden, *Jonathan Edwards*.

21. Jn. 3.7: "'You must be born anew.'"

22. Peeling bark from trees becomes increasingly difficult with the reduction in the flow of sap as fall approaches.

23. Sun-drying blueberries, or placing them next to a fire to dry, a common practice of northeastern Indian people, may have appeared familiar to the Moravians. In Europe, blueberries were dried in ovens in preparation for baking tarts and making other foods. ([Kalm], *Travels*, 262).

24. The date of Aaron's death was 21 August 1751.

25. "*Backen*": here, probably shallow, elongated bowls made of wood.

26. "We have such a high priest, one who is seated on the throne of the Majesty, a minister in the sanctuary and the true tent." After Heb. 8.1–2.

27. September 7 is a festival day in the Moravian Church, a day of prayer and covenanting for the married brethren and sisters. Büninger may have intended to write "of my dear brethren and sisters in Bethlehem."

28. "Corn"—that is, maize—is not mentioned in the Bible; the allusion is to other types of grain.

29. Or "relatives."

30. "I pray to the God of my life, soul of souls, and the body's potter."

31. Mt. 22.2: "'The kingdom of heaven may be compared to a king who gave a marriage feast for his son.'"

32. Or "related to."

33. Heb. 12.4: "[His] blood that speaks more graciously than the blood of Abel."

34. Or "related to him."

35. "A Lamb goes uncomplaining forth," by Paul (Paulus) Gerhardt. See Julian, *Dictionary of Hymnology*, 1:409–12.

36. The Reverend Gilbert Tennent (1703–1764), a leader of the First Great Awakening, wrote the anti-Moravian tract *Some account of the principles of the Moravians: chiefly collected from several conversations with Count Zinzendorf: and from some sermons preached by him at Berlin, and published in London: being an appendix to a treatise on the necessity of holding fast to the truth* (London, 1743).

37. Or "relatives."

38. Balsam, a fragrant, oily exudate from various trees and plants, here possibly the balsam fir, *Abies balsamea*. It is used in topical preparations to treat, for example, skin irritations. Various parts of this tree have been used as folk remedies for bronchitis, burns, catarrh, consumption, dysentery, earache, gonorrhea, heart ailments, rheumatism, scurvy, and a host of other ailments. See, generally, Duke and Wain, *Medicinal Plants*. Twentieth-century Iroquois medical practitioners suggest its use for colds, coughs, cuts, sores, and leg ulcers (Herrick, *Medical Botany*, 108).

39. "Christ's blood and righteousness."

40. "Seek the right food for yourselves."

41. Or "relatives."

42. Is. 1.18: "[T]hough your sins are like scarlet," etc. "He who found salvation in the wounds of Jesus will become as blessed as Jesus' wounds."

43. "To you it has been given to lie in the blood of the Lamb and to be victorious in all your wars."

44. Here and elsewhere Büninger uses the verb "*stribben*," apparently a Germanized form of the English verb "to strip." The Indians are probably husking (shucking) corn.

45. "*Rothe ruhr*," in modern German "*rote Ruhr*" (bloody flux). This is dysentery, here probably bacillary dysentery, an acute disease caused by bacteria of the genus Shingella found in food and water contaminated by infected fecal matter.

46. "The Lord has given us the Sabbath." After Ex. 16.29.

47. Jn. 1.29: "'Behold the Lamb of God, who takes away the sin of the world!'"

48. "Side hole[d], Side hole[d]."

49. See the glossary of Latin terms and abbreviations.

50. Jn. 3.16: "For God so loved the world."

51. This is an indication that none of the Moravians then at Pachgatgoch—Büninger, Sensemann, or Post—had sufficient control of the Indians' language to preach without the services of an interpreter.

52. This is Zinzendorf, from *Advocatus et Ordinarius Fratrum*, the position he held in

the Moravian Church by which his "unlimited powers of management and oversight" were acknowledged (Hamilton and Hamilton, *History of the Moravian Church*, 97).

53. November 13 is one of the immovable festivals of the Moravian Church. Instituted in Germany in 1741, it commemorates the acknowledgment of Jesus Christ as the head of the church. The reference here, however, is to the 1748 synod in Bethlehem, where the American church committed itself to the same doctrine (De Schweinitz, *Moravian Manual*, 113; Hamilton and Hamilton, *History of the Moravian Church*, 139).

54. "He who believes in me has eternal life." After Jn. 6.47.

55. Connecticut had proclaimed days of thanksgiving in the colony, which were intended to take place annually in the months of September, October, or November, as early as 1639 (PRCC, 1:33).

56. The office Nitschmann held would once again be occupied by Augustus Gottlieb Spangenberg.

57. Johann Wolfgang Michler (b. Wurtemberg, d. 1785), a weaver, ordained a deacon of the church in 1762, and Rosina Schneider Michler (1715–1755), from Moravia (W. Reichel, "Register of Members," 362).

58. Spangenberg returned to the colonies to resume leadership of the American branch of the Church of the United Brethren. His tasks included "removing the traces and effects of the 'Time of Sifting.'" See "Translation and Editorial Comments"; Hamilton and Hamilton, *History of the Moravian Church*, 170.

Sensemann: 6 December 1751 to 15 April 1752

1. RMM 3/114/5/1. Written by Joachim Sensemann, this diary covers the period from 6 December 1751 to 15 April 1752. There are vertical lines and brackets in ink as well as in pencil in the margins of this document. A cross drawn at intervals in the text indicates the death of a person and, in one case, the union of a couple. These marks do not appear to have originated with Sensemann and are not reproduced here. Sensemann provided marginalia and interlinear text to be inserted in his diary entries, which are noted.

2. Latin, "in abundance," although the intention here might be "completely" or "in its entirety."

3. The preceding text is written in a different hand on a separate page.

4. "'[H]e shall grow up in his place, and he shall build the temple of the Lord.'" "The church where He is the Chief Elder."

5. "He led His people like a flock of sheep." After Ps. 77.20.

6. Rom. 15.10: "'Rejoice, O Gentiles, with his people.'"

7. Ex. 19.6: "'[Y]ou shall be to me a kingdom of priests.'"

8. *"Flinte"*: gun, also flintlock or light musket.

9. Here and elsewhere the Moravians use the verb *"fahren,"* generally "to ride" or "to drive," to describe how the Indians maneuvered their sleds or sledges up and down the mountain. In this example, the sleds were drawn and controlled by the Indians using ropes. Given the terrain, it is doubtful that they would have employed horses in this task.

10. Is. 45.11: "'Will you question me about my children, or command me concerning the work of my hands?'"

11. Jn. 3.16: "For God so loved the world that he gave his only Son."

12. Probably deer hides.

13. See the glossary.

14. Zinzendorf.

15. For insertion here: "we told the brethren and sisters that they should stay at home because of the speaking" [of the brethren and sisters in preparation for Communion].

16. Acknowledging sinfulness carries with it a positive connotation in Moravian theology and represents an important step toward receiving the Savior's forgiveness.

17. In the margin: "In the evening the dear heart Grube and Sensemann had a love feast; they thought of our dear Bethlehem a great deal. Br. Grube read delightful news until 12 o'clock."

18. Wampano, here Wompona, was the language spoken by the Indians at Pachgatgoch. An eastern dialect of Munsee, it exhibited at least one non-Munsee phonological feature that must have diffused from Mahican or Quiripi-Naugatuck-Unquachog, the Algonquian language of western Connecticut and central Long Island (Goddard, Review of *Mahican Language Hymns*).

19. "O how does my heart weep." "Press us to your heart, to your wounds."

20. This may be the local Indian-language word for "Savior." See Masthay, *Schmick's Mahican Dictionary*, 75, 80, 118, 181.

21. "Jesus hung on the cross."

22. "At the bottom of our heart, p[p]., appear to us in that same form, p[p]." This translated verse and the two mentioned earlier became part of the letters and greetings that the Pachgatgoch Indians sent to Zinzendorf (RMM 34/319/4/4, 27 Dec. 1751). For these and other hymns translated into Indian languages to be used at Pachgatgoch, see Masthay, *Mahican Language Hymns*, 12–16.

23. "'Stay with us.'" "There you have heart and hands that until the end we want to be your faithful souls."

24. Sensemann refers to himself in the third person; thus, he and Grube are "they."

25. 2 Cor. 6.2: "Behold, now is the acceptable time."

26. Lk. 2.21: "He was called Jesus."

27. "Simeon took him up in his arms, p[p]." After Lk. 2.28.

28. For insertion here: "[and] of which this sick child too, by her request and petition, shall partake."

29. For insertion here: "may let flow into this water."

30. "Fuß" (foot), a measurement of length that varied from region to region in Germany, from about nine to slightly more than twelve inches.

31. For insertion here: "from the winter huts."

32. Rom. 8.31: "If God is for us, who is against us?"

33. For insertion here: "Witthry."

34. See "Translation and Editorial Comments."

35. The apparent absence of any ceremony attached to this marriage, at least as recognized by the Moravians, may have reflected native practice. It is nonetheless possible that there first had been an exchange of gifts between families, as suggested elsewhere in the diaries. See entry of 5 November 1753. There is no record of a Moravian uniting any of the Indian residents of Pachgatgoch. The only marriage known to have been performed in the area was at Shekomeko on 24 August 1743, but this was for Brother Christian Frederick Post and Rachel, an Indian woman from Pachgatgoch (RMM 26/211/5/1).

36. This is one of several instances where, with the encouragement of the Moravians, the Indians resolved to plant more crops, with the intention of reaping larger harvests, so that they would not have to depend on surrounding colonial farmers for a part of their sustenance. Hiring themselves out not only reduced the time they could spend in their own fields, but it put the Indians at risk of becoming indebted to local merchants and others (through having easy access to alcohol, and by placing themselves at a distance from the supportive influence of the Moravians).

37. "Side hole^d, side hole^d, side hole^d, she is yours."

38. That is, the mill races and wheels had frozen.

39. In the order of Moravian choirs, that is, in groups segregated by sex, age, and marital status.

40. "Give us our eternal bread." For the complete verse, see Masthay, *Mahican Language Hymns*, 13.

41. "Läfel," elsewhere "lefel," "löffeln"; in modern German "Löffel": a utensil for spooning or ladling.

42. A pipe of tobacco, a smoke.

43. "Press us to your heart."

44. Rudolphus van Dyck and Jacob Reed. The first Moravian marriage ceremony held in New York City united Reed and the widow Jane Taylor. Van Dyck also was a church member there (Stocker, *History of the Moravian Church in New York City*, 78, 82).

45. Is. 12.3: "With joy you will draw water from the wells of salvation."

46. "And you beloved brethren."

47. Macedonia Brook at Kent.

48. "*Luft*": air. Sensemann seems to imply that, as a result of the fire, the general atmosphere in Gideon's house had improved; that is, Gideon and Martha had resolved their differences over the behavior of Martha's son Jonathan. See entry for 17 December.

49. "The Lord Jesus Christ with all His red wounds, bruises, and welts; this resounds and adheres in the hearts."

50. See [Indian Papers], 1st ser., 2:76, for the text of the Indians' petition, and 2:75 for the associated assembly resolution. See also PRCC, 10:108. A determination of sorts on this question would not be reached for five years. See entry for 23 June 1757.

51. Or "relatives."

52. Gen. 49.11: "[H]e washes his garments in wine and his vesture in the blood of grapes."

53. Is. 27.6: "In days to come Jacob shall take root, Israel shall blossom and put forth shoots."

54. "*Kannen*," also tankards, containers made of wood.

55. "*Freunde*," also "relatives." Implied is that the Indians should focus their love on the Savior rather than on just their family and friends. In her discussion of the choir system in *Moravians in Two Worlds*, Gollin writes: "It was made quite clear that the survival of the family system, even in modified form, was dependent on the subordination of family to choir. In more personal terms, this meant that the individual's duty to the welfare of his soul and to the religious development of his choir was placed above and beyond his duty to family" (85).

56. See [Indian Papers], 1st ser., 2:75, and PRCC, 10:108, for a description of the lands conveyed to the Indians at Pachgatgoch.

57. Gen. 24.31: "'Come in, O blessed of the Lord.'"

58. "April 1752" is written at the top of the following manuscript page.

59. Sensemann writes "*Beuchme*," presumably for "*Beumche*" or "*Bäumchen*," the diminutive for "trees," which marked the property line.

Rundt: 15 April to 22 May 1752

1. RMM 3/114/6/1. The first part of this diary, until his departure on 18 April, was heavily edited by August Gottlieb Spangenberg, and to a much lesser degree by Carl Gottfried Rundt, the diary's author. Unless otherwise noted, marginalia, word insertions, and substitutions for some of Rundt's wording, evidently made to shorten sentences or for emphasis, are by Spangenberg. Other signs of Spangenberg's editing include: (1) backslashes scattered throughout the text, which in some cases indicate insertion points for comments, but at other times seem to have no discernable significance; (2) brackets of varying length used to set off portions of text, also of unknown significance; and (3) intertextual parentheses that appear to mark sections of the text for deletion, perhaps to create a shorter version of the diary. Other than retaining parentheses that were clearly meant to set off a statement, none of these devices has been reproduced.

2. By Rundt, for insertion here: "(in New England this place is called Scatticock)"; in his personal diary, he writes "Scattikok" (RMM 29/221/8/1, 15 Apr. 1752). "Scatticock" (various spellings, later standardized to "Schaghticoke") is the first documented use by a Moravian of the alternate name for Pachgatgoch. See the gazetteer. What may be the earliest English-language record of this place-name, dated 1750, contains "Caticock" and "Scaticook" ([Indian Papers], 2nd ser., 2:44). Linguistically, "Pachgatgoch" is Eastern Munsee [Wapanoo] or Mahican. "Schaghticoke" more resembles a southern New England form of Eastern Algonquian, possibly influenced by a Mahican dialect. Both signify "the confluence of two streams" (Ives Goddard, personal communication, 2002; Trumbull, *Indian Names*, 43). The evidence suggests that these place-names were applied, apparently at the same time, to two different geographic areas. The first was at the junction of the Tenmile and Housatonic Rivers, about one mile south of Bulls Bridge, as described in the 1749 petition of "Capt. Chickins" and "worups Chickins Sone [son]": "above Newmilford at a Place Call'd Scatecook . . . it being Bounded Easterly by the Great River at the Great Falls (where there is Good Fishing) and westerly by the Mountains where there is Good hunting, and no likelihoods of any English Setteling So near as to Interrupt us for a long time" ([Indian Papers], 1st ser., 2:32). Confirming this location is a 1748 document that names the Tenmile River in describing Chickins's land, and one from 1762 that puts Chickins on land near Isaac Bull's house, that is, at Bulls Bridge ([Indian Papers], 1st ser., 2:31, 126). The second is described in the entry for 18 February 1752. Sensemann writes that he is on his way to visit John Mills, who lived in Kent, and that he "came to the creek from which Pachgatgoch [the Indian community] derives its name." This is

Macedonia Brook, which flows into the Housatonic at Kent, thus, at "the confluence of two streams."

3. This is the first instance in the records where the Moravians identify the river by name. See the gazetteer.

4. In the margin: "and was welcomed most heartily."

5. As did several other diarists, Rundt writes in the third person.

6. Word inserted.

7. Rundt arrived in the colonies with Bishop Spangenberg, the head of the American church, five months earlier. Pachgatgoch was his first mission assignment; moreover, Spangenberg, his superior, introduced Rundt to his duties. These two factors may help explain both the instructional editing of the diary and Rundt's efforts to provide a very detailed account, which at times is wordy and stilted in its phrasing.

8. Inserted: "[I]n the evening."

9. Word inserted.

10. Inserted: "[T]hen we."

11. Word inserted.

12. Inserted: "[T]here were."

13. Inserted: "[T]his is . . . the Indians."

14. Word inserted.

15. Inserted: "Br. Joseph."

16. Word inserted.

17. Phrase inserted.

18. Inserted: "[T]hink that," "would stay," and "for a period of time."

19. In the margin: "Br. Joseph talked to them about their children and their upbringing and related to them how it went with that in Gnadenhütten."

20. In the margin: "He also informed them of the upcoming *synodum*."

21. Rundt does not finish this sentence. Spangenberg rewords the paragraph thus: "Moreover, he advised the brethren and sisters to plant more Welsh corn. If they did this, they could stay home more and better enjoy the occasions and all that is good at this place, and then."

22. Spangenberg rewords this paragraph thus: "Thus they would not need to solicit here and there the one thing or other that they need from such people who are harmful to them."

23. Inserted: "had a mind to [*word crossed out*] such to plant more."

24. Inserted: "[It] pleased us to hear."

25. The preceding discussion is a further example of the Moravians encouraging the Indians to become more self-sufficient by planting more crops and, in turn,

reducing their dependence on—and importantly, their interactions with—colonial farmers and merchants.

26. Inserted: "could work at home in the meantime."

27. "Certain wicked" substituted for "those white."

28. "Become" substituted for "were."

29. "Some" substituted for "the white."

30. Inserted: "for the Indians would very much like an English school instead of the German [school], because they do understand English, but not German."

31. Parenthetical statement by Spangenberg.

32. There is no indication previous to this entry that, at Pachgatgoch, the Moravians had been teaching the Indian children German.

33. The Delaware headman married to Esther. See entries beginning 8 June 1751.

34. In the margin: "Then consideration was given to a love feast to be celebrated tomorrow."

35. Word inserted.

36. Inserted: "and thus her parents were spoken with on her account."

37. For insertion: "With regard to the conference."

38. Word inserted.

39. Word inserted.

40. For insertion: "and could continue to be in the future."

41. For insertion: "The conference having disbanded, we shortly thereafter retired blissfully to the wounds of our Lamb[d], for it [the conference] had lasted quite a long time."

42. The preceding paragraph is marked for insertion here.

43. Spangenberg rewords this paragraph thus: "Because they intend to go before the court to acquire a little more land—given that they are unable to sustain themselves and their many families any longer on the little land that they have—this matter was thus reflected upon together by them; whether they perhaps had a good friend to whom they could turn with respect to this matter, and who had some knowledge of how their affair is to be handled before the court."

44. In October 1750, the colony of Connecticut had appointed a committee to look into the purchase from Indians of lands west of the Housatonic River by "persons living in New York Province." The committee was empowered to "warn all persons that are on any part of said lands claiming in opposition to, or not holding or claiming under this government, to remove off from the same or to take a lease or leases under this government for a short time, not exceeding the term of two years, with covenant to surrender at the end of said term" (PRCC, 9:566). Rundt's reporting of what

Spangenberg had heard suggests that Gideon had sold land to certain persons without the knowledge or consent of the colony, which in turn repossessed these lands and denied the purchasers compensation.

45. There is an abbreviation at this point in the text that is not clearly legible. It may be an l followed by a superscript *e*, perhaps for "*Liebe*" (love or kindness).

46. Although it leaves out the third line, a translation of this verse is provided in Eberhardt's journal entry for 8 May 1756: "Bless both my Thought & Action, afford me thy Direction, [bless thou bleeding hands], Beginning, Mid[d]le, Ending."

47. "Christ's blood and righteousness."

48. Jn. 6.7: "[F]or each of them to get a little."

49. The shingles may have been made from northern white cedar (*Thuya orientalis*), a relatively uncommon tree in southern New England.

50. This is Samuel Canfield. See the introduction.

51. "Sidehole^d, Sidehole^d."

52. A side-blown flute, as opposed to one that is end-blown.

53. Word inserted.

54. Although there are variations among the German states that used this measurement, a "shoe" (German: *Schuh*) equals approximately one U.S. foot. In a letter to Johann Nitschmann dated 15 April 1750, Büninger reported on the building of the log house to which the new construction described here is being attached: "When I arrived [at Pachgatgoch] I right away made preparations for a sum[m]er house, for nothing had been done to that end other than that the wood was cut [and lying] in the woods. However, now it [the house] is stacked up to the rafters. It is 16 F [Fuß] long and 14 F wide" (RMM 4/115/15/1).

55. Rundt, of course, is being playful, talking about feathers for their beds when dried grass was the reality.

56. The timberwork framing for this house may have been post and beam.

57. "*Mulden*": shallow, probably elongated carved wooden bowls.

58. The list begins with number 2.

59. In the margin: "and in the process found himself in great danger; the Savior too assisted in this!"

60. "Thou bloody wounds / and great cleft in the side / remain sweet to our Indians / always and by day and night. / Yea, thou sidehole^d / bleed on every soul / here at this place of grace / evermore. / Render them blissful, here and there." The suffixes indicating the diminutive in "*Höhle*" and "*Seele*" were crossed out, possibly by Spangenberg.

61. The words "was presented" and "a" were added.

62. Zinzendorf. See entry for 10 November 1751.

63. A hardened mass of entangled materials sometimes found in the stomachs and intestines of animals, usually formed of hair, hair and vegetable matter, or food. Bezoar is generally used in folk medicines as an antidote for suspected poisons.

64. "Albanien."

65. That is, the likelihood of finding a roast at a hospital equaled that of finding corn at Pachgatgoch.

66. "*Hochdeutsch*": High German or German.

67. "*Äkker*," in modern German "*Acker*," can also be translated as "acres." In the entry that follows, reference is made to two pieces of land that together made up two acres.

68. This letter is not in the collection of materials from Pachgatgoch; however, one in German from Spangenberg, addressed to the missionaries at Pachgatgoch and dated 24 April 1752, most probably arrived at the same time as that in English for the Indians. In it Spangenberg mentions enclosing a letter from Eberhardt to Rundt, along with one from Post to the Indians. He also writes that he included a "reminder," which also is not in this collection (RMM 4/115/15/4).

69. Jonathan, one of the drunken Indians, is Gideon's wife's son.

70. The battle of Chotusice, in what is today the Czech Republic, took place during the first Silesian War (1740–42). Details about Rundt's time as a soldier are found in his personal diary (RMM 29/221/8/1).

71. "Matthew" is written above this name in an unknown hand.

72. "*Now annoint heart and house with a smearing of blood*."

73. The four-page enclosure to which Rundt refers is not found at the end of the manuscript. Instead, it was inserted five pages before this parenthetical notation. However, to avoid interrupting the flow of the narrative, it has been placed at the end of the diary.

74. "The wisest ruler / dispatches hither Brother Führer / and has word sent to him: Come back / come, and experience new happiness." This is Brother Rundt's recall to Bethlehem.

75. Marked for insertion here by Rundt: "that Br. Gottfried is to return to Bethlehem right away; yet Br. Christian is to remain alone in Pachgatgoch until Br. Sensemann's return."

76. A copy of this petition, absent the marks of the Indian signatories, is in RMM 4/115/15/5, 12 May 1762. See appendix 4, "Lists and Correspondence."

77. See "The Humble Petition of sundry Indians inhabitants of Pachgatgoch or Scaticook near Kent," 12 May 1752, [Indian Papers], 1st ser., 2:76. See also 2:75; and PRCC, 10:108.

78. "Why! So let Him continue to act and do not interfere."

79. Inserted here: "*Unsere Geschw. in Bethl. feyerten heute das Pfingst-Fest.*"

Sensemann: 7 August 1752 to 18 February 1753

1. RMM 3/114/7/1. This line is in another hand. This diary, written by Joachim Sensemann, Christian Fröhlich's relief, begins on 7 August 1752, some ten weeks after Rundt's last entry in the previous diary. Whether Fröhlich kept a diary in the interim is not known. There has been some editing of the diary, and in places, brackets line the margins of the text. As their significance is unknown, they have not been reproduced. A number of the insertions are in a hand other than Sensemann's, and are so noted. As did several other Moravians, Sensemann occasionally wrote in the third person.

2. Priscilla was the mother of the late Rachel Post, Brother Christian Frederick Post's wife.

3. This verb is singular.

4. Here Sensemann writes "*Klaben.*" Referring to the same task in the entry that follows, he writes phonetically in English "*Klaborts.*"

5. "Bless us from out of your holy wounds."

6. Jn. 6.29: "'This is the work of God, that you believe in him whom he has sent.'"

7. Tree bark.

8. For insertion here: "the gable."

9. There appears to be an H before this name, possibly an abbreviation for *Herr* "Mister."

10. For insertion here: "to a doctor for [the treatment of] his late wife."

11. John Sackett, MD, was a son of Richard Sackett (d. 1749), one of the Little Nine Partners patentees and a major landholder in the region. See the introduction.

12. A line is drawn through the word "*Schwit,*" and "weet" is written above in another hand, suggesting "schweet" or "sweet."

13. Perhaps for "*mistig*" (misty), possibly to suggest "murky" or "bleak." This word was crossed out and "*critisch*" (critical) was written above the line in another hand.

14. For an account of this journey into Iroquois country, see "Diary of J. Martin Mack's, David Zeisberger's and Gottfried Rundt's Journey to Onondaga in 1752," in Beauchamp, *Moravian Journals*, 112–52. The incident to which Sensemann is referring appears on pages 113–14.

15. A reference to Brother Mack's visit to the seaside in 1743, where he encountered a number of Indians, including one of Gideon's sons (RMM 1/111/3/2, 4 Mar. 1743).

16. Sensemann is applying the designation "church" to the wood-frame addition made to the Moravians' log house in the spring of 1752. See the introduction.

17. The six Iroquois nations.

18. Written above this crossed-out word in what appears to be another hand: "and Gottfried" [a reference to Rundt].

19. "The Soul of Christ you sanctify." The hymn's title, as it appears in a 1742 Moravian hymn book, is "The Soul of Christ me sanctify" (Julian, *Dictionary of Hymnology*, 1:70).

20. In the margin: "She is not an unfit person; I have hopes."

21. A line is drawn through the words "Süßen korn," and "*sweet corn*" is substituted in an unknown hand.

22. "[V]*origen platz*." The location is unclear.

23. Sensemann refers to this activity as "*aufblocken*" (to stack up), a reference to laying up logs in constructing Gihorn's house.

24. "Christel" is a reference to Christian Renatus von Zinzendorf, the twenty-seven-year-old son of Zinzendorf and Erdmuth Reuss, who had died in Westminster Abbey on 28 May 1752 (Fries, *Moravian Heroes*, 54).

25. Sensemann was likely reading from a letter, prepared by Moravians in Pennsylvania, that described the meaning behind the belts and strings of wampum that Nathanael had brought with him; he was not reading the wampum.

26. Quaker Hill, a hamlet on the eastern edge of the town of Pawling, Dutchess County, New York, about ten miles from Pachgatgoch. See the gazetteer.

27. For insertion here in another hand: "shall be authorized to hand out *belte of wampon* in the name of the nation." The belt in question here signified the conferral of headman status on Abraham, previously Shabash, at Gnadenhütten.

28. This line is in another hand.

29. For insertion before "Brothers": "The Indian."

30. Mt. 5.3: "'Blessed are the poor in spirit, for theirs is the kingdom of heaven.'"

31. "Into the soft bed of your side."

32. Substituted in another hand: "*blanquets*."

33. "*Canuhn*" changed to "*canous*" in another hand.

34. See Atwater, *History of Kent*, 49–51, for a brief commentary on Marsh and his sometimes difficult relationship with Kent's Congregational church.

35. Inserted in another hand.

36. The numbers 1 through 4 are written above this line in another hand, changing the syntax in German to agree with the crossed out "that."

37. This and the previous word are in another hand.

38. This and the previous word are in another hand.

39. The location of the winter huts.

40. See Atwater, *History of Kent*, 30. "Lieutenant" is substituted in another hand.

41. Inserted in another hand.

42. "Give us our eternal bread."

43. "Sweet" is substituted in another hand.

44. A fetus that dies in utero might remain in place for days or perhaps weeks.

45. This and the three preceding words are inserted in another hand.

46. Most likely a reference to the *Gemeinnachrichten*. See the glossary.

47. For insertion here in another hand: "from Bethlehem."

48. Word inserted in another hand.

49. "Day" is added in another hand. In a third hand is *x* in Latin script, significance unknown.

50. For a brief account of their visit, see UAH, *Kurze Relation von Br. Nathanaels und Dav. Zeisbergers Besuch nach New York, Pachgatgoch und Dutches County*, R.15.H.I.a.5.14b, 4–27 Jan. 1753.

51. Word inserted in another hand.

52. Inserted in another hand.

53. The word order here is marked with the superscribed numbers 2 and 3; there is no number 1.

54. "Saltzbery" is changed to "Salisbery" in another hand. See the gazetteer.

55. This last part of this sentence is reworded in another hand thus: "and that the brethren were coming to them for that reason."

56. See W. Reichel, *Memorials*, 66–68, for a discussion of this event and the full text of the letter mentioned. This congregation is later referred to as Sichem. On their visit the brethren lodged with Jonathan Moore in Dutchess County (UAH, *Kurze Relation von Br. Nathanaels und Dav. Zeisbergers Besuch nach New York, Pachgatgoch und Dutches County*, R.15.H.I.a.5.14b, 4–27 Jan. 1753).

57. "*Jünger*" is a reference to Zinzendorf, and "Mother" to Anna Caritas Nitschmann (1715–1760), his second wife. See [Neisser], *History of Moravian Work*, 108–10; and the glossary.

58. Candidates for baptism in the Moravian Church are dressed in white, although this practice is only infrequently mentioned at Pachgatgoch. When the Thorps, the last missionaries stationed there, were recalled, they carried with them, among other things, two shirts used in baptisms (UAH, unsigned letter to Brother Lucius, M. Dep. [*Missions-Deputation*], 1.3.2., 30 Nov. 1770).

59. Word inserted in another hand.

60. "Ejd. ai.": abbreviation for the Latin *ejusdem anni* (of the same year).

61. In the margin: "at 1 o'clock at night."

62. "The soul of Christ us sanctify," a variation of "The soul of Christ me sanctify" (Julian, *Dictionary of Hymnology*, 1:70).

63. This comment suggests that the Indians may have intended to plant, or had been planting, winter wheat or perhaps winter rye.

64. "*Bad stoffen.*"

65. Jonathan was baptized on 10 October 1742; his Indian name had been Tennis (RMM 1/111/1/1).

66. "Gate," "Thor." A variation on an idiom, meaning that the Wechquadnach Indians would be received well, they would be welcome.

67. In the margin in another hand: "NB" (nota bene).

Sensemann: 19 February 1753 to 27 February 1754

1. RMM 3/114/8/1. The above is written in another hand. The date of the diarist's last entry was later changed from the 11th to the 10th.

2. This diary was written by three Moravians: Christian Fröhlich (19 February to 10 April 1753); Joachim Sensemann (9 April to 29 November); and Carl Gottfried Rundt (30 November to 11 December). The concluding entries, 12 December to 27 February 1754, are also by Sensemann. Fröhlich's diary was edited by an unidentified person, in large part to make clear his Hessian dialect. We note only those changes having to do with word meaning. As in a number of other diaries, brackets of unknown significance line the margins of the text. They are not reproduced.

3. The Moravians' log house, to which the wood-frame "church" mentioned here had been added in the spring of 1752, was furnished with a fireplace. See the introduction.

4. In another hand: "*Geschwister Dafitz*" changed to "*Geschwister David*"; that is, David Warop (var.) and his wife Rebecca.

5. Word corrected from "blood" to "bloody" in another hand.

6. Inserted in another hand.

7. This sentence is modified in another hand to read thus: "First there was the sermon about Domas, how he had placed his fingers into the beloved Savior's nail marks and the hand into His side, and what power the dear Savior's blood holds."

8. "[O]ccasion" is substituted for "meeting" in another hand.

9. Changed to "Philippus" in another hand.

10. Marsh is referring to the arrest and questioning of the Moravians Martin Mack, Joseph Shaw, and Johann Pyrlaeus by local authorities in June 1743. See the introduction.

11. Inserted in another hand.

12. These boards are to be used to finish the interior walls of the "church." See the introduction.

13. Corrected to "Gideon" in another hand.

14. "Matts" inserted in another hand.

15. This paragraph is rewritten in another hand to read thus: "First there was the early service, wherein Br. Nathanael informed the brethren and sisters about the visit of the Nantegock [Nanticokes] and Schawanos [Shawnees] to Bethlehem, relating to them everything in detail. Then we readied ourselves for our journey to New York, taking a heartfelt leave of the brethren and sisters. Br. Sensemann went with us for 2 miles and then we parted from one another with tender love." Spangenberg's complete record of the visit of these Indians, which took place between 17 and 26 March 1753, is in R M M 35/323/1. During the several days of meetings, the Nanticokes and Shawnees, speaking for the Iroquois, invited the Indians at Gnadenhütten to move north to Wyoming. Although they voiced approval, the Moravians left it up to the Delaware and Mahican residents of the mission town to decide for themselves; furthermore, they assured all of the Indian parties present that they would remain united with those who would leave.

16. Date changed from the 10th in another hand.

17. See August Gottlieb Spangenberg, "Account of the visit of the Indians in Bethlehem March 1753," R M M 40/3500/16/1.

18. The son of the Indian Solomon Waunaupaugus was shot and killed while chasing two white men allegedly in the act of stealing horses near Stockbridge. Although one of the men was later found guilty of manslaughter, the incident caused considerable resentment among the Indians, and led colonial families to fear for their safety (Frazier, *Mohicans of Stockbridge*, 105–6).

19. Or "relatives."

20. Although it is not known if the parcels were the same, five years later Samuel and his brother Jeremias were asked to go to Potatuck to receive payment owed them for land they had inherited from their father, but that nevertheless had been sold to colonists (UAH, *Diarium des Indianer-Häufleins in Pachgatgoch Seit Geschw. Schmicks Daseyn vom 25ten Mart. bis 12ten Oktobr. 1758*, R.15.H.I.b.5.15.a, 9, 15 May 1758).

21. It is unclear whether "it" refers to the land or to the fact that Samuel intended to sell it.

22. Above the date in another hand: "this week."

23. This congregation was later named Sichem by Bishop Spangenberg, in memory of Brother Bruce. Abraham Reincke was stationed there for two months in 1753 (UAH, Johannes (John) Ettwein, R.14.A.40.1.m, n.d.).

24. Jeanette/Johannette Rau, Martin Mack's wife, who had died in 1749.

25. Neither Fröhlich nor Sensemann left a record describing the Indians' transgressions.

26. At the beginning of this sentence in another hand: "NB" (nota bene).

27. "But what can I say?" Is. 38.15: "That He shall perform unto me what He has sworn."

28. "Lift up your eyes [. . .] they all [. . .] come to you."

29. "*Veter*" for "*Vetter*." See entry for 27 March 1751.

30. John and Jane Mills had three daughters: Lydia (1734–1755), Jane (1735–1829), and Sarah (1747–1767) (Johnson, *Register of Some of the Families*).

31. It is unclear whether this section, bracketed in the margin, was placed in parentheses by Sensemann or someone else.

32. "*Kriedl.*," i.e., "*kriedlich*," perhaps for "*kricklich*" (irritable).

33. See the glossary.

34. The last of the residents of Wechquadnach were reported to have left on 2 July.

35. RMM 30/225/3/1, Dec. 1748.

36. "[A]nd the God [. . .] of peace will be with you." 2 Cor. 13.11.

37. Date inserted in another hand.

38. Sensemann and Anna Catherine were married in Marienborn on this date in 1741 ([Neisser], *History of Moravian Work*, 174).

39. The *Irene* was one of three ships that the Moravians owned, operated, and manned with their own crews. The others were *Catherine* and *The Little Strength*. The *Irene* "was built on Staten Island, between 1745 and 1748, under the direction of Abraham Boemper and Timothy Horsfield, agents of the Moravian Church, in New York. . . . The cost of her building was defrayed almost entirely by Bishop Spangenberg, from a legacy left him individually by Thomas Noble, a merchant of New York." In 1757 the *Irene* was captured by a French privateer and accidentally wrecked by her prize crew off Cape Breton. She had made twenty-four trans-Atlantic voyages and one from New York to the Moravian mission in Greenland (W. Reichel, "Register of Members," 329).

40. It is unclear whether this section, bracketed in the margin, was placed in parentheses by Sensemann or someone else.

41. Sekes's family.

42. Johannan was the name given to Zinzendorf by Indians in contact with the Moravians.

43. This is a reference to Gideon's son Chuse.

44. "*Kannen*," also "tankards": containers made of wood.

45. Word inserted in another hand.

46. Sensemann writes this entry twice.

47. "Princes and great men rule; His disciples are spared this great squandering of time."

48. This was the suspect and only partly realized agreement made earlier in the year authorizing Abraham and the Delaware headman Teedyuscung to lead a party of Christian Delawares and Mahicans from eastern Pennsylvania north to the Wyoming Valley, and once there, to be under the supervision of the Iroquois. See entry for 9 April (Wallace, *King*, 47–55; Weslager, *Delaware Indians*, 210–12).

49. Jn. 10.9: "I am the door."

50. Thamar and Petrus's daughter.

51. "For you are all sons of light." 1 Th. 5.5: "As the blood of the Lamb keeps the garments clean."

52. An expression of approval, similar forms of which are found in other Eastern Algonquian, but also Northern Iroquoian, languages. See, for example, Gehring and Starna, *Journey*, 14–15, 44n100, 45n103.

53. Maria and Theodora are sisters; Caritas is Maria's granddaughter.

54. If Sensemann's observation is accurate, this is a snowshoe hare (*Lepus americanus*); otherwise, it is either a New England cottontail (*Sylvilagus transitionalis*) or Eastern cottontail (*S. floridanus*).

55. After Ex. 16.13.

56. Word inserted in another hand.

57. It is unclear whether this section, bracketed in the margin, was placed in parentheses by Sensemann or someone else. This may be an example of bride wealth, the practice of offering gifts or compensation to the family/kin group of the future bride by the family/kin group of the future husband, thus legitimizing the marriage.

58. "*Pünktchen*," literally "point" (diminutive), a reference to what Zinzendorf understood to be the pivotal point of the theology of the New Testament, here the acknowledgment that a person can become blessed by recognizing himself/herself as a sinner and accepting Jesus' gracious act of having made sinners righteous before God through His death. In other instances, Jesus' wounds, for example, may be identified as the "*Hauptpünktchen*," literally "main point" (diminutive). See Hahn, "*Theologie*," 288–90.

59. Or "her."

60. That is, sold into bondage.

61. "'You did not choose me, but I chose you.'"

62. A phonetic rendering of the French "*gouvernement*" (government). Laws enacted

in seventeenth-century New England banned outright the celebration of Christmas. Although they were soon overturned, Connecticut and its religious lobby nevertheless disapproved of and discouraged keeping this holiday until the nineteenth century.

63. The referent for "it" is unclear. Sensemann may have wanted to express that the girl had attended her last love feast on Christmas Day.

64. That is, "up" from the winter huts to the cemetery, which was located on a plot of land upriver from the modern Schaghticoke Indian reservation. See the introduction.

65. "Feb." is written here in another hand.

Rundt: 2 March to 14 May 1754

1. RMM 3/114/9/1. This diary is by Carl Gottfried Rundt. The month is written on the upper right-hand corner of a number of pages, notations that are not reproduced here. The previous diary ended on 27 February 1754.

2. Jonathan is probably Abraham's son, formerly known as Tennis.

3. Although descriptions of their neighbors in Wechquadnach and Stockbridge were provided, there is no mention of the Indians at Pachgatgoch tapping maple trees to make sugar. Here girls from the community are going out to collect birch sap, probably from the black or sweet birch (*Betula lenta*), perhaps for a treat. The original root beer was made from the fermented sap of this tree.

4. Rundt's statement is suggestive of the use of the lot to decide whether to baptize the child. See the introduction.

5. Rundt writes two separate entries on the same day.

6. Jn. 6.68: "'Lord, to whom shall we go?'"

7. "Pilgrim's Letter," written by Zinzendorf and published in London in 1742 as *My Dear Fellow-Traveller, Here hast Thou a Letter, which I have wrote to Thee out of the Fulness of my Heart, and with many Tears for Thy Salvation's Sake; and the Lamb of God hath sprinkled it with His Blood, that it will be profitable for Thee, if Thou abidest by thy Heart, or now findest thy Heart.*

8. Jn. 13.13: "'You call me Teacher and Lord; and you are right.'"

9. 2 Th. 3.18: "The grace of our Lord Jesus Christ be with you all."

10. "We were quiet on the Sabbath, taking our enjoyment from the fullness of the Lamb: These offerings, which one needs to enjoy at all times, indeed taste exceptionally good on the Sabbath."

11. "'Blessed are the dead who die in the Lord.'"

12. "In their order," that is, by choir.

13. "Oh, wounds of Jesus! in which we are buried, receive this brown tabernacle[d]."

14. Jn. 21.17: "Do you love me?"

15. 1 Cor. 2.2: "For I decided to know nothing among you except Jesus Christ and him crucified."

16. Mt. 23.8: "You are all brethren."

17. Mt. 23.9: "You have one Father."

18. Tit. 2.11: "For the grace of God has appeared for the salvation of all men."

19. Pr. 31.17: "She girds her loins." "And ran thus through the world."

No. A. Appendix to the Bethlehem *Diario*

1. These two lines are in a second hand.

2. Nelson, *Guide to the Records*, 23, lists Johann Christopher Pyrlaeus and "Other" as authors for these two documents, items 1 and 2, dated 1747 and 1749 (RMM 3/114/10/1–2). Note: Personal names are transcribed as they appear in the originals.

3. Christian names written on the far right side of the original manuscript page are here separated by dashes. This document—item 2—is in a different hand than item 1. Note: Petrus and Schermann, or Shermann, are the same person.

4. Perhaps an attempt to write phonetically the English "conch."

Rauch: 17 June to 27 July 1754

1. RMM 4/115/1/1. By the time Rauch arrived at Pachgatgoch on 2 July 1754, there had been a six-week break in the reporting on the mission. The previous diary, written by Carl Gottfried Rundt, ended on 14 May 1754. It is not known whether Abraham Büninger, who relieved Rundt at Pachgatgoch, kept a diary in the interim.

2. This may be the grist mill at Pittstown, New Jersey, built by Edward Rockhill, a Quaker, before 1748.

3. There apparently were four men named David Nitschmann living at this time. See "List of Moravian and Colonial Participants." This man, however, is probably Bishop David Nitschmann (b. 1696).

4. This name appears as Jakes Catiliau, Catilieau, and Catileau (Hamilton and Madeheim et al., *Bethlehem Diary*, 2:176, 404).

5. Rau's home had first served as the mission house at Shekomeko, the construction of which had begun on 9 October 1742. Built of logs, it replaced a bark-and-pole house that Gottlob Büttner had described as being cold and smoky (RMM 1/III/1/1, 1/III/2/8, 25 Dec. 1743; see also DHNY, 3:614). In early 1743, this was home for Büttner and his wife Margarete, Martin and Jeannette/Johannette Mack, Joachim and Anna Sensemann, and Frederick Post (RMM 1/III/2/8, Feb. 1743). A twenty-by-thirty-foot

bark-and-pole "church" was added to the mission house in July 1743, which was reported to be "completely gone" by 1748 (RMM 26/211/5/1; W. Reichel, *Memorial of the Dedication*, 39; see also sketch of Shekomeko at 63; RMM 30/225/3, 15 Dec. 1748).

6. "*Weissagen*": prophecy, in a biblical sense; inspired preaching.

7. "Thus it remains the truth, He can do whatever He wills, in heaven and on earth, and through people He so happens to seize."

8. "Disciple," a reference to Zinzendorf.

9. This may be the Reverend Cotton Mather Smith (1731–1806), who graduated from Yale College in 1751 and was ordained in Sharon, Connecticut, on 28 August 1755 (Barber, *Historical Collections*, 495).

10. "*Schwiz-ofen*": sweating oven.

11. This is probably Michael, a.k.a. Hendrick, baptized by Büttner in Shekomeko in 1742 and buried in Bethlehem in 1758 (W. Reichel, *Memorials*, 153–54). In an account written on the occasion of his death, he is identified as a Minisink Indian, about seventy years of age. Of interest is the description of his facial tattoos, a physical detail that is not mentioned for any of the Indians at Pachgatgoch about whom the Moravians wrote: "He also had (as one still sees on the very old Indians) a face with figures painted in gunpowder so that it [*sic*] would not to come off, and his cheerful look with the figures gave a pleasing appearance in the coffin. The figures that he had on his face were a large snake on the ~~one~~ right side at the temple, and ~~from~~ starting at the lips a pole that [ran] between the eyes and nose and up the forehead onto the head, on which pole there was every quarter of an inch something of a round figure, like a *scalp*. On the left cheek he had two spears cross-wise, one over the other, and at the jaw line the head of a wild boar. All of it done very neatly" (MAB, Bethlehem Diary, 1758, 19:56).

12. "*Böstern Mann*" may be "*Boston Mann*" (a man from Boston), an Englishman, or perhaps "*böser Mann*" (wicked man).

13. 2 Cor. 5.17: "Therefore, if any one is in Christ, he is a new creation."

Büninger and Rauch: 25 July to 31 December 1754

1. RMM 4/115/2/1. The previous diary, written by Rauch, ends on 27 July 1754. The diary here consists of three parts: Büninger wrote the first, dated 25 July to, and including, a portion of the entry for 18 August; Rauch wrote the second, from 18 August to 21 September; and Büninger the third, from 24 September to 31 December 1754. On a number of pages the month is written in the upper right-hand corner, notations that are not reproduced here.

2. "*Plan*." See the glossary.

3. This is one of several indications that entries in the diaries sent to Bethlehem were not always made on a daily basis but were at times written after the fact or copied from earlier drafts.

4. Dt. 33.28. "[I]n safety [. . .] alone."

5. "Now no enemy can any longer harm us."

6. "Ind." is written above this word in another hand.

7. The choir house for the single sisters. Christina had gone to Bethlehem in December 1748 after the visit of Bishops von Watteville and Cammerhoff to Pachgatgoch. Given that she was twenty years old in 1748, and Martha did not marry Gideon until 1744, it seems that Christina was Gideon's daughter through a previous union.

8. "Vetter." See entry for 27 March 1751.

9. Erdmuth and her daughter Martha are from Potatuck.

10. Acknowledging sinfulness is a positive gesture in Moravian theology and an important step toward receiving the Savior's forgiveness. Joshua, along with his wife Elisabeth mentioned later, is a member of the conference. Ensuring that both are in a proper spiritual state is evidently of particular concern to the resident missionaries.

11. "Do not love the world."

12. "Bedeckung": here, intending the forgiveness of sins.

13. Magdalena is living six miles from Pachgatgoch, presumably near Gaylordsville. See entry for 16 August.

14. This date commemorates the spiritual beginnings of the Renewed Church of the Brethren at Berthelsdorf in 1727. See De Schweinitz, Moravian Manual, 113, 165.

15. This rhyme may be translated as follows: "Hence it's true. At the definite end, all falls indeed into His hands."

16. The following entries are by Christian Heinrich Rauch.

17. Gideon is concerned about the treatment of his grandchild by the stepmother. In July 1747 Andreas, his wife Leah, who was Gideon's daughter, and their two sons had gone to Bethlehem and then to Gnadenhütten with a party of Indians from Pachgatgoch, but then returned. Leah died in Pachgatgoch in early spring 1749, and sometime afterward, Andreas went back to Gnadenhütten (MAB 3/114/10/1, 3/114/1/2, 23 Mar. 1749).

18. Anna Rauch's statement is suggestive of a general sentiment that the Pachgatgoch Indians apparently had expressed about themselves and the Indians at Gnadenhütten—that they enjoyed a kind of freedom that the Gnadenhütten Indians did not. Gnadenhütten was a mission town whose Indian residents were subject to rules and regulations imposed by the Moravians. Moreover, one of the reasons the Pachgatgoch Indians had left Gnadenhütten and then Nazareth in 1747—after only a short

stay—was that they were not permitted to own land that could then be passed on to family members. Another was evidently the lack of autonomy that they experienced while under Moravian supervision. See the introduction.

19. Reference to Lk. 17.11–19.

20. "*Frohnen dienst,*" in modern German "*Frondienst,*" also, "socage." This is a reference to the Indians' having been forced to be part of the search party.

21. Possibly Benjamin Chase.

22. Jeremias, born in Potatuck, was baptized in March 1743 at Shekomeko, where Rauch had been a missionary.

23. Rauch writes "*geschalbt,*" a Germanized version of the English "scalped," with the letter k written above the line, possibly for insertion after the s.

24. On 1 September 1754, Indians allied to the French killed either three or four colonists, including a child and an infant, near Stockbridge, causing great panic in the area and problems for the people at Pachgatgoch (Frazier, *Mohicans of Stockbridge*, 107–9).

25. From all accounts, Pyrlaeus had last been to Connecticut in 1743, when he, along with Martin Mack and Joseph Shaw, was arrested, taken to court, and then forced to leave the colony. See the introduction. The hostility directed at Rauch is perhaps an expression of continued anti-Moravian sentiments in the colony related to their presumed pro-French leanings.

26. The Leightons were on their way to serve the congregation at Sichem, where they remained until early 1755 (UAH R.14.A.40.1.m., n.d.).

27. "*Hirsche*": stag or hart, both references to a male deer, in particular the European red deer.

28. Rauch writes "*Martin u. seine Justina,*" although he only refers to Justina in this sentence.

29. Or "friends."

30. Zech. 13.1: "'[A] fountain opened [. . .] to cleanse them from sin and uncleanness.'"

31. There is no known record of the incident to which Joshua is referring.

32. Latin: "Lord have mercy."

33. Although the symbol and date appear as is in the manuscript, no diary entry follows.

34. The diary that follows was written by Abraham Büninger. A check mark and the initials "Sp." (for Spangenberg) appear on the upper left-hand corner of this manuscript page. In the right-hand corner, initialed by Spangenberg and in his hand, is the following: "p. Sk. [*post scriptum:*] I believe this *diarium* should be sent to the Jünger [Zinzendorf] *in copia*" (Latin: in copy).

35. One of the immovable festivals of the Moravian Church — St. Michael and All Angels — a remembrance day for those engaged in the instruction of children and youth.

36. "'If any man would come after me, let him deny himself.'"

37. See entry of 1 September on these killings.

38. This would place the initial planting of the land in 1737. The Indians were reported to have first taken up residence on the west side of the Housatonic River in May 1736 (PRCC, 8:38–39).

39. It was several weeks before the Indians at Stockbridge were absolved of blame for these killings.

40. For insertion here: "had been seen."

41. This "incident" is reported in depositions taken by a magistrate in Sharon on 14 and 15 October 1754. Several colonists reported that Indians had been seen and heard "hooping and whistling" at night near the homes of Thomas Jones and Thomas Barnes, striking at one of these with their hatchets or clubs and pelting the other with stones. One evening, while several men were standing watch at the Jones house, an Indian stuck his head in the doorway and then ducked away. Spotting the Indian in the distance, the men fired shots and apparently wounded him, but in spite of their best efforts, he eluded capture ([Indian Papers], 1st ser., 2:82–88). There is no known Indian version of this event. According to Büninger's diary entry of 22 February 1755, the Indian in the night was in fact an unnamed colonist playing a prank meant to frighten local settlers. However, given the involvement of Barnes, who in 1750 and 1752 had purchased Indian land in Sharon under questionable circumstances, and also the fact that there was no further mention of the person who had been wounded, it is not unreasonable to suggest that the entire affair had been concocted by the men who had given the depositions, perhaps with the hope of arousing opposition to Indian claims to the land. Indeed, the visit to Pachgatgoch by the party of colonials may well have been made to intimidate. For early accounts that place the blame squarely on the Indians, and specifically the Indian Timotheus, see De Forest, *History*, 403–5; and Sedgwick, *General History*, 39–41. Frazier, *Mohicans of Stockbridge*, 109, repeats De Forest's version.

42. Possibly John Williams (Sedgwick, *General History*, 161).

43. This list has not been located.

44. The American eel (*Anguilla rostrata*).

45. Samuel's house was on the road running along the west side of the Housatonic River from Macedonia Brook to the vicinity of Bulls Bridge, roughly following today's Schaghticoke Road.

46. The restive atmosphere ushering in the Seven Years' War is making itself felt. Büninger's request is an indicator that colonial officials and neighbors are keeping close tabs on the Indians.

47. The implication is that, should the hunt not produce enough to eat, the Indians could make and sell or exchange canoes for food.

48. This date in November is one of the immovable festivals of the Moravian Church, commemorating the formal acknowledgment that Jesus Christ is the head of the church (De Schweinitz, *Moravian Manual*, 113).

49. This apparently is a reference to an act passed by the colonial assembly in May 1752 granting the Indians land "for their improvement and for the cutting of wood and timber for their own use only" (PRCC, 10:108).

50. This is Post's Indian name, which may be Mahican, given the apparent nasalized vowel (Ives Goddard, personal communication, 2003).

51. This section of the diary is initialed by Spangenberg and given his check mark.

52. Or "relatives." Post was related to Priscilla and her family through his marriage to Rachel, who was from Pachgatgoch.

53. Büninger speaks of himself in the third person.

54. The "*Nachtwache*" (night watch) was observed by a person or small groups of persons who remained awake through the night engaged in prayer and devotion; it could also include watchman duties. The night watch service on New Year's Eve was introduced in the church in 1733. See Hamilton and Madeheim et al., *Bethlehem Diary*, 2:391; Hamilton and Hamilton, *History of the Moravian Church*, 37.

55. Jn. 14.6: "'I am the way, and the truth, and the life.'"

56. "*Wunden*" (wounds) is added in another hand.

Büninger and Rundt: 1 January to 7 December 1755

1. RMM 4/115/3/1. This diary, written by Abraham Büninger and Carl Gottfried Rundt, continues without interruption from that previous. Büninger wrote the first section, dated 1 January to 9 March 1755. Rundt's entries begin on 10 March and continue until the end of the diary on 7 December 1755. On 8 December Rundt departed Pachgatgoch to return to Bethlehem by way of New York, leaving behind Brothers Seidel and Utley, as well as the Jungmanns. During Rundt's absence from 4 August until 6 September, the diary was kept by Johann Georg Jungmann. That translated here, however, is in Rundt's hand, suggesting that it is a later draft made perhaps from Jungmann's notes. Büninger's habit of inscribing the month at the top of almost every manuscript page is not repeated here. A check mark and the initials "Sp." appear in the upper left-hand corner of this and other pages, indicating that

Spangenberg read the diary; they are not reproduced. Spangenberg's occasional marginalia are noted.

2. "*Nerven gichter.*"

3. Masthay, *Schmick's Mahican Dictionary*, 181, offers Mahican "*Pachtamuus*" (Savior), and "*Pachtamáwaas*" (var.) (God, Savior, Lord).

4. In this and the following sentence the child is identified as female.

5. Büninger sometimes writes in the third person.

6. Eph. 5.14: "Awake, O sleeper."

7. Jn. 11.51–52: "Jesus should die for the nation, and not for the nation only, but to gather into one the children of God."

8. The Reverend John Graham (b. ca. 1693, d. 1774), the first minister of Southbury (Barber, *Historical Collections*, 251–52).

9. Is. 53.5: "With his stripes we are healed."

10. Acts 16.31: "'Believe in the Lord Jesus, and you will be saved.'"

11. "[S]weat house." See entries in Masthay, *Schmick's Mahican Dictionary*, 136.

12. The immediate question in respect to the disposition of the lands of the Wechquadnach Indians begins with a transaction that had taken place almost thirty years earlier. In 1726 Richard Sackett (d. Amenia NY, 1746), a partner in the Little Nine Patent of New York, entered into an agreement with Metoxson (var.), alleged to be "ye Chiefe Sachem of the indians in these parts," and other Indians, for a large tract of land that included the western part of Sharon. With the final adjustment of the New York–Connecticut boundary in 1731, a portion of Sackett's land that now lay in Connecticut was confiscated. In 1738 Thomas Lamb, acting as an agent for the colony, repurchased from the same Metoxson and others the land that had been deeded to Sackett. The Indians at Wechquadnach, however, insisted that they should retain the right to live where they were, that is, in the northwest corner of the purchase. Thus, in 1742 the colony appointed Daniel Edwards to "Secure and Settle in a proper manner" fifty acres of land for the Indians from the proprietors of Sharon, and in return, to convey to the proprietors 100 acres lying south of these lands, "they making the purchase of the native right, if not yet done" ([Indian Papers], 1st ser., 1:244, 244b, 245; PRCC, 8:502–3). However, upon his arrival in Sharon, Edwards learned that the proprietors did not find the suggested one-for-two exchange of acreage satisfactory, maintaining that the lands set aside for the Indians actually amounted to some eighty-nine acres. In addition, they argued, the Indians had told them that this was well short of the amount of land to which they actually laid claim, and moreover, was insufficient for their needs; nonetheless, the Indians added, having the benefit of 200 acres would permit them to "Keep together undispersed" ([Indian Papers], 1st

ser., 1:246). The matter remained unresolved. In a petition to the colonial assembly in 1747, the Indians, recalling past attempts to settle the question of their lands, requested some 246 acres at "The Indian ponds" in the northwest corner of the town of Sharon, "which: Tho: Small yet will: be to us a Sufficient accommodation" ([Indian Papers], 2nd ser., 1:103).

13. 1 Jn. 2.2: "He is the expiation for our sins."

14. Jn. 3.16: "For God so loved the world that he gave his only Son, that [etc.]."

15. The discussion in respect to the Wechquadnach lands continues later; the concluding diary entry is dated 22 February.

16. Dt. 6.5: "You shall love the Lord your God with all your heart." Lev. 19.18: "[And] your neighbor as yourself."

17. "Christ's blood and righteousness."

18. That is, the Holy Spirit. See the glossary.

19. Title of the hymn: "O Sacred Head! now wounded" (Julian, Dictionary of Hymnology, 1:835).

20. Mk. 9.24: "'I believe; help my unbelief!'"

21. The "trick" alluded to is the incident mentioned in Büninger's diary entry of 16 October 1754. On 20 February 1755, Timotheus is said to have agreed that "in Case Sd Barns would give him Two pounds & ten Shillings Lawfull money of New York and Eight pounds in Old Tenor Bills of Credit, he would give to the Governor & Company of his Majesties English Colony of Connecticutt in New England a quit Claim of all his Right in the Lands Lying in the Township of Sharon," which was done ([Indian Papers], 1st ser., 2:89–89c). There is a considerable discrepancy between the amount paid to Timotheus as reported by Büninger, and that which appears in the Indian Papers.

22. Jn. 3.14–15: "And as Moses lifted up the serpent in the wilderness, so must the Son of Man be lifted up, that whoever believes in Him."

23. A reference to Satan.

24. "Christ will be portrayed before your eyes."

25. "Geschwister," elsewhere "brethren and sisters," is written in Rundt's hand.

26. There appears to be a name missing here.

27. The entries that follow are in Rundt's hand.

28. In the margin in Rundt's hand, for insertion here: "Because the minister in Kent, Mr. Marsh, had expressed to Br. Büninger the desire to read something from our Gem[ein] Schrifften, Br. Jungmann, on this occasion, delivered the 2 small pieces, The plain case of the Repraesentatives, pp., to the house of the minister; he himself was not at home."

29. In the margin in Rundt's hand, for insertion here: "We had our Br. Gideon join us today for the midday meal."

30. A subset of a choir. Small groups of persons who would meet for fellowship or devotional purposes.

31. The Annunciation, Festival of all the Choirs.

32. "*Acker*" can be a unit of land measurement or simply a reference to a parcel of land of unspecified size.

33. In the bottom margin, for insertion here: "(as far as 4 1/2 miles from here)."

34. Kihor and Wenemo are Leah's father and brother.

35. "Father, Who on high."

36. W. Reichel, "Register of Members," 356, notes that Jungmann was a miller by trade. Here and elsewhere, however, it is evident that he also possessed carpentry skills, which he may have learned from his father, a cooper (Faull, "Jungmann," 179).

37. This may be the Reverend Benajah Case (b. ca. 1710), New Fairfield's first minister (Barber, *Historical Collections*, 387).

38. Heb. 4.12: "[He is] discerning the thoughts and intentions of the heart."

39. The use of the plural suggests, however, that all three women had returned.

40. Rom. 5.5: "God's love has been poured into our hearts through the Holy Spirit."

41. There is no "enclosure" with this document. However, RMM 4/115/14/6 contains a "*Catalogus*," dated May 1755, that lists the baptized and unbaptized Indians residing at Pachgatgoch at this time. See appendix 4, "Lists and Correspondence."

42. Spangenberg's comment in the margin: "Who intends to continue the Indian *catal[og]*?"

43. See figure 4. Spangenberg's comment in the margin: "This, too, is to be added to the *catalogo* [catalog]. The *diaspora* of the Indians should be noted as well."

44. Also, Alworth (b. ca. 1715), a farmer in Amenia, New York, and a signatory to a 1752 letter requesting a Moravian minister. He was a member of the congregation at Sichem (W. Reichel, *Memorial of the Dedication*, 67–68n1).

45. In the margin in Rundt's hand: "Br. Christian [took] a heartfelt leave of the baptized and unbaptized, kissing all of the brethren."

46. Plural of "*Bande.*" See the glossary.

47. Spangenberg's comment in the margin, "How are matters proceeding with the *Banden?*" (RMM 115/14/7, 20 May 1755), contains a list of persons organized into *Banden* by Christian Seidel. See appendix 4, "Lists and Correspondence."

48. We are unable to identify this individual, whose name appears in a number of subsequent diary entries as Hays, Heys, Heas, and Heass.

49. Spangenberg's comment in the margin: "This frost occurred in Wachovia as well, on the same day." Wachovia was a tract of nearly 100,000 acres near present Winston-Salem, North Carolina, purchased by the Moravian Church from John Carteret, 1st Earl Granville (1690–1763), in 1753. From the German "*Wachau,*" the name of Zinzendorf's estate in the region of the same name in Austria.

50. Buckwheat can be milled into flour, and the straw used as food for livestock.

51. 1 Cor. 1.18: "For the word of the cross is folly to those who are perishing, but to us who are being saved it is the power of God."

52. An indication that Indian people continued to live in the vicinity of this former settlement and the mission that had once been there.

53. Spangenberg's comment in the margin: "Oh, if only one would hereby learn to understand the saying: To fill someone's hands that he may be able to give to J.C."

54. The Connecticut General Assembly passed a resolution in May 1755 asking the governor to proclaim a day of fasting and prayer in supplication for God's protection against the threat of war with the French (PRCC, 10:395).

55. "*Heidelbeeren.*"

56. In the margin in Rundt's hand, for insertion here: "(That which she threatened she made come true the next night, but regrettably! has not done us any injury, but has done harm to herself and to many other baptized who she drew into her affair.)"

57. "*Camin.*"

58. Spangenberg's note in the margin: "[D]*er Reinigung born nach* 1. *Joh.* 2 *so*[*l*]*ches schreibe ich euch, daß ihr nicht sündigt; hatte aber iemand gesündigt, so haben wir einen heyland pp.*" (The cleansing [by the fountain of water] according to 1 Jn. 2[:] I am writing this to you so that you may not sin; but if anyone does sin, we have a Savior, pp.).

59. Spangenberg's comment in the margin: "Ay! Do they do this?"

60. The printed text of this resolution is found in PRCC, 10:108. An earlier draft and the petition of the Indians at "Pachgatgoth or Scatticook" is in [Indian Papers], 1st ser., 2:75, 76. The "copy" of the text mentioned in the entry appears on the succeeding manuscript page (see later).

61. As do several other Moravian diarists, Rundt often writes in the third person.

62. Spangenberg's comment in the margin: "Break bread for the hungry. Will not the Savior do so?"

63. Christian is enlisted in the militia.

64. This is Lititz, Pennsylvania. See the gazetteer.

65. Although identified as Jungmann's diary, the text continues in Rundt's handwriting. Written above this heading in Spangenberg's hand are the following notations: "Scatticock N. 1.," a check mark, the initials "Sp.," and "1755."

66. The Reverend Cyrus Marsh was a captain in the local militia.

67. "My God! and was a poor human being like me."

68. "*Reisse*," probably for "*Reis*" (twig, sprig), or "*Reisig*" (brushwood).

69. "My God"; "Dear Father"; Jer. 3.4: "'[T]hou art the friend of my youth'"; Jer. 22.18: "'Ah, my brother!'"; "My beloved"; 1 Pet. 1.18: "You know that you were ransomed [. . .] not with perishable things such as silver or gold."

70. Jn. 19.28: "'I thirst!'"

71. Two series of sermons delivered by Zinzendorf in Berlin in 1738, published as Berliner Reden (Hamilton and Hamilton, *History of the Moravian Church*, 69–70, 154, 156).

72. The Reverend Solomon Palmer was the first resident Episcopal minister in New Milford, arriving there in 1754 (Barber, *Historical Collections*, 478).

73. The notation "hl." is probably an abbreviation for "*hochlöblich*" (very laudable or worshipful).

74. Graf von Zinzendorf, Count Zinzendorf.

75. Lindsey House, Chelsea, London, was purchased by Zinzendorf in 1750 and used as his headquarters (Hamilton and Hamilton, *History of the Moravian Church*, 107).

76. This is Gerhard Winegar's grist mill.

77. 1 Jn. 3: "See what love the Father has given us, that we should be called children of God."

78. There is no other known report or record of this earthquake (John E. Ebel, Weston Observatory, Boston College, personal communication, 2003).

79. "O, my Savior! Please allow me to feel your presence throughout this day. Please keep the image of you on the cross before my eyes and heart at all times."

80. "Our most favorite place[d] to be sure is the shrine in His side."

81. Above this heading, in Spangenberg's hand: "Scatticock num. 8."

82. "He is the great prophet."

83. In the margin in Rundt's hand, for insertion here: "their names were: Gideon, Joshua, Gottlieb, and Simon; and Martha, Elisabeth, Magdalena, Justina, Erdmuth, [and] Benigna, Simon's daughter, as well as Priscilla."

84. Written above this heading, in Spangenberg's hand: "Scatticock n. 1[?]" and two check marks.

85. Spangenberg's comment in the margin: "Alas, but not without need!"

86. "*Geschriebene Schrifft*," perhaps as opposed to a printed text.

87. "Jacob prayed."

88. "*Anstalten*": institutes, educational institutions, schools.

89. Johann Michael Sauter (d. Bethabara NC, 1765), a Moravian, arrived in Wachovia, North Carolina, in 1755.

90. Four manuscript pages of verses composed by Brother Rundt on the occasion of this festival day (November 13) are included with this entry. To avoid interrupting the flow of the text, they have been moved to the end of the diary.

91. Spangenberg's comment in the margin: "Can this not be prevented."

92. Spangenberg's comment in the margin: "This must be communicated to them frequently, yet warmly, because this running about is like poison for them."

93. "Post-Bericht."

94. Spangenberg's comment in the margin: "Hence it occurred earlier in New England than in Bethlehem, also stronger and longer."

95. Rundt reports what is today known as the Cape Ann earthquake of 18 November 1755. Centered east of Cape Ann, Massachusetts, and with an estimated magnitude of 6.0 to 6.3 on the Richter scale, it caused damage in Boston and other coastal cities north to southern Maine. Its effects were felt in the region stretching from Halifax, Nova Scotia, to South Carolina. Although Rundt's entry is dated the seventeenth, the time of the shock was about 4:30 a.m. on the eighteenth (John E. Ebel, personal communication, 2003).

96. Spangenberg's comment in the margin: "If only I had a list of these people."

97. This is the well-documented aftershock of the 18 November earthquake (John E. Ebel, personal communication, January 2003).

98. Spangenberg's comment in the margin: "Is Stockbridge not the place where the murders happened this year?"

99. In the margin in Rundt's hand, for insertion here: "This happened right after our brethren and sisters had recently gone to Wachovia."

100. Spangenberg's comment in the margin begins in Latin, "*Fama malum quo non velocius ullum*"; he was probably intending to write "*Fama malum quo non aliud velocius ullum*" (nothing travels faster than scandal). He continues in German: "In the evening of the 24th, the murderous deed occurs on the Mahoning. On the 26th, it [the news] is in Schaghticoke." Spangenberg is referring to the Indian raid on Gnadenhütten, where ten adult Moravians and an infant were killed. William C. Reichel neglects to include Sr. Nitschmann in his list of people killed (*Memorials*, 201). Also among the dead was Anna Catherine Sensemann, a person very familiar to the Indians at Pachgatgoch. Her husband, Joachim Sensemann, along with four other persons, escaped. In his report, Spangenberg indicated that it was some consolation that the Moravians had suffered the first blow; otherwise, the widespread suspicion that they were in league with the French or their Indian allies might have been

reinforced ("Br. *Josephs Bericht von der Begebenheit an der Mahony am 24ten Nov.* 55," MAB, Bethlehem Diary, September–December 1756, 15:329–31).

101. In the margin in Rundt's hand, for insertion here: "They had met Brother and Sister Jungmann and had lodged with them the previous night at Azariah Smith's [house] in Salisbury."

102. Spangenberg's comment in the margin: "The English *statuta* [Latin: statutes] indeed belong especially in Schaghticoke."

103. Written above this heading in Spangenberg's hand: "Scatticock N 14."